MOON

NEW ENGLAND HIKING

KELSEY PERRETT & MILES HOWARD

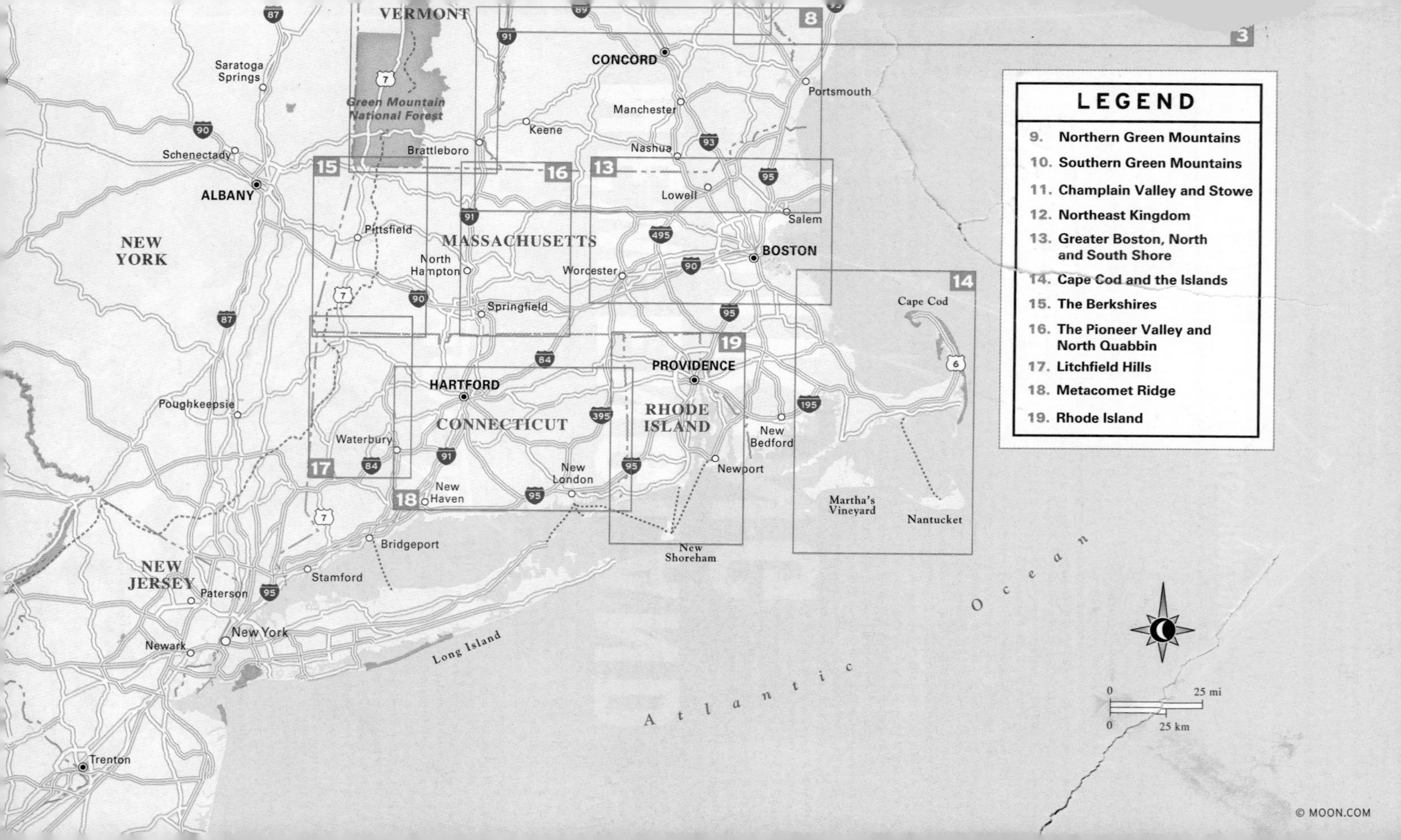
LEGEND
9. Northern Green Mountains
10. Southern Green Mountains
11. Champlain Valley and Stowe
12. Northeast Kingdom
13. Greater Boston, North and South Shore
14. Cape Cod and the Islands
15. The Berkshires
16. The Pioneer Valley and North Quabbin
17. Litchfield Hills
18. Metacomet Ridge
19. Rhode Island
VERMONT
Green Mountain National Forest
NEW YORK
MASSACHUSETTS
CONNECTICUT
RHODE ISLAND
NEW JERSEY
CONCORD
ALBANY
BOSTON
HARTFORD
PROVIDENCE
Saratoga Springs
Schenectady
Brattleboro
Keene
Manchester
Nashua
Portsmouth
Lowell
Salem
Pittsfield
North Hampton
Worcester
Springfield
Poughkeepsie
Waterbury
New Haven
New London
New Bedford
Newport
Cape Cod
Martha's Vineyard
Nantucket
New Shoreham
Bridgeport
Stamford
Paterson
New York
Newark
Trenton
Long Island
Atlantic Ocean
0 25 mi
0 25 km
© MOON.COM

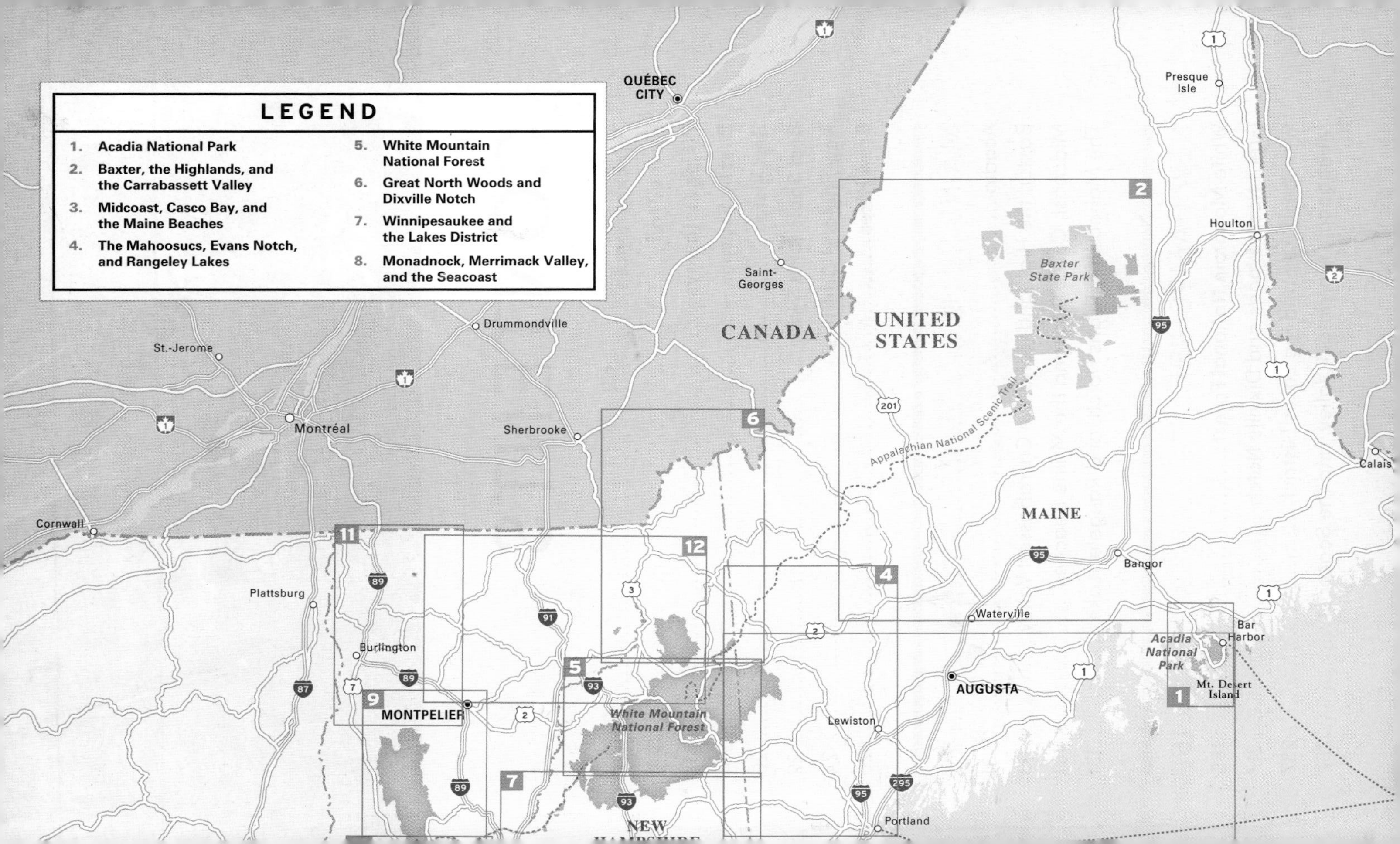

LEGEND
1. Acadia National Park
2. Baxter, the Highlands, and the Carrabassett Valley
3. Midcoast, Casco Bay, and the Maine Beaches
4. The Mahoosucs, Evans Notch, and Rangeley Lakes
5. White Mountain National Forest
6. Great North Woods and Dixville Notch
7. Winnipesaukee and the Lakes District
8. Monadnock, Merrimack Valley, and the Seacoast
QUÉBEC CITY
Saint-Georges
CANADA
UNITED STATES
Baxter State Park
Presque Isle
Houlton
Calais
Drummondville
St.-Jerome
Montréal
Sherbrooke
Cornwall
Plattsburg
Burlington
MONTPELIER
Appalachian National Scenic Trail
MAINE
Bangor
Waterville
AUGUSTA
Lewiston
Portland
Acadia National Park
Bar Harbor
Mt. Desert Island
White Mountain National Forest
NEW

CONTENTS

NEW ENGLAND HIKING
TOP EXPERIENCES

1 Feel the spray from majestic waterfalls (pages 82, 276, and 460).

2 Take in Classic New England views (page 373, page 413, and page 522).

3 Spot waterfowl and shorebirds (pages 252 and 285).

4 Admire wildflowers and fall foliage (pages 134 and 379).

5 Watch the sun set (pages 34 and 540).

6 Reach new heights on high-elevation hikes (pages 56, 210, and 255).

7 Wander secluded paths (pages 207, 226, and 422).

8 Reward yourself with tasty local brews (page 26).

9 Enjoy ocean breezes (pages 119, 432, and 567).

10 Catch a glimpse of elusive wildlife (pages 69 and 322).

HIT THE TRAIL

Chiaroscuro birch trees. Chuckling streams. Mossy slabs of granite. These are the ancient woodlands that Hawthorne's characters wandered, the waters that the Abenaki Native Americans charted by canoe, and the mountains on which generations of American peak-baggers have left their sweat, blood, and tears.

These regal yet rugged places are the backbone of New England, largely untouched by the breakneck pace of modern life. The forests are thick with curious sounds, lush colors, and inquisitive furry faces. The trails can get steep enough to leave even the most dedicated athletes longing for an ice bath. The alpine zone—where only the toughest flowers and vegetation can grow—is home to some of the most spectacular sunsets, wind gusts, and thunderstorms in the world.

There's something for every adventurer in New England—verdant valleys, roller-coaster ridges, crystal cascades, acres of wildflowers, 17th-century villages—and almost all of it is conveniently located within a day's drive of Boston, the region's largest city and air hub. Every enclave of New England wilderness offers not only natural beauty, but also the opportunity to experience everyday life in such an arresting place. Here you can chase a good day's hike with a bowl of lobster stew, a mug of locally brewed dunkelweizen, or a performance by an outdoor puppet circus famous for its civil rights-era activism. And yet, diverse as these amenities are, all of them are grounded by the serenity, rigor, and timeless quality of the New England scenery.

Taking a walk in the woods in New England is both exhilarating and humbling. Hiking here has always been an act of discovery, of sublime wonder, and of hill-or-high water, rain-or-shine grit. You will get wet. Your muscles may feel the mileage and at times, the elevation. But the longer you spend clomping around here and savoring every beguiling sight and sound, the more you'll begin to feel unstuck from time itself.

This is New England. We wouldn't have it any other way.

▼ THE BOARDWALK THROUGH WELLS RESERVE

HIKING GETAWAYS

Long Strange Coast

Experience the magic of the northern New England seacoast in two nights and three days.

DAY 1

Start your expedition by admiring the ecological diversity of New Hampshire along the **Sweet Trail**. From there, head north to Portland, Maine, to explore the city's renowned food and nightlife circuit and spend the night.

DAY 2

In the morning, take a jaunt over to the city forest and hike to **Fore River and Jewell Falls.** Then jump on US-1, grab a bite to eat at any of the lobster and clam shacks near Wiscasset, and continue north to Rockport for an afternoon climb up **Ragged Mountain.** Decamp in nearby Rockland or Belfast for dinner, drinks, and lodging.

DAY 3

Wake up early the next morning, enjoy a nice local breakfast, and make your way to nearby Camden Hills State Park and climb **Mount Megunticook** for a final ocean vista. If you find yourself pining for the beauty of the seacoast as you begin the journey home, stop by **Wells Reserve** or **Odiorne Point State Park** for a lush, meditative stroll alongside the Atlantic before it's time to hang up your boots.

Alpine Trilogy

Challenge yourself to three mountain summits in three New England states in three days!

DAY 1

Get a good night's sleep and rise at dawn to drive north through the greenery of Vermont to **Camel's Hump** (aim to summit before 2pm). Balance the adrenaline rush with a hearty locally sourced dinner and a few craft beers in Montpelier, and spend the night in Vermont's capital.

DAY 2

Get up early the next morning and head east into New Hampshire where—depending on how tired you are after yesterday's formidable ascent—you can work your way up the moderately difficult **Welch** and **Dickey,** or the easier and shorter **Mount Willard.** Knock both off if you feel like it! Then drive to either **North Conway** or **Gorham** for another round of decadent cooking and craft libations. But don't stay up too late. You'll finish big on day 3.

DAY 3

For on the third and final day, you'll drive north across the Maine border and climb the mighty **Old Speck**—one of the most thrilling hikes in this book. At least, that's the ideal finale. If you're feeling beat after two days of summits, you can easily swap Old Speck for **Mount Agamenticus** on Maine's southwestern oceanside, a two-hour drive from the White Mountains.

▲ OLD SPECK

Island Hopper

Hike three of New England's scenic offshore islands on this easygoing tour around the Atlantic seaboard.

DAY 1

Head east through Massachusetts and cross over the bridged canal marking your arrival in idyllic Cape Cod. Park at the Steamship Authority lot in Hyannis and enjoy a leisurely ferry ride to Nantucket. Take a bus or taxi a few minutes outside Nantucket town to explore the varied local terrain at **Sanford Farm**, **Ram Pasture**, and **The Woods**. Stay and play on the island, or hop back on the ferry to spend the night in Hyannis.

DAY 2

Wake up and drive approximately 25 miles southwest to Woods Hole, where you can pick up the Steamship Authority ferry to Martha's Vineyard. From either Vineyard Haven or Oak Bluffs, where the ferries drop off, catch a ride to pastoral Chilmark, about 15 miles away, and spend some time admiring the sweeping ocean views at **Menemsha Hills Reservation**. Treat yourself to a night on the Vineyard, or return to Falmouth for dinner and a good night's sleep.

DAY 3

Get up early to beat the Cape Cod traffic and get a jump on your 2-hour (85 miles) drive to Rhode Island. From Falmouth, make your way west around Buzzards Bay. After a scenic crossing of Narragansett Bay, you'll arrive in Narragansett, where the ferry to Block Island departs. The pleasant ferry cruise will deliver you just a few minute's drive from **Clay Head Preserve**, an easy walk around the beach and the imposing clay cliffs of Block Island.

BEST BY SEASON

Fall

MAINE

- **South Bubble and Jordan Pond:** The forests around Jordan Pond are shimmering with gold once October rolls around, and the rocky peak of South Bubble makes for a fine overlook (page 40).
- **Mount Kineo:** Jutting up from an island on Moosehead Lake, this isolated peak features sheer cliffs and a fire tower with stunning views of the autumnal Maine frontier woods (page 76).
- **Caribou Mountain:** The 360-degree vista from the top of Caribou Mountain is already one of the finest in New England, but when you add a palette of fall colors, it's unforgettable (page 134).

NEW HAMPSHIRE

- **Zealand Valley and Thoreau Falls:** A long stroll through Zealand Valley's vast beaver marshes during fall foliage season is pure New England ecstasy (page 184).
- **Mount Lafayette and Franconia Ridge:** Summiting Mount Lafayette is an uncommonly scenic ascent, with spectacular views of Franconia Notch—and the ridge traverse ups the ante (page 174).
- **Table Rock:** The pinnacle of this dizzyingly sheer 700-foot-tall rock formation is the perfect crow's nest from which to admire the autumn forests of the remote, quiet Dixville Notch (page 223).

VERMONT

- **Bald Mountain:** Vermont views do not get any better than those during peak foliage season from this impressive fire tower overlooking Lake Willoughby and the Northeast Kingdom (page 391).
- **Mount Horrid:** Survey a sea of fall color from the Great Cliff of Mount Horrid, an easily reached ledge overlooking a marsh and a series of rolling hills (page 300).

MASSACHUSETTS

- **Mount Greylock:** Stony Ledge, a secluded vista overlooking the Greylock Range, pops with fall color in mid- to late October (page 460).
- **Bartholomew's Cobble:** The expansive view from Hulburt's Hill looks out on the Berkshires draped in fall color—all for the price of just a short, leisurely hike (page 471).

CONNECTICUT

- **Undermountain Trail:** The highest peak in Connecticut, Bear Mountain is the best place to watch the leaves turn with views across three states (page 522).
- **Sleeping Giant State Park:** This commanding mountain in central Connecticut reveals vista after vista as hikers move along its colorful ridgeline (page 537).

A WINTER HIKE

Winter

MAINE

- **Androscoggin Riverlands:** When the woods of Androscoggin Riverlands get nice and snowy, winter hikers, cross-country skiers, and even snowmobilers head here to play (page 152).
- **Mount Agamenticus:** This prominent peak at the southern tip of Maine (complete with ruins of an old ski resort) draws visitors year-round thanks to its views and easy trails (page 104).

NEW HAMPSHIRE

- **Arethusa Falls:** New Hampshire's tallest waterfall somehow manages to look even more dramatic when it freezes for the winter—tempting not only hikers, but ice climbers (page 190).
- **Sweet Trail:** Even when its flora and fauna are buried under snow, the Sweet Trail still makes for a charming woodland stroll to the Great Bay Estuary (page 285).
- **Mount Willard:** A family favorite for all seasons, Mount Willard offers a gentle ascent, a frozen cascade, and a view of Crawford Notch that would make Robert Redford weep (page 187).
- **Mount Chocorua:** Take the Champney Falls Trail to visit two gorgeous frozen waterfalls, and if you're feeling adventurous, keep climbing to summit the mighty Chocorua itself (page 199).

VERMONT

- **Abbey Pond Trail:** The easy elevation of this short trail makes it ideal for winter hiking, and the peaceful pond is an idyllic place to spot Vermont wildlife (page 303).
- **Stratton Pond Trail:** A long, scenic walk through flat forest culminates in great views of Stratton Pond, a secluded lake at the base of the mountain of the same name (page 340).

MASSACHUSETTS

- **Tully Trail:** Experience the magic of a frozen waterfall—or three—on this relatively flat trail along the Tully River and its nearby cascades (page 487).
- **Carriage Paths, Worlds End:** This wind-whipped park, designed by Frederick Law Olmsted, is particularly scenic in the snow, with frosty vistas of the Boston skyline (page 413).

CONNECTICUT

- **Housatonic River Walk:** A flat, gentle section of the Appalachian Trail along the Housatonic River is welcoming even in wintertime (page 506).

RHODE ISLAND

- **Tillinghast Pond:** Stroll the banks of this quiet Nature Conservancy pond with terrain that alternates between quiet forests and snowy fields (page 573).

Spring

MAINE

- **Fore River and Jewell Falls:** For a magical day in Portland, take a walk through the woods of Fore River Sanctuary, where you'll find wildflowers, great blue herons, and a waterfall (page 110).
- **Cadillac Mountain:** Beat the summer hordes and take the beautiful Gorge Path up Acadia's highest mountain for one of the most sweeping seacoast vistas anywhere in Maine (page 46).

NEW HAMPSHIRE

- **Purgatory Falls:** Spring comes sooner in southern New Hampshire, and the brookside hike to Purgatory Falls is the perfect way to kick off a new season of backcountry exploring (page 276).
- **Markus Wildlife Sanctuary:** New Hampshire's iconic loons get restless during the spring season, and you might catch one taking flight around this mossy lakeside sanctuary (page 252).
- **Giant Falls:** This aptly named yet little-known cascade just north of the White Mountains becomes a rip-roaring 80-foot monster during spring snowmelt (page 207).

VERMONT

- **Hamilton Falls:** Catch this spectacular waterfall at its finest, when spring rains and snowmelt amp up its flow (page 342).
- **Lye Brook Falls Trail:** Snowmelt from the peaks of the Green Mountains builds to a rush during spring at this 125-foot waterfall, one of the tallest in Vermont (page 337).

▲ PINK LADY SLIPPER

- **Sterling Pond:** Your boots will get muddy, your quads might quake, but the climb to Vermont's highest-elevation trout pond will leave you feeling serene and rejuvenated (page 361).

MASSACHUSETTS

- **High Ledges:** Featuring some of the finest displays of wildflowers—including rare orchids—to be found in New England, High Ledges is a must-see in spring (page 492).

CONNECTICUT

- **Rand's View:** Hike to a meadow dotted with wildflowers and emerging greenery on this lovely destination along the Appalachian Trail (page 511).
- **Devil's Hopyard:** A shroud of misty spring rain adds to the mystique of this lore-steeped trail that includes a waterfall, vista, and strange rock formations (page 534).

RHODE ISLAND

- **Arcadia Management Area:** This lush path along the Falls River looks best in the spring colors of fresh greenery and blooming wildflowers (page 555).

mmer

AINE

- **Lane's Island Preserve:** This enchanting hike on the island of Vinalhaven—replete with wildflowers and pebble beaches—might make you reconsider your return to the mainland (page 119).
- **Tumbledown Mountain:** Few things are more romantic than catching a golden summer sunset on the banks of Tumbledown Mountain's summit pond or its rolling granite ridge (page 156).
- **Mount Katahdin:** The window for summiting New England's toughest mountain is a short one—August and September are your best bets for glorious weather and panoramic views (page 94).

NEW HAMPSHIRE

- **Mount Washington via Tuckerman Ravine:** Scaling the steep and waterfall-festooned bowl of Tuckerman Ravine surpasses the thrill of summiting New England's highest peak (page 203).
- **The Flume:** This 800-foot-deep natural gorge is the perfect misty environment in which to cool off during the height of summer, as well as take in some spectacular waterfalls and mossy cliffs (page 178).

VERMONT

- **Falls of Lana:** Enjoy a vista of lush greenery from the Rattlesnake Cliffs before descending to the Falls of Lana, where you can find multiple swimming holes along the river (page 313).
- **Mount Pisgah:** Beat the heat after a hike up Mount Pisgah with a swim in the scenic, cliff-bound blue waters of Lake Willoughby (page 388).
- **Chazy Fossil Reef:** Searching for fossils along Vermont's Chazy Reef is best done when nearby fields of wildflowers are blooming and fireflies are dancing in the dusk (page 379).

MASSACHUSETTS

- **Great Island Trail:** Extraordinary sunsets and swimmable waters make this long beach-and-dune hike a great destination for summer (page 438).
- **Castle Neck, Crane Beach:** Crane is one of the most scenic beaches in the Northeast, and while the dunes are quite hot in summertime, a jump in the ocean is never far away (page 419)!

RHODE ISLAND

- **Clay Head Preserve:** Summer on Block Island is made even more magical with a hike along this scenic clay bluff, which hikers can follow with a dip in the Atlantic Ocean (page 578).
- **Sachuest Point:** Marvel at the beach rose in bloom on this short hike around the tip of the Rhode Island coast, then spend the rest of the day at one of many nearby beaches (page 567).

BEST VISTAS

MAINE

- **Mount Katahdin:** The Penobscot Native Americans were right—when it comes to panoramic views of verdant wilderness and crystal-blue lakes, the craggy and titanic Katahdin is truly "the Greatest Mountain" in Maine, and arguably New England (page 94).
- **Caribou Mountain:** The bumpy granite summit of Caribou might sound modest at only 2,850 feet above sea level, but hikers who make the climb are amply rewarded with views of the Carter, Mahoosuc, and Presidential Ranges and the Cold River valley (page 134).

NEW HAMPSHIRE

- **Mount Carrigain:** The view from Carrigain's observation tower is worth the trek into the vast Pemigewasset Wilderness—you'll begin your hike in the depths of those woods and finish with a 360-degree vista of the "Pemi" and the neighboring Presidential and Sandwich Ranges (page 193).
- **Mount Washington:** On a clear day, you can glimpse the Atlantic Ocean from the notoriously windy pinnacle of New England's tallest mountain—or you might find yourself looking down at a sea of thick white clouds flowing past the summit cone (page 203).

VERMONT

- **Mount Horrid:** "The Great Cliff" is a short hike, and not particularly high, but it overlooks the wide valley of Brandon Gap where the Green Mountains roll out toward Lake Champlain (page 300).
- **Mount Abraham:** After climbing endless granite slabs towards the 4,017-foot summit of Mount Abraham, hikers are rewarded with 360-degree views from the Champlain Valley to the Adirondack Mountains (page 297).
- **Bald Mountain:** One of the finest fire tower views in New England, this less-traveled trail in Willoughby State Park features an expansive vista of the Northeast Kingdom (page 391).
- **White Rocks Cliffs:** This drop-off overlooking glacial ice beds is a unique mountainside vista named for its alabaster-hued Cheshire quartzite (page 330).
- **Mount Mansfield:** The tip-top of Vermont's tallest mountain offers sterling views of Stowe and the Northeast Kingdom to the east, and the exposed descent down Sunset Ridge is set against the backdrop of Lake Champlain and New York's distant Adirondacks (page 364).

▸ THE WHITE ROCKS CLIFFS

▲ THE SUMMIT OF CARIBOU MOUNTAIN

MASSACHUSETTS

- **Alander Mountain:** The vistas are nonstop as you wander across the long ridgeline of Alander Mountain, which boasts a strategic vantage point at the corners of Massachusetts, New York, and Connecticut (page 466).
- **Stony Ledge, Mount Greylock:** A lesser-known vista on the west slopes of Mount Greylock, this secluded overlook of the Greylock Range and the cavernous Hopper cirque rivals the mountain's summit (page 460).
- **Buck Hill, Blue Hills Reservation:** The iconic Boston skyline is the highlight of the Buck Hill vista, but jetliners cruising toward Logan Airport add an air of excitement (page 410).

CONNECTICUT

- **Rand's View:** Enjoy the spaciousness of an open meadow hemmed by the Berkshire Range on this gem of a hike along the Appalachian Trail (page 511).
- **Ragged Mountain:** Overlook the Hartford skyline and pristine forests surrounding crystal reservoirs from the red traprock outcroppings of the Metacomet Range (page 528).
- **Bear Mountain:** The tallest peak in Connecticut offers iconic views across three states on this last stop before the Appalachian Trail plunges north into Massachusetts (page 522).

RHODE ISLAND

- **Long and Ell Pond Trail:** This beloved vista overlooking a glassy pond from a stone bluff was featured in the Wes Anderson hit Moonrise Kingdom (page 562).
- **Nelson Pond Trail:** Admire marsh, beach, and the great Atlantic Ocean from the finger-like rock formations of the Nelson Bird Sanctuary (page 570).

BEST SPOTS FOR A SWIM

MAINE

- **Blueberry Ledges:** This little-known curiosity in Baxter State Park is a natural wonder where Katahdin Stream spills down a series of gently sloped granite ledges to form natural waterslides and potholes. Chances are you'll encounter thru-hikers at the ledges, cooling off and celebrating their soon-to-be-completed pilgrimage north (page 91).
- **Ocean Path:** In coastal Maine, most roads (and trails) lead to the Atlantic, but Acadia's famous Ocean Path begins at Sand Beach, where you can take an invigorating dip in one of the prettiest coves in the Pine Tree State before or after your oceanside hike (page 34).

NEW HAMPSHIRE

- **Bridal Veil Falls:** The ovular pool at the base of Bridal Veil Falls is vast and brimming with ice-cold White Mountain water from the falls themselves—and the Coppermine Trail literally delivers you to the rocky brink of this grade A swimming hole (page 171).
- **Arethusa Falls:** Take the Bemis Brook cutoff trail to Coliseum Falls, where you can follow the flow of the brook a short distance to arrive at Fawn Pool—an idyllic little swimming hole that's guaranteed to shock you back to life on a stupefyingly hot day (page 190).

VERMONT

- **Owl's Head Town Forest:** Though there isn't any swimming directly off the trails of Owl's Head, you'll want to follow up your hike with a plunge in the famous Dorset Quarry (page 332).
- **Hamilton Falls:** Swimming in the falls themselves is discouraged (too dangerous), but there is a great swimming hole right at the trailhead where hikers can cool off in the West River (page 342).
- **Falls of Lana:** These impressive falls form pools all the way down the mountainside where you can relax in the cold waters after a jaunt to Rattlesnake Cliffs (page 313).

MASSACHUSETTS

- **Crane Beach:** The sun-scorched trails of Castle Neck get hot during summertime, but hikers can cool off in the Atlantic post-hike while enjoying one of the finest stretches of sand in New England (page 419).
- **Great Island Trail:** Explore Jeremy Point at low tide, then revitalize your legs with a dip in Cape Cod Bay (page 438).
- **Walden Pond:** When in New England, do as the transcendentalists did and follow your stroll around Walden Pond with a dunk in a kettle-hole lake that stays warm well into fall (page 416).
- **Sanford Farm:** Enjoy the solitude of a quiet Nantucket beach by hiking the Ocean Walk trail through Sanford Farm (page 435).

▲ HAMILTON FALLS

CONNECTICUT

- **Mashamoquet Brook:** The pond at Mashamoquet Brook State Park is a nice spot for hikers (especially families with kids) to splash around in a scenic setting (page 543).
- **Steep Rock Preserve:** Keep an eye out for swimming holes as you hike along the Shepaug River—you may find your new favorite spot to cool off in Connecticut (page 516).

RHODE ISLAND

- **Clay Head and the Maze:** After wandering "The Maze" and capturing the incredible views from the top of Clay Head bluff, you can descend through the dunes to a pristine beach and watch the ferries come in while you float (page 578).
- **Walkabout Trail:** The best part about the Walkabout Trail is that it begins and ends at the beach of Bowdish Reservoir—a gorgeous body of sparkling blue water (page 565).

NEW ENGLAND ODDITIES

MAINE

- **Debsconeag Ice Caves:** Nestled deep in a preserve of pristine forests and glacial lakes, these caves retain a foundation of thick ice through the summer months—the entrance resembles a hole in the forest floor, and the ice itself serves as natural air-conditioning when the outside temperatures become punishing (page 88).
- **Perpendicular and Razorback Trails:** This off-the-beaten-path loop hike begins with a steep climb up hundreds of carved stone stairs to the top of Mansell Mountain, and concludes with a wild descent down an exposed granite ridge where the natural contours resemble the spiky back of a dinosaur (page 50).

NEW HAMPSHIRE

- **Madame Sherri's Forest:** These lush woods in southwestern New Hampshire hide the ruins of a castle once owned by a hedonist fashion designer named Madame Antoinette Sherri—who, legend has it, would drive into town wearing nothing but her fur coat (page 279).
- **Devil's Den Mountain:** This unshakably creepy peak near Merrymeeting Lake not only looks like the kind of stone pyre on which a human sacrifice might be conducted, but it also contains a hidden slit cave that's rumored to be haunted by monstrous presence (page 246).

VERMONT

- **Mount Abraham:** Follow the Long Trail just past the summit of Mount Abraham to where a small side path leads to the wreckage of a casualty-free 1973 plane crash (page 297).
- **Peacham Bog:** Visit this unique boardwalk to peek inside a pitcher plant and see what insects and other creatures these carnivorous plants have captured to digest with liquid enzymes (page 398).
- **Chazy Fossil Reef:** Far north on the Champlain Islands, you'll encounter exposed sections of an ancient fossilized reef that contains the fragmented remnants of little gastropods and cephalopods (page 379).

▸ THE CRUMBLING STAIRS IN MADAME SHERRI'S FOREST

▲ HERMIT'S CASTLE

MASSACHUSETTS

- **Hermit's Castle:** This rock formation along the New England Trail was home to the Scottish hermit John Smith for 32 years (page 489).
- **Bartholomew's Cobble:** Among the many wonders of the Bartholomew's Cobble trail system is an enormous cottonwood tree, widely believed to be the largest in Massachusetts (page 471).

CONNECTICUT

- **Mine Hill Preserve:** This unique trail takes visitors past relics of the mining industry, including several grated air shafts that have been repurposed as bat hibernacula (page 520).
- **Mashamoquet Brook:** Visit the site where the last wolf in Connecticut lived and died. The wolf was shot for preying upon livestock by Israel Putnam, who would later become a major general in the Revolutionary War (page 543).

RHODE ISLAND

- **Ninigret National Wildlife Refuge:** Before this refuge became one of the top bird-watching spots in Rhode Island, it was the Naval Auxiliary Air Station Charlestown, where pilots, including former U.S. president George H. W. Bush, trained for World War II. Runways are still visible today (page 560).
- **Walkabout Trail:** This trail has one of the strangest origin stories in New England. It was built by a group of Australian sailors who were stranded in Rhode Island while awaiting the arrival of their new destroyer. In just six weeks the men completed this 8-mile trail and named it for the Australian tradition of the walkabout (page 565).

BREW HIKES

MAINE

- **Gulf Hagas:** Once you're done sizing up the waterfalls and slate cliffs in "the Grand Canyon of Maine," drive east through the KI-Jo Mary Forest (past the Katahdin Iron Works ruins) to nearby Milo and reflect with a liberally hopped IPA or jet-black stout at Maine craft beer favorite **Bissell Brothers** (157 Elm St., Milo, 207/808-8258, http://bissellbrothers.com, 3pm-8pm Fri., noon-6pm Sat, noon-5pm Sun.).
- **Cadillac Mountain:** The coastal vista from Cadillac's summit seems to stretch on forever, but it's only a short drive to **Atlantic Brewing Company** (15 Knox Rd., Bar Harbor, 207/288-2337, http://atlanticbrewing.com, late-May-mid-October, hours vary seasonally), which not only offers a mouthwatering roster of seasonal beers but also some of the finest barbecue in northern Maine.

NEW HAMPSHIRE

- **Sweet Trail:** After a day of ambling through mixed woods and past reptile-rich vernal pools, keep the biodiversity coming by driving over to **Earth Eagle Brewings** (175 High St., Portsmouth, 603/502-2244, http://eartheaglebrewings.com, 11:30am-10pm Sun.-Thurs., 11:30am-midnight Fri.-Sat.) for a beer or *gruit* made with locally foraged ingredients—and then treat yourself to a meal from the inventive brewpub menu.
- **Mount Chocorua:** Scrambling up the steep summit cone of Chocorua is a rush, and once you've finished the hike, you'll want to relax—so head straight to nearby **Tuckerman Brewing** (66 Hobbs St., Conway, 603/447-5400, http://tuckermanbrewing.com, noon-6pm Sun.-Thurs., noon-7pm Fri.-Sat.) for a flight of German-style brews and special-batch beers that you won't find in stores.

VERMONT

- **Killington Peak:** A trip up the long, tough Bucklin Trail to 4,236-foot Killington Peak is best followed with a visit to **Long Trail Brewing Company** (5520 US-4, Bridgewater Corners, 802/672-5011, http://longtrail.com, 10am-7pm daily, hours vary seasonally), where handcrafted beers are paired with a seasonal comfort-food menu.
- **Falls of Lana:** A perfect day in Middlebury? Hike and swim at Rattlesnake Cliffs and the Falls of Lana before stopping into **Otter Creek Brewing** (793 Exchange St., Middlebury, 802/388-0727, http://ottercreekbrewing.com, 11am-6pm Sat.-Thurs., 11am-7pm Fri.) for hoppy beers and a tasty pub menu.
- **Mount Ascutney:** Climb to the viewing platform of Mount Ascutney for views stretching as far at the White Mountains, and then stop into Windsor's **Harpoon Brewery** (336 Ruth Carney Dr., Windsor, 802/674-5491, http://harpoonbrewery.com, 10am-6pm Sun.-Wed., 10am-9pm Thurs.-Sat.) for a burger and a pint in the beer garden.

- **Sterling Pond:** Sterling Pond might be one of the most meditative places in Vermont, but there's nothing understated about the deliciously hoppy ales down the road at **The Alchemist** (100 Cottage Club Rd., Stowe, 802/882-8165, http://alchemistbeer.com, 11am-7pm Mon.-Sat., 10am-4pm Sun.)—especially Heady Topper, a double IPA that is one of the most coveted craft beers in America.

MASSACHUSETTS

- **Mount Tom:** Survey the Pioneer Valley from the peak of Mount Tom, then dip into Easthampton where you can admire views of the mountain with a flight from the tasting room at **Fort Hill Brewery** (30 Fort Hill Rd., Easthampton, 413/203-5754, http://forthillbrewery.com, 4pm-7pm Thurs.-Fri., 2pm-8pm Sat., 2pm-6pm Sun.).
- **Sanford Farm:** Fun on Nantucket doesn't get any better than a walk in the fresh ocean air at Sanford Farm followed by music, brews, and food truck offerings in the lively outdoor courtyard at **Cisco Brewers** (5 Bartlett Farm Rd., Nantucket, 508/325-5929, http://ciscobrewers.com, noon-7pm Mon.-Thurs., 11am-7pm Fri.-Sat., noon-6pm Sun.).

CONNECTICUT

- **People's State Forest:** Follow a hike in Peoples State Forest with a visit to **Brewery Legitimus** (283 Main St. b3, New Hartford, 860/238-7870, http://brewerylegitimus.com, 4pm-9pm Wed.-Thurs., 3pm-10pm Fri., noon-10pm Sat., noon-7pm Sun.), a craft brewery featuring interesting ales, food trucks, and a variety of live music and other events.
- **Housatonic River Walk:** After a day on the Appalachian Trail, unwind at **Kent Falls Brewing Company** (33 Camps Road, Kent, 860/398-9645, http://kentfallsbrewing.com, 2pm-7pm Thurs.-Fri., noon-5pm Sat.), a tasting room that holds events and offers tours of its brewery and farm.

RHODE ISLAND

- **Arcadia Management Area:** Explore this notable section of Rhode Island's North South Trail, then head over to **Tilted Barn Brewery** (1 Hemsley Place, Exeter, http://tiltedbarnbrewery.com, noon-8pm Fri., 1pm-4pm Sat.), featuring tours of a historic barn and fresh-off-the-farm brews.
- **Ninigret National Wildlife Refuge:** Work up a thirst wandering the trails of the Ninigret National Wildlife Refuge, and then stop into South Kingstown's **Whalers Brewing Company** (1174 Kingstown Rd., South Kingstown, 401/552-0002, http://whalers.com, 4pm-10pm Tues.-Thurs., 1pm-10pm Fri., 11:30am-10pm Sat., 11:30am-7pm Sun.) for some of Rhode Island's favorite beers.
- **Sachuest Point:** Ocean views, shorebirds, and windswept rocks make Sachuest Point a top hike in the Newport area, and there are plenty of great options nearby for a post-hike drink. **Taproot Brewing** (909 E. Main Rd., Middletown, 401/848-5161, http://newportvineyards.com/taproot-brewing, hours vary seasonally) in Middletown is a favorite.

▲ VIEW FROM CADILLAC MOUNTAIN IN AUTUMN

MAINE

ACADIA

On a little slice of the Maine coast called Mount Desert Island, a secluded universe of exposed peaks, serene beaches, and unrivaled biodiversity welcomes millions each year. Acadia National Park is one of the oldest and most beloved parks in America. One look at a map illustrates why: The waterlocked wonder contains more than 120 miles of trails for every taste. You can wander around lagoons and fjords, search the woods for more than 40 species of mammalian wildlife, or scale cliffs steep enough to make you feel like a sponsored athlete. To top it off, the villages of Bar Harbor and Southwest Harbor are your ticket for freshly caught sustenance including lobsters, bluefish, and good old Maine steamers.

▲ the wooded cove of Ship Harbor

▲ the view near the summit of Cadillac Mountain

◂ THE SILVERY TUMULT OF HADLOCK FALLS

1 Ocean Path

DISTANCE: 3.6 miles round-trip
DURATION: 1.5 hours
EFFORT: Easy

2 The Beehive

DISTANCE: 1.6 miles round-trip
DURATION: 1 hour
EFFORT: Moderate

3 South Bubble and Jordan Pond

DISTANCE: 3.6 miles round-trip
DURATION: 3 hours
EFFORT: Moderate

4 Hadlock Falls

DISTANCE: 2 miles round-trip
DURATION: 1 hour
EFFORT: Easy

5 Cadillac Mountain

DISTANCE: 4.6 miles round-trip
DURATION: 2.5 hours
EFFORT: Strenuous

6 Perpendicular and Razorback Trails

DISTANCE: 2.6 miles round-trip
DURATION: 2.5 hours
EFFORT: Moderate

7 Ship Harbor

DISTANCE: 1.4 miles round-trip
DURATION: 45 minutes
EFFORT: Easy

8 Penobscot Mountain

DISTANCE: 3.3 miles round-trip
DURATION: 2 hours
EFFORT: Strenuous

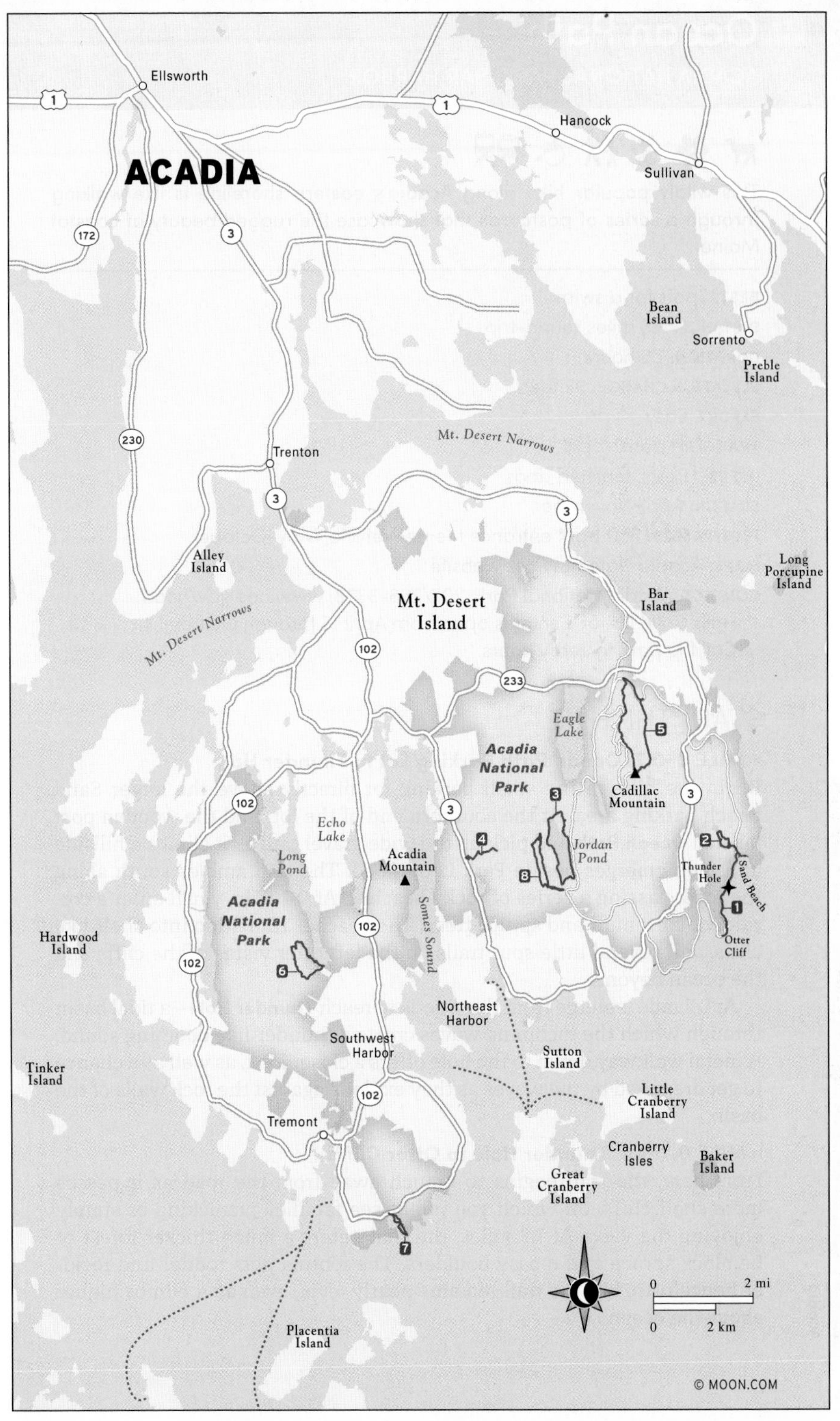
ACADIA
Ellsworth
Hancock
Sullivan
Bean Island
Sorrento
Preble Island
Mt. Desert Narrows
Trenton
Alley Island
Long Porcupine Island
Bar Island
Mt. Desert Island
Mt. Desert Narrows
Eagle Lake
Acadia National Park
Cadillac Mountain
Echo Lake
Long Pond
Acadia Mountain
Jordan Pond
Thunder Hole
Sand Beach
Otter Cliff
Somes Sound
Acadia National Park
Hardwood Island
Northeast Harbor
Southwest Harbor
Sutton Island
Tinker Island
Little Cranberry Island
Tremont
Cranberry Isles
Baker Island
Great Cranberry Island
Placentia Island
0 2 mi
0 2 km
© MOON.COM

1 Ocean Path

ACADIA NATIONAL PARK, BAR HARBOR

This wildly popular hike along Acadia's eastern shoreline is like walking through a series of postcards that showcase the rugged beauty of coastal Maine.

BEST: Spots for a swim

DISTANCE: 3.6 miles round-trip

DURATION: 1.5 hours

ELEVATION CHANGE: 92 feet

EFFORT: Easy

TRAIL: Dirt path, rocks

USERS: Hikers, leashed dogs

SEASON: April-November

FEES/PASSES: $30 park entrance fee per vehicle, May-October

MAPS: Acadia National Park website

CONTACT: Acadia National Park, 207/288-3338, www.nps.gov/acad. Hulls Cove Visitor Center is open from April 15 through October 31. Call the park to verify hours.

START THE HIKE

▸ MILE 0-0.7: Ocean Path Parking Lot to Thunder Hole

Begin the hike in the small parking lot directly above the larger Sand Beach parking area. At the southern end of the lot, find the wooden post labeled **Ocean Path** and pick up the wide gravel trail as it climbs a hillside and then emerges beside Park Loop Road. The trail ambles south along the road, passing a series of rocky beaches. At 0.4 mile, you'll enter a corridor of balsam fir and spruce trees. The beaches transition into shelf-like cliffs, and several little spur trails on the left offer vistas of the cliffs and the ocean beyond.

At 0.7 mile, emerge from the woods to reach **Thunder Hole**—a tidal basin through which the incoming waves create a thunder-like booming sound. A metal walkway down to the hole offers a closer look, as well as a chance to get drenched by the waves as they explode against the rock walls of the basin.

▸ MILE 0.7-1.4: Thunder Hole to Otter Cliffs

From here, the trail begins to branch away from the road as it passes more shelf cliffs, on which you might see families picnicking or simply enjoying the view. At 1.2 miles, the trail enters a much thicker forest of hemlock-spruce and mossy boulders. The footing gets rootier and rockier henceforth, but the trail remains nearly level, even as it climbs higher above the ocean.

▲ THE OCEAN PATH

At 1.4 miles, the trees open up once again as the trail reaches **Otter Cliffs**—a destination for rock climbers, who can often be seen scaling the craggy rock faces here.

▸ MILE 1.4–3.6: Otter Cliffs to Ocean View Vista

Climb a set of stone stairs to reach an observation walkway that hugs Park Loop Road, walk to the end of the walkway, and descend another staircase to return to the woods. At 1.6 miles, right after descending this staircase, take a moment to look behind you for an incredible view of the Beehive and Champlain Mountain framed by the sea and the sky. Continue as the trail curves southwest through a thick grove of ferns before it delivers you to a final vista that overlooks the ocean at 1.8 miles. Return the way you came.

DIRECTIONS

From Bangor, drive southeast on US-1A E for 25 miles. After crossing the bridge onto Mount Desert Island, turn left at the fork onto ME-3 E. Continue driving along ME-3 E for about 10 miles into the town of Bar Harbor, and then drive straight onto Kebo Street. Take Kebo Street south until its terminus and then veer left onto Park Loop Road. Drive along this road to the Sand Beach entrance station and then continue south to the sign for Sand Beach parking, which will be on your left. The entrance to the larger lot comes first and the turnoff for the small lot (from which the Ocean Path begins) comes immediately after. If both lots are full, roadside parking on the right side is allowed.

GPS COORDINATES: 45°53'11.7"N 68°59'59.1"W, 45.886588, -68.999748

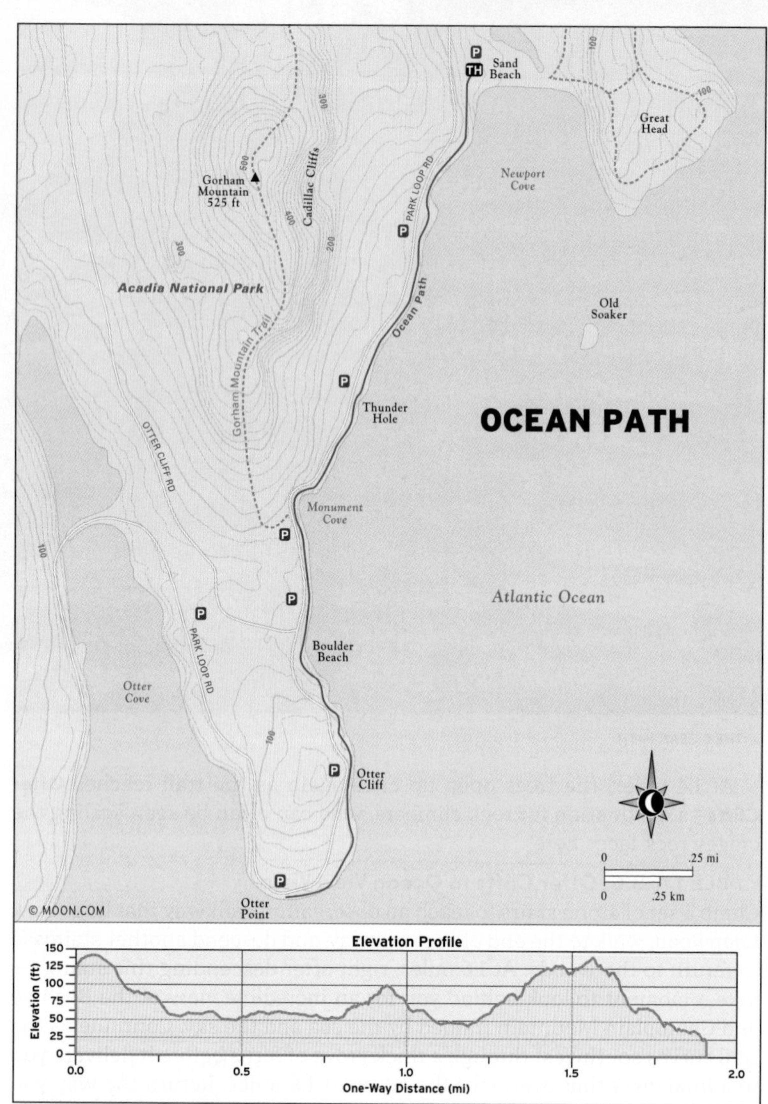

BEST NEARBY BITES

Replicate the serene beauty of your hike with locally sourced and French-inspired cuisine such as duck confit and braised scallops at **Mache Bistro** (321 Main St., Bar Harbor, 207/288-0447, www.mache-bistro.com, 5:30pm-10pm Tues.-Sat.). Or try any of the wildly creative extra-butterfat ice cream flavors at **Mount Desert Island Ice Cream** (7 Firefly Ln., Bar Harbor, 207/801-4007, www.mdiic.com, summer 10am-11pm daily, fall 11am-10pm daily).

2 The Beehive

ACADIA NATIONAL PARK, BAR HARBOR

The hike up Beehive isn't for the faint of heart, but it offers pretty views and a glacial lake to anyone up for the challenge.

DISTANCE: 1.6 miles round-trip

DURATION: 1 hour

ELEVATION CHANGE: 505 feet

EFFORT: Moderate

TRAIL: Dirt path, rocks, iron rungs, wooden bog bridges

USERS: Hikers

SEASON: June-October

FEES/PASSES: $30 park entrance fee per vehicle, May-October

MAPS: Acadia National Park website

CONTACT: Acadia National Park, 207/288-3338, www.nps.gov/acad. Hulls Cove Visitor Center is open from April 15 through October 31. Call the park to verify hours.

The Beehive might be the most perfectly named peak in Acadia—not only is this handsome little mountain shaped like a hive, but a closer look at its exposed cliffs on a summer day reveals intrepid hikers scaling the mountain like little worker bees. It's another Acadia hike with lots of iron ladder rungs and handrails to aid your perilous journey. If it's wet, or if you have a fear of heights, skip this hike. The ledges and sheer drops make this hike scary for anyone, at any time of year—people have fallen and been injured and killed. Be sure to watch your footing and have both hands free for the duration of the hike.

START THE HIKE

▸ MILE 0-0.2: Trailhead at Park Loop Road to Beehive Trail

Begin the hike at the wooden post along Park Loop Road that reads Beehive Trail. (The post is on the side of the road just north of the entrances to the Sand Beach parking lots.) Hike west up a stone path through the woods before reaching a clearing with a signpost for the **Beehive Trail** at 0.2 mile.

▸ MILE 0.2-0.3: Beehive Trail to Split Ledge and Metal Grate

Make a right turn onto the trail, which heads north and immediately begins climbing the Beehive by way of narrow stone stairs. Enjoy the wide ledges and early views here. Follow blue blazes on the trees and cliffs as the trail becomes a series of switchbacks and arrives as a section of split ledge that's bridged with a metal grate at 0.3 mile. Crossing this narrow grate is one of the scarier parts of the hike.

▸ MILE 0.3-0.5: Split Ledge and Metal Grate to Beehive Summit

Continue past the grate and carefully make your way up the first round of iron rungs and handrails, noting the placement of your feet as you climb.

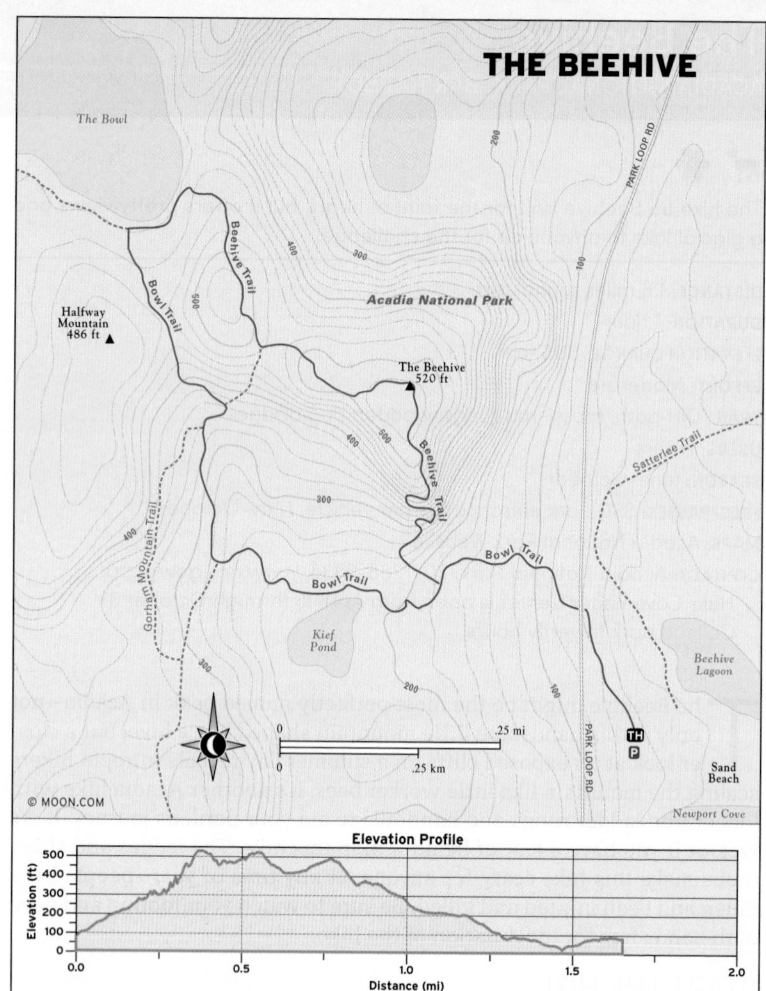

The smooth rungs can sometimes be slippery due to being handled by lots of hikers who've applied sunscreen recently. Squeeze behind some balsam firs and watch your footing as the trail becomes a much higher and narrower ledge that overlooks **Sand Beach.** Take a minute to enjoy the vista and calm your nerves. Beyond this ledge, the trail ascends its most complex series of rungs. Scramble up this final series of ledges, and you'll be standing atop **The Beehive**'s rocky summit at 0.5 mile.

‣ MILE 0.5-0.7: Beehive Summit to The Bowl

Once you're ready for a soothing return journey, follow the blue blazes into a grove of balsams and down some rock stairs. At just under 0.6 mile, veer right onto the **Bowl Trail** and amble over a secondary summit before descending into the forest on a rocky dirt path. Listen for the lapping of water as you approach the shores of **The Bowl** at 0.7 mile, and enjoy the stillness of this little glacial lake as the trail continues along its eastern shoreline.

▲ THE BEEHIVE'S EXPOSED SOUTH FACE

MILE 0.7-1.1: The Bowl to Beehive Trail

After crossing a swampy area on some bog bridges, make a left at the Champlain Mountain Trail junction to stay on the Bowl Trail and descend a few gentle log stairs into boreal forest. At 0.9 mile, the trail intersects the Beehive Trail again; turn right onto Beehive and make your way down more log stairs, keeping left to stay on Beehive at the next two junctions for Gorham Mountain.

MILE 1.1-1.6: Beehive Trail to Sand Beach

Enjoy a final view of the Beehive cliffs as the trees open up and the trail returns to the first Beehive Trail cutoff at 1.2 miles. Backtrack down the stone path to Park Loop Road to conclude the hike at 1.6 miles. For a cooldown, cross the road and descend the stairs to Sand Beach.

DIRECTIONS

From Bangor, drive southeast on US-1A E for 25 miles. After crossing the bridge onto Mount Desert Island, turn left at the fork onto ME-3 E. Continue driving along ME-3 E for about 10 miles into the town of Bar Harbor, and then drive straight onto Kebo Street. Take Kebo Street south until its terminus and then veer left onto Park Loop Road. Drive along this road to the Sand Beach park entrance station, and then continue south briefly until you see the sign for Sand Beach parking on your left. The entrance to the larger lot comes first and the turnoff for a smaller lot comes immediately after. If both lots are full, roadside parking on the right side of the road is allowed.

GPS COORDINATES: 44°19'53.6"N 68°11'07.1"W, 44.331559, -68.185297

BEST NEARBY BITES

Once you're done savoring flat ground again, head into Bar Harbor for a stacked wood-fired pizza at **Sweet Pea's Café** (854 ME-3, Bar Harbor, 207/801-9099, www.sweetpeascafemaine.com, 11am-9pm Wed.-Sun.). If you're in the mood for something more adventurous, enjoy tapas and flame-seared meats and veggies from the Argentinian-style wood-fired grill at **Parrilla** (318 Main St., Bar Harbor, 207/288-2822, www.havanamaine.com, 4:30pm-9pm Tues.-Sat.).

3 South Bubble and Jordan Pond

ACADIA NATIONAL PARK, BAR HARBOR

This fun hike along Jordan Pond visits the summit of South Bubble, offering vistas, rock climbing, and bog bridges along the way.

BEST: Fall hikes
DISTANCE: 3.6 miles round-trip
DURATION: 3 hours
ELEVATION CHANGE: 498 feet
EFFORT: Moderate
TRAIL: Dirt path, rocks, wooden bog bridges, water crossings on stones
USERS: Hikers
SEASON: June-October
FEES/PASSES: $30 park entrance fee per vehicle, May-October
MAPS: Acadia National Park website
CONTACT: Acadia National Park, 207/288-3338, www.nps.gov/acad. Hulls Cove Visitor Center is open from April 15 through October 31. Call the park to verify hours.

START THE HIKE

▸ MILE 0-0.3: Jordan Pond House to Carriage Road

Begin the hike at the end of the observation lawn at Jordan Pond House, on the southern shore of the pond. Looking straight out to the pond and the Bubbles, you'll be standing on a groomed gravel path; this is the **Jordan Pond Trail.** Head right and stroll through some wildflowers and into the cedar and spruce woods on the pond's eastern shore. Continue north along the shoreline on this gentle section, passing several boat launches and some little rocky beaches. As you circle a larger cove, the forest transitions to hemlocks and passes a cutoff for the Carriage Road at 0.3 mile.

▸ MILE 0.3-1.3: Carriage Road to Bubbles Trail

Keep left here and check out the views of the cliffs on neighboring Penobscot Mountain on the western side of the pond. Follow signs for Bubble Rock as the smooth path veers close to the water—close enough to spot trout swimming beneath the surface on a sunny day! One mile in, you'll cross a wooden footbridge over a creek before approaching the foot of South Bubble. Cross a second bridge to reach a junction for the **Bubbles Trail** at 1.3 miles; pick up the trail and warm up your quads with a moderately graded ascent up rock stairs and through the woods. Blue blazes mark the path.

▸ MILE 1.3-1.5: Bubbles Trail to South Bubble

As the stairs become rougher and steeper, the trail emerges from the trees and slabs dramatically up the southern face of the mountain. One trickier section requires passing through a tight crevice of rock. A few iron rungs are placed here and there to help hikers bypass the steeper parts of the climb, which soon levels off and reaches the globular rocky summit of

▲ THE BULBOUS PROFILE OF THE BUBBLES AT THE NORTH END OF JORDAN POND

South Bubble at 1.5 miles. There are views of Jordan Pond to the south and Pemetic Mountain to the east.

▸ MILE 1.5–1.6: South Bubble to Summit Rock
Before continuing onward, scramble down the rock slopes on the eastern edge of the summit to find the mountain's famous glacial erratic—a house-sized rock that's precariously placed on the edge of a cliff!

▸ MILE 1.6–2.1: Summit Rock to Bubbles Divide Trail
Hike north past the summit proper and dip back into the woods and down some log stairs to reach the wooded col (gap) between the two Bubbles. Turn left at the Bubbles Divide junction at 1.8 miles to take Bubbles Divide Trail and descend a steep and winding rock staircase that becomes more like a boulder field as you approach the waters of Jordan Pond again.

▸ MILE 2.1–2.3: Bubbles Divide Trail to Jordan Pond Trail
At 2.1 miles, make a right to link back up with the **Jordan Pond Trail.** Pass a large pebbly beach and cross a larger wooden footbridge to reach the Deer Brook junction at 2.2 miles. Veer left to stay on Jordan Pond and return along the pond's more densely forested western shores.

▸ MILE 2.3–3.6: Jordan Pond Trail to Jordan Pond House
The woods on this side of the pond are a lot rockier and darker. The trail stays near the water but makes use of the rougher landscape by rock-hopping across watery sections and weaving between some massive boulders. The grand finale—a long, meandering boardwalk of wooden bog bridges—begins at roughly 2.7 miles. These bridges, many of which are new, traverse a mossy bog-like area of forest. Some of them are a couple of feet above the ground or water, so be sure to watch your balance. After the last bridge, the trail reaches the Carriage Road at 3.6 miles. Merge onto the road and take an immediate left onto the Jordan Pond Path, which delivers you back to the Pond House after just a few yards.

DIRECTIONS
From Bangor, drive southeast on US-1A E for 25 miles. After crossing the bridge onto Mount Desert Island, turn right at the fork and continue south

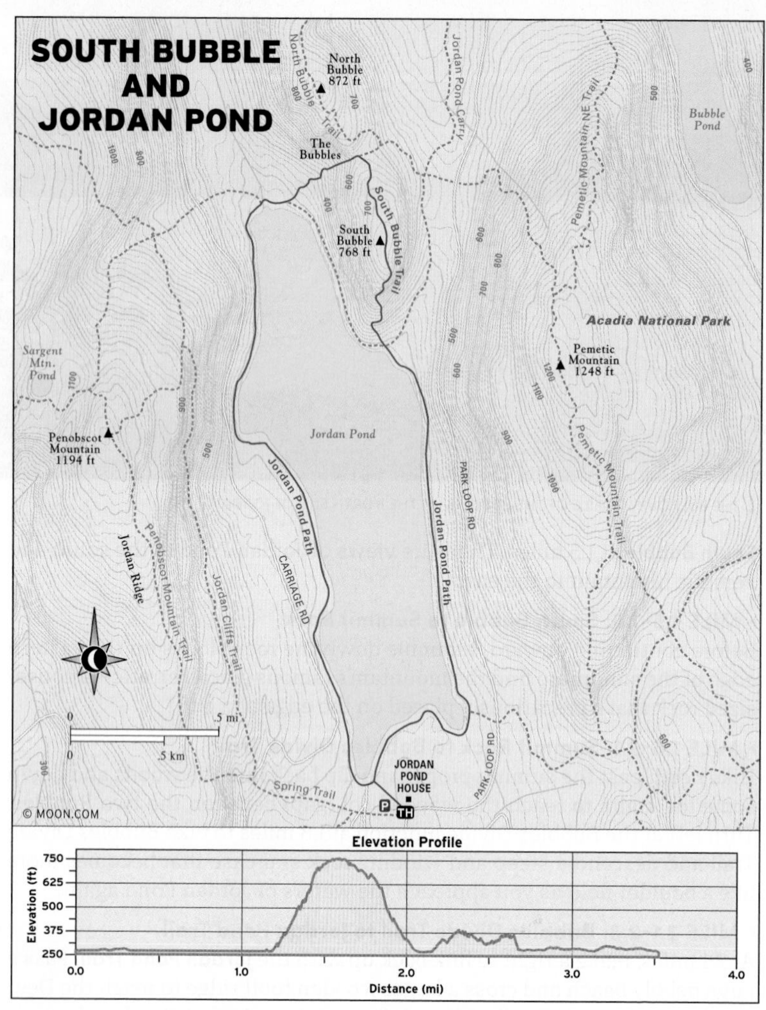

along ME-102 S for about 4 miles before swinging left onto ME-3 W. Drive southwest for another 5 miles, make a left turn to stay on ME-3 W, and then take a left at the Stanley Brook entrance for Acadia. Take this road to its terminus, make a slight left onto Park Loop Road, and drive north until you see the Jordan Pond House entrance on your left. If the lot here is full (which it usually is), continue north past the Pond House and turn left to access the overflow parking areas.

GPS COORDINATES: 44°19'22.5"N 68°15'13.4"W, 44.322917, -68.253715

BEST NEARBY BITES

Make a reservation before your visit and enjoy a spread of freshly baked popovers with jam, tea, coffee, and more on the sunny pondside patio of the legendary **Jordan Pond House Restaurant** (2928 Park Loop Rd., Seal Harbor, 207/276-3316, www.jordanpondhouse.com, 11am-7pm daily).

4 Hadlock Falls

ACADIA NATIONAL PARK, BAR HARBOR

This quiet and meditative hike to Acadia's prettiest waterfall is a chance to stroll along the famous carriage roads that wind through the island's woods.

DISTANCE: 2 miles round-trip
DURATION: 1 hour
ELEVATION CHANGE: 146 feet
EFFORT: Easy
TRAIL: Gravel path, optional rock stairs
USERS: Hikers, cyclists, horseback riders
SEASON: May-October
FEES/PASSES: $30 park entrance fee per vehicle, May-October
MAPS: Acadia National Park website
CONTACT: Acadia National Park, 207/288-3338, www.nps.gov/acad. Hulls Cove Visitor Center is open from April 15 through October 31. Call the park to verify hours.

The modest yet beautiful 40-foot-tall Hadlock Falls is among the park's lesser-known attractions (most tourists are focused on the mountain and coastline). If you're on foot, the only way to reach it is to take a walk along Acadia's carriage roads as they meander along the southern flanks of Parkman Mountain and Sargent Mountain. The falls are most impressive during the late spring and early summer, when the flow is more dramatic.

START THE HIKE

▸ MILE 0-0.4: Parkman Mountain Parking Lot to Junction 12

Begin the hike at the north side of the Parkman Mountain parking lot by the large wooden information kiosk for the carriage road. Walk northeast past the sign and make an immediate right turn onto the carriage road. Briefly take the road south through a mixed forest of spruce and birch before turning left at the 13 junction. (Look for a little sign bearing the number 13 on a tree—all the carriage road junctions are marked numerically like this.)

The road sharply veers northwest and climbs a duet of switchbacks through mossy, boulder-strewn woods. As you pass several cliff faces, note how the baby cedar trees explode out of the rifts in the cliff. As the sound of auto traffic fades away, the road curves northeast and reaches **Junction 12** at 0.4 mile.

▸ MILE 0.4-0.9: Junction 12 to Arched Stone Bridge

Turn right here and continue hiking along the road as it meanders through a denser corridor of hemlock and balsams. The nearby ripple of a stream offers a teaser of things to come, and the cliffs start to tower over the road in places. Pass by the Bald Mountain Trail cutoff at 0.6 mile, then enjoy a

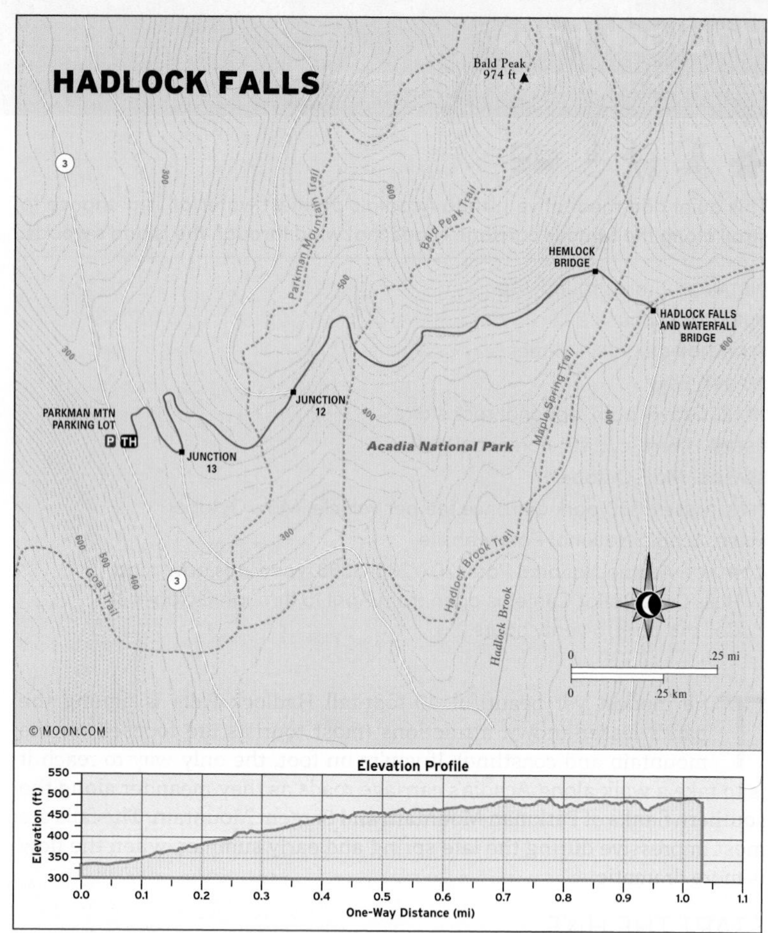

few glimpses of **Penobscot Mountain** ahead. Suddenly cedar and balsam fir become the dominant trees here. Also take a look along the side of the trail for wildflowers such as asters and goldenrods, especially in late summer or early fall. Continue hiking east for 0.3 mile.

▸ MILE 0.9–2.0: Arched Stone Bridge to Hadlock Falls

At 0.9 mile, the road crosses an arched stone bridge over a creek. Hike past the Maple Springs Trail before arriving at a second arched bridge overlooking **Hadlock Falls.** The bridge is outfitted with a little cleft from which visitors can view the falls, but a set of rock stairs on the left side of the road allows hikers to descend closer to the cascade—which is complemented by a little observation terrace that would be a hell of a place to propose to someone. The rocks at the foot of the falls can get very slick from the moss and water, but as long as you watch your footing, it doesn't take much effort to scramble close enough to feel the cooling mist of Hadlock Falls—the perfect finale to a heavenly hike. Return the way you came.

▲ STONE BRIDGE ALONG ACADIA'S CARRIAGE ROADS

DIRECTIONS

From Bangor, drive southeast on US-1A E for 25 miles. After crossing the bridge onto Mount Desert Island, turn right at the fork and continue south along ME-102 S for about 4 miles before swinging left onto ME-3 W. Drive southwest for another 4 miles and then take a sharp left at the sign for the Parkman Mountain parking lot.

GPS COORDINATES: 44°19'45.5"N 68°17'34.8"W, 44.329301, -68.292985

BEST NEARBY BITES

Just a few minutes north of the Hadlock Falls trailhead, you can dig into a Maine lobster or a heaping bucket of steamers while enjoying a pretty view of Somes Sound at **Abel's Lobster Pound** (13 Abels Ln., Mt. Desert, 207/276-5827, www.abelslobsterpound.com, noon-9pm daily).

5 Cadillac Mountain via the Gorge Path

ACADIA NATIONAL PARK, BAR HARBOR

This hidden gem of a mountain hike reaches the highest summit in Acadia by negotiating the rocky recesses of an atmospheric gorge complete with waterfalls.

BEST: Spring hikes, brew hikes

DISTANCE: 4.6 miles round-trip

DURATION: 2.5 hours

ELEVATION CHANGE: 1,240 feet

EFFORT: Strenuous

TRAIL: Dirt path, rocks, water crossings by rocks, wooden bog bridges

USERS: Hikers

SEASON: June-October

FEES/PASSES: $30 park entrance fee per vehicle, May-October

MAPS: Acadia National Park website

CONTACT: Acadia National Park, 207/288-3338, www.nps.gov/acad. Hulls Cove Visitor Center is open from April 15 through October 31. Call the park to verify hours.

No trip to Acadia is complete without the superlative climb up Cadillac Mountain, the tallest point on the island at 1,529 feet above sea level. Most visitors take the well-worn North Ridge Trail to the summit, but a better option is to take Gorge Path—a lesser-known, more sublime experience—to the top and then descend via North Ridge.

START THE HIKE

▸ MILE 0-0.4: Gorge Path Parking Lot to Hemlock Trail Junction

Begin the hike at the Gorge Path parking lot on the side of Park Loop Road. Walk toward the east side of the stone bridge, where a wooden trail post reads "Gorge Path." Descend some stone stairs to the bottom of the bridge, cross the stream, ascend another set of stairs, and then turn left onto the **Gorge Path.** The trail begins as a dirt path that burrows south through a thick and dark hemlock forest. Blue blazes mark the way. After passing into a sunnier stretch of white birch forest, the trail crosses creek beds and wooden bog bridges over muddy areas before reaching the Hemlock Trail junction at 0.4 mile.

▸ MILE 0.4-1.6: Hemlock Trail Junction to A. Murray Young Path

Keep right to stay on Gorge. Cross another pebbly creek bed as the trail becomes a smooth highway of well-placed stones. The grade of the surrounding forest steepens on both sides of the trail. Around 0.6 mile, the severe rock cliffs of the gorge itself begin to appear, as well as a pretty, silvery cascade. Continue hiking south along the rock pathway past several smaller cascades as the trail gradually steepens. One mile in, you'll pass a jumble of mossy boulders just before the trail makes a sharp, lung-busting

▲ CADILLAC MOUNTAIN

climb out of the gorge with the help of some winding rock staircases. The trail gets sunnier, with some views of Cadillac Mountain's upper slopes through the trees on the right. The trail grade becomes gentler as it arrives at the Dorr Mountain Trail junction at 1.3 miles. Turn right to continue on the Gorge Path as it curves toward the summit of Cadillac Mountain, and take another right to stay on Gorge at the junction with the A. Murray Young Path.

▸ MILE 1.6-1.8: A. Murray Young Path to Cadillac Mountain Summit

The trail emerges from the woods by climbing a series of boulders and ledges, revealing the first primo view of Bar Harbor as well as a stunning perspective of the rocky western face of Dorr Mountain. Look for blue blazes on the rocks as you tunnel through some spruce and pine trees before cresting a ridge from which the summit of Cadillac—dotted with the silhouettes of people and vehicles—comes into focus. Follow cairns along the exposed upper reaches of the mountain for another 0.2 mile, cross the paved summit observation footpath, and bound up some modest rocks to the summit proper of **Cadillac Mountain** at 1.8 miles. Most summit visitors tend to stick to the footpath, so you should have the true summit all to yourself for views, pictures, and meditation.

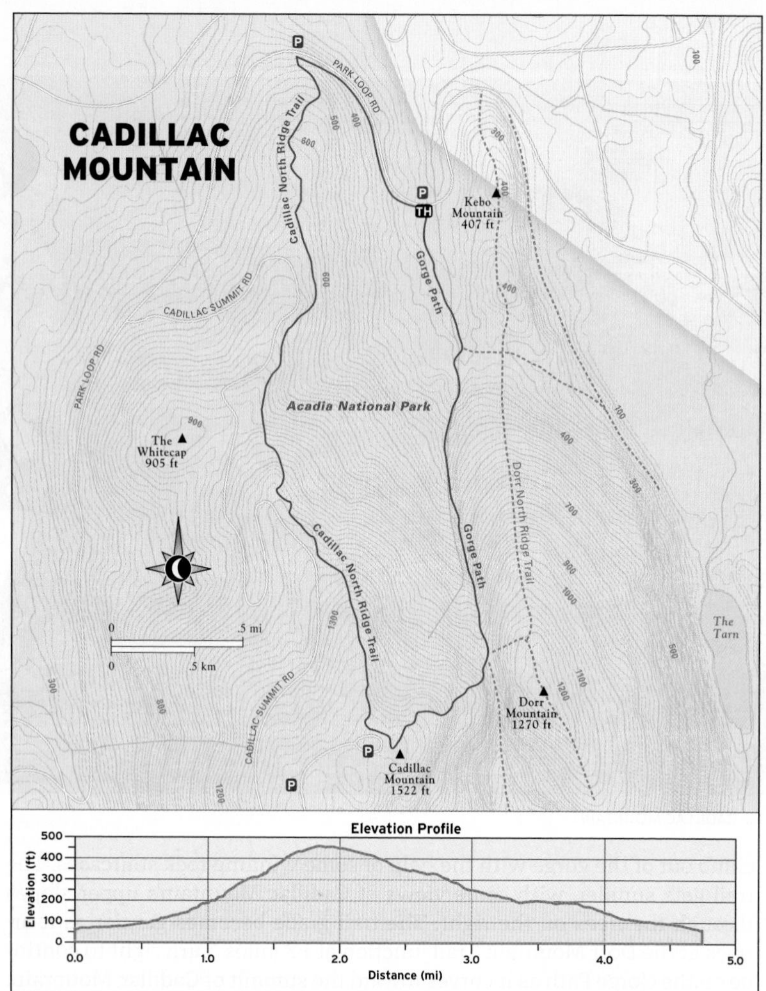

‣ MILE 1.8–3.9: Cadillac Mountain Summit to North Ridge Trailhead

To descend the mountain by way of the popular **North Ridge Trail,** walk north across the summit parking lot and find the trail sign on a wooden post. The trail descends gently across a long and exposed ridgeline that offers an incredible panorama of the north side of Mount Desert Island and, on a clear day, the verdant landscapes of mainland Maine. Most of the North Ridge Trail is pure rock, which can be slippery when wet. After traversing the exposed ridge for nearly 1 mile, the trail dips into the woods on rock stairs and passes several sunlit clearings before making a final exciting descent down a series of sloped rock faces to reach the North Ridge trailhead and parking area at 3.9 miles.

‣ MILE 3.9–4.6: North Ridge Trailhead to Gorge Path Parking Area

Take a right here and walk east along the **Park Loop Road** for another 0.7 mile until you reach the Gorge Path parking area at 4.6 miles.

▲ THE GORGE PATH

DIRECTIONS

From Bangor, drive southeast on US-1A E for 25 miles. After crossing the bridge onto Mount Desert Island, turn left at the fork onto ME-3 E. Continue driving along ME-3 E for about 9 miles and then turn right onto Paradise Hill Road. Follow this road for 3 miles as it climbs into the hills near Bar Harbor. As the road ends and merges with Park Loop Road, pull a sharp left and then a right onto Park Loop Road. Drive north and then southeast along Park Loop Road for roughly 1 mile until you see the sign for Gorge Path on your right.

GPS COORDINATES: 44°22'21.6"N 68°13'19.0"W, 44.372663, -68.221936

BEST NEARBY BREWS

Who said the South has a monopoly on barbecue? Cap off your hike with smoky pulled pork, chicken, ribs, and more at **Mainely Meat BBQ on Dreamwood Hill** (369 ME-3, Bar Harbor, 207/288-1100, www.atlanticbrewing.com/mainly-meat-bbq, 6:30am-9pm daily) and wash it down with a local microbrew from **Atlantic Brewing,** which owns and runs the Mainely Meat restaurant.

6 Perpendicular and Razorback Trails

ACADIA NATIONAL PARK, SOUTHWEST HARBOR

Climb hundreds of exquisitely carved stone stairs up the side of Mansell Mountain, then scramble down an exposed rock formation with nice views of Mount Desert Island's southwest woods.

BEST: New England oddities

DISTANCE: 2.6 miles round-trip

DURATION: 2.5 hours

ELEVATION CHANGE: 868 feet

EFFORT: Moderate

TRAIL: Dirt path, rocks, iron rungs, wooden bog bridges

USERS: Hikers, leashed dogs

SEASON: June-October

FEES/PASSES: $30 park entrance fee per vehicle, May-October

MAPS: Acadia National Park website

CONTACT: Acadia National Park, 207/288-3338, www.nps.gov/acad. Hulls Cove Visitor Center is open from April 15 through October 31. Call the park to verify hours.

START THE HIKE

▸ MILE 0-0.2: Spring Trail to Perpendicular Trail

Begin the hike in the parking lot beside the southern end of Long Pond. Walk west toward the pumphouse and look for a wooden post for **Long Pond Trail.** A gravel path along the shore of the pond takes you into the forest. Keep right at the first junction and continue along the pond until you reach the turnoff for **Perpendicular Trail** at 0.2 mile; turn left and start climbing a series of low, gentle rock stairs.

▸ MILE 0.2-0.3: Perpendicular Trail to Long Pond View

As you climb through a breezy grove of spruce woods, following blue blazes on the tree trunks, the stairs become switchbacks and then emerge from the trees into an expansive rockslide at around 0.3 mile. Check out the view of Long Pond below, then continue the ascent. From here, the staircases become steeper, narrower, and more winding.

▸ MILE 0.3-0.9: Long Pond View to Mansell Mountain Summit

As the stairs reenter the woods, climb a small set of iron rungs installed into a rock slab that separates two sections of stairs. Cedar trees overtake the spruce as the stairs get rougher and bypass some small boulders. At 0.5 mile, enter a mossier patch of forest and enjoy a brief break from the stairs as the trail hobbles along a sheer cliff face that's often trickling with water runoff. The trail becomes a level wooded ledge for a few hundred yards before transitioning back to stairs. Continue your climb and watch your footing as the trail becomes rougher and ascends several large rock formations flanked by birch trees. After passing a small ravine full of

▲ THE WINDING STAIRS OF THE PERPENDICULAR TRAIL

blowdowns, you'll climb a more open wooded slope from which you can glimpse the mountains and forest to the east.

At 0.9 mile, turn left at the junction and climb a few wet crags to reach the **Mansell Mountain** summit at 1 mile. Pause here, then press on—the greatest views are yet to come.

▸ MILE 0.9–1.5: Mansell Mountain Summit to Razorback Trail

Continue past the summit cairn and head into the woods, cross some bog bridges, and turn right at the junction at 1.2 miles. The trail descends a steep, eroded, and rooty section of trail. From the bottom of this doozy, ascend some rock slabs to reach the junction with the **Razorback Trail** at 1.5 miles.

▸ MILE 1.5–2.1: Razorback Trail to Gilley Trail

Turn left onto Razorback and hike (or scramble) your way down a series of sawtooth rock faces that can be quite slippery when wet. The outlooks along this section have photo-worthy views of Mount Desert Island's southwest woods.

Keep scrambling along rock faces for another quarter mile before heading back into the woods, where the trail makes a moderately graded descent down a combination of rock stairs and rooty path. At 2 miles, turn left at the **Gilley Trail** junction and follow Gilley to the roundabout at 2.1 miles.

▸ MILE 2.1–2.6: Gilley Trail to Long Pond Trail

Walk straight across the roundabout and pick up the **Cold Brook Trail,** which cruises through the woods past young balsams at a near-level grade. Cross a wooden footbridge over a creek to rejoin the Long Pond Trail at 2.5 miles. Turn right and backtrack to the parking lot to complete the loop at 2.6 miles.

DIRECTIONS

From Bangor, drive southeast on US-1A E for 25 miles. After crossing the bridge onto Mount Desert Island, turn right at the fork onto ME-102 S. Continue south along this road for 10 miles and then swing right onto Seal

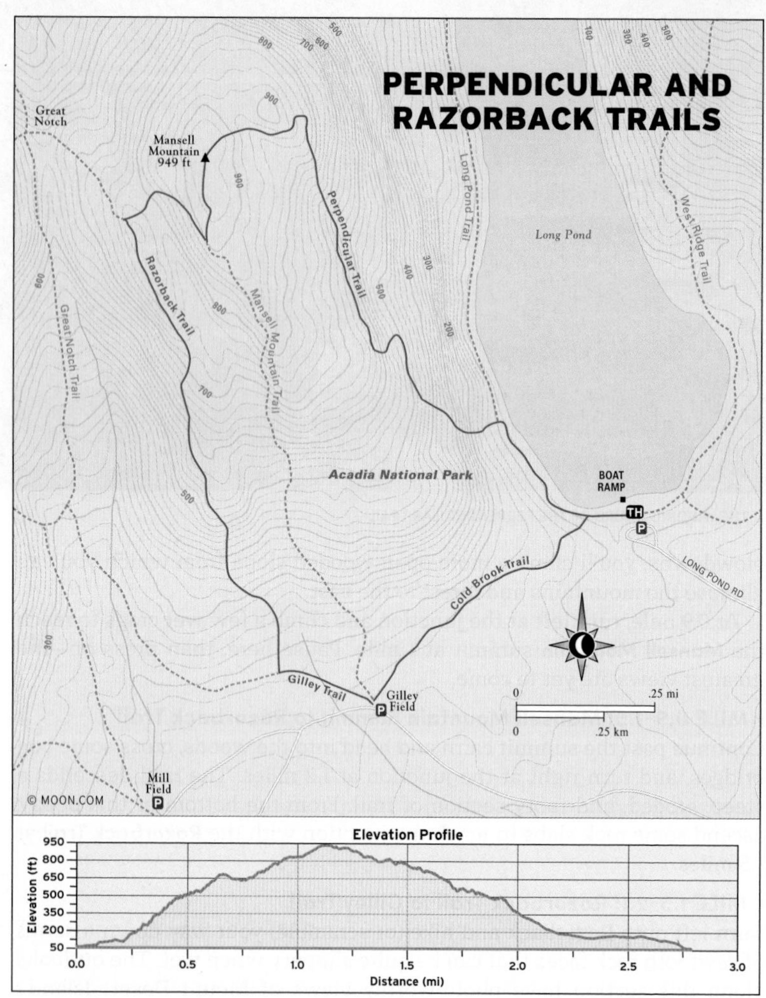

Cove Road. After roughly half a mile, turn right onto Long Pond Road and follow it to its terminus at the southern shore of Long Pond, where you'll see the visitors parking lot. If the lot is full, park alongside the road near the pond.

GPS COORDINATES: 44°18'00.8"N 68°21'01.0"W, 44.300208, -68.350266

BEST NEARBY BITES

Start the day by supporting a good cause and wolfing down some incredible popovers with maple walnut butter at Southwest Harbor's donation-based **Common Good Soup Kitchen** (19 Clark Point Rd., Southwest Harbor, 207/244-3007, www.commongoodsoupkitchen.org, 7:30am-11:30am Tues.-Sun.). Cap off your evening with creative Maine-sourced New American fare and an impressive wine list at **Red Sky** (14 Clark Point Rd., Southwest Harbor, 207/244-0476, www.redskyrestaurant.com, 5:30pm-8:30pm Thurs.-Sat.).

7 Ship Harbor

ACADIA NATIONAL PARK, SOUTHWEST HARBOR

This secluded ocean hike takes visitors through an otherworldly landscape of pink granite, mixed forests, and that classic Maine fog that regularly envelops the coast.

DISTANCE: 1.4 miles round-trip
DURATION: 45 minutes
ELEVATION CHANGE: 81 feet
EFFORT: Easy
TRAIL: Dirt path, rocks, wooden bog bridges
USERS: Hikers
SEASON: May-October
FEES/PASSES: $30 park entrance fee per vehicle, May-October
MAPS: Acadia National Park website
CONTACT: Acadia National Park, 207/288-3338, www.nps.gov/acad. Hulls Cove Visitor Center is open from April 15 through October 31. Call the park to verify hours.

START THE HIKE

▸ MILE 0-0.6: Ship Harbor Parking Lot to Mount Desert Island

Begin the hike in the **Ship Harbor** parking lot. Pick up the gravel path and briefly descend south into a meadow before veering slightly east and passing a trail information kiosk for Ship Harbor. Continue southeast through a tunnel of ferns, wildflowers, and mixed trees before the forest widens into rich green wonderland of massive spruce trees. Keep an eye out for deer, which are active here, and hike southeast to the fork at roughly 0.1 mile. It's all the same trail, but for the most compelling sequence of sights, take a left here.

As you continue southeast through the woods, the trail passes through verdant blankets of moss. Reach another fork at 0.4 mile, and this time, swing right. Listen for the gentle lapping of the ocean as the trail partially emerges from the woods and meanders along Ship Harbor itself—a shallow, pool-shaped inlet. On your right, you'll notice a few sets of log stairs that offer hikers the chance to descend to a stony beach at the water's edge. The trail becomes rockier and climbs some log stairs to pass into a new forest zone of abundant and very skinny hemlocks. Cross some wooden bog bridges, minding your footing during wet weather, and prepare for another transition as the trail suddenly leaves the woods behind at 0.6 mile and arrives at the southern edge of **Mount Desert Island**—a gorgeous landscape of pink granite rocks and gentle waves.

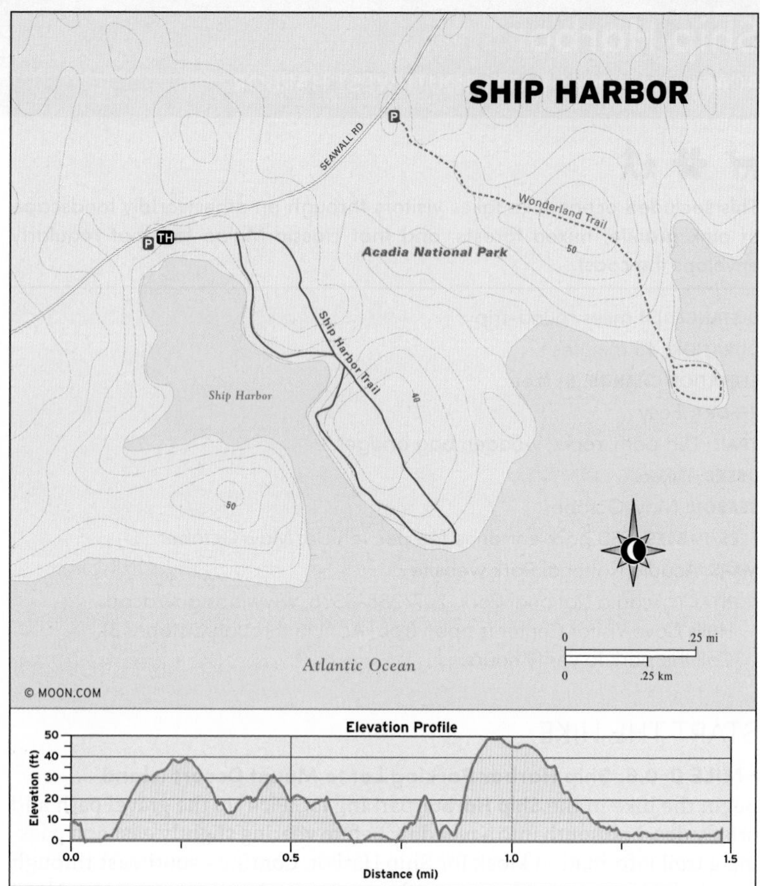

▸ MILE 0.6–1.0: Mount Desert Island to Rock Stairs

From here, hikers can choose to scramble around the rocks or stick to the path, which is now flanked by spruce trees small enough to allow for an unobstructed view of the coast. As the trail veers left into some bushes and crosses a few more bog bridges, the pattering of the waves becomes quieter and the trail reenters the forest at 0.7 mile. Continue walking northwest through the forest over more bog bridges and down some spacious **rock stairs** to arrive at a familiar-looking fork at 1 mile. Turn left.

▸ MILE 1.0–1.4: Rock Stairs to Ship Harbor Trailhead

The concluding lap of the hike—which resembles a figure-eight—returns to the inlet, ambling along the water from a higher position. The hemlocks here are even more majestic than the ones in the woods. A final winding descent delivers you to the first fork at 1.3 miles. Take a left turn here and backtrack northwest to the **trailhead** to complete the hike at 1.4 miles.

▲ BASS HARBOR HEAD LIGHTHOUSE

DIRECTIONS

From Bangor, drive southeast on US-1A E for 25 miles. After crossing the bridge onto Mount Desert Island, turn right at the fork onto ME-102 S. Continue south along this road through the town of Southwest Harbor for 13 miles and then take a slight left onto ME-102A N. Drive south and then east along this road for another 2 miles; shortly after, the parking lot and trailhead for Ship Harbor will be on your right. If the parking lot is full, you can park along the side of the road.

GPS COORDINATES: 44°13'56.0"N 68°19'22.4"W, 44.232217, -68.322900

BEST NEARBY BITES

Double down on the maritime theme with a classic oceanside Maine lobster dinner. Head over to Bass Harbor to check out **Thurston's Lobster Pound** (9 Thurston Rd., Bernard, 207/244-7600, www.thurstonforlobster.com, 11am-8pm Mon.-Sat.) or drive east to Seawall and visit **Charlotte's Legendary Lobster Pound** (465 Seawall Rd., Southwest Harbor, 207/244-8021, www.charlotteslegendarylobsters.com, 11am-8:30pm daily).

8 Penobscot Mountain via the Jordan Cliffs Trail

ACADIA NATIONAL PARK, BAR HARBOR

Climb one of Acadia's most popular mountains via a series of dramatic cliff faces for awe-inspiring views of the coast.

DISTANCE: 3.3 miles round-trip
DURATION: 2 hours
ELEVATION CHANGE: 1,027 feet
EFFORT: Strenuous
TRAIL: Dirt path, rocks, iron rungs, wooden bog bridges
USERS: Hikers
SEASON: June-October
FEES/PASSES: $30 park entrance fee per vehicle, May-October
MAPS: Acadia National Park website
CONTACT: Acadia National Park, 207/288-3338, www.nps.gov/acad. Hulls Cove Visitor Center is open from April 15 through October 31. Call the park to verify hours.

The most unforgettable way up Penobscot is the Jordan Cliffs Trail—a wildly scenic climb across the rock walls that form the eastern flank of the peak. The trail is not especially steep, but its iron ladders and narrow ledges can make sections of this hike feel like a training run for American Ninja Warrior. If the weather is wet, take a different trail to the top. The trail is also occasionally closed if peregrine falcons have been spotted in the area (there is a nesting zone along the trail).

START THE HIKE

▸ MILE 0-0.3: Jordan Pond House to Jordan Cliffs Trail

Begin the hike by the restroom entrance outside the Jordan Pond House. Veer left at the wooden trail post to pick up a gravel path that descends into the forest. Cross the carriage road and continue east over a wooden bridge that crosses a creek. Amble through the woods briefly and then turn right at the junction for **Jordan Cliffs Trail,** which follows blue blazes through a mossier stretch of forest.

The trail swings north and climbs some gentle stone stairs to reach another junction at roughly 0.3 mile. Keep right here as the trail crosses the carriage road once more and continues into the forest on the opposite side.

▸ MILE 0.3-1.0: Carriage Road to Sheer Cliff Face

Climbing gradually through airier spruce-and-fir woods, the dirt trail quickly transitions to sloped slabs of rock with a notable peach hue. A few fleeting views of Penobscot's summit appear through the trees on the left. At 0.7 mile, the trail levels out and continues north. Suddenly, the woods on your right will open to reveal the expanse of Jordan Pond several

▲ THE SUMMIT MARKER OF PENOBSCOT MOUNTAIN

hundred feet below. The footing gets rockier, and the trail climbs higher with the help of steep rock stairs. One mile in, the trail traverses the first sheer cliff face and becomes much skinnier—watch your step here.

▸ MILE 1.0-1.6: Sheer Cliff Face to Penobscot East Trail

After dipping in and out of the woods, the trail arrives at the first obstacle at 1.1 miles: a large boulder that hikers must climb over with the help of a single iron rung and a bar installed in the rock. (Consider this your last chance to turn back.) The trail continues north but becomes much rougher, with lots of exposed tree roots. At 1.3 miles, you'll cross a long balance beam-like wooden bridge with handrails. Descend the stairs at the end of the bridge and prepare to tread carefully—the trail traverses a much longer stretch of exposed cliff here with the help of iron rungs in the rock, including one vertical rung climb of at least 15 feet that requires the use of handholds in the surrounding rock. Be sure that your boots have a good grip on each rung before stepping onto the next rung.

At the top of this scary stretch, the trail swerves into the woods and climbs a gentler stony path to the junction with the **Penobscot East Trail** at 1.6 miles.

▸ MILE 1.6-1.9: Penobscot East Trail to Penobscot Mountain Summit

Swing left onto Penobscot East Trail and hoist your way up some boulders and rock ledges onto the upper heights of Penobscot. The trail meanders

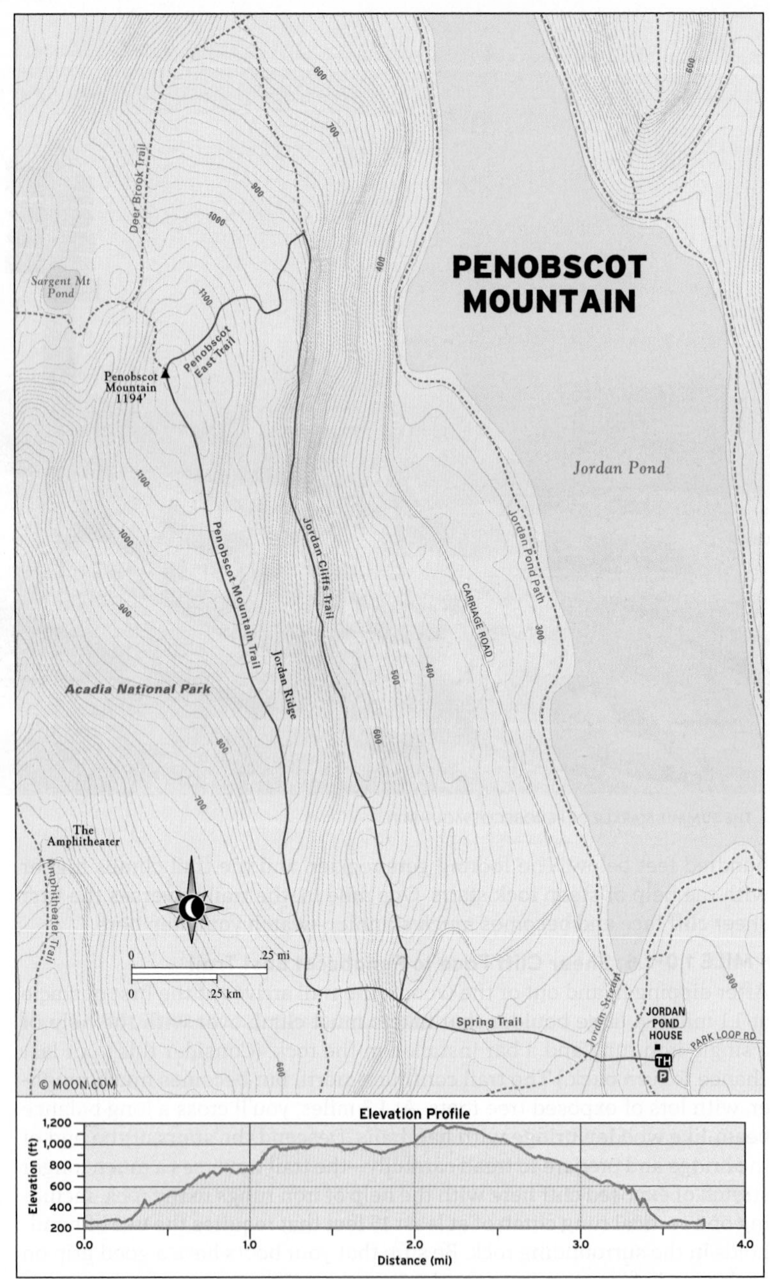

across the alpine landscape, following blue-blazed cairns, before climbing to a final height of land and reaching the **Penobscot Mountain** summit signpost at 1.9 miles.

▸ MILE 1.9–2.8: Penobscot Mountain Summit to Spring Trail

Enjoy the views while beginning your return journey down the **Penobscot Mountain Trail** from the summit post. The initial descent is a dreamy stroll

▲ THE JORDAN CLIFFS TRAIL

down the mountain's broad summit, with the south coast of Mount Desert Island serving as an epic backdrop. Continue south for 0.9 mile as the crops of young spruce trees segue into full-on forest. At 2.8 miles, take a left at the junction onto **Spring Trail.**

▸ MILE 2.8-3.3: Spring Trail to Jordan Cliffs Trail and Jordan Pond House

The descent becomes very steep after this point, with rock steps, some slabs, and even a wooden boardwalk that hugs a series of sheer cliff faces. It's hair-raising, but short-lived. The trail reaches the carriage road again at 3 miles. Cross to the other side and make your way down some rugged rock stairs before reaching the **Jordan Cliffs Trail junction** at 3.1 miles. Turn right, backtrack to the Jordan Pond House, and complete your hike at a hearty 3.3 miles.

DIRECTIONS

From Bangor, drive southeast on US-1A E for 25 miles. After crossing the bridge onto Mount Desert Island, turn right at the fork and continue south along ME-102 S for about 4 miles before swinging left onto ME-3 W. Drive southwest for another 5 miles, make a left turn to stay on ME-3 W, and then take another left turn at the Stanley Brook entrance for Acadia. Take this road to its terminus, make a slight left onto Park Loop Road, and drive north until you see the Jordan Pond House entrance on your left. If the lot here is full (which it usually is), continue north past the Pond House and turn left to access the overflow parking areas.

GPS COORDINATES: 44°19'13.5"N 68°15'15.1"W, 44.320428, -68.254180

NEARBY CAMPGROUNDS

NAME	LOCATION	FACILITIES	SEASON	FEE
Hadley's Point Campground	33 Hadley Point Rd., Bar Harbor, ME 04609	Tent sites, RV sites, cabins, toilets, showers, potable water, laundry, swimming pool, camp store, Wi-Fi	late June through mid-October	$29-90
207/288-4808, www.hadleyspoint.com				
Bar Harbor Campground	409 ME-3, Bar Harbor, ME 04609	Tent sites, RV sites, toilets, showers, potable water, laundry, swimming pool, camp store, Wi-Fi	late May through mid-October	$34-46
207/288-5185, www.thebarharborcampground.com				
Blackwoods Campground	155 Blackwoods Dr., Otter Creek, ME 04660	Tent sites, RV sites, toilets, potable water	May through mid-October	$30-60
207/288-3274, www.recreation.gov				
Somes Sound View Campground	5 Spinnaker Way, Mt Desert, ME 04660	Tent sites, cabin tents, RV sites, cabins, toilets, showers, potable water, swimming pool, camp store, Wi-Fi	late May through mid-October	$30-90
207/244-3890, www.ssvc.info				
Bar Harbor/ Oceanside KOA Campground	136 County Rd., Bar Harbor, ME 04609	Tent sites, RV sites, cabins, toilets, showers, potable water, laundry, camp store, Wi-Fi	mid-May through mid-October	$45-221
207/288-3520, www.koa.com				
Smuggler's Den Campground	20 Main St., Southwest Harbor, ME 04679	Tent sites, RV sites, cabins, toilets, showers, potable water, laundry, swimming pool, camp store, Wi-Fi	late May through mid-October	$25-175
207/244-3944, www.smugglersdencampground.com				

NEARBY CAMPGROUNDS (continued)				
NAME	**LOCATION**	**FACILITIES**	**SEASON**	**FEE**
Quietside Campground & Cabins	397 Tremont Rd., Bernard, ME 04612	Tent sites, RV sites, cabins, toilets, showers, potable water, laundry, camp store, Wi-Fi	mid-June through mid-October	$20-75
207/244-0566 , www.quietsidecampground.com				
Bass Harbor Campground	342 Harbor Dr., Bass Harbor, ME 04653	Tent sites, RV sites, cabins, yurts, toilets, showers, potable water, laundry, swimming pool, camp store; Wi-Fi	May through October	$24-172
207/244-5857, www.bassharbor.com				
Seawall Campground	668 Seawall Rd., Southwest Harbor, ME 04679	Tent sites, RV sites, toilets, potable water	mid-May through mid-October	$22-60
207/244-3600, www.recreation.gov				

▲ DELUXE GLAMPING TENT AT BAR HARBOR/OCEANSIDE KOA CAMPGROUND

BAXTER, THE HIGHLANDS, AND THE CARRABASSETT VALLEY

Northern Maine is a land of superlatives. The tallest mountain, biggest lake, and longest river in the state are all here. The region contains thousands of miles of trails, all of which are surrounded by acre after acre of evergreen frontier. To amble through Maine's northern forests is to experience the Pine Tree State at its most rugged and majestic. For hikers who make the considerable journey here, three wild and wooded wonderlands await: Baxter State Park, the Maine Highlands, and the Carrabassett Valley. Each contains relics of Maine's unique blend of logging and geological history—from old sawmills to older caves, cascades, and remote peaks that seem to poke the sky.

▲ the headwaters of Gulf Hagas

▲ the Orono Bog boardwalk

◂ VIEWS FROM MOUNT KATAHDIN

1 **Poplar Stream Falls**
DISTANCE: 4.4 miles round-trip
DURATION: 2 hours
EFFORT: Easy

2 **Mount Bigelow**
DISTANCE: 10 miles round-trip
DURATION: 6.5 hours
EFFORT: Strenuous

3 **Gulf Hagas**
DISTANCE: 8.2 miles round-trip
DURATION: 5 hours
EFFORT: Strenuous

4 **Mount Kineo**
DISTANCE: 3.5 miles round-trip
DURATION: 2 hours
EFFORT: Moderate

5 **Orono Bog**
DISTANCE: 1.6 miles round-trip
DURATION: 45 minutes
EFFORT: Easy

6 **Little and Big Niagara Falls**
DISTANCE: 2.4 miles round-trip
DURATION: 1.5 hours
EFFORT: Easy

7 **South Turner Mountain**
DISTANCE: 3.6 miles round-trip
DURATION: 2.5 hours
EFFORT: Moderate/strenuous

8 **Debsconeag Ice Caves**
DISTANCE: 2 miles round-trip
DURATION: 1 hour
EFFORT: Easy

9 **Blueberry Ledges**
DISTANCE: 3.6 miles round-trip
DURATION: 1.5 hours
EFFORT: Easy

10 **Mount Katahdin**
DISTANCE: 9.4 miles round-trip
DURATION: 8.5 hours
EFFORT: Strenuous

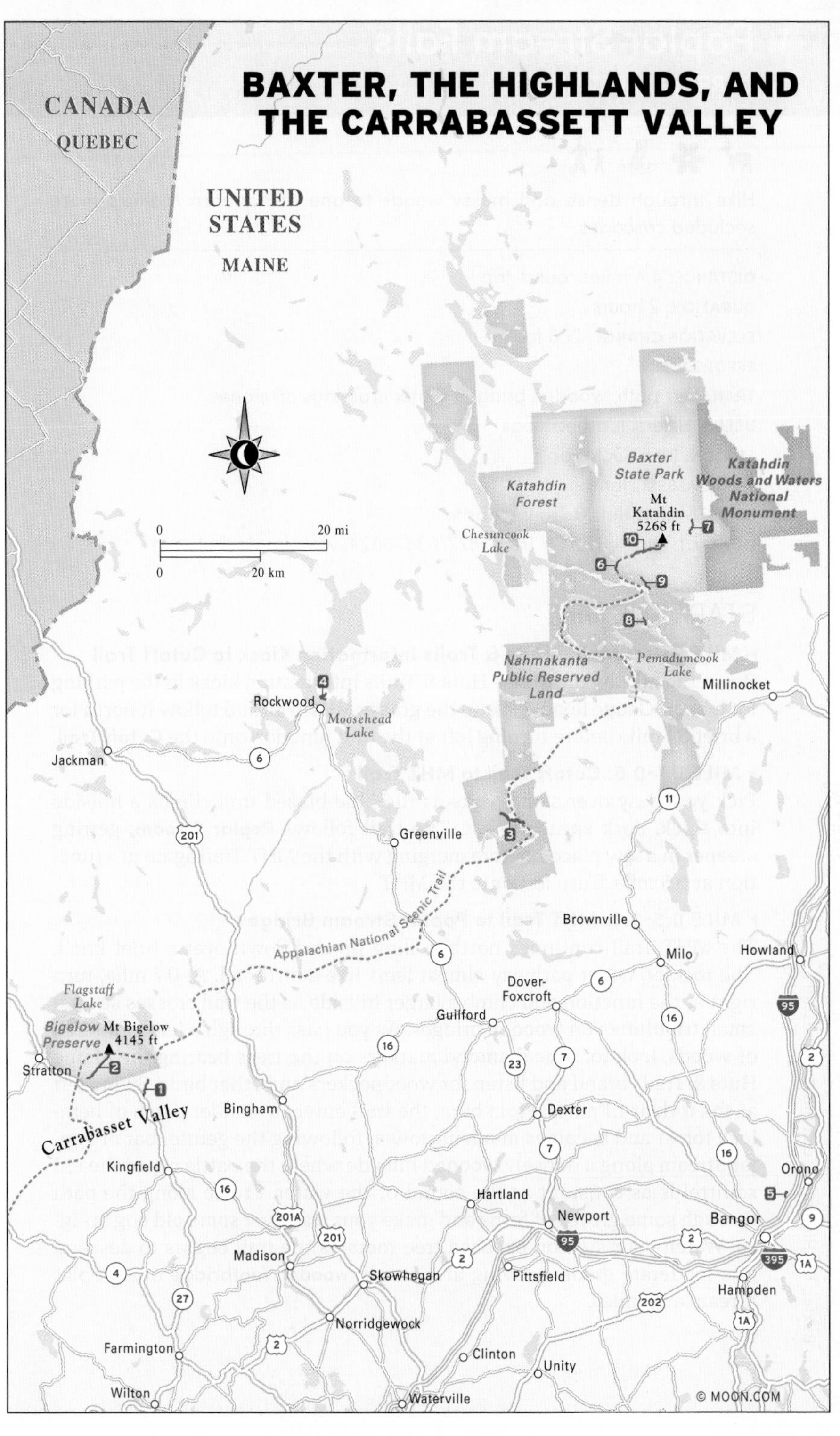
BAXTER, THE HIGHLANDS, AND THE CARRABASSETT VALLEY
CANADA
QUEBEC
UNITED STATES
MAINE
0
20 mi
0
20 km
Baxter State Park
Katahdin Woods and Waters National Monument
Katahdin Forest
Mt Katahdin 5268 ft
Chesuncook Lake
Nahmakanta Public Reserved Land
Pemadumcook Lake
Millinocket
Rockwood
Moosehead Lake
Jackman
Greenville
Appalachian National Scenic Trail
Brownville
Milo
Howland
Dover-Foxcroft
Guilford
Flagstaff Lake
Bigelow Preserve
Mt Bigelow 4145 ft
Stratton
Carrabasset Valley
Bingham
Dexter
Kingfield
Orono
Hartland
Newport
Bangor
Madison
Skowhegan
Pittsfield
Hampden
Norridgewock
Farmington
Clinton
Unity
Wilton
Waterville
© MOON.COM

1 Poplar Stream Falls

CARRABASSETT VALLEY

Hike through dense and mossy woods to one of northern Maine's more secluded cascades.

DISTANCE: 4.4 miles round-trip

DURATION: 2 hours

ELEVATION CHANGE: 268 feet

EFFORT: Easy

TRAIL: Dirt path, wooden bridges, water crossings on stones

USERS: Hikers, leashed dogs

SEASON: June-October

FEES/PASSES: None

MAPS: Maine Huts & Trails website

CONTACT: Maine Huts & Trails, 877/634-8824, www.mainehuts.org

START THE HIKE

▸ MILE 0-0.1: Maine Huts & Trails Information Kiosk to Cutoff Trail

Begin the hike by the Maine Huts & Trails information kiosk in the parking lot just off Gauge Road. Pick up the grassy **MHT Trail** and follow it north for a brief 0.1 mile before turning left at the first junction onto the **Cutoff Trail.**

▸ MILE 0.1-0.5: Cutoff Trail to MHT Trail

Pick your way over some rocks as the blue-blazed trail climbs a hillside into thick, dark spruce forest. The trail follows **Poplar Stream,** getting steeper in a few places, before merging with the MHT Trail again at a junction at 0.5 mile. Turn left onto the MHT.

▸ MILE 0.5-2.0: MHT Trail to Poplar Stream Bridge

The MHT Trail continues north, rolling up and down over a brief knoll. The rockier, wider pathway almost feels like a dirt road. At 0.7 mile, turn right at the junction and climb a larger hillside as the trail crosses several small tributaries on wooden bridges. As you pass through a leafier stretch of woods, look for blue diamond markers on the trees bearing the Maine Huts & Trails brand and listen for woodpeckers and other birds. Swing left at the fork at 1.1 miles. From here, the trail enters a shadier patch of hemlock forest and becomes much narrower, following the gentle roar of Poplar Stream along a densely wooded hillside where the battle cry of the red squirrel is as constant as the sound of the water. Cruise along the path through some groves of ferns and make your way over some old bog bridges. Watch your step on exposed tree roots as the trail begins to descend at a moderate grade, arriving at a sturdy **wooden footbridge** over Poplar Stream at 2 miles.

▲ THE ROARING TUMULT OF POPLAR STREAM FALLS

MILE 2.0-4.4: Poplar Stream Bridge Poplar Stream Falls and Poplar Hut

After crossing the bridge, you'll hear the sound of crashing water echoing through the forest on your right. Continue north along the path until you reach a steep series of stone stairs; turn right here to stay on level ground, skipping the stairs, and continue a few more yards. At 2.2 miles, you'll reach **Poplar Stream Falls,** a roaring chute of water that tumbles 50 feet into a stunningly pretty pool. The deep, reflective pool is cold but swimmable in the summer. Hikers interested in checking out nearby Poplar Hut can backtrack to the stone stairs and head up them to the junction for the hut. The hut offers comfy overnight lodging and locally sourced meals by reservation, and day hikers can purchase lunch here from 11:30am to 1:30pm on Saturday and Sunday during the full-service season (June 21-September 1). Otherwise, return the way you came.

DIRECTIONS

From Portland, it's about 2.5 hours to the trailhead. Take I-295 N and I-95 N to ME-3 and ME-27 N until it intersects with US-2 W. Turn left onto US-2 W and continue to West Farmington, where you'll turn right onto ME-27 N once again. Drive north to Carrabassett Valley, turn right onto Carriage Road, and then take the first left to reach the Carrabassett Valley Town Office parking lot. (This is where you'll leave your car.) To reach

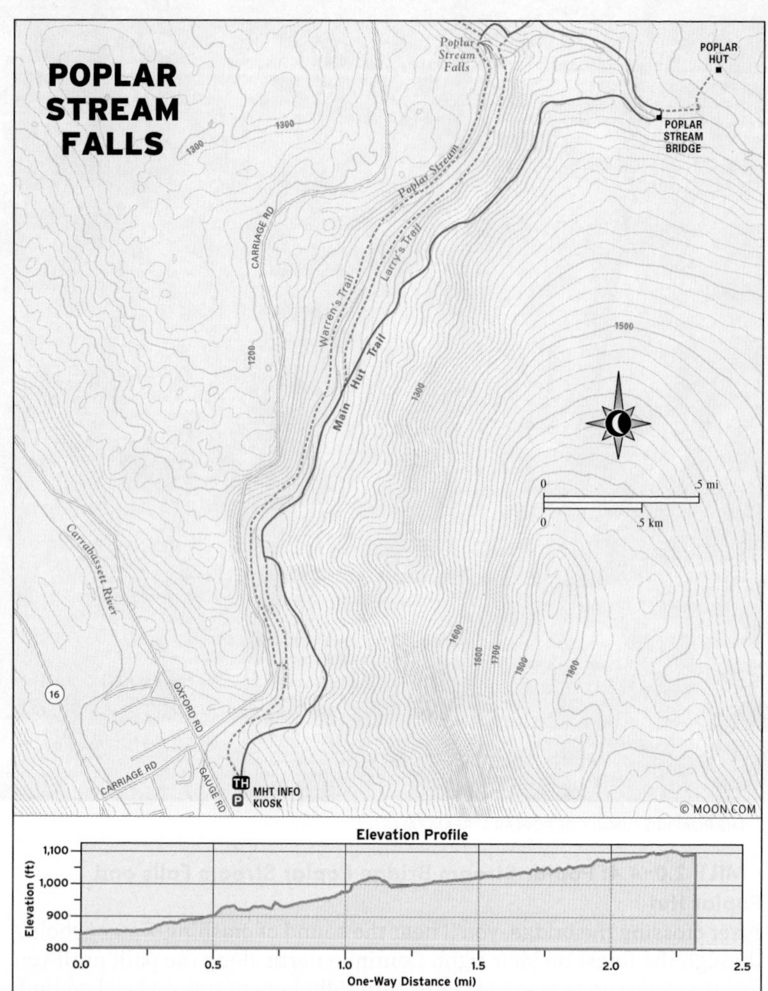

the trailhead, walk back to Carriage Road, turn left, and continue walking northeast along the road to Gauge Road. Make a right onto Gauge Road, cross a wooden footbridge over Poplar Stream, and take the first left to arrive at the Poplar Stream Falls trailhead.

GPS COORDINATES: 45°04'44.4"N 70°12'27.7"W, 45.078993, -70.207693

BEST NEARBY BITES

Feel like injecting some more fun into your day after a serene waterfall hike? Devour a bacon-laden cheeseburger, sip some suds from an impressive Maine craft beer list, and roll a few games of bowling at **The SugarBowl** (1242 Carrabassett Dr., Carrabassett Valley, 207/235-3300, www.sugarbowlmaine.com, 3pm-10pm Mon.-Fri., noon-10pm Sat.-Sun.).

2 Mount Bigelow

BIGELOW PRESERVE, STRATTON

Venture deep into the woods to visit a pair of peaks with incredible views of one of Maine's tallest mountains.

DISTANCE: 10 miles round-trip

DURATION: 6.5 hours

ELEVATION CHANGE: 2,615 feet

EFFORT: Strenuous

TRAIL: Dirt path, rocks, wooden bridges, water crossings on stones

USERS: Hikers, leashed dogs

SEASON: June-September

FEES/PASSES: None

MAPS: Maine Department of Agriculture, Conservation, and Forestry website

CONTACT: Maine Bureau of Parks and Lands, 207/778-8231, www.maine.gov/bigelowpreserve

Mount Bigelow, one of the highest summits in Maine, is a remote and immense heap of granite that offers multiple peaks. The highest point on Bigelow—West Peak, at 4,145 feet—is best paired with the nearby Avery Peak for an unforgettable two-for-one climb.

START THE HIKE

▸ MILE 0-0.7: Trail Information Kiosk to Firewarden's Trail

Walk to the trail information kiosk at the north end of the parking lot and pick up a rugged logging road, which climbs and then descends a small hill to reach a wooden bridge over Stratton Brook. Cross the bridge and keep right at the junction as the logging road ambles along the brook. Enjoy pretty views of a nearby marshy area and Sugarloaf Mountain in the distance. At 0.7 mile, turn left onto the **Firewarden's Trail** to leave the brook behind and venture into the Bigelow Preserve.

▸ MILE 0.7-3.1: Firewarden's Trail to Moose Falls Campsite

Climbing steadily at a gentle grade, the trail heads northeast with few deviations over the next mile. After climbing a steep, rocky ridge for 0.3 mile, you'll descend into a boggy stretch of boreal pine and spruce forest at 1.7 miles. Watch your footing on the many bog bridges. Continue ascending into thicker, more deciduous woods where black bears and deer are known to wander. At 2.1 miles, keep right at the Horns Pond Trail junction to stay on the Firewarden's Trail. Rock-hop across a creek and keep heading northeast, deeper into the woods—the trees are spaced apart just enough to allow you to admire the depth of color and texture in this forest. The footing slowly becomes rockier and steeper, and the occasional gust of wind through the trees hints at what lies ahead.

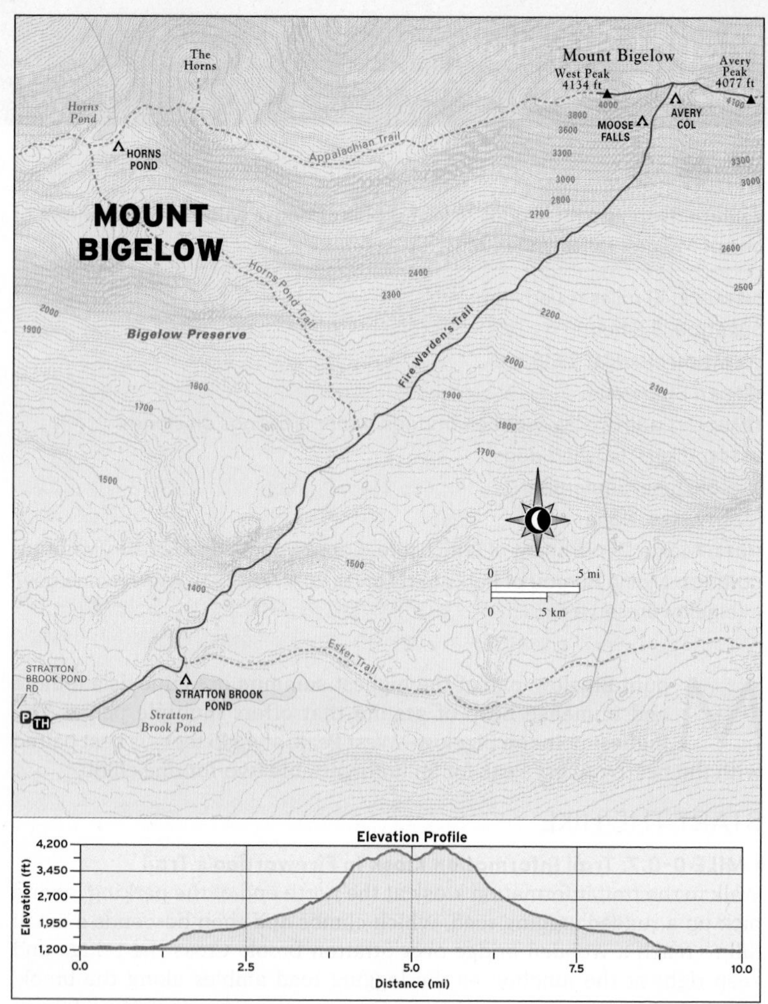

At 3.1 miles, the trail climbs a set of rock stairs to reach **Moose Falls Campsite,** a bare-bones tenting site that is first come, first served and used by hikers doing longer overnight treks in the Bigelow Range.

‣ MILE 3.1-4.2: Moose Falls Campsite to Avery Memorial Campsite

From here, the gradual ascent through the woods comes to an end. The trail crosses a nearby creek and becomes very steep and rocky, ascending a series of winding granite stairs and slabs to break through the foliage. As the boreal trees get thinner and smaller, the green expanse of northern Maine becomes partially visible, making the brutal ascent just a little more bearable. Keep climbing northeast, keeping left at the junction for **Avery Memorial Campsite** at 4.2 miles (this is another tenting area for overnight hikers) to stay on Firewarden's.

‣ MILE 4.2-10.0: Avery Memorial Campsite to West Peak and Avery Peak Summits

Enjoy a sudden blast of alpine exposure as you step onto the open ridgeline between **West Peak** and **Avery Peak** at just over 4.2 miles, where the

▲ ROUGH-HEWN MAINE BOG BRIDGES AID HIKERS' PASSAGE ALONG THE FIREWARDEN'S TRAIL

trail finally (mercifully) levels off a bit and concludes at the Appalachian Trail, which visits both summits. From this beautiful juncture, hikers can choose to turn left or right to either peak. The climbs are similar—rocks, boulders, tundra, and abundant views of the Rangeley Lakes, the Carrabassett Valley, and even the Quebec wilderness. Avery Peak also has the stone foundations of an old fire tower. From the AT/Firewarden's junction, it's about 0.4 mile round-trip to each summit. Ascend both summits for maximum victory points, then return the way you came.

DIRECTIONS

From Portland, drive northeast on I-295 N for 46 miles and then merge onto I-95 N to continue northeast to Exit 113 for ME-3 toward Augusta/Belfast. At the end of the off-ramp, enter the traffic circle and take the third exit to get on ME-3 N. Another traffic circle will appear just ahead. Take the first exit to stay on ME-3 N and drive north for a mile before turning right onto ME-27 N/Civic Center Drive. Follow this road to its terminus and then make a left onto US-2 W. After a mile, turn right onto Weeks Mill Road, drive northwest for another 6 miles, and then make a very sharp right onto ME-43 E. At the fork a mile ahead, veer left onto Mosher Hill Road, continue for 3 miles, and swing left onto Ramsdell Road. Follow this road to its end and turn right onto ME-27 N. Drive north for another 33 miles and then take a right onto Stratton Brook Road at the sign for Bigelow Preserve. Follow the road to the hiker parking area.

GPS COORDINATES: 45°06'35.6"N 70°20'14.0"W, 45.109879, -70.337209

BEST NEARBY BITES

What good is a mountain hike without a decadent dinner to conclude the day? For locally sourced gourmet international cooking, get thee to the **Coplin Dinner House** (8252 Carrabassett Rd., Stratton, 207/246-0016, www.coplindinnerhouse.com, 4:30pm-9pm Wed.-Thurs., 4:30pm-9:30pm Fri.-Sat., 4:30pm-9pm Sun.). If you're feeling like something heavier, meatier, and saucier, you'll find what you're craving at **The Rack BBQ** (5016 Access Rd., Carrabassett Valley, 207/237-2211, www.therackbbq.com, 4pm-1am Mon.-Sat., 4pm-midnight Sun.).

3 Gulf Hagas

KI JO-MARY MULTIPLE USE MANAGEMENT FOREST, BROWNVILLE

Hike through the isolated Maine wilderness into the majestic Gulf Hagas, a breathtaking canyon with an abundance of waterfalls.

BEST: Brew hikes

DISTANCE: 8.2 miles round-trip

DURATION: 5 hours

ELEVATION CHANGE: 1,154 feet

EFFORT: Strenuous

TRAIL: Dirt path, rocks, wooden bog bridges, water crossings on stones

USERS: Hikers, leashed dogs

SEASON: June–September

FEES/PASSES: $15 day-use fee per person for nonresidents, $10 for Maine residents

MAPS: North Maine Woods Inc. website

CONTACT: North Maine Woods Inc., 207/435-6213, www.northmainewoods.org

Deep in the Maine wilderness that once housed the Katahdin Iron Works furnaces, you'll find Gulf Hagas, often referred to as "the Grand Canyon of Maine." But this moniker doesn't do the canyon justice—the dark gray slate cliffs are uncharacteristically sheer, the waters of the Pleasant River surge through the canyon with a monotone roar, and the curious glacial rock formations have created an abundance of pretty waterfalls.

START THE HIKE

▸ MILE 0-0.2: Trail Information Kiosk to Pleasant River

Begin the hike in the parking area and walk north to the trail information kiosk. Pick up the **Appalachian Trail** as it leads into the deciduous forest. At 0.2 mile, you'll ford the Pleasant River, Oregon Trail-style—this crossing is too deep and wide to rock-hop, so either bring water shoes or consider removing your boots for this "initiation" into the realm of Gulf Hagas.

▸ MILE 0.2-1.5: Pleasant River to Appalachian Trail

On the other side of the river, veer right and follow white blazes on the trees. The trail curves away from the river and crosses some bog bridges before reaching a T-intersection at 0.4 mile. Turn left to stay on the AT and follow the trail for roughly 1 mile as it gradually climbs west through the woods over rocks and roots.

▸ MILE 1.5-1.8: Appalachian Trail to Rim Trail

At 1.5 miles, cross a stream to reach the junction for the Rim Trail and the Pleasant River Tote Road. Take a left onto the **Rim Trail** and make a rooty descent toward the sound of rushing water to reach your first cascade, **Screw Auger Falls,** at 1.7 miles. A few spur trails on the left lead to

▲ WATERFALL IN GULF HAGAS

overlooks from which you can admire the cascade. (The Rim Trail is replete with such spur paths to canyon vistas, almost all of which are worth checking out.)

▸ MILE 1.8–3.0: Rim Trail to The Jaws

Continue gently descending through the woods for another 0.5 mile. As the trail begins to climb the north rim of Gulf Hagas, huff and puff your way up some winding rock staircases for another 0.2 mile. At 2.5 miles, keep left to stay on Rim Trail at the Tote Road connector junction. Enjoy your first stunning view of the canyon by taking a spur path at 2.6 miles. Over the next half mile, the Rim Trail becomes a rocky and root-festooned roller coaster with a few steep sections that require a bit of scrambling. Check out **The Jaws**—a teeth-like rock formation through which the Pleasant River flows—at 3 miles.

▸ MILE 3.0–3.4: The Jaws to Buttermilk Falls

As the hemlock forest gets mossier, the trees start to become more spread out and the trail gets sunnier. Pass several exposed ledges that offer killer perspectives of the canyon. At 3.4 miles, you'll reach **Buttermilk Falls,** and the trail climbs steadily onward.

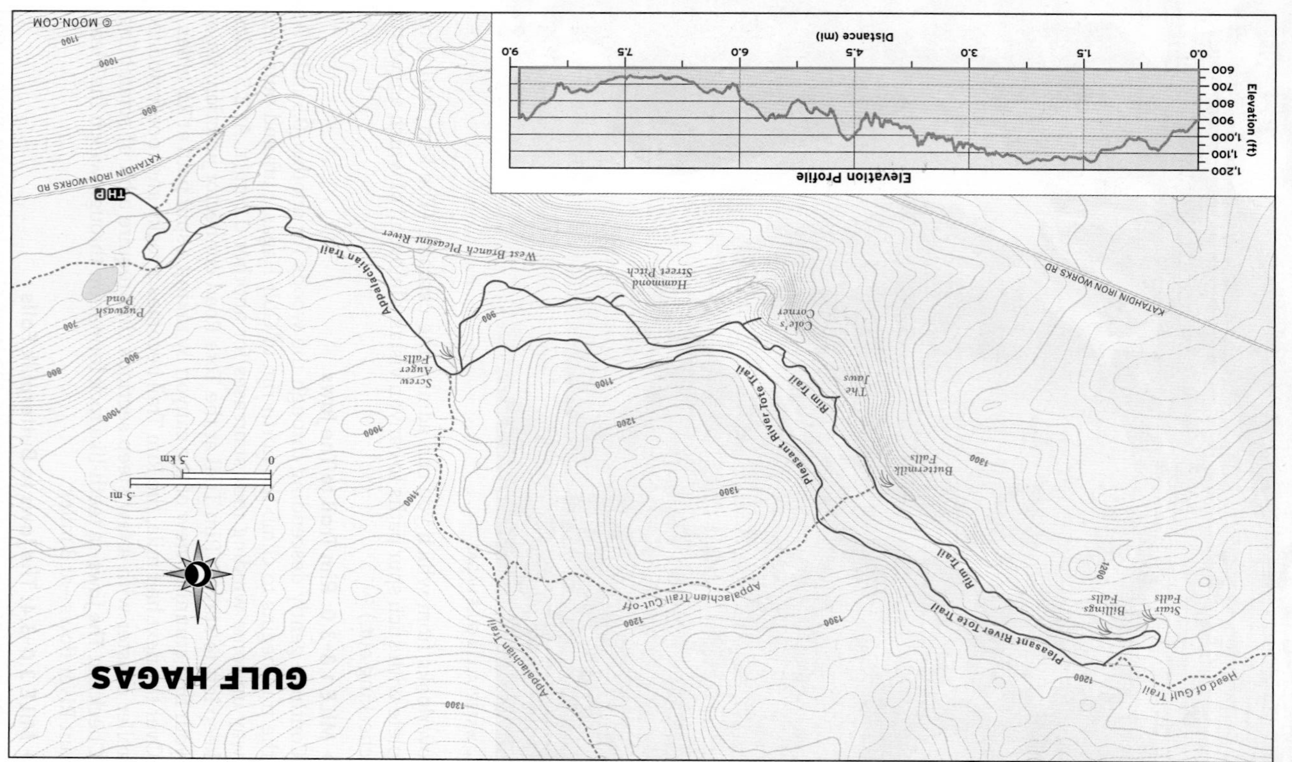
GULF HAGAS
Elevation Profile
Elevation (ft)
1,200
1,100
1,000
900
800
700
600
0.0
1.5
3.0
4.5
6.0
7.5
9.0
Distance (mi)
Head of Gulf Trail
Stair Falls
Billings Falls
Pleasant River Tote Trail
Rim Trail
Buttermilk Falls
The Jaws
Cole's Corner
Appalachian Trail Cut-off
Hammond Street Pitch
West Branch Pleasant River
Screw Auger Falls
Appalachian Trail
KATAHDIN IRON WORKS RD
Pugwash Pond
TH P
0
.5 mi
.5 km
© MOON.COM

▸ **MILE 3.4-4.2: Buttermilk Falls to Billings Falls and Stair Falls**

Keep left to stay on Rim at the second junction for the Tote Road. The trail swings in and out of the forest onto more rocky ledges and ambles past overlook points for **Billings Falls** at 4.1 miles and **Stair Falls** at 4.2 miles.

▸ **MILE 4.2-4.3: Stair Falls to Head of Gulf Hagas**

As the sound of the river dissipates, the Rim Trail dips deeper into the forest before arriving at the **Head of the Gulf** at 4.3 miles. This is the gorgeous delta of waterways that "feed" Gulf Hagas. Here, on a sunny day, you'll find swimmers, fishermen, photographers, and maybe even a few thru-hikers taking a scenic detour.

▸ **MILE 4.3-4.5: Head of Gulf Hagas to Pleasant River Tote Road**

The return path seems specifically designed for those tuckered out from the exhausting climb. From the Head, take the **Rim Trail** north to its terminus at the junction with the **Pleasant River Tote Road** at 4.5 miles.

▸ **MILE 4.5-8.2: Pleasant River Tote Road to Katahdin Iron Works Road**

Turn right onto the Tote Road, which cruises through the woods on a smooth dirt path and over lots of bog bridges at a gradual downhill grade for 2.2 miles. The path effortlessly delivers you back to the beginning of the Rim Trail at 6.7 miles. Turn left onto the **Appalachian Trail,** recross the stream, and backtrack to reach **Katahdin Iron Works Road** at 8.2 miles.

DIRECTIONS

From Bangor, drive north on I-95 N for 13 miles and take Exit 199 for ME-16 toward Alton/Lagrange/Milo. At the bottom of the off-ramp, turn left onto ME-16 W and follow it for 15 miles before making a slight left onto ME-16 W/ME-6 W as you pass through Lagrange. Drive northwest into Milo and turn right onto Main Street. Take an immediate slight left onto ME-11 N/ Park Street and continue for another 12 miles. As you reach Prairie, veer left onto Ebermee Road, which will soon become Katahdin Iron Works Road. After the road transitions to dirt, you'll reach the KI gatehouse. Stop here to register and pay the fee before continuing west along the road. The Gulf Hagas parking lot is clearly marked on your right.

GPS COORDINATES: 45°28'26.4"N 69°17'39.8"W

BEST NEARBY BREWS

Those approaching Gulf Hagas from the Greenville (western) side can enjoy a hearty old-school diner breakfast at **Auntie M's** (13 Lily Bay Rd., Greenville, 207/695-2238, 5am-3pm Sun.-Sat.); if you're departing Gulf Hagas by heading east to Brownville, reward yourself with a dizzyingly hazy Maine IPA or pale ale at **Bissell Brothers Three Rivers** (157 Elm St., Milo, 207/808-8258, www.bissellbrothers.com, 3pm-8pm Fri., noon-6pm Sat., noon-5pm Sun.).

4 Mount Kineo

MOUNT KINEO STATE PARK, ROCKWOOD

Take a boat ride to an island on Maine's largest lake to climb an arrestingly steep and gorgeous mountain.

BEST: Fall hikes

DISTANCE: 3.5 miles round-trip

DURATION: 2 hours

ELEVATION CHANGE: 724 feet

EFFORT: Moderate

TRAIL: Dirt path, rocks, wooden bog bridges

USERS: Hikers

SEASON: May-October

FEES/PASSES: $12 (cash only) per adult round-trip ferry ride from Rockwood to Mount Kineo Golf Course, $3 day-use fee for the trail (honor system)

MAPS: $2 at golf course clubhouse

CONTACT: Mount Kineo Golf Course, 207/534-9012, www.mooseheadlakegolf.com; clubhouse address: 223 Young Road, Rockwood, ME

FERRY HOURS: Every 2 hours, on the hour, 9am-3pm May-June; Every hour, on the hour, 8am-6pm July-August; Every hour, on the hour, 9am-4pm September-October

Rising above the choppy waters of Moosehead Lake like a behemoth creature carved out of stone, Mount Kineo is a spellbinding sight—the mountain is legendary for its massive rhyolite cliffs, from which Native American tribes once harvested rock for arrowheads. The way to get to the trailhead is by taking a ferry ride from the village of Rockwood to the Mount Kineo Golf Course, which sits in the shadow of the mountain.

START THE HIKE

▸ MILE 0-1.0: Trailhead to Indian Trail

Begin your hike to the left of the ferry dock by the large trailhead sign, featuring a map of the island. Pick up the **Carriage Trail** and stroll northwest along a wide gravel path that meanders along the shore of the island. In the summer, the trail is flanked by wildflowers that sprout from the tallgrass. As you enjoy the sound of water lapping at the shoreline, notice how the cliffs on your right become taller and more sheer. Within minutes, you'll be heading up there.

Turn right at a signed junction for the **Indian Trail** at 0.6 mile and begin the steep, root-festooned climb up Kineo's ledges. Blue blazes and red arrows mark the path, which heads northeast, passing a few ledges that offer spectacular views of the shoreline and the golf course. The trail becomes steeper over the next 0.3 mile, climbing over several rocky steps and ledges that require handholds. A few of the ledges are narrow and skirt perilously close to the tops of the cliffs, so tread slowly and carefully here.

▲ MOUNT KINEO

▸ MILE 1.0–1.9: Indian Trail to Mount Kineo Summit

About 1 mile in, the Indian Trail reaches a grassy height of land that offers the best view yet. Enter the mountaintop forest for the final push to the summit. At 1.1 miles, keep right at the junction for Bridle Trail to stay on Indian Trail, continuing to amble through boreal woods with lots of moss and rocks. A final brief climb delivers you to the proper summit of **Mount Kineo** at 1.8 miles. The summit is wooded but it features a six-story viewing tower that can be climbed for an unbeatable view of Moosehead Lake. The tower is higher than it looks, and climbing it is easily the scariest part of the hike, but it's well worth the effort.

▸ MILE 1.9–2.2: Mount Kineo Summit to Bridle Trail

To return, backtrack down the Indian Trail to the junction for the **Bridle Trail** at 2.2 miles and turn right onto the Bridle Trail. Descend the western haunch of Kineo at a pleasant grade for just over half a mile (blue blazes mark this path too). The path is gentler than the Indian Trail, but no less rocky and rooty.

▸ MILE 2.2–3.5: Bridle Trail to Carriage Trail

After passing through a grove of hemlock and spruce, the trail crosses some bog bridges and rejoins the **Carriage Trail** at 2.9 miles. Veer left onto the Carriage Road, keep right at the Indian Trail junction just ahead to stay on the Carriage Road, and retrace your steps along the shore until you reach the trailhead at 3.5 miles.

DIRECTIONS

From Portland, drive northeast on I-295 N for 46 miles and then merge onto I-95 N to continue heading northeast. Take Exit 150 for Somerset Avenue toward Pittsfield/Hartland. Turn left onto Somerset Avenue at the end of the off-ramp and then take a right onto Spring Road. Follow the road to its terminus and veer left onto ME-152. Drive north on ME-152 until the highway concludes in Cambridge, where you'll make a right turn onto ME-150. Continue along ME-150 to the town of Guilford and turn left onto ME-15 N/ME-6 W. Drive northwest to Greenville, veer left onto Pritham Avenue, and then take a right at the road's end to continue along ME-15 N/

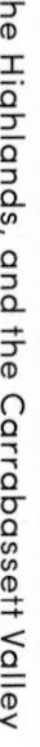

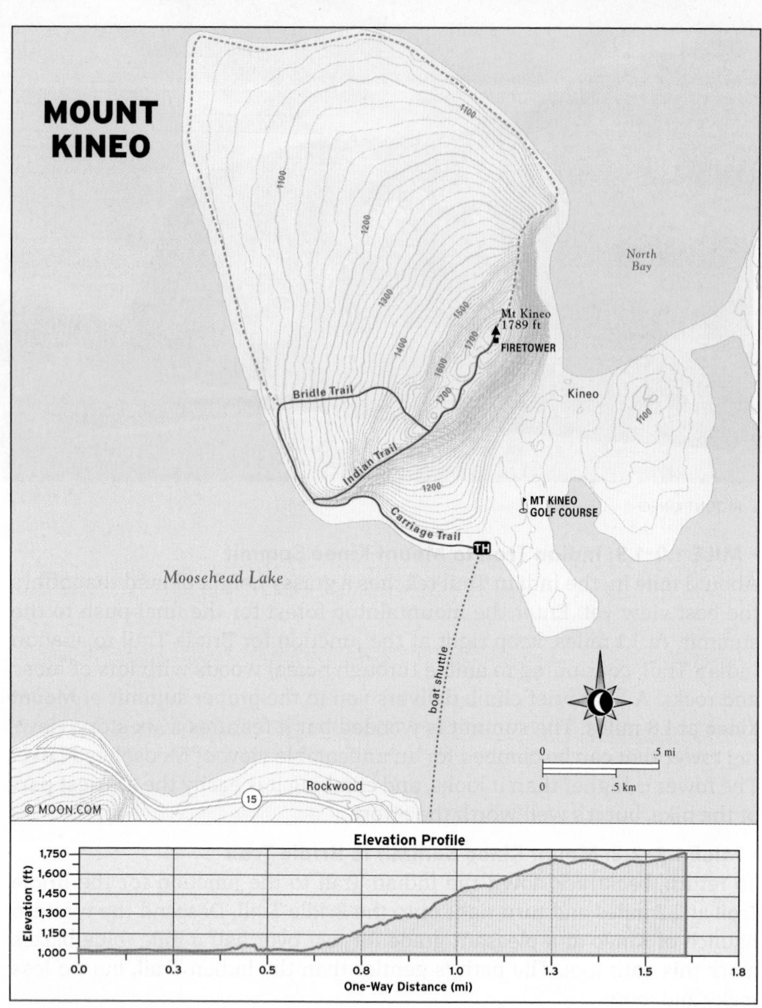

ME-6 W. Head northwest along the shores of Moosehead Lake for another 17 miles, enter the village of Rockwood, and make a final right turn onto Village Road, which descends to the parking lot for the Kineo shuttle ferry. Walk to the nearby dock to catch the boat.

GPS COORDINATES: 45°40'36.5"N 69°44'18.8"W, 45.676793, -69.738555

BEST NEARBY BITES

A gargantuan and smoky chopped pork sandwich is just one of many hunger-sating choices at the delectably quirky **Spring Creek Bar-B-Q** (26 Greenville Rd., Monson, 207/997-7025, www.springcreek-bar-b-qmaine.com, 11am-7pm Thurs., 11am-8pm Fri.-Sat., 11am-5pm Sun.). If you're craving something lighter and greener, you'll find tasty sandwiches, salads, and a stellar view of Moosehead Lake at the **Farmhouse Café** (143 Moosehead Lake Rd., Greenville, 207/695-2167, www.farmhousecafeatmooseheadlake.com, 7am-2pm Tues.-Sun.).

5 Orono Bog

BANGOR CITY FOREST, BANGOR, AND ORONO BOG, ORONO

This boardwalk loop through a beautiful bog is especially nice for bird-watchers, families, and couples on a sunset stroll.

DISTANCE: 1.6 miles round-trip
DURATION: 45 minutes
ELEVATION CHANGE: 27 feet
EFFORT: Easy
TRAIL: Dirt path, boardwalk
USERS: Hikers
SEASON: May-November
FEES/PASSES: None
MAPS: University of Maine Orono Bog Walk website
CONTACT: University of Maine, 207/581-1865, www.umaine.edu/oronobogwalk

Tucked away in Bangor's public forest is Orono Bog—a 616-acre conservation area that's teeming with wildlife and vivid green peat moss so thick that it actually constitutes a small height of land at the center of the bog. This walk is especially nice during the evening "magic hour" when the lighting is softer.

START THE HIKE

▸ MILE 0-0.4: East Trail to Orono Bog Boardwalk

Walk to the northeast end of the parking area to the wooden sign for the **East Trail.** Go 0.3 mile northeast along this gravel path that meanders through an airy forest of spruce and cedar trees. Upon reaching a clearing with picnic tables and an information kiosk, take a right turn onto the **Orono Bog Boardwalk** entrance.

▸ MILE 0.4-0.6: Orono Bog Boardwalk to Orono Bog

Continue northeast along the first section of boardwalk as it takes you through a much thicker, diverse stretch of forest. Some pieces of the boardwalk are actually resting on the bog surface, so don't be worried if they bounce like a floating dock. Colorful signs are placed throughout the boardwalk to give visitors an idea of the many bird, mammal, and reptile species that call the bog home. The boardwalk splits at 0.5 mile; bear right and keep heading northeast through an airier grove of spruce. The landscape suddenly opens up into an panorama of peat moss in countless shades of green. You're officially in **Orono Bog** now.

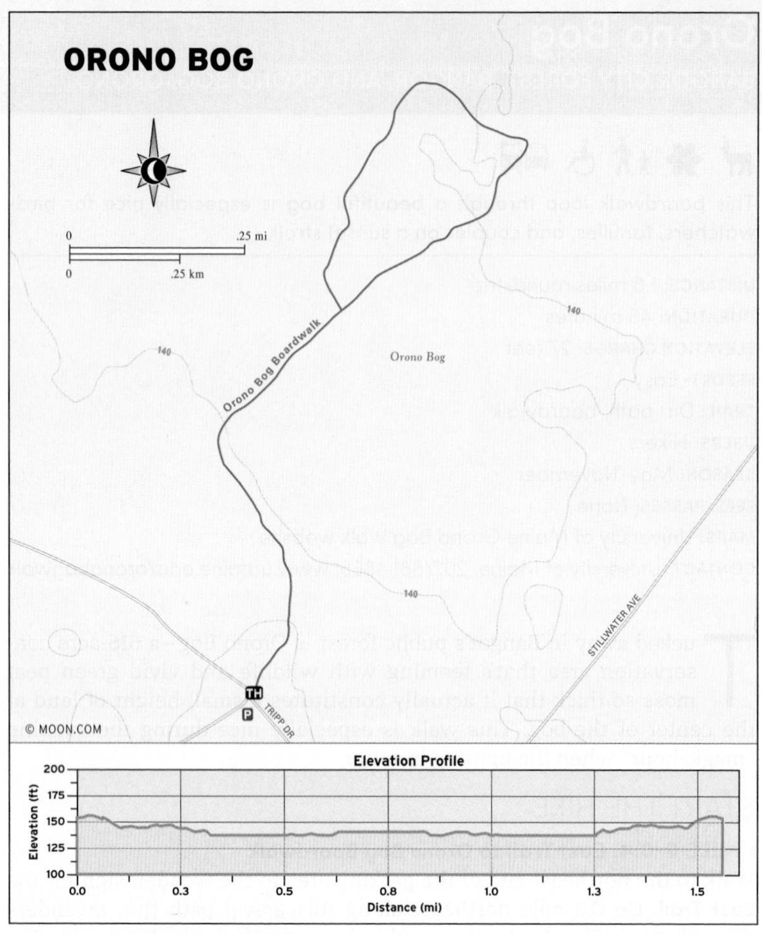

▸ MILE 0.6–1.0: Orono Bog

As the bog boardwalk curves north and then northwest over the next 0.3 mile, watch the sky for northern harriers. Not only do these medium-size raptors make regular appearances around the bog, but the trees and shrubs here are less than 10 feet tall, offering birders a prime view. The boardwalk starts to turn west and passes through a stretch of young spruce. Around here the boardwalk is slightly more raised, but it's still close enough to the peat for hikers to spot a northern leopard frog hopping around on the surface.

▸ MILE 1.0–1.6: Orono Bog to Orono Bog Boardwalk

The trail heads southeast for 0.3 mile as the boardwalk loop draws toward its close. Be sure to take a good final whiff of the air—some of the herbs that grow around here are bog variations of laurel and rosemary. The boardwalk loop enters forest again, reaching its origin point at 1.1 miles. From here, you can turn left and backtrack to the parking lot or explore more of the Bangor City Forest trails.

▲ THE BOARDWALK THROUGH ORONO BOG

DIRECTIONS

From Portland, take I-95 north to the Bangor area. Take Exit 186 for Stillwater Avenue and then turn right onto Stillwater Avenue. Take Stillwater Avenue northeast for 2.6 miles and then make a left turn onto Tripp Drive. The Bangor City Forest parking lot is at the end of this quiet road.

GPS COORDINATES: 44°51'46.1"N 68°43'42.1"W, 44.862799, -68.728366

BEST NEARBY BREWS

The nearby city of Bangor is teeming with restaurants and watering holes, but in Orono, right near the bog, you can get a representative taste of Maine's craft beers and some seriously loaded hot dogs at **The Family Dog** (6 Mill St., Orono, 207/866-2808, www.thefamilydogorono.com, 7am-10pm Mon.-Sat., 9am-9pm Sun.).

6 Little and Big Niagara Falls

BAXTER STATE PARK, MILLINOCKET

This forest hike visits two explosive waterfalls that spill from the height of Baxter State Park into the valley below.

DISTANCE: 2.4 miles round-trip
DURATION: 1.5 hours
ELEVATION CHANGE: 185 feet
EFFORT: Easy
TRAIL: Dirt path, rocks, wooden bog bridges
USERS: Hikers
SEASON: June-October
FEES/PASSES: $15 park entrance fee per vehicle
MAPS: Baxter State Park website
CONTACT: Baxter State Park, 207/723-5140, www.baxterstatepark.org

START THE HIKE

▸ MILE 0-0.2: Trail Kiosk to Daicey Pond Nature Trail Junction

Begin the hike at the southwest corner of the parking lot by the trails kiosk. Look for the wooden **Appalachian Trail** sign for Little and Big Niagara on a nearby tree; briefly walk east along a dirt path through tall grass, then turn left as the trail veers into a mixed forest of beech and pine. Look for white blazes on trees. The footing quickly becomes rockier and muddier but is made easier by lots of wooden bog bridges. Turn right at the two junctions with the Daicey Pond Nature Trail to continue your hike toward the falls.

▸ MILE 0.2-0.9: Daicey Pond Nature Trail Junction to Little Niagara Falls Cutoff Path

Listen for the sound of rushing water before the trail reaches **Nesowadehunk Stream** at 0.3 mile.

As you continue south beside the water, the trail begins to descend through the increasingly mossy and rocky forest at a gentle grade. Big glacial boulders are visible in the surrounding woodland, rich with those classic Maine ferns. The roar of the stream gradually grows louder, and at 0.9 mile the trail reaches a sign for the cutoff path to **Little Niagara Falls.**

▸ MILE 0.9-1.0: Little Niagara Falls Cutoff Path to West Peak and Doubletop Mountain Viewpoint

Turn right onto the cutoff and emerge onto an open rock slab that the falls spill around. This cascade resembles a sloped series of rapids, but in times of high water they take on a powerful frothing appearance. The falls outlook point also offers a killer view of nearby West Peak and Doubletop Mountain to the north.

▲ LITTLE NIAGARA FALLS

▸ MILE 1.0–1.2: West Peak and Doubletop Mountain Viewpoint to Big Niagara Falls Cutoff Path

To reach the grand finale, backtrack to the AT and turn right to continue the hike. The trail veers away from the stream and descends at a more moderate grade, with plenty of exposed roots—be careful of these during soggy conditions. As the hemlock woods become more spacious and sunlit, the trail descends several rock stairs to reach the cutoff path for **Big Niagara Falls** at 1.2 miles.

▸ MILE 1.2–2.4: Big Niagara Falls Cutoff Path to Big Niagara Falls

Turn right here and briefly walk through the undergrowth to reach a ledge that overlooks the gargantuan waterfall. Big Niagara Falls lives up to its name, exploding outward in great torrents and spilling down several 20-foot cliffs to form a larger stream below that contains several rock islands on which trees have managed to grow. Chances are you'll be sharing the ledge with some thru-hikers. Return the way you came.

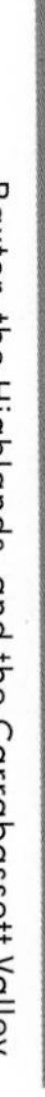

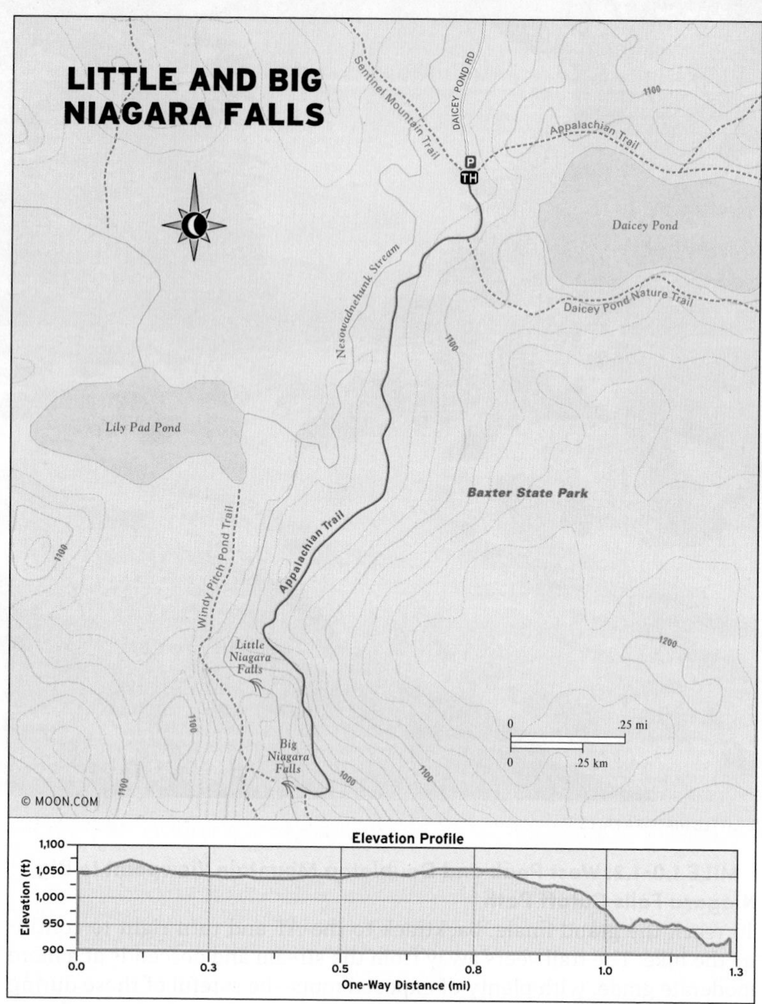

DIRECTIONS

From Bangor, drive north on I-95 N for roughly 58 miles and then take Exit 144-244 for ME-157 toward Medway/Millinocket. Turn left at the bottom of the off-ramp, drive northwest along ME-157 W/Medway Road until its terminus, and then take a right onto Katahdin Road. Turn left onto Bates Street and drive northwest for 8 miles as Bates Street becomes Millinocket Road and then Baxter Park Road. Continue north to the Togue Pond Gate House for Baxter State Park, pay the $15 entrance fee, and turn left at the fork onto Park Tote Road. Drive along the winding dirt road for roughly 10 miles and then make a left onto Daicey Pond Road. You'll arrive at the parking lot in an exposed grassy area just over half a mile ahead.

GPS COORDINATES: 45°52'57.5"N 69°01'54.6"W, 45.882644, -69.031825

7 South Turner Mountain

BAXTER STATE PARK, MILLINOCKET

Traverse a swampy forest and ascend a bald-faced peak for top-notch views of Katahdin.

DISTANCE: 3.6 miles round-trip
DURATION: 2.5 hours
ELEVATION CHANGE: 1,558 feet
EFFORT: Moderate/strenuous
TRAIL: Dirt path, rocks, wooden bog bridges, water crossings via stones
USERS: Hikers
SEASON: May-October
FEES: $15 park entry fee per vehicle
MAPS: Baxter State Park website
CONTACT: Baxter State Park, 207/723-5140, www.baxterstatepark.org

Located directly east of the iconic Katahdin, South Turner offers a challenging climb and scenic vistas without taking up a whole day. It's a perfect choice for hikers who are preparing for a Katahdin expedition or forgoing the big one altogether. Note that weekend visitors should reserve a parking spot at the Roaring Brook Campground parking lot two weeks in advance by using the Baxter State Park online reservations system. Many trails start from this lot, and it's almost always full on Saturdays and Sundays.

START THE HIKE

▸ MILE 0-0.3: Ranger Cabin to South Turner Mountain Trail

Begin the hike just beyond the ranger cabin at the north end of the parking lot. Cross a large wooden footbridge over **Roaring Brook**. At the nearby trail junction, turn right onto the **South Turner Mountain Trail**. Enjoy a brief, gravelly stretch of level pathway and follow blue blazes as you saunter northeast through a moist and mossy forest. At 0.3 mile, a section of boardwalk takes you deeper into the forest before it transitions into rough-hewn bog bridges.

▸ MILE 0.3-0.5: South Turner Mountain Trail to Sandy Stream Pond

Continue northeast as the trail swings past **Sandy Stream Pond** and passes several little spur trails that lead to scenic points on the edge of the pond. Listen for the twang of local frogs—and, if you choose to check out any of the scenic cutoffs, watch the shoreline for moose, especially in the late afternoon or evening.

▸ MILE 0.5-0.7: Sandy Stream Pond to South Turner Mountain Trail

The trail leaves the pond behind and ascends gradually before reaching the junction with the Sandy Stream Pond Trail at 0.7 mile. Veer right to stay on the South Turner Mountain Trail. Mind your footing as the trail crumples into a jumble of big mossy rocks.

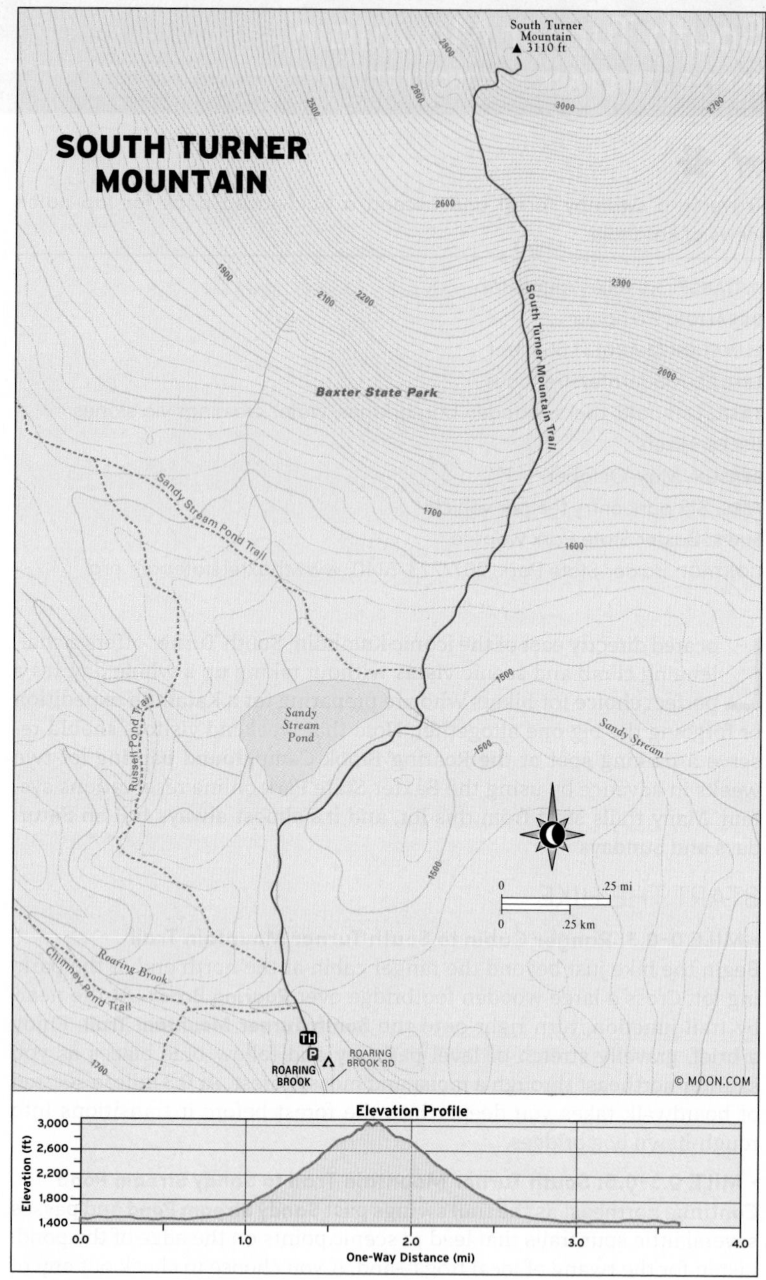

SOUTH TURNER MOUNTAIN
South Turner Mountain
3110 ft
South Turner Mountain Trail
Baxter State Park
Sandy Stream Pond Trail
Sandy Stream Pond
Sandy Stream
Russell Pond Trail
Roaring Brook
Chimney Pond Trail
TH
P
ROARING BROOK
ROARING BROOK RD
0
.25 mi
.25 km
© MOON.COM
Elevation Profile
Elevation (ft)
One-Way Distance (mi)

▲ SOUTH TURNER MOUNTAIN'S SUMMIT

▸ **MILE 0.7–1.7: South Turner Mountain Trail to South Turner Knife Edge Ridge**

Pick your way over the rocks and note the vernal pools on both sides of the trail. One mile in, the trail steepens considerably and ascends a series of rock stairs that slab northward up the mountainside. A few fleeting views through the birch and pine trees will give you a sense of how much elevation you're gaining within less than a mile (it's a lot). As the trees begin to shrink and the ground becomes much more eroded, the trail pops out onto the sun-kissed southern shoulder of **South Turner** at 1.7 miles. Enjoy a spectacular panorama of Katahdin's eastern heights—which include the notorious, razor-thin Knife Edge ridge where hikers go to test their self-preservation instincts.

▸ **MILE 1.7–1.8: South Turner Knife Edge Ridge to South Turner Summit**

To continue to the summit proper, head northeast and ascend an alternating series of rock stairs and large boulders (some of which necessitate scrambling). You'll reach the barren, knob-shaped summit at 1.8 miles. Return the way you came.

DIRECTIONS

From Bangor, drive north on I-95 N for roughly 58 miles and then take Exit 144-244 for ME-157 toward Medway/Millinocket. Turn left at the bottom of the off-ramp, drive northwest along ME-157 W/Medway Road until its terminus, and then take a right onto Katahdin Road. Turn left onto Bates Street and drive northwest for 8 miles as Bates Street becomes Millinocket Road and then Baxter Park Road. Continue north to the Togue Pond Gate House for Baxter State Park, pay the entrance fee, and veer right at the fork onto Roaring Brook Road. Drive along the winding dirt road for about 8 miles to reach the Roaring Brook Campground parking lot.

GPS COORDINATES: 45°55'10.8"N 68°51'26.5"W, 45.919667, -68.857352

8 Debsconeag Ice Caves

DEBSCONEAG LAKES WILDERNESS AREA, MILLINOCKET

This gentle wooded path has an awesome surprise at the end—a series of caves that retain their natural ice throughout the year.

BEST: New England oddities
DISTANCE: 2 miles round-trip
DURATION: 1 hour
ELEVATION CHANGE: 158 feet
EFFORT: Easy
TRAIL: Dirt path, rocks, wooden bridges, river crossings on stones, metal ladders
USERS: Hikers
SEASON: May-September
FEES/PASSES: None
MAPS: The Nature Conservancy website
CONTACT: The Nature Conservancy, 207/729-5181, www.nature.org

Hidden deep in the forest of the Debsconeag Wilderness Area, the Debsconeag Ice Caves are chock-full of ice that can last beyond July. Hikers will want to have boots with good tread, and parents with small children might want to skip this one. Traction isn't necessary for exploring the ice caves—boots with good grip, and a healthy dose of caution, will suffice.

START THE HIKE

▸ MILE 0-0.6: Trailhead to Glacial Boulders

Begin the hike by walking toward the red gate at the south end of the parking lot. Cross a large wooden bridge, then make a left as the dirt trail veers into the woods. Blue blazes mark the path forward. The trail crosses a few creeks on stones and ambles south through deciduous forest with plenty of young spruce and cedar trees. Look out for bear and moose scat—the woods here have a very active mammal population.

As the trail starts to ascend gradually, the trees on your left will begin to part and offer fleeting views of the Debsconeag Wilderness expanse, including the Penobscot River. Abundant ferns add some color along the trail. Continue hiking south as the trail narrows into a ledge and takes you along the flank of a broad hillside. Note the glacial boulders that begin to appear around 0.6 mile.

▸ MILE 0.6-1.0: Glacial Boulders to Debsconeag Ice Caves

After another 0.2 mile, the trail reaches a junction with a sign for the ice caves. Turn left here, descend through a dreamy, mossy stretch of woods, and then turn right at a second junction (also affixed with a sign for the ice caves). Walk west toward a looming garden of glacial boulders and reach the entrance to the **Debsconeag Ice Caves** at 1 mile.

▲ DESCEND INTO DEBSCONEAG ICE CAVES.

▸ **MILE 1.0-2.0: Debsconeag Ice Caves and Return to Trailhead**

You can climb down into the caves by using the metal rungs that are installed in the rock walls, but be careful upon reaching the bottom: The floor of the cave is sheer ice and very slippery. A guide rope affixed to the right wall of the cave offers some support. If you feel like venturing deeper into the abyss, you'll want to have a reliable light source. Solo hikers should take extra caution when exploring the cave. When you're done exploring, return the way you came.

DIRECTIONS

From Bangor, drive north on I-95 N for roughly 58 miles and then take Exit 144-244 for ME-157 toward Medway/Millinocket. Turn left at the bottom of the off-ramp, drive northwest along ME-157 W/Medway Road until its terminus, and then take a right onto Katahdin Road. Turn left onto Bates Street and drive northwest for 8 miles as Bates Street becomes Millinocket Road and then Baxter Park Road. After passing the Big Moose Inn, take a left and then turn right to merge onto Golden Road. Drive carefully along this pothole-filled logging road for another 10 miles. Immediately after crossing Abol Bridge, turn left onto the dirt road flanked by a large Nature Conservancy sign. Drive south for about 3 miles. Veer left at the fork and continue for another mile until you reach the Debsconeag Ice Caves parking lot on the right side.

GPS COORDINATES: 45°47'29.2"N 68°58'41.4"W, 45.791449, -68.978171

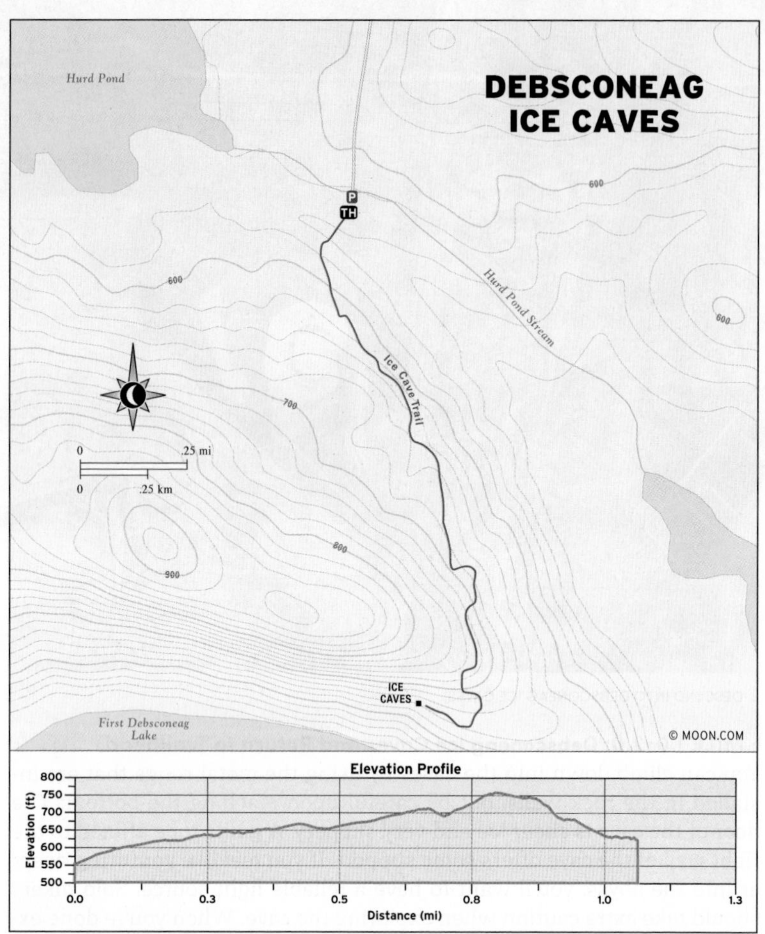

BEST NEARBY BITES

Tuck into a nourishing burger or sandwich in the middle of the Millinocket backwoods by making a pit stop at Abol Bridge Campground's rustic on-site eatery, **The Northern Restaurant** (3969 Golden Rd., Mile 19, Millinocket, 207/447-5803, www.greatnorthernvacations.com, call for hours).

9 Blueberry Ledges

BAXTER STATE PARK, MILLINOCKET

Hike through forest to visit one of the most wonderous places in Maine—a massive exposed rock slab decorated with rivulets of rushing water.

BEST: Spots for a swim
DISTANCE: 3.6 miles round-trip
DURATION: 1.5 hours
ELEVATION CHANGE: 263 feet
EFFORT: Easy
TRAIL: Dirt path, rocks, wooden bridges
USERS: Hikers
SEASON: May-September
FEES/PASSES: None
MAPS: Baxter State Park website
CONTACT: Baxter State Park, 207/723-5140, www.baxterstatepark.org

Blueberry Ledges is a rolling expanse of exposed rock cuts on the southern border of Baxter State Park. What makes this place special are the chutes of water that spill down the rocky ledges—putting the "blue" in blueberry. In spring and early summer, the snowmelt turns the entire mess of slides into a big torrent of rushing water, which funnels into watery chutes that hikers can ride into pools of (very cold) water. This feature makes Blueberry Ledges a popular stop for thru-hikers who've just finished the trail and are craving a celebratory cool-down.

START THE HIKE

▶ MILE 0-0.3: Twin Woodsheds to Baxter State Park

Begin the hike by the **twin woodsheds** in the north end of the parking lot. Walk toward the Northern Outdoors sign, pass through the trees, and turn left onto a dirt road. Walk north along the road to an open marsh area and cross a wooden log bridge over a creek. This bridge marks your official entry point into **Baxter State Park.**

▶ MILE 0.3-0.6: Baxter State Park to Blueberry Ledges Trail

Enter the forest on the other side of the bridge and continue northwest to the trail information kiosk at 0.4 mile. Make a right turn here onto the **Abol Pond Trail.** The trail climbs a hill before leveling off and reaching a junction for the Blueberry Ledges Trail at 0.6 mile.

▶ MILE 0.6-1.8: Blueberry Ledges Trail to Blueberry Ledges

Turn left onto the Blueberry Ledges Trail and enjoy a meandering stroll through a hall of beautiful white birch trees. The undergrowth is rich with multiple fern species, but the trail remains wide and smooth. As the trail begins to ascend at a gradual grade, the surrounding woods become more diverse, with cedar trees making appearances.

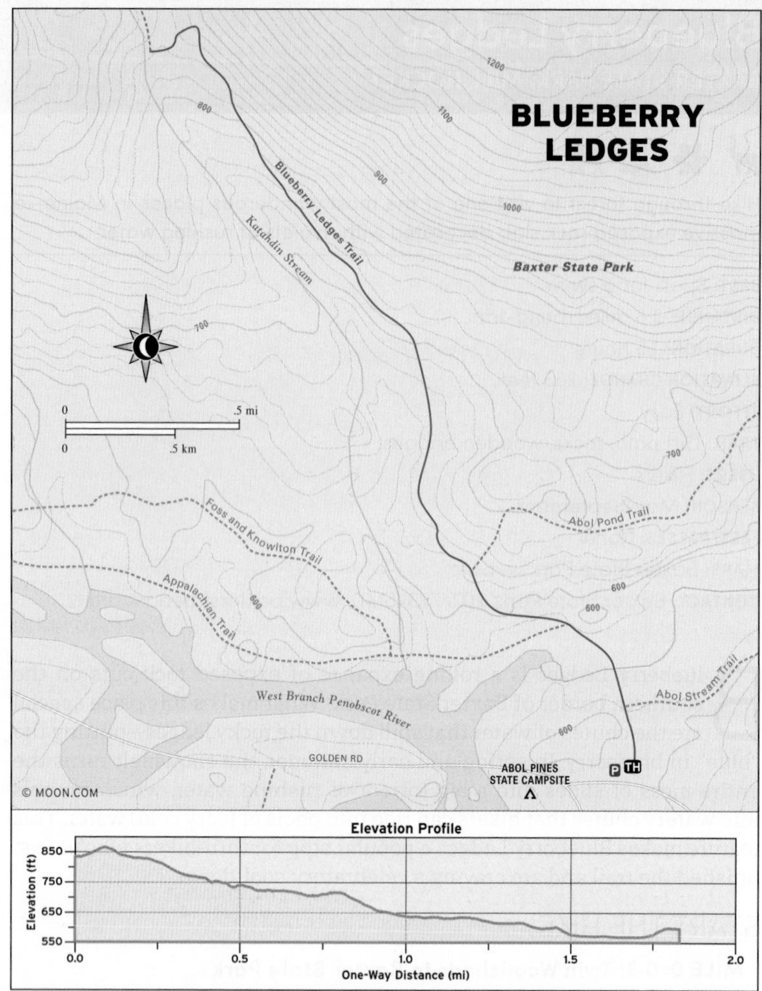

At 1.1 miles, keep an eye out for a dirt cutoff path on the left. This little spur leads down to the bottom of the Blueberry Ledges, where hikers can admire some seasonal cascades during the wettest months. To continue to the real deal, keep hiking northwest along the main trail as it becomes narrower and rockier. Cross several muddier sections on wooden bog bridges and stones. As the trail ascends, small cairns begin to appear. Emerge onto an open rock face dotted with balsam firs and climb to a large rock straight ahead, where the ground becomes level. Take a sharp left here and enjoy the full grandeur of **Blueberry Ledges,** which appears before you as a hilly landscape of exposed rock, water, and spare groves of trees and vegetation. Even from afar, the chutes of water are visible as they wind their way down the expanse. Descend another sloped rock face as you head toward the ledges. Watch your step, as the rock gets wet in places—especially where black moss is growing.

▲ BLUEBERRY LEDGES POOLS

▸ MILE 1.8–3.6: Blueberry Ledges to Blueberry Ledges Pools

At 1.8 miles, the trail reaches a swirling pool fed by chutes. From here, hikers can scramble up and across the ledges to explore them further. There are several choice swimming holes in the vicinity, though hikers should be careful to note the presence of large tree branches and blowdowns before taking a dip. Some of the larger rivulets can carry woodland debris down the ledges, adding to the otherworldly appearance of this place. Return the way you came.

DIRECTIONS

From Bangor, drive north on I-95 N for roughly 58 miles and then take Exit 144-244 for ME-157 toward Medway/Millinocket. Turn left at the bottom of the off-ramp, drive northwest along ME-157 W/Medway Road until its terminus, and then take a right onto Katahdin Road. Turn left onto Bates Street and drive northwest for 8 miles as Bates Street becomes Millinocket Road and then Baxter Park Road. After passing the Big Moose Inn, take a left and then turn right to merge onto Golden Road. Drive carefully along this pothole-filled logging road for another 10 miles. As you approach the Abol Bridge Campground store, pull a U-turn-esque right onto a dirt road, then make another left onto a dirt road. Ahead, on your left, you'll see a gravel parking area with twin woodsheds.

GPS COORDINATES: 45°50'08.5"N 68°57'35.7"W, 45.835687, -68.959929

10 Mount Katahdin

BAXTER STATE PARK, MILLINOCKET

The tallest mountain in Maine and the northern terminus of the Appalachian Trail is a once-in-a-lifetime climbing experience that will take your breath away.

BEST: Summer hikes, vistas
DISTANCE: 9.4 miles round-trip
DURATION: 8.5 hours
ELEVATION CHANGE: 4,077 feet
EFFORT: Strenuous
TRAIL: Dirt path, rocks, iron rungs, wooden bridges
USERS: Hikers
SEASON: June-September
FEES/PASSES: $15 park entrance fee, optional $5 parking reservation fee
MAPS: Baxter State Park website
CONTACT: Baxter State Park, 207/723-5140, www.baxterstatepark.org

Various trails lead to the summit, all of which require you to climb hundreds of rock stairs through boreal forests, scale perilous ledges, and scramble through mazes of boulders. Because Katahdin is the northern terminus of the Appalachian Trail, the route below follows the Hunt Trail—the official AT ascent route.

Baxter State Park limits the number of hikers on Katahdin each day. There are three parking lots from which the Katahdin trails depart and most of the spaces in those lots are reserved by hikers in advance. (A limited number of first-come, first-served spots are handed out when the park opens at 6am each morning, and people will line up to grab them.)

Reservations can be made online or by phone. Maine residents can book summer parking spots in advance starting in April and non-Mainers can reserve their spots two weeks before their hiking date. Weekends are far more competitive and there is no parking allowed on the sides of the roads in the park.

START THE HIKE

▸ MILE 0-1.0: Hunt Trail Trailhead to The Owl

Begin the hike in the clearing beside the day-use parking lot. The Hunt Trail begins on the north end of the clearing by a post with a white blaze. Check the trailhead for bridge closure notices. If the bridge is out and you're comfortable crossing Katahdin Stream on wet rocks, take the Hunt Trail north along a gentle stony path. Veer right at the junction for **The Owl** at 1 mile and carefully cross Katahdin Stream. If you don't want to risk getting wet, take the Katahdin Stream bypass route from the trailhead by crossing a large wooden bridge over Katahdin Stream, walking east along a gravel road, and picking up the signed bypass trail on your left. Just like the original Hunt

▲ MOUNT KATAHDIN

Trail, it lumbers north through the woods at a patient grade until it converges with the Hunt Trail. (Note the outhouse beside Katahdin Stream: this is your last chance to relieve yourself in relative comfort.)

▸ MILE 1.0–2.5: The Owl to Boulders

From here, the trail ascends a series of sloped rock faces that emerge from the trees and passes the beautiful **Katahdin Stream Falls** at 1.1 miles. Keep following the white blazes as the trail becomes a sequence of rock stairs that grow progressively steeper and rougher for the next mile. Gradually, the stairs transition to dicier rock scrambles, and the trees open up a bit to reveal some killer views of The Owl, a craggy peak that sits to Katahdin's west. Then, quite suddenly, the trail fully emerges from the trees at 2.5 miles and arrives at a jumble of house-sized boulders.

▸ MILE 2.5–2.8: Boulders to Hunt Spur

This is where the hike truly becomes a climb, as the Hunt Trail scales the boulders with the assistance of some iron rungs and pegs that have been installed along the trail to help hikers pull themselves over the gargantuan rocks. This is a tough and often scary section of trail that requires concentration, caution, and considerable upper-body strength. After bypassing the last of the boulders, the trail levels out and reaches **Hunt Spur** at 2.8 miles. This is one of the most incredible parts of the hike. The upper heights of Katahdin are now in sight, but to get there, you must scale the exposed and dizzyingly steep ridge of Hunt Spur.

▸ MILE 2.8–3.7: Hunt Spur to Katahdin Tableland

For the next half mile, the trail works its way up the spur, over all manner of crags and cliffs. (Don't stray from the white-blazed climbing route.) Take

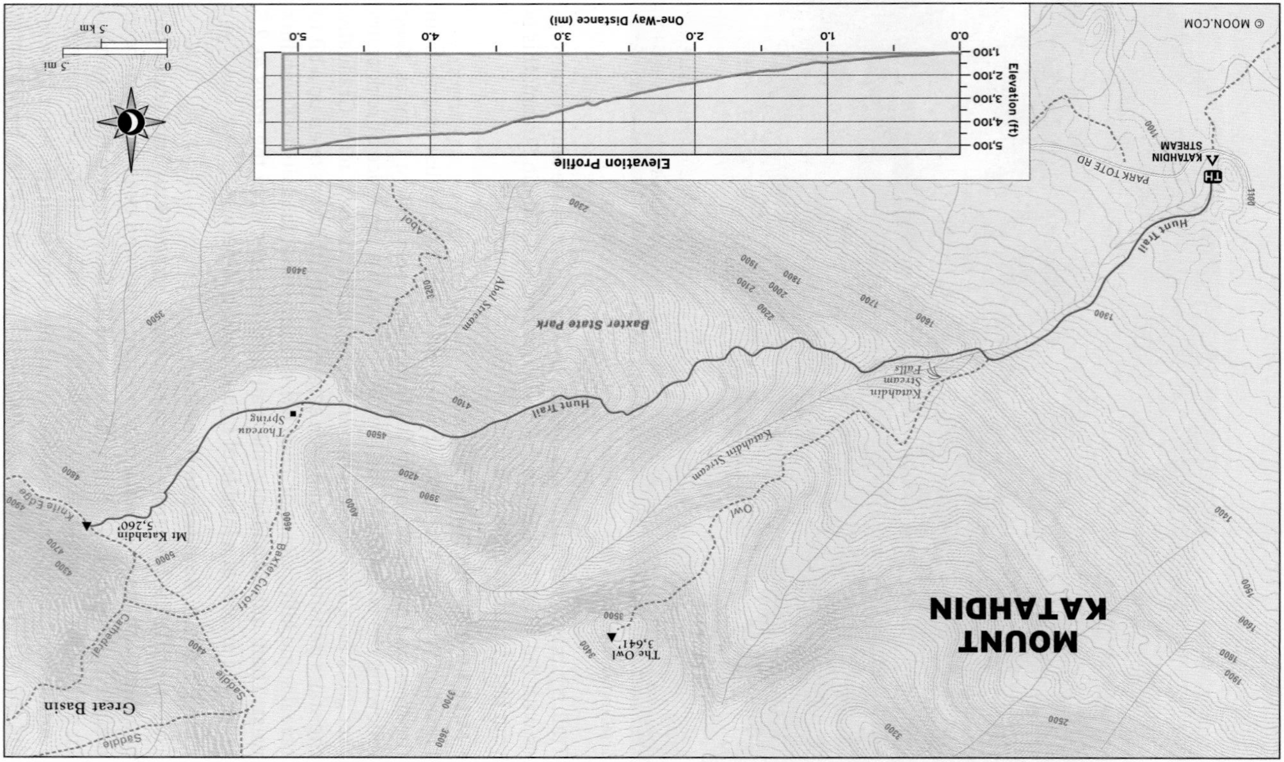
MOUNT KATAHDIN
© MOON.COM
KATAHDIN STREAM
PARK TOTE RD
Hunt Trail
Katahdin Stream Falls
Katahdin Stream
Owl
The Owl 3,641'
Baxter State Park
Abol Stream
Abol
Thoreau Spring
Baxter Cut-off
Saddle
Cathedral
Great Basin
Mt Katahdin 5,260'
Knife Edge
Elevation Profile
Elevation (ft)
5,100
4,100
3,100
2,100
1,100
0.0
1.0
2.0
3.0
4.0
5.0
One-Way Distance (mi)
0
.5 mi
0
.5 km

a break to recover your breath and drink in the beauty of the surrounding landscape: a sea of green trees and blue lakes. After a final stretch of ledges, the trail reaches the tableland of Katahdin at 3.1 miles and segues into a gorgeous amble across a windswept plateau of tundra and rocks.

MILE 3.7-9.4: Katahdin Tableland to Mount Katahdin Summit

Veer left at the junction with the Abol Trail at 3.7 miles to stay on Hunt. Slather on some sunscreen here—it will be at least another hour or two before you're back in the shade of the trees. The trail curves to the northeast and climbs a series of rock steps. Just ahead, you'll likely notice a gaggle of hikers. At 4.7 miles, you will arrive at the summit of **Mount Katahdin,** which offers an awe-inspiring panoramic view of Maine's deep green northern wilderness. Take your time at the top and assess your physical condition before making your descent. For hikers uncomfortable with the prospect of venturing down the technical portions of the boulder field, the Abol Trail offers a less tricky (but relentlessly steep) alternative descent that finishes roughly 2.4 miles down the road from the Katahdin Stream Campground. Otherwise, returning by way of the Hunt Trail is the "easiest" way back down.

DIRECTIONS

From Bangor, drive north on I-95 N for roughly 58 miles and then take Exit 144-244 for ME-157 toward Medway/Millinocket. Turn left at the bottom of the off-ramp, drive northwest along ME-157 W/Medway Road until its terminus, and then take a right onto Katahdin Road. Turn left onto Bates Street and drive northwest for 8 miles as Bates Street becomes Millinocket Road and then Baxter Park Road. Continue north to the Togue Pond Gate House for Baxter State Park, pay the $15 entrance fee, and turn left at the fork onto Park Tote Road. Drive along the winding dirt road for roughly 8 miles and then turn right at the sign for Katahdin Stream Campground parking.

GPS COORDINATES: 45°53'11.7"N 68°59'59.1"W, 45.886588, -68.999748

BEST NEARBY BREWS

Down the road from Togue Pond Gate House, you'll find killer burgers, salads, pastas, and Maine craft beers at the **Loose Moose Bar & Grille** (Big Moose Inn, Main St., Millinocket, 207/723-8391, www.bigmoosecabins.com, 5pm-10pm Sun.-Sat.). Head further into town for a nice selection of bars and home-style eateries such as the **Scootic In Restaurant** (70 Penobscot Ave., Millinocket, 207/723-4566, www.scooticin.com, 11am-9pm Mon.-Thurs., 11am-10pm Fri.-Sat.); be sure to make time for a few homemade baked goods and some conversations with thru-hikers at the **Appalachian Trail Café** (210 Penobscot Ave., Millinocket, 207/723-6720, www.appalachiantraillodge.com, 5am-2pm daily).

NEARBY CAMPGROUNDS

NAME	LOCATION	FACILITIES	SEASON	FEE
Wilderness Edge Campground	71 Millinocket Lake Rd., Millinocket, ME 04462	Tent sites, rental tents, cabin tents, RV sites, RV rentals, toilets, showers, potable water, laundry, camp store, Wi-Fi	early May through mid-October	$14-69
207/447-8485, www.wildernessedgecampground.com				
Big Moose Inn Cabins & Campground	5 Frederickas Way, Millinocket, ME 04462	Tent sites, lean-tos, RV sites, cabins, hotel rooms, toilets, showers, potable water, camp store, restaurant, Wi-Fi	June-late October	$13-840
207/723-8391, www.bigmoosecabins.com				
Katahdin Stream Campground	Appalachin Trail/Katahdin Stream, Millinocket, ME 04462	Tent sites, lean-tos, toilets	mid-May through late October	$32 (plus $15 park entry fee)
207/723-5140, www.baxterstatepark.org				
Roaring Brook Campground	Chimney Pond Trail, Millinocket, ME 04462	75 RV sites	mid-April–October	$20
207/723-5140, www.baxterstatepark.org				
Abol Bridge Campground	3969 Golden Rd., Mile 19, Millinocket, ME 04462	Tent sites, RV sites, cabins, toilets, showers, camp store, restaurant, Wi-Fi	late May through September	$25-250
207/447-5803, www.abolcampground.com				
Big Eddy Cabins & Campground	Golden Rd., Millinocket, ME 04462	Tent sites, cabins, RV sites, toilets, showers, potable water, Wi-Fi	early May through mid-October	$13-96
207/882-7323, www.bigeddy.chewonki.org				
Moosehead Family Campground	312 Moosehead Lake Rd., Greenville, ME 04441	Tent sites, RV sites, toilets, showers, potable water, camp store, Wi-Fi	mid-May through mid-October	$30-54
207/695-2210, www.mooseheadcampground.com				

NEARBY CAMPGROUNDS (continued)

NAME	LOCATION	FACILITIES	SEASON	FEE
Balsam Woods Campground	112 Pond Rd., Abbot, ME 04406	Tent sites, RV sites, cabins, toilets, showers, potable water, laundry, swimming pool, camp store, Wi-Fi	late May through mid-October	$32-135
207/876-2731, www.balsamwoods.com				
Deer Farm Camps	495 Tufts Pond Rd., Kingfield, ME 04947	Tent sites, RV sites, cabins, toilets, showers, potable water, laundry, camp store	mid-May through mid-October	$18-60
207/265-4599, www.deerfarmcamps.com				
Cathedral Pines Campground	945 The Arnold Trl., Eustis, ME 04936	Tent sites, RV sites, toilets, showers, potable water, laundry, Wi-Fi	mid-May through September	$32-40
207/246-3491, www.gopinescamping.com				

▲ THE OUTLOOK LEDGE ATOP MOUNT KINEO

MIDCOAST, CASCO BAY, AND THE MAINE BEACHES

The beauty of the Maine coast is in its seamless pairing of hills and sea. This is the Maine that people dream of—cerulean seas crackling with whitecaps, towering pines rocked by the wind, and the aroma of golden-fried shrimp wafting down the shore. Nowhere else in New England can you scale steeplechase cliffs (flanked with blueberry bushes!) while breathing in that salty sea breeze. The sheer number of islands that speckle the Maine coast—more than 4,500 of them—imbues some local hiking destinations with an expeditionary thrill. And when it's time to refuel, Maine's coastal communities offer an unparalleled smorgasbord of classic maritime and New American culinary delights, plus a booming craft beer scene.

▲ Mirror Lake and Rockland from the slopes of Ragged Mountain

▲ a path into the eastern woods of Wells Reserve

◂ A LONE HIKER ALONG THE ROCKY, FLOWERING SHORELINE OF LANE'S ISLAND

1 **Mount Agamenticus**
DISTANCE: 2.5 miles round-trip
DURATION: 2 hours
EFFORT: Easy/moderate

2 **Wells Reserve**
DISTANCE: 2.8 miles round-trip
DURATION: 1.5 hours
EFFORT: Easy

3 **Fore River Sanctuary and Jewell Falls**
DISTANCE: 3.3 miles round-trip
DURATION: 1.5 hours
EFFORT: Easy

4 **Harpswell Cliff Trail**
DISTANCE: 2.2 miles round-trip
DURATION: 1.5 hours
EFFORT: Easy

5 **Oven's Mouth Preserves**
DISTANCE: 3.1 miles round-trip
DURATION: 1.5 hours
EFFORT: Easy

6 **Lane's Island**
DISTANCE: 1 mile round-trip
DURATION: 30 minutes
EFFORT: Easy

7 **Ragged Mountain**
DISTANCE: 4.8 miles round-trip
DURATION: 3.5 hours
EFFORT: Moderate/strenuous

8 **Mount Megunticook**
DISTANCE: 2.8 miles round-trip
DURATION: 2 hours
EFFORT: Moderate

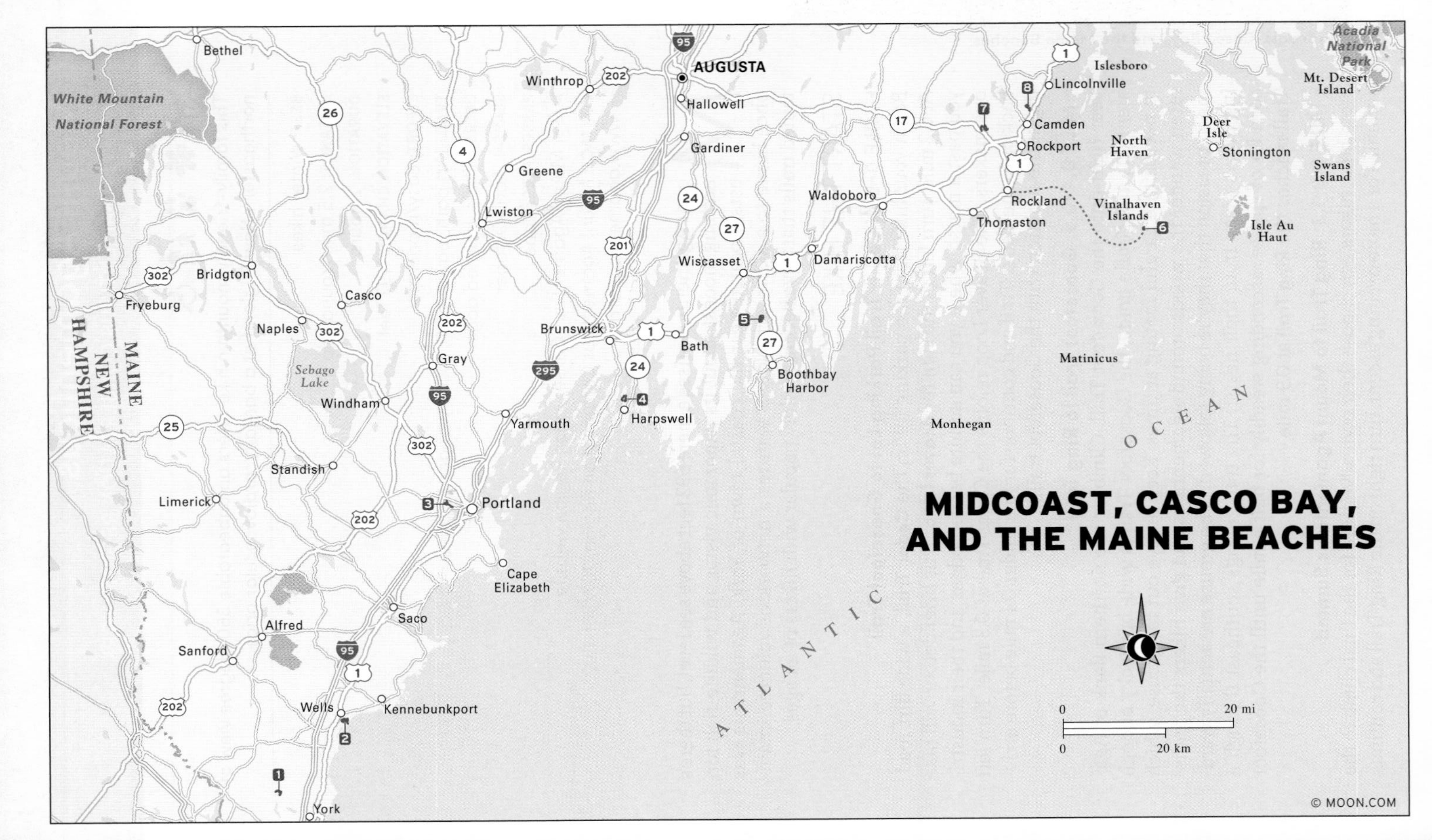
MIDCOAST, CASCO BAY, AND THE MAINE BEACHES
White Mountain National Forest
Acadia National Park
MAINE
NEW HAMPSHIRE
Bethel
AUGUSTA
Winthrop
Hallowell
Gardiner
Greene
Lwiston
Bridgton
Fryeburg
Casco
Naples
Sebago Lake
Gray
Windham
Brunswick
Bath
Wiscasset
Damariscotta
Waldoboro
Thomaston
Rockland
Rockport
Camden
Lincolnville
Islesboro
North Haven
Vinalhaven Islands
Deer Isle
Stonington
Mt. Desert Island
Swans Island
Isle Au Haut
Boothbay Harbor
Harpswell
Yarmouth
Portland
Cape Elizabeth
Standish
Limerick
Saco
Alfred
Sanford
Wells
Kennebunkport
York
Matinicus
Monhegan
ATLANTIC OCEAN
0 20 mi
0 20 km
© MOON.COM

1 Mount Agamenticus

MOUNT AGAMENTICUS CONSERVATION REGION, YORK

This family-friendly mountain hike offers an unbeatable 360-degree view of northeastern New England at a bargain cardiovascular price.

BEST: Winter hikes

DISTANCE: 2.5 miles round-trip

DURATION: 2 hours

ELEVATION CHANGE: 492 feet

EFFORT: Easy/moderate

TRAIL: Dirt path, paved path, rocks, wooden bridges

USERS: Hikers, leashed dogs

SEASON: April-October

PASSES/FEES: None

MAPS: Mount Agamenticus Conservation Region website

CONTACT: Mount Agamenticus Conservation Region, 207/361-1102, www.agamenticus.org

Mount Agamenticus rises a mere 692 feet above sea level, but there's nothing modest about its panoramic vistas and wildlife-rich forests. Located near the coastal town of York, Agamenticus was once home to a ski resort. Now it features a network of volunteer-maintained trails that have become wildly popular with hikers of all ages.

START THE HIKE

▸ MILE 0-0.4: Cedar Trail Parking Lot to Goosefoot Trail

Begin your hike from the parking lot on the **Cedar Trail,** a wide dirt road. At 0.2 mile, turn left at the sign for **Beaver Loop.** This brief detour will take you past a marsh where you can admire beaver lodges and their industrious makers. The Beaver Loop rejoins the Cedar Trail at 0.3 mile. Turn left back onto the Cedar Trail and continue for just under 0.1 mile before arriving at the junction with the Goosefoot trail.

▸ MILE 0.4-0.9: Goosefoot Trail to Ring Trail

Veer right onto the Goosefoot Trail. Climbing the northern flank of Agamenticus at a gentle grade, the Goosefoot Trail is wide but rocky enough to necessitate careful footing at times. Keep an eye out for grouse, which often wander the woods around Agamenticus and give hikers the amusing impression that they're being followed. (The grouse are actually warding hikers away from their nests!) The trail zigzags southeast through a corridor of spruce, ascending steadily for half a mile until the Goosefoot Trail reaches the **Ring Trail** at 0.9 mile.

▸ MILE 0.9-1.3: Ring Trail to Mount Agamenticus Summit

From here, hikers can choose their own adventure for the final climb to the summit. For a more exciting ascent, turn right on the Ring Trail and continue

▲ VIEW FROM THE MOUNT AGAMENTICUS SUMMIT

west past an old rusted ski lift tower, until you reach the **Sweetfern** connector trail after less than 0.1 mile. Take a left onto Sweetfern and scramble up a series of exposed rock slabs. (Watch your step—the lower slabs are very smooth.) At 1.1 miles, Sweetfern flattens and emerges onto the vast open summit of Mount Agamenticus. The second option for reaching the summit is to turn left onto the Ring Trail (back at the terminus of Goosefoot) and climb steadily along Agamenticus's eastern slope for 0.2 mile before swinging right onto the Big A cutoff and making a short final push to the summit. The Sweetfern route is the more fun and scenic of the two; no matter which you choose, the summit offers a grand bouffe of attractions.

▸ MILE 1.3-1.6: Mount Agamenticus Summit to Big A Path and Observation Tower

Continue on Sweetfern for 0.1 mile until you reach the wheelchair-accessible Big A summit path (also accessible via the Agamenticus auto road). Take a right onto the **Big A path,** cross a wooden bridge, and enjoy the north-facing views of New Hampshire and Maine as you amble along the path in a southwesterly direction. On clear days, Mount Washington is visible from here. Big A soon curves north and passes a rocky overlook point called Blueberry Bluff before delivering you to the summit proper and its nearby **observation tower** at 1.6 miles. From the tower, you can gaze out to the Atlantic Ocean and spot the Isles of Shoals.

▸ MILE 1.6-2.5: Observation Tower to Cedar Trail Parking Lot (via Big A Path)

For a more interesting return journey, pick up the Vultures View Trail from the Big A path—back by the wooden summit bridge—and descend some sunny stone stairs into the woods. Vultures View intersects with Goosefoot at 2.2 miles. Keep left at this final junction and retrace your steps to the parking lot.

DIRECTIONS

From Boston, drive north on I-93. Take Exit 37A to merge onto I-95 N. Continue through New Hampshire and into Maine until you reach Exit 7

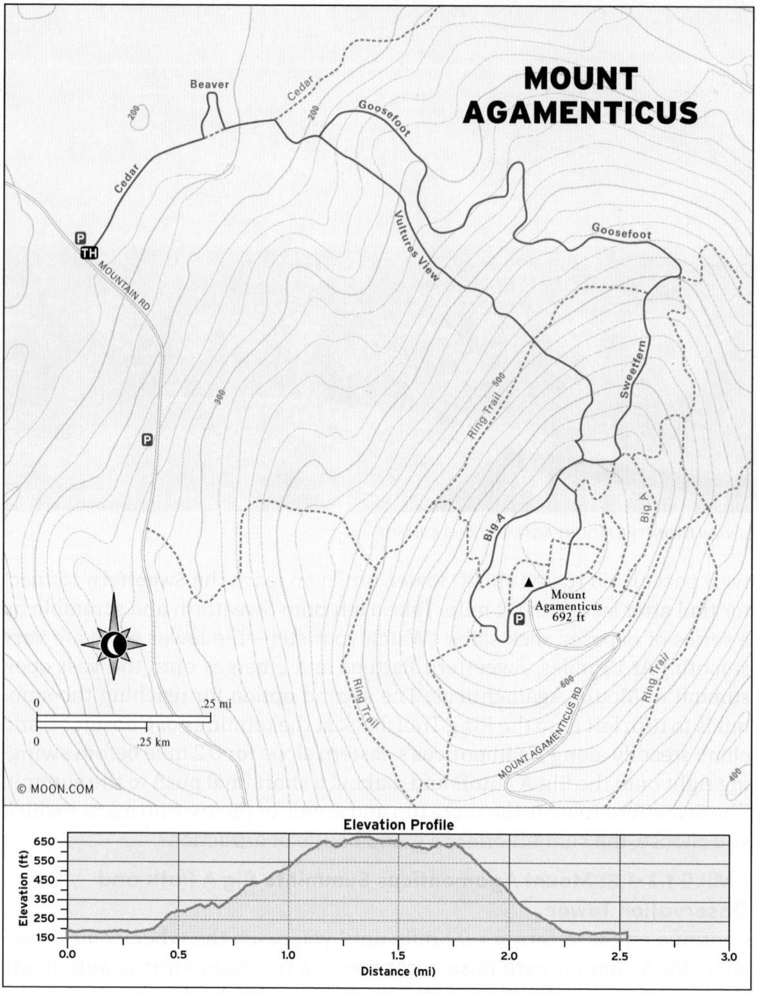

MOUNT AGAMENTICUS

Beaver
Cedar
Goosefoot
Vultures View
Sweetfern
Ring Trail
Big A
MOUNTAIN RD
MOUNT AGAMENTICUS RD
Mount Agamenticus 692 ft
0 .25 mi
0 .25 km
© MOON.COM

Elevation Profile

Elevation (ft)
Distance (mi)

toward ME-91. Turn left at the top of the exit ramp, then take an immediate right onto Chases Pond Road. Drive north on Chases Pond Road as it curves northwest and becomes Mountain Road. Continue past the Mount Agamenticus auto road. The paved road becomes a dirt road and the Cedar Trail parking lot is ahead on the right. If the Cedar Trail lot is full, there's also a hiker parking lot back by the auto road entrance.

GPS COORDINATES: 43°13'39.3"N 70°42'06.0"W, 43.227589, -70.70166

BEST NEARBY BREWS

If you have a soft spot for craft beer, prepare to go weak in the knees when you try the oyster stout and farmhouse saisons at **Tributary Brewing Company** (10 Shapleigh Rd., Kittery, 207/703-0093, www.tributarybrewingcompany.com, noon-7pm Wed.-Sat., 1pm-6pm Sun.).

2 Wells Reserve

WELLS RESERVE AT LAUDHOLM, WELLS

Explore one of the most biodiverse coastal environments in Maine, with mixed woods, estuaries, and a windswept beach.

DISTANCE: 2.8 miles round-trip

DURATION: 1.5 hours

ELEVATION CHANGE: 63 feet

EFFORT: Easy

TRAIL: Dirt path, wooden bridges

USERS: Hikers

SEASON: May-October

FEES/PASSES: $5 adult, $1 ages 7-16, free ages 6 and under

MAPS: Wells Reserve website

CONTACT: Wells Reserve, 207/646-1555, www.wellsreserve.org. The visitors center is open daily 10am-4pm from Memorial Day weekend through mid-October, and then 10am-4pm in late October, November, April, and May.

The Maine coast is a melting pot of flora and fauna. The mixed woods here are alive with the cries of gulls and red squirrels. The spiny spruce trees give way to salty estuaries where tallgrass blows in the wind. This biodiversity is best experienced by taking a jaunt through Wells Reserve—a 2,250-acre estuarine research area with a vast network of trails that meander through fields, forests, beaches, boardwalk, and tidal marshes.

START THE HIKE

▸ MILE 0-0.4: Wells Reserve Visitors Center to Muskie Trail Boardwalk

Begin the hike on the north side of the visitors center. Walk east down the grassy hill to the right of the visitors center and pick up the **Muskie Trail,** which cuts through a sunny meadow speckled with flowers and buzzing with insects. (Be sure to do a tick check after the hike.) Shortly after the trail begins, you'll cross an access road and walk along a stretch of boardwalk that tunnels through a forest of pine and sugar maple before popping back out into a larger meadow.

▸ MILE 0.4-0.8: Muskie Trail Boardwalk to Webhannet Estuary

Continue hiking east as the trail segues from boardwalk to a flat grassy path at 0.5 mile. The trail curves north through a red oak and spruce corridor and concludes at a cutoff trail for **Webhannet Estuary** at 0.8 mile. To visit the estuary lookout, keep right and take a brief northward stroll to reach a wooden deck that overlooks the briny marsh.

▸ MILE 0.8-1.6: Webhannet Estuary to Barrier Beach Connector

To continue deeper into the reserve, turn left at the junction to pick up the **Pilger Trail,** which heads west into a shrubbier stretch of woods with lots

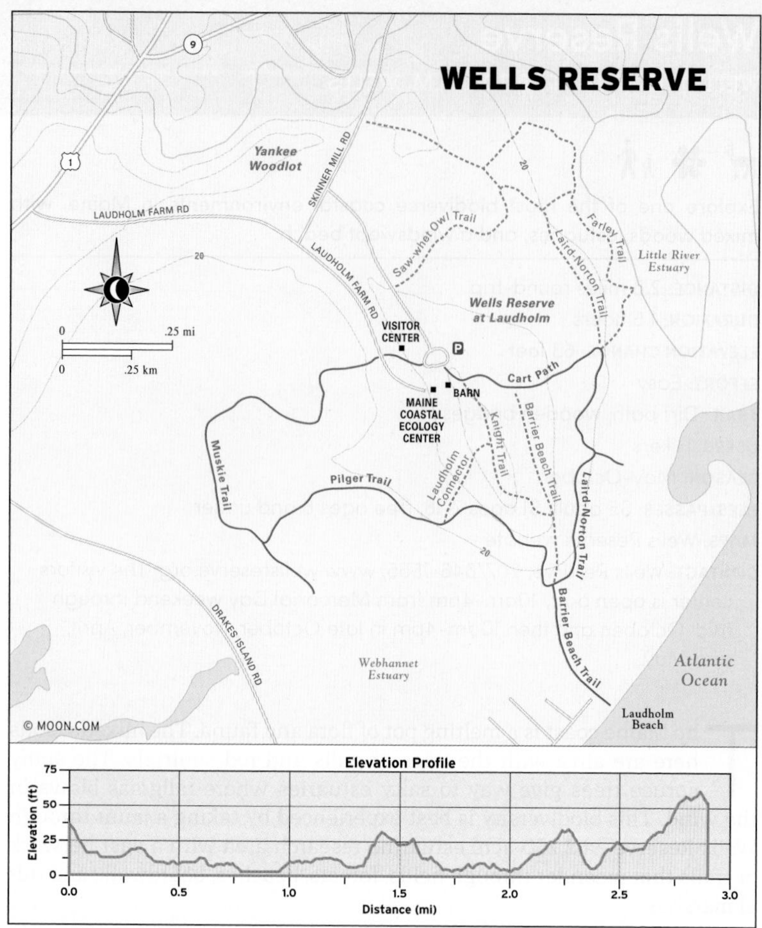

of sunlight and fruit trees bearing black cherries and apples. At 1.3 miles, turn right at the junction with Laudholm Connector and make a brief descent through groves of slender trembling aspen trees. At 1.6 miles, reach a four-way intersection and turn right onto the **Barrier Beach Connector,** a spacious dirt road that emerges from the woods to bisect two estuaries.

▸ MILE 1.6-2.0: Barrier Beach Connector to Laird-Norton Trail

Continue north through a stone gate and pass some houses. A boardwalk takes you down to the dune-like sprawl of **Laudholm Beach** at 1.8 miles. (This beach is much quieter and more pristine than the heavily trafficked ones closer to Wells.) Once you've had your fill of surf and sand, backtrack south along the Barrier Beach Connector; at the junction, swing right onto the **Laird-Norton Trail.**

▸ MILE 2.0-2.8: Laird-Norton Trail to Cart Path

Head southwest for another 0.3 mile as the Laird-Norton Trail transitions from dirt to a gorgeous highway of boardwalk that weaves through towering maples and yellow birches; there are plenty of wooden benches along the boardwalk for taking in the scenery. At 2.3 miles, the trail passes a cutoff for the Little River Estuary observation deck and continues southwest

▲ ESTUARIES WITHIN THE WELLS RESERVE ECOSYSTEM

through vividly green ferns and sphagnum moss. At 2.5 miles, turn left onto the **Cart Path** and walk east along a gravel trail that takes you out of the hemlocks and up a gentle exposed hillside to return to the visitors center at 2.8 miles.

DIRECTIONS

From Portland, take I-295 S to merge onto I-95 S and then drive south for 23 miles. Take Exit 25 toward ME-35/Kennebunk/Kennebunkport. Swing left onto Alewife Road and then make a right turn onto ME-35 S/Fletcher Street. Continue to the traffic circle, take the first exit onto Storer Street, and follow it to the four-way intersection with US-1 S/York Street and Water Street. Turn right onto US-1 S/York Street, drive south for another 3 miles, and make a left onto Laudholm Farm Road. Shortly ahead, veer left onto Skinner Mill Road and take the first turnoff on your right to reach the parking lot for Wells Reserve.

GPS COORDINATES: 45°53'11.7"N 68°59'59.1"W, 45.886588, -68.999748

BEST NEARBY BREWS

Wet your whistle with any of the renowned IPAs and seasonal beers at **Hidden Cove Brewing Co.** (73 Mile Rd., Wells, 207/646-0228, www.hiddencovebrewingcompany.com, 3pm-8pm Mon.-Thurs., noon-9pm Fri.-Sat., noon-5pm Sun.).

3 Fore River and Jewell Falls

FORE RIVER SANCTUARY, PORTLAND

Hike through bird-filled salt marsh and mixed woods to a beautiful waterfall—all within the city limits of Portland.

BEST: Spring hikes
DISTANCE: 3.3 miles round-trip
DURATION: 1.5 hours
ELEVATION CHANGE: 147 feet
EFFORT: Easy
TRAIL: Dirt path, wooden bridges
USERS: Hikers, leashed dogs
SEASON: May-November
FEES/PASSES: None
MAPS: Portland Trails website
CONTACT: Portland Trails, 207/775-2411, www.trails.org

START THE HIKE

▸ MILE 0-0.2: Parking Lot to Fore River Estuary

Begin the hike in the north end of the parking lot. Pick up the trail, which begins as a few sections of wooden boardwalk that run parallel to the parking lot before dipping into a grove of trees. Follow white blazes down a hillside to reach the mouth of the Fore River. Cross a long wooden bridge at 0.2 mile, take a good whiff of salty air, and enter the Fore River estuary.

▸ MILE 0.2-1.0: Fore River Estuary to Fore River Bridge

The trail heads north along the river on sandy footing, which is helpful for minimizing your audible impact and thereby improving your chance of spotting a heron traipsing through the tall grass.

Curving west into a more wooded region, the trail crosses a few small wooden bridges before taking a sharp right and crossing a much larger bridge at 0.8 mile. A brief climb up a sandy hillside takes you into the cool, verdant depths of a spruce and pine forest. Keep right at the trail junction at the top of the hill. One mile in, you'll reach another junction where a rickety wooden bridge crosses the Fore River.

▸ MILE 1.0-1.5: Fore River Bridge to Jewell Falls Junction

Turn left here (skipping the bridge) and continue deeper into the woods, following blue blazes. The trail meanders through a boggier stretch of forest and crosses some mudflats on bog bridges—the distant rumble of city traffic pairs surprisingly well with the croaking of frogs.

At 1.2 miles, veer right at the trail split to climb a larger hill. (The blazes become red at this point.) Cross into a sun-splashed zone of woods, where the trail levels off and passes some industrial buildings on the edge of the forest. At 1.5 miles, turn left at a signed junction to Jewell Falls; follow blue blazes down some wooden stairs to a railroad crossing.

▲ JEWELL FALLS

▸ MILE 1.5–1.8: Jewell Falls Junction to Jewell Falls

The trail descends from the tracks into a wooded ravine and reaches a final junction at 1.7 miles. Make a left at this split, follow white blazes once again, and gently descend a hillside before the trail transitions to a charming stretch of wooden boardwalk. Schlep your way up to a small, eroded height of land and arrive at the resplendent 30-foot-tall **Jewell Falls** at 1.8 miles.

▸ MILE 1.8–3.3: Jewell Falls to Fore River Estuary

Hikers can view the cascade from a terrace-like outlook with a bench, continue up the trail to a wooden bridge that spans the falls, or scramble down the embankment to the pool at the bottom of the main cascade. To begin the return journey, backtrack to the last junction and go left. Follow the path along a ridge with pretty birch trees and keep right at the fork at 2.1 miles (follow the sign for Congress Street). The trail crosses the railroad tracks and enters the estuary again on a longer and more scenic boardwalk. Take a right at the next junction to climb a knoll with nice partial views of the marshy area. At the top of the hill, veer left and descend to a familiar-looking rickety wooden bridge across the Fore River at 2.3 miles. Cross the bridge, make a left on the other side, and backtrack to the trailhead at 3.3 miles.

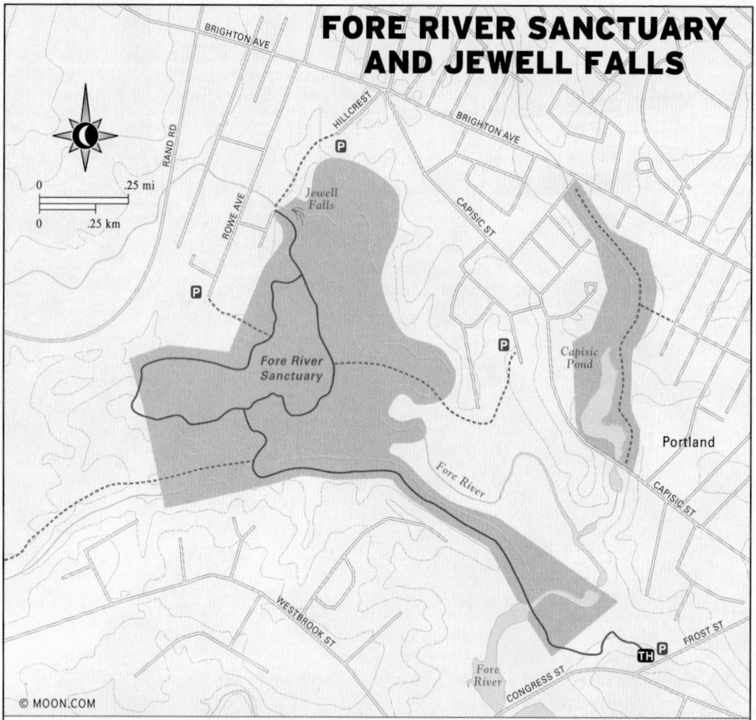

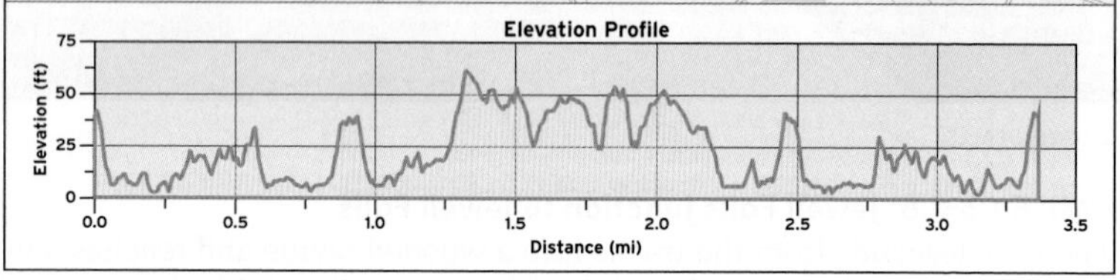

FORE RIVER SANCTUARY AND JEWELL FALLS

BRIGHTON AVE
HILLCREST
RAND RD
ROWE AVE
CAPISIC ST
Jewell Falls
Fore River Sanctuary
Capisic Pond
Portland
Fore River
WESTBROOK ST
FROST ST
CONGRESS ST
0 .25 mi
0 .25 km

Elevation Profile
Elevation (ft)
Distance (mi)

DIRECTIONS

The Southern Maine Pediatrics Dentistry building and parking lot, from which the trail begins, is located at 1601 Congress Street in Portland, but the entrance to the lot is actually off of Frost Street, which connects to Congress. If the designated hiker parking spots are full, there are plenty of nearby residential streets where hikers can park their vehicles.

GPS COORDINATES: 43°39'37.6"N 70°18'24.7"W, 43.660441, -70.306858

BEST NEARBY BREWS

Portland was named one of Bon Appetit's top restaurant cities in 2018, which gives you an idea of the plethora of dining and drinking options you'll find in neighborhoods like Old Port, Back Cove, and Munjoy Hill. But if you want to keep your forays extra local, take a 20-minute stroll east from the Fore River trailhead and pay a visit to what many consider the best microbrewery in Maine—the seriously hopped-up **Bissell Brothers** (4 Thompsons Point #108, Portland, www.bissellbrothers.com, noon-8pm Tues.-Sat., noon-7pm Sun.).

4 Harpswell Cliff Trail

HARPSWELL HERITAGE LAND TRUST, HARPSWELL

Wander through a magical woodland full of handmade fairy houses to reach some of the most dramatic coastal cliff faces in the region.

DISTANCE: 2.2 miles round-trip
DURATION: 1.5 hours
ELEVATION CHANGE: 329 feet
EFFORT: Easy
TRAIL: Dirt path, rocks, wooden bridges
USERS: Hikers, leashed dogs
SEASON: May-November
FEES/PASSES: None
MAPS: Harpswell Heritage Land Trust website
CONTACT: Harpswell Heritage Land Trust, 207/721-1121, www.hhltmaine.org

START THE HIKE

▸ MILE 0-0.4: Harpswell Town Office Parking Lot to Old Town Road Intersection

Begin the hike in the northwest corner of the parking lot. Pick up the dirt trail and cross a wooden footbridge into the forest, where you'll quickly arrive at a sign for the **Harpswell Cliff Trail.** Follow white blazes north as the rooty path snakes through hemlock and spruce trees, occasionally skirting the edge of the woods for some sightings of **Strawberry Creek.** As the creek becomes marshier, the trail itself gets softer under your feet. Continue north as the trail veers away from Strawberry Creek and crosses a gulch on another footbridge. Keep straight at the three-way intersection with Old Town Road at 0.4 mile and cross another bridge to reach a series of seasonal cascades.

▸ MILE 0.4-0.9: Old Town Road Intersection to Harpswell Cliffs

Around this point, you may start seeing **fairy houses** along the trail. (Fairy houses are pretty little model dwellings made of twigs, stones, shells, moss, and other natural materials found in the woods. Stop and build one of your own, if inspired!) Continue strolling north through the woods as chipmunks and red squirrels rustle through the branches overhead. At 0.6 mile, make a right turn at the **Henry Creek Lookout junction**. The trail crosses some bog bridges and ascends a mossy hillside. (In the evening, this part of the trail is alive with the sound of peepers.) A brief descent down the opposite side of the hill delivers you to the first of the cliffs at 0.9 mile.

▸ MILE 0.9-1.4: Harpswell Cliffs to Orr's Island Overlook

The trail transforms into a wooded ledge and heads south along the cliffs, rolling up and down. The views of the ocean are stunning, and the trail itself never feels perilous or vertigo-inducing. A rockier and slightly steeper ascent leads to the ultimate cliff overlook at 1.4 miles, where hikers can

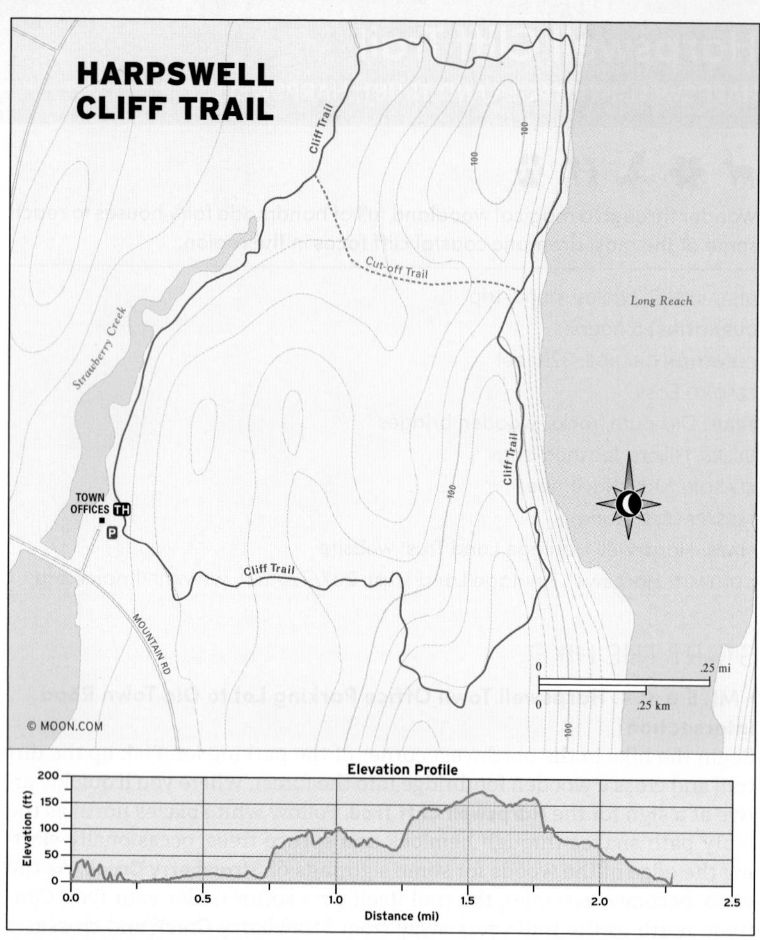

gaze out at nearby Orr's Island. Savor this concluding vista before returning south back into the forest.

▸ MILE 1.4–2.0: Orr's Island Overlook to Community Road
Pass through another fairy house building zone and descend gradually down the slopes of a large hillside known as Long Reach Mountain. The trail soon flattens and meanders through a shrubbier patch of woods before emerging onto the shoulder of Community Road at 2 miles.

▸ MILE 2.0–2.2: Community Road to Harpswell Town Office Parking Lot
Turn right onto the road and make an immediate left into the parking lot for the Harpswell Transfer Station. Walk northwest across the lot and down a grassy embankment to a grove of trees; walk through the grove to the Harpswell Town Office parking lot to complete the loop at 2.2 miles.

▲ LOOKING BACK FROM THE PINNACLE OF THE HARPSWELL CLIFFS

DIRECTIONS

From Portland, drive northeast on I-295 N for 17 miles and take Exit 24 for US-1 toward Freeport. Make a left onto US-1 N at the end of the off-ramp and continue northeast for roughly 3 miles before swinging right onto Highland Road. At the four-way intersection, turn left onto Pleasant Hill Road and take it east to its terminus at Maine Street. Make a right onto Maine Street and then make a slight right to stay on Maine Street, which becomes Mere Point Road. Shortly ahead, veer slightly left onto Middle Bay Road and then turn right onto ME-123 S. Drive south along this road for 3.5 miles and then swing left onto Mountain Road. The Harpswell Town Offices parking lot will be on your left just over a mile ahead.

GPS COORDINATES: 43°48'51.6"N 69°56'34.7"W, 43.814342, -69.942972

BEST NEARBY BITES

Gaze out over Casco Bay while tucking into parmesan-crusted haddock or seafood lasagna at **The Dolphin** (515 Basin Point Rd., Harpswell, 207/833-6000, www.dolphinmarinaandrestaurant.com, 11:30am-8pm Wed.-Sun.) or enjoy classic New England chowder, golden-fried clams, and some incredible natural rock formations at **Giant Stairs Seafood Grille** (2118 Harpswell Islands Rd., Bailey Island, 207/833-5000, 7am-3pm Thurs., 7am-8:30pm Fri.-Sun.).

5 Oven's Mouth Preserve

BOOTHBAY REGION LAND TRUST, BOOTHBAY

This coastal forest hike follows a saltwater channel to reach a beautiful tidal basin where warships used to hide.

DISTANCE: 3.1 miles round-trip
DURATION: 1.5 hours
ELEVATION CHANGE: 248 feet
EFFORT: Easy
TRAIL: Dirt path, rocks, wooden bridges
USERS: Hikers, leashed dogs
SEASON: May-October
FEES/PASSES: None
MAPS: Boothbay Region Land Trust website
CONTACT: Boothbay Region Land Trust, 207/633-4818, www.bbrlt.org

A few centuries ago, British and American ships needed a place to hide along the northeastern seaboard during the American Revolutionary War. One of the safe havens in which those vessels took cover is accessed by Oven's Mouth—a narrow yet deep waterway that leads to an expansive tidal basin with several coves large enough to hold seacraft of considerable size. The surrounding forests, wetlands, and twin peninsulas now known as Oven's Mouth Preserve offer a mixed coastal ecosystem home to deer and otters.

START THE HIKE

▸ MILE 0-0.2: Oven's Mouth Preserve Trailhead to Back River

Begin the hike on the west side of the parking area. Pick up the **White Trail** and enter a lush pine forest on a rooty dirt path. Veer right at the fork and follow white blazes north toward the sound of lapping water. At 0.2 mile, the trail emerges from the thicker greenery onto a wooded yet sunny hillside on the shores of the **Back River.**

▸ MILE 0.2-0.9: Back River to Oven's Mouth Bridge

This "river" is actually one of the coves that formerly sheltered warships. Continue north along the Back River as the trail rolls up and down the hillside, occasionally descending close enough to the water for hikers to veer off-trail and immerse their feet. The trail curves west around the tip of the east peninsula, following a narrower channel with lots of rushing water.

Pass through a grove of spruce trees to reach an outlook clearing with a wooden bench at 0.6 mile. The great aqua-hued basin of water you're looking at is the divide between the dual peninsulas of **Oven's Mouth**. The trail curves south and hugs the shoreline before arriving at a handsome wooden bridge at 0.9 mile. This bridge connects the east and west peninsulas.

▲ THE BRIDGE BETWEEN THE EAST AND WEST PENINSULAS AT OVEN'S MOUTH PRESERVES

▸ MILE 0.9–1.1: Oven's Mouth Bridge to White Trail

Turn right onto the bridge, cross over to the west peninsula, and then turn right again to enter the rockier and more densely wooded part of the preserve. The trail climbs steeply to a ridge that curves to the west, offering a pretty overhead perspective of the channel. At 1.1 miles, keep right at the **Blue Trail junction** to stay on White Trail and descend toward the water.

▸ MILE 1.1–2.2: White Trail to Blue Trail

Hike south for half a mile along a smaller cove on the far edge of the west peninsula. The footing becomes much softer—a classic Maine foundation of pine needles and soil. At 1.6 miles, a series of steeper and much rockier climbs and dips begins. The spruce woods around here are darker and thicker (and the red squirrels are especially feisty). As the cove narrows into something resembling a creek, the trail slabs up a larger hillside and climbs gradually to a height of land that's covered in ferns, spruce, and beech trees. At 2.2 miles, turn left onto the **Blue Trail**, following blue blazes on a level walk across a broader wooded ridge.

▸ MILE 2.2–2.8: Blue Trail to Oven's Mouth Bridge

Descend an especially fertile slope of ferns and wildflowers to reach a set of closely interspersed junctions at 2.4 miles. Turn right at the first split and follow combined blue and yellow blazes to the second junction at 2.6 miles; turn left onto this cutoff trail, which heads north and quickly merges with the **White Trail** again, making a steep and rocky descent to return to the Oven's Mouth bridge at 2.8 miles.

▸ MILE 2.8–3.1: Oven's Mouth Bridge to Ice House Cove

Cross the bridge, turn right this time, and enjoy a final victory lap through **Ice House Cove**—a sprawling marsh where eagles and herons are sometime spotted. As you hike south along the marsh, a series of bog bridges will deliver you back to the fork at the beginning of your hike. Turn right to reach the parking lot at 3.1 miles.

DIRECTIONS

From Portland, drive northeast on I-295 N for 22 miles and take Exit 28 to merge onto US-1 N toward Coastal Route/Brunswick/Bath. Continue northeast along US-1 N for another 21 miles and then, after crossing a large bridge in Wiscasset, make a right turn onto ME-27 S. Drive south along this

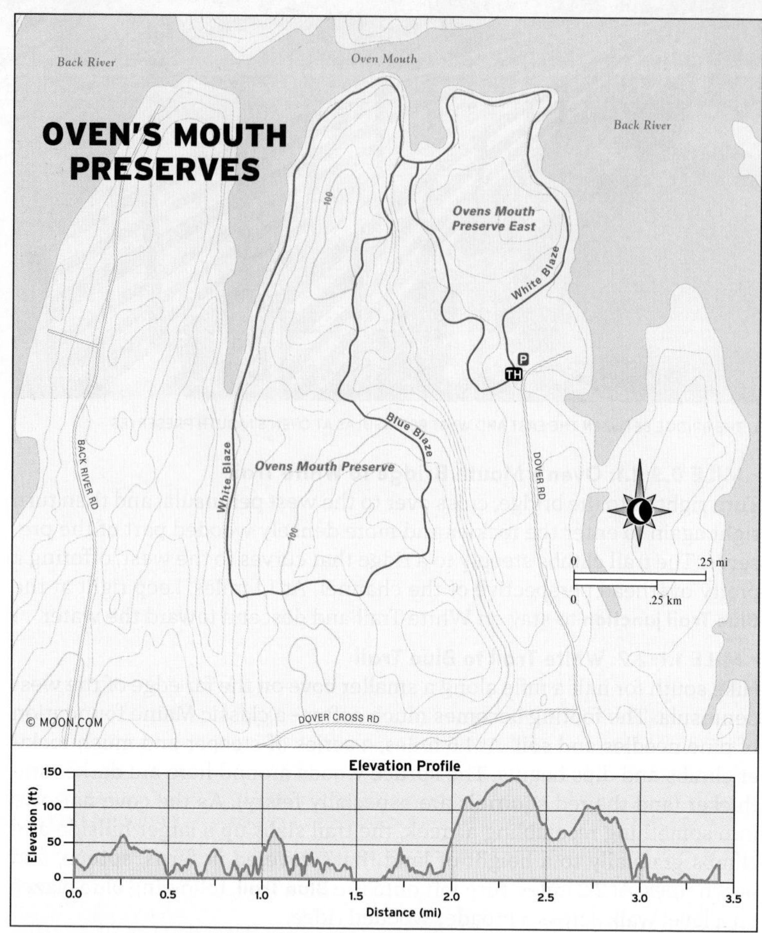

road for 7 miles, turn right onto Adams Pond Road, and then take a right onto Dover Road. Continue north and keep right at the fork to stay on Dover Road. The Oven's Mouth parking lot will be on your left less than half a mile ahead.

GPS COORDINATES: 43°55'45.9"N 69°38'24.4"W, 43.929413, -69.640112

BEST NEARBY BITES

If you want the pinnacle of classic no-frills Maine seafood, head into Wiscasset, brave the long take-out line, and enjoy the biggest, most meaty and buttery lobster roll of your life at **Red's Eats** (41 Water St., Wiscasset, 207/882-6128, www.redseatsmaine.com, 11am-5pm Mon.-Thurs., 11am-8pm Fri.-Sun.). If you'd rather savor something finer and more potent, head slightly north of Oven's Mouth and try the organic rum, vodka, and whiskey at **Split Rock Distilling** (16 Osprey Point Rd., Newcastle, 207/563-2669, www.splitrockdistilling.com, noon-5pm Wed.-Sat.).

6 Lane's Island Preserve

LANE'S ISLAND PRESERVE, VINALHAVEN

The ferry trip to Vinalhaven is worth it for this dreamy hike that's bursting with wildflowers and gorgeous ocean views.

BEST: Summer hikes

DISTANCE: 1 mile round-trip

DURATION: 30 minutes

ELEVATION CHANGE: 95 feet

EFFORT: Easy

TRAIL: Dirt path, rocks

USERS: Hikers, leashed dogs

SEASON: May–November

FEES/PASSES: Round-trip ferry fares $11 adult, $5.50 child 11 and under, $20 adult with bike, $10 child with bike, $30 adult with vehicle less than 20 feet, $2.50/foot for vehicles over 20 feet

MAPS: MainTrailFinder.com, http://vinalhaven.org/20142015brochure.pdf

CONTACT: Town of Vinalhaven, 207/863-4471, www.townofvinalhaven.org; Rockland Ferry Services, 517A Main Street, Rt. 1, Rockland, ME, 207/596-5400. Summer hours: First ferries depart both Rockland and Vinalhaven at 7am, last ferries at 4:30pm.

Just an hour off the midcoast of Maine, the island of Vinalhaven beckons travelers who prefer mossy glens and Zen-like rocky beaches to the hubbub of resorts and coastal country clubs. The village of Carver's Harbor is an affable working enclave where you'll encounter lobstermen tucking into pancakes and bacon each morning before heading out for a long day's work. South of the village is Lane's Island Preserve, a little peninsula with an incredible scenic amble with ocean views worthy of landscape paintings.

START THE HIKE

▸ MILE 0–0.2: Lane's Island Preserve Trailhead to Trail Junction

Begin the hike in the south end of the parking lot by the metal bike rack. Pick up the dirt path and walk south through some tallgrass before emerging into a vast clearing with some picnic tables and views of the ocean. Ahead, to your right, you'll see a wooden trail register box. Sign your name if you wish and pick up the grassy path to begin your loop around the peninsula. You'll start by walking through a field with a small **cemetery** on your left, where members of the Lane family are buried. Spot Indian paintbrushes and even wild raspberries in the field. Pass under a large apple tree and into a grove of spruce and then veer left at the unmarked trail junction at 0.2 mile.

▸ MILE 0.2–0.4: Trail Junction to Ocean Overlook

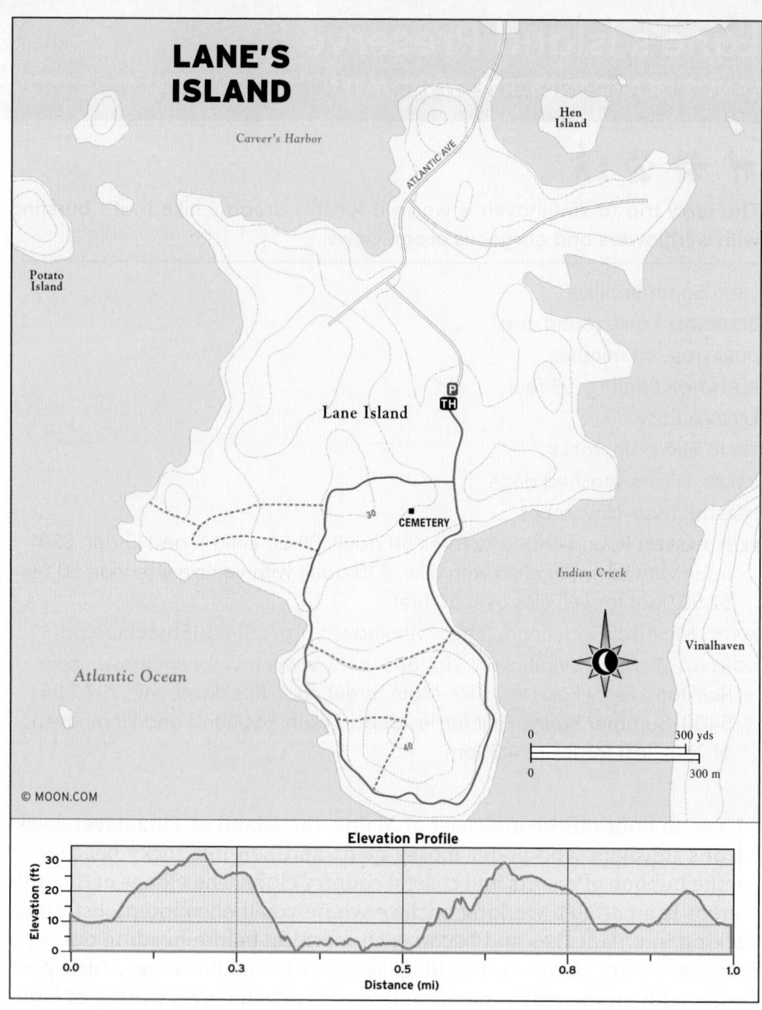

The trail becomes rockier here and passes through immense ferns. The roar of the ocean becomes louder as the trail reaches a viewpoint from which hikers can admire Green's Island to the southwest. This stretch of Lane's Island is also known for its Rosa rugosa—bright pink roses that are native to East Asia but are known to pop up in certain parts of coastal Maine. Continue hiking east along the coast past several **pebbly beaches** that can easily be reached. As the trail enters another pocket of woods, turn right at the junction at 0.4 mile.

Make a brief climb up a rocky and rooty hill to arrive a grassy height of land with a wooden bench for looking out at the ocean.

▸ MILE 0.4-0.5: Ocean Overlook to Cove Overlook

The trail rolls up and down along some vegetation-rich cliffs and starts to curve northeast. Make another right at a junction at 0.5 mile, pass through some more spruce trees, and ascend a small ledge to a sunny ridge. From here, the trail dips in and out of pockets of trees, with constant ocean

▲ COVE

views to the east. Finally, at 0.7 mile, the trail reaches a slabby open **clifftop** that overlooks a cove with its own beach.

MILE 0.5-1.0: Cove Overlook to Lane's Island Preserve Trailhead
Pick your way down rocks as the trail descends to the beach and stroll along the sand, past some more roses. On your left, you'll soon reach a spur that immediately brings you back to the big clearing from which you began the hike. To close the loop, walk north across the clearing and backtrack down the short dirt path that delivers you back to the parking lot at 1 mile.

DIRECTIONS

From Portland, drive northeast along I-295 N for 22 miles and then take Exit 28 to merge onto US-1 N toward Coastal Route/Brunswick/Bath. Continue northeast on US-1 N for 55 miles into the town of Rockland and then make a left turn onto Main Street. After a few blocks, you'll see the large ferry terminal and parking lot on your right. Turn right to enter the terminal area. If you're bringing your car to the island, head inside to buy a ticket and park your car in the appropriate queue for ferry loading. (Schedules for the ferry can be found at www.maine.gov/mdot/ferry/vinalhaven.) If you'd prefer to leave your car in Rockland, day parking is available in the terminal lot for $10. The ferry ride takes roughly one hour. After disembarking on Vinalhaven, turn right onto Main Street and drive 0.5 mile before swinging right onto Water Street. Head south, making a slight right onto Atlantic Avenue, and cross the stone bridge connecting Lane's Island to Vinalhaven; turn left onto the road marked Lane's Island Preserve. The parking lot is just ahead.

GPS COORDINATES: 44°02'15.5"N 68°49'56.7"W, 44.037643, -68.832427

BEST NEARBY BITES

Start your day on Vinalhaven by living like a lobsterman and enjoying a classic breakfast of pancakes or eggs right on the water at **Surfside** (35 W Main St., Vinalhaven, 207/863-2767, 4am-10:30am daily). Once you've concluded your visit to Lane's Island, spend the afternoon exploring the village of Carver's Harbor, where you can stock up on penny candy at **Go Fish** (56 Main St. #12, Vinalhaven, 207/863-4193, call for hours) and enjoy a loaded lobster roll from the local food truck known as **Greets Eats** (11am-2pm Wed.-Sun.), which you'll find right next to the Fisherman's Co-Op at 11 West Main Street.

7 Ragged Mountain

GEORGES RIVER LAND TRUST, ROCKPORT

Weave through a boulder-strewn forest and scale a ragged mountainside to enjoy the views from one of coastal Maine's tallest peaks.

DISTANCE: 4.8 miles round-trip

DURATION: 3.5 hours

ELEVATION CHANGE: 1,102 feet

EFFORT: Moderate/strenuous

TRAIL: Dirt path, rocks, wooden bridges, water crossings on stones

USERS: Hikers, leashed dogs

SEASON: May-November

FEES/PASSES: None

MAPS: Georges River Land Trust website

CONTACT: Georges River Land Trust, 207/594-5166, www.georgesriver.org/ragged-mountain

START THE HIKE

▸ MILE 0-0.5: Ragged Mountain Parking Lot to Georges Highland Path

Begin the hike at the north end of the parking lot by the trail information kiosk. Descend a small set of wooden stairs into the forest and amble down a stony path to a nearby stream, which you'll cross on a wooden bridge. The **Georges Highland Path** follows blue blazes as it gently rolls through mixed maple and pine woods, cresting a series of knolls with occasional views of Ragged Mountain towering ahead. The sections of ancient stone walls along the path add some historical seasoning.

▸ MILE 0.5-1.3: Georges Highland Path to Mirror Lake

After reaching the top of a knoll with a good view of Ragged Mountain's more elongated north face, the trail descends to reach the **Oyster River** (really more of a small brook) at 0.7 mile. Rock-hop across the water and past a big boulder slide as the trail heads southeast beneath the cliffs on Ragged Mountain's west face. As the footing gets rockier and more slippery in places, the trail veers away from the Oyster River briefly but rejoins just before it spills into **Mirror Lake.** Before you reach the shores of the lake, the trail suddenly veers east at 1.3 miles and climbs at a steeper grade right up the western haunch of Ragged Mountain. From here, you've officially left the foothills behind.

▸ MILE 1.3-1.8: Mirror Lake to Ragged Mountain Ridgeline

Continue climbing east, enjoying some partial views of Mirror Lake and the nearby coast through the trees on your right. The trail is wider here, but the exposed tree roots can become slippery with rain. As the grade starts to level out a bit, the trail reaches a wooded height of land at 1.6 miles with a new vista perspective—this time, you can gaze out at the Camden Hills and the northern coastline of Downeast Maine. From here,

▲ VIEW FROM THE SLOPES OF RAGGED MOUNTAIN

the trail climbs north at a more gradual rate up the ridgeline of Ragged Mountain. A series of exposed, rocky ledges at 1.8 miles offer the best views yet, and a great chance to get a face full of that inimitable Maine sea breeze.

▸ MILE 1.8–2.4: Ragged Mountain Ridgeline to Ragged Mountain Summit

A brief descent into a wooded col (gap) brings you to the final stretch of rocky trail, which is more eroded and rougher on the feet. Ahead, through the trees, you'll see the summit communications tower. Climb north around a bulbous piece of ridgeline and emerge onto a much more thoroughly exposed granite landscape at 2.1 miles. Little cairns and blue blazes spray-painted on the rock mark the way as you scramble up some slabs and breeze through a few thin stretches of alpine forest to reach the summit "cone." Muscle your way up the concluding lichen-covered rock slabs and step onto the spacious summit of **Ragged Mountain** at 2.4 miles. The summit overlooks Mirror Lake and beyond to the pretty coastal enclaves of Rockport and Rockland. Return the way you came.

DIRECTIONS

From Portland, drive northeast on I-295 N for 22 miles and take Exit 28 to merge onto US-1 N toward Coastal Route/Brunswick/Bath. Continue northeast along US-1 N for another 42 miles; after passing through Waldoboro, turn left onto ME-90 E. Take this road for 8 miles and make another left turn onto ME-17 W. The Georges Highland Path parking lot will be on your right just over 2 miles ahead.

GPS COORDINATES: 44°12'07.1"N 69°09'32.0"W, 44.201963, -69.158897

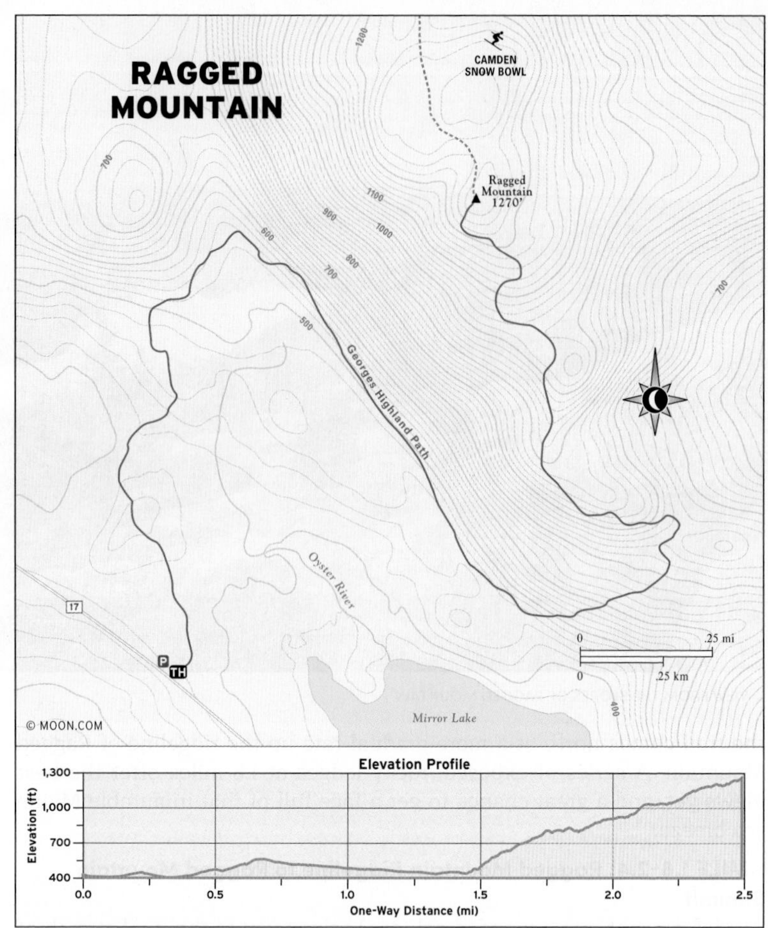

BEST NEARBY BITES

Ragged Mountain is a stone's throw from Rockland, where no palates are left unsatisfied. Start or conclude the hike with a robust cup of locally roasted espresso and a house-baked pastry at **Rock City Coffee Roasters** (252 Main St., Rockland, 207/594-5688, www.rock-city-coffee.myshopify.com, 7am-4pm Mon.-Fri.). When you're ready for something more lavish, take your pick of Rockland's classic seafood and modern American restaurants: the hottest joint in town is chef Melissa Kelly's **Primo Restaurant** (2 Main St., Rockland, 207/596-0770, www.primorestaurant.com, 5pm-10pm Thurs.-Sun.). Primo was featured on Anthony Bourdain's No Reservations, but have no illusions: you'll definitely need one!

8 Mount Meguntícook

CAMDEN HILLS STATE PARK, CAMDEN

Climb alongside a pretty stream and past miniature cascades to reach a breathtaking ocean overlook.

DISTANCE: 2.8 miles round-trip

DURATION: 2 hours

ELEVATION CHANGE: 1,019 feet

EFFORT: Moderate

TRAIL: Dirt path, rocks, wooden bog bridges, water crossings on stones

USERS: Hikers, leashed dogs

SEASON: June–October

FEES/PASSES: $4 entrance fee per vehicle for Maine residents, $6 for nonresidents

MAPS: Camden Hills State Park website

CONTACT: Camden Hills State Park, 207/236-3109, www.maine.gov/dacf/parks

Mount Megunticook, the tallest mountain on the Maine coast, rises 1,385 feet above the town of Camden, but the best vista actually precedes the summit. The Ocean Overlook is an exposed shelf-like granite cliff from which hikers can gaze out at the Atlantic and more—on a clear day, Mount Washington is visible to the west!

START THE HIKE

▶ MILE 0–0.3: Camden Hills State Park Entrance to Megunticook Trail

Begin the hike on the west side of the hikers parking lot just beyond the entrance of Camden Hills State Park. Pick up the rooty dirt path by the trail information kiosk and head northwest across a series of wooden bog bridges through balsam fir and hemlocks. You'll soon arrive at a T-intersection. Turn right onto the **Nature Trail** and head north along a dirt path that crosses a brook and ascends a small hillside by way of stone stairs to reach the **Megunticook Trail** at 0.3 mile.

▶ MILE 0.3–1.3: Megunticook Trail to Ocean Overlook

Make a left and begin your climb up the eastern slopes of the mountain as the trail switchbacks through the forest, following blue blazes on the trees. The trail starts to ascend beside a brook on stone stairs that wind up the mountainside at a steeper grade. Continue hiking north as the trail crests the top of the stairs and veers away from the brook onto a rockier ledge-like path across the mountainside. Keep right at the junction for Adam's Lookout at 0.9 mile to stay on Megunticook. Watch your step as the trail becomes soggier and muddier and the deciduous trees transition to much darker spruce and hemlocks.

The trail curves northeast and hops across some little streams to reach a series of miniature cascades that spill alongside the trail. During rainy weather, the cascades can overflow and transform this stretch of trail into

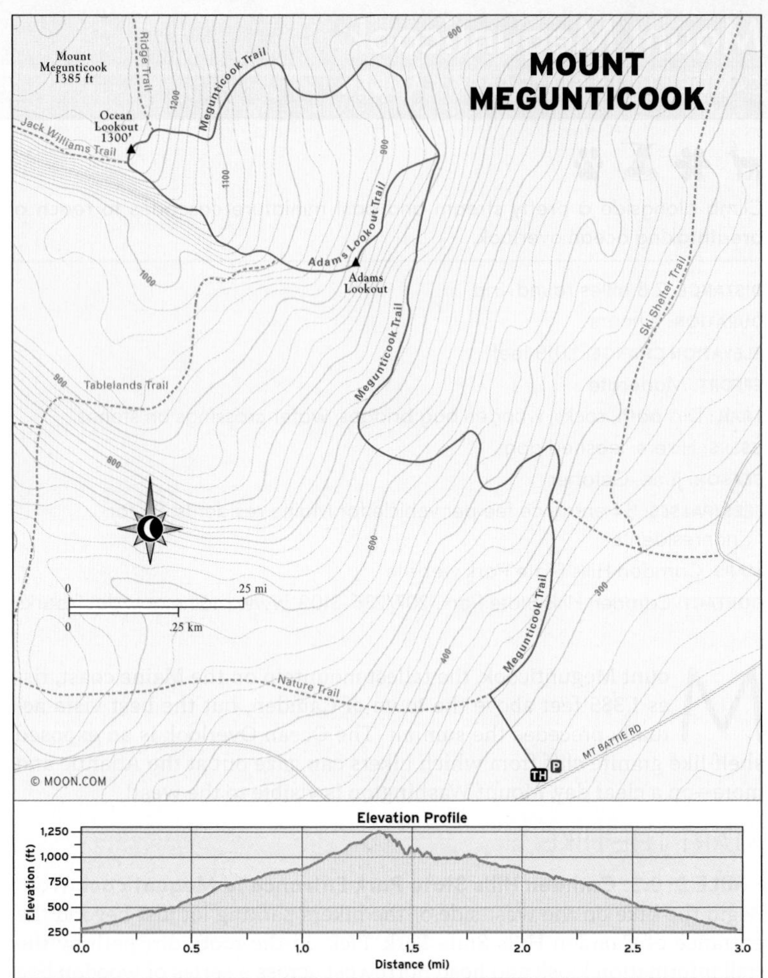

something of a waterway itself. Continue your northerly ascent up more stone stairs and some sloped rock slabs that become bigger and steeper as the spruce trees get shorter. The salty breeze that brushes through the trees hints at what lies ahead. The trail levels off at a grassy clearing and passes through a grove of trees to arrive at **Ocean Overlook** at 1.3 miles.

▸ MILE 1.3–1.4: Ocean Overlook to Megunticook Mountain Summit

Take a few moments to enjoy the ocean vista and the overhead perspective of nearby Mount Battie. Hikers who wish to see the wooded (and mostly view-less) summit proper of **Megunticook Mountain** can continue north up the Megunticook Trail.

▸ MILE 1.4–1.5: Ocean Overlook to Ridge Trail

Otherwise, pick up the **Ridge Trail** by following blue blazes that lead southeast down the lichen-crusted rock slabs of Ocean Overlook.

▸ MILE 1.5–1.8: Ridge Trail to Adam's Lookout Trail

The Ridge Trail scrambles back into the woods and reaches a junction that can be somewhat easy to miss at 1.6 miles. (If you arrive at a big cliff face

▲ THE VIEW FROM MOUNT MEGUNTICOOK

on your right, you've gone too far.) Turn left onto the **Adam's Lookout Trail** and descend a snug dirt path that soon delivers you to **Adam's Lookout**—an exposed ledge flanked by twisted white birches that stand out from the other trees glimpsed along the trail.

▸ **MILE 1.8-2.8: Adam's Lookout Trail to Megunticook Trail**

Take in your final ocean vista before continuing east and then northeast down a more rugged set of rock stairs. Reach the **Megunticook Trail** again at 1.9 miles. Veer right and backtrack to the parking lot to complete the hike at 2.8 miles.

DIRECTIONS

From Portland, drive northeast on I-295 N for 22 miles and take Exit 28 to merge onto US-1 N toward Coastal Route/Brunswick/Bath. Continue northeast along US-1 N for another 42 miles; after passing through Waldoboro, turn left onto ME-90 E. Take this road for 10 miles; upon reaching downtown Rockport, turn left to merge back onto US-1 N. The entrance to Camden Hills State Park is just over 3 miles ahead on your left. Once you've paid the entrance fee, drive past the ranger station, make a left onto Mount Battie Road, and then take your first right into the hikers parking lot.

GPS COORDINATES: 44°13'48.2"N 69°03'05.4"W, 44.230060, -69.051501

BEST NEARBY BITES

The beauty of Megunticook's Ocean Overlook is best followed by exquisite Southeast Asian-inspired cuisine such as spicy Thai basil-minced chicken and Chiang Mai curry noodles at **Long Grain** (20 Washington St., Camden, 207/236-9001, www.longgraincamden.com, 11:30am-2:45pm, 4:30-9pm Tues.-Sat.) or a glass of locally made wine and even a vineyard tour at **Cellardoor Winery** (367 Youngtown Rd., Lincolnville, 207/763-4478, www.mainewine.com, 11am-5pm Thurs.-Sun.).

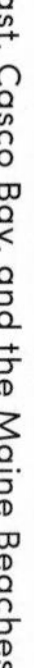

NEARBY CAMPGROUNDS

NAME	LOCATION	FACILITIES	SEASON	FEE
Megunticook Campground	620 Commercial St., Rockport, ME 04856	Tent sites, RV sites, cabins, toilets, showers, potable water, laundry, swimming pool, camp store, Wi-Fi	mid-May through mid-October	$32-79
207/594-2428, www.megunticookcampgrounds.com				
Camden Hills Campground	30 Applewood Rd., Rockport, ME 04856	Tent sites, RV sites, toilets, showers, potable water, laundry, swimming pool, camp store, Wi-Fi	mid-May through mid-October	$28-48
207/236-2498, www.camdenhillscampgrounds.com				
Lobster Buoy Campsite	280 Waterman Beach Rd., South Thomaston, ME 04858	Tent sites, RV sites, toilets, showers, potable water, camp store	mid-May through mid-October	$29
207/594-7546, www.wixsite.com				
Chewonki Campground	235 Chewonki Neck Rd., Wiscasset, ME 04578	Tent sites, RV sites, toilets, showers, potable water, swimming pool, camp store, Wi-Fi	mid-May through mid-October	$45-88
207/882-7426, www.chewonkicampground.com				
Thomas Point Beach & Campground	29 Meadow Rd., Brunswick, ME 04011	Tent sites, RV sites, toilets, showers, potable water, laundry, camp store, Wi-Fi	mid-May through September	$27-42
207/725-6009, www.thomaspointbeach.com				

NEARBY CAMPGROUNDS (continued)				
NAME	**LOCATION**	**FACILITIES**	**SEASON**	**FEE**
Wolfe's Neck Oceanfront Camping	134 Burnett Rd., Freeport, ME 04032	Tent sites, RV sites, cabin tents, cabins, toilets, showers, potable water, laundry, camp store, restaurant, Wi-Fi	May through October	$20-250
207/865-9307, www.freeportcamping.com				
Sandy Pines Campground	277 Mills Rd., Kennebunkport, ME 04046	Tent sites, rental tents, RV sites, cabin tents, cabins, toilets, showers, potable water, laundry, swimming pool, camp store, Wi-Fi	mid-May through mid-October	$50-380
207/967-2483, www.sandypinescamping.com				
Wells Beach Resort Campground	1000 Post Rd., Wells, ME 04090	Tent sites, RV sites, toilets, showers, potable water, laundry, swimming pool, camp store, Wi-Fi	mid-May through mid-October	$41-98
207/646-7570, www.wellsbeach.com				
Dixon's Campgrounds	1740 US-1, Cape Neddick, ME 03902	Tent sites, RV sites, yurts, toilets, showers, potable water, swimming pool, camp store, Wi-Fi	mid-May through late September	$36-135
207/363-3626, www.dixonscampground.com				
Libby's Oceanside Camp	725 York St., York, ME 03909	Tent sites, RV sites, toilets, showers, potable water, laundry, Wi-Fi	mid-May through mid-October	$65-103
207/363-4171, www.libbysoceancamping.com				

THE MAHOOSUCS, EVANS NOTCH, AND RANGELEY LAKES

If New Hampshire's White Mountains had wilder, quieter, more artsy cousins, the mountains and forests of western Maine would fit the bill. Everything about this part of the state feels starker. The trees here come in darker shades of green. The rocks are more jagged and the boulders more unwieldy. The lonesome peaks that tower above the valleys here are too remote to be spoiled by the cacophony of summer and fall tourism. And western Maine's lakes and rivers are the stuff of legend for canoeing enthusiasts. In other words, western Maine is what hikers and outdoor adventurers live for—pure, isolated wilderness, far from the madding crowds and bountiful for those who make the pilgrimage.

▲ the vast forests of Androscoggin Riverlands

▲ one of several pretty pools near the Bickford Slides

◀ VIEW OF GRAFTON NOTCH

1 **Caribou Mountain**
DISTANCE: 6.7 miles round-trip
DURATION: 4.5 hours
EFFORT: Strenuous

2 **Bickford Slides**
DISTANCE: 2.3 miles round-trip
DURATION: 1 hour
EFFORT: Easy/moderate

3 **Lord Hill**
DISTANCE: 4.3 miles round-trip
DURATION: 2 hours
EFFORT: Easy

4 **Old Speck**
DISTANCE: 7.6 miles round-trip
DURATION: 4.5 hours
EFFORT: Strenuous

5 **Table Rock**
DISTANCE: 2.1 miles round-trip
DURATION: 1.5 hours
EFFORT: Moderate/strenuous

6 **Angel Falls**
DISTANCE: 1.4 miles round-trip
DURATION: 1 hour
EFFORT: Easy

7 **Androscoggin Riverlands**
DISTANCE: 7.2 miles round-trip
DURATION: 3.5 hours
EFFORT: Moderate

8 **Tumbledown Mountain**
DISTANCE: 5.8 miles round-trip
DURATION: 4 hours
EFFORT: Strenuous

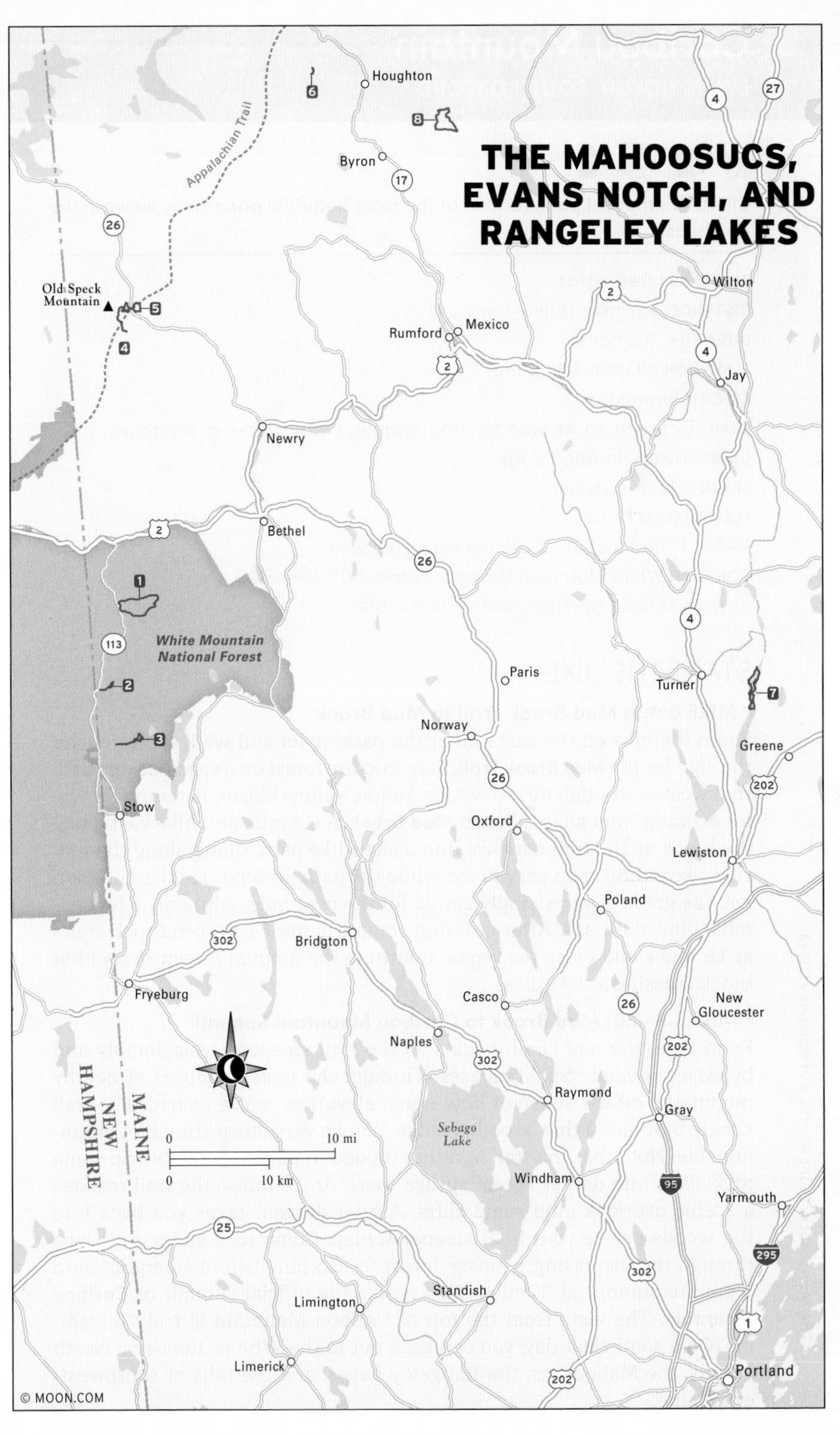

THE MAHOOSUCS, EVANS NOTCH, AND RANGELEY LAKES
Houghton
Byron
Appalachian Trail
Old Speck Mountain
Wilton
Mexico
Rumford
Jay
Newry
Bethel
White Mountain National Forest
Paris
Turner
Norway
Greene
Stow
Oxford
Lewiston
Poland
Bridgton
Fryeburg
Casco
New Gloucester
Naples
Raymond
Gray
Sebago Lake
MAINE
NEW HAMPSHIRE
0
10 mi
0
10 km
Windham
Yarmouth
Standish
Limington
Limerick
Portland
1
2
3
4
5
6
7
8
2
4
17
26
27
113
202
302
25
95
295
© MOON.COM

1 Caribou Mountain

EVANS NOTCH, SOUTH OXFORD

Climb this modest peak for one of the most beautiful panoramic views in the Northeast.

BEST: Fall hikes, vistas

DISTANCE: 6.7 miles round-trip

DURATION: 4.5 hours

ELEVATION CHANGE: 1,898 feet

EFFORT: Strenuous

TRAIL: Dirt path, rocks, wooden bog bridges, water crossings on stones

USERS: Hikers, leashed dogs

SEASON: June–October

FEES/PASSES: None

MAPS: White Mountain National Forest website

CONTACT: White Mountain National Forest, 603/536-6100, www.fs.usda.gov/recarea/whitemountain

START THE HIKE

▸ MILE 0–1.9: Mud Brook Trail to Mud Brook

Begin the hike on the east end of the parking lot and walk south toward the sign for the **Mud Brook Trail.** Step into the forest on a spacious dirt path that weaves through mixed woods. Follow yellow blazes, listening for water echoing from ahead. Reach **Mud Brook** at 0.3 mile and hike east along the brook as the trail narrows into a shelf-like path. Climb along the hillside, ascending at an easy grade while the path becomes rockier and rootier. The grade is surprisingly gentle for the next mile, with only a few notable dips and rises. After crossing some tributaries, descend rock stairs at 1.6 miles and cross the brook. Continue the gradual ascent to another brook crossing at 1.9 miles.

▸ MILE 1.9–3.0: Mud Brook to Caribou Mountain Summit

From here, the real climb begins as the trail steepens considerably and bypasses several rock staircases. Through the trees, glimpses of nearby mountains offer a sense of how much elevation you've gained. The trail slowly becomes a thin, wooded ledge along a very steep stretch of mountainside. Note that the trail is rather eroded in places. Scramble up some rock slabs into darker boreal spruce trees. At 2.8 miles, the trail reaches a scenic overlook atop some cliffs. A brief descent takes you back into the woods before your final steeper schlep. Climb rock stairs and slabs through the increasingly mossy forest for 0.3 mile before emerging onto a granite summit at 3 miles. This marks the official summit of **Caribou Mountain.** The vista from the top of Caribou Mountain is truly incredible. On a semi-clear day, you can gaze out to the Whites, the Great North Woods, the Mahoosucs, the Rangeley Lakes, and the hills of southwestern Maine.

▲ CARIBOU MOUNTAIN SUMMIT

▸ MILE 3.0–4.0: Caribou Mountain Summit to Caribou Trail

To continue the loop, follow little cairns on the summit and look for yellow blazes on the rocks. The path alternates between exposed rock and a ribbon-like trail through the boreal forest and tundra, skirting northeast along the broad upper slopes of the mountain. After descending a longer stretch of granite, the trail dips back into the forest and descends some steep slabs and slippery rock stairs to reach the Caribou Trail junction at 3.7 miles. Turn left onto the **Caribou Trail** and descend through a strange section of forest with lots of blowdowns and unusually high sun exposure before entering a more deciduous ravine.

▸ MILE 4.0–6.7: Caribou Trail to Trailhead

At 4 miles, a stream presents the first of many crossings on the way down. As the trail grade becomes more gradual, passing several cascades along the stream, the forest transitions to tall spruce and hemlocks. Mind your footing on the rockier sections of the descent. At 5.3 miles, the trail levels, becoming a cruise through the woods. At 5.7 miles, make another stream crossing, after which the trail becomes wider and smoother before reaching the final and largest of the stream crossings at 6.4 miles; some ruins of an **old wooden bridge** remain here. (The water level at this crossing can become high enough to saturate boots.) On the other side, climb a few sets of stone stairs, pick your way over some exposed roots, and then descend to the trailhead parking lot at 6.7 miles.

DIRECTIONS

From Portsmouth, New Hampshire, drive north on NH-16 N to the town of Conway. Keep right at the junction for NH-16 N and NH-113 E to continue driving east on NH-113 E. After 2 miles, turn left onto US-302 W and then make a right onto East Conway Road. Drive northeast for 6 miles and

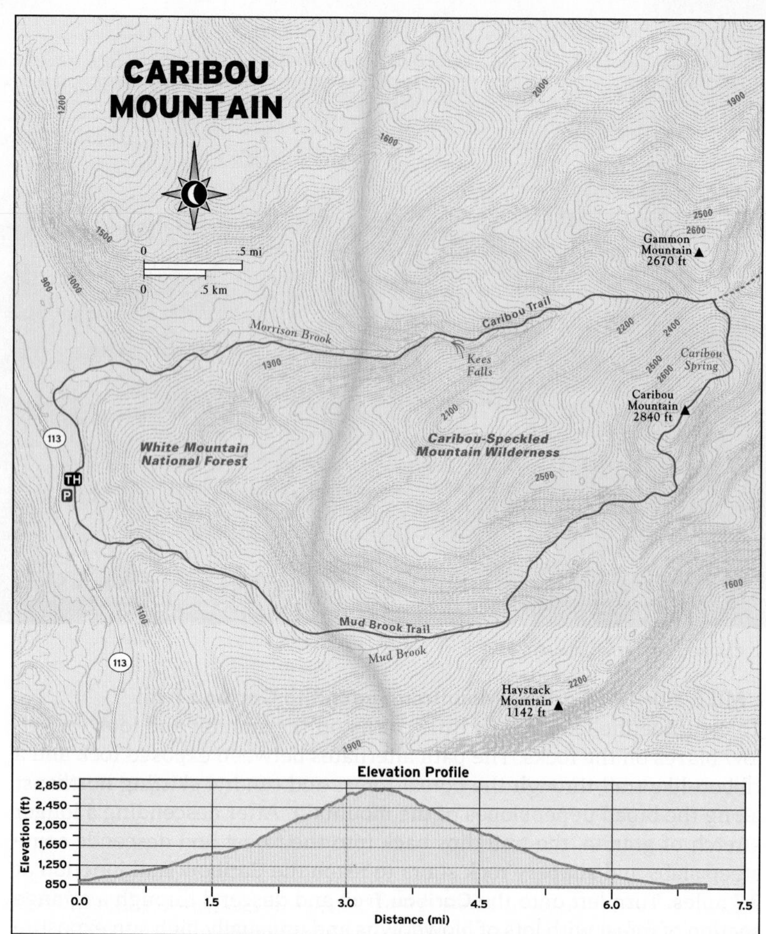

then swing a right onto West Fryeburg Road. Here you'll briefly cross into Maine as you continue north along West Fryeburg Road, which eventually becomes Stow Road. At the junction with ME-113B, veer slightly right to stay on Stow Road and follow it north for another 11 miles through Evans Notch. After passing Bull Brook Campground on the left, look for a hiker sign on the right and turn onto the cutoff road here to reach the parking lot for Caribou Mountain.

GPS COORDINATES: 44°20'09.0"N 70°58'31.8"W, 44.335833, -70.975511

BEST NEARBY BITES

Coming down from a view as splendorous as Caribou's can be hard, so make the transition easier with a sumptuous dinner of teriyaki steak tips, scallops with herbed risotto, or one of many other indulgent options at **Brian's** (43 Main St., Bethel, 207/824-1007, www.briansbethel.com, 4pm-9pm Thurs.-Mon.).

2 Bickford Slides

EVANS NOTCH, STOW

Visit a pretty series of cascades that tumble through a dark and densely forested ravine.

DISTANCE: 2.3 miles round-trip

DURATION: 1 hour

ELEVATION CHANGE: 609 feet

EFFORT: Easy/moderate

TRAIL: Dirt path, water crossings on stones

USERS: Hikers, leashed dogs

SEASON: June-October

FEES/PASSES: $5 day-use fee (per vehicle)

MAPS: White Mountain National Forest website

CONTACT: White Mountain National Forest, 603/536-6100, www.fs.usda.gov/recarea/whitemountain

Some of the best-kept secrets of the White Mountains are housed in ravines—those wooded, rocky clefts sandwiched between the more heavily trafficked mountains. On the southern end of Evans Notch, a splendid series of waterfalls known as the Bickford Slides await hikers curious enough to venture into the narrow space between Sugarloaf Mountain and Blueberry Mountain.

START THE HIKE

▸ MILE 0-0.4: Brickett Place Historical Site to Bickford Brook Trail

Begin the hike in the parking lot for Brickett Place—a historic site where the original buildings of an old settlers farmstead are open to visitors from late May through early October (call the Saco Ranger Station at 603/447-5448 to verify operating hours). Find the wooden sign for the **Bickford Brook Trail** at the east side of the parking lot. Pick up the dirt trail as it enters an airy birch forest. The trail, rooty and rocky at first, climbs a hillside at a moderate grade heading northeast before leveling out briefly and then resuming the climb at a gentler angle. Continue your ascent, stepping over some rock water bars.

▸ MILE 0.4-0.6: Bickford Brook Trail to Blueberry Ridge Trail

The trail gets smoother and more spacious as the mixed trees transition into much taller hemlocks. Listen for the promising sound of rippling water as the trail climbs into the ravine between Sugarloaf and Blueberry along a wooded hillside. Down the slope to your right, you can see and hear **Bickford Brook.** At 0.6 mile, turn right onto **Blueberry Ridge Trail.**

▸ MILE 0.6-0.9: Blueberry Ridge Trail to Bickford Slides Trail

A brief descent to Bickford Brook delivers you to another junction with the Bickford Slides Trail. The positioning of the sign here is slightly confusing—to continue in the right direction, make a slight left toward the

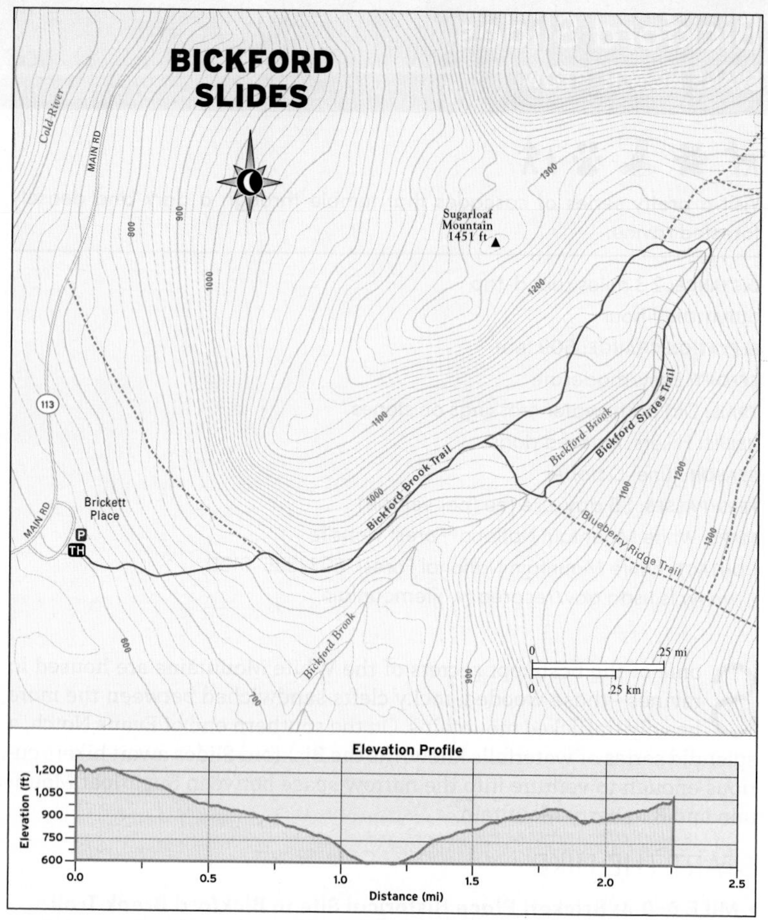

smaller sign that reads "Trail," attached to a tree just beyond the Bickford Slides sign, and cross Bickford Brook on rocks. On the other side of the brook, veer left to take the **Bickford Slides Trail.** Amble along the brook on a much skinnier dirt path that bypasses several little tributaries and a few muddier zones. Continue hiking northeast along the increasingly lively brook as the woods get mossier, denser, and darker.

▸ MILE 0.9–1.1: Bickford Slides Trail to Bickford Waterfalls

A set of miniature cascades at 0.9 mile marks the beginning of the slides. Make a steeper ascent along a more eroded stretch of trail, catching glimpses of more silvery slides before reaching a reflecting pool into which a big, beautiful **40-foot-tall waterfall** spills. The trail passes above the pool, but you can scramble down the embankment to your left to reach the water for a better view. The trail climbs alongside the falls at a steep grade; watch your footing as you make this ascent. A small wooden arrow confirms that you're on the right track. Once you reach the top of the big slide, enjoy a gentler stroll along the rim of a little "canyon" through which even more slides shoot and slosh. The trail here becomes quite narrow and ledge-like in places, with plenty of exposed roots, so exercise caution here during soggy conditions.

▲ THE TALLEST OF THE BICKFORD SLIDES

▸ MILE 1.1–2.3: Bickford Waterfalls to Bickford Brook Trail

A quick descent delivers you back to Bickford Brook at 1.3 miles. Rock-hop your way across and climb away from the brook for a few beats along a gentle wooded connector path that concludes at **Bickford Brook Trail** at 1.4 miles. Make a left here and gently descend southwest for 0.3 mile to reach the fork you initially took to reach Bickford Slides. Keep right and backtrack to Brickett Place at 2.3 miles.

DIRECTIONS

From Portsmouth, New Hampshire, drive north on NH-16 N to the town of Conway. Keep right at the junction for NH-16 N and NH-113 E to continue driving east on NH-113 E. After 2 miles, turn left onto US-302 W and then make a right onto East Conway Road. Drive northeast for 6 miles and then swing right onto West Fryeburg Road. You'll briefly cross into Maine as you continue north along West Fryeburg Road, which eventually becomes Stow Road. At the junction with ME-113B, veer slightly right to stay on Stow Road and follow it north for another 7 miles as you cross back into New Hampshire. After passing a large sign for The Basin on your left, a sign for Brickett Place will appear on your right almost immediately. Turn right onto the cutoff road here and park in the lot beside the preserved farmhouse.

GPS COORDINATES: 44°16'01.5"N 71°00'14.5"W, 44.267090, -71.004036

3 Lord Hill

WHITE MOUNTAIN NATIONAL FOREST, STONEHAM

Hike past ruins and through two distinct forest areas to a pretty pond vista.

DISTANCE: 4.3 miles round-trip

DURATION: 2 hours

ELEVATION CHANGE: 811 feet

EFFORT: Easy

TRAIL: Dirt path, rocks, wooden bridges, river crossings on stones, metal ladders

USERS: Hikers, leashed dogs

SEASON: May–October

FEES/PASSES: None

MAPS: White Mountain National Forest website

CONTACT: White Mountain National Forest, 603/536-6100, www.fs.usda.gov/recarea/whitemountain

A stroll up Lord Hill offers a unique and enchanting walk from a traditional New Hampshire forest zone to a traditional Maine one. Along the way, you'll encounter backcountry relics such as crumbling stone walls, a graveyard, and even an abandoned mining site that awaits hikers near the top of the 1,257-foot-tall "hill."

START THE HIKE

▶ MILE 0-1.2: Conant Trail to Mine Loop Junction

Begin your like in the parking lot and walk south toward the trailhead sign. Turn left onto the **Conant Trail,** which is really a rocky, eroded road. The road ambles east through an open stretch of marshland before tunneling into a deciduous forest of beech trees. Climb gently through the woods as the road passes an **A-frame house** and some **cottages.** Veer right at the sign for **Lord Hill** at 0.4 mile and walk on. The trail continues east and swings by a small graveyard before arriving at an unmarked junction at 0.6 mile. Take a left here to stay on the Conant Trail and ascend a steeper hillside.

As the road curves left, continue straight as the Conant Trail becomes narrower and rockier and enters a darker stretch of forest. The trail follows an old creek bed as it begins a steady, occasionally steep climb through spruce and birch trees (look for yellow blazes henceforth). Turn left at the Mine Loop junction at 1.2 miles to stay on the Conant Trail.

▶ MILE 1.2-2.3: Mine Loop Junction to Lord Hill Summit

Continue a gentler ascent, meandering past some old stone walls that have been reclaimed by the forest. After rolling up and down mildly for a bit, the trail suddenly enters an airier stretch of pine and spruce forest around 1.8 miles. The greenery of the trees and the abundant moss is dizzying, and the breeze foreshadows what's just ahead.

▲ THE BEGINNING OF THE HIKE UP LORD HILL

At 2.1 miles, turn right at the Horseshoe Pond Trail junction to stay on the Conant Trail. Climb a steeper pitch, arriving at the top of **Lord Hill** at 2.3 miles. On a clear day, the summit offers a primo view of **Horseshoe Pond,** which is shaped exactly like you'd might expect.

▸ MILE 2.3–2.7: Lord Hill Summit to Mine Loop Trail

Once you've had your fill, pick up the **Mine Loop Trail** at the sign on the summit and hike west along the top of the hill. Check out the abandoned mining site just a couple of steps beyond the summit; this dugout of rocks is rich with glittering feldspar specimens. The Mine Loop Trail veers south and makes a moderate rocky descent into the woods before arriving at a grassy clearing with a junction at 2.7 miles.

▸ MILE 2.7–4.3: Mine Loop Trail to Conant Trail

Turn right to stay on the Mine Loop and stroll through an emerald corridor of ferns, tallgrass, and white birch trees. You'll make several creek crossings on stones before the trail enters darker spruce woods once again. Make a brief, steep descent to reach the **Conant Trail** again at 3.2 miles. Turn left onto Conant here and retrace your steps for a little over a mile back to the parking area to finish the loop at 4.3 miles.

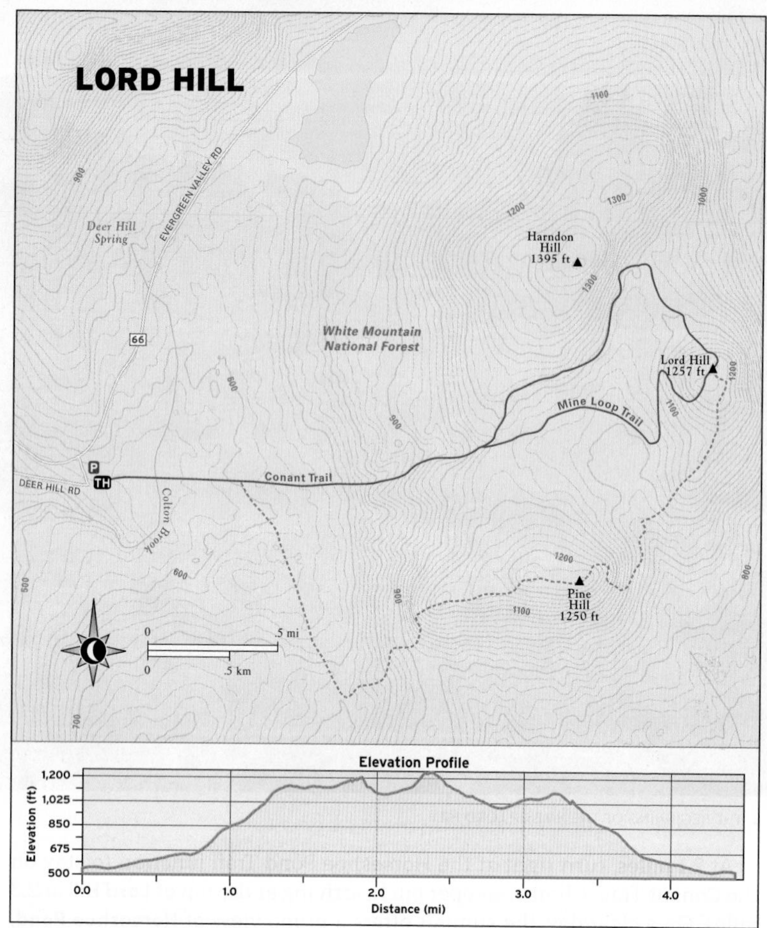

DIRECTIONS

From Portland, take ME-22 W to its junction with ME-14 N. Turn right onto ME-14 N and then, at the traffic circle, take the second exit onto ME-112 S. Continue straight through the next traffic circle to stay on ME-112 S; at the subsequent circle, take the second exit onto ME-25 W/Ossipee Trail E. Drive northwest for around 8 miles, veer right onto ME-113 N, and follow the road northwest to its terminus in Fryeburg. Turn right onto ME-5 N/Main Street and drive north for 4 miles before taking a left onto Fish Street. Follow Fish Street to its end, turn right onto North Fryeburg Road, and drive north for 2.5 miles, as North Fryeburg Road becomes Stow Road. Take a slight right to stay on Stow Road and continue north for about 5 miles to reach the turnoff for Deer Hill Road. Turn right onto Deer Hill Road and rumble along a dirt road with some potholes. Swing left at the first fork and then take a right at the next junction. Drive southeast and look for a sign on the right pointing to the Conant Trail. Take this final right turn onto a cutoff road. The parking area and trailhead will be just ahead on your left.

GPS COORDINATES: 44°13'12.0"N 70°59'08.3"W, 44.219999, -70.985643

Old Speck

GRAFTON NOTCH STATE PARK, NEWRY

Maine's third-tallest mountain has it all—alpine flowers, cascades, and gorgeous vistas.

DISTANCE: 7.6 miles round-trip

DURATION: 4.5 hours

ELEVATION CHANGE: 2,913 feet

EFFORT: Strenuous

TRAIL: Dirt path, rocks, iron rungs, wooden bog bridges, water crossings on stones

USERS: Hikers

SEASON: June-October

FEES/PASSES: $3 day-use fee for Maine residents, $4 for nonresidents

MAPS: Maine State Parks website

CONTACT: Grafton Notch State Park, 207/824-2912, www.maine.gov/graftonnotch

"Old Speck" might sound like something you'd hear from a grizzled old mountaineer in a smoky bar after midnight. But it's a fitting name for the third-tallest mountain in Maine at 4,170 feet, which rises high above the craggy Grafton Notch and can be seen from many miles away on a clear day. The hike to the top is challenging, with some rock climbing up and across the exposed cliffs on the lower eastern face of the mountain, but the reward at the top is worth it. Just be sure to save Old Speck for a clear day—it gets slippery during rainy weather.

START THE HIKE

▸ MILE 0-0.9: Appalachian Trail to Grafton Notch Overlook

Begin the hike in the parking lot by the trail information kiosk. Pick up the **Appalachian Trail** and walk along a stony path into birch and beech woods. Turn right onto the **Eyebrow Trail** at 0.1 mile. Follow orange blazes as the trail crosses several bog bridges before climbing some steep and winding rock stairs. Ascend into a denser and greener stretch of spruce woods before reaching an obstacle of sorts at 0.5 mile. The trail climbs an extremely steep series of rock slabs with the aid of steel cables anchored into the rock on posts. Use the cables as handholds as you ascend the slabs to arrive at a sloped and exposed cliff face. Carefully cross the cliff face with the aid of metal rungs affixed to the rock and reach a small ladder on the other side that takes you back into the woods. Climb a final set of iron rungs up the steep and mossy wooded hillside to reach surer footing.

Continue ascending steeply along the rocky trail as it ascends the eastern face of the mountain. Partial views of Grafton Notch through the trees will try to fool you into thinking you're almost there—you're not, but a beautiful reward lies ahead at 0.9 mile, where the trail reaches a height of

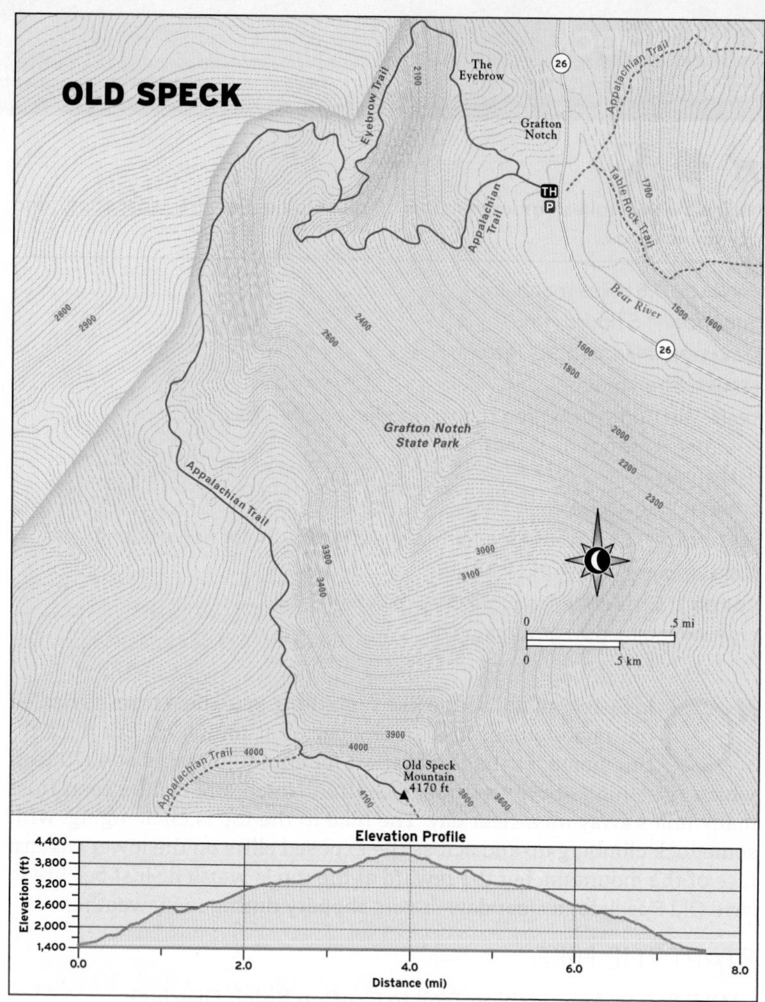

land with a stunning and picturesque **Grafton Notch overlook.** The dome-like summit of Old Speck looms ahead to the south.

▸ MILE 0.9–3.6: Grafton Notch Overlook to Grafton Loop Trail and Old Speck Summit

The trail ambles up and down a wooded ridge with lots of boreal spruce trees. At 1.2 miles, turn right onto the **Appalachian Trail.**

After briefly heading north, the AT shifts south to begin the long and steady 2.4-mile climb up Old Speck's elongated northern slopes. The rock up here glitters with traces of mica and feldspar, which is noticeable even on gray, foggy days. Follow white blazes and cairns up rock stairs and slabs as the trail dips in and out of the trees. Check out the views to the west to see Maine's Table Rock and to the east to see the boglands of northern New Hampshire. Here the exposure and alpine tundra become constant. At 3.5 miles, turn left onto **Grafton Loop Trail** and stroll up the gently graded summit spur to arrive at the **Old Speck summit** at 3.6 miles. The 360-degree view from the mossy and exposed peak is one for the ages,

▲ ALONG THE EYEBROW TRAIL

with sweeping views into northern New Hampshire, Maine, and Canada. Brave hikers can climb the ladder up the 40-foot-tall summit fire tower for an even wilder view. (This rickety, steep climb is not for the faint of heart.)

MILE 3.6-7.6: Old Speck Summit to Appalachian Trail

To begin the return journey, backtrack along the Grafton Loop Trail, turn right onto the AT again, and retrace your steps down the north ridge to the junction with **Eyebrow Trail** at 6.1 miles. This time turn right to stay on the AT, which descends rock stairs beside a series of chuckling cascades that spill and swirl beside the trail. As the grade and the ground conditions soften, the trail crosses a creek on rocks, then segues to a rooty dirt path that meets the Eyebrow Trail again at 7.5 miles. Keep right on the AT and continue to the parking lot to conclude the loop at 7.6 miles.

DIRECTIONS

From Portland, drive southwest on I-295 S and take Exit 1 for I-95 N. Merge onto I-95 N and drive north for 17 miles. Take Exit 63 for US-202/ME-115/ME-4 toward ME-26/Gray/New Gloucester. At the bottom of the off-ramp, turn left onto US-202 W and then make an immediate right onto ME-26A N. Continue north along this road as it becomes ME-26 N and take it all the way to the town of Bethel, where you'll turn right onto US-2 E. Drive north to Newry and then make a left turn onto ME-26 N. Continue northwest for 12 miles as the road enters Grafton Notch State Park and watch for the Old Speck parking lot on your left.

GPS COORDINATES: 44°35'23.4"N 70°56'49.9"W, 44.589834, -70.947180

BEST NEARBY BREWS

Believe it or not, some seriously fine Italian cooking is happening in the woods near Grafton Notch; if you're looking for a celebratory feast after coming down Old Speck, change your shirt and drive south to **22 Broad Street Restaurant & Martini Bar** (22 Broad St., Bethel, 207/824-3496, www.22broadstreet.com, 4:30pm-9pm Sun.-Sat.). If you prefer your victory dance in liquid form, try the maibock, red ale, and black porter over at **Sunday River Brewing Company** (29 Sunday River Rd., Bethel, 207/824-4253, www.sundayriverbrewingcompany.com, 6am-10pm Mon.-Thurs., 6am-11pm Fri.-Sun.).

5 Table Rock

GRAFTON NOTCH STATE PARK, NEWRY

Maneuver through some boulder fields to the top of a uniquely shaped rock formation overlooking Grafton Notch.

DISTANCE: 2.1 miles round-trip

DURATION: 1.5 hours

ELEVATION CHANGE: 881 feet

EFFORT: Moderate/strenuous

TRAIL: Dirt path, rocks, iron rungs, wooden bog bridges

USERS: Hikers

SEASON: June-October

FEES/PASSES: $3 day-use fee for Maine residents, $4 nonresidents

MAPS: Maine State Parks website

CONTACT: Grafton Notch State Park, 207/824-2912, www.maine.gov/graftonnotch

Thru-hikers often cite the Mahoosucs of western Maine as comprising one of the most brutal sections of the Appalachian Trail because of how relentlessly rocky they are. To get a brief taste of the formidable terrain, climb Table Rock. Located directly across the road from Old Speck mountain, Table Rock is exactly what it sounds like: a rock formation with a flat surface that stands roughly 2,300 feet above the valley.

START THE HIKE

▸ MILE 0-0.4: Appalachian Trail to Table Rock Trail

Begin the hike in the parking lot for Old Speck Mountain. Cross the road, walk northeast toward the large wooden "A" sculpture (the symbol for the Appalachian Trail), and pick up the **Appalachian Trail** as it ventures into the woods. Cross several skinny bog bridges before turning right onto the **Table Rock Trail.** Follow orange blazes as you hike south through a sumptuous forest of ferns and beech trees. The surrounding forest becomes increasingly rocky as the trail climbs a hillside at a gradual grade. At 0.4 mile, the trail swerves east, and the climb begins in a sudden and jarring fashion.

▸ MILE 0.4-0.9: Table Rock Trail to Table Rock Summit

Make your way up winding rock staircases before reaching a brief section of ladder rungs on a sloped rock face. (The rungs here aren't really necessary, but they're fun.) As the stairs get steeper and rougher, notice lots of tiny yellow mushrooms growing along the trail in places. At 0.6 mile, transition into boreal forest and schlep your way over some big Maine boulders as the trail continues climbing east.

▲ VIEW OF THE MAHOOSUC RANGE FROM THE SUMMIT OF TABLE ROCK

Watch your balance as the rocky stairs become even steeper. The parting trees offer some solid views of Old Speck and the valley below. At 0.7 mile, the trail reaches a massive rock overhang; instead of climbing straight up, the trail turns right, makes a brief descent, and then worms up through a rockfall. A few thoughtfully placed iron rungs aid this part of the climb. Squeeze your body between a few tight places, ascend a final set of stone stairs, and swing left at 0.8 mile as the Table Rock Trail ends at a junction with the blue-blazed AT connector cutoff route. The summit of **Table Rock** is just a few meters ahead. Enjoy an epic view of the Mahoosuc Range and note the distinctly flat shape of the rocky summit.

▸ MILE 0.9–1.3: Table Rock Summit to Appalachian Trail

To begin your return journey, backtrack down the blue-blazed AT connector route and keep left at the junction with the trail that you came up. Descend a large sloped rock face with ladder rungs. Continue down the moderately graded rocky trail until you reach the Appalachian Trail at 1.3 miles. Veer left onto the official AT and continue your descent through leafy deciduous woods, crossing a few streams on stones.

▸ MILE 1.3–2.1: Appalachian Trail to Table Rock Trail

Watch your footing as the trail becomes steeper and somewhat eroded in places before transitioning to bog bridges. Arrive at the Table Rock Trail junction again at 2 miles. Turn right and backtrack to the road to complete your hike at 2.1 miles.

DIRECTIONS

From Portland, drive southwest on I-295 S and take Exit 1 for I-95 N. Merge onto I-95 N and drive north for 17 miles. Take Exit 63 for US-202/ME-115/

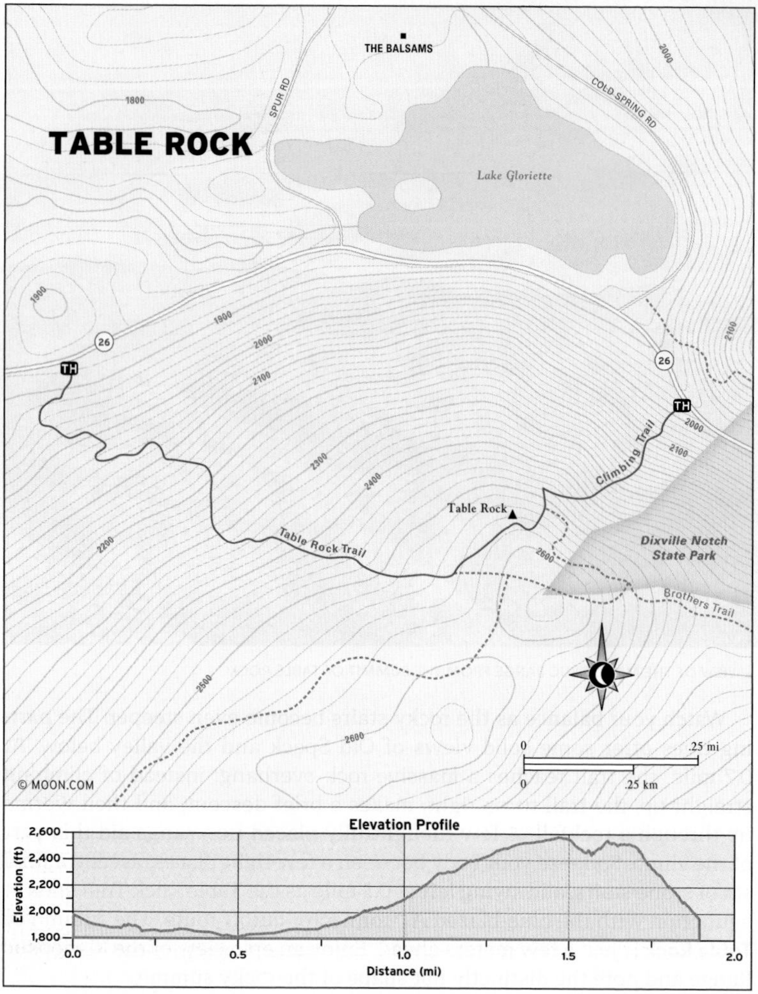

TABLE ROCK

THE BALSAMS
SPUR RD
COLD SPRING RD
Lake Gloriette
26
TH
Table Rock Trail
Table Rock
Climbing Trail
Dixville Notch State Park
Brothers Trail
© MOON.COM

Elevation Profile

Elevation (ft)
Distance (mi)

ME-4 toward ME-26/Gray/New Gloucester. At the bottom of the off-ramp, turn left onto US-202 W and then make an immediate right onto ME-26A N. Continue north along this road as it becomes ME-26 N and take it all the way to the town of Bethel, where you'll turn right onto US-2 E. Drive north to Newry and then make a left turn onto ME-26 N. Continue northwest for 12 miles as the road enters Grafton Notch State Park and watch for the Old Speck parking lot on your left.

GPS COORDINATES: 44°35'25.3"N 70°56'46.7"W, 44.590373, -70.946293

BEST NEARBY BREWS

If you're looking to sample some artisanal Maine suds, be sure to try the honey-infused Belgian ale and the toasty American stout at **Steam Mill Brewery** (7 Mechanic St., Bethel, 207/824-1264, www.steammill-brew.com, 4pm-8pm Fri., noon-8pm Sat.-Sun.).

6 Angel Falls

PRIVATE LAND, TOWNSHIP D

Feel like a frontier explorer as you journey through an isolated timber forest and ford multiple waterways to a rip-roaring cascade.

DISTANCE: 1.4 miles round-trip

DURATION: 1 hour

ELEVATION CHANGE: 192 feet

EFFORT: Easy

TRAIL: Dirt path, rocks, water crossings on stones

USERS: Hikers, leashed dogs

SEASON: May-October

FEES/PASSES: None

MAPS: USGS Map for Houghton, ME

CONTACT: Wagner Forest Management, 603/795-2002, www.wagnerforest.com

Was that a bear rustling around in the undergrowth? What mushroom species are these? Am I the only human being out here? These are questions you might find yourself asking on the hike to Angel Falls—this is as backcountry as Maine hiking gets. While it's a short hike, the route involves fording several waterways. A walking stick or trekking poles would be really handy for this one.

START THE HIKE

▸ MILE 0-0.3: Angel Falls Trailhead to Berdeen Stream

Begin the hike at the southern edge of the parking area. A wooden sign with the word "trail" painted on it will be nailed to a tree, with an arrow pointing to your left. Hike south past a logged stretch of forest, following red blazes on the trees. Enjoy a few yards of smooth, sandy footing as the trail curves into the forest and arrives at **Berdeen Stream** at 0.2 mile. During low to moderate water conditions, it's possible to cross the stream on stones with some finesse, but after rain and especially in late spring, the water will be high enough to soak even the tallest pair of boots—which will leave no option but to walk through the water.

▸ MILE 0.3-0.5: Berdeen Stream to Mountain Brook

Pick up the trail on the other side of the stream and continue following red blazes as the trail transitions into something of a stony road. The road is flanked with wildflowers and a variety of trees including beech, white birch, and spruce. After passing an open grassy area, the trail veers southwest into a much darker and thicker section of spruce woods and climbs gradually. The footing becomes twisted with roots and quite rocky in places. After popping out onto an exposed and slippery ledge, the trail arrives at **Mountain Brook** at 0.5 mile. The water level isn't quite as high here but the "stepping" stones are rough and ragged.

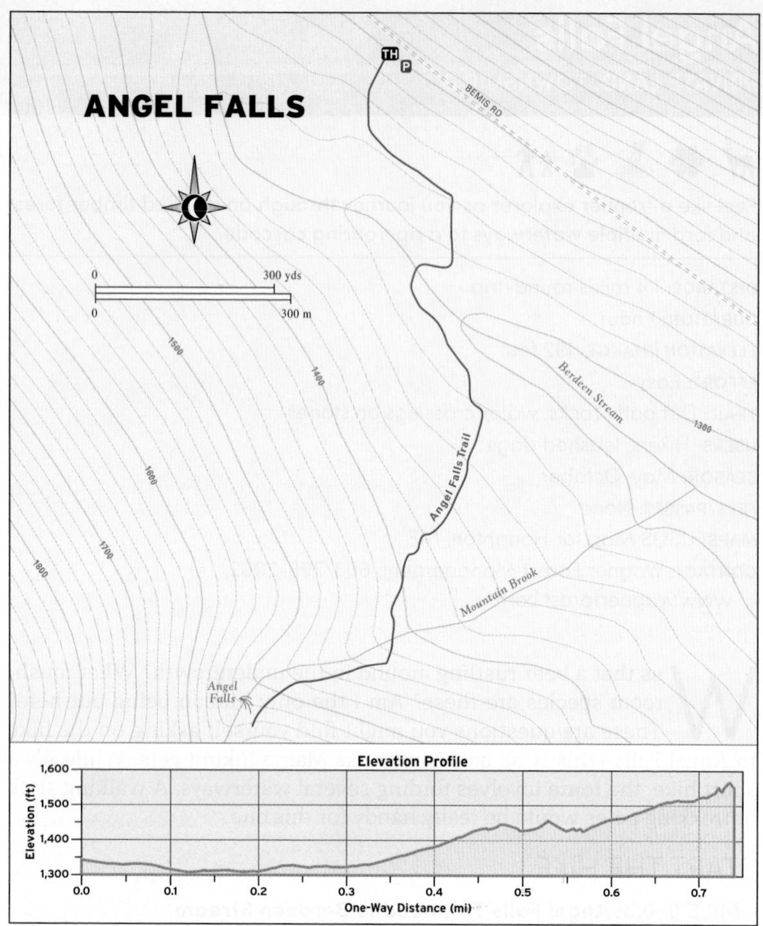

▸ MILE 0.5–0.7: Mountain Brook to Angel Falls Observation Deck

Hike west alongside Mountain Brook and watch your footing as the trail crosses the brook two more times, with comparably treacherous footing in places. After the third crossing, the trail climbs the bank of the brook at a steeper grade and bypasses some boulders. A dull roar from up ahead grows louder. Navigate a final pitch of rock slabs and you'll find yourself at a rough-hewn observation "deck" at 0.7 mile. Here you can admire and even feel the misty majesty of **Angel Falls,** a 90-foot-tall cascade that crashes down a sheer cliff. Daredevil hikers might be tempted to scramble further up the rocky embankment toward the top of the falls, but this is essentially bushwhacking and is neither recommended nor permitted by the landowner. Scrambling over to the base of the falls, while no less tricky, is a better option. After enjoying the falls, return the way you came.

▲ ANGEL FALLS

DIRECTIONS

From Portland, drive northeast on I-95 N for 29 miles and take Exit 75 toward US-202/ME-4/ME-100/Auburn. At the end of the off-ramp, turn left onto US-202 E/ME-4 N/ME-100 N and drive north through Lewiston and Turner before veering left onto ME-108 W. Continue along this road for 16 miles and then, upon reaching the town of Dixfield, turn right onto North Main Street to cross the Androscoggin River; take a left onto US-2 W. Drive west into the town of Mexico and make a right turn onto ME-17 W. Continue northwest for another 17 miles, make a left turn onto Houghton Road, and then turn right onto Bemis Road. The route becomes a dirt logging road. Drive northwest for 2 miles or so until you reach a Y-junction where you'll see a crude sign for the falls nailed to a tree. Turn left at this junction and arrive at the parking area.

GPS COORDINATES: 44°47'18.4"N 70°42'29.6"W, 44.788440, -70.708220

BEST NEARBY BITES

If the isolation of Angel Falls gets to you, drive over to Andover and bump shoulders with Mainers as you indulge in house-baked pies, muffins, breakfast skillets, and more at **The Little Red Hen Diner** (28 S Main St., Andover, 207/392-2253, www.littleredhendiner.com, 7am-2pm Wed.-Thurs., 7am-9pm Fri.-Sat., 7am-2pm Sun.).

7 Androscoggin Riverlands

ANDROSCOGGIN RIVERLANDS STATE PARK, TURNER AND LEEDS

Explore the lush and wildlife-rich woodlands along the Androscoggin River while bypassing the ruins of old farms and settlements that once existed here.

BEST: Winter hikes
DISTANCE: 7.2 miles round-trip
DURATION: 3.5 hours
ELEVATION CHANGE: 662 feet
EFFORT: Moderate
TRAIL: Dirt path, rocks, wooden bridges
USERS: Hikers, leashed dogs, cyclists, ATV riders
SEASON: June–October
FEES/PASSES: None
MAPS: Maine Department of Agriculture, Conservation, and Forestry website
CONTACT: Range Pond State Park, 207/998-4104, www.maine.gov/dacf

The Androscoggin Riverlands, one of the Maine's newer state parks, is a mixed-use recreational forest on the western banks of the big, blue Androscoggin River. It's home to hundreds of bird and mammal species, as well as ruins of the farms and outposts that once operated here. The park's abundant trails are popular with long-distance runners (the Riverlands 100—Maine's first 100-mile endurance race—is held here), mountain bikers, and ATV riders.

START THE HIKE

▸ MILE 0–0.5: Old River Road to Homestead Trail

Begin the hike by the entrance to the day-use parking lot. Find the wooden trail information kiosk, pick up **Old River Road** (a dirt ATV trail), and walk south through the orange gate and up a small hill. Immediately after, you'll see a wooden sign for the Homestead Trail on your left. Veer left onto the **Homestead Trail** and leave the road behind as you enter a vast, resplendent forest of pine, spruce, and beech.

▸ MILE 0.5–1.2: Homestead Trail to Androscoggin River

Follow blue blazes as the trail rolls up and down over the hills and keep your ears open for the songs of hermit thrushes and pine warblers. You'll reach the mossy foundations of an ancient house at 0.6 mile.

Continue south through the forest for half a mile, passing crumbling stone walls and rock-hopping across streams. Cross a slatted wooden footbridge to reach the Harrington Path junction at 1.1 miles. Continue straight to stay on the Homestead Trail, which shortly reaches the **Androscoggin River** and ambles along a sandier path near the water.

▲ THE RIVER'S EDGE

▸ MILE 1.2–2.2: Androscoggin River to Old River Road

Veer left at the unmarked fork ahead to reach **Picnic Meadow** at 1.3 miles; walk south across this pretty clearing. Cross Old River Road to pick up the Homestead Trail on the other side (look for a wooden sign).

After crossing a wooden footbridge, the trail passes a lush cove before gently climbing a ferny hillside with a lively salamander population. The greenery you see on this portion of the trail is the Maine woods at their finest. Continue south as the Homestead Trail veers away from the river and concludes at Old River Road at 2.2 miles.

▸ MILE 2.2–2.8: Old River Road to Ridge Trail

Hikers who've had their fill can turn right and take the road back to the parking lot. Those who want more should turn left and briefly continue along **Old River Road** to its junction with the Ridge Trail. Turn right onto the **Ridge Trail** and follow blue blazes as the ribbon-like dirt trail ascends a lumbering, mossy hillside. At 2.8 miles, keep left at the unmarked junction.

▸ MILE 2.8–3.9: Ridge Trail to Ledges Trail and Old River Road

Continue your ascent of the hill, enjoying the breeze and views of the river. Amble across the gentler, rocky hilltop until you reach the Ledges Trail junction at 3.5 miles. Turn left onto the **Ledges Trail** and watch your step as you descend a thrillingly steep switchback of rock stairs. Continue through the woods and down a final staircase to rejoin Old River Road at 3.9 miles.

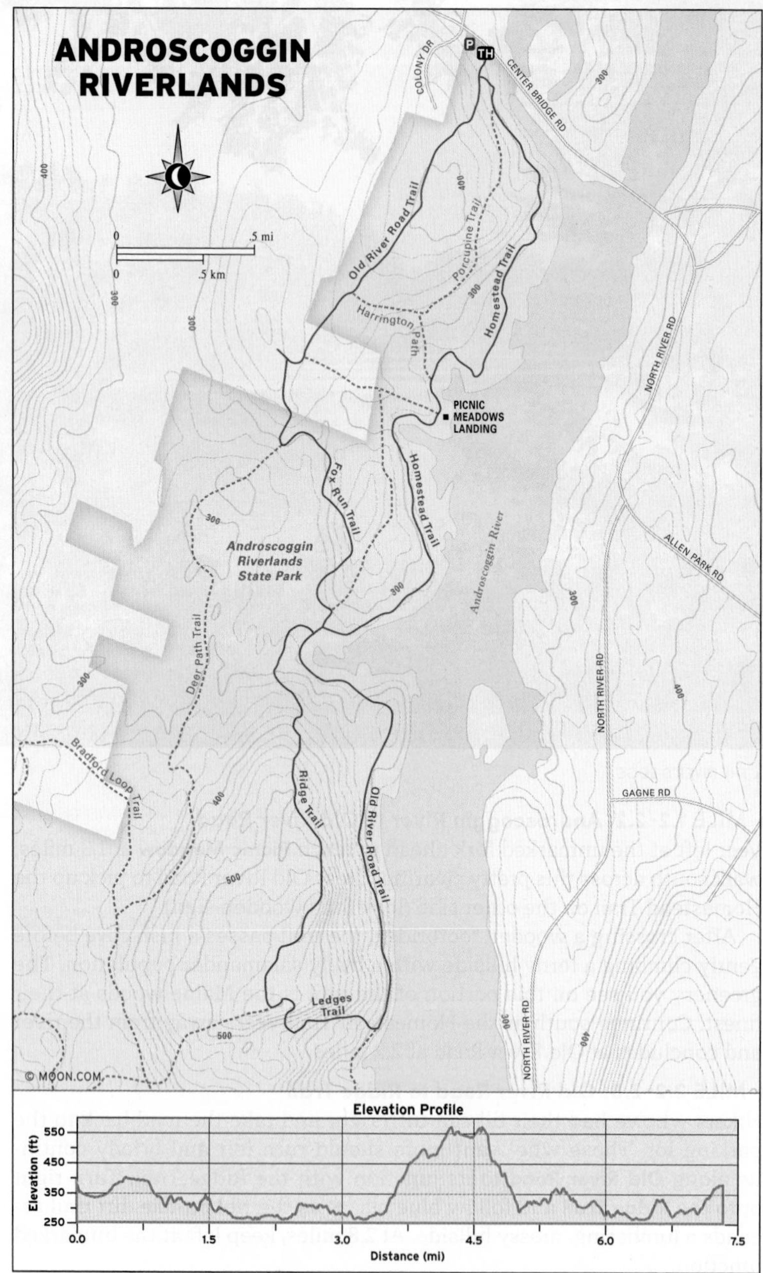
ANDROSCOGGIN RIVERLANDS
0
.5 mi
0
.5 km
COLONY DR
P
TH
CENTER BRIDGE RD
Old River Road Trail
Porcupine Trail
Homestead Trail
Harrington Path
PICNIC MEADOWS LANDING
Fox Run Trail
Homestead Trail
Androscoggin Riverlands State Park
Androscoggin River
NORTH RIVER RD
ALLEN PARK RD
Deer Path Trail
Bradford Loop Trail
Ridge Trail
Old River Road Trail
GAGNE RD
NORTH RIVER RD
Ledges Trail
NORTH RIVER RD
300
400
500
© MOON.COM
Elevation Profile
Elevation (ft)
550
450
350
250
0.0
1.5
3.0
4.5
6.0
7.5
Distance (mi)

▸ **MILE 3.9-5.3: Old River Road to Fox Run Trail**

Turn left onto the road and walk for just over a mile, past the Ridge Trail sign and a marshy area, until you reach the Fox Run Trail at 5.2 miles. Turn left onto **Fox Run Trail** and head back into dense forest, ambling past some meadows where deer sightings are a regular occurrence.

▸ **MILE 5.3-5.9: Fox Run Trail to Deer Run Trail**

Cross a rickety wooden bridge to reach the junction with the appropriately named Deer Run Trail at 5.9 miles. Turn right onto the **Deer Run Trail.**

▸ **MILE 5.9-7.2: Deer Run Trail to Old River Road**

Ascend a small rocky hillside on a sandier path. Turn right at an unmarked junction and pass a jumble of boulders before arriving at an ATV trail roundabout at 6.2 miles. Walk north across the roundabout to pick up **Old River Road** one last time. Continue north along the road for about a mile as it climbs a series of knolls before descending back to the trailhead sign at 7.2 miles.

DIRECTIONS

From Portland, drive south on I-295 S for roughly 4 miles and take Exit 1 to merge onto I-95 N. Drive north on I-95 toward Lewiston/Augusta and take Exit 75. At the end of the off-ramp, turn left onto ME-100 N/ME-4 N/US-202 E. Drive north through Lewiston for 12 miles and then take a right onto Upper Street. Follow this hillside road to its terminus at Center Bridge Road and make a left onto Center Bridge Road. The turnoff for the Androscoggin Riverlands State Park parking area will be on your right just over 1.5 miles ahead. Look for an easily missed dark brown wooden sign by the side of the road.

GPS COORDINATES: 44°15'40.7"N 70°11'18.4"W, 44.261292, -70.188445

BEST NEARBY BREWS

If you're driving through Lewiston, take a few minutes to sample an indelible Maine IPA and many other admirable brews at **Baxter Co.** (120 Mill St., Lewiston, 207/689-3830, www.pubatbaxter.com, 3pm-10pm Tues.-Thurs., 3pm-midnight Fri., noon-midnight Sat., noon-10pm Sun.). Make your foodie friends jealous and experience a farm-to-table breakfast or lunch on an actual Maine farm by visiting **Nezinscot Farm** (284 Turner Center Rd., Turner, 207/225-3231, www.nezinscotfarm.com, 7am-3pm Thurs.-Sun.).

8 Tumbledown Mountain

TUMBLEDOWN PUBLIC LANDS, WELD

Make an exciting ascent—complete with cave spelunking—to an otherworldly summit with amazing views and an alpine pond.

BEST: Summer hikes

DISTANCE: 5.8 miles round-trip

DURATION: 4 hours

ELEVATION CHANGE: 1,899 feet

EFFORT: Strenuous

TRAIL: Dirt path, rock scrambling, ladder climb, water crossings via stones and bog bridges

USERS: Hikers

SEASON: June–October

MAPS: Maine Department of Agriculture, Conservation and Forestry website

CONTACT: Maine Bureau of Parks and Lands, 207/778-8231, www.maine.gov/dacf

Standing tall and defiant in the modest hills of Franklin County, Tumbledown Mountain, at 3,054 feet, is a dramatic sight. Hikers can reach this enchanting summit by two routes: the short, easier Brook Trail, or the more exciting Loop Trail, which is recommended for those who aren't afraid of heights, rock scrambling, and mild spelunking. Note that the Loop Trail should not be hiked during wet weather.

START THE HIKE

▸ MILE 0–0.7: Loop Trail to Tumbledown Boulder

Begin your hike in the parking area along Byron Road. Cross the road to the trailhead sign for the **Loop Trail** and enter a thick deciduous forest. Follow blue blazes as the rock-strewn trail snakes north through the woods for 0.2 mile. After crossing a creek, the trail starts to climb at a moderate grade before reaching the absurdly massive **Tumbledown Boulder** at 0.7 mile.

▸ MILE 0.7–1.2: Tumbledown Boulder to Fat Man's Misery Cave

From here, the real workout begins as the trail immediately climbs steeply up the lower haunch of Tumbledown Mountain through a jumble of boulders and roots. Catch your breath at a clearing at 1 mile that offers a primo view of Tumbledown's sheer south face. Briefly descend into a patch of boreal forest before climbing straight up a rift in the south face at an even steeper grade than before. The trail here is somewhat eroded and bypasses rock slabs, some of which require handholds. At 1.2 miles, you'll come upon the infamous **Fat Man's Misery,** a narrow and damp chimney cave through which hikers must hoist themselves with the help of three iron rungs that are attached to the interior walls. This doesn't require much upper-body strength but it's a tricky maneuver, so take your time.

▲ THE SHORE OF TUMBLEDOWN POND

‣ MILE 1.2–1.8: Fat Man's Misery Cave to Tumbledown Mountain Summit

After exiting the cave, the worst is over. Continue briefly up some rocks and at 1.6 miles, turn left onto **Tumbledown Mountain Trail** and hike west up a series of sloped slabs. You'll reach the summit of **Tumbledown Mountain** at 1.8 miles.

‣ MILE 1.8–2.3: Tumbledown Mountain Summit to Tumbledown Mountain Trail

After gazing across the lush panorama of western Maine, backtrack east to the junction of the Loop Trail and the Tumbledown Mountain Trail and veer left to continue along the Tumbledown Mountain Trail, which meanders across a windswept ridgeline for 0.5 mile. (Notice how the metamorphic rock contains visible flows of sediment!)

‣ MILE 2.3–2.4: Tumbledown Mountain Trail to Tumbledown Pond

A pleasant descent delivers you to the shores of **Tumbledown Pond**—a heavenly body of cerulean water with its own lightly forested island.

‣ MILE 2.4–4.4: Tumbledown Pond to Brook Trail

At 2.4 miles, pick up the **Brook Trail** beside the pond. Hike southeast down a mess of rocks strewn throughout the woods for about 0.6 mile, before the trail softens and widens into an old streambed at 3 miles. Continue along the path through corridors of white birches, rock-hopping your way across a series of streams, over the next 1.4 miles. Mind your step: tiny eastern American toads are active here.

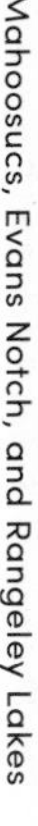

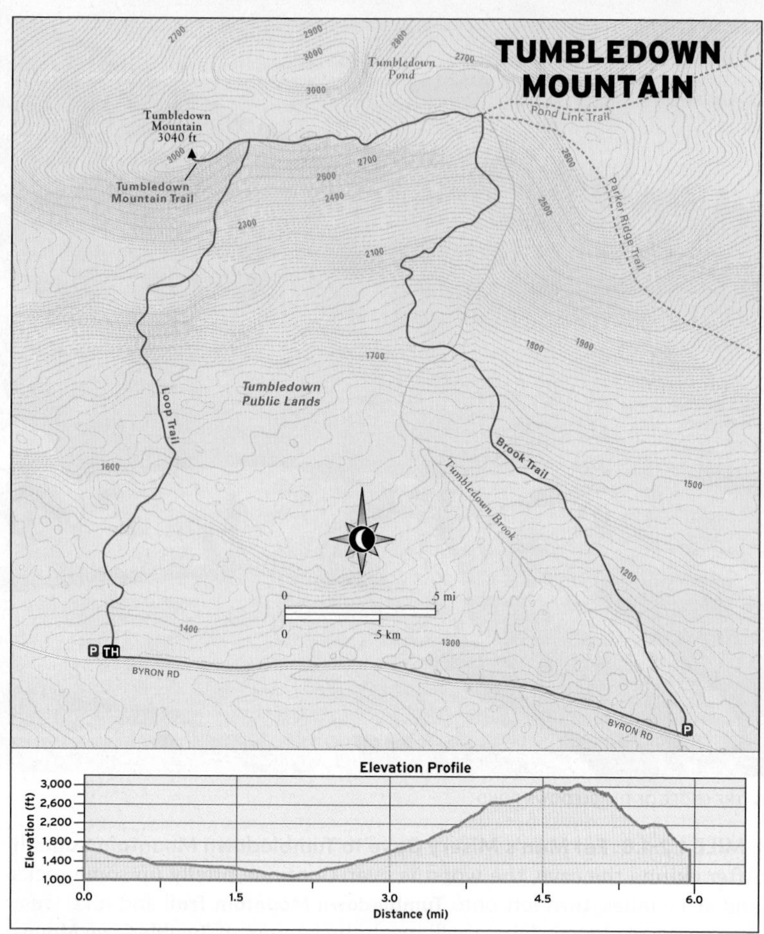

▸ **MILE 4.4-5.8: Brook Trail to Byron Road**

The Brook Trail reaches **Byron Road** at 4.4 miles. Turn right and walk west along the sunlit road for an easy 1.4 miles back to the Loop Trail parking area, completing the hike at 5.8 miles.

DIRECTIONS

From Boston or Portland, drive north on I-95 toward Lewiston/Augusta. Take Exit 75 and turn left onto ME-100 N/ME-4 N/US-202 E. Drive into Lewiston and continue straight onto ME-4 N. Take this road north for 20 miles and then turn left onto ME 108-W. Drive northwest for another 16 miles to Dixfield and then take a right onto Main Street over the bridge; then make another right onto US-2 E. Head east briefly before taking a left onto ME-142 N and continuing north into Carthage. Turn left onto West Road and continue north past Webb Lake until you reach Byron Road. Take a final left onto Byron Road and follow the dirt road west past the Brook Trail parking lot to the nearby Loop Trail parking area.

GPS COORDINATES: 44°43'52.8"N 70°33'17.4"W, 44.731335, -70.554843

▲ THE RIDGELINE TRAVERSE

BEST NEARBY BREWS

After gazing out at Webb Lake from the top of Tumbledown, take in the lake from a different perspective at **Kawanhee Inn** (12 Anne's Way, Weld, 207/585-2000, www.kawanheeinn.com), where you'll find hearty comfort food and Maine beers at the **in-house pub** (5pm-9pm Tues.-Sun. summer.) Call the inn to inquire about limited dining hours during the fall.

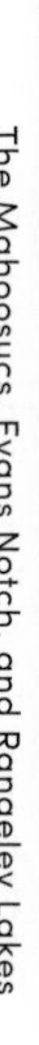

NEARBY CAMPGROUNDS

NAME	LOCATION	FACILITIES	SEASON	FEE
Grafton Notch Campground	1472 Bear River Rd., Route 26, Newry, ME 04261	Tent sites, RV sites, toilets, showers, potable water	mid-May to mid-October	$28
207/824-2292, www.campgrafton.com				
Stony Brook Recreation & Camping	42 Powell Pl., Hanover, ME 04237	Tent sites, lean-tos, RV sites, cabins, toilets, showers, potable water, laundry, swimming pool, camp store, Wi-Fi	year-round	$28-100
207/824-2836, www.stonybrookrec.com				
Bethel Outdoor Adventure	121 Mayville Rd., Bethel, ME 04217	Tent sites, RV sites, toilets, showers, potable water, laundry, camp store, Wi-Fi	mid-May to mid-October	$24-39
207/824-4224, www.betheloutdooradventure.com				
Pleasant River Campground	800 W Bethel Rd., Bethel, ME 04217	Tent sites, RV sites, cabins, toilets, showers, potable water, swimming pool, camp store, Wi-Fi	May through October	$28-40
207/836-2000, www.pleasantrivercampground.com				
Hastings Campground	State Rte 113, Bethel, ME 04217	Tent sites, toilets, potable water	late May through mid-October	$18
www.recreation.gov				
Basin Campground	ME/NH border, Basin Rd, Chatham, NH 03813	Tent sites, toilets, potable water	late May through mid-October	$20
603/447-5443, www.recreation.gov				

NEARBY CAMPGROUNDS (continued)				
NAME	**LOCATION**	**FACILITIES**	**SEASON**	**FEE**
Mount Blue State Park Campground	187 Webb Beach Rd., Weld, ME 04285	Tent sites, lean-tos, toilets, showers, potable water	mid-May through September	$20-30
207/585-2347, www.maine.gov				
Coos Canyon Campground	445 Swift River Rd., Byron, ME 04275	Tent sites, lean-tos, RV sites, cabins, toilets, showers, potable water, laundry, camp store, Wi-Fi	late May through early October	$25-125
207/364-3880, www.cooscanyoncamping.com				
Silver Lake Campground	261 Main St., Roxbury, ME 04275	Tent sites, RV sites, cabins, toilets, showers, potable water, laundry, Wi-Fi	mid-May through mid-October	$25
207/545-0416, www.silverlakecampground.com				

▲ RED SQUIRREL

▲ THE VIEW FROM MOUNT WILLARD

NEW HAMPSHIRE

WHITE MOUNTAIN NATIONAL FOREST

New Hampshire's White Mountains dominate the Northeast like the Beatles once ruled pop music. These craggy peaks—including Mount Washington, the tallest in New England—are wildly popular, scenically diverse, and, sometimes, a bit dangerous. The abundance of 4,000-plus-foot mountains here is unparalleled by anything in New England, and there's something for everyone. Whether you fancy a gentle stroll to some hidden waterfalls or following cairns up a bumpy ridge, you'll find it. The trails here range from meditatively gentle to relentlessly steep. You'll share the woods with deer, pine martens, beavers, and bears. And come sundown, you can pair your hike with award-winning cuisine and artisanal libations.

▲ the path along Whitewall rockslide

▲ the trail along Upper Greeley Pond

◂ A BRIEF REVERIE OF SMOOTH TRAIL BEFORE THE NEXT ROCKY RIDGE CLIMB

1 **Mount Moosilauke**
DISTANCE: 7.6 miles round-trip
DURATION: 5 hours
EFFORT: Strenuous

2 **Bridal Veil Falls**
DISTANCE: 4.4 miles round-trip
DURATION: 2.5 hours
EFFORT: Easy/moderate

3 **Mount Lafayette and Franconia Ridge**
DISTANCE: 8.4 miles round-trip
DURATION: 5.5 hours
EFFORT: Strenuous

4 **The Flume**
DISTANCE: 2 miles round-trip
DURATION: 1 hour
EFFORT: Easy

5 **Greeley Ponds**
DISTANCE: 4.2 miles round-trip
DURATION: 2.5 hours
EFFORT: Easy/moderate

6 **Zealand Valley and Thoreau Falls**
DISTANCE: 9.4 miles round-trip
DURATION: 4.5 hours
EFFORT: Moderate

7 **Mount Willard**
DISTANCE: 3 miles round-trip
DURATION: 1.5 hours
EFFORT: Easy

8 **Arethusa Falls via Bemis Brook**
DISTANCE: 2.8 miles round-trip
DURATION: 2 hours
EFFORT: Easy/moderate

9 **Mount Carrigain**
DISTANCE: 10.4 miles round-trip
DURATION: 6 hours
EFFORT: Strenuous

10 **Basin Rim**
DISTANCE: 4.4 miles round-trip
DURATION: 3 hours
EFFORT: Moderate

11 **Mount Chocorua**
DISTANCE: 7.4 miles round-trip
DURATION: 4.5 hours
EFFORT: Moderate/strenuous

12 **Mount Washington via Tuckerman Ravine**
DISTANCE: 8.2 miles round-trip
DURATION: 8 hours
EFFORT: Strenuous

13 **Giant Falls**
DISTANCE: 3 miles round-trip
DURATION: 1.5 hours
EFFORT: Easy

14 **Mount Adams**
DISTANCE: 8.6 miles round-trip
DURATION: 7 hours
EFFORT: Strenuous

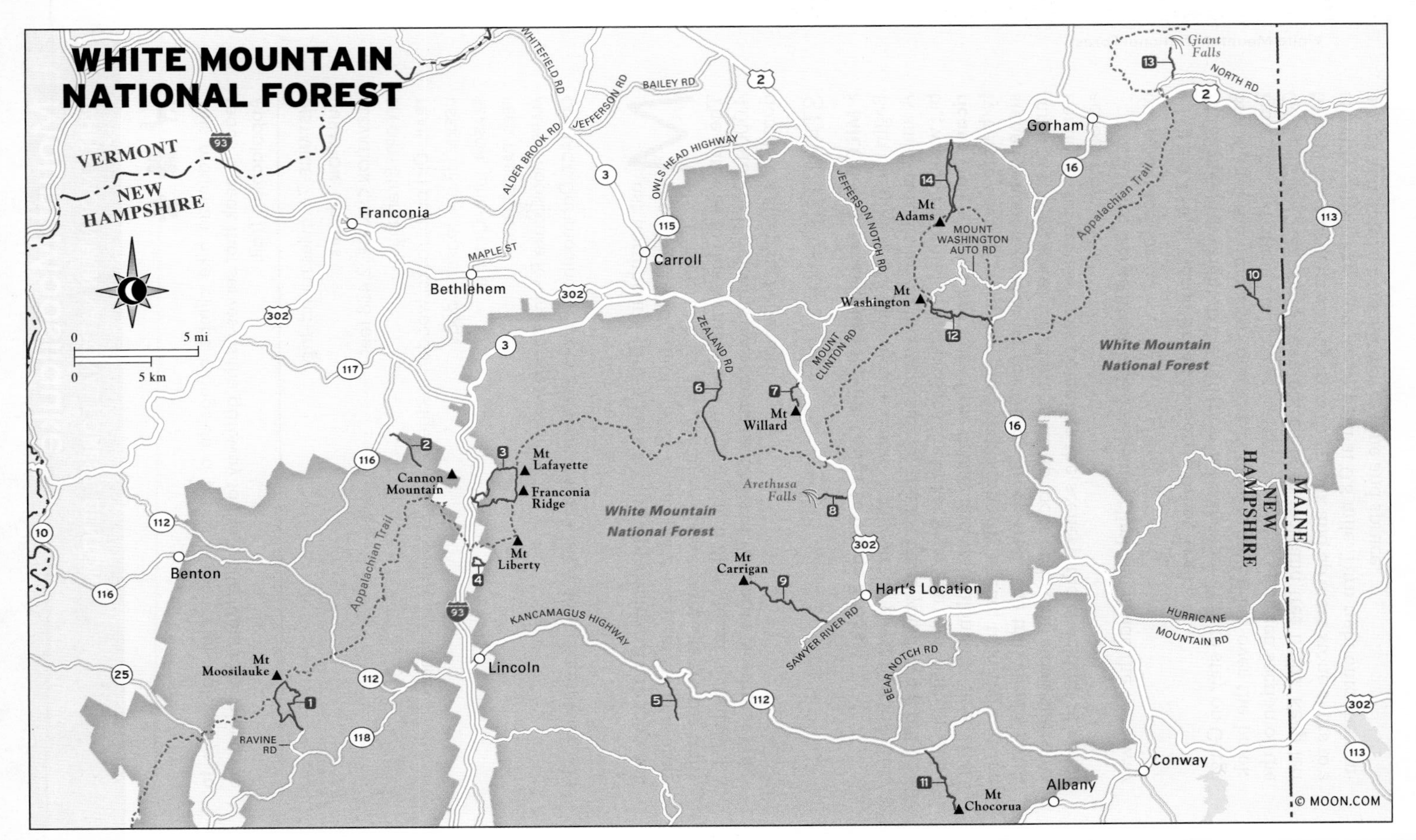

WHITE MOUNTAIN NATIONAL FOREST
VERMONT
NEW HAMPSHIRE
MAINE
0
5 mi
0
5 km
Franconia
Bethlehem
MAPLE ST
Carroll
Gorham
Benton
Lincoln
Hart's Location
Conway
Albany
WHITEFIELD RD
JEFFERSON RD
BAILEY RD
ALDER BROOK RD
OWLS HEAD HIGHWAY
JEFFERSON NOTCH RD
ZEALAND RD
MOUNT CLINTON RD
MOUNT WASHINGTON AUTO RD
NORTH RD
Giant Falls
Mt Adams
Mt Washington
Mt Willard
Arethusa Falls
Mt Lafayette
Franconia Ridge
Cannon Mountain
Mt Liberty
Mt Carrigan
Mt Moosilauke
Mt Chocorua
RAVINE RD
KANCAMAGUS HIGHWAY
SAWYER RIVER RD
BEAR NOTCH RD
HURRICANE MOUNTAIN RD
Appalachian Trail
White Mountain National Forest
© MOON.COM

1 Mount Moosilauke

WHITE MOUNTAIN NATIONAL FOREST, BENTON

This mountain hike climbs alongside a series of peaceful waterways to reach a peak that serves as the gateway to the White Mountains along the Appalachian Trail.

DISTANCE: 7.6 miles round-trip

DURATION: 5 hours

ELEVATION CHANGE: 2,438 feet

EFFORT: Strenuous

TRAIL: Dirt path, rocks, wooden bridges, water crossings on stones

USERS: Hikers, leashed dogs

SEASON: June–October

FEES/PASSES: None

MAPS: Moosilauke Ravine Lodge website

CONTACT: Dartmouth Outdoors, 603/646-2428, www.outdoors.dartmouth.edu

Most northbound thru-hikers on the Appalachian Trail approach the White Mountains with equal parts excitement and anxiety. The vistas here are relentlessly sweeping—as are the trails. The gateway to this formidable stretch of the trail is Mount Moosilauke, a 4,000-footer that looms over the rolling hills of Vermont's Northeast Kingdom like a sleeping behemoth.

START THE HIKE

▸ MILE 0–0.4: Moosilauke Ravine Lodge to Gorge Brook

Begin the hike at the Moosilauke Ravine Lodge in the guest parking area. A small cutoff trail on the west side of the lot takes you down a hill to a big wooden footbridge that crosses the **Baker River.** Turn left onto the **Hurricane Trail** on the other side of the bridge and walk along the river briefly before veering right into the woods. Shortly ahead, turn right at the signed junction to pick up the **Gorge Brook Trail.** The trail climbs north through the woods at a patient grade up rocks and some stone stairs. As hemlock and spruce trees dominate the scenery, the chuckling of water echoes from ahead.

You'll reach **Gorge Brook** at 0.4 mile and climb alongside the waterway on rockier footing.

▸ MILE 0.4–0.8: Gorge Brook to Gorge Brook Trail

At 0.5 mile, veer right at the junction with Snapper Trail to stay on Gorge Brook, and then cross an ominously creaky footbridge over the brook. From the end of the bridge, the trail passes a discontinued section of the Gorge Brook Trail that's been barred with rock and tree limbs. Keep left here as the trail climbs away from the brook and up more stone stairs to a recently constructed connector path at 0.8 mile. Turn right onto the connector and enter a boreal forest of pine and spruce.

▲ THE UMMISTAKABLE TITANIC PROFILE OF MOUNT MOOSILAUKE

▸ MILE 0.8–3.7: Gorge Brook Trail to Moosilauke Summit

The trail becomes a gulch-like ribbon that weaves through the woods, merging with the original Gorge Brook Trail again.

At 1.3 miles, you'll reach the brook again, where another bridge crossing awaits. Hop across some tributaries that feed the brook and climb north at a steeper grade alongside the brook. This rugged ascent continues for roughly 1 mile up the eastern shoulder of Moosilauke. The trees get smaller with each twist and turn.

At 3 miles, emerge from the woods and enter the exposed alpine zone, where the trail transforms into a rocky road across the upper slopes of the mountain, with plenty of krummholz and tundra. (Moosilauke is one of the broader and gentler summits in the Whites.) A final ascent up some rock stairs delivers you to the pinnacle of the mountain at 3.7 miles, where hikers can size up the Presidentials to the east and the Green Mountains to the west. You're also likely to encounter a few thru-hikers hanging out and taking in the territory ahead.

▸ MILE 3.7–7.6: Moosilauke Summit to Snapper Trail

Descend southwest from the summit by following signs for the **Moosilauke Carriage Road,** which is part of the Appalachian Trail. What begins as an exposed ridge walk segues into a stroll down a sunlit rocky road flanked by modest spruce trees. It's a nice change of pace from the usual rock-hopping. Keep left at the four-way junction with South Peak Spur and Glencliff Trail at 4.7 miles, continue southwest along the Carriage Road to the junction with **Snapper Trail** at 6 miles, and make a left to take Snapper down the lush and densely wooded south side of Moosilauke. After passing through several groves of ferns and crossing some streams on rocks, Snapper Trail concludes at the Gorge Brook Trailhead at 7.1 miles. Retrace your steps to Moosilauke Ravine Lodge to complete the loop at 7.6 miles.

DIRECTIONS

From Concord, drive north on I-93 for 61 miles and take Exit 32 for NH-112 toward Lincoln/North Woodstock. Turn right onto NH-112 W at the bottom

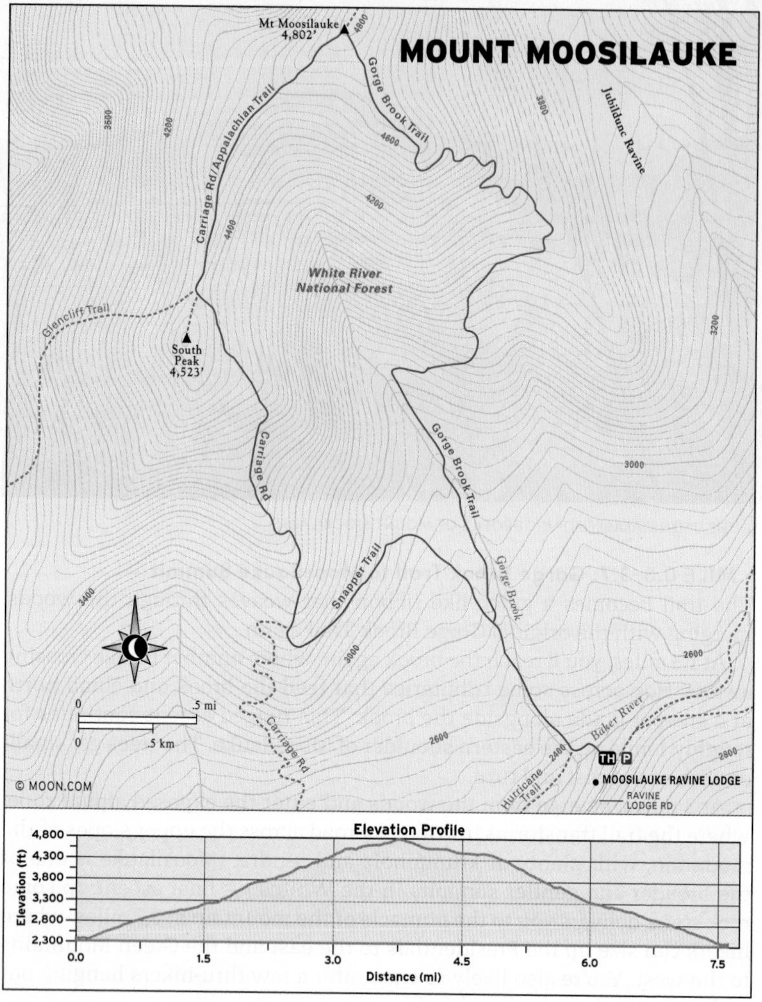

MOUNT MOOSILAUKE

of the off-ramp and head west for 3 miles. At the fork, veer left onto NH-118 S and drive southwest for another 7 miles. Turn right onto Ravine Road and drive to the first parking area, which is located in a clearing. This is where day hikers should park their vehicles. The lodge parking lot from which the trail itself begins is just under a mile's walk up the gently graded dirt road.

GPS COORDINATES: 43°59'37.5"N 71°48'53.7"W, 43.993759, -71.814919

BEST NEARBY BREWS

Replenish your spent calories post-hike by heading to North Woodstock and tucking into a multicourse comfort food dinner and a flight of seasonal craft beers at the **Woodstock Inn Station & Brewery** (135 Main St., North Woodstock, 603/745-3951, www.woodstockinnbrewery.com, 11am-11pm Sun.-Thurs., 11:30am-1am Fri.-Sat.).

2 Bridal Veil Falls

WHITE MOUNTAIN NATIONAL FOREST, FRANCONIA

This forest hike features one of New Hampshire's most elegant cascades, a sumptuous swimming hole, and a haunting memento of Hollywood history.

BEST: Spots for a swim
DISTANCE: 4.4 miles round-trip
DURATION: 2.5 hours
ELEVATION CHANGE: 966 feet
EFFORT: Easy/moderate
TRAIL: Dirt path, rocks, wooden bridge, water crossings via rocks
USERS: Hikers, leashed dogs
SEASON: May-October
PASSES/FEES: None
MAPS: White Mountain National Forest website
CONTACT: White Mountain National Forest, 603/536-6100, www.fs.usda.gov/whitemountain/

One of New Hampshire's most elegant and aptly named cascades, Bridal Veil Falls spills from a pitcher-like cleft of rock in a ravine on Cannon Mountain's western haunch. The top of this 80-foot-tall cascade resembles the silky veil of a bride, and the access route to the falls—the Coppermine Trail—makes for a breezy day hike with enough climbing to get the blood pumping. The trail is rustling with deciduous vegetation and critters, and it also contains a mystery that has bamboozled visitors for decades.

START THE HIKE

▸ MILE 0-1.0: Bridal Veil Falls Parking Area to Coppermine Brook

Begin your hike in the parking area for Bridal Veil Falls on Coppermine Road. Turn left and walk east on Coppermine Road. Keep right at the fork with Beechwood Lane and at 0.2 mile look for a metal hiker sign on a tree on your left. Turn left onto the dirt path by the sign. This is the start of the **Coppermine Trail.** As you step into a thick forest of pine trees, the trail curves southeast (following yellow blazes) and ambles upward at a gentle grade. The footing gets rockier and rootier, but the generous trail width makes the going pleasant. Around 0.6 mile, you'll start to hear the promising sound of rushing water.

Passing through some white birch trees, the trail reaches **Coppermine Brook** at 1 mile. Before you continue southeast along the water, take a minute to pick your way down to the brook from the trail: one of the boulders here contains a bronze plaque memorializing Arthur Farnsworth, a local innkeeper who became the second husband of Hollywood icon Bette Davis. Local legend has it that Davis herself had the plaque placed there.

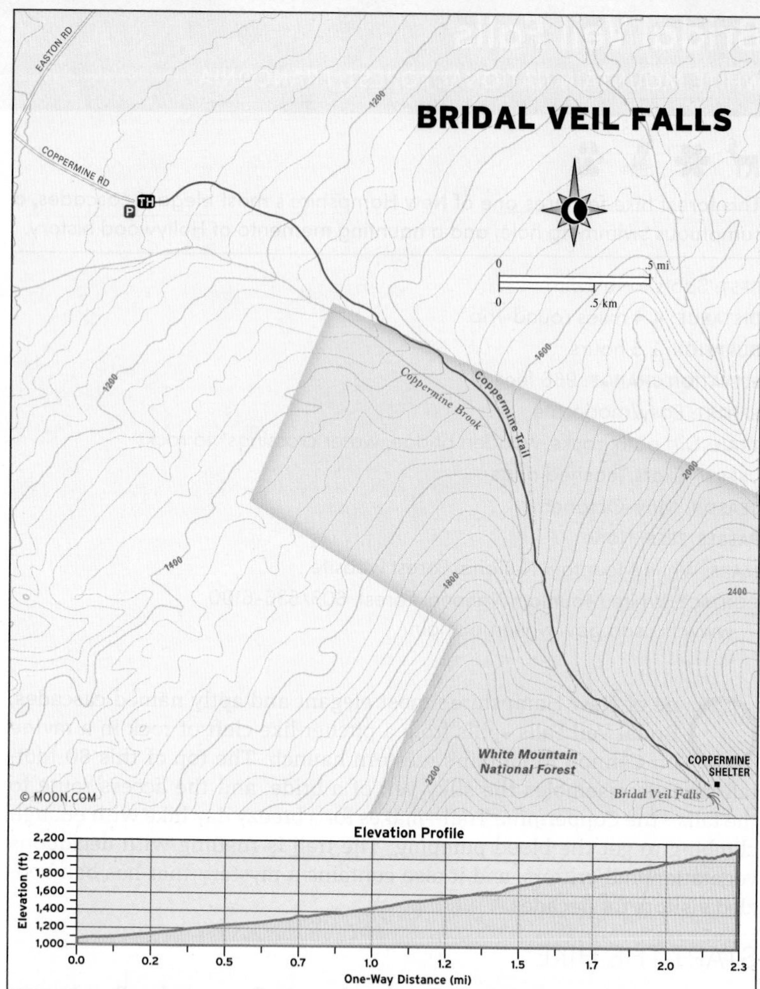

(The plaque, which refers to Farnsworth as "The Keeper Of Stray Ladies," cites Davis as "A Grateful One.")

▸ MILE 1.0–2.1: Coppermine Brook to Coppermine Shelter

Once you've either found the plaque or given up, continue along the brook and savor this final stretch of laid-back terrain, for the Coppermine Trail steepens at 1.4 miles and begins to veer away from the brook. After climbing the western flank of Cannon Mountain for roughly half a mile—passing into a mixture of deciduous and boreal forest—the trail rejoins Coppermine Brook and crosses the brook on a wooden bridge at 1.9 miles. Shortly after, at 2.1 miles, you'll arrive at Coppermine Shelter—a grungy lean-to for overnight hikers.

▸ MILE 2.1–2.2: Coppermine Shelter to Bridal Veil Falls

The Coppermine Trail continues past the shelter and crosses the brook on stones one final time. Listen for the sound of crashing water; at 2.2 miles, emerge from the forest at the foot of Bridal Veil Falls' bottom half—a

▲ THE ARC OF BRIDAL VEIL FALLS

waterslide that tumbles down an open slope of granite. The pool at the base of the slide is ideal for a brisk swim before scrambling up the rocks and roots along the left side of the lower falls (the trail concludes at the pool) and reaching the upper half of **Bridal Veil Falls**—the veil-like part for which it's named. There are plenty of nearby rocks for sitting and admiring the view. Return the way you came.

DIRECTIONS

From Boston, drive north on I-93. Once you've crossed the New Hampshire border, continue north and take Exit 34C. Turn left onto NH 8 N. Veer left at the junction with Profile Road, after which NH 8 becomes Wells Road. Continue to the end of Wells Road and turn right on NH 116. Coppermine Road is half a mile ahead. Turn left on Coppermine Road and park in the hiker parking area that you'll see on your immediate left.

GPS COORDINATES: 44°10'49.0"N 71°45'13.9"W, 44.180285, -71.753850

BEST NEARBY BREWS

Start the day with a stack of maple syrup-coated flapjacks at **Polly's Pancake Parlor** (672 NH-117, Sugar Hill, 603/823-5575, www.pollys-pancakeparlor.com, 7am-3pm Fri.-Mon.). After your hike, hop over to Littleton and reflect with a roasty Baltic porter or any of the other European-inspired artisanal brews at **Schilling Beer Company** (18 Mill St., Littleton, 603/444-4800, www.schillingbeer.com, 3pm-10pm Mon.-Thurs., noon-10pm Fri.-Sun.).

3 Mount Lafayette and Franconia Ridge

FRANCONIA NOTCH STATE PARK, LINCOLN

Summit the tallest mountain on the Franconia Ridge along with two others and make a thrillingly steep descent of several large waterfalls.

BEST: Fall hikes

DISTANCE: 8.4 miles round-trip

DURATION: 5.5 hours

ELEVATION CHANGE: 3,812 feet

EFFORT: Strenuous

TRAIL: Dirt path, rocks, wooden bog bridges

USERS: Hikers

SEASON: June–October

FEES/PASSES: None

MAPS: Franconia Notch State Park website

CONTACT: Franconia Notch State Park, 603/823-8800, www.nhstateparks.org/visit/state-parks

Mount Lafayette greets visitors to the White Mountains as they approach from the south on Interstate 93. It's the tallest point along the breathtaking Franconia Ridge, which also contains comparably mighty mountaintops such as Mount Lincoln and Little Haystack. Ascending to Lafayette by way of the Old Bridle Path is one of the most generously scenic ridge climbs in New Hampshire. But the fun doesn't stop there—as any peak-bagger worth their salt would say, why summit just one mountain when you could experience a trilogy? That's exactly what this loop offers—an opportunity to climb Lafayette, Lincoln, and Haystack in one fell swoop.

START THE HIKE

▸ MILE 0–2.1: Old Bridle Path to The Three Agonies

Begin the hike on the I-93 N side of the Lafayette Place parking lot. Pick up the **Old Bridle Path** by the trail sign and step into the forest on a rocky path that ambles over to **Walker Brook.** Veer left at the junction for Falling Waters Trail at 0.2 mile to stay on Old Bridle Path and hike northwest as the trail meanders up the foothills of Lafayette at a pleasant grade. As the footing becomes rockier and steeper, the trail ascends a series of slabby switchbacks. At 1.5 miles, you'll reach the first of many exposed ledges on Lafayette's curvy southern ridgeline. Lafayette and the Franconia ridgeline beckon beyond this lookout point.

From here, the Old Bridle Path roller-coasters up and down the Lafayette ridgeline. The views of Franconia Ridge and the deep deciduous valley below are constant, with only a few forays into the trees. At just over 2 miles, you'll reach "The Three Agonies"—a trio of very steep and rocky

▲ A GENTLER STRETCH OF TRAIL ALONG THE OTHERWISE ROCKY AND PUNISHING RIDGE

ledge climbs. (The first Agony consists of smooth red rock that can become super slippery when wet.)

▸ MILE 2.1-2.8: The Three Agonies to Greenleaf Hut

After this trifecta of obstacles, the trail levels off and emerges from boreal forest into the alpine zone. Here, at 2.8 miles, you'll reach **Greenleaf Hut,** where you can buy soup, tea, or—if so desired—a bunk bed and a five-course dinner. (Reservations are recommended and can be made at www.outdoors.org.)

▸ MILE 2.8-3.8: Greenleaf Hut to Mount Lafayette Summit

Continue past the hut by picking up the Greenleaf Trail, which descends some rocks briefly to skirt around the swampy southern shore of **Eagle Lake.** Then, ignite your quads as the trail climbs the barren cone of Lafayette on winding rock stairs that follow cairns that seem to go on forever. At 3.8 miles, a stone foundation (an old hiker hut that burned down) marks your arrival on the summit of Mount Lafayette. An unobstructed panoramic view of the Whites is your reward here, and to the south, you'll see the rolling expanse of Franconia Ridge beckoning you.

▸ MILE 3.8-5.5: Mount Lafayette Summit to Little Haystack

Once you've caught your breath, take a moment to assess the weather, as the ridgeline ahead offers few escape routes. Head south from the summit on the **Franconia Ridge Trail,** which is marked with more cairns. The trail descends from Lafayette into a patch of krummholz before emerging again and traveling up and down along the verdant, exposed, and often very narrow ridgeline to visit Mount Lincoln at 4.7 miles and Little Haystack at 5.5 miles.

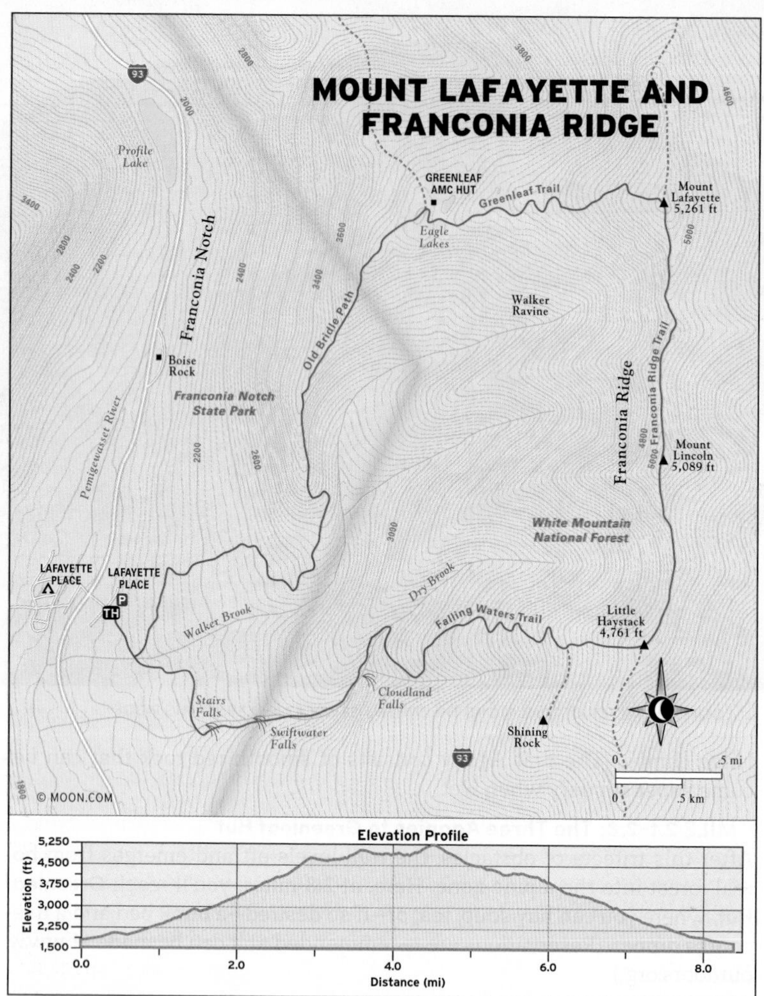

‣ MILE 5.5-6.8: Little Haystack to Dry Brook

The path is alternately rocky and smooth, weaving along and over the bumpy ridgeline like a dirt ribbon. Complemented by the rich green moss and krummholz, it's one of the most beautiful and dreamy trails in New England—with no trees to obstruct the view.

Your return journey begins from the top of Little Haystack. From the summit, turn right onto the **Falling Waters Trail, which is clearly marked with a sign on the summit. Follow blue blazes and** descend west back into the boreal spruce forest at a steep grade down rock slabs and some very rough stairs before entering more deciduous woods. The churning of water precedes your first crossing of the ironically named **Dry Brook** at 6.8 miles.

‣ MILE 6.8-8.2: Dry Brook to Walker Brook

Rock-hop across the brook a few more times to arrive at **Cloudland Falls**—an 80-foot-tall behemoth of a waterfall that the trail descends alongside at a steep grade. The trail stays close to the brook and passes two more

▲ FRANCONIA RIDGE FROM A LOOKOUT LEDGE ON THE OLD BRIDLE PATH

cascades before leveling out, making a final crossing, and heading north to a bridge across the familiar Walker Brook at 8.2 miles.

▸ MILE 8.2-8.4: Walker Brook to Old Bridle Path

Turn left onto **Old Bridle Path** after the bridge and backtrack to Lafayette Place to complete the hike at 8.4 miles.

DIRECTIONS

From Concord, drive north on I-93 N for 69 miles into Franconia Notch. Take the Trailhead Parking exit for Lafayette Place. If the lot is full, continue north on I-93, take Exit 34B, turn left at the bottom of the off-ramp, drive under the highway, and then pull an immediate left to merge back onto I-93, heading south this time. Backtrack to Lafayette Place and take the Trailhead Parking exit off I-93 S. The two lots are connected by a pedestrian tunnel underneath the highway. The outhouses are up a short concrete path that ascends east from the lot.

GPS COORDINATES: 44°08'30.6"N 71°40'51.4"W, 44.141820, -71.680939

BEST NEARBY BITES

Before hitting the trail, carbo-load with a house-made bagel or two at **White Mountain Bagel Co.** (25 Main St., Lincoln, 603/745-8576, www.whitemtnbagel.com, 6:30am-3pm daily). Later, once you've hobbled off the trail and taken off your boots, head back to Lincoln and savor some decadent Italian cooking and wines at **La Vista** (22 S. Mountain Dr., Lincoln, 603/745-7555, www.lavistaitalian.com, 8am-11:30am and 5pm-9pm Mon.-Wed., 5pm-9pm Thurs., 8am-11:30am and 5pm-11pm Fri., 7am-11:30am and 5pm-11pm Sat., 7am-11:30am and 5pm-9pm Sun.). If you're feeling extra ravenous, rip into a loaded Angus burger at **Black Mtn Burger Co.** (264 Main St., Lincoln, 603/745-3444, www.blackmtnburger.com, 11:30am-9pm Thurs.-Tues.).

4 The Flume

FRANCONIA NOTCH STATE PARK, LINCOLN

This waterfall hike takes visitors through a misty gorge with plenty of cascades, boardwalks, covered bridges, and views of the Franconia ridgeline.

BEST: Summer hikes

DISTANCE: 2 miles round-trip

DURATION: 1 hour

ELEVATION CHANGE: 527 feet

EFFORT: Easy

TRAIL: Dirt path, wooden bridges and staircases

USERS: Hikers

SEASON: June-October

FEES/PASSES: $12 adult, $8 child ages 6-11, free ages 5 and under

MAPS: New Hampshire State Parks website

CONTACT: Franconia Notch State Park, 603/823-8800, www.nhstateparks.org, Visitors center 8am-5pm daily, mid-May to late Oct.; these are the hours when the trail is "open" to hikers.

Discovered in 1808 by a 93-year-old woman who was looking for a good place to fish, The Flume is one of New Hampshire's most popular natural wonders. This 800-foot-deep gorge sits at the base of Mount Liberty and contains an eye-popping series of waterfalls that hikers can glimpse up close thanks to the ingeniously constructed boardwalk system that runs through The Flume and links up with a path that traverses a forest of wildflowers, moss, and glacial boulders above the gorge itself.

START THE HIKE

▸ MILE 0-0.2: Great Boulder to Flume Trail

Begin the hike by the Great Boulder—a massive rock that's a short walk up the road from the visitors center. Turn right to pick up the **Flume Trail,** which begins as a wide gravel path that descends a broad hillside to a handsome covered bridge over the **Pemigewasset River.**

▸ MILE 0.2-0.4: Flume Trail to Table Rock Falls

From the bridge, the trail climbs gradually through a beech forest and reaches **Flume Brook** at 0.3 mile. Continue climbing east alongside the brook past several miniature cascades before ascending a rockier and slightly steeper pitch to arrive at **Table Rock Falls.** This waterfall spills down a vast sloped rock face and marks your arrival to the gorge at 0.4 mile.

▸ MILE 0.4-0.9: Table Rock Falls to Avalanche Falls

Staying eastward, the trail enters **The Flume** and transitions to boardwalk at 0.5 mile, just as the damp walls of the gorge are becoming more

▲ THE FLUME BOARDWALK

pronounced. Stroll along the boardwalk and up flights of precariously tilted wooden stairs, beneath which Flume Brook crashes and spills down several miniature cascades. You'll notice that the air in The Flume is remarkably moist and cool—this contributes to the many species of moss you'll observe growing on the walls. A final round of stairs delivers you to **Avalanche Falls** at 0.9 mile.

Take a moment to admire this thundering 45-foot-tall torrent of water before stepping off the last stretch of the boardwalk and onto a level gravel path. You'll leave the gorge and head into the rim forest.

▸ MILE 0.9-1.6: Avalanche Falls to Wolf's Den

The trail ambles through the trees for a few beats. This is a good place for hikers to take in partial views of the Kinsman mountains to the west and to look for local birds such as white-throated sparrows. Pass the outlook cutoff for Liberty Falls (worth the brief detour) and hike northwest as the trail descends gradually toward a covered bridge at 1.6 miles that crosses high above several waterfalls on **Cascade Brook.** The bridge also offers a great perspective down into **The Pool,** a deep, reflective body of water into which the brook falls spill. On the other side of the bridge, a lemon-squeezer-style cave known as the **Wolf's Den** offers a brief but exciting side trip for hikers who aren't afraid of tight spaces. (It's a quick subterranean detour and no spelunking gear is required.)

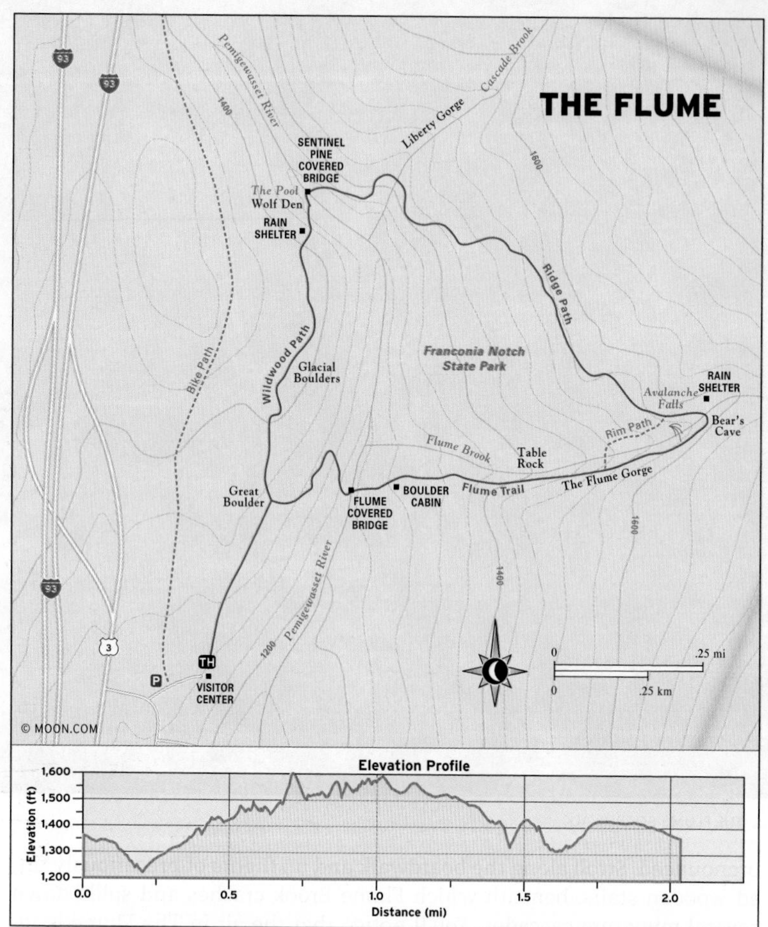

▸ MILE 1.6-2.0: Wolf's Den to Flume Loop Trail and Great Boulder

Whether you choose the main trail or the cave, you'll continue hiking west and eventually pass into a much rockier stretch of forest that's chock-full of glacial erratics at 1.7 miles. This final portion of the hike feels like a stroll through a sculpture park. Enjoy a bit of light climbing and descending through these knoll-y woods and reemerge at Great Boulder to complete your Flume loop at 2 miles.

DIRECTIONS

From Concord, drive north on I-93 N for 66 miles and take Exit 34A to merge onto US-3 N toward the Flume Gorge. Turn right at the first sign for the Flume Gorge Information Center and park in the visitors lots ahead. Enter the information center to buy your ticket, pass through the admission gate to the back end of the information center, and walk up the road into the woods, following signs for the Flume hiking trails. This will deliver you to Great Boulder, where the hike begins.

GPS COORDINATES: 44°05'53.2"N 71°40'45.5"W, 44.098118, -71.679317

5 Greeley Ponds

WHITE MOUNTAIN NATIONAL FOREST, WOODSTOCK

This forest hike passes through the southern reaches of the Pemigewasset Wilderness and into Mad River Notch to visit two of the most beautiful bodies of water in New Hampshire.

DISTANCE: 4.2 miles round-trip
DURATION: 2.5 hours
ELEVATION CHANGE: 378 feet
EFFORT: Easy/moderate
TRAIL: Dirt path, rocks, wooden bog bridges, water crossings on stones
USERS: Hikers, leashed dogs
SEASON: June-October
FEES/PASSES: None
MAPS: White Mountain National Forest website
CONTACT: White Mountain National Forest, 603/536-6100, www.fs.usda.gov/main/whitemountain/

In a state as compact yet bustling with hiker activity as New Hampshire, certain outdoor experiences can be trickier to achieve—say, standing beside a quietly rippling boreal pond as the setting sun fills the sky with shades of violet. But Greeley Ponds offers that sumptuous mix of beauty and isolation, and that's why these twin bodies of water are a New England hiking classic for folks who regularly visit the Whites. Nestled in Mad River Notch—which serves as kind of a border zone between the Pemi and the Sandwich Range—the ponds are ideal for picnicking, birding, and meditating. The upper pond is deep enough for swimming (though you may have to contend with muck and possibly some leeches) and both ponds are stocked with trout, which are fair game for anyone willing to bring a rod and tackle box into the backcountry.

START THE HIKE

▸ MILE 0-1.2: Greeley Ponds Trailhead to Mount Osceola Trail Junction

Begin the hike at the south end of the Greeley Ponds Trail parking lot by the wooden trail sign. Climb south up a small rocky hillside festooned with exposed tree roots—you'll be walking on a lot of these—and enter a thickly vegetated pine forest. Follow yellow blazes on the trees as the trail crosses a series of trickling creeks before entering a stretch of evergreen woods with more "breathing room" and better opportunities for bird sightings. (Woodpeckers often add to the natural soundtrack around here.) The footing is consistently rooty but mostly dirt otherwise, and the trail ascends at a very patient grade through the forest.

The sound of rushing water precedes your arrival at a stream crossing at 0.3 miles. Pick your way over the water on rocks and step onto the first of many wooden bog bridges that take you over some muddier patches of the trail. After passing some mossy boulders, the trail climbs a hillside at a slightly steeper grade to arrive at the junction with the Mount Osceola Trail at 1.2 miles.

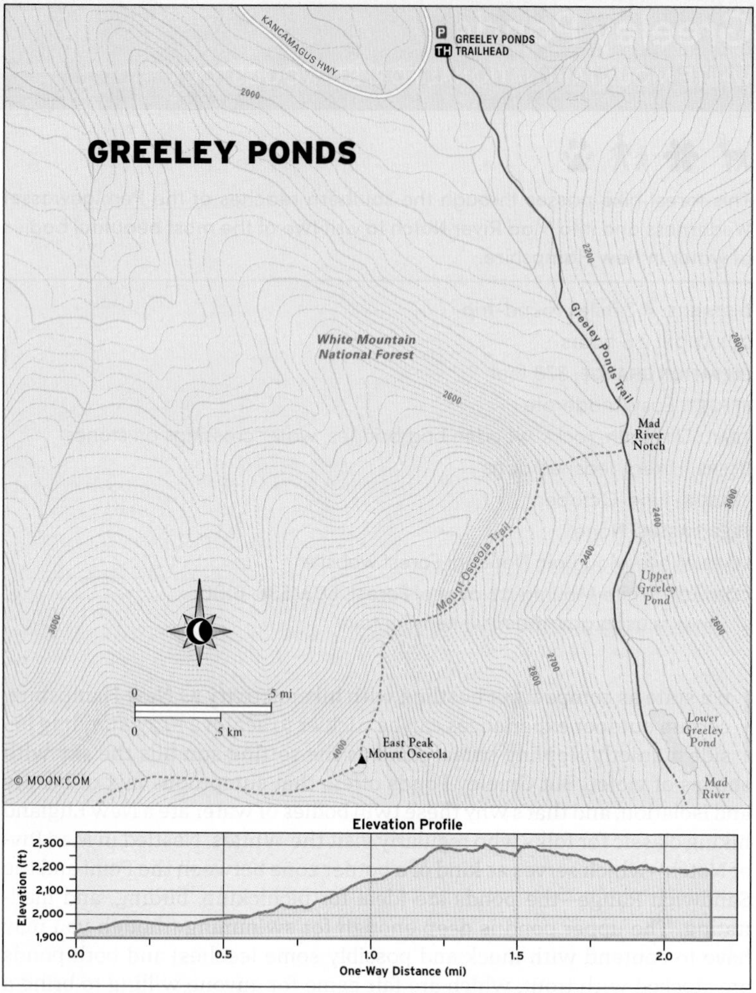

‣ MILE 1.2-1.6: Mount Osceola Trail Junction to Mount Osceloa Lookout

Take a left turn to stay on the Greeley Ponds Trail and enjoy some softer, sandier footing—a hint of what lies ahead. Pass an enormous fortress-like rock the size of a garage and reach a second junction at 1.4 miles, where you can go right to stay on Greeley Ponds Trail or take a left to follow a brief ski path to a pebbly beach on Upper Greeley Pond. (The ski path-to-beach approach is much more scenic and gets you closer to the water.) Upper Greeley Pond is deeper and less boggy than Lower Greeley, which makes it the better pond for aquatic activities. To hike along the pond from the pebbly beach, walk to the right across the beach and up a small hill to link back up with the Greeley Ponds Trail. Amble along the pond's western shore, which is replete with young spruce trees. As you approach the

▲ LOWER GREELEY POND

southern edge of the pond, keep an eye out for a dirt cutoff on your left, which leads to a scenic lookout from which you can see the cliff faces of nearby Mount Osceola.

▸ MILE 1.6-1.9: Mount Osceola Lookout to Lower Greeley Pond
The main trail continues south and descends through the forest by way of a rocky former streambed before reaching some more bog bridges. Emerging from the woods, the trail arrives at Lower Greeley Pond at 1.9 miles and ambles through a rich landscape of ferns and maple trees along the western shore.

▸ MILE 1.9-2.1: Lower Greeley Pond to Observation Bench
Look for a spur cutoff on your right at 2.1 miles. This will take you to a beautiful little beach surrounded by hemlocks and complete with an observation bench made from logs. It also marks the conclusion of your hike!

DIRECTIONS

From Concord, drive north on I-93 N for 60 miles and then take Exit 32 for NH-112 toward Lincoln/North Woodstock. Turn left onto NH-112 E at the bottom of the off-ramp. Drive east along the Kancamagus Highway for roughly 9 miles. The Greeley Ponds trailhead parking lot will be on your right.

GPS COORDINATES: 44°01'53.0"N 71°31'00.5"W, 44.031397, -71.516810

6 Zealand Valley and Thoreau Falls

CRAWFORD NOTCH STATE PARK, BETHLEHEM

This long yet gentle waterfall hike winds through a beaver bog and traverses a breathtaking white rockslide before concluding with one of the prettiest waterfalls in New Hampshire.

BEST: Fall hikes
DISTANCE: 9.4 miles round-trip
DURATION: 4.5 hours
ELEVATION CHANGE: 425 feet
EFFORT: Moderate
TRAIL: Dirt path, rocks, wooden bog bridges, water crossings via stones
USERS: Hikers, leashed dogs
SEASON: June-October
FEES: $5 day-use fee per vehicle
MAPS: White Mountain National Forest website
CONTACT: White Mountain National Forest, 603/536-6100, www.fs.usda.gov/recarea/whitemountain

It's no secret that Henry David Thoreau had a hankering for beautiful and isolated places, so it's fitting that he got his very own cascade right in the thick of New Hampshire's Pemigewasset Wilderness. Thoreau Falls, which spills 80 feet down a series of ledges that overlook the verdant "Pemi" woods, is a classic.

START THE HIKE

▸ MILE 0-2.3: Zealand Trail to A-Z Trail Junction

Walk toward the trailhead sign at the south end of the parking lot and pick up the **Zealand Trail** as it heads south through a tight corridor of birch and pine trees before entering a more spacious deciduous forest. After gentle ups and downs over a rocky hillside, the smooth dirt trail crosses a wooden footbridge at 0.3 mile and follows an old railroad bed through the forest. The trail ambles along the **Zealand River** for a bit before veering deeper into the woods and crossing several streams on wooden bridges and rocks.

Curving southwest, the trail suddenly emerges into a vast bogland at 1.7 miles and crosses a long stretch of boardwalk that marks your entrance into the Zealand Valley. Continue through the bogland as the trail alternates between forest and tallgrass. (Look out for the resident beavers and moose here.) The trail traverses two more streams on rocks and reaches the A-Z Trail junction at 2.3 miles.

▸ MILE 2.3-2.5: A-Z Trail Junction to Zealand Falls

Keep right to stay on the Zealand Trail and enjoy the view of Zealand Mountain from a wooden footbridge just ahead. Listen for the roar of a nearby waterfall as you reenter the forest and pass **Zealand Pond** on your

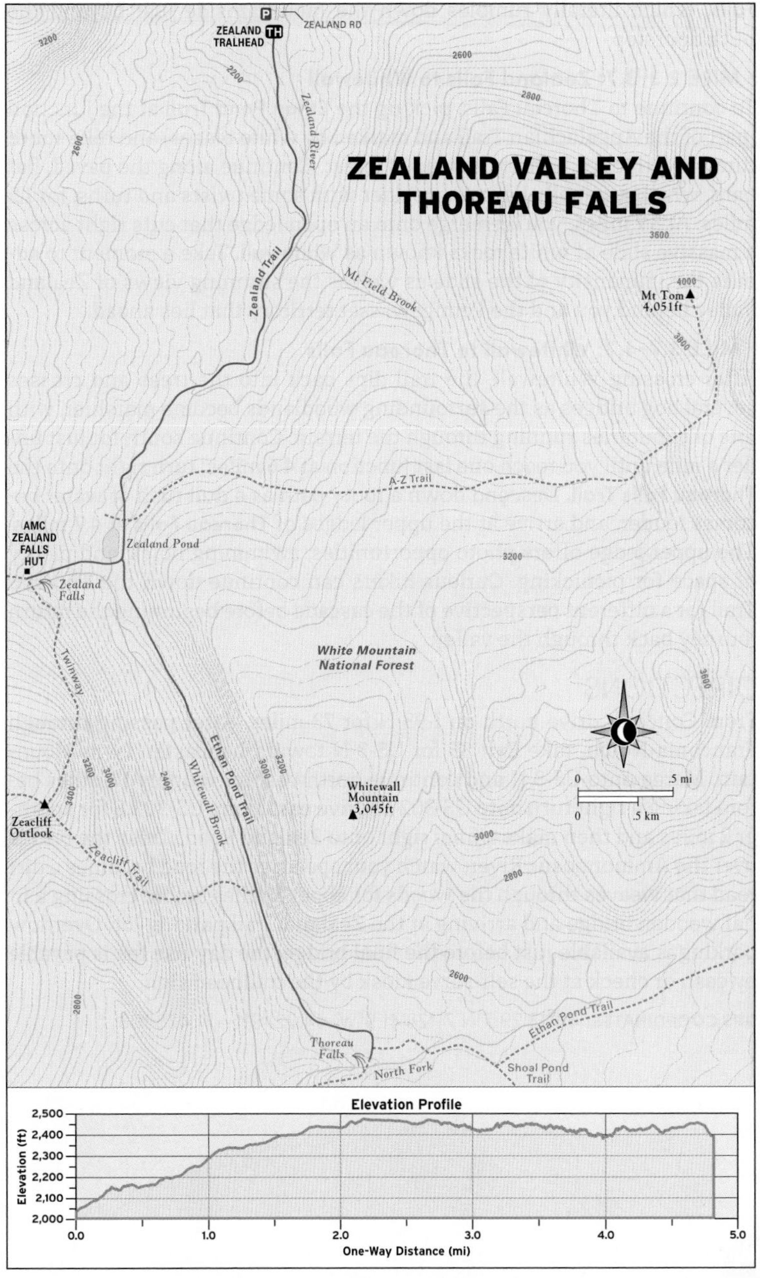

right. At 2.5 miles, a huge glacial boulder marks the junction with the Ethan Pond Trail and the Twinway Trail. If you feel like a bowl of soup and a scenic vista, turn right onto the Twinway and scramble up a steep rock staircase to **Zealand Falls Hut,** one of the Appalachian Mountain Club's mountain huts, which offers fresh food and a front-row seat to **Zealand**

Falls, which literally rumbles down the mountainside just beyond the hut's doorstep.

MILE 2.3-3.7: Zealand Falls to Whitewall

To continue to Thoreau Falls, pick up the **Ethan Pond Trail** at the junction (part of the Appalachian Trail and marked by white blazes) and hike south through a thicker, tighter deciduous forest. Continue along the paved, flat path, which gradually becomes rockier with some twists and turns, for 1.2 miles. At 3.7 miles, you'll emerge onto an open ledge that cuts right across a massive slide of white rocks known as **Whitewall.** Take a moment to admire the immensity of the slide as well as the stunning views of Zealand Valley behind you and the Pemigewasset territory that lies ahead.

MILE 3.7-4.7: Whitewall to Thoreau Falls

After crossing Whitewall, the trail dips back into the trees and crosses several bog bridges as the surrounding woodlands become marshier, with lots of tributaries running through the terrain. Continue south for just under a mile until you reach one last junction at 4.6 miles; turn right onto the **Thoreau Falls Trail.** Descend down a rooty path as a dull rush of water becomes louder, and arrive at the upper ledges of **Thoreau Falls** at 4.7 miles. The upper ledge offers photo opportunities, swimming holes, and plenty of space for picnicking. Curious hikers can continue down the Thoreau Trail for a different perspective of the cascade before beginning the return journey back through the valley.

DIRECTIONS

From Concord, drive north on I-93 N for 73 miles. After passing through Franconia Notch, take Exit 35 for US-3 N toward Lancaster/Twin Mountain. Merge onto US-3 N and continue northwest for roughly 10 miles before taking a right turn onto US-302 E. Drive east along US-302 E for another 2 miles and then make a final right onto Zealand Road. Cross the bridge over the Ammonoosuc River; watch your speed, as the road becomes a dirt road that weaves through the woods for about 3 miles before crossing a final wooden bridge and arriving at the Zealand Trail parking lot. Overflow parking is available just before the final bridge; the day-use fee is payable by cash or check at the self-serve kiosk by the trailhead sign.

GPS COORDINATES: 44°13'29.7"N 71°28'41.9"W, 44.224911, -71.478308

BEST NEARBY BREWS

Cool off with a nitro stout or West Coast IPA at **Rek-Lis Brewing** (2085 Main Street, Bethlehem, 603/869-9696, www.reklisbrewing.com, 4pm-9pm Thurs., 4pm-10pm Fri., 11am-10pm Sat., 11am-9pm Sun., 4pm-9pm Mon.).

7 Mount Willard

CRAWFORD NOTCH STATE PARK, CARROLL

A rite of passage for New Englanders, this classic family-friendly mountain hike ascends to an exposed lookout ledge that offers the most awe-inspiring view of Crawford Notch.

BEST: Winter hikes
DISTANCE: 3 miles round-trip
DURATION: 1.5 hours
ELEVATION CHANGE: 874 feet
EFFORT: Easy
TRAIL: Dirt path, rocks, water crossings on stones
USERS: Hikers, leashed dogs
SEASON: June-October
FEES/PASSES: None
MAPS: Crawford Notch State Park website
CONTACT: Crawford Notch State Park, 603/374-2272, www.nhstateparks.org/visit/state-parks

For those who are just getting started with hiking, the little tuft-like Mount Willard is the equivalent of a bicycle with training wheels. The ascent itself is a gentle and pleasant walk in the woods, offering a lively waterfall along the way to Willard's upper slopes. But the summit of Mount Willard is a legend—a windy, exposed ledge with sheer drops and an amazing panoramic view of Crawford Notch that's too vast and epic to be contained within most camera frames.

START THE HIKE

▸ MILE 0-0.2: Cross Notch Depot to Mount Willard Trail

Begin the hike by the boarding area at Crawford Notch Depot. Cross the railroad tracks and pick up the dirt trail on the other side. Walk west through a small field into the woods and turn left onto the yellow-blazed **Mount Willard Trail.** Head south through the rich birch and spruce forest, snaking through the forest at a level grade and crossing a series of streams on rocks.

▸ MILE 0.2-0.5: Mount Willard Trail to Centennial Pool

The trail begins to curve southwest, ascending the northern haunch of Mount Willard up stone stairs at a relaxed grade. Up ahead, the hulking profile of nearby Mount Avalon looms through the boreal spruce trees as the trail continues climbing gradually, meeting up with a stream that spills beside the trail.

Continue west along the stream until you reach **Centennial Pool** at 0.5 mile. This little cascade is worth a look—the water spatters down a beautifully carved cliff into a reflective basin that you can scramble down to.

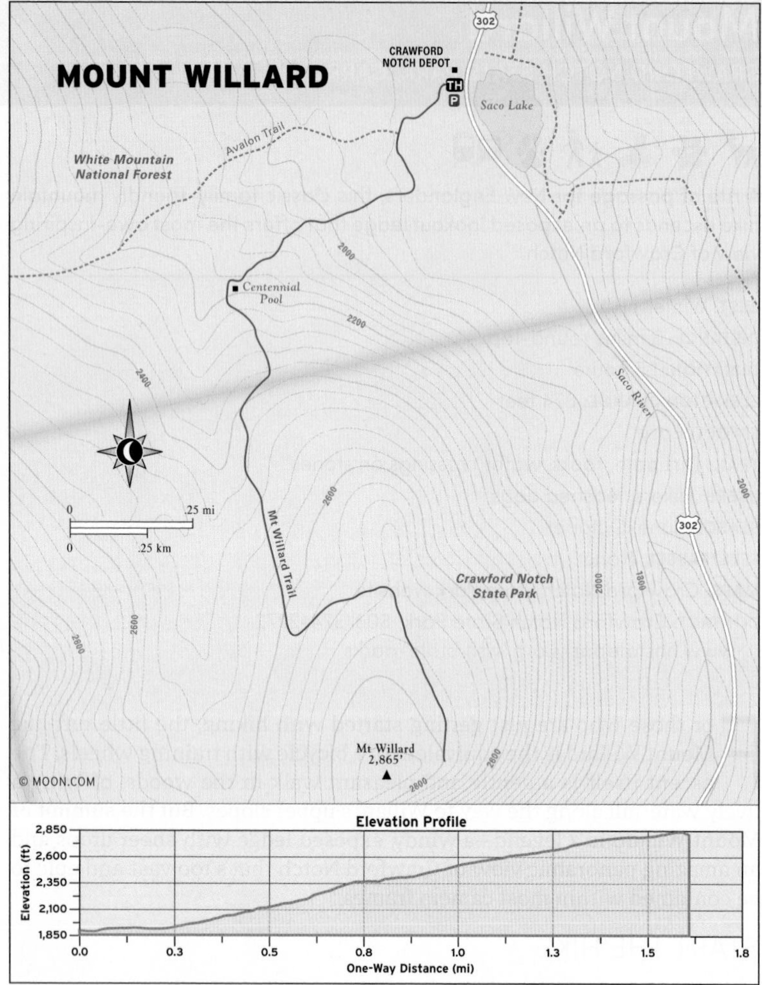

‣ MILE 0.5-1.5: Centennial Pool to Ledges of Mount Willard

The Mount Willard Trail climbs south from here and ascends some taller rock stairs before transitioning into a wider and rockier path that's often bisected by ancient concrete water pipes. The strong pine aroma here foreshadows the forests of the upper slopes. At 1.1 miles, you'll reach the slopes, as the trail flattens and swerves east into dark, mossy woods.

A brief series of moist, sloped rock slabs through the boreal pine woods delivers you to a long corridor of trees where the path becomes a much smoother dirt highway across the mountaintop. Far ahead, a distant orb of daylight shines like the metaphorical "light at the end of the tunnel." Head south again toward the light and step out onto the famous ledges of **Mount Willard** at 1.5 miles. Watch your step around the rim of the ledge, especially on a gusty day, and enjoy one of the most disarmingly beautiful vistas in New Hampshire. The notch—a vast glacial gorge filled with woodlands—is framed by Mount Webster on the left and Mount Willey on

▲ THE VIEW FROM MOUNT WILLARD

the right. Beyond, well-known peaks such as Carrigain and Chocorua tickle the clouds. Return the way you came—if you can bring yourself to leave.

DIRECTIONS

From Concord, drive north on I-93 N for 73 miles. After passing through Franconia Notch, take Exit 35 for US-3 N toward Lancaster/Twin Mountain. Merge onto US-3 N and continue northwest for roughly 10 miles before taking a right turn onto US-302 E. Drive east along US-302 E for another 8 miles. You'll then see the Appalachian Mountain Club's Highland Center lodge on your right. Turn right into the Highland Center parking lot, where hikers can park their vehicles. The Crawford Notch Depot train station is next to the Highland Center and accessible by a short dirt path that cuts across a field.

GPS COORDINATES: 44°13'04.1"N 71°24'40.8"W, 44.217810, -71.411324

8 Arethusa Falls via Bemis Brook

CRAWFORD NOTCH STATE PARK, HART'S LOCATION

This popular hike to New Hampshire's tallest waterfall takes a rugged detour to visit a series of hidden cascades along Bemis Brook.

BEST: Winter hikes, spots for a swim

DISTANCE: 2.8 miles round-trip

DURATION: 2 hours

ELEVATION CHANGE: 928 feet

EFFORT: Easy/moderate

TRAIL: Dirt path, rocks, wooden bridges, water crossings on stones

USERS: Hikers, leashed dogs

SEASON: May-October

PASSES/FEES: None

MAPS: Crawford Notch State Park website

CONTACT: Crawford Notch State Park, 603/374-2272, www.nhstateparks.org

A trip to the Whites wouldn't be complete without gawking at the towering wonder that is Arethusa Falls. At nearly 200 feet tall, this silvery cascade tumbles down a sheer cliff face right in the heart of Crawford Notch State Park. The direct-access route, the Arethusa Falls Trail, is popular during all seasons—even winter, when ice climbers tempt fate by scaling the frozen falls. But the coolest way to reach Arethusa Falls is taking the lesser-known Bemis Brook Trail cutoff, which features a gorgeous pair of smaller waterfalls that spill through the forest in which Arethusa Falls is tucked away.

START THE HIKE

▸ MILE 0-0.1: Arethusa Falls Trailhead Parking Lot to Bemis Brook Trail Junction

Begin your hike in the Arethusa Falls parking lot, directly off Route 302. Walk up the concrete road to the railroad tracks and look for the Arethusa Falls trailhead to your left. Cross the tracks and pick up the trail as it gently climbs west into a forest of birches and pine. Follow the blue-blazed trail up a root-festooned path for a few minutes before quickly reaching the Bemis Brook Trail junction.

▸ MILE 0.1-0.3: Bemis Brook Trail to Coliseum Falls

Turn left here and pick up the Bemis Brook Trail as it efficiently descends to Bemis Brook itself. After reaching the stream, the yellow-blazed trail follows the boulder-strewn brook while ascending at a modest grade.

The dynamic rush of water announces your arrival at Coliseum Falls at roughly 0.3 miles. The lower portion of this lively 25-foot-tall cascade spatters down a series of natural rock steps that resemble a miniature amphitheater.

▲ ARETHUSA FALLS ON A SUNNY AFTERNOON

MILE 0.3–0.5: Coliseum Falls to Bemis Falls

Continue along the brook for another 0.2 miles before reaching Bemis Falls, a larger trifecta of falling waters with a wonderful outlook ledge. From here, the trail takes a sharp right and makes a steep, rocky climb back up to the main trail.

MILE 0.6–1.1: Coliseum Falls to Bemis Falls to Arethusa Falls Trail

Upon reaching the junction at 0.6 miles, continue left on the Arethusa Falls Trail, which weaves west through the woods at an agreeable grade for 0.5 miles and widens into a smoother, gravelly path with occasional stone stairs. Cross two wooden footbridges at 1.1 miles and keep an eye out for lady's slippers, which bloom here during the spring and early summer.

MILE 1.1–1.5: Arethusa Falls Trail to Arethusa Falls

After ascending a series of log steps, the Arethusa Falls Trail reaches a junction with the Arethusa-Ripley Falls Trail at 1.3 miles.

Veer left toward the nearby roar of water and make your way southeast down a more eroded path before arriving at the mist-sprayed base of Arethusa Falls at 1.4 miles. The base has plenty of sun-kissed stones for picnicking and little potholes that double as foot baths. Hikers can also scramble closer to the falls and dip their heads under the torrent for a cooldown like no other.

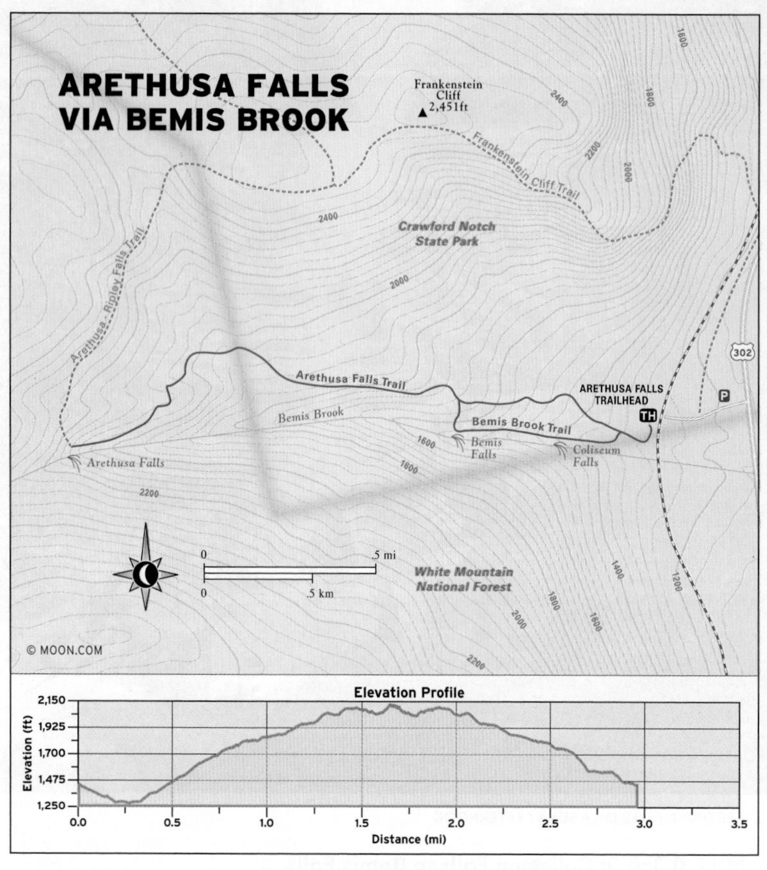

▸ **MILE 1.5-2.8: Arethusa Falls to Trailhead**

Once you feel optimally serene, backtrack east along the Arethusa Falls Trail and this time, when you reach the Bemis Brook Trail junction, take a left to stay on the main trail, which descends at a moderate grade through the woods for roughly half a mile over exposed roots and small rocks before delivering you back to the Arethusa Falls trailhead at 2.8 miles.

DIRECTIONS

From Boston, drive north on I-93 N for 139 miles across the New Hampshire border and into the White Mountains. Take Exit 35 for US-3 N toward Lancaster/Twin Mountain and continue until you reach the junction with US-302 E. Turn right onto US-302 E and drive southeast for roughly 15 miles as you pass the sign for Crawford Notch State Park and descend into the notch itself. A sign on your right clearly marks the turnoff for the Arethusa Falls parking area.

GPS COORDINATES: 44°08'53.3"N 71°21'59.1"W, 44.148142, -71.366406

9 Mount Carrigain

WHITE MOUNTAIN NATIONAL FOREST, HART'S LOCATION

Venture deep into the isolated Pemigewasset Wilderness to ascend the long, scenic ridgeline of this cone-shaped peak, which has a lookout tower offering the finest vista in New Hampshire.

BEST: Vistas
DISTANCE: 10.4 miles round-trip (out-and-back)
DURATION: 6 hours
ELEVATION CHANGE: 3,474 feet
EFFORT: Strenuous
TRAIL: Dirt path, rocks, wooden bog bridges, water crossings on stones
USERS: Hikers, leashed dogs
SEASON: June-October
FEES/PASSES: None
MAPS: White Mountain National Forest website
CONTACT: White Mountain National Forest, 603/536-6100, www.fs.usda.gov/whitemountain/

START THE HIKE

▸ MILE 0-0.5: Signal Ridge Trail to Whiteface Brook

Begin the hike at the entrance to the parking lot for Mount Carrigain. Cross Sawyer River Road and head for the wooden trailhead sign to pick up the yellow-blazed **Signal Ridge Trail.** Head northwest, warming up your quads as the trail gently ascends a hemlock-spruce forest. Watch your step on the abundant roots and rocks. To your right, the constant rippling of **Whiteface Brook** provides a soothing soundtrack. The trail heads directly northeast alongside the brook, crossing the occasional log bridge and passing some little sputtering cascades at 0.5 mile.

▸ MILE 0.5-1.7: Whiteface Brook to Carrigain Brook

As the woods become sunnier and breezier, a moderately graded stone staircase takes you away from the brook to a higher stretch of beechwood forest. Continue northeast as the trail transitions into smoother expressway of rock and stone that cruises through the woods. Up ahead, the titanic mass of Carrigain looms through the trees. At 1.5 miles, the trail passes a fork with an unmarked side path. Veer right here to stay on Signal Ridge—note that the yellow blazes become less frequent henceforth. At 1.7 miles, the trail arrives on the stony banks of **Carrigain Brook**. Shortly ahead, the trail crosses the brook on rocks. The water level here can easily get high enough to cover the stepping-stones and saturate a boot, so be prepared to ford barefoot if you don't want to squelch your way to the top of Carrigain.

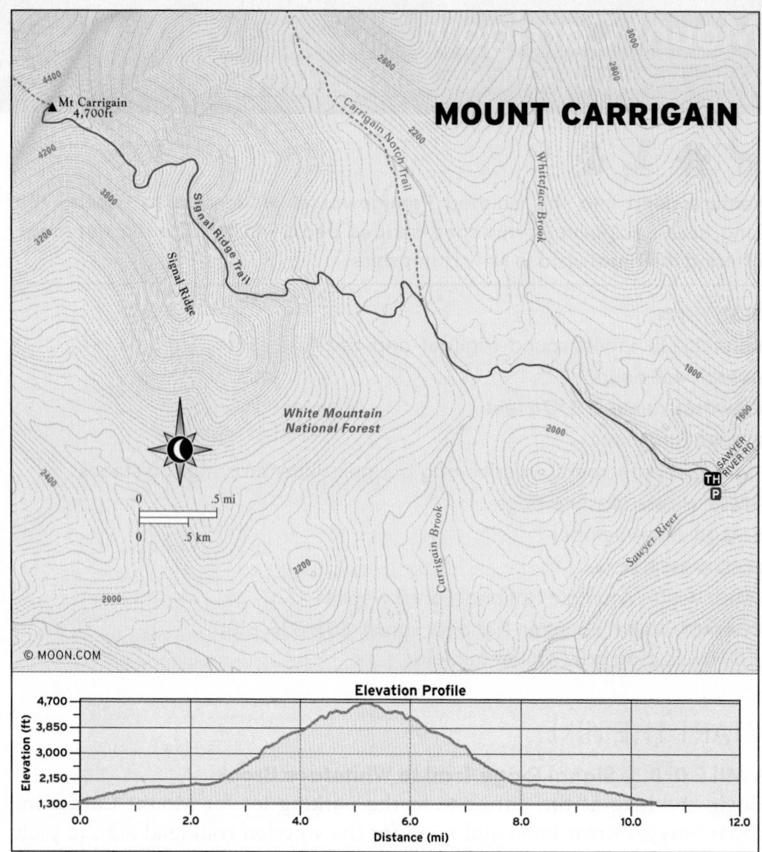

▸ **MILE 1.7–3.2: Carrigain Brook to Signal Ridge**

Shortly after the brook crossing, the trail passes through a beaver marsh before reaching the junction with Carrigain Notch Trail at 2.2 miles. Make a left here to stay on Signal Ridge Trail as it approaches the mountain base. Then, quite suddenly, the terrain changes from level ambling to steep rock stairs and slabs through mossier boreal woods. Consider this the "toll booth" to reach the more exposed and scenic ridgeline. Be sure to pause and enjoy the partial views of nearby peaks such as Mount Lowell, especially as the forest thins out and the trees start to shrink. The trail climbs steadily and steeply, heading northeast before reaching the gustier and sunnier southern end of **Signal Ridge** at roughly 3.2 miles.

▸ **MILE 3.2–5.2: Signal Ridge to Mount Carrigain Observation Tower**

Over the next mile, the climb is a much more gradual and enjoyable saunter across the wooded ridgeline. The evergreen trees up here are small enough to offer near-constant views of the vast Pemi wilderness, as well as the Presidentials and the Sandwich Range. The footing is a mixture of dirt and rocks as the trail closes in on the summit. A brief dip into the trees at 4.7 miles takes you to the final ascent—a steeper and rockier pitch that slabs up to the top of the summit cone before fully emerging from the alpine woods and reaching the famous summit **observation tower** at 5.2 miles. Unlike the other, more terrifying lookout towers in the Whites, this

▲ A STRETCH OF MIXED WOODS ALONG THE SIGNAL RIDGE TRAIL, BEFORE THE CLIMB BEGINS

one is short enough for almost anyone to scramble up and enjoy. On a clear day, you can gaze out at Mount Washington and Co. to the north and the craggy Sandwich Range to the south. Return the way you came.

DIRECTIONS

From Concord, drive north on I-93 N for 73 miles. After passing through Franconia Notch, take Exit 35 for US-3 N toward Lancaster/Twin Mountain. Merge onto US-3 N and continue northwest for roughly 10 miles before taking a right turn onto US-302 E. Drive east along US-302 E for another 19 miles and then make a right turn onto Sawyer River Road. Follow this dirt road up into the woods for roughly 1 mile. The parking lot for Mount Carrigain hikers will be on your left immediately after crossing a bridge over Whiteface Brook. Hikers should check the White Mountain National Forest website to ensure that Sawyer River Road is open. If the road is closed, hikers should park alongside the road at the access gate and walk up the road to the Signal Ridge Trailhead. This will add about 4 miles to the already taxing round-trip distance.

GPS COORDINATES: 44°04'11.8"N 71°23'01.4"W, 44.069947, -71.383733

BEST NEARBY BREWS

Enjoy some of the finest internationally inspired gourmet cooking in the north country, along with several varieties of craft cider, at the **White Mountain Cider Co.** (207 US-302, Glen, 603/383-9061, www.ciderconh.com, 7:30am-9pm Sun.-Thurs., 7:30am-10pm Fri.-Sat.).

10 Basin Rim

EVANS NOTCH, CHATHAM

This forest hike bypasses a spellbinding glacial lake and a waterfall before climbing to exposed cliffs with excellent views into western Maine.

DISTANCE: 4.4 miles round-trip

DURATION: 3 hours

ELEVATION CHANGE: 1,251 feet

EFFORT: Moderate

TRAIL: Dirt path, rocks, wooden bridges, water crossings on stones

USERS: Hikers, leashed dogs

SEASON: June-October

FEES/PASSES: None

MAPS: White Mountain National Forest website

CONTACT: White Mountain National Forest, 603/536-6100, www.fs.usda.gov/recarea/whitemountain

Straddling east New Hampshire and western Maine, Evans Notch is a mysterious and under-visited place where multiple mountain ranges converge. One of the most memorable oddities found here is The Basin—a glacial cirque, a feature that hikers normally encounter at much higher elevations in places like the Rockies. This gorgeous lake sits in a dugout, surrounded by cliffs and mountains. And lucky for hikers, it's relatively easy to get from the lake to the top of those cliffs, thanks to the Basin Trail.

START THE HIKE

▸ MILE 0-0.7: Basin Boat Launch to Basin Brook

Begin the hike in the west end of the Basin boat launch parking lot by the wooden Basin Trail sign. Step into a deciduous forest on the rooty dirt path of the **Basin Trail,** marked by yellow blazes. Warm up with some gentle ups and downs along the southern shore of the lake as the trail chugs west, crossing several pretty tributaries that feed into the lake. After climbing a larger hill and veering away from the lake briefly, the trail descends some rock stairs and emerges from the woods at 0.7 mile by the edge of **Basin Brook,** which you'll have to cross on stones. The water here can get high enough to fully saturate a boot, so consider removing your hiking shoes for the crossing.

▸ MILE 0.7-1.4: Basin Brook to Hermit Falls

Pick up the trail on the other side of Basin Brook and hike northwest along an old streambed. Cross another tributary on a wooden footbridge and then venture deeper into a vast forest replete with glacial boulders. The grade here is almost flat, with fewer roots and rocks. At 1.3 miles, you'll reach a junction for **Hermit Falls**; turn left and follow a creek along a narrower stony path as a rush of water echoes from ahead. The trail steepens

▲ THE BASIN'S SOUTH SHORE

considerably before reaching **Hermit Falls** at 1.4 miles. This spattering cascade tumbles 30 feet along a series of cliffs, and the trail climbs alongside the falls by way of rock slabs and exposed roots.

▸ MILE 1.4-2.0: Hermit Falls to The Rim and The Basin

Continue climbing the steep hillside beyond the falls. At 1.5 miles, take a left at the junction to remerge with the **Basin Trail.**

Now the hike becomes a more labored, rocky ascent up the southwestern haunch of West Royce Mountain. Climb through the woods for a half mile, hopping across several tiny streams—watch the ground for toads, which are often seen hopping around here. The exposed tree roots almost serve as stairs in places along this section; be careful when the roots are wet.

At 2 miles, give your calves a rest; the trail becomes much steeper after this point, with foot-tall rock stairs that are rough and sloped in places. As the trees open up around you, the trail passes several sheer cliffs with natural white streaks, a sight seldom seen in the region. A final winding set of rock stairs takes you up a cleft in **The Rim.** At the top of the stairs, take a cutoff trail on your left to an exposed ledge that overlooks **The Basin** and offers a tantalizing glimpse of western Maine's hills and farmlands.

▸ MILE 2.0-2.2: The Rim and The Basin to Trail Junction and Return to Trailhead

The Basin Trail continues past the viewpoint cutoff and concludes at a five-way trail junction at 2.1 miles. Gluttons for punishment can push on to the summits of West Royce or Ragged Jacket, but for hikers who fancy a more pleasant and relaxed day hike, this is where the backtracking begins.

DIRECTIONS

From Portsmouth, drive north on NH-16 N to the town of Conway. Keep right at the junction for NH-16 N and NH-113 E to continue driving east on NH-113 E. After 2 miles, turn left onto US-302 W and then make a right onto East Conway Road. Drive northeast along this road for 6 miles and then swing right onto West Fryeburg Road. Here you'll briefly cross into Maine as you continue north along West Fryeburg Road, which eventually becomes Stow Road. At the junction with ME-113B, veer slightly right

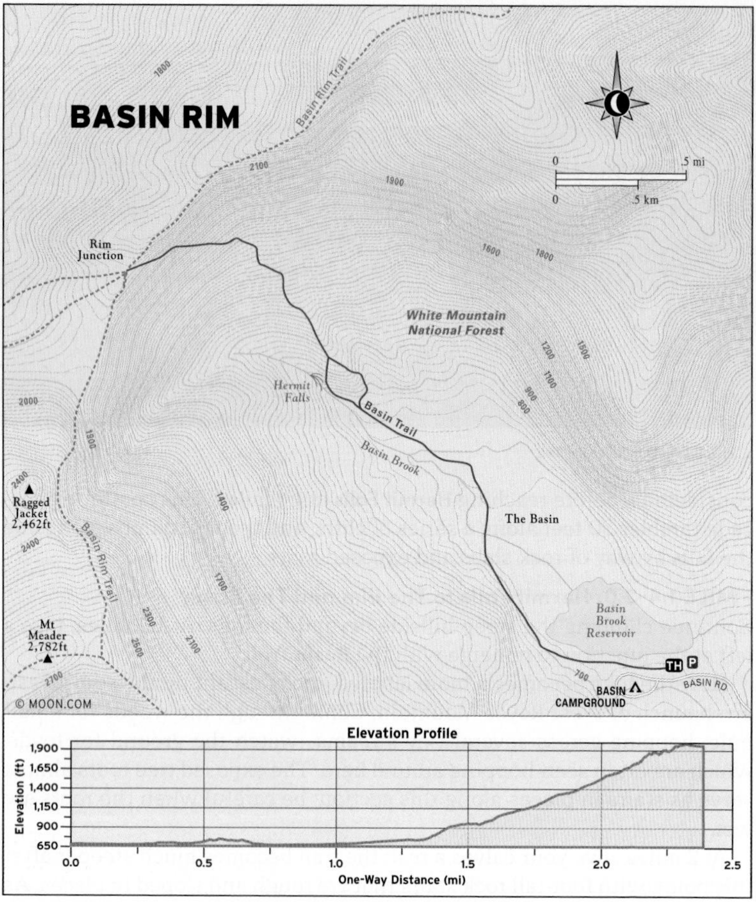

BASIN RIM

Rim Junction
Basin Rim Trail
White Mountain National Forest
Hermit Falls
Basin Trail
Basin Brook
The Basin
Basin Brook Reservoir
Ragged Jacket 2,462ft
Mt Meader 2,782ft
BASIN CAMPGROUND
BASIN RD
TH P
0 .5 mi
0 .5 km
© MOON.COM

Elevation Profile
Elevation (ft): 650, 900, 1,150, 1,400, 1,650, 1,900
One-Way Distance (mi): 0.0, 0.5, 1.0, 1.5, 2.0, 2.5

to stay on Stow Road and follow it north for another 7 miles as you cross back into New Hampshire. A large sign for The Basin will soon appear on your left. Turn left here onto Basin Road and drive west until you reach a large clearing, where the boat launch road will soon appear on your right. Turn right here. The Basin will be straight ahead, with a parking lot on your right.

GPS COORDINATES: 44°16'09.0"N 71°01'12.1"W, 44.269176, -71.020025

BEST NEARBY BREWS

Make the most of your afternoon in this quiet corner of the White Mountains by swinging down to Fryeburg, Maine, for some seriously hopped-up ales at **Saco River Brewing** (10 Jockey Cap Lane, Fryeburg, 207/256-3028, www.sacoriverbrewing.com, 3pm-7pm Thurs.-Fri., noon-7pm Sat., noon-5-pm Sun.). If you're feeling extra indulgent, dig into a mountain of ribs and pulled pork with southern fixins at **302 West Smokehouse & Tavern** (636 Main St., Fryeburg, 207/935-3021, www.302west.com, 11am-11pm Mon.-Sat., 9am-11pm Sun.).

11 Mount Chocorua

WHITE MOUNTAIN NATIONAL FOREST, ALBANY

This hike to one of New Hampshire's sharpest and most recognizable peaks features some of the prettiest waterfalls in the state—and a thrilling finale of steep climbing.

BEST: Winter hikes, brew hikes
DISTANCE: 7.4 miles round-trip
DURATION: 4.5 hours
ELEVATION CHANGE: 2,125 feet
EFFORT: Moderate/strenuous
TRAIL: Dirt path, rocks, wooden bog bridges
USERS: Hikers, leashed dogs
SEASON: June-October
FEES/PASSES: $5 day-use fee per vehicle
MAPS: White Mountain National Forest website
CONTACT: White Mountain National Forest, 603/536-6100, www.fs.usda.gov/recarea/whitemountain

When you look at the Sandwich Range of the White Mountains from afar, one sharp horn-like peak stands out from the rest. Mount Chocorua's distinctive peak has a relatively modest height of 3,478 feet compared to the 4,000-footers, but it's still a formidable climb, and the Champney Brook Trail makes it a fun one. With lush forest, crashing waterfalls, gorgeous vistas, and some seriously steep rock scrambling near the top, this is one of the most enjoyable hikes in the state.

START THE HIKE

▸ MILE 0-0.5: Champney Brook Trail to Champney Brook

Begin your trail by the outhouses at the **Champney Brook Trail** parking lot. A trailhead sign marks the starting point. Follow yellow blazes as the trail enters deciduous forest, crosses a brook on stones, and turns southeast. Hike through the trees along a wide dirt path with plenty of exposed roots, and listen for the sound of rushing water echoing through the undergrowth. At 0.5 mile, the trail reaches **Champney Brook.**

▸ MILE 0.5-1.4: Champney Brook to Champney Falls Loop Trail

Continue along the brook as the trail begins to ascend the northeastern flank of Mount Chocorua at a patient grade. After climbing higher above Champney Brook for about a mile, you'll reach a wooden sign for the **Champney Falls Loop Trail** at 1.4 miles.

▸ MILE 1.4-1.8: Champney Falls Loop Trail to Champney Brook Trail

Take a left onto this trail and briefly descend some wet rock stairs to the foot of **Champney Falls**, a stunning 70-foot-tall cascade that can become quite explosive after rain. Just beyond these falls to the left of the trail, an

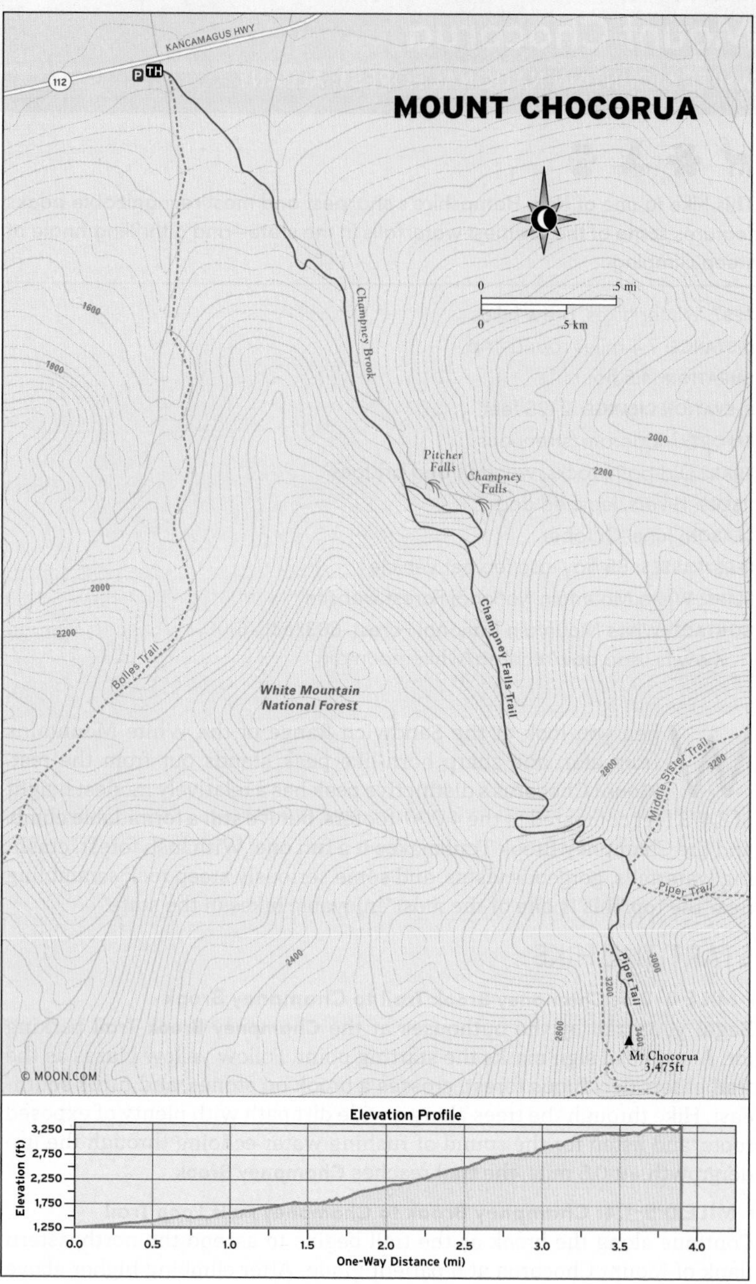
MOUNT CHOCORUA
KANCAMAGUS HWY
112
P
TH
0
.5 mi
0
.5 km
1600
1800
Champney Brook
Pitcher Falls
Champney Falls
2000
2200
2000
2200
Champney Falls Trail
Bolles Trail
White Mountain National Forest
2800
3200
Middle Sister Trail
Piper Trail
2400
3000
3200
Piper Trail
2800
3400
Mt Chocorua 3,475ft
© MOON.COM
Elevation Profile
Elevation (ft)
3,250
2,750
2,250
1,750
1,250
0.0
0.5
1.0
1.5
2.0
2.5
3.0
3.5
4.0
One-Way Distance (mi)

▲ THE ETHEREAL CHAMPNEY FALLS

even more remarkable cascade **Pitcher Falls**—lives up to its name, spilling 50 feet from the top of a sheer rock wall in a long, thin stream. Champney Falls Loop Trail ascends the side of Champney Falls by way of exquisitely carved rock stairs before turning back into the woods and rejoining the **Champney Brook Trail** at 1.8 miles.

▸ MILE 1.8–2.9: Champney Brook Trail to Mount Chocorua Scenic Vista
Make a left back onto the main trail and feel your quads burn as the once-gentle path becomes a rockier series of stairs and slabs. Yard by yard, the trees open up, offering glimpses of the valley below and the Three Sisters mountains to the north of Chocorua. Traverse some switchbacks with exposed rock faces before entering a boreal forest. At 2.9 miles, you'll come upon a sign for a scenic **vista** on the right. The ledge beyond this sign offers a fine view of the northern Presidentials and an even better look at the pointy peak of Chocorua itself, which is now startlingly close.

▸ MILE 2.9–3.1: Mount Chocorua Scenic Vista to Piper Trail
Shortly after this viewpoint, the Champney Brook Trail passes the Champney Falls Cutoff and the Middle Sister Trail (keep right at both) and ends at the junction for the **Piper Trail** at 3.1 miles. Turn right onto the Piper Trail and make a left at the nearby West Side Trail junction. Keep looking for yellow blazes as the trail tunnels through more boreal forest before popping out onto the rocky upper reaches of Chocorua.

▸ **MILE 3.1–3.8: Piper Trail to Chocorua Summit**

From this point, the trail becomes an exciting climb up very steep rock slabs and ledges. You truly "feel" the sharpness of the peak here. Some sections may require the use of handholds for balance, but the rock also has plenty of natural steps to make the ascent easier. Turn left at the junction with the Brook Trail at 3.7 miles to stay on Piper Trail, scramble up a final pitch of rock faces, and plant your boots on the Chocorua summit at 3.8 miles. (It's a very small and raised summit, so keep low to the rock if it's especially windy.)

▸ **MILE 3.8–5.8: Chocorua Summit to Champney Falls Trail**

The return journey is a simple backtrack along the Piper Trail to Champney Falls Trail. That said, at the Champney Falls Loop Trail junction at 5.8 miles (remember, this is the cutoff loop path that you took to view the falls) hikers can go left and stick to the Champney Brook Trail on the way down for a shorter, less rocky descent.

▸ **MILE 5.8–7.4: Champney Falls Trail to Trailhead Parking Lot**

The Champney Falls Trail passes the start of the falls observation loop at 6 miles and the remainder of the return is an easy amble through the deciduous woods, finishing at the parking lot at 7.4 miles.

DIRECTIONS

From Concord, drive north on I-93 N for 60 miles and take Exit 32 for NH-112 toward Lincoln/North Woodstock. Turn left onto NH-112 E at the bottom of the off-ramp and then drive along the famous Kancamagus Highway for about 24 miles. The Champney Brook trailhead will be on your right.

GPS COORDINATES: 43°59'24.4"N 71°17'57.5"W, 43.990123, -71.299312

BEST NEARBY BREWS

Kick back like a local and pair your hike with an afternoon or evening glass of dark brown altbier or a nice golden IPA at **Tuckerman Brewing Company** (66 Hobbs St., Conway, 603/447-5400, www.tuckermanbrewing.com, noon-6pm Sun.-Thurs., noon-7pm Fri.-Sat.).

12 Mount Washington via Tuckerman Ravine

WHITE MOUNTAIN NATIONAL FOREST, PINKHAM NOTCH

Hike through a gigantic bowl-like ravine filled with waterfalls, wildflowers, and glacial boulders to reach the highest summit in New England.

BEST: Summer hikes, vistas

DISTANCE: 8.2 miles round-trip (loop)

DURATION: 8 hours

ELEVATION CHANGE: 4,265 feet

EFFORT: Strenuous

TRAIL: Dirt path, rocks, wooden bridges

USERS: Hikers

SEASON: June-September

FEES/PASSES: None

MAPS: White Mountain National Forest website

CONTACT: Appalachian Mountain Club Pinkham Notch Visitor Center, 603/466-2721, www.outdoors.org. Summer and fall visitors center hours are 6:30am-9:30pm daily.

You haven't really hiked in New England until you've pulled yourself over the lip of Mount Washington's peak only to find yourself surrounded by tourists in flip-flops clutching chili dogs and struggling to stay upright against the wind. The highest summit in all of New England is definitely an attraction—it has its own weather observatory, a museum, and a cafeteria where you can buy fast food. It's reachable by foot, car, and even train.

The most epic route to the top of Mount Washington is the Tuckerman Ravine Trail, which scrambles straight up the sloped walls of Tuckerman Ravine. In the summer, the ravine blooms into a paradise of cascades and alpine flora, and it's arguably better than the peak itself.

START THE HIKE

▸ MILE 0-0.4: Tuckerman Ravine Trail to Crystal Cascade

Begin the hike to the left of the entrance to the Appalachian Mountain Club's Pinkham Notch Visitor Center. Walk toward the large wooden sign for the **Tuckerman Ravine Trail** and turn right to pick up the stony trail as it ventures into the woods behind the visitors center. Cross the **Ellis River** on a wooden footbridge. As the trail begins to climb a hillside at a moderate grade, you'll pass a rock staircase that leads to a lookout spot at 0.4 mile, from which you can view the **Crystal Cascade**—a shimmering 100-foot-tall waterfall that's a promising sign of things to come.

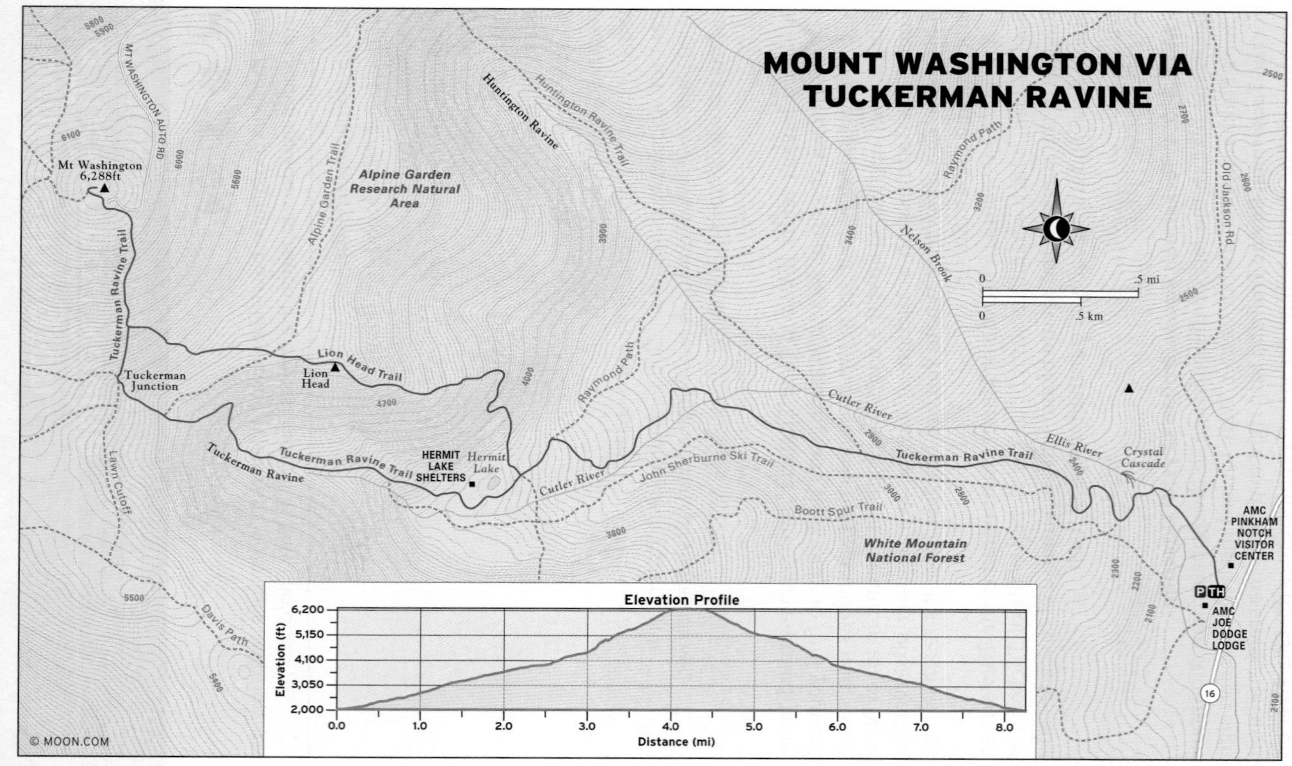
MOUNT WASHINGTON VIA TUCKERMAN RAVINE
Mt Washington 6,288ft
MT WASHINGTON AUTO RD
Alpine Garden Trail
Alpine Garden Research Natural Area
Huntington Ravine
Huntington Ravine Trail
Raymond Path
Nelson Brook
Old Jackson Rd
0 .5 mi
0 .5 km
Tuckerman Ravine Trail
Tuckerman Junction
Lion Head Trail
Lion Head
Lawn Cutoff
Tuckerman Ravine
Tuckerman Ravine Trail
HERMIT LAKE SHELTERS
Hermit Lake
Cutler River
John Sherburne Ski Trail
Boott Spur Trail
Ellis River
Crystal Cascade
White Mountain National Forest
AMC PINKHAM NOTCH VISITOR CENTER
AMC JOE DODGE LODGE
P TH
16
Davis Path
© MOON.COM
Elevation Profile
Elevation (ft)
6,200
5,150
4,100
3,050
2,000
0.0
1.0
2.0
3.0
4.0
5.0
6.0
7.0
8.0
Distance (mi)

▲ THE GRUELING CLIMB UP TUCKERMAN RAVINE'S HEADWALL

▸ MILE 0.4-2.4: Crystal Cascade to Hermit Lake Shelter

Climb west along the rocky trail, navigating moderately steep switchbacks for roughly 2 miles. With each turn, the trail becomes sunnier and the skyline offers flashes of Mount Washington's distant upper slopes. At 2.4 miles, take a water break and slather on some sunscreen when you reach **Hermit Lake Shelter**. The bowl of the ravine lies straight ahead in all its glory.

▸ MILE 2.4-3.4: Hermit Lake Shelter to Alpine Garden Trail Junction

From **Hermit Lake,** continue for 0.7 mile as the trail becomes steeper, climbing several rock stairs to reach the floor of the bowl at 3.1 miles. Here, you might encounter a looming ice arch that can last well into the summer. Don't walk near the arch, as chunks of ice the size of boulders regularly break off.

Continue past several misting waterfalls that spill down the bowl of the ravine, and get your quads ready. The trail begins to scramble up the headwall at a very steep grade; there are surprisingly few ledges with drop-offs here, but the trail is rough and maintaining your balance is crucial. After skirting around the rim of the headwall, the trail climbs a modest jumble of rocks, breaking through the tree line and reaching the junction for the Alpine Garden Trail at 3.4 miles.

▸ MILE 3.4–4.2: Alpine Garden Trail Junction to Mount Washington Summit

Turn left to stay on Tuckerman Ravine and be sure to take a look behind you—the view of the Carter-Wildcat Range from here is incredible.

Continue up a mess of rocks and make a right at the second junction at 3.6 miles to stay on the Tuckerman Ravine Trail. With the cone of Washington towering ahead, the trail steepens and navigates its way across larger lichen-crusted boulders and rock slabs. Well-placed cairns keep hikers on the correct trajectory. At 3.7 miles, veer left at the Lion's Head Trail junction to stay on Tuckerman and carefully schlep your way up the final rocks until you step onto the Mount Washington Auto Road at 4 miles. Turn left, walk up the road to the parking lot, and climb two wooden staircases to reach the summit of Washington at 4.2 miles.

▸ MILE 4.2–5.9: Mount Washington Summit to Lion's Head Trail

Hikers can choose to come back the way they came, but a less brutal option is to backtrack to the Lion's Head Trail junction at 4.7 miles and then turn left to take **Lion's Head Trail** down the northern flank of the ravine. The trail is steep with plenty of rock stairs and slabs, but it's not as dizzying as the headwall itself. (An added bonus: the upper stretches of Lion's Head are rich with alpine wildflowers in the summer.)

▸ MILE 5.9–8.2: Lion's Head Trail to Tuckerman Ravine Trail

Arrive back at Hermit Lake Shelter at 5.9 miles and hop back on the **Tuckerman Ravine Trail** to return to Pinkham Notch Visitor Center, completing the loop at 8.2 miles.

DIRECTIONS

From Concord, drive north on I-93 N for 74 miles and take Exit 35 for US-3 N toward Lancaster/Twin Mountain. Merge onto US-3 N and take it for 11 miles before veering right onto NH-115 N. Drive along this local highway until its terminus at US-2. Make a right onto US-2 E and drive northeast into the town of Gorham. As you pass the town common, turn right onto NH-16 S and continue south into Pinkham Notch for a final 10 miles. After you pass the Wildcat Mountain ski lift, look for the entrance to Pinkham Notch Visitor Center on your right and make a final right turn into the facility parking lot.

GPS COORDINATES: 44°15'26.2"N 71°15'11.6"W, 44.257273, -71.253224

BEST NEARBY BREWS

Once you've completed the hike, drive to North Conway and reward yourself with a frothy mug of Czech-style pilsner and a flatbread pizza or pile of barbecue at **Moat Mountain Smokehouse & Brewing Co.** (3378 White Mountain Hwy., North Conway, 603/356-6381, www.moatmountain.com, 11:30am–11:45pm daily).

13 Giant Falls

PEABODY FOREST, SHELBURNE

This seldom-traveled waterfall hike leads you to the foot of a towering cascade that spills from the hills just north of the White Mountain National Forest.

BEST: Spring hikes
DISTANCE: 3 miles round-trip
DURATION: 1.5 hours
ELEVATION CHANGE: 685 feet
EFFORT: Easy
TRAIL: Dirt path, wooden bridges, water crossings on stones
USERS: Hikers
SEASON: May–October
FEES/PASSES: None
MAPS: New Hampshire Fish and Game website (USGS topo map of Shelburne, NH)
CONTACT: Society for the Protection of New Hampshire Forests, 603/224-9945, www.forestsociety.com

One of the joys of New England hiking is stumbling upon an epic natural treasure that's somehow managed to avoid the tourists' detection. Giant Falls, a 200-foot-tall behemoth of a waterfall on the northern edge of the White Mountains, is unknown to most visitors who've come here to climb Mount Washington and gaze at Arethusa Falls. Even the trailhead for Giant Falls is so nondescript that this writer had to pull two U-turns and double back twice before finally spotting the sign.

START THE HIKE

▸ MILE 0–0.2: Peabody Brook Trail to Peabody Brook

Begin your hike by the white Peabody Brook Trail sign on the shoulder of North Road. Pick up the blue-blazed **Peabody Brook Trail**, which starts off on a rocky, eroded road. Head north into the woods through a tunnel of white birch trees and past several residences. After passing around a metal gate, take a right turn at a trail sign affixed to a tree. Watch your step as you cross a rickety old wooden footbridge that passes **Peabody Brook** at 0.2 mile. Stroll through a verdant field and enter the cool shade of Peabody Forest as the trail gently climbs along the eastern shores of the brook through the hemlock woods.

▸ MILE 0.2–1.2: Peabody Brook to Giant Falls Cutoff Trail

The trail here alternates between a smooth dirt path lined with ferns and wider stretches that are bursting with tallgrass. (Be sure to do a tick check after completing the hike.) You may also notice the abundance of colorful wild mushrooms that grow along the path. At 0.8 mile, take a left turn at the Peabody Brook Trail sign and continue your ascent as the trail becomes

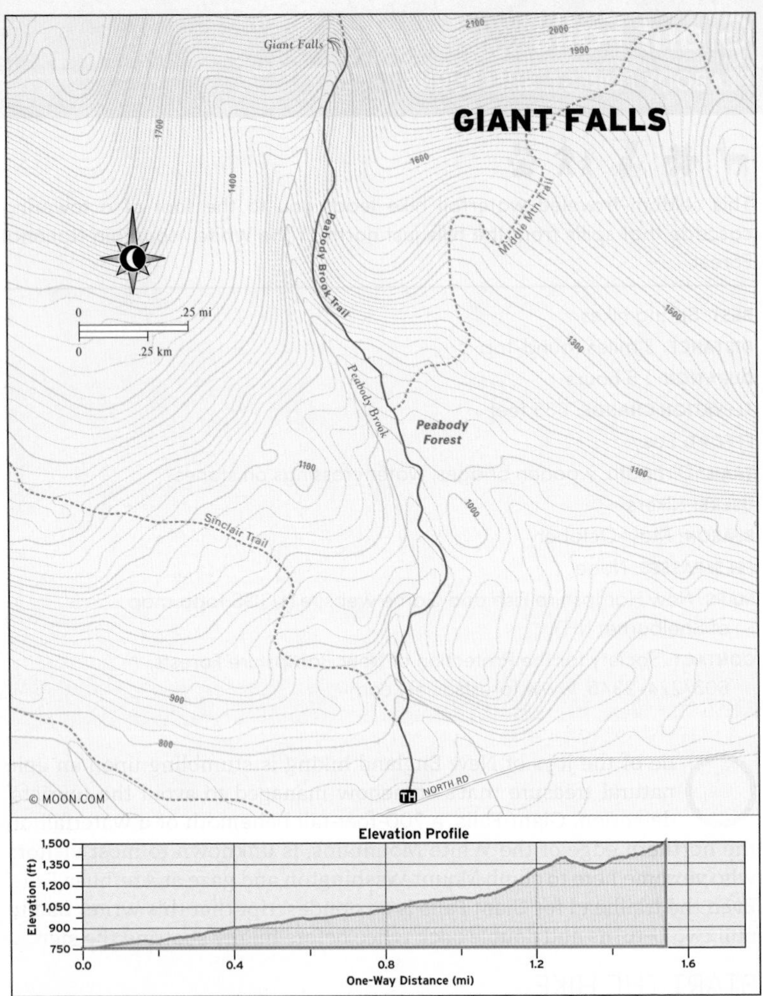

rockier and steeper with each step. Climb higher above Peabody Brook and work your way up stone staircases past a series of glacial boulders and some sheer cliff faces. The trail grade eventually softens and reaches a signed cutoff trail **for Giant Falls** at 1.2 miles.

▸ MILE 1.2-1.5: Giant Falls Cutoff Trail to Giant Falls

Turn left at the sign, descending a rooty dirt path to Peabody Brook at a moderate grade. The cutoff reaches the brook at 1.4 miles and climbs north alongside some small cascades. A dull roar beckons from just ahead. After scrambling up a final steeper pitch, the trail arrives at a rocky perch at 1.5 miles that offers a pristine view of **Giant Falls.** Nimble hikers can carefully make their way down from the perch and reach the base of the falls, but the rocks here can be quite slippery, especially during the spring when snowmelt turns the falls into a rip-roaring monster that's as beautiful as it is dangerous. Return the way you came.

▲ GIANT FALLS

DIRECTIONS

From Concord, drive north on I-93 N to the White Mountain National Forest. After passing through Franconia Notch, take Exit 35 and merge onto US-3 N to Lancaster/Twin Mountain. Continue north on US-3 N for 12 miles before turning right onto NH-115 N. Take this road northeast to its terminus and then take a right onto US-2 E. Drive east into Gorham and turn right onto US-2 E/Main Street. Continue for roughly 7 miles and then take a left onto Meadow Road. Cross a bridge over the Androscoggin River and take your final right turn onto North Road. The Peabody Brook Trailhead will be on your left, just past 267 North Road.

GPS COORDINATES: 44°24'47.7"N 71°06'15.5"W, 44.413249, -71.104293

14 Mount Adams

WHITE MOUNTAIN NATIONAL FOREST, RANDOLPH

This mountain hike ascends a beautiful and narrow rocky ridgeline to reach the summit of New Hampshire's second-tallest peak and returns by way of a lush forest trail with waterfalls.

DISTANCE: 8.6 miles round-trip (loop)
DURATION: 7 hours
ELEVATION CHANGE: 4,465 feet
EFFORT: Strenuous
TRAIL: Dirt path, rocks
USERS: Hikers
SEASON: June-September
FEES/PASSES: None
MAPS: White Mountain National Forest website
CONTACT: White Mountain National Forest, 603/536-6100, www.fs.usda.gov/recarea/whitemountain

Mount Adams is arguably the most thrilling summit in the White Mountains—a barren and dizzyingly high tower of rocks that seems to poke the cosmos. At 5,794 feet above sea level, it's the second-highest mountain in the Granite State. It's everything that Mount Washington (a more developed and lumbering peak) would seem to be, given its moniker at the tallest peak. Adams is a beauty and a beast of a climb, no matter which route you take.

START THE HIKE

▸ MILE 0-1.0: Airline Trail to Randolph Path

Begin the hike on the south side of the Appalachia parking lot by the trail information kiosk. Follow a dirt path into a meadow through which power lines run, then turn right at the junction to pick up the blue-blazed **Airline Trail** as it heads south into a dense deciduous forest full of mossy boulders and twittering birds. The footing is rooty and rocky as the Airline crosses a stream on rocks and then ascends through ferns at a steady grade. Keep straight to stay on Airline as Sylvan Way bisects the trail, turn right at the nearby junction with Beechwood Way, and then make a left at the Short Line Trail fork.

After reaching the **Randolph Path** crossing at roughly 1 mile, keep straight as the Airline steepens considerably and transitions from dirt to large and unwieldy stone stairs. It soon becomes a ledge-like path that climbs sharply up the north spur of Mount Adams.

▸ MILE 1.0-2.0: Randolph Path to Mount Adams's North Ridge

After ascending more stairs through a breezier and sun-broiled stretch of deciduous woods, enter a darker boreal pine forest and climb several steep rock slabs that occasionally require scrambling. Continue north as the trail

▲ MOUNT ADAMS (THE MIDDLE PEAK)

breaks out from the trees at roughly 2 miles and delivers you to the "foot" of Mount Adams's north ridge.

The pointy summit looms tall straight ahead, but a long tumult of boulders—with serious drops on both sides—is your next obstacle. Hike south along this ridgeline, following cairns and scrambling over the bulbous rocks.

▸ MILE 2.0–3.6: Mount Adams's North Ridge to Gulfside Trail Junction

Enjoy views of the boulder-strewn basin of King Ravine to your right and the emerald ravine between Adams and Mount Madison to your left. Some of the more elongated boulders hang precariously over the abyss of King Ravine, making for killer landscape photos. Along the way, you'll pass numerous junctions for trails that descend to the left and right, but keep straight to stay on Airline.

At 3.6 miles, you'll reach the windswept junction with the **Gulfside Trail**, which Airline merges with briefly.

▸ MILE 3.6–4.2: Gulfside Trail Junction to Mount Adams Summit

Turn right onto Gulfside and enjoy a brief, more level walk across big lichen-crusted rocks as you curve around the summit cone. Shortly ahead, take a left as Airline splits off again and climbs at a much tougher grade straight up the final pitch of the Adams summit. Here you'll truly feel the severe angle of the summit cone, which has a horn-like shape. A final pitch leads you to small crow's nest of rocks and boulders surrounded by an ocean of green hills. You've officially arrived at Mount Adams's summit at 4.2 miles.

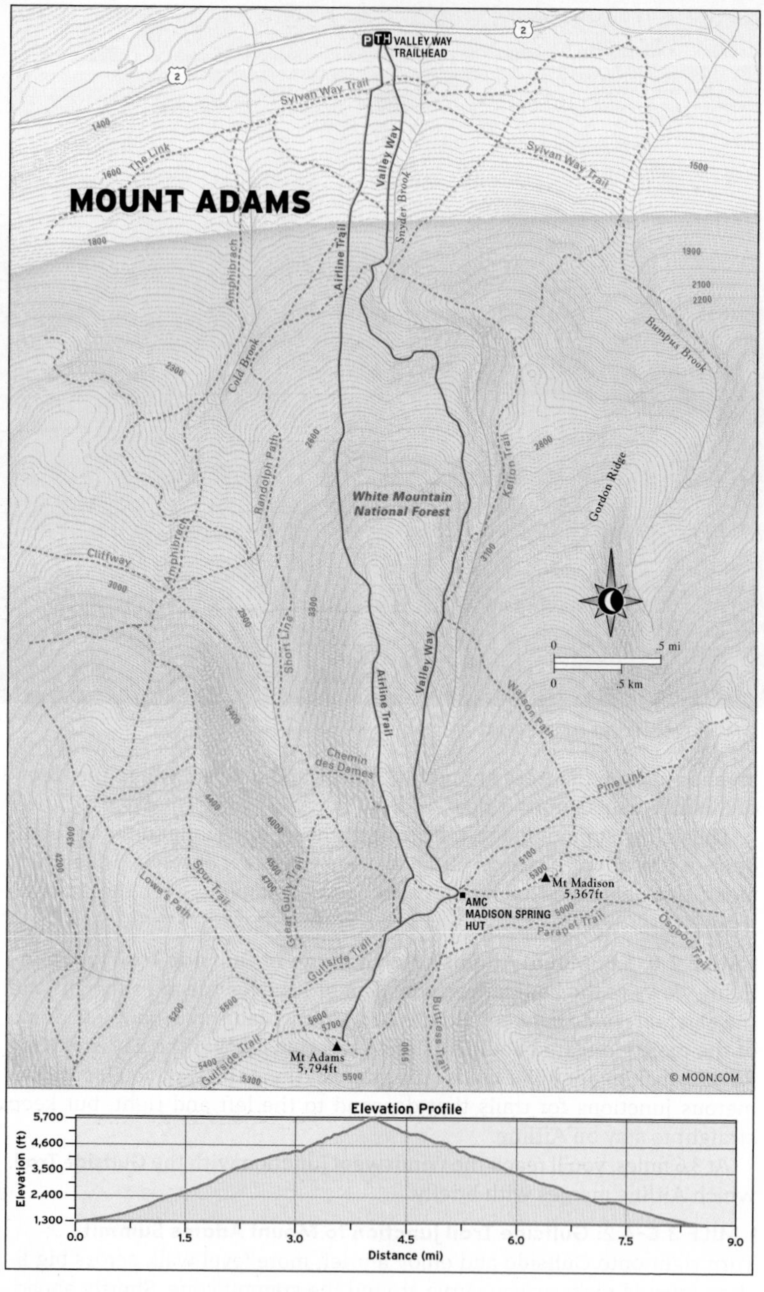
MOUNT ADAMS
VALLEY WAY TRAILHEAD
P TH
2
Sylvan Way Trail
The Link
Valley Way
Snyder Brook
Airline Trail
Amphibrach
Cold Brook
Randolph Path
Kelton Trail
Gordon Ridge
Bumpus Brook
White Mountain National Forest
Cliffway
Short Line
Watson Path
Chemin des Dames
Pine Link
Spur Trail
Lowe's Path
Great Gully Trail
Gulfside Trail
Buttress Trail
Parapet Trail
Osgood Trail
Mt Madison 5,367ft
AMC MADISON SPRING HUT
Mt Adams 5,794ft
0 .5 mi
0 .5 km
© MOON.COM
Elevation Profile
Elevation (ft)
5,700
4,600
3,500
2,400
1,300
0.0
1.5
3.0
4.5
6.0
7.5
9.0
Distance (mi)

MILE 4.2-4.8: Mount Adams Summit to Madison Spring Hut

Have a snack, rest your legs, and enjoy being on top of New England. To start your descent, backtrack to the **Gulfside Trail,** turn right, and keep right at the Airline junction as Gulfside descends a rockslide into the gap between Mount Adams and Madison, where **Madison Spring Hut** is reached at 4.8 miles. (A post-summit bowl of soup here is ideal fuel for the journey ahead.)

MILE 4.8-5.9: Madison Spring Hut to Valley Way Trail

From the hut, pick up the **Valley Way Trail,** marked by blue blazes, and hike north as it makes a very rocky and steep descent into boreal forest before segueing to a more manageable dirt path at 5.5 miles with plenty of knee-creaking rock stairs. Continue north and keep straight as you pass several marked cutoffs that branch off to the left and right of the Valley Way trail. The trail is flanked with plenty of moss tuffets in places, which can make for a nice place to rest your legs and enjoy a partial view of the valley below.

MILE 5.9-7.9: Valley Way Trail to Snyder Brook

A final series of stone staircases into deciduous woods leads to the junction with Brookside Trail at 7.7 miles. Turn left here, then right at the Beechwood Way fork, continuing on Valley Way at both junctions. Enjoy a gentler dirt path that ambles along several chuckling cascades on **Snyder Brook**—a great place to take a shockingly rejuvenating dip.

MILE 7.9-8.6: Snyder Brook to Airline Trail Junction

The trail soon levels and leaves the brook behind to pass through a grove of ferns and hemlocks. Keep straight as Valley Way bisects Sylvan Way and emerge into the meadow with the Airline junction at 8.5 miles. Stroll (or drag your tired carcass) to the parking lot ahead to complete the hike at 8.6 miles!

DIRECTIONS

From Concord, drive north on I-93 N. After passing through Franconia Notch, take Exit 35 and merge onto US-3 N to Lancaster/Twin Mountain. Continue north on US-3 N for 12 miles before turning right onto NH-115 N. Take this road northeast to its terminus and then take a right onto US-2 E. Drive east for another 7 miles. The Appalachia parking lot will be on your left. If it's a busy summer day, you may have to park off the shoulder of the road before or after the parking lot.

GPS COORDINATES: 44°22'16.5"N 71°17'20.7"W, 44.371247, -71.289093

BEST NEARBY BITES

Prepare for your climb by stopping in Gorham for a breakfast sandwich, hot coffee, or a smoothie at the **White Mountain Café & Bookstore** (212 Main St, Gorham, 603/466-2511, www.whitemountaincafe.com, 7am-4pm daily). When the sun goes down and you're (hopefully) off the mountain, circle back for a hearty dinner of nut-crusted chicken, Cambodian pasta ragu, or many other delicacies at **Libby's Bistro & SAaLT Pub** (111 Main St., Gorham, 603/466-5330, www.libbysbistro.org, 5pm-10pm Wed.-Sun.).

NEARBY CAMPGROUNDS

NAME	LOCATION	FACILITIES	SEASON	FEE
Lafayette Place Campground	2 Franconia Notch State Park, Franconia, NH 03580	Tent sites, toilets, showers, potable water, camp store	year-round (no services in winter)	$25
603/823-9513, www.nhstateparks.org				
Hancock Campground	133 Hancock Campground, Lincoln, NH 03251	Tent sites, toilets, potable water	year-round (no services in winter)	$24
603/536-6100, www.fs.usda.gov				
Fransted Family Campground	974 Profile Rd., Franconia, NH 03580	Tent sites, RV sites, toilets, showers, potable water, laundry, camp store, Wi-Fi	mid-May through early October	$40-55
603/823-5675, www.franstedcampground.com				
Sugarloaf Campground	Campground Rd. and Zealand Rd., Jefferson, NH 03583	Tent sites, toilets, potable water	mid-May-mid-October	$20
603/536-6100, www.fs.usda.gov				
Dry River Campground	2057 US-302, Bartlett, NH 03812	Tent sites, lean-tos, toilets, showers, potable water, laundry	mid-May-mid-October	$25-29
603/374-2272, www.nhstateparks.org				
Jigger Johnson Campground	Kancamagus Hwy., Albany, NH 03818	Tent sites, toilets, potable water	mid-May through mid-October	$24
www.fs.usda.gov				
Eastern Slope Camping Area	03818, 584 White Mountain Hwy., North Conway, NH 03860	Tent sites, RV sites, cabins, toilets, showers, potable water, laundry, swimming pool, camp store, Wi-Fi	May through October	$49-110
603/447-5092, www.easternslopecamping.com				

NEARBY CAMPGROUNDS (continued)

NAME	LOCATION	FACILITIES	SEASON	FEE
Glen Ellis Family Campground	Route 302, Glen, NH 03838	Tent sites, RV sites, toilets, showers, potable water, laundry, camp store, swimming pool	late-May-mid-October	$48-165
603/383-4567, www.glenelliscampground.com				
Barnes Field Campground	Dolly Copp Rd., Gorham, NH 03581	Tent sites, toilets, potable water	year-round	$15-70
603/466-2713, www.recreation.gov				
Timberland Campground	809 US-2, Shelburne, NH 03581	Tent sites, RV sites, RV rentals, cabins, toilets, showers, potable water, laundry, swimming pool, camp store, Wi-Fi	mid-May through mid-October	$26-139
603/466-3872, www.timberlandcampgroundnh.com				

▲ DIAPENSIA FLOWERS

GREAT NORTH WOODS AND DIXVILLE NOTCH

Beyond the hubbub of the Whites lies a remote and pristine territory where even the most active New England hikers rarely venture. The Great North Woods and Dixville Notch are New Hampshire at its most rugged and eerily beautiful. Getting here is a hike itself, but the trails are worth the pilgrimage. You'll step back in time on quiet paths that take you deep into New Hampshire's logging capital to otherworldly sights such as the origin of the Connecticut River, or the scariest precipice in the Granite State. Plus, the lack of human activity will magnify your chances of having an unforgettable encounter with some of New England's rarest (and endangered) creatures—such as the golden eagle or the Canada lynx.

▲ New Hampshire fungi growing on trees near Devil's Hopyard

▲ the spire of Table Rock

◂ LITTLE HELLGATE FALLS

1 **The Devil's Hopyard**
DISTANCE: 2 miles round-trip
DURATION: 1 hour
EFFORT: Easy

2 **Table Rock**
DISTANCE: 1.4 miles round-trip (out-and-back) or 1.7 miles round-trip (loop)
DURATION: 1 hour
EFFORT: Moderate/strenuous

3 **Magalloway Mountain**
DISTANCE: 1.8 miles round-trip
DURATION: 1.5 hours
EFFORT: Moderate

4 **Little Hellgate Falls**
DISTANCE: 1.5 miles round-trip
DURATION: 1 hour
EFFORT: Easy

5 **Fourth Connecticut Lake**
DISTANCE: 2.1 miles round-trip
DURATION: 2 hours
EFFORT: Moderate

▲ RED-TAILED HAWK

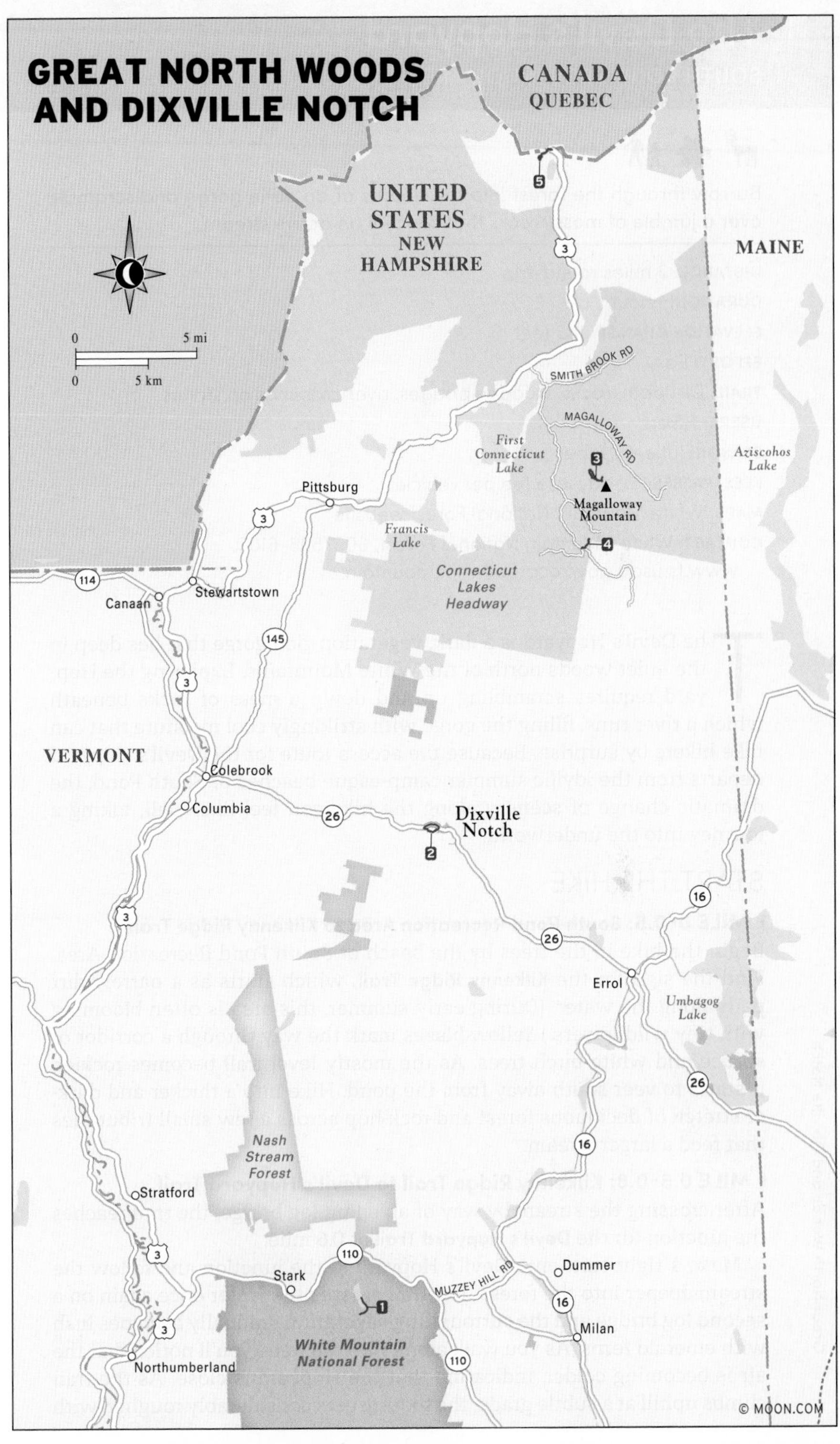
GREAT NORTH WOODS
AND DIXVILLE NOTCH
CANADA
QUEBEC
UNITED
STATES
NEW
HAMPSHIRE
MAINE
VERMONT
0
5 mi
0
5 km
SMITH BROOK RD
MAGALLOWAY RD
First
Connecticut
Lake
Magalloway
Mountain
Aziscohos
Lake
Pittsburg
Francis
Lake
Connecticut
Lakes
Headway
Canaan
Stewartstown
Colebrook
Columbia
Dixville
Notch
Errol
Umbagog
Lake
Nash
Stream
Forest
Stratford
Stark
Dummer
MUZZEY HILL RD
Milan
Northumberland
White Mountain
National Forest
114
145
3
26
16
110
1
2
3
4
5
© MOON.COM

1 The Devil's Hopyard

SOUTH POND RECREATION AREA, STARK

Burrow through the forest into the depths of an eerie gorge and scramble over a jumble of mossy rocks that conceal an active stream.

DISTANCE: 2 miles round-trip
DURATION: 1 hour
ELEVATION CHANGE: 145 feet
EFFORT: Easy
TRAIL: Dirt path, rocks, wooden bridges, river crossings on stones
USERS: Hikers
SEASON: June-October
FEES/PASSES: $7 day-use fee per vehicle
MAPS: White Mountain National Forest website
CONTACT: White Mountain National Forest, 603/536-6100, www.fs.usda.gov/recarea/whitemountain

The Devil's Hopyard is a dark, vegetation-rich gorge that lies deep in the quiet woods north of the White Mountains. Exploring the Hopyard requires scrambling up and down a mess of rocks beneath which a river runs, filling the gorge with strikingly cool moisture that can take hikers by surprise. Because the access route for the Devil's Hopyard departs from the idyllic summer camp-esque beaches of South Pond, the dramatic change of scenery along the hike can feel like, well, taking a journey into the underworld.

START THE HIKE

‣ MILE 0-0.5: South Pond Recreation Area to Kilkenny Ridge Trail

Begin the hike in the trees by the beach at South Pond Recreation Area. Find the sign for the **Kilkenny Ridge Trail,** which starts as a narrow dirt path along the water. (During early summer, this area is often blooming with tiny wildflowers.) Yellow blazes mark the way through a corridor of spruce and white birch trees. As the mostly level trail becomes rockier, it starts to veer south away from the pond. Hike into a thicker and darker stretch of deciduous forest and rock-hop across a few small tributaries that feed a larger stream.

‣ MILE 0.5-0.8: Kilkenny Ridge Trail to Devil's Hopyard Trail

After crossing the stream by way of an aging log bridge, the trail reaches the junction for the **Devil's Hopyard Trail** at 0.6 mile.

Make a right turn onto Devil's Hopyard at the junction and follow the stream deeper into the forest. The trail crosses the water once again on a second log bridge and the surrounding vegetation gradually becomes lush with emerald ferns. As you walk along the trail here, you'll notice that the air is becoming colder, indicating that the Hopyard is close. As the trail climbs uphill at a subtle grade, the footing gets considerably rougher, with

▲ MOSSY ROCKS FOUND IN THE DEVIL'S HOPYARD

lots of loose rocks that can become quite slick during rainy weather due to the growth of moss and algae. Then, quite suddenly, the crumbling walls of the gorge appear at 0.8 mile, marking your entry into the Hopyard.

▸ MILE 0.8–2.0: Devil's Hopyard Trail to Gorge

From here, you'll scramble up a jumble of rocks and boulders through the recesses of the gorge. As you carefully make your way through the gorge, streams of chilly and moist air will blast upward through the gaps between the rocks. And, if you listen closely, you can hear the rushing of water beneath the rocks; that's the sound of the stream that you've followed to this point. The gorge walls get taller, darker, and more dramatic as the trail climbs the rockfall. Finally, the trail reaches its terminus at a looming vertical cliff at roughly 1 mile. Return the way you came.

DIRECTIONS

From Concord, drive north along I-93 N through Franconia Notch and then take Exit 35 for US-3 N toward Lancaster/Twin Mountain. Continue north along US-3 N to the town of Northumberland and then turn right onto NH-110 E. Drive along this road for 10 miles and then swing a right onto South Pond Road. Keep right at the forks for Short Road and Normand Road, and then take a sharper right to stay on South Pond Road. Follow the road past a gate to its end at the South Pond Recreation Area. The gate is usually opened for the season in mid-June and closes in October, but off-season visitors can park before the closed gate and walk down the final stretch of road to the South Pond Recreation area.

GPS COORDINATES: 45°53'11.7"N 68°59'59.1"W, 45.886588, -68.999748

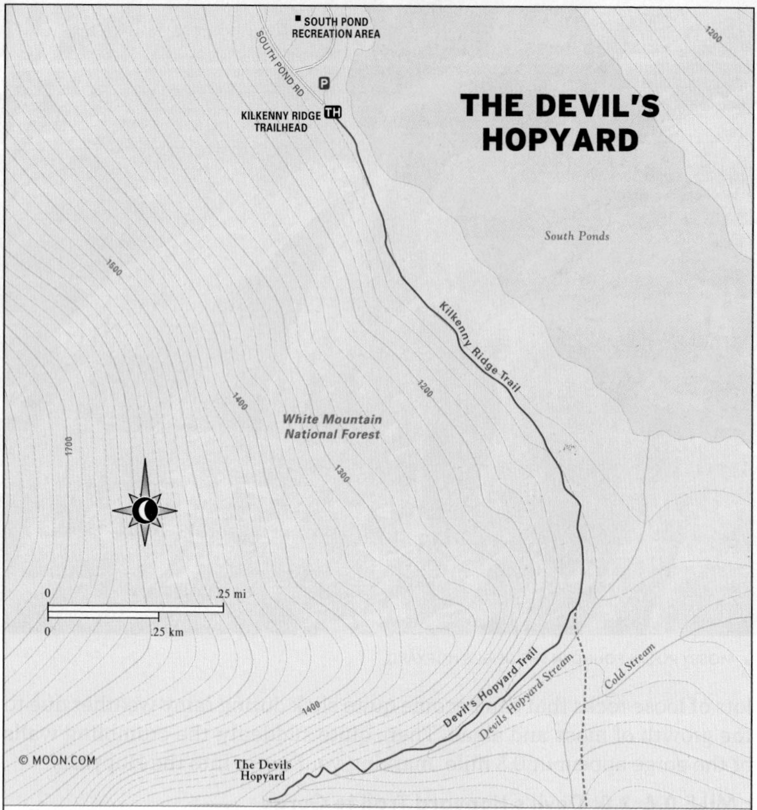

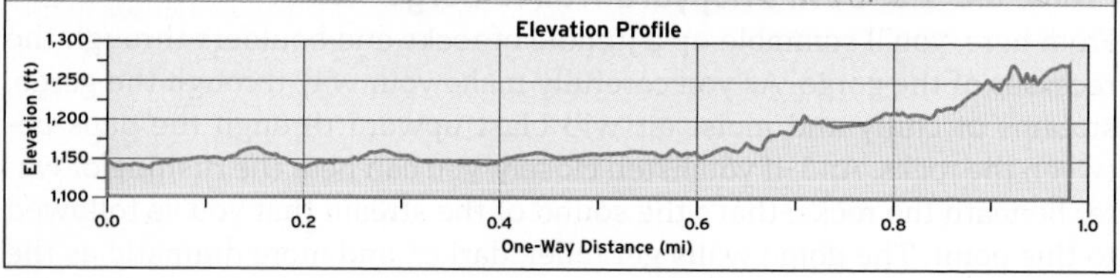

THE DEVIL'S HOPYARD

SOUTH POND RECREATION AREA
SOUTH POND RD
P
KILKENNY RIDGE TRAILHEAD
TH
South Ponds
Kilkenny Ridge Trail
White Mountain National Forest
Devil's Hopyard Trail
Devils Hopyard Stream
Cold Stream
The Devils Hopyard
1200
1300
1400
1600
1700
0 .25 mi
0 .25 km
© MOON.COM

Elevation Profile
Elevation (ft): 1,100 1,150 1,200 1,250 1,300
One-Way Distance (mi): 0.0 0.2 0.4 0.6 0.8 1.0

BEST NEARBY BREWS

The Devil's Hopyard might not be the toughest hike in the book, but that's no reason to turn down a Irish red ale or any of the other microbrews you'll find at **Copper Pig Brewery** (1 Middle St., Lancaster, 603/631-2273, www.copperpigbrewery.com, 5pm-9pm Thurs., 4pm-9pm Fri., noon-9pm Sat., noon-6pm Sun.).

2 Table Rock

DIXVILLE NOTCH STATE PARK, DIXVILLE TOWNSHIP

Hike to the top of one of New England's most beautiful (and scary) natural attractions.

BEST: Fall hikes

DISTANCE: 1.4 miles round-trip (out-and-back) or 1.7 miles round-trip (loop)

DURATION: 1 hour

ELEVATION CHANGE: 754 feet

EFFORT: Moderate/strenuous

TRAIL: Dirt path, rocks, river crossings on stones

USERS: Hikers, leashed dogs

SEASON: May-October

FEES/PASSES: None

MAPS: USGS topo map of Coos County, New Hampshire

CONTACT: Dixville Notch State Park, 603/538-6707, www.nhstateparks.org

North of the White Mountains in the isolated wild of Dixville Notch, Table Rock awaits the bold traveler. This spire of crumbling granite looms 700 feet above the road through Dixville Notch, erupting from the forest like a wizard's tower in Lord of the Rings. And luckily for hikers, there are two different ways to reach the top of Table Rock. The first trail—the Climbing Trail, which is the more popular of the two routes—is a near-vertical scramble through the woods on the east side of Table Rock. You'll gain a dizzying 754 feet in less than half a mile! The second, lesser-known route, the Table Rock Trail, takes a more gradual and civilized approach to the payoff. Both trails are located on NH-26, roughly 20 minutes apart by foot, and they can be combined for a fun loop hike.

Note that this trail should not be attempted in wet weather.

START THE HIKE

CLIMBING TRAIL

▸ MILE 0-1.4: NH-26 S to Table Rock

Begin the hike on the shoulder of NH-26 S directly behind the "Welcome to Dixville Notch State Park" sign. **The Climbing Trail** up to Table Rock is marked with a wooden sign on a tree. Warm up your leg muscles by ascending a series of stone stairs that wind through a mossy, boulder-strewn forest. The trail grade steepens considerably with each little twist and turn, and you might have to pick your way up and over blowdowns here and there.

As the trail climbs above the floor of Dixville Notch—with fleeting views through the trees to measure your progress—the footing becomes more eroded in places, with lots of exposed tree roots. In some places, you may even find yourself using the roots themselves as handholds. The pine and spruce trees start to shrink and the trail becomes more sunlit. A few

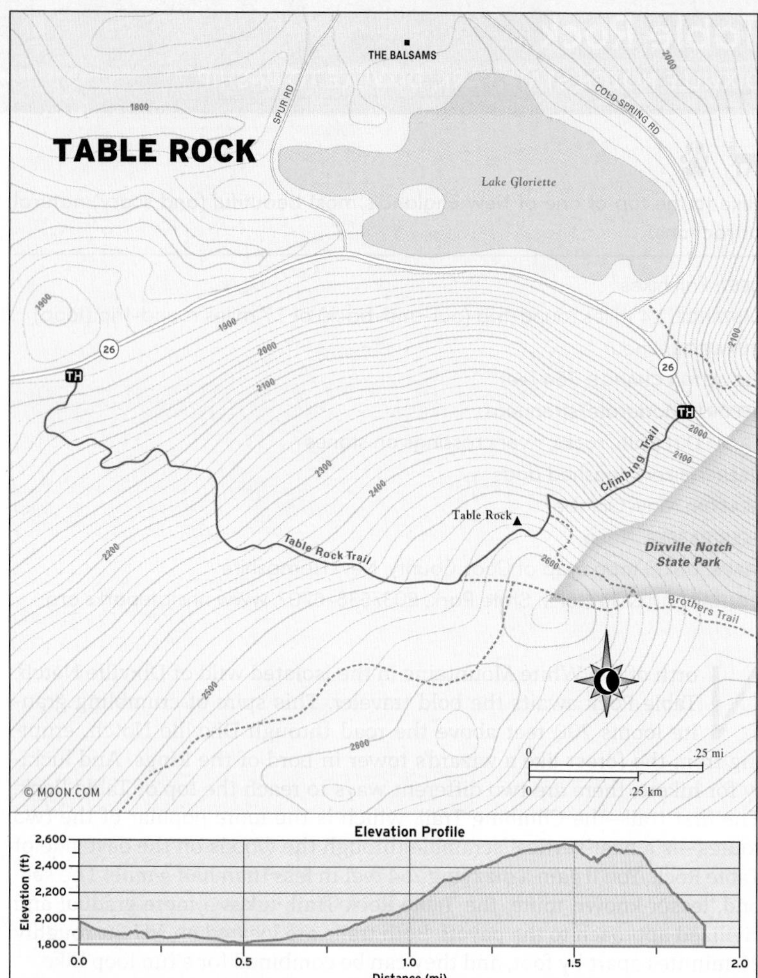

glimpses of Table Rock's sheer pinnacle offer hope as the Climbing Trail approaches its terminus.

After reaching a rocky height of land at 0.25 miles, the Climbing Trail arrives at an unmarked trail junction. Take a right turn and tread carefully as the trail emerges onto the tip-top of Table Rock. Hikers can decide how far out they wish to venture onto the "summit," which is barely 7 feet wide at its farthest point—with a 700-foot vertical drop on three sides! The views of Dixville Notch are unbeatable, and the vertigo is similarly unique. Return via the Table Rock Trail.

TABLE ROCK TRAIL

‣ MILE 0-1.7: Table Rock Parking Area to Table Rock

Begin your hike in the parking area for the Table Rock Trail—a small dugout on the shoulder of NH-26 S, immediately west of the now-closed Balsams resort. Enter a deciduous forest of beech and white birches and climb gradually up a series of switchbacks. The trail then crosses a trickling

▲ THE SPIRE OF TABLE ROCK

creek and begins to ascend southeast at a moderate grade. Watch for loose rocks in some of the more eroded sections, especially during rain or soggy conditions. The trail steepens considerably at 0.4 mile for several yards before merging with, and then crossing, another creek.

As you continue your climb, notice the shards of dark gray stone that litter the trail—these slick, sometimes glittering rocks are native to the far north of New Hampshire. The ferns that line the trail thicken as the forest transitions into a boreal mixture of pine, spruce, and birch. The trail grade starts to soften at 0.6 mile and curves southeast through the upper woods before reaching an unmarked four-way junction at 0.7 mile. Turn left and descend a sunny knoll to arrive at the junction with the Climbing Trail. Veer left here to reach the top of Table Rock. Return the way you came.

DIRECTIONS

From Concord, drive north on I-93 N. After passing through Franconia Notch, take Exit 35 for US 3-N toward Lancaster/Twin Mountain. Merge onto US-3 N and continue north to the town of Colebrook. Take a right turn onto NH-26 E and drive east for roughly 10 miles. The Table Rock Trail parking area will be on your right just before you reach the Balsams resort property. To reach the Climbing Trail, continue east along NH-26E past the Balsams resort and pull into one of the dugouts on the right side of the road. Park here and walk east along the road to the nearby "Welcome to Dixville Notch" sign.

CLIMBING TRAIL GPS COORDINATES: 44°51'53.5"N 71°18'03.3"W, 44.864872, -71.300914

TABLE ROCK TRAIL GPS COORDINATES: 44°51'55.1"N 71°18'47.8"W, 44.865306, -71.313285

BEST NEARBY BITES

Meat is a big deal in far northern New Hampshire, and you'll find melt-in-your-mouth heaps of it at **Hawg Trauf Restraunt** (30-40 East Side Rd., Errol, 603/482-3665, 11:30am-7:30pm Wed.-Thurs., 11:30am-8:30pm Fri.-Sat., 11:30am-7:30pm Sun.). Just up the road in Colebrook, you'll find roasted beet and goat cheese canapes, pistachio-crusted salmon, and many more fine-dining temptations at **Parsons Street** (1 High St., Colebrook, 603/331-3190, www.parsonsstreetnh.com, 5pm-8pm Tues.-Thurs., 5pm-8:30pm Fri.-Sat.).

3 Magalloway Mountain

PITTSBURG

This hike to the highest peak in far northern New Hampshire offers sweeping views of Quebec and the Connecticut Lakes—as well as a profound feeling of true isolation.

DISTANCE: 1.8 miles round-trip

DURATION: 1.5 hours

ELEVATION CHANGE: 901 feet

EFFORT: Moderate

TRAIL: Dirt path, rocks, wooden bridges

USERS: Hikers, leashed dogs

SEASON: June–September

FEES/PASSES: None

MAPS: A basic map is accessible at Trails.com, but that's essentially it.

CONTACT: NH Division of Forests and Lands, 603/271-2214, www.nhdfl.org

Magalloway Mountain is a remote heap of granite and boreal forest that stands high above the Great North Woods landscape, looking straight into the agrarian hills of Quebec. At 3,383 feet tall, Magalloway isn't a giant, but in a way, that adds to the mountain's quiet and austere beauty. Speckled with spruce trees and complete with an old 40-foot-tall fire tower and watchman's cabins at the summit, Magalloway has a ghostly atmosphere that can make hikers feel like they've stumbled across the ruins of a lost civilization. It's a long drive to get there and the rocky road to the trailhead is an adventure in and of itself, but the sensation of being dropped in the middle of a most wonderous nowhere is worth it.

START THE HIKE

▸ MILE 0-0.8: Coot Trail to Magalloway Fire Tower

Begin the hike on the east end of the small parking area for Magalloway Mountain by the outhouse, to the right of which is a wide dirt path, **the Coot Trail.** Hike south along the trail as it climbs at a moderate grade into spruce and birch woods and passes an old red-shingled house. After crossing a wooden footbridge over a creek, the trail starts to climb the northern haunch of the mountain on rockier ground with an alternately moderate and steep grade. Stop and look behind you for some early views toward Quebec.

At 0.4 mile, you'll pass a logged area as the trail becomes narrower and steeper, climbing into a much thicker section of boreal forest. After crossing some water bars and ascending a very steep pitch of loose rocks, the Coot Trail passes a signed cutoff for the Bobcat Trail on the right at around 0.6 mile (easy to miss when you're ascending but easy to spot when descending). Keep left and climb the last few yards of the steep pitch to

▲ THE SUMMIT OF MAGALLOWAY MOUNTAIN

emerge onto a grassy wooded ridge. The trail curves through the forest at a level grade here before finally reaching a vast clearing at 0.8 mile where the Magalloway **fire tower** looms tall.

▸ MILE 0.8-1.0: Magalloway Fire Tower to Magalloway Mountain Overlook

Technically, you've reached the summit proper, but the best view is ahead. Hike straight past the tower and the watchman's cabins, turning left after the last cabin (look for a fire pit here) to pick up a skinny dirt path that descends through some mossy woods. You'll reach a stunning **overlook** point at 0.9 mile. From here, you can gaze out at the sheer cliffs of the mountain's eastern side and the American and Canadian wilderness beyond.

▸ MILE 1.0-1.2: Magalloway Mountain Overlook to Bobcat Trail

Once you've had your fill, backtrack to the fire tower and pick up the Coot Trail again. Backtrack until you reach the Bobcat Trail sign again at 1.2 miles; turn left onto Bobcat. Compared to the Coot Trail, the Bobcat Trail is more forested and grown-in, but the trees part just often enough to offer pretty views of the surrounding countryside.

▸ MILE 1.2-1.8: Bobcat Trail to Tower Road

The trail descends the western slope of Magalloway at a moderate grade, with some steep sections. There are some slippery rock slabs, as well as some eroded sections, so step delicately as you approach the valley. After a rockier stretch of path through ferns and spruce trees, the trail levels out a bit and crosses some mud patches on wooden bog bridges before suddenly spilling out onto **Tower Road** at 1.7 miles. Turn right onto the road and you'll see the parking lot straight ahead, concluding at 1.8 miles.

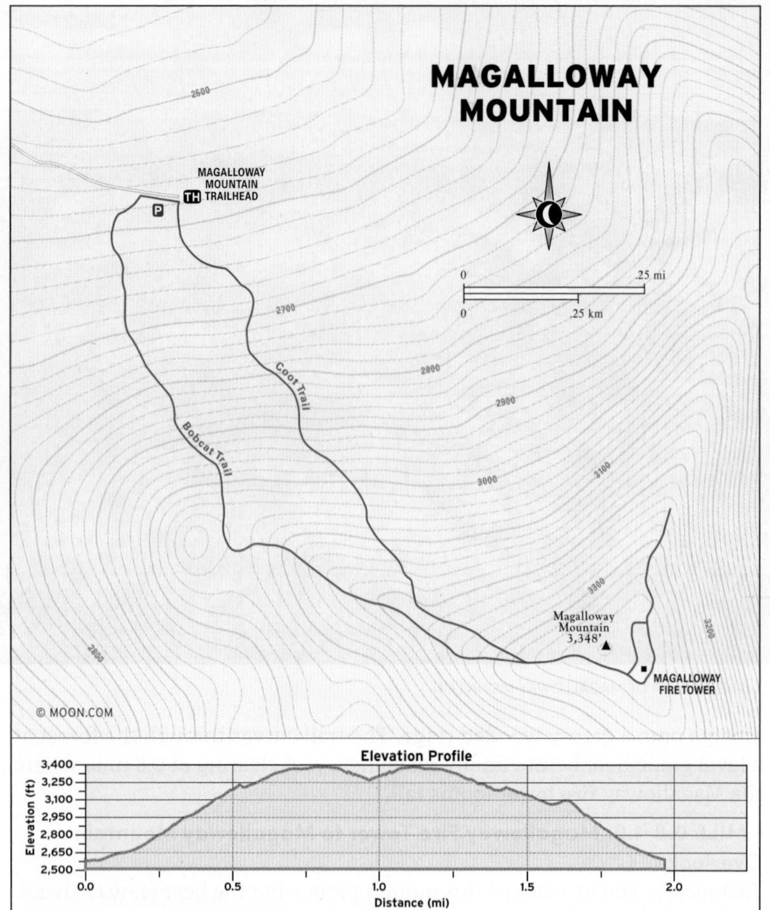

DIRECTIONS

From Concord, drive north along I-93 N through Franconia Notch and then take Exit 35 for US-3 N toward Lancaster/Twin Mountain. Continue north along US-3 N to the town of Colebrook and then turn right onto NH-145 N. Drive north for 13 miles to the road's terminus and then turn right onto US-3 N again. Take this road through the town of Pittsburg for another 11 miles and then make a right onto Magalloway Road, a well-maintained dirt road. Drive southeast along this road for 5 miles, then make the first right after the Mile 5 marker onto Tower Road. Tower Road is much narrower and quite rocky, with some potholes in places, but it can be safely traversed with a standard low-clearance vehicle as long as you take things nice and slow. Continue south along Tower Road for a final 3 miles to its terminus at the parking area for Magalloway Mountain.

GPS COORDINATES: 45°04'10.0"N 71°10'19.5"W, 45.069435, -71.172093

▲ VIEWS OF NEARBY QUEBEC FROM MAGALLOWAY MOUNTAIN

BEST NEARBY BITES

Sit by a roaring fireplace, savor a glass of red wine, and cut into a juicy Angus strip steak at **Murphy's Steakhouse** (3329 US-3, Pittsburg, 603/538-9995, www.atbeartree.com, 5pm-9pm Wed.-Sun.). Down the road a little farther, you can attempt to finish one of the many creative pizzas dished out at **the burg** (8 Back Lake Rd., Pittsburg, 603/538-7400, 5pm-9pm Wed.-Fri., noon-9pm Sat., 5pm-9pm Sun.). But whatever you do, be sure to stop for a home-style made-to-order breakfast sandwich at **Treats & Treasures Store & Gift Shop** (3316 US-3, Pittsburg, 603/538-7472, www.treatsandtreasuresnh.com, 7am-5pm Sun.-Thurs., 7am-7pm Fri.-Sat.).

4 Little Hellgate Falls

CLARKSVILLE

Traverse a remote and very underexplored forest to reach a towering cascade with a dark and tragic history.

DISTANCE: 1.5 miles round-trip

DURATION: 1 hour

ELEVATION CHANGE: 322 feet

EFFORT: Easy

TRAIL: Dirt path, rocks, log stairs

USERS: Hikers, leashed dogs

SEASON: June-September

FEES/PASSES: None

MAPS: A basic map is accessible at Trails.com, but that's essentially it.

CONTACT: NH Division of Forests and Lands, 603/271-2214, www.nhdfl.org

Not too long ago, thousands of loggers spent the peaks of their lives cutting timber in the Great North Woods. Quite often, this occupation caused their demise. Little Hellgate Falls is a particularly infamous place in local logging history. This crashing 40-foot-tall cascade is fed by a mighty brook that served as a natural "flume" for logs. But the narrow opening at the top of the falls caused frequent logjams, and more than a few loggers died while trying to restart the flow of timbers—hence the name "Hellgate." The hike to this pretty and mostly unknown waterfall might feel like a dreamy jaunt through evergreen woods, but even the local wood itself is an ode to what happened here.

START THE HIKE

▶ MILE 0-0.1: Trail Information Kiosk to Falls Trail

Begin the hike by the wooden trail information kiosk on the shoulder of Cedar Stream Road. A few yards south of the kiosk, you'll see a snowmobile junction for trails 20 and 137. Take a left turn here onto the unnamed dirt road that branches off from Cedar Stream Road. Walk around the orange access gate ahead and cross a wooden bridge over Rowell Brook. Continue east along the road past a clear-cut (logging still happens in the Great North Woods). A small wooden sign that says "**Falls Trail" will soon appear** on your left just beyond the clear-cut. Turn left here to leave the road behind and begin your true foray to Little Hellgate Falls.

▶ MILE 0.1-0.6: Falls Trail to Little Hellgate Falls

Follow the winding dirt path northeast through a rich forest of spruce and pine trees—a testament to nature's ability to make a comeback after decades of ravaging. As the trail climbs a sun-splashed hillside on notched and beautifully carved log stairs, you'll reach the edge of the rejuvenated forest and pass by a much larger logging zone at 0.3 mile. After skirting this border between the two forest zones briefly, the trail descends more

▲ LITTLE HELLGATE FALLS

log stairs into a wooded ravine. The rush of water that you hear echoing from below is **Hellgate Brook.** Continue northeast through the ravine, following the sound of the brook, and make another brief climb past mossy boulders and tuffets into a hemlock forest. Once again, the trail emerges from the woods to make a quick foray through the logging zone before returning to the greenery of the trees and moss—the latter of which is truly abundant here, lending the forest a distinctly Scandinavian feel.

Turn right onto the spur path at 0.6 mile; quite suddenly, you'll find yourself standing on a dirt ledge that overlooks **Little Hellgate Falls.** A little log picnic table and bench nearby offers a great place to have a snack, while hikers who don't mind a bit of bushwhacking can carefully descend the steep overlook slopes to the falls' base. To reach the top of the falls, pick up the main trail again and continue hiking northeast as it climbs above the cascade at a moderate grade before reaching a height of land.

▸ MILE 0.6–1.5: Little Hellgate Falls to Hellgate Brook

Make a final descent down some more log stairs to reach a sunny little beach beside Hellgate Brook at 0.7 mile. To your right, a few yards down the brook, you'll see the narrowing rock walls that caused all those deadly logjams not so long ago. This spot marks the finish of your hike. Dip your feet in the water and reflect before returning the way you came.

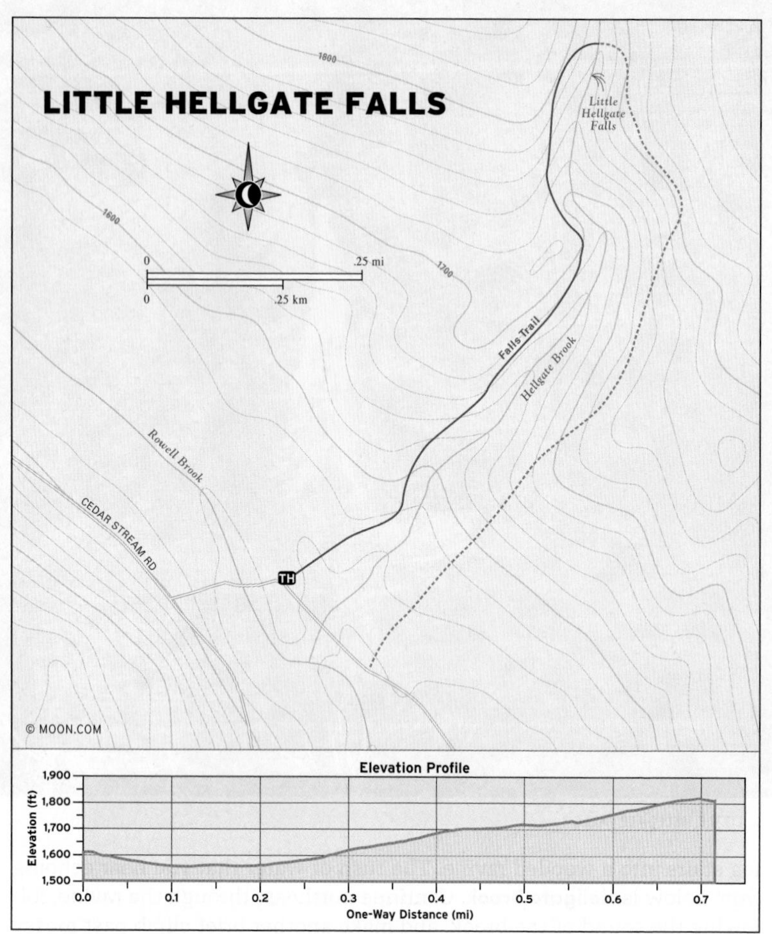

DIRECTIONS

From Concord, drive north along I-93 N through Franconia Notch and then take Exit 35 for US-3 N toward Lancaster/Twin Mountain. Continue north along US-3 N to the town of Colebrook and then turn right onto NH-145 N. Drive north for 13 miles to the road's terminus and then turn right onto US-3 N again. Take this road through the town of Pittsburg for another 11 miles and then make a right onto Magalloway Road, a well-maintained dirt road with numerical mile marker signs. Drive southeast along this unmarked road for 3 miles and make the first right onto Buckhorn Road. Follow Buckhorn Road for a few miles to a juncture where another unmarked road intersects; stay straight to continue onto Cedar Stream Road. Drive along this road for a final 2-3 miles, past two cabins, and you'll see the trail kiosk on your left. Park on the side of the road.

GPS COORDINATES: 45°01'27.8"N 71°10'47.2"W, 45.024378, -71.179775

5 Fourth Connecticut Lake

FOURTH CONNECTICUT LAKE PRESERVE, PITTSBURG

Hike along the U.S.-Canadian border to reach the heavenly Fourth Connecticut Lake, origin of the Connecticut River.

DISTANCE: 2.1 miles round-trip

DURATION: 2 hours

ELEVATION CHANGE: 387 feet

EFFORT: Moderate

TRAIL: Dirt path, rocks, wooden bridges, water crossings via stones

USERS: Hikers

SEASON: June–October

MAPS: The Nature Conservancy website

CONTACT: The Nature Conservancy, 603/224-5853, www.nature.org

The Connecticut River is a mighty waterway that cuts through some of rural New England's most popular destinations, but it begins at a humble little lake in the forests at the very top of New Hampshire. Hikers who are willing to go the distance can get to Fourth Connecticut Lake by taking a unique, little-known trail that traipses along the U.S.-Canada border. The lake is known to attract moose, black bears, and other amazing wildlife. The Nature Conservancy suggests bringing along your passport, but odds are you won't encounter a soul here.

START THE HIKE

▸ MILE 0–0.5: Nature Conservancy Sign to Fourth Connecticut Lake Trail

Begin your hike in the designated parking area by the large Nature Conservancy sign. Approach the border station and look for the signs marked "Hiking Trail." You'll follow these signs along a chain-link fence before veering left at a set of dual U.S. and Canadian flags to cross the road via a crosswalk. Continue up a small grassy knoll to the official wooden trailhead sign for **Fourth Connecticut Lake Trail.** Pick up the dirt trail to the right of this sign and enter a thick stretch of tallgrass and ferns as the trail heads west through a clear-cut that marks the border between the United States and Canada.

▸ MILE 0.5–0.8: Fourth Connecticut Lake Trail to Fourth Connecticut Lake

Begin climbing at a steep grade up some smooth rocks that can be slippery even in dry conditions. As the grade becomes somewhat more gradual, look down for small metal discs in the ground that mark the split between the two countries. After bypassing some muddier sections, climb a final steep pitch before reaching a height of land at 0.6 mile, where the trail transitions from dirt to pure granite. At 0.7 mile, you'll reach a wooden sign for **Fourth Connecticut Lake;** veer left into the thick spruce and white

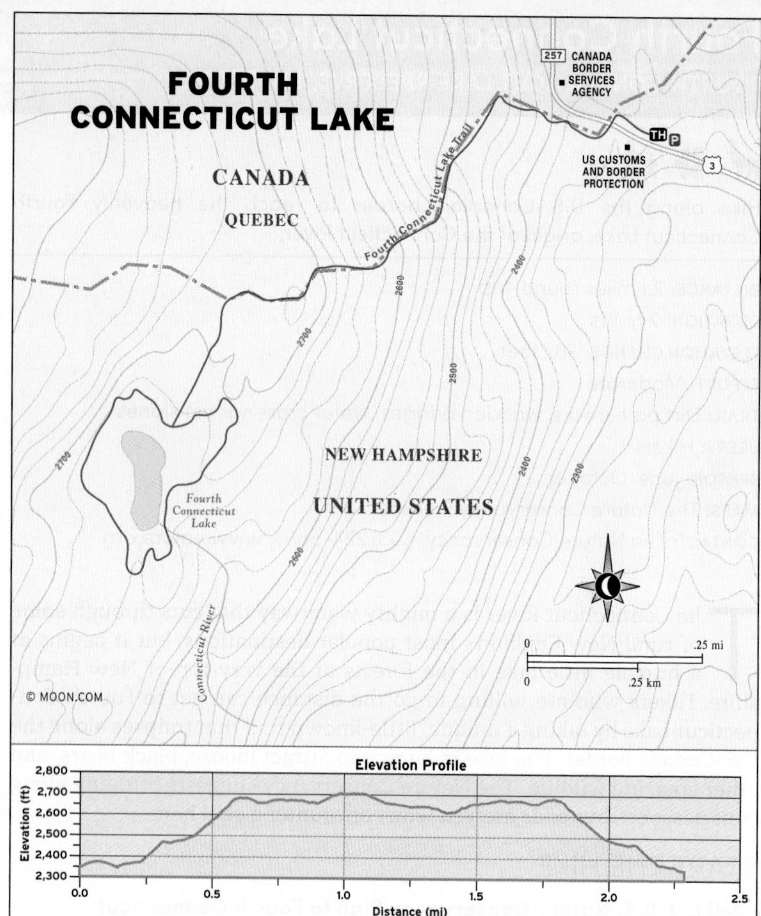

birch forest and cross a few wooden bog bridges as the trail gently descends into the preserve area. Look for green diamond-shaped signs bearing yellow arrows on the trees. Watch for flashes of blue water through the trees ahead.

▸ MILE 0.8–1.2: Fourth Connecticut Lake to Lake Overlook

At 0.8 mile, you'll arrive at a scenic **overlook** on the northern banks of Fourth Connecticut Lake. From the overlook, the trail loops around the lake. Turn right at the overlook and notice how the trail begins to resemble a dirt ribbon weaving in and out of the mossy forest, never straying too far from the water. After crossing several aging bog bridges at 1 mile, enjoy the finest lake views yet on your left. Watch your footing beyond here as the trail becomes bumpier and more grown-in. Make your way through a marshier area for 0.2 mile.

▸ MILE 1.2–2.1: Lake Overlook to Connecticut River

At 1.2 miles, arrive at a stream that flows from the lake down into the nearby woods. This little trickle of water is nothing less than the start of the Connecticut River, which flows 400 miles south to Long Island! Cross the stream on stones and continue along the trail as it becomes rockier and

▲ ALONG THE MOSSY SHORES OF THE LAKE

curves away from the lake. After briefly meandering up and down through the woods, you'll reach the lake overlook point again at 1.4 miles. Turn right, backtrack to the clear-cut marking the borders, and then make a right turn to retrace your steps back to the border station and complete the hike at 2.1 miles.

DIRECTIONS

From Concord, drive north along I-93 N through Franconia Notch and then take Exit 35 for US-3 N toward Lancaster/Twin Mountain. Continue north along US-3 N to the town of Colebrook and then turn right onto NH-145 N. Drive north for 13 miles to the road's terminus and then turn right onto US-3 N again. Take this road through the town of Pittsburg, past the larger Connecticut Lakes, and into the northern foothills of the area until the road finishes at the U.S.-Canada border station. Park by the big Nature Conservancy sign.

GPS COORDINATES: 45°15'10.0"N 71°12'17.4"W, 45.252772, -71.204845

NEARBY CAMPGROUNDS

NAME	LOCATION	FACILITIES	SEASON	FEE
Percy Lodge and Campground	338 Percy Rd., Stark, NH 03582	Tent sites, RV sites, hotel rooms, toilets, showers, potable water, camp store, Wi-Fi	late May-October	$20-125
603/636-1662				
Clear Stream Campground	33 Chabot Rd., Errol, NH 03579	Tent sites, RV sites, toilets, showers, potable water	late May-mid-September	$28-35
603/482-3888, www.clearstreamcampground.com				
Notch View Resort Inn & Campground	54 Forbes Hill Rd., Colebrook, NH 03576	Tent sites, RV sites, RV rentals, hotel rooms, toilets, showers, potable water, laundry, swimming pool, camp store, Wi-Fi	year-round	$30-50
603/237-4237, www.notchviewresort.com				
Mountain View Cabins & Campground	2787 N Main St., Pittsburg, NH 03592	Tent sites, RV sites, cabins, toilets, showers, potable water, laundry, camp store, restaurant, Wi-Fi	year-round	$25-170
603/538-6305, www.mountainviewcabinsandcampground.com				
Ramblewood Cabins & Campground	Daniel Webster Hwy., Pittsburg, NH 03592	Tent sites, lean-tos, RV sites, cabins, toilets, showers, potable water, laundry, camp store, Wi-Fi	year-round	$25-250
603/538-6948, www.ramblewoodcabins.com				
Lake Francis State Park	439 River Rd., Pittsburg, NH 03592	Tent sites, RV sites, toilets, showers, potable water, camp store	late May-early October	$25-35
603/538-6965, www.nhstateparks.org				
Deer Mountain Campground	5309 North Main St., Pittsburg, NH 03592	Tent sites, toilets, potable water	mid-May-early November	$23
603/538-6965, www.nhstateparks.org				

WINNIPESAUKEE AND THE LAKES DISTRICT

Most of us have heard illustrious tales of summers on Lake Winnipesaukee, but in New Hampshire, the famed lake is just the start. The Lakes District is home to many such bodies of water, all of which provide the type of aquatic bliss that's worth traveling for. Just as essential are the local trails that can make a swim more refreshing. In the Lakes District, you can climb a mountain without completely wearing out your calves, glimpse wild animals and birds without disappearing into wild territory, and enjoy old-school cooking and shopping in towns such as Tamworth and Sandwich. And if your heart desires, you can even rent a boat and do your best *Miami Vice* impression on New Hampshire waters.

▲ the vista from West Rattlesnake

▲ the exposed face of lower Welch

1 **Belknap Mountain**
DISTANCE: 2.5 miles round-trip
DURATION: 1.5 hours
EFFORT: Moderate

2 **Lake Solitude**
DISTANCE: 3.8 miles round-trip
DURATION: 2 hours
EFFORT: Easy/moderate

3 **Devil's Den Mountain**
DISTANCE: 5.4 miles round-trip
DURATION: 2.5 hours
EFFORT: Easy/moderate

4 **West and East Rattlesnake**
DISTANCE: 3.8 miles round-trip
DURATION: 2 hours
EFFORT: Easy/moderate

5 **Markus Wildlife Sanctuary**
DISTANCE: 2 miles round-trip
DURATION: 1 hour
EFFORT: Easy

6 **Welch and Dickey**
DISTANCE: 4.2 miles round-trip
DURATION: 3 hours
EFFORT: Moderate/strenuous

7 **Welton Falls**
DISTANCE: 2.6 miles round-trip
DURATION: 2 hours
EFFORT: Easy

8 **Mount Cardigan**
DISTANCE: 3.4 miles round-trip
DURATION: 3 hours
EFFORT: Moderate/strenuous

▲ LAKE SOLITUDE, TUCKED JUST BENEATH THE SUMMIT OF MOUNT SUNAPEE

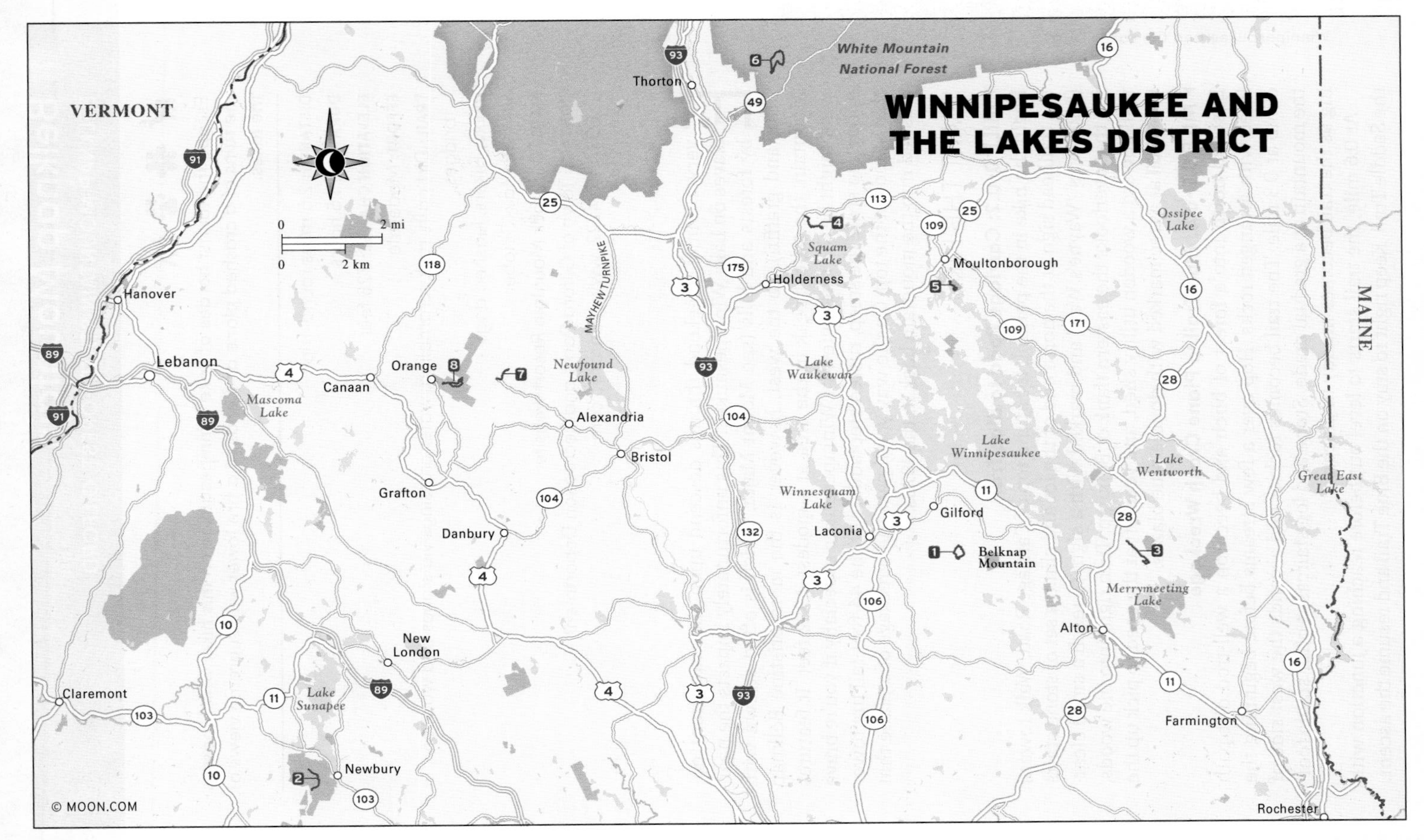
WINNIPESAUKEE AND THE LAKES DISTRICT
VERMONT
MAINE
White Mountain National Forest
Thorton
Hanover
Lebanon
Canaan
Orange
Grafton
Danbury
Alexandria
Bristol
Newfound Lake
MAYHEW TURNPIKE
Mascoma Lake
Squam Lake
Holderness
Moultonborough
Lake Waukewan
Lake Winnipesaukee
Winnesquam Lake
Laconia
Gilford
Belknap Mountain
Ossipee Lake
Lake Wentworth
Merrymeeting Lake
Alton
Farmington
Rochester
Great East Lake
New London
Lake Sunapee
Newbury
Claremont
0
2 mi
0
2 km
© MOON.COM

1 Belknap Mountain

BELKNAP MOUNTAIN STATE FOREST, GILFORD

Escape the tourist hordes of Lake Winnipesaukee on this hike, which passes the ruins of a crashed plane and ends at a fire tower with supreme views of the lakes.

DISTANCE: 2.5 miles round-trip

DURATION: 1.5 hours

ELEVATION CHANGE: 726 feet

EFFORT: Moderate

TRAIL: Dirt path, rock scrambling, water crossings via stones and wooden bridges

USERS: Hikers, leashed dogs

SEASON: May-October

MAPS: Gunstock Mountain Resort website

CONTACT: Town of Gilford Parks and Recreation Department, 603/527-4722, www.gilfordrec.com

Every summer, weekend throngs descend upon the waterfront enclaves on Lake Winnipesaukee. This unfortunately impacts the nearby forests and hills (see Mount Major, which is often strewn with litter and graffiti). To the west, however, is the more pristine Belknap Mountain, the tallest peak in the area at a modest 2,382 feet. It features what might be the finest view of Winnipesaukee especially if you're brave enough to scale the steep, rusted stepladders of the 44-foot-tall fire tower that stands at the top. On the way you'll pass the wreckage of a plane that crashed into the mountain back in the 1970s.

START THE HIKE

▸ MILE 0-0.2: Carriage Road to Blue Trail

Begin the hike in the parking lot at the top of Carriage Road. Walk toward the trailhead sign at the north end of the lot and climb a set of stone stairs (known as "Wayne's Way" and marked with a sign) to reach a small clearing that overlooks the eastern flank of Belknap. Turn right into the woods, walk toward a wooden utility shed, and veer left at the shed to pick up the **Blue Trail** at a tree marked with double blue blazes.

▸ MILE 0.2-0.8: Blue Trail to Plane Crash Wreckage

Descend north into a forest of birch and beech on a well-trod dirt path lined with arranged rocks. Hop over a few streams before beginning the climb at 0.3 mile. The trail becomes rockier and ascends the west side of the mountain at a gradual grade. Stone and log staircases offer stable footing as the trail becomes muddy in places.

At 0.6 mile, the trail starts to level out before reaching a junction with the Saddle Trail. Keep right to stay on the Blue Trail and resume the ascent.

▲ FIRE TOWER ON BELKNAP MOUNTAIN

Climb a steeper set of stone stairs and emerge into a sloped, sunny meadow with tiny white starflowers. The trees start to transition from birch to pine around here, and blue cairns begin to appear on the trail. Around 0.8 mile, look for a piece of colored tape tied to a tree branch on the left. You can find the plane crash **wreckage** just off the trail from this point—if you don't mind a little bushwhacking.

▸ MILE 0.8-1.1: Plane Crash Wreckage to Belknap Mountain Summit
Continue northeast for 0.3 mile into an airier boreal forest before arriving at the summit of **Belknap Mountain** at 1.1 miles.

A fire tower looms at the summit, and while it's safe to climb—and the glorious view of the Lakes District from the top is worth it—be aware that the staircases are quite steep, and the railings are low. Exercise caution on the up-and-down.

▸ MILE 1.1-1.3: Belknap Mountain Summit to Yellow/White Trail
To begin the return journey, pick up the **Yellow/White Trail** (marked with yellow and white blazes, naturally) on the east side of the tower and walk along the power lines that run across the ridge of Belknap before descending into a mossier swath of forest.

▸ MILE 1.3-1.6: Yellow/White Trail to White Trail
At 1.3 miles, reach a rocky clearing and turn right onto the **White Trail** as it heads south across an exposed ridge with cairns. Follow white blazes down into the woods and mind your footing on the numerous slippery rock slabs.

Descend a ramp-like stone ledge at around 1.6 miles with a killer view of Winnipesaukee, then continue south down a larger rock face.

▸ MILE 2.0-2.5: White Trail to Three-Way Junction and Carriage Road
At 2.0 miles, you'll reach a three-way junction; take a right and enjoy the final stretch of the trail as it winds through deciduous beech and delivers you back to the carriage road at 2.3 miles. Turn right and walk up the carriage road to the parking lot to finish the loop at roughly 2.5 miles.

DIRECTIONS

From Concord, drive north on NH-106 N for 20 miles. Merge right onto the ramp for NH-11 E/US-3 N/Laconia-Gilford Bypass and then take the NH-11A

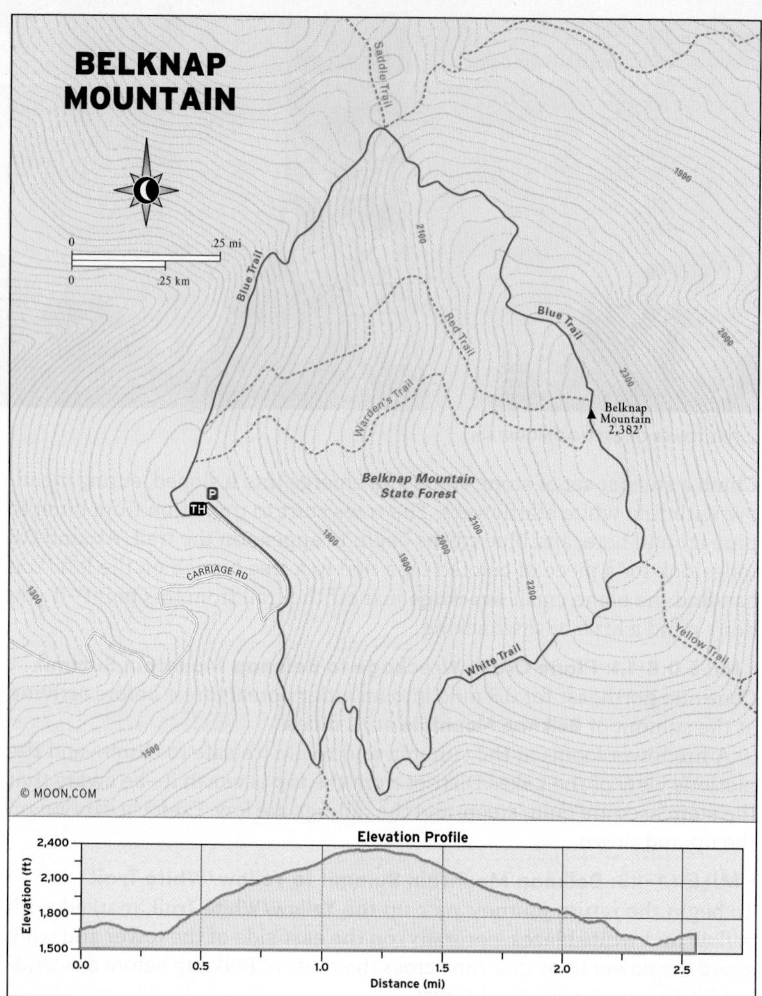

exit toward Gilford/Laconia. Turn right onto NH-11A and continue northwest for just over a mile before making a right onto Hoyt Road. Drive south for another 2 miles as Hoyt Road merges with Belknap Mountain Road. Make a final left onto Carriage Road and watch your speed as the road transitions to dirt, enters the forest, and climbs the eastern slope of Belknap. The road is narrow, winding, and steep, with several bridge crossings. As you reach the end of Carriage Road, the trail parking lot will be on your left.

GPS COORDINATES: 43°30'55.8"N 71°22'36.9"W, 43.515503, -71.376929

BEST NEARBY BITES

If you've never dined on blackened salmon salad or chicken Florentine inside a regal 19th-century barn, give it a try at **Ellacoya Barn & Grille** (2667 Lake Shore Rd., Gilford, 603/293-8700, www.barnandgrille.com, 11:30am-9pm daily).

2 Lake Solitude

MOUNT SUNAPEE STATE PARK, NEWBURY

Hike through the secluded woods on the north slopes of Mount Sunapee to a beautiful lake that lies just below the summit.

DISTANCE: 3.8 miles round-trip

DURATION: 2 hours

ELEVATION CHANGE: 948 feet

EFFORT: Easy/moderate

TRAIL: Dirt path, rocks, wooden bog bridges

USERS: Hikers, leashed dogs

SEASON: June-October

FEES/PASSES: $5 day-use fee per adult

MAPS: Mount Sunapee Resort website

CONTACT: Mount Sunapee State Park, 603/763-5561, www.nhstateparks.org

START THE HIKE

MILE 0-0.7: Park Road to Rim Trail

Begin the hike at the end of Park Road in a clearing festooned with pieces of old ski lift machinery. Pick up the **Rim Trail** at the trail sign on the edge of the forest and follow yellow blazes into the woods heading southeast. Rock-hop across **Johnson Brook** and climb a series of gently graded stone steps through the beech trees. The stone stairs are older and some of them might be a bit loose. Listen to the chattering of red squirrels and gray jays in the branches overhead.

MILE 0.7-1.0: Rim Trail to Newbury Trail

The trail levels off a bit before reaching a junction with Newbury Trail at 0.8 mile; make a right onto **Newbury Trail** (marked by orange blazes) and climb south up a steep and eroded stretch that quickly delivers you to an exposed rocky ledge called **Eagle's Nest Outlook,** which has a stunning view out to Lake Sunapee. From here, the trail ascends the north side of Sunapee for a little while before flattening at roughly 1 mile and peacefully weaving through an unusually lush ridge forest that's bursting with ferns and wildflowers.

MILE 1.0-1.8: Newbury Trail to Jack and June Junction

The footing gets rockier and rootier as the trail goes up and down some knolls before reaching the four-way "Jack and June Junction" at 1.8 miles. Here, you can choose between a waterside view of the lake or an overhead vista.

MILE 1.8-1.9: Jack and June Junction to Lake Solitude

For the former, turn left onto the Mount Sunapee Greenway South and descend a rocky trail for 0.1 mile that cuts through deciduous woods before arriving quite suddenly on the northern banks of **Lake Solitude.** Stop here

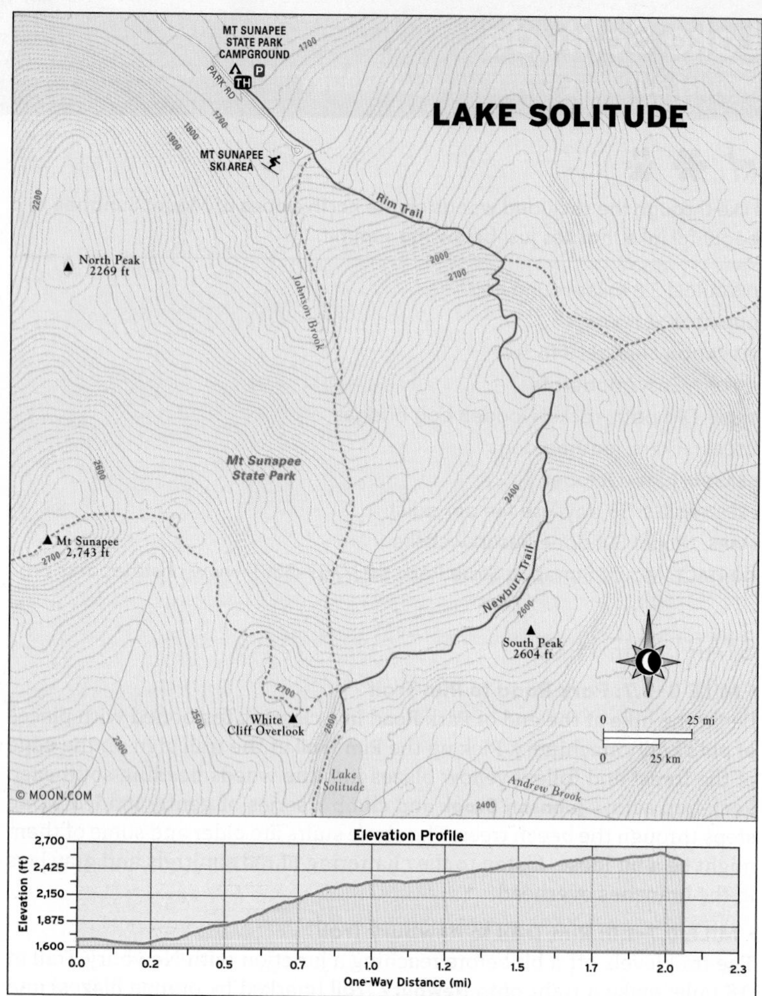

or continue south on the trail for a little while as it follows the western shore of the lake.

▸ MILE 1.9–3.8: Lake Solitude to White Cliff Overlook

To reach the overhead vista, backtrack to Jack and June Junction and take the Mount Sunapee Greenway North up a comparably rocky trail for 0.2 to reach **White Cliff Overlook**—a shelf-like ledge perched just above the lake. If you still have some gas in the tank, you can continue up the Mount Sunapee Greenway North to the summit of Mount Sunapee itself, roughly 0.8 mile up the trail. Otherwise, return the way you came.

DIRECTIONS

From Concord, take I-93 S briefly and merge onto I-89 N toward Lebanon/White River Junction VT. Drive northeast for 20 miles and then take Exit 9 for NH-103 toward Warner/Bradford. Follow this local highway for another 16 miles to reach the entrance to Mount Sunapee Resort. Upon reaching the entrance, turn left onto NH-103B S and continue straight onto Sunapee

▲ THE EAGLE'S NEST OUTLOOK

Road to enter the resort itself. Shortly ahead, make a left turn onto Park Road, a rugged dirt road that climbs the north slopes of the mountain. Follow the road for about a mile and you'll reach the entrance to Mount Sunapee State Park Campground on your left. Park on the right side of the road here, across from the campground entrance. Continue on foot beyond the gate to the end of Park Road.

GPS COORDINATES: 43°19'27.4"N 72°03'53.2"W, 43.324290, -72.064774

BEST NEARBY BITES

Treat yourself to a scenic Lake Sunapee dinner cruise by stepping aboard the **MV Kearsarge Restaurant Ship** (1 Lake Ave., Sunapee, 603/938-6465, www.sunapeecruises.com, 6:30pm-8:30pm Tues.-Sun.), or stick to the land and indulge in some peppery beef brisket and baby back ribs at **Wildwood Smokehouse** (45 Main St., Sunapee, 603/763-11787, www.wildwoodsmokehousebbq.com, 4pm-9pm Tues.-Sat.).

3 Devil's Den Mountain

PRIVATE LAND, ALTON

This spooky, little-known hike visits a desolate mountaintop with a cave that's rumored to be haunted by a monstrous presence.

BEST: New England oddities
DISTANCE: 5.4 miles round-trip
DURATION: 2.5 hours
ELEVATION CHANGE: 478 feet
EFFORT: Easy/Moderate
TRAIL: Dirt path, rocks
USERS: Hikers
SEASON: May-October
MAPS: USGS Strafford County Topo Map
CONTACT: LandVest Inc., 603/227-2414, www.landvest.com

Hidden in a relatively quiet corner of the Lakes District and rising 1,050 feet above sea level, the craggy Devil's Den Mountain offers a killer view of Lake Winnipesaukee—but its moody atmosphere is what makes it unique. The trail to the mountaintop, while easy to follow, is mostly unmarked, and the mountain's most infamous feature—a slit cave from which locals have reported hearing ferocious hissing sounds—requires a bit of hunting around the summit area.

START THE HIKE

▸ MILE 0-1.3: Dirt Access Road to T-Intersection

Begin your hike by picking up the dirt access road just beyond the gate and heading southeast into the forest. This road will be your trail for most of the hike. Walk along the road as it cuts southeast through a forest of pine, birches, and stone walls. At 0.3 mile, take a left at the fork and continue onward as the road ascends at a very gentle grade. The pine trees here are green and numerous enough to make you feel like you've stepped into an episode of Twin Peaks.

As the road becomes sandier, you can often glimpse fresh animal tracks cutting across the ground. At 0.7 mile, keep straight at the split and hike past a clearing full of young trees. Look out for a partial glimpse of the Devil's Den Mountain summit just ahead, around 0.9 mile. Continue hiking southeast for another 0.4 mile before reaching a T-intersection at 1.3 miles; take a left and start to climb the northwest haunch of Devil's Den Mountain. Look to your right and you'll glimpse a series of granite cliffs and boulders in the woods. This is where the infamous haunted cave is located.

▸ MILE1.3-1.8: T-Intersection to Devil's Den Mountain Cave

To find the **cave,** keep an eye peeled for a rough-hewn and slightly overgrown side path that appears on your right at roughly 1.7 miles (marked

▲ THE SUMMIT OF DEVIL'S DEN MOUNTAIN

with felled tree trunks). Continue for roughly 0.1 mile to reach the cliffs, then look for a red arrow spray-painted on a jumble of boulders. Scramble up the jumble and you'll find the opening to the cave on a ledge that overlooks the forest. The interior of the cave is damp and tight—and then there are the accounts of hissing and a large shadow moving on the walls. So, proceed at your own risk.

▸ MILE 1.8–2.7: Devil's Den Mountain Cave to Devil's Den Mountain Summit

Backtrack to the road and continue southeast for another 0.3 mile before taking a right and climbing the mountain at a steeper grade. At. 2.3 miles, you'll reach the height of land; pick up a well-tread side trail into the woods here and look for red blazes on the trees henceforth. The rocky "tower" of the summit looms ahead as the trail cuts around the south side of the summit on a series of ledges before curving to the right. Ascend a brief series of granite slabs and arrive at the top of Devil's Den Mountain at 2.7 miles. Enjoy the lake views before returning the way you came.

DIRECTIONS

From Boston, take I-93 N to Exit 37A and merge onto I-95 N toward Peabody. Drive east for 8 miles and keep right at the fork to stay on I-95 N toward Portsmouth, New Hampshire. Continue north into New Hampshire and then take Exit 4 to merge onto NH-16 N toward the White Mountains.

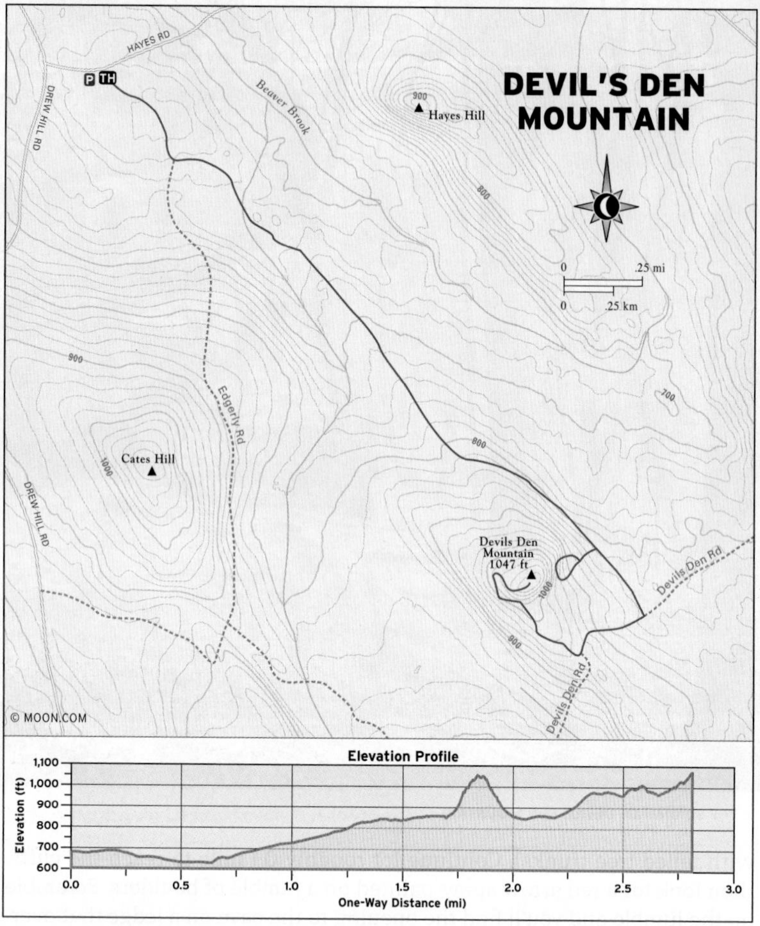

DEVIL'S DEN MOUNTAIN

© MOON.COM

Drive along NH-16 N for roughly 16 miles before taking Exit 15 for NH-11 W toward Farmington/Alton. Keep driving northwest until you reach downtown Alton and then merge right onto NH-28 N. Drive north on NH-28 N for a few minutes, turn right onto Drew Hill Road, and then turn left onto Hayes Road. The gated road for Devil's Den Mountain will be on your immediate right. Open the gate and park in any of the small clearings on either side of the road just after the gate. Do not park on the road itself—it must remain clear for emergency vehicles.

GPS COORDINATES: 43°31'45.9"N 71°11'38.8"W, 43.529415, -71.194104

BEST NEARBY BREWS

Try a farmhouse ale or Belgian-style tripel at **Lone Wolfe Brewing Company** (36 Mill St., Wolfeboro, 603/515-1273, www.thelonewolfe.com, noon-9pm Tues.-Thurs., 11am-11pm Fri.-Sat., noon-5pm Sun.).

West and East Rattlesnake

ARMSTRONG NATURAL AREA, HOLDERNESS

This family-friendly mountain hike visits two neighboring peaks with views of Squam Lake that would make Ansel Adams weep.

DISTANCE: 3.8 miles round-trip
DURATION: 2 hours
ELEVATION CHANGE: 609 feet
EFFORT: Easy/moderate
TRAIL: Dirt path, rocks
USERS: Hikers, leashed dogs
SEASON: June-October
FEES/PASSES: None
MAPS: New Hampshire Division of Forests and Lands website
CONTACT: New Hampshire Natural Heritage Bureau, 603/271-2215, www.nhdfl.org

Rising from the northern shores of Squam Lake, the modest West and East Rattlesnake Mountains form a popular destination for families with small children and couples making proposals. A gentle ascent up West Rattlesnake leads to a vast, heavily visited lookout ledge with one of the most awe-inducing panoramic lake views anywhere in New England. The neighboring East Rattlesnake is more quiet and rugged, but it features a comparably beautiful vista with a more romantic ambience.

START THE HIKE

▸ MILE 0-0.4: Trail Information Kiosk to Old Bridle Path

Begin the hike in the south end of the parking lot, where you'll see a wooden trail information kiosk. Pick up the **Old Bridle Path** by the kiosk and head southeast up log stairs into the forest. The trail is wide and mostly dirt, with a few odd rocks scattered about. Follow yellow diamond markers on the trees as the trail flows through oaks and beech, gradually curving south and ascending some gently sloped rock slabs near the entrance to a University of New Hampshire revegetation area at 0.4 mile (UNH manages portions of the land here).

▸ MILE 0.4-0.9: Old Bridle Path to West Rattlesnake Lookout

Climbing steadily up the western flank of West Rattlesnake, the trail passes into an airy stretch of red pines, where the terrain alternates between flat stony floor and rock stairs. Glimpses of blue through the trees hint at the nearby lookout. At 0.8 mile, turn left at the junction with the Ramsey Trail to stay on Old Bridle. Ascend a series of exposed and sloping rock faces to reach another set of log stairs that delivers you to the scenic **West Rattlesnake lookout** at 0.9 mile. The rock here has a deep glowing tan that's reminiscent of landscapes in the American Southwest, and the view is spectacular. The lookout ledge is generally a bit crowded.

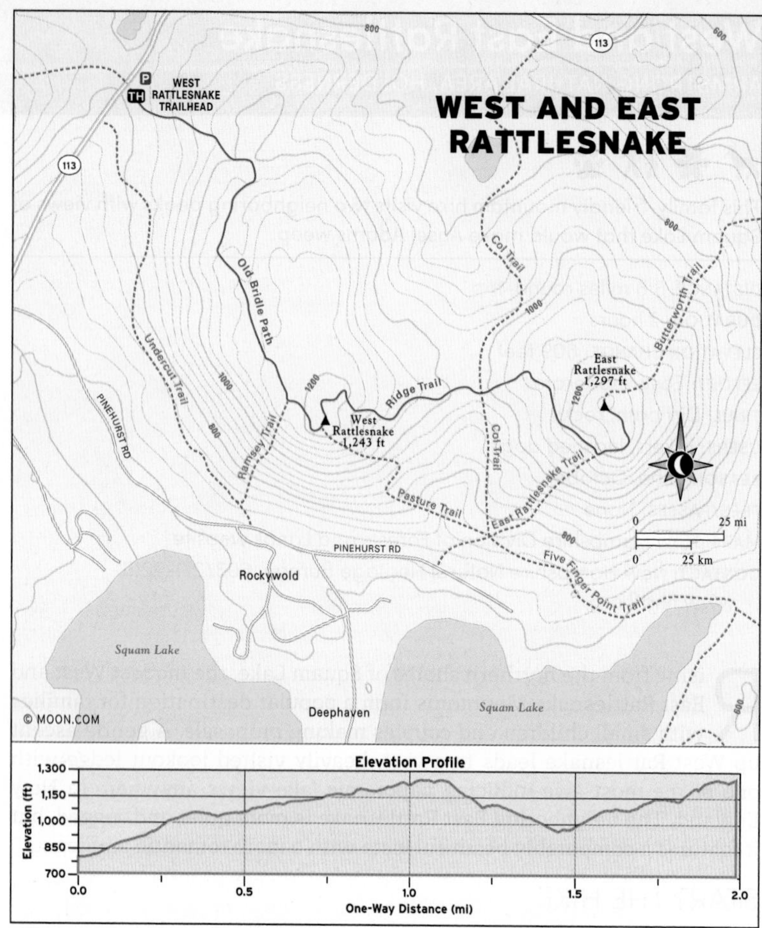

‣ MILE 0.9-1.5: West Rattlesnake Lookout to Ridge Trail

To continue onward to more peaceful surroundings, pick up the **Ridge Trail** by the junction sign on the ledge and head northeast back into the woods, where you'll quickly reach the wooded summit of West Rattlesnake at 1 mile. The narrower dirt trail, marked by green diamond markers, plows through a breezy ridge forest before making a steeper descent into a much darker forest in the col (gap) between the two mountains. A rugged climb out of the col brings you to the junction with the aptly named **Col Trail** at 1.4 miles. Turn left here, and then take an immediate right at a second junction ahead to stay on the Ridge Trail.

‣ MILE 1.5-1.7: Ridge Trail to East Rattlesnake Trail

Climb northeast along the sunnier southern slopes of East Rattlesnake for another 0.3 mile. Watch your step on the countless exposed roots along this stretch of trail, which can become quite eroded during drier summer conditions. At 1.7 miles, you'll reach the junction for **East Rattlesnake Trail;** veer left to take East Rattlesnake and continue along a narrow ledge-like path.

▲ THE VISTA FROM WEST RATTLESNAKE

▸ MILE 1.7–3.8: East Rattlesnake Trail to East Rattlesnake Lookout

Climb steadily up the mountain before reaching the gorgeous **East Rattlesnake lookout** at 1.8 miles. The lookout ledge is perfectly framed by trees that have bent to form a circular opening in the woods. (The intimate scale of this ledge, paired with the beauty of Squam Lake, would make this a fine place to propose.) The wooded summit of East Rattlesnake is 0.1 mile farther up the trail, which continues north from the ledge into the woods. Top off the summit and then return the way you came.

DIRECTIONS

From Concord, drive north on I-93 N for 36 miles and take Exit 24 for US-3/NH-25 toward Ashland/Holderness. At the bottom of the off-ramp, turn right onto NH-25 E/US-3 S and continue along this road for 4 miles. As you enter downtown Holderness, pull a left onto NH-113 and drive northeast and then north for another 5 miles. The Rattlesnake parking lot will be on your right at the top of a hill.

GPS COORDINATES: 43°47'19.8"N 71°32'54.3"W, 43.788831, -71.548407

BEST NEARBY BITES

Fresh Maine lobster, roasted beet and pear salad, and grilled flat iron pork tenderloin are just a few of the gourmet line items you'll find in the lakeside dining room at **Walter's Basin** (859 US-3, Holderness, 603/968-4412, www.waltersbasin.com, 11:30am-9:30pm Sun.-Thurs., 11:30am-10pm Fri.-Sat.).

5 Markus Wildlife Sanctuary

MARKUS WILDLIFE SANCTUARY, MOULTONBOROUGH

This wildlife-rich hike takes hikers through a lush forest, wetlands, and along the shores of Lake Winnipesaukee to visit an active loon nest.

BEST: Spring hikes
DISTANCE: 2 miles round-trip
DURATION: 1 hour
ELEVATION CHANGE: 75 feet
EFFORT: Easy
TRAIL: Dirt path, rocks, wooden bridges
USERS: Hikers
SEASON: May-October
FEES/PASSES: None
MAPS: Loon Preservation Committee website
CONTACT: Loon Preservation Committee, 603/476-5666, www.loon.org/markus-wls.php

Countless mammal, bird, and reptile species reside along the waterfront woodlands in the Lakes District. The Markus Wildlife Sanctuary is a lush preserve that offers hiking trails through the conjoined ecosystems of Lake Winnipesaukee. The "crown jewel" of the sanctuary is the loon nest, a special place that draws native loons each year. Midsummer is the best season to hear their distinct cry.

START THE HIKE

▸ MILE 0-0.2: Loon Center to Forest Loop Trail

Begin your hike in the parking lot by the Loon Center building. Find the Trails sign and walk east, toward a large wooden bridge that spans a brook. Cross the bridge into the woods, pick up the Loon's Nest Trail for a few yards, and then take an immediate left onto the **Forest Trail Loop.** Stroll through a corridor of pine trees marked with red blazes and keep an ear open for birdsong.

▸ MILE 0.2-0.5: Forest Loop Trail to Loon's Nest Trail

Upon reaching the end of the Forest Trail Loop, turn left back onto **Loon's Nest Trail,** following yellow blazes along a smooth dirt path that weaves through the woods along the brook. At 0.3 mile, cross a second wooden footbridge as the trail curves away from the brook. Continue along some sections of wooden boardwalk through a wetter area of the forest and enjoy a few glimpses of Lake Winnipesaukee between the trees. The trail passes through a patch of bogland, becoming rockier with each yard, before entering a darker forest of pine.

▲ THE NARROW ROCK CORRIDOR NEAR THE LOON'S NEST

▸ **MILE 0.5–1.2: Loon's Nest Trail to Loon's Nest Trail Loop and Lookout Point**

After crossing a stream on rocks, you'll reach a trail junction at 0.7 mile; the Loon's Nest Trail diverges in two directions to form a loop. Make a left and note how intensely green the forest becomes. The abundance of moss here feels more like the Pacific Northwest. As the path rolls up and down mildly through the woods, you'll really hear the melodies of native bird species. At 1.1 miles, emerge from the forest by a marsh and hike northwest along the banks of the lake until you reach a bench at 1.2 miles. This is the lookout point for the loon nest.

▸ **MILE 1.2–2.0: Lookout Point to Boardwalk**

Take a seat, watch the reeds of the marsh for rustling, and listen for that unmistakable cry that the White Mountains are famous for. From the lookout, the trail turns back into the woods, passing some muddier terrain before arriving at a massive glacial **rock formation** that hikers must squeeze their way through. The trees around here are often speckled with wild discus-shaped mushrooms that grow on the bark and can become quite large. Continue along the rocky, rooty path for another 0.2 mile before reaching the end of the Loons Nest Trail loop at 1.4 miles. Turn left and backtrack over the boardwalk and along the brook to return to the trailhead and end your hike at 2 miles.

DIRECTIONS

From Concord, drive north on I-93 N for 30 miles and take Exit 23 for NH-104/NH-132 toward Meredith/New Hampton. Turn right onto NH-104 E/

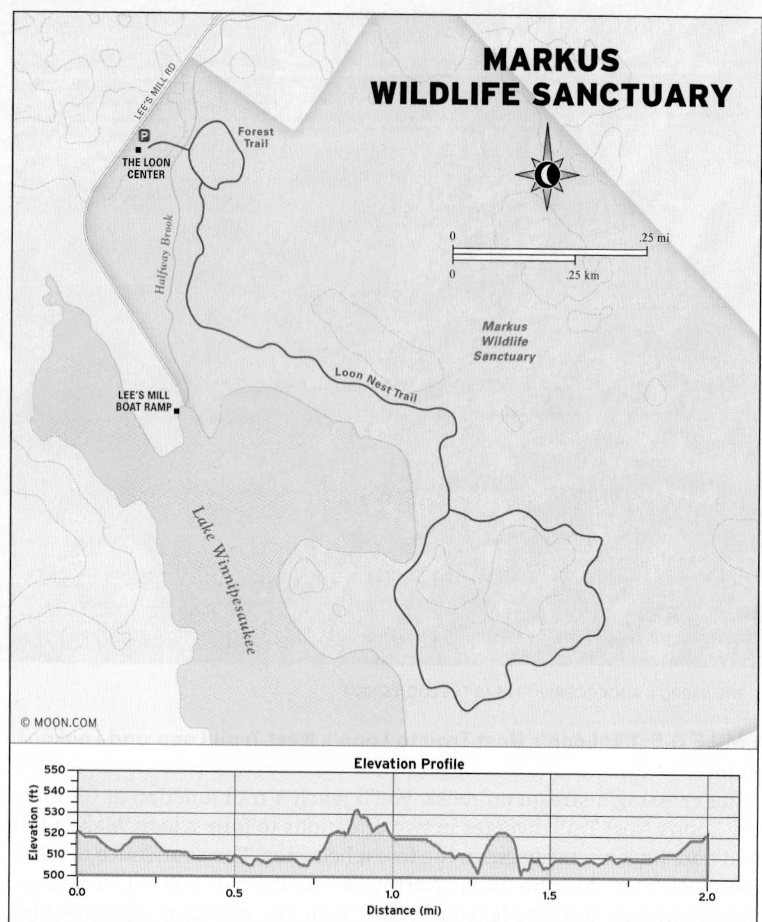

NH-132 N at the bottom of the off-ramp and drive east for 8 miles. Veer right onto US-3 N and then make another right onto NH-25 E/Winnipesaukee Street. Take this road northeast for another 9 miles before turning right onto Blake Road. Follow the road to its terminus and then turn right onto Lee's Mill Road. The Loon Center visitors building and parking area will be on your left shortly after this turn.

GPS COORDINATES: 43°44'15.2"N 71°23'27.1"W, 43.737557, -71.390856

BEST NEARBY BITES

Enjoy fine patio dining with a killer lake view at the nearby Castle in the Clouds historic preservation site's in-"house" restaurant, **The Carriage House** (586 Ossipee Park Rd., Moultonborough, 603/476-5900, www.castleintheclouds.org, 4pm-8:30pm Fri., 10:30am-4pm Sat., 9am-2:30pm Sun.). Be sure to check out the little trails and waterfalls on the property while you're there.

6 Welch and Dickey

WHITE MOUNTAIN NATIONAL FOREST, THORNTON

This two-in-one mountain hike has plenty of broad and exposed slabs that offer sweeping views of the Waterville Valley.

DISTANCE: 4.2 miles round-trip

DURATION: 3 hours

ELEVATION CHANGE: 1,711 feet

EFFORT: Moderate/strenuous

TRAIL: Dirt path, rocks, water crossings on stones

USERS: Hikers, leashed dogs

SEASON: June-October

FEES/PASSES: $5 day-use fee per vehicle

MAPS: White Mountain National Forest website

CONTACT: White Mountain National Forest, 603/536-6100, www.fs.usda.gov/main/whitemountain

Plopped on the northern border of the Lakes District, the conjoined Welch and Dickey Mountains are well known for their steep and mostly treeless rock faces.

START THE HIKE

▸ MILE 0-1.1: Trail Information Kiosk to Welch-Dickey Loop Trail

Begin the hike in the north end of the parking lot by the trail information kiosk. Pick up the stony **Welch-Dickey Loop Trail,** marked by yellow blazes, and veer right at the first fork. The trail kicks off on a root-festooned note, gradually climbing Welch Mountain through a hemlock forest. Cross a brook on rocks at 0.2 mile. As the grade steepens, the spacious path transitions to a rotating series of log and rock stairs that lead to a darker boreal forest with some exposed slabby sections—a small taste of what's ahead.

▸ MILE 1.1-2.0: Welch-Dickey Loop Trail to Welch Mountain Summit

Quite suddenly, at around 1.2 miles, the trail emerges onto a wide and exposed clearing with nice views toward Sachem and Jennings Peaks. The tundra here is protected with felled tree trunks that have been placed as natural barriers. The trail continues north up some sparsely wooded rock slabs on the southern side of Welch before reaching a vaster, steeper, and more exposed rock face at 1.5 miles. Now the climb begins. Scramble your way up the epic rock face and hoist yourself up some boulders to reach the summit of **Welch Mountain** at 2 miles. Look out to see the pinnacle of the larger Dickey Mountain directly ahead.

▸ MILE 2.0-2.4: Welch Mountain Summit to Dickey Mountain Summit

Continue on the trail to descend into the col (gap) between the two mountains. At the bottom of the col, pass by an enormous cairn at 2.1 miles and make a brief foray back into boreal woods before scaling an even steeper and more exposed section of slabby rock faces. At 2.4 miles, step onto the

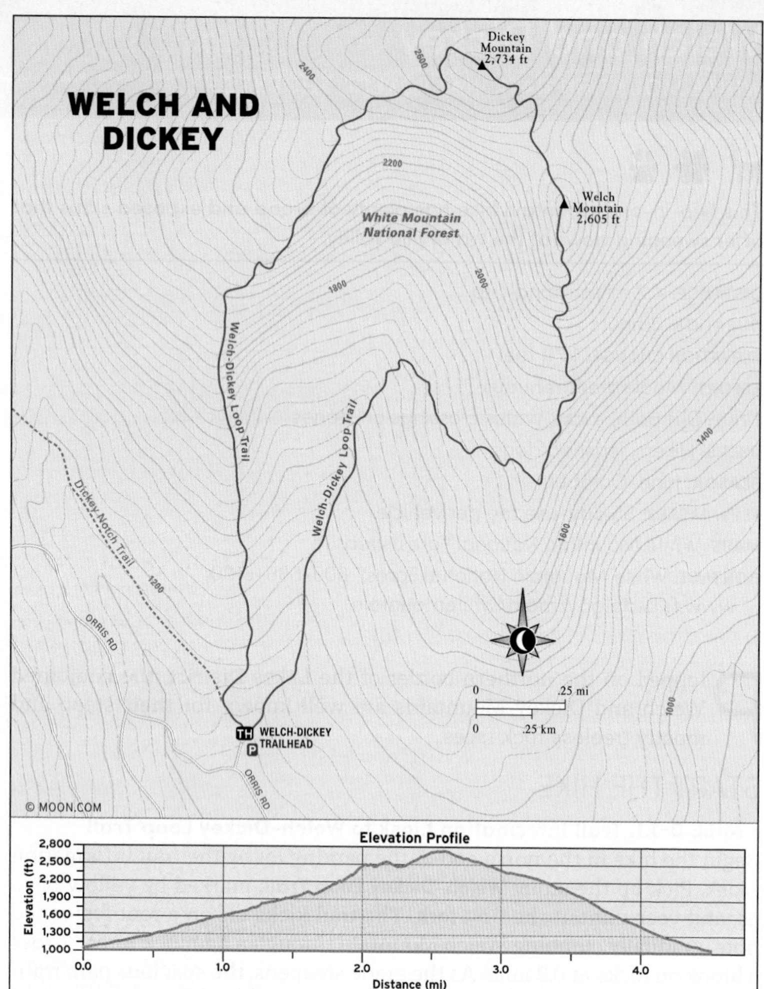

summit of **Dickey Mountain,** where you can savor a view of the deep green Pemigewasset Wilderness to the north.

‣ MILE 2.4–4.2: Dickey Mountain Summit to Dickey Notch Trail

As you begin your descent of the mountain's southern haunch, get ready for the best part yet—a long walk down a barren rock shelf with a sheer drop on one side, and killer views of Welch. This shelf is a great place to appreciate the grandeur of the Whites. The smooth rock here can get slippery in wet weather.

As you near the end of the shelf descent, segue back into deciduous forest at 3.3 miles. The trail narrows considerably and heads south, descending the remainder of Dickey by way of winding rock stairs and a dirt path that's somewhat eroded in places from heavy hiker traffic. The grade is consistently moderate, with only a few steeper pitches. Swing left at the **Dickey Notch Trail** junction at 4.1 miles to stay on the Welch-Dickey Loop Trail and amble through the forest to meet back up with the loop trailhead fork and parking lot at 4.2 miles.

▲ THE EXPOSED FACE OF UPPER WELCH

DIRECTIONS

From Concord, drive north on I-93 N for 48 miles and take Exit 28 toward NH-175/Campton/Waterville Valley. At the end of the off-ramp, turn right onto NH-49 E and continue northeast for another 5 miles before making a left turn onto Upper Mad River Road. Head west along this road for half a mile and pull a final right onto Orris Road. The Welch and Dickey trailhead parking lot is another half mile ahead on your right.

GPS COORDINATES: 43°54'14.8"N 71°35'19.9"W, 43.904116, -71.588864

BEST NEARBY BITES

The Mad River region offers several solid options for a pre-summit breakfast. For a damn fine cup of locally roasted coffee and a decadent egg sandwich, head to **Mad River Coffee Roasters Coffee House** (18 Six Flags Rd., Campton, 603/726-7793, www.madrivercoffeeroasters.com, 6am-4pm Mon.-Thurs., 6am-6pm Fri.-Sun.). If you're craving something more rustic and old-fashioned—say, a tower of blueberry pancakes—check out **Benton's Sugar Shack** (2010 NH-175, Thornton, 603/726-3867, www.bentonssugarshack.com, 8am-2pm Sat.-Sun.).

7 Welton Falls

WELTON FALLS STATE FOREST, ALEXANDRIA

Follow a pretty brook through the forest to a cascade that spills from a rift in the cliffs.

DISTANCE: 2.6 miles round-trip
DURATION: 2 hours
ELEVATION CHANGE: 472 feet
EFFORT: Easy
TRAIL: Dirt path, water crossings via stones
USERS: Hikers, leashed dogs
SEASON: May–October
FEES: None
MAPS: Appalachian Mountain Club Southern New Hampshire Trail Map
CONTACT: Appalachian Mountain Club Cardigan Lodge, 603/744-8011, www.outdoors.org

START THE HIKE

▸ MILE 0-0.3: Shem Valley Road to Manning Trail

Begin the hike from the shoulder of Shem Valley Road; look for the wooden sign for **Lower Manning Trail** and walk east into a hemlock forest past several tent sites and a pair of outhouses. Yellow blazes mark the way as the path crosses a ski trail and descends a series of log stairs into the forest. Rock-hop your way across a chuckling stream and listen for the roar of **Clark Brook** as the air suddenly becomes much cooler and moist.

▸ MILE 0.3-1.0: Manning Trail to Clark Brook

At 0.3 mile, the trail reaches the first viewpoint of the brook and then turns sharply to the north. Make your way down a few more sets of log and stone stairs and enjoy a more agreeable grade as you follow Clark Brook, which flows north alongside the trail. Watch your footing on several more stream crossings—some of them quite muddy—and take a moment to admire the brook from a few more outlook points. After a brief, higher climb above the brook, the trail descends and crosses Clark Brook on rocks at 1 mile. Be sure to exercise caution crossing here, especially during the late spring when snowmelt can cause the water level to rise. Look for a double yellow blaze on a tree on the opposite side of the brook to stay along the trail.

▸ MILE 1.0-1.3: Clark Brook to Welton Falls

Continue hiking north as the trail veers deeper into the woods and starts to scramble up a steeper series of knolls with lots of exposed tree roots. Crest a height of land and mind your footing as the trail suddenly makes a steep, winding descent and arrives at the top of **Welton Falls** at 1.3 miles For a unique perspective of the 30-foot-tall cascade, take the marked viewpoint path onto a ledge that wraps around a large cliff to an **overlook**

▲ A CHUCKLING STREAM ALONG THE TRAIL

where you can view the falls from above. An old cable fence offers some measure of protection from the drop, but it's best not to test its limits.

▸ MILE 1.3-2.6: Welton Falls to Lower Manning Trail

To reach the bottom of the falls, continue down the Lower Manning Trail as it wraps around the rim of a ravine before making a final descent. While descending, you'll get multiple viewpoints of the falls, which pour from a little slot in the cliffs into the ravine that you just bypassed. The actual base of the falls can be tricky to reach—the swimming holes that lie just beyond the base of the falls are far more popular. Return the way you came after taking a refreshing dip.

DIRECTIONS

From Concord, drive north on I-93 N for 30 miles and take Exit 23 for NH-104/NH-132 toward Meredith/New Hampton. Turn left onto NH-104/NH-132 and drive west into Bristol. Continue straight onto Lake Street and then veer left onto Bristol Hill Road. Drive northwest and make another left onto Plumer Hill Road. Swing a left onto Thissell Road, then turn right onto Town Pound Road. Keep right at the fork with Washburn Road and continue heading northwest as Town Pound Road becomes Mount Cardigan Road. After 3 miles, turn right to stay on Mount Cardigan Road, which becomes the dirt Shem Valley Road. (Be careful driving this road in spring—it can get muddy enough to trap low-clearance vehicles.) Continue until you arrive at the Appalachian Mountain Club's Cardigan Lodge. Park on the left side of the road.

GPS COORDINATES: 43°38'56.7"N 71°52'35.5"W, 43.649073, -71.876534

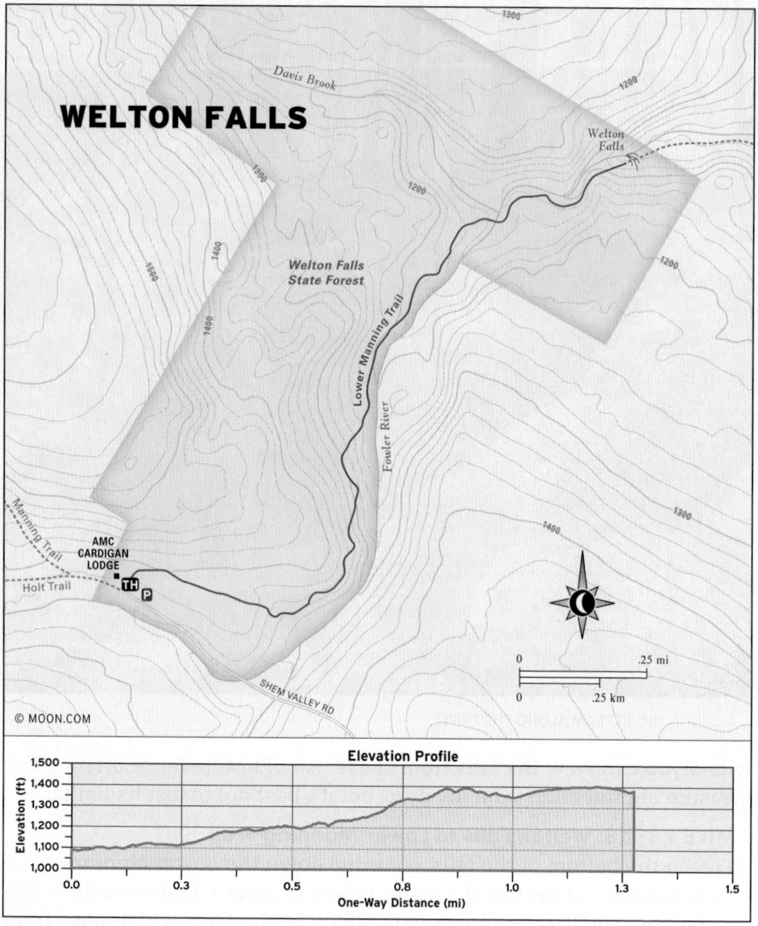

WELTON FALLS

Davis Brook

Welton Falls

Welton Falls State Forest

Lower Manning Trail

Fowler River

Manning Trail

AMC CARDIGAN LODGE

Holt Trail

SHEM VALLEY RD

© MOON.COM

Elevation Profile

Elevation (ft)

One-Way Distance (mi)

BEST NEARBY BREWS

Welton Falls might feel remote, but the relatively nearby town of Bristol offers plenty of sustenance, whether it's a rich rye wheat ale at **Shackett's Brewing Company** (26 Central Sq., Bristol, 603/217-7730, 2pm-8pm Fri.-Sat., noon-5pm Sun.) or a good, hearty country scramble or triple-decker sandwich with fries at the diner-esque **Gina's Place** (15 Pleasant St., Brisol, 603/744-0688, www.ginasplace.biz, 5am-2pm Thurs.-Fri., 5am-noon Sat., 6am-noon Sun., 5am-2pm Mon.).

8 Mount Cardigan

CARDIGAN MOUNTAIN STATE PARK, ORANGE

This tough but short mountain hike is a rock scrambler's paradise—and the beautiful views into Vermont aren't bad either.

DISTANCE: 3.4 miles round-trip

DURATION: 3 hours

ELEVATION CHANGE: 1,191 feet

EFFORT: Moderate/strenuous

TRAIL: Dirt path, rocks, wooden bridges, water crossings on stones

USERS: Hikers, leashed dogs

SEASON: June-October

FEES/PASSES: None

MAPS: Cardigan Mountain State Park website

CONTACT: Cardigan Mountain State Park, 603/227-8745, www.nhstateparks.org

In the 1950s, a devastating forest fire ripped across western New Hampshire. The blaze was so strong that it left some mountains stripped of vegetation at their highest points, including Mount Cardigan. The boreal forest has grown back, but the upper cone of the mountain is still a steep, treeless heap of granite. This makes for an exhilarating climb to the top, with panoramic vistas of the surrounding wilderness and plenty of smooth rock slabs to be scaled.

START THE HIKE

▸ MILE 0-0.4: Mount Cardigan Trail Information Sign to West Ridge Trail

Begin the hike on the east side of the parking lot by the wooden trail information sign. Climb a set of log stairs into the woods and head northwest up **West Ridge Trail,** marked by orange blazes. The trail begins as a well-worn stone path that snakes through the spruce and birch trees on Cardigan's western slopes. Step carefully on the abundant tree roots that squiggle across the trail and look out for some prized plant species such as lady's slippers. Cross a winding stream on rocks before reaching a junction with South Ridge Trail at 0.4 mile; keep left to stay on West Ridge Trail.

▸ MILE 0.4-1.4: West Ridge Trail to Cardigan Mountain Summit Dome

Continuing northwest up the mountain, the trail becomes rockier and steeper as the surrounding woods transition into a more boreal collection of trees. Craggy rocks and boulders around the trail foreshadow what awaits. A brief and more level reprieve from the climb leads to a wooden bridge at 0.8 mile.

From here, the ascent resumes at a steep grade almost immediately and ascends sloped slabs and rock stairs to the Skyland Trail junction at 1 mile. Make a left turn to stay on West Ridge and keep left again at the Ranger

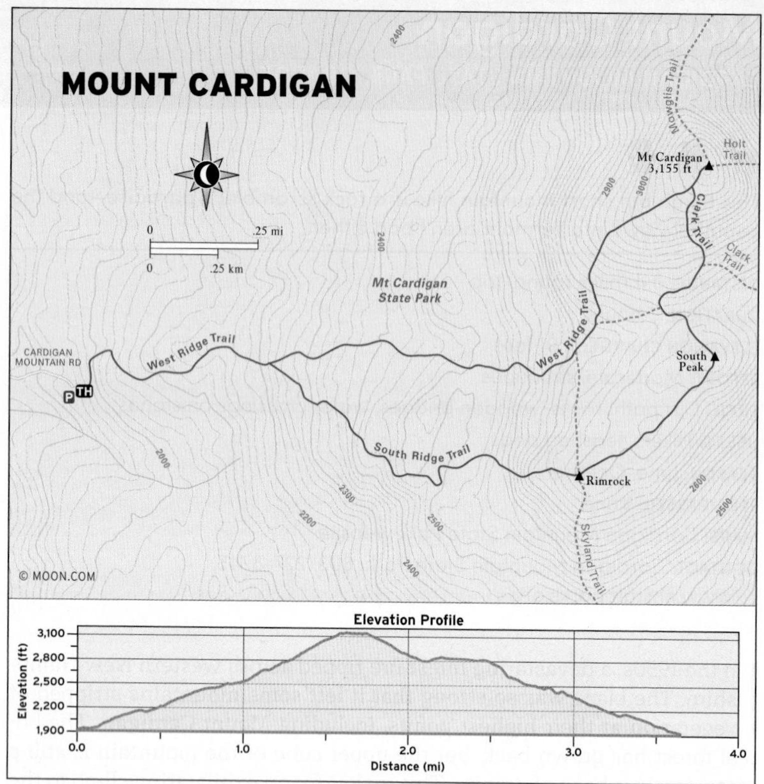

Cabin Trail junction shortly ahead. Then, quite suddenly, emerge from the woods at 1.4 miles onto the massive and exposed summit dome of Cardigan Mountain.

▸ MILE 1.4–1.6: Cardigan Mountain Summit Dome to Cardigan Mountain Summit

The home stretch of the West Ridge Trail is a thrilling climb straight up the barren granite slopes of Cardigan's summit. Follow the cairns and watch out for algae on the rock during wet weather. Be sure to take a look behind you and gaze out toward White River Junction, Mount Killington, and Camel's Hump in nearby Vermont. Climb a final and less sheer pitch of stone before reaching the victory point at 1.6 miles—the summit of **Cardigan Mountain.** Scale the **fire tower** and look to the east to see the mighty Presidentials looming like a gathering of green giants. Just northeast of Cardigan's summit lies **The Firescrew**—a partially wooded ridge where the fire that ravaged Cardigan in the 1800s left a spiral-shaped section of exposed rock amid the trees.

▸ MILE 1.6–2.3: Cardigan Mountain Summit to South Ridge Trail

Once you're ready to head back, pick up the **Clark Trail** by following cairns that head south from the summit to the junction with South Ridge Trail at 1.7 miles. Turn right here to pick up the South Ridge Trail and descend an even steeper side of the exposed dome. (Scrambling on your hands and knees may prove necessary.) Keep left at the fork for the old Cardigan ranger cabin and make another right at the Hurricane Gap Trail junction at

▲ A VIEW OF THE VALLEY FROM MOUNT CARDIGAN'S BARREN SUMMIT CONE

1.9 miles to stay on South Ridge. Hike across a wooded ridge to the South Cardigan summit and then down to the nearby Rimrock peak at 2.3 miles. Here you'll reach a four-way intersection with Skyland Trail; stay straight on South Ridge and continue down into the boreal forest.

▸ **MILE 2.3-3.4: South Ridge Trail to Mount Cardigan Trailhead**

The descent continues through the mossy woods on Cardigan's south face at an increasingly gradual grade. Hike for another 0.5 mile, crossing some streams on rocks and passing through wildflowers and berry bushes. At 3 miles, link back up with the **South Ridge Trail.** Make a left and backtrack to the trailhead to complete your loop at 3.4 miles.

DIRECTIONS

From Concord, drive north on I-93 N for 5 miles and take Exit 17 for US-4 toward US-3/NH-132/Boscawen/Penacook. Merge onto US-4/Hoit Road and drive to the traffic circle, where you'll take the first exit, US-4 W. At the fork ahead, make a slight left to stay on US-4 W and continue for 15 miles. Make a right turn onto US-4 and drive north for another 11 miles. Pull a right onto Turnpike Road and then a second right onto Millbrook Road. Follow this road to its terminus and then turn left onto Burnt Hill Road. Drive north for 2 more miles and make a final right turn onto Cardigan Mountain Road, which leads to the hiker parking lot and trailhead.

GPS COORDINATES: 43°38'38.9"N 71°56'06.4"W, 43.644133, -71.935104

BEST NEARBY BITES

The town of Hanover—less than 30 minutes west of Cardigan—is an edible mecca of dining options. But if you'd rather stay local, you can't go wrong with the old-school diner comforts and made-to-order breakfast counter classics at **Dishin' It Out** (1194 US-4, Canaan, 603/523-9500, 7am-2pm Wed.-Sun.).

NEARBY CAMPGROUNDS

NAME	LOCATION	FACILITIES	SEASON	FEE
AMC Cardigan Campsites	774 Shem Valley Rd., Alexandria, NH 03222	Tent sites, toilets, potable water	year-round	$32-62
603/744-8011, www.outdoors.org				
Mascoma Lake Campground	92 US Route 4A, Lebanon, NH 03766	Tent sites, RV sites, cabins, cottages, tiny houses, toilets, showers, potable water, laundry, camp store, Wi-Fi	early May through mid-October	$30-95
603/448-5076, www.mascomalake.com				
Mount Sunapee State Park	86 Beach Access Rd., Newbury, NH 03255	Tent sites, lean-tos, toilets, potable water	late May through mid-October	$23-29
603/763-5561, www.nhstateparks.org				
Harbor Hill Camping Area	189 NH-25, Meredith, NH 03253	Tent sites, RV sites, cabin tents, cabins, toilets, showers, potable water, laundry, swimming pool, camp store, Wi-Fi	late May through mid-October	$37-72
603/279-6910, www.hhcamp.com				
Baker River Campground & Resort	56 Campground Rd., Rumney, NH 03266	Tent sites, RV sites, toilets, showers, potable water, camp store	mid-May through mid-October	$35-42
603/786-9707, www.bakerrivercampground.com				
Long Island Bridge Campground	29 Long Island Rd., Moultonborough, NH 03254	Tent sites, RV sites, toilets, showers, potable water, laundry, Wi-Fi	mid-May through mid-October	$32-50
603/253-6053, longislandbridgecampgroundnh.com				

NEARBY CAMPGROUNDS (continued)				
NAME	**LOCATION**	**FACILITIES**	**SEASON**	**FEE**
Clearwater Campground	556 NH-104, Meredith, NH 03253	Tent sites, RV sites, toilets, showers, potable water, laundry, camp store, Wi-Fi	mid-May through early October	$31-184
603/279-7761, www.clearwatercampground.com				
Wolfeboro Campground	61 Haines Hill Rd, Wolfeboro, NH 03894	Tent sites, RV sites, toilets, showers, potable water, camp store, Wi-Fi	late May through early October	$32-35
603/569-9881, www.wolfeborocampground.com				

▲ NORTH AMERICAN PORCUPINE

MONADNOCK, MERRIMACK VALLEY, AND THE SEACOAST

Southern New Hampshire is the delta for northern New England's famous mountains, forests, and seacoast. Far from being just a place between Boston and popular summer destinations like the White Mountains and Acadia, the southern reaches of New Hampshire are a taster's menu of adventures for first-time hikers and experienced backcountry trekkers. The numerous suburbs and small cities of the region are surrounded by mile after mile of sunny forests, angular hills, and coastal marshes and beaches that are often singing with visiting birds and native wildlife. In southern New Hampshire, you can saunter past a farm, over hills, and through swamps before arriving at a secluded beach. It's just that easy.

▲ Mount Monadnock

▲ a climactic walk across the jetty near Odiorne Point

1 **Monte Rosa and Mount Monadnock**
DISTANCE: 4.6 miles round-trip
DURATION: 3.5 hours
EFFORT: Strenuous

2 **Odiorne Point State Park**
DISTANCE: 3.3 miles round-trip
DURATION: 2 hours
EFFORT: Easy

3 **Purgatory Falls**
DISTANCE: 5 miles round-trip
DURATION: 2.5 hours
EFFORT: Easy/moderate

4 **Madame Sherri's Forest**
DISTANCE: 4.0 miles round-trip
DURATION: 3 hours
EFFORT: Easy/moderate

5 **Skatutakee Mountain and Thumb Mountain**
DISTANCE: 5.0 miles round-trip
DURATION: 4 hours
EFFORT: Moderate

6 **Sweet Trail**
DISTANCE: 5.6 miles round-trip
DURATION: 2.5 hours
EFFORT: Easy

▲ ODIORNE TIDEPOOLS

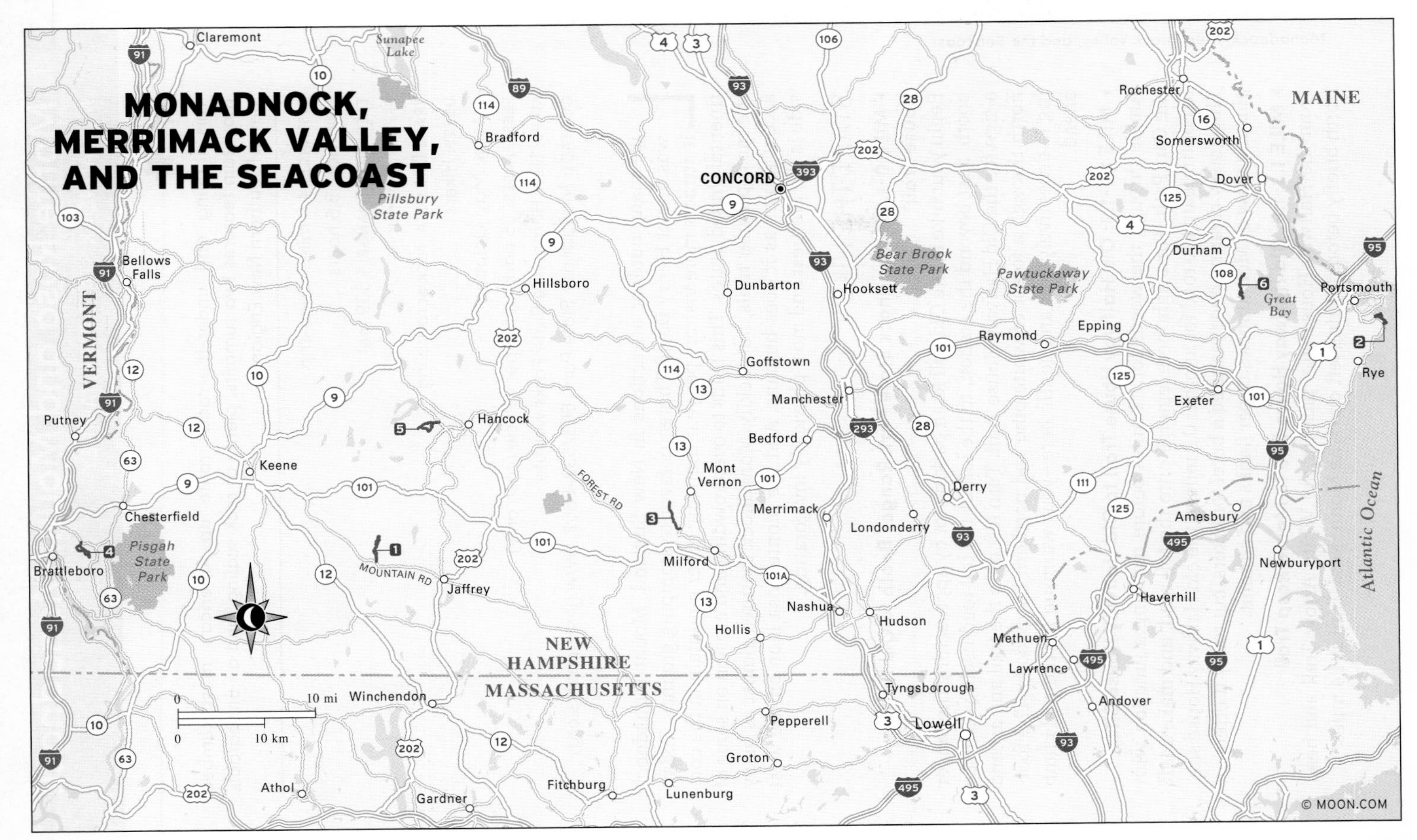
MONADNOCK, MERRIMACK VALLEY, AND THE SEACOAST
VERMONT
NEW HAMPSHIRE
MASSACHUSETTS
MAINE
Atlantic Ocean
CONCORD
Claremont
Sunapee Lake
Bradford
Pillsbury State Park
Bellows Falls
Hillsboro
Dunbarton
Hooksett
Bear Brook State Park
Pawtuckaway State Park
Rochester
Somersworth
Dover
Durham
Great Bay
Portsmouth
Rye
Epping
Raymond
Goffstown
Manchester
Exeter
Putney
Hancock
Bedford
Derry
Keene
Mont Vernon
Merrimack
Londonderry
Amesbury
Chesterfield
FOREST RD
Brattleboro
Pisgah State Park
MOUNTAIN RD
Jaffrey
Milford
Newburyport
Haverhill
Nashua
Hudson
Hollis
Methuen
Lawrence
Tyngsborough
Andover
Winchendon
Pepperell
Lowell
Groton
Athol
Fitchburg
Lunenburg
Gardner
0
10 mi
0
10 km
© MOON.COM

1 Monte Rosa and Mount Monadnock

MONADNOCK STATE PARK, JAFFREY

This thrilling and under-the-radar route up America's most climbed mountain features two summits, plenty of rock scaling, and an unbeatable view of southern New England.

DISTANCE: 4.6 miles round-trip
DURATION: 3.5 hours
ELEVATION CHANGE: 1,509 feet
EFFORT: Strenuous
TRAIL: Dirt path, rock scrambling
USERS: Hikers
SEASON: May-October
FEES/PASSES: $5 parking fee per vehicle (cash only)
MAPS: New Hampshire State Parks website
CONTACT: Monadnock State Park, 603/532-8862, www.nhstateparks.org

Like many outdoor attractions in New England, Mount Monadnock was one of Henry David Thoreau's favorite stomping grounds. Today, it attracts more visitors per year than any other mountain in the continental United States. This leads to overcrowding and erosion on some of the most popular trails, but luckily, Monadnock features almost as many ascent routes as it does humans. And the Monte Rosa loop on the west side is the prettiest and most physically invigorating.

START THE HIKE

▸ MILE 0-1.2: Monadnock State Park Ranger Booth to Old Halfway House Trail

Begin your hike in the Old Toll Road parking lot by approaching the ranger booth. Just beyond the station, to the left of the toll road itself, you'll see a sign for the Old Halfway House Trail. Turn left onto the trail and ascend north through a forest of white pine and northern hardwoods. The footing is deceptively soft and gentle here—your warm-up for the real climb ahead.

▸ MILE 1.2-1.3: Old Halfway House Trail to Old Halfway House Site

Amble through the woods for 1.2 miles before reaching a junction with the Cart Path. Turn right here, emerge onto the toll road, and make a left to continue up the road for another 0.2 mile to the old Halfway House site. This grassy clearing once featured a hotel for hikers, but today it offers an alluring view of Monadnock's upper flanks and summit.

▸ MILE 1.3-1.6: Old Halfway House Site to Monte Rosa Trail

From the Halfway House site, pick up the White Arrow Trail and head north briefly before turning left onto the Monte Rosa Trail at 1.4 miles.

MOUNT MONADNOCK

The trail steepens dramatically here, climbing straight up a torrent of roots, rocks, and loose soil. A few lush groves of wildflowers offer a contrast to the brutishness of the trail.

MILE 1.6–1.8: Monte Rosa Trail to Monte Rosa Summit

Keep climbing for 0.2 mile past the Fairy Spring Cutoff until you reach a rocky height of land at 1.8 miles where the trees recede to shrub-like krummholz. This is the summit of Monte Rosa, marked by a weathervane on a steel post.

MILE 1.8–2.4: Monte Rosa Summit to Mount Monadnock Summit

Once you've had a chance to drink in the vista here, pick up the Great Pasture Trail, make a left turn onto the Smith Summit Trail just a few yards ahead, and climb northeast up the west face of Monadnock. (Look for white S's spray-painted on the rock.) Watch your footing on the well-worn rock slabs as you scramble upward for 0.6 mile before arriving at the summit of Mount Monadnock at 2.4 miles. Odds are you'll have to wait in line to stand at the highest point, but the 360-degree views of Massachusetts, the Green Mountains, and New Hampshire's Lakes District should be more than enough to satisfy.

MILE 2.4–4.6: Mount Monadnock Summit to Old Halfway House Site

To begin your descent, briefly backtrack down the Smith Summit Trail and turn left onto the White Arrow Trail. For the next 0.4 mile, you'll lower yourself down steep, craggy rock faces marked with white arrows before transitioning back into the woods and enjoying easier, less sheer footing. Continue through the forest as you pass the Monte Rosa Trail entrance (keep left here) and arrive back at the Old Halfway House site at 3.3 miles. Depending on your energy level, you can take the Old Halfway House Trail again or descend the final 1.3 miles by staying on the smoother old toll road itself.

DIRECTIONS

From Boston, drive to Cambridge's Alewife Station and pick up MA-2 W/Concord Turnpike. Head northwest along MA-2 for 39 miles and then merge onto MA-140 N in Westminster. Keep heading northwest as MA-140 merges with MA-12 N near Winchendon. Take a sharp right onto US-202 and continue north into New Hampshire. Once you reach the town of Jaffrey, turn left onto NH-124 W and drive west for 5 miles. The Old Toll House parking lot will be on your right.

GPS COORDINATES: 42°50'07.7"N 72°06'53.8"W, 42.835482, -72.114955

MONTE ROSA AND MOUNT MONADNOCK

BEST NEARBY BREWS

Once you've rehydrated after the hike, enjoy a second round of liquid replenishment with a java stout or raspberry sour ale at **Granite Roots Brewing** (244 N Main St., Troy, 603/242-3435, www.graniterootsbrewing.com, 4pm-7pm Thurs.-Fri., noon-6pm Sat.-Sun.).

2 Odiorne Point State Park

ODIORNE POINT STATE PARK, RYE

This seaside stroll across one of New Hampshire's finest coastal conservation areas bypasses sandy and rocky beaches, tidepools, spooky World War II-era bunkers, and a drowned forest.

DISTANCE: 3.3 miles round-trip

DURATION: 2 hours

ELEVATION CHANGE: 74 feet

EFFORT: Easy

TRAIL: Dirt path, sandy beaches, rocks, wooden bridges

USERS: Hikers

SEASON: March-November

PASSES/FEES: $4 adult, $2 child ages 6-11 (late May through October)

MAPS: Odiorne Point Seacoast Science Center website

CONTACT: Odiorne Point State Park, 603/436-7406, www.nhstateparks.org

Roughly 30 minutes north of the casinos and clam shacks that occupy Hampton Beach lies one of the Granite State's premier coastal preserves. Odiorne Point State Park—named for the family who settled the land in the mid-17th century—offers a colorful palette of natural environments that includes white pine and hemlock woods, beaches, and the ruins of ancient forest that has since been swallowed by the sea. The park also contains a marine science center and some abandoned bunkers and artillery batteries that were built to defend the New England coast during World War II.

The trails around the park—while numerous, very short, and interconnected—are not always marked or even named, so it's best to print a map of the park before your visit.

START THE HIKE

▸ MILE 0-0.2: Odiorne Point Boat Launch to Heritage Trail

Begin your hike in the Odiorne Point Boat Launch parking lot at the northwest end of the park. Cross the wooden bridge by the Trails sign and then immediately take a right onto a dirt path that passes through a thicket of briars before reaching the Heritage Trail. Turn right onto the Heritage Trail and hike south through the forest at an even grade.

▸ MILE 0.2-0.6: Heritage Trail to Memorial Point

The Heritage Trail ends at Frost Point Road at 0.3 mile. Turn left onto the road and then make an immediate right onto the Sugar Maple Trail at 0.3 mile; the first bunker will appear on your right. Continue southeast on the Sugar Maple Trail through a sun-splashed corridor of hemlocks until you reach Memorial Point at 0.6 mile. This grassy clearing has grade A ocean views, stone walls, and a monument to New Hampshire's earliest settlers.

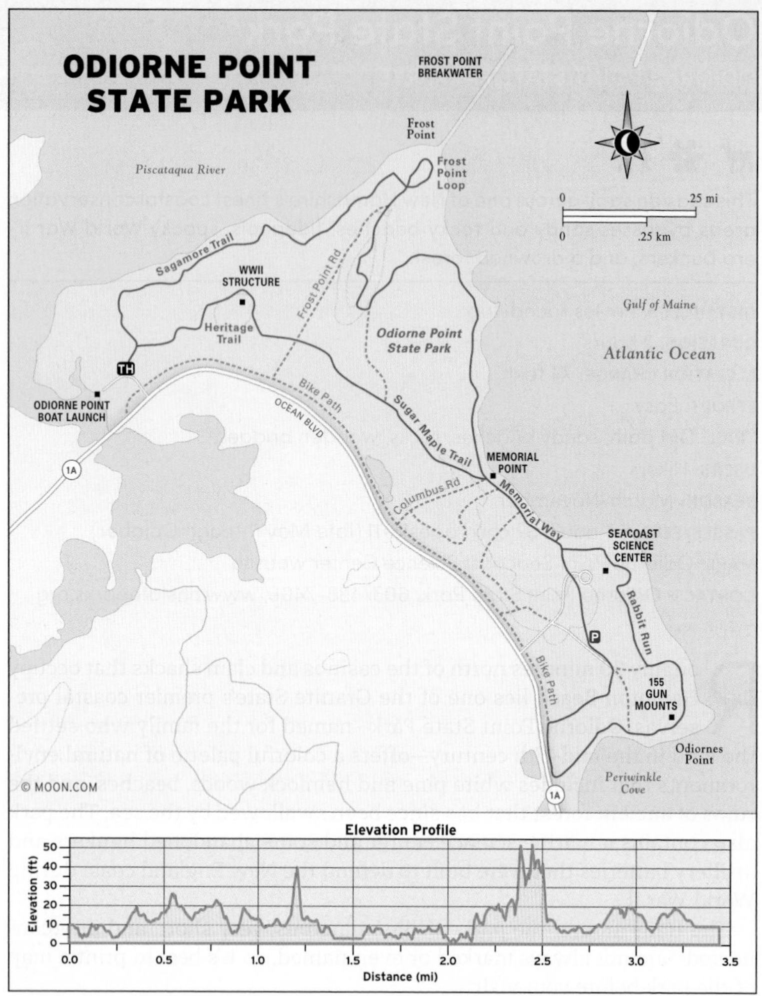

▸ MILE 0.6-1.3: Memorial Point to Periwinkle Cove

Head south along Monument Way for 0.2 mile. Upon reaching the Odiorne Point Seacoast Science Center parking lot, you'll see a hill in front of you with wooden stairs. Climb these stairs to reach another bunker and descend the hill toward the science center. From here, walk south across the parking lot and turn right on the spur trail at its end. This trail will immediately deliver you to the Odiorne Point bike path. Take a left onto the bike path; just a few moments later, you'll reach the beach known as Periwinkle Cove at 1.2 miles.

Veer left to enter the beach. At low tide, you can observe the ancient decaying stumps of trees that once stood tall here—Odiorne Point's "drowned forest."

▸ MILE 1.3-2.7: Periwinkle Cove to Frost Point Outlook

Head northwest along the pebble-strewn beach, cutting back up to the grassier upper shore when the going gets too rocky; maintain your northerly shoreline hike with the ocean on your right. The beach becomes

▲ ODIORNE POINT'S COASTLINE

sandier at 1.7 miles and passes several tidepools and a large meadow where white-tailed deer make regular appearances.

When you reach a beached dock wreck at 2.2 miles, take a sharp left and pick up a narrow sandy path at the top of the beach. Hike west back into the forest briefly before reaching a massive gun battery built into a hillside at 2.5 miles. A small path to the right will take you up the hill to the final bunker. From here, turn right and descend the hill on an eroded, wooded path that delivers you to the grassy, gusty Frost Point outlook at 2.7 miles. A stone jetty extends far into the Atlantic for the intrepid to explore, and the picnic tables at Frost Point make for an ideal lunch spot.

▸ MILE 2.7-3.3: Frost Point Outlook to Sagamore Trail

Once you've had your fill of the maritime vista, finish your hike by picking up the Sagamore Trail from Frost Point. Head west through the white pines along the shoreline for just under half a mile before reaching a salt marsh and arriving back at the bridge from which you began your adventure.

DIRECTIONS

From Boston, head north on I-93 N and continue 9 miles to Exit 37A for I-95 N. Merge onto I-95 N toward Peabody. Keep right at the fork to stay on I-95 N toward Portsmouth, New Hampshire, and continue for another 32 miles. After crossing the New Hampshire border, take Exit 3 for NH-33. Turn right at the bottom of the exit ramp and briefly drive east on NH-33 E/ Greenland Road before taking a right onto Peverly Hill Road. Keep driving east to the traffic circle and continue straight onto NH-1A. After a just over a mile, you'll see the Odiorne Point Boat Launch lot on your left.

GPS COORDINATES: 43°02'55.1"N 70°43'37.9"W, 43.048627, -70.727191

BEST NEARBY BREWS

Local oysters, littleneck clams, and salmon tartare are just a few of the raw-bar treats you'll find at **The Carriage House** (2263 Ocean Blvd., Rye, 603/964-8251, www.carriagehouserye.com, 5pm-9pm Mon.-Sat., 11am-2pm and 5pm-9pm Sun.). Nearby in Hampton, you can sample award-winning craft beers and have a hearty lunch or dinner at the prolific **Smuttynose Brewing Company** (105 Towle Farm Rd., Hampton, 603/436-4026, www.smuttynose.com, noon-7pm Mon.-Fri., 11am-7pm Sat.-Sun.).

3 Purgatory Falls

PURGATORY BROOK WATERSHED, MONT VERNON

This relaxing and refreshing hike visits two gorgeous waterfalls by way of a brook that weaves and tumbles through the western woods of the Merrimack River valley.

BEST: Spring hikes

DISTANCE: 5 miles round-trip

DURATION: 2.5 hours

ELEVATION CHANGE: 317 feet

EFFORT: Easy/moderate

TRAIL: Dirt and gravel paths, wooden bridges, water crossings via stones and logs

USERS: Hikers, leashed dogs

SEASON: April-October

PASSES/FEES: None

MAPS: Mont Vernon Conservation Commission website

CONTACT: Mont Vernon Conservation Commission, 603/673-6080, www.montvernonnh.us

Tucked away in the hills north of Nashua, the Purgatory Brook Trail is an under-the-radar gem compared to the heavily trafficked trails of the nearby Monadnocks. While this makes for serene hiking, it also means that the trail can be overgrown. For a confusion-free trip, bring a printout of the trail map found on the Mont Vernon Conservation Commission website and watch the tree trunks for the yellow plastic strips that mark the path. If you're hiking in late May or June, throw some bug spray in your day pack too: those 4-5 weeks are blackfly season in New Hampshire, and blackflies love running water.

START THE HIKE

▸ MILE 0-0.3: Purgatory Brook Trail to Lower Purgatory Falls

Begin your hike in the Lower Purgatory Falls parking lot by the trailhead sign and pick up the **Purgatory Brook Trail** heading west. Bear left at a Y-junction to stay on the main dirt path, which ambles through hemlocks at an even grade. After passing several reptile-rich vernal pools, the trail curves northwest and makes a quick descent to **Lower Purgatory Falls** at 0.3 mile. The shoreline that circles the pool of the explosive 25-foot-tall cascade is ideal for picnickers and landscape photographers, making this a popular place.

▸ MILE 0.3-1.7: Lower Purgatory Falls to Purgatory Brook

Leaving the crowds behind, the trail climbs the right side of the lower falls and flattens into a narrow, rockier path through mossy woods. Hugging the shore of **Purgatory Brook,** continue north and cross several mud patches on wooden plank bridges and logs. At 0.8 mile, turn right to avoid

▲ LOWER PURGATORY FALLS

a bridge over Purgatory Brook. Continue for 0.9 mile as the forest expands into a great hall of deciduous hardwoods. Occasionally the trees part wide enough to offer pleasant views of Purgatory Brook, which are often complemented by rock slabs and boulders large enough to host a small group of picnickers.

▸ MILE 1.7–2.5: Purgatory Brook to Upper Purgatory Falls

The trail briefly merges with a gravel access road at 1.75 miles before veering sharply to the right to avoid another wooden bridge. Note that the markings on this right turn are a little tough to see if you're not looking for them, especially since the intuitive thing to do when hikers encounter a bridge is to cross it. Bottom line: Don't cross the bridge. Turn right instead.

Now it's time for the final climb. The trail ascends a wooded ravine at a moderate grade for 0.7 mile. Be mindful of slippery exposed roots and loose rocks. Keep an ear open for the rumble of Upper Purgatory Falls and look for a small wooden sign; the falls can be viewed from an outlook just beyond this sign at 2.5 miles. The crashing 50-foot-tall falls are surrounded by sheer walls of granite. Extra-curious hikers can get a closer look by carefully scrambling down a steep gully to the pool. Return the way you came.

DIRECTIONS

From Boston, drive north on I-93 to exit 37B. Merge onto I-95 S and drive 5.5 miles before turning right onto US-3 N. Continue north on US-3 N for

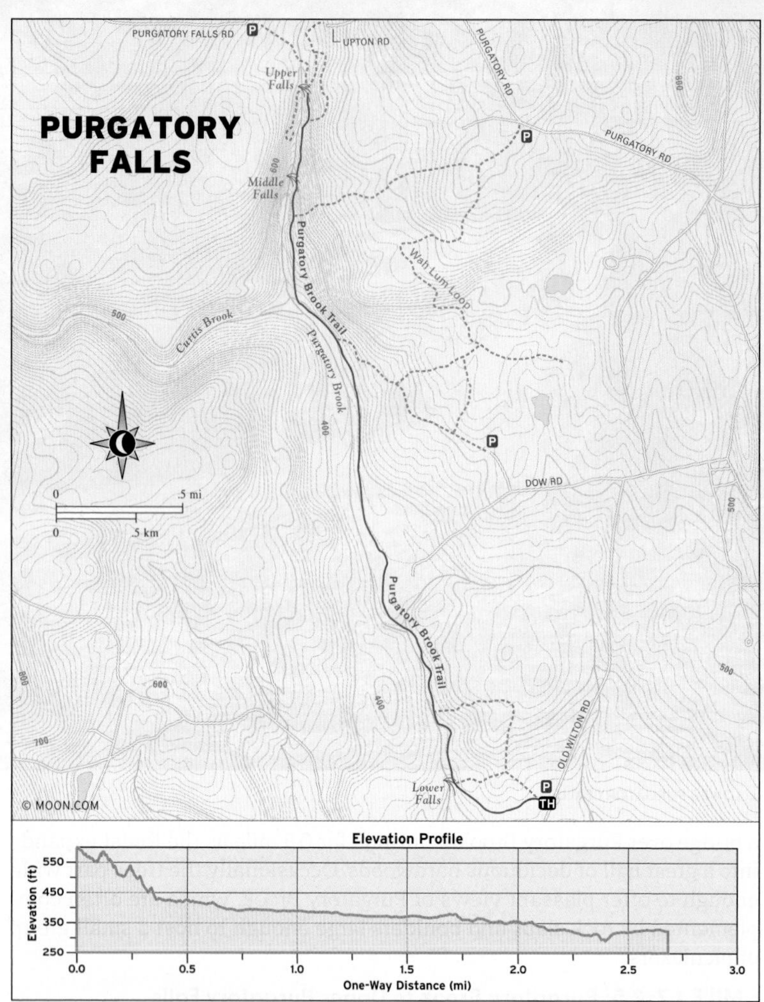

27.6 miles into New Hampshire. Take exit 8 toward Somerset Parkway and turn right onto NH-101A W. Drive 7 miles and turn left onto NH-101 W at the junction. Continue as the road curves north and look for the Lower Purgatory Falls parking lot on the left. If the parking lot is full, park alongside Purgatory Falls Road.

GPS COORDINATES: 42°51'31.6"N 71°41'40.1"W, 42.858790, -71.694483

BEST NEARBY BITES

Take a walk on the chic side of southern New Hampshire with wine tastings, a vineyard tour, and farm-to-table bistro fare at **LaBelle Winery** (345 NH-101, Amherst, 603/672-9898, www.labellewinerynh.com, 11am-9pm Wed.-Sat., 10am-5pm Sun.).

4 Madame Sherri's Forest

MADAME SHERRI'S FOREST, CHESTERFIELD

Hike through lush forest and past the ruins of an old castle to a romantic vista overlooking the hills of Massachusetts.

BEST: New England oddities
DISTANCE: 4.0 miles round-trip
DURATION: 3 hours
ELEVATION CHANGE: 531 feet
EFFORT: Easy/moderate
TRAIL: Dirt path, rocks, wooden bridges
USERS: Hikers, leashed dogs
SEASON: May–October
PASSES/FEES: None
MAPS: Chesterfield Conservation Commission website
CONTACT: Town of Chesterfield, 603/313-1416, www.chesterfield.nh.gov

Back in the Gilded Age, a New York costume designer named Antoinette Sherri laid claim to this thick pocket of woods in the southwest tip of New Hampshire. Today, the ruins of her old forest castle form one of the region's most evocative sights. Beyond the castle is vivid emerald foliage, amphibian-rich wetlands, and the wooded knoll known as Daniels Mountain. The park is a paradise for hikers who appreciate grown-in trails and the ambience of undeveloped (and under-visited) woodlands.

START THE HIKE

▸ MILE 0–0.7: Madam Sherri's Forest Trailhead to Anne Stokes Loop

Begin your hike in the Madam Sherri's Forest parking lot by crossing a wooden bridge and picking up the **Anne Stokes Loop.** Immediately, you'll encounter a sign for the castle ruins. Veer right up a small hill to take a good gander at the ruins before merging back onto the Anne Stokes Loop, which is marked with brown diamonds bearing the name of the loop. Hike southeast past a marsh into a denser section of northern hardwood conifers. Turn left at the loop junction sign at 0.2 mile and continue 0.5 mile as the trail becomes rockier and rootier. Watch your step—frogs and garter snakes make regular crossings along this stretch of the trail.

▸ MILE 0.7–1.2: Anne Stokes Loop to Daniels Mountain Loop

As the trail begins to ascend, turn left at the junction with the **Daniels Mountain Loop** at 0.7 mile. Head north briefly before the trail takes a sharp right and slabs up the northern flank of Daniels Mountain at a moderate grade. The footing contains many exposed roots, so be mindful of your footing during wet weather. An exposed ledge offers a stunning view of the forest at 0.8 mile. Continue for another 0.4 mile on the final ascent to the top of Daniels Mountain.

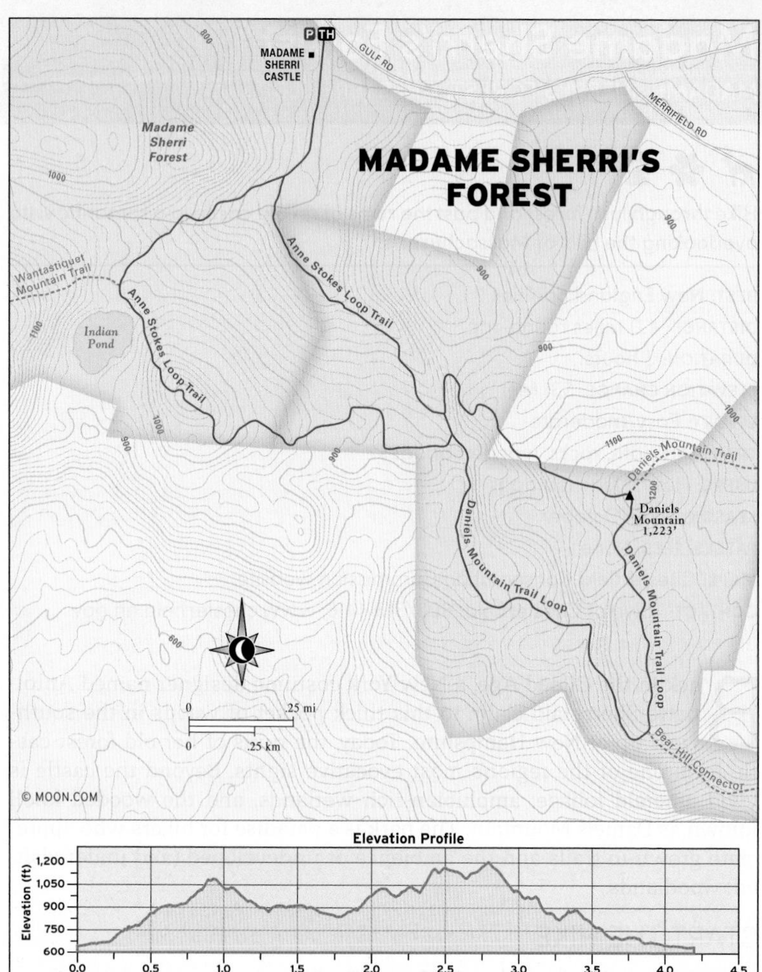

▸ MILE 1.2–1.6: Daniels Mountain Loop to Daniels Mountain Summit

At 1.2 miles, you'll be at the summit. Ironically, though, the best view is just below the summit. Turn right at the summit junction to continue along the loop trail and descend for 0.4 mile until you reach the sign for **Moon Ledge.** Here, at 1.6 miles, you'll be treated to a vista of Massachusetts's Pioneer Valley that could easily be the subject of a painting, especially near sunset.

▸ MILE 1.6–4.0: Daniels Mountain Summit to Anne Stokes Loop

Continue down the mountain on the Daniels Mountain Loop trail for another 0.7 mile and enjoy a brief foray through some wooded hollows before hooking up with the **Anne Stokes Loop** again at 2.3 miles. Take an immediate left onto the Anne Stokes Loop and ascend a rocky knoll called East Hill. The trail is steep in a few places but it quickly transitions from granite into lush vegetation. Enjoy a view of the nearby Indian Pond from the pinnacle of East Hill at 3.1 miles before concluding the loop hike with a gentle descent back into the forest. Upon reaching the end of the Anne

▲ WESTERN MASSACHUSETTS FROM MOON LEDGE

Stokes Loop at 3.8 miles, turn left onto the familiar starter trail and backtrack past the castle ruins to the trailhead.

DIRECTIONS

From Boston, drive to Cambridge's Alewife Station and pick up MA-2 W/ Concord Turnpike. Head northwest along MA-2 for 65 miles. After entering the town of Erving, turn right onto Church Street. Drive north as Church Street becomes North Street and then Gulf Road. Stay on this road until it ends at NH-63. Turn right onto NH-63 and drive north into New Hampshire. At the terminus of NH-63 in Hinsdale, turn left onto Main Street and then turn right onto Plain Road. Continue north along Plain Road for 5 miles until you reach Merrifield Road. Turn left onto Merrifield Road and then take a left onto Gulf Road. The Madam Sherri's Forest trailhead and parking lot will be on your left, and a spillover parking area is located directly across the road on the right side.

GPS COORDINATES: 42°51'53.0"N 72°31'05.2"W, 42.864723, -72.518114

BEST NEARBY BREWS

Traipse over the nearby New Hampshire-Vermont border to enjoy the restaurant scene in Brattleboro, and be sure not to miss the phenomenal New American sour ales at **Hermit Thrush Brewing** (29 High St. #101C, Brattleboro, 802/257-2337, www.hermitthrushbrewery.com, 3pm-8pm Mon.-Thurs., noon-9pm Fri.-Sat., 11am-6pm Sun.).

5 Skatutakee Mountain and Thumb Mountain

HARRIS CENTER FOR CONSERVATION EDUCATION, HANCOCK

This family-friendly hike traverses a forest with an active bobcat population and visits two neighboring peaks that offer views of the Monadnocks and the Wapack Range.

DISTANCE: 5.0 miles round-trip
DURATION: 4 hours
ELEVATION CHANGE: 892 feet
EFFORT: Moderate
TRAIL: Dirt path, rocks, water crossings by stones
USERS: Hikers, leashed dogs
SEASON: May-October
PASSES/FEES: None
MAPS: Harris Center website
CONTACT: Harris Center for Conservation Education, 603/525-3394, www.harriscenter.org

START THE HIKE

▸ MILE 0-0.2: Harris Center to Harriskat Trail

Begin your hike in the parking lot for the Harris Center by the Trails sign. Follow a dirt path down to the adjacent road (Kings Highway) and cross the road to pick up the **Harriskat Trail,** marked with white rectangles on trees. The trail begins with a pleasant meander through mossy, boulder-strewn woods with plenty of vernal pools and a few creeks to hopscotch across. Some of the hemlocks here are riddled with woodpecker holes.

▸ MILE 0.2-1.7: Harriskat Trail to Skatutakee Summit

Continue along this stretch for 0.6 mile before reaching the intersection of Harriskat and the Thumbs Down Trail. Turn left to continue on Harriskat. The trail segues into a series of switchbacks that ascend the northeastern haunch of Skatutakee Mountain at a surprisingly laid-back grade. As the trees start to thin out and the trail becomes rockier, the trail reaches the summit of Skatutakee at 1.7 miles, which is marked with a massive cairn. The summit resembles a high-altitude meadow with panoramic views of Keene, the Monadnocks, and the Wapack Range just across the state border in Massachusetts.

▸ MILE 1.7-2.3: Skatutakee Summit to Thumbs Up Trail

To continue the loop, turn right onto the **Thumbs Up Trail** at the summit junction with the Harriskat and Cadot Trails. (Look for white triangles on this section.) After a brief and relaxing descent from the top of Skatutakee, the trail veers west and begins its ascent to Thumb Mountain at 2.3 miles. The grade is somewhat gentler, but with more rocks and exposed roots.

▲ THE ELUSIVE BOBCAT IN THE HARRIS CENTER WOODS

▸ MILE 2.3–2.9: Thumbs Up Trail to Thumb Mountain Summit

Climb until you reach a junction with the **Thumbs Down Trail** at 2.6 miles. Turn left to stay on Thumbs Up and continue at a steeper angle for 0.3 mile before arriving at the summit proper at 2.9 miles. The top of Thumb is more grown-in with foliage than Skatutakee, but a clearing—complete with a stone victory bench—offers a direct and superior view of Mount Monadnock.

▸ MILE 2.9–3.3: Thumb Mountain Summit to Thumbs Down Trail

Begin the return journey by backtracking down the Thumbs Up Trail to the junction and turning left onto the Thumbs Down Trail, which is marked with yellow rectangles. The descent grade is moderate but the trail here is more rugged and less traveled. Keep an eye peeled for any of the local forest's resident bobcats, which occasionally make brief but unforgettable appearances in the presence of lucky hikers.

▸ MILE 3.3–5.0: Thumbs Down Trail to Harriskat Trail

Continue the descent for roughly half a mile. The grade smoothens once the trail passes **Jack's Pond at 3.9 miles,** and the remaining half mile is nearly level. At 4.4 miles, the Thumbs Down Trail concludes at the **Harriskat Trail**. Turn left onto Harriskat to return to the parking lot.

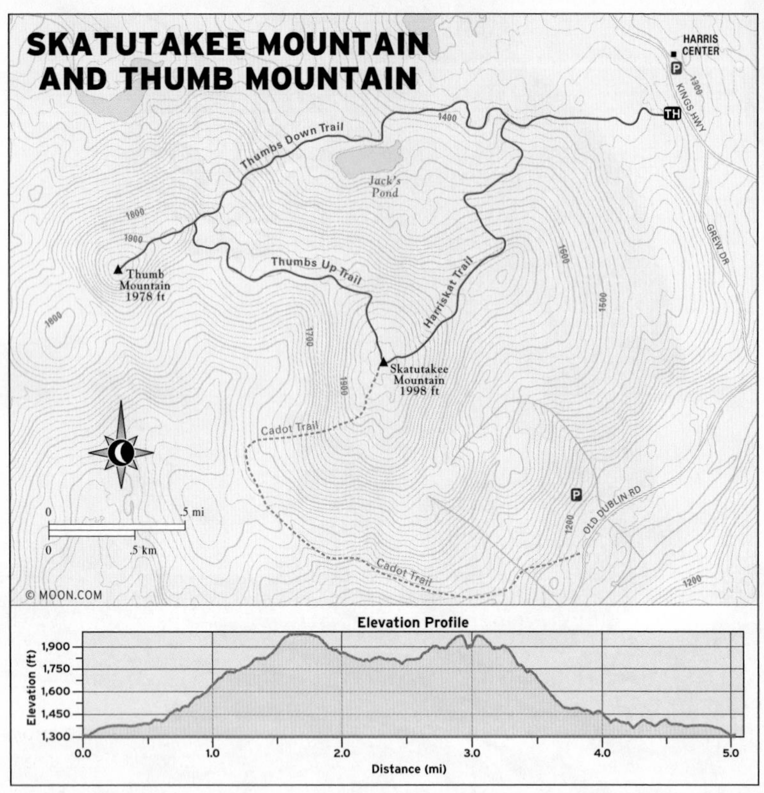

DIRECTIONS

From Boston, pick up I-93 N and drive north for 73 miles into New Hampshire. Shortly after passing through the toll booth, take Exit 5 to merge onto I-89 N. Drive north for 9 miles and use the left lane to take Exit 5 onto US-202 W/NH-9 toward Henniker/Keene. Continue heading west and then southwest along NH-9 for 27 miles before taking a left onto NH-123. Turn right onto Hunts Pond Road and take it to its end, where you'll turn left onto Kings Highway. The road transitions from concrete to dirt and the Harris Center parking lot will be on your left.

GPS COORDINATES: 42°58'41.9"N 72°01'13.8"W, 42.978309, -72.020505

BEST NEARBY BITES

Reward yourself for a solid double mountain hike by trucking up to nearby Harrisville and enjoying a few house-made doughnuts or a piping-hot bowl of seasonal vegetable soup at the historic **Harrisville General Store** (29 Church St., Harrisville, 603/827-3138, www.harrisvillegeneralstore.com, 8am-6pm Mon.-Sat., 8am-4pm Sun.).

6 Sweet Trail

CROMMET CREEK CONSERVATION AREA, DURHAM

This gentle and wildlife-rich hike takes you from the middle of the New Hampshire woods through a series of wetlands to the salty and serene estuaries of Great Bay.

BEST: Winter hikes, brew hikes
DISTANCE: 5.6 miles round-trip
DURATION: 2.5 hours
ELEVATION CHANGE: 88 feet
EFFORT: Easy
TRAIL: Dirt path, wooden bridges, water crossings via stones
USERS: Hikers, leashed dogs
SEASON: April-October
PASSES/FEES: None
MAPS: Great Bay Resource Protection Partnership website
CONTACT: Great Bay Resource Protection Partnership, 603/659-2678, www.greatbaypartnership.org

New Hampshire's seacoast is an ecosystemic melting pot of deciduous forest and windswept coastal preserves. The Sweet Trail goes through both of these natural environments, making for a wondrous, family-friendly shrub-to-sea jaunt. Better yet, the protected forest and wetlands through which the Sweet Trail meanders are teeming with birds, amphibians, and beavers. From April to May, the entire area becomes a symphony hall for spring peepers.

START THE HIKE

▸ MILE 0-0.6: Sweet Trail to Footbridge

Begin your hike at the Crommet Creek parking lot by the trailhead sign and turn right onto the **Sweet Trail,** heading south. Blue-and-white diamond-shaped signs mark the trail. Descend through a thick stretch of hemlock forest for 0.3 mile before arriving at Dame Road. Take a left here and walk south along the dirt road until you reach a small parking lot on your left. From here, the Sweet Trail continues deeper into the woods. Watch your footing as the trail skirts a series of boulders beside a bog and crosses a creek on a precarious-looking but sturdy **wooden footbridge.** The bridge is a great outlook for spotting beavers, which can often be glimpsed fortifying their lodges in the boggy area that's visible from this point of the trail.

▸ MILE 0.6-1.8: Footbridge to Sweet Trail

Leaving the bog and creek behind, the trail continues south and crosses a smaller stream on rocks at 0.9 mile before curving to the southeast and widening into a smoother dirt path. The trail ambles through a hall of hemlocks and birches before skirting a second, larger series of wetlands.

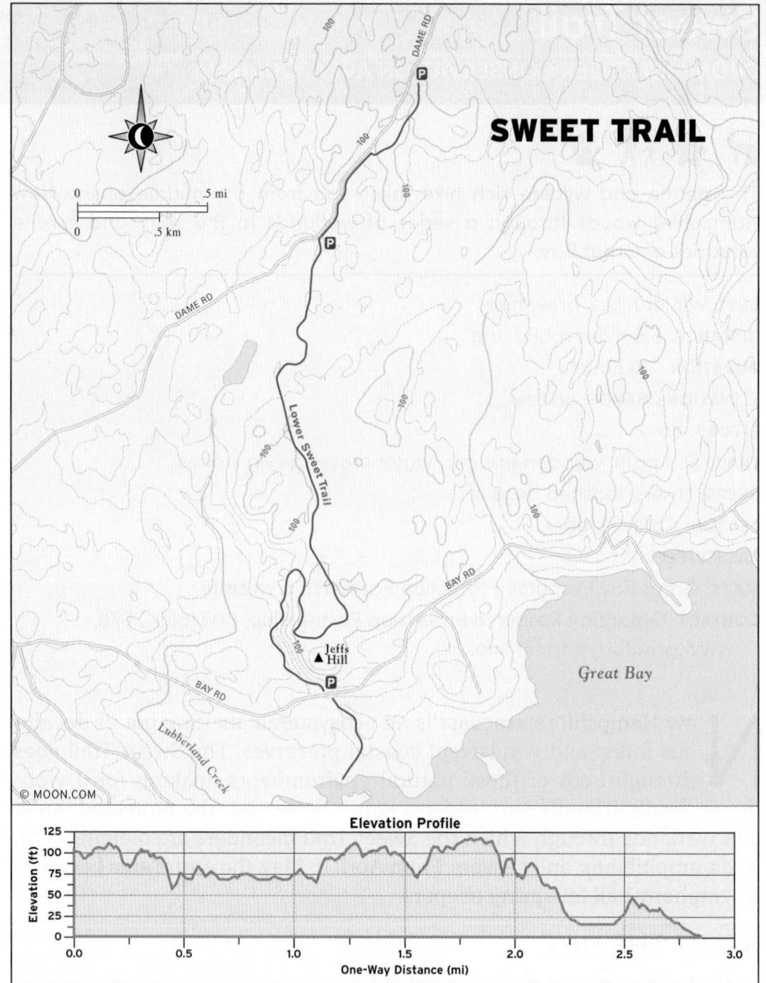

Tread lightly and quietly here: not only do spotted salamanders and wood frogs regularly cross the forest floor, but the dead white pine snags of the nearby wetlands are the nesting grounds for a small group of great blue herons who occasionally make appearances. Keep an ear open for their deep-throated croak as you pass through here.

At 1.8 miles, the Sweet Trail reaches the upper flank of Jeff's Hill. At this junction, hikers can choose to continue over the hill or stick with the Sweet Trail.

▸ MILE 1.8-2.8: Sweet Trail to Great Bay Estuary

Turn right to continue on the Sweet Trail as it takes a sharp curve north before turning south again and descending into one final wetland that partially engulfs the trail itself. Avoid the muck here by staying on the wooden bog bridges. The trail crosses Bay Road at 2.4 miles and ambles through a roomier stretch of hemlocks.

The trail finally emerges at the edge of the woods and reaches its end at the Great Bay estuary at 2.8 miles. Take a deep whiff of the briny sea

▲ WOOD FROG ALONG THE SWEET TRAIL

breeze and plop down on the circular stone bench, which offers a splendid view of the coastal tides, before heading back the way you came.

DIRECTIONS

From Boston, drive north on I-93 to exit 37B. Merge onto I-95 N. Continue north on I-95 for 25 miles and cross into New Hampshire. Take Exit 2 toward NH-101 to Hampton/Manchester. Follow the signs to State Route 101 W to Manchester/Concord. Merge onto 101 W and continue to Exit 10 for NH-85 to Exeter/Newfields. Turn right at the bottom of the exit ramp and head north on NH-85 for 3 miles before turning left onto NH-108. Drive north on 108 for another 3 miles and take a right onto Dame Road. The road soon goes from concrete to dirt and the trailhead parking is on your right at 65 miles. There is no fee or permit required for parking.

GPS COORDINATES: 43°06'01.4"N 70°54'16.3"W, 43.100386, -70.904540

BEST NEARBY BREWS

The nearby towns of Durham and Dover have plenty of dining options, from savory burgers to Southeast Asian cuisine, but before you make your decision, stop for a hazy wheat IPA or a tart Berliner weisse at **Deciduous Brewing Company** (12 Weaver St., Newmarket, 603/292-5809, 4pm-7pm Thurs., 2pm-8pm Fri., noon-8pm Sat., 1pm-6pm Sun.).

NEARBY CAMPGROUNDS

NAME	LOCATION	FACILITIES	SEASON	FEE
Ashuelot River Campground	152 Pine St., Swanzey, NH 03446	Tent sites, RV sites, cabins, toilets, showers, potable water, laundry, camp store, Wi-Fi	May-October	$45-70
603/357-5777, www.ashuelotrivercampground.com				
Shir-Roy Camping Area	136 Athol Rd., Richmond, NH 03470	Tent sites, RV sites, toilets, showers, potable water, laundry, camp store, Wi-Fi	late May-mid-October	$33-44
603/239-4768, www.shir-roy.com				
Gilson Pond Campground	116 Poole Rd., Jaffrey, NH 03452	Tent sites, toilets, showers, potable water	May-October	$18-25
www.nhstateparks.org				
Seven Maples Campground	24 Longview Rd., Hancock, NH 03449	Tent sites, RV sites, cabins, toilets, showers, potable water, laundry, swimming pool, camp store, Wi-Fi	mid-May-mid-October	$49-129
603/525-3321, www.sevenmaples.com				
Oxbow Campground	8 Deering Center Rd., Deering, NH 03244	Tent sites, RV sites, cabins, toilets, showers, potable water, laundry, camp store, Wi-Fi	mid-May-mid-October	$30-65
603/464-5952, www.oxbowcampground.net				
Autumn Hills Campground	285 S Stark Hwy., Weare, NH 03281	Tent sites, RV sites, toilets, showers, potable water, laundry, camp store, Wi-Fi	May-mid-October	$33-49
603/529-2425, www.autumnhillscampground.com				

NEARBY CAMPGROUNDS (continued)				
NAME	**LOCATION**	**FACILITIES**	**SEASON**	**FEE**
Sunset Park Campground	104 Emerson Ave., Hampstead, NH 03841	Tent sites, RV sites, yurts, toilets, showers, potable water, Wi-Fi	late May-early October	$30-75
603/329-6941, www.sunsetparknh.com				
Wakeda Campground	294 Exeter Rd., Hampton Falls, NH 03844	Tent sites, RV sites, cabins, toilets, showers, potable water, laundry, camp store, restaurant, Wi-Fi	mid-May-September	$43-92
603/772-5274, www.wakedacampground.com				

▲ THE MONTE ROSA WEATHERVANE ON MOUNT MONADNOCK

▲ THE LONG POND TRAIL

VERMONT

NORTHERN GREEN MOUNTAINS

The northern region of the 399,151-acre Green Mountain National Forest and its surrounding parks contain some of the most prized wildlands in the Northeast. Here, the Long Trail traverses the bald granite "backbone" of Vermont, where views of rolling hills unfold and plunge into swaths of rich farmland. Additional paths lead to sparkling ponds and cascading falls, many secluded within pristine wilderness areas. Hikes range from challenging all-day climbs to easygoing jaunts that can be completed in a few hours. Many of these routes are an easy drive from the Middlebury area, which is a great jumping-off point for adventures of all types.

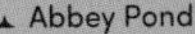

▲ Abbey Pond

▲ along Bucklin Trail

◀ THE GREAT CLIFF OF MOUNT HORRID

1 **Long Trail: Lincoln Gap to Mount Abraham**
DISTANCE: 4.8 miles round-trip (with optional additions)
DURATION: 3.25 hours
EFFORT: Strenuous

2 **Long Trail: Brandon Gap to Mount Horrid Great Cliff and Cape Lookout**
DISTANCE: 1.8 miles round-trip (with optional additions)
DURATION: 2.5 hours
EFFORT: Moderate/strenuous

3 **Abbey Pond Trail**
DISTANCE: 4.4 miles round-trip
DURATION: 2 hours
EFFORT: Easy/moderate

4 **Skylight Pond Trail and Long Trail to Breadloaf Mountain**
DISTANCE: 6.9 miles round-trip
DURATION: 4 hours
EFFORT: Moderate

5 **Bucklin Trail to Killington Peak, Coolidge State Forest**
DISTANCE: 7.4 miles round-trip
DURATION: 4 hours
EFFORT: Strenuous

6 **Upper Meadow Road, Mountain Road, Mount Tom Road, and Precipice Trail to Mount Tom**
DISTANCE: 3.6 miles round-trip
DURATION: 1.75 hours
EFFORT: Moderate

7 **Falls of Lana and Rattlesnake Cliffs**
DISTANCE: 4.9 miles round-trip
DURATION: 2.5 hours
EFFORT: Moderate

▲ INDIAN PIPE

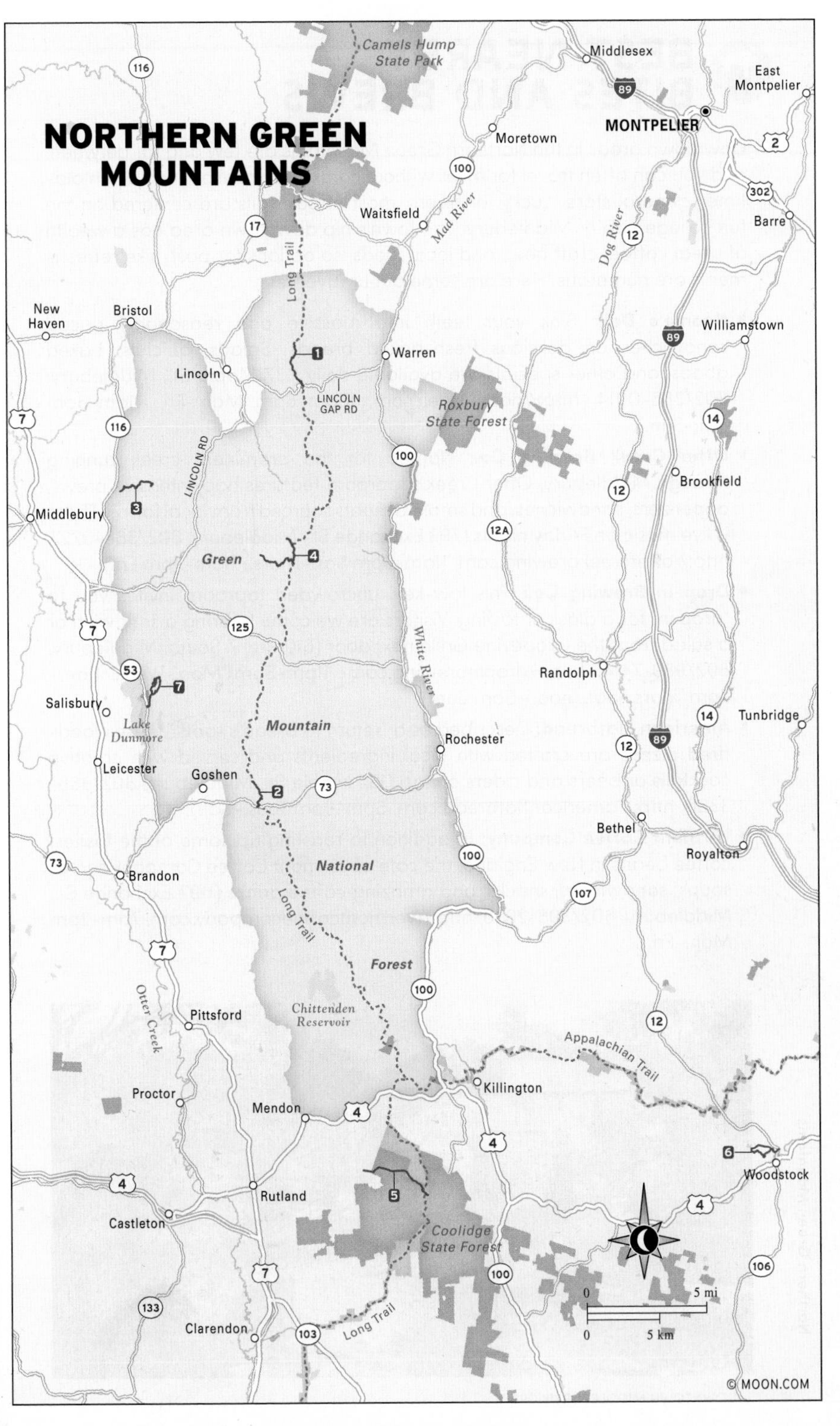
NORTHERN GREEN MOUNTAINS
Camels Hump State Park
Middlesex
East Montpelier
MONTPELIER
Moretown
Waitsfield
Mad River
Dog River
Barre
Long Trail
New Haven
Bristol
Williamstown
Warren
Lincoln
LINCOLN GAP RD
Roxbury State Forest
LINCOLN RD
Brookfield
Middlebury
Green
Mountain
National
Forest
White River
Randolph
Salisbury
Lake Dunmore
Tunbridge
Rochester
Leicester
Goshen
Bethel
Royalton
Brandon
Otter Creek
Pittsford
Chittenden Reservoir
Appalachian Trail
Killington
Proctor
Mendon
Woodstock
Rutland
Castleton
Coolidge State Forest
Clarendon
0
5 mi
5 km
© MOON.COM

BEST NEARBY BITES AND BREWS

Downtown areas in the Northern Green Mountains are few and far between, and you can often travel for miles without coming across so much as an old-timey general store. Lucky for hikers, most of our trails are centered on the fun college hub of Middlebury. The town's hip downtown area has a wealth of great coffee, craft beer, and local foods, so options for post-hike refreshments are numerous. Here are some of our favorites.

- **Noonie's Deli:** Sink your teeth into massive and reasonably priced sandwiches on delicious fresh-baked breads. Salads, quiches, baked goods, and other specials are available daily (137 Maple St., Middlebury, 802/388-0014, http://nooniesdeli.com, 10am-6pm Mon.-Fri., 11am-6pm Sat.-Sun.).
- **Otter Creek Brewing Co.:** Named for the prominent creek running through Middlebury, Otter Creek's taproom features hop-intensive brews, appetizers, sandwiches, and smoked meats sourced from local farms. There is live music on Friday nights (793 Exchange St., Middlebury, 802/388-0727, http://ottercreekbrewing.com, 11am-6pm Sat.-Thurs., 11am-7pm Fri.).
- **Drop-In Brewing Co.:** This low-key, uncrowded taproom invites you to "drop in" for a glass or tasting. Visitors are welcome to bring a sandwich or a salad from the Grapevine Grille next door (610 Rte. 7 South, Middlebury, 802/989-7414, http://dropinbrewing.com, 11pm-5pm Mon.-Wed., 11am-7pm Thurs.-Sat., noon-5pm Sun.).
- **American Flatbread:** Described as a "return to bread's roots," these wood-fired pizzas are crafted with local ingredients and served with creative cocktails or beers and ciders on tap (137 Maple St., Middlebury, 802/388-3300, http://americanflatbread.com, 5pm-9pm Tues.-Sat.).
- **Vermont Coffee Company:** In addition to roasting up some of the tastiest coffee beans in New England, the café of Vermont Coffee Company serves soups, sandwiches, snacks, and amazing coffee drinks (1197 Exchange St., Middlebury, 802/398-2038, http://vermontcoffeecompany.com, 7am-2pm Mon.-Fri.).

▲ DOWNTOWN MIDDLEBURY'S CREEK

1 Long Trail: Lincoln Gap to Mount Abraham

GREEN MOUNTAIN NATIONAL FOREST, LINCOLN

Hike to 360-degree views from a rare alpine meadow and visit the ruins of 1973 plane crash on the summit of 4,017-foot Mount Abraham.

BEST: Vistas, New England oddities
DISTANCE: 4.8 miles round-trip (with optional additions)
DURATION: 3.25 hours
ELEVATION CHANGE: 1,617 feet
EFFORT: Strenuous
TRAIL: Dirt/rock singletrack
USERS: Hikers, leashed dogs
SEASON: May-October
PASSES/FEES: None
MAPS: Green Mountain National Forest
CONTACT: Green Mountain National Forest, Rochester Ranger Station, 99 Ranger Road, Rochester, VT, 800/767-4261, http://fs.usda.gov

START THE HIKE

▸ MILE 0-1.7: Long Trail Trailhead to Battell Shelter

Find the signed trailhead for the Long Trail northbound on the north side of Lincoln Gap Road. Follow the white blazes west as the trail climbs uphill into the woods and winds around a gorge. The trail may be slick and rocky, but the surrounding forest is lush with moss and secluded in the shade of dense conifers. In 1.6 miles, reach the signed intersection with the **Battell Trail** and turn right (east) to stay on the Long Trail. Reach the **Battell Shelter** and tent area at 1.7 miles.

▸ MILE 1.7-2.4: Battell Shelter to Summit

Follow the **Long Trail** as it turns left (north) away from the camping area. From this point on, the trail surface changes to steep rock slabs where hikers may need to climb with their hands for extra support. This section may be especially slippery after rain. Pay attention to your footing even as the tree line falls away and views start to unfold in every direction. Reach the summit at 2.4 miles in. From this fifth-tallest peak in Vermont at 4,017 feet, hikers can take in vistas of the Lake Champlain valley and the Adirondacks to the west, Sugarbush ski area to the east, Lincoln Gap to the south, and the rolling green peaks of Mount Ellen and the Monroe Skyline to the north. Enjoy the 360-degree views from the trail only—the roped-off area protects a delicate alpine meadow that can be damaged by foot traffic.

▸ MILE 2.4-4.8: Summit to Plane Crash Detour

Hikers can simply backtrack down from the summit when ready, but if you want to explore further, take a quick detour to view the site of a small **plane crash.** This lesser-known point of interest on the mountain

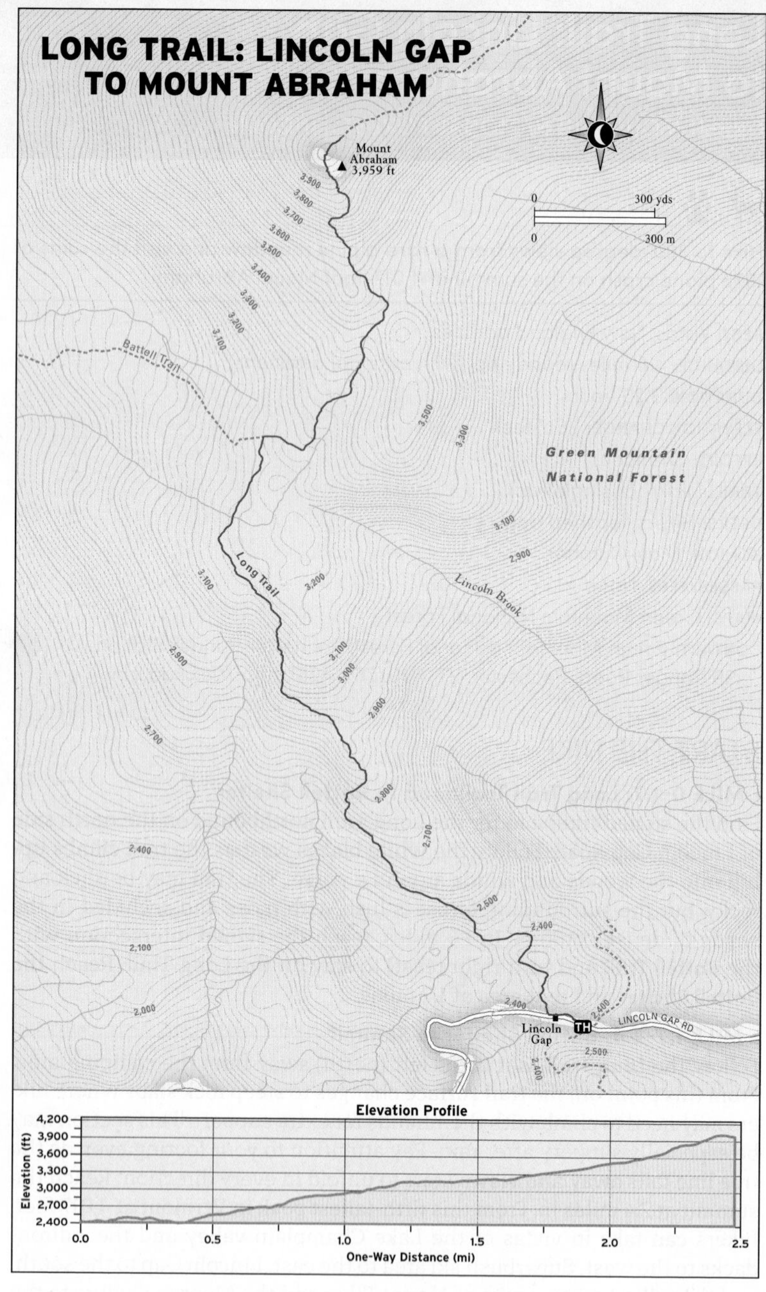

LONG TRAIL: LINCOLN GAP TO MOUNT ABRAHAM
Mount Abraham 3,959 ft
0
300 yds
0
300 m
Battell Trail
Green Mountain National Forest
Long Trail
Lincoln Brook
Lincoln Gap
TH
LINCOLN GAP RD
Elevation Profile
Elevation (ft)
One-Way Distance (mi)

▲ SUMMIT OF MOUNT ABRAHAM

is a testament to the power of Vermont's high peaks—and the dangers of navigating them. In June of 1973, the lone pilot was traveling from Vermont to New York when cloud cover on Mount Abraham obscured his vision and sent him crashing through the trees. The pilot survived relatively unscathed, but large parts of the Cessna 182N aircraft can still be found on the mountain. To view the wreckage, continue straight north from the summit on the Long Trail for about 400 feet. A small cairn on the left side of the trail designates the path to the site. Turn left (east) and follow it for about 100 feet to find the orange and white fuselage, a detached wing, and other parts scattered across the forest. If you do decide to visit the plane crash site, return to the summit of Mount Abraham, then backtrack on the Long Trail southbound to Lincoln Gap.

DIRECTIONS

From VT-116, turn onto Lincoln Road, which becomes West River Road through the center of Lincoln. Continue east as it becomes East River Road, then continue straight on Lincoln Gap Road. The trailhead and parking lot is about 3.5 miles up the road on the right, and is marked by signs for the Long Trail.

GPS COORDINATES: 44°05'41.7"N 72°55'44.5"W

2 Long Trail: Brandon Gap to Mount Horrid Great Cliff and Cape Lookout

GREEN MOUNTAIN NATIONAL FOREST, GOSHEN

This short hike to one of the Green Mountains' most prized vistas can be extended with a trek through lush forests to Cape Lookout Mountain.

BEST: Fall hikes, vistas

DISTANCE: 1.8 miles round-trip (with optional additions)

DURATION: 2.5 hours

ELEVATION CHANGE: 1,195 feet

EFFORT: Moderate/strenuous

TRAIL: Dirt/rock singletrack

USERS: Hikers, leashed dogs

SEASON: May-October. This trail may be closed between March and August to protect nesting peregrine falcons. Please heed posted signs.

PASSES/FEES: None

MAPS: Green Mountain National Forest

CONTACT: Green Mountain National Forest, Rochester Ranger Station, 99 Ranger Road, Rochester, VT, 800/767-4261, http://fs.usda.gov

START THE HIKE

▸ MILE 0-0.1: Long Trail Trailhead to Joseph Battell Wilderness

From the parking lot, cross to the north side of Brandon Mountain Road (VT-73) and find the narrow path and sign for the **Long Trail** northbound. Reach a larger trailhead sign in about 0.1 mile, then turn left (north) through a tangle of raspberry and blackberry bushes and into the woods, where you'll enter the **Joseph Battell Wilderness.**

▸ MILE 0.1-0.9: Joseph Battell Wilderness to Great Cliff

The trail quickly steepens, ascending switchbacks and stone staircases through a birch forest. Reach a sign for the **Great Cliff** at 0.8 mile and stay straight (east). The cliff is another 0.1 mile down the trail. This steep granite face perched above Brandon Gap has great views of the deep valley, stretching east to west. Glimpses of the Champlain Valley peer out from the west, while wildlife can often be spotted in the marsh directly below the cliff. Many hikers, fulfilled by this impressive vista, will turn around here.

▸ MILE 0.9-1.4: Great Cliff to Mount Horrid Summit Detour

For a longer hike, backtrack 0.1 mile to the sign for the Great Cliff and continue right (north) for 0.4 mile toward the summit of **Mount Horrid.** The summit is enclosed by trees, so there are not any vistas here, but this lightly traveled section of trail snakes through a dense, shady forest where hikers are likely to stumble across wildlife prints in the muddy singletrack.

▲ VIEW FROM THE GREAT CLIFF OF MOUNT HORRID

▸ MILE 1.4–2.0: Mount Horrid Summit to Cape Lookout Summit

Continue over the summit and dip in and out of several rolling hills for 1 mile to **Cape Lookout Mountain**. This summit features a narrower yet peaceful vista, stretching west into the Champlain Valley. Backtrack to the Great Cliff sign and then head southbound on the Long Trail to return to the parking area.

DIRECTIONS

From US-7 or VT-100, turn onto VT-73 (Gap Road/Brandon Mountain Road) toward Goshen. The Brandon Gap parking area is marked with a large sign on the south side of the road.

GPS COORDINATES: 43°50'22.9"N 72°58'03.3"W

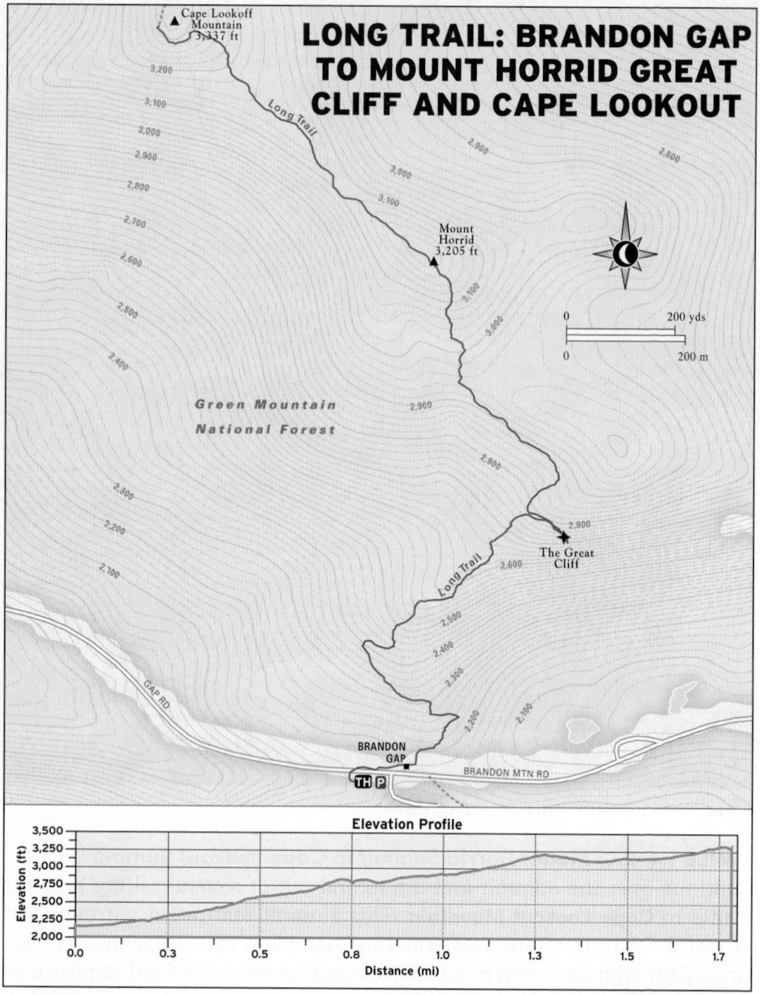

LONG TRAIL: BRANDON GAP TO MOUNT HORRID GREAT CLIFF AND CAPE LOOKOUT

Cape Lookoff Mountain 3,337 ft
Long Trail
Mount Horrid 3,205 ft
Green Mountain National Forest
The Great Cliff
BRANDON GAP
GAP RD
BRANDON MTN RD
TH P
0 200 yds
0 200 m

Elevation Profile

Elevation (ft): 2,000, 2,250, 2,500, 2,750, 3,000, 3,250, 3,500
Distance (mi): 0.0, 0.3, 0.5, 0.8, 1.0, 1.3, 1.5, 1.7

▲ THE GREAT CLIFF OF MOUNT HORRID

3 Abbey Pond Trail

GREEN MOUNTAIN NATIONAL FOREST, MIDDLEBURY

This easygoing trail leads past cascades and slightly uphill to tranquil Abbey Pond, a great spot for wildlife viewing.

BEST: Winter hikes
DISTANCE: 4.4 miles round-trip
DURATION: 2 hours
ELEVATION CHANGE: 1,173 feet
EFFORT: Easy/moderate
TRAIL: Dirt/rock singletrack
USERS: Hikers, leashed dogs
SEASON: May–October
PASSES/FEES: None
MAPS: Green Mountain National Forest
CONTACT: Green Mountain National Forest, Rochester Ranger Station, 99 Ranger Road, Rochester, VT, 802/767-4261, http://fs.usda.gov

START THE HIKE

▸ MILE 0–0.3: Abbey Pond Trailhead to Abbey Cascades

Hike east from the parking lot on a wide gravel path that slopes gradually uphill. Follow the blue blazes around some large rock formations and pass a gravel **quarry** on your left (west). There is also a quarry to the right, which may be heard but not seen from the trail. The fern-lined trail, shaded by a mixed hardwood forest, reaches a bridge crossing over the upper and lower **Abbey Cascades** at 0.3 mile. The upper falls plunge through a tumble of high granite boulders to the right (east), pass under the bridge to the left (west), and fall across a slide of mossy rocks before the stream rushes around the corner to the north. In warm weather, the lower falls are a fine place to dunk your feet, while in winter the upper falls freeze into dramatic icicles.

▸ MILE 0.3–1.0: Abbey Cascades to Stream Crossing

From the falls, the rocky path steepens and continues east upstream to the music of rushing water. In another 0.3 miles, the trail crosses the stream at a narrow junction where hikers can hop across. There are some more steep sections and rolling hills as the trail climbs upward, but the terrain evens out after about 0.4 mile.

▸ MILE 1.0–2.2: Stream Crossing to Abbey Pond

After it flattens, the trail meanders through a deciduous forest along the stream then crosses the stream again on a line of large flat stepping stones in 0.3 mile. Use caution during or after wet weather as the rocks may be slick. Arrive on the quiet banks of **Abbey Pond** after another 0.9 mile. The trail ends on the rocky shore of the pond, which is surrounded by reeds and marsh grasses that serve as the nesting area for Great Blue Herons.

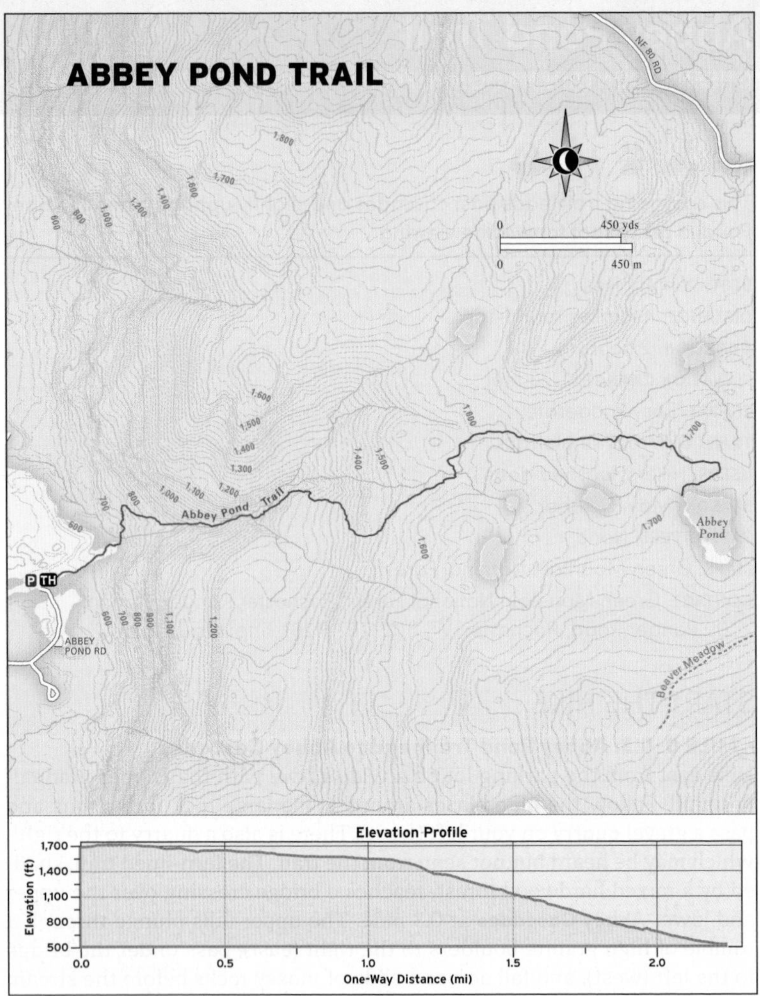

The rocky perch is a great spot to sit quietly and scope out wildlife across the pond, especially at the prime feeding hours of dawn and dusk. Enjoy the view from the rocks where the trail ends, then backtrack the same route to return to the start.

DIRECTIONS

From Middlebury, travel south on US-7 for 4 miles until it intersects with VT-125. Travel east on VT-125 for approximately 0.5 mile to the intersection with VT-116. Turn left onto VT-116 and continue 4.5 miles until the sign for the Abbey Pond Trail on the right. Turn onto the gravel road and follow it to the parking area at the end.

GPS COORDINATES: 44°01'51.5"N 73°05'17.3"W

4

Skylight Pond Trail and Long Trail to Breadloaf Mountain

GREEN MOUNTAIN NATIONAL FOREST, MIDDLEBURY

This climb to a secluded pond and vista is the jewel of the Green Mountains' pristine Breadloaf Wilderness.

DISTANCE: 6.9 miles round-trip
DURATION: 4 hours
ELEVATION CHANGE: 1,902 feet
EFFORT: Moderate
TRAIL: Dirt/rock singletrack
USERS: Hikers, leashed dogs
SEASON: May-October
PASSES/FEES: None
MAPS: Green Mountain National Forest
CONTACT: Green Mountain National Forest, Rochester Ranger Station, 99 Ranger Road, Rochester, VT, 802/767-4261, http://fs.usda.gov

START THE HIKE

▸ MILE 0-0.4: Skylight Pond Trailhead to Middlebury River Footbridge

Go east from the parking lot to reach the trailhead and pass a sign marking the entrance to the **Breadloaf Wilderness.** The tree-lined dirt track heads straight east, briefly paralleling a stream, and reaches a crossing at 0.2 mile. When water is low, hikers should be able to hop right over this crossing, but the stream widens after rain so waterproof boots are a good idea. After the stream crossing, the wide double-track trail is marked with blue blazes. Continue straight (southeast) for another 0.2 mile and cross the Middle Branch of the Middlebury River on a wooden footbridge.

▸ MILE 0.4-2.2: Middlebury River Footbridge to Skylight Pond

The path narrows into a single track through a thick forest and over several rolling hills as it makes its way east toward the slopes of Battell Mountain. The trail steepens after 1.0 mile, then climbs northeast for 1.1 miles to a hemlock-bound ridgeline. Follow the trail southeast along the ridge to reach the signed four-way intersection with the **Long Trail** at 2.2 miles. Continue straight (east) through the intersection and downhill to **Skylight Pond.**

▸ MILE 2.2-2.4: Skylight Pond to Long Trail

The pond sits below the **Skyline Lodge** cabin/shelter at 2.3 miles. Hikers can explore this peaceful, boggy oasis with views of distant ridgelines before backtracking 0.1 mile to the **Long Trail** intersection.

▲ SKYLIGHT POND

▸ **MILE 2.4–6.9: Long Trail to Breadloaf Mountain Summit**
Turn right (north) onto the Long Trail northbound. This section of trail can be muddy, and includes some stretches of slick rocks as it climbs gradually through an evergreen forest. At the top of the long stone staircase, the trail evens out atop a mossy ridgeline leading to **Breadloaf Mountain.** The true summit is 1 mile from the Long Trail intersection, but for the best views, take a brief detour; turn left (west) where the trail forks and continue 0.1 mile to the vista. Continue the 1 mile to the summit. When you are ready to return, backtrack from the summit 1.1 miles to the Long Trail intersection, then turn right (west) onto the Skylight Pond Trail, following it 2.2 miles back to the parking area.

DIRECTIONS

From Middlebury, travel south on US-7 for 4 miles until it intersects with VT-125. Travel east on VT-125 for approximately 6.5 miles, then turn left onto Forest Road 59 (Steam Mill Road). The free parking area for Skylight Pond is marked with a small sign on the right after 6.6 miles.

GPS COORDINATES: 43°59'23.2"N 72°57'56.6"W

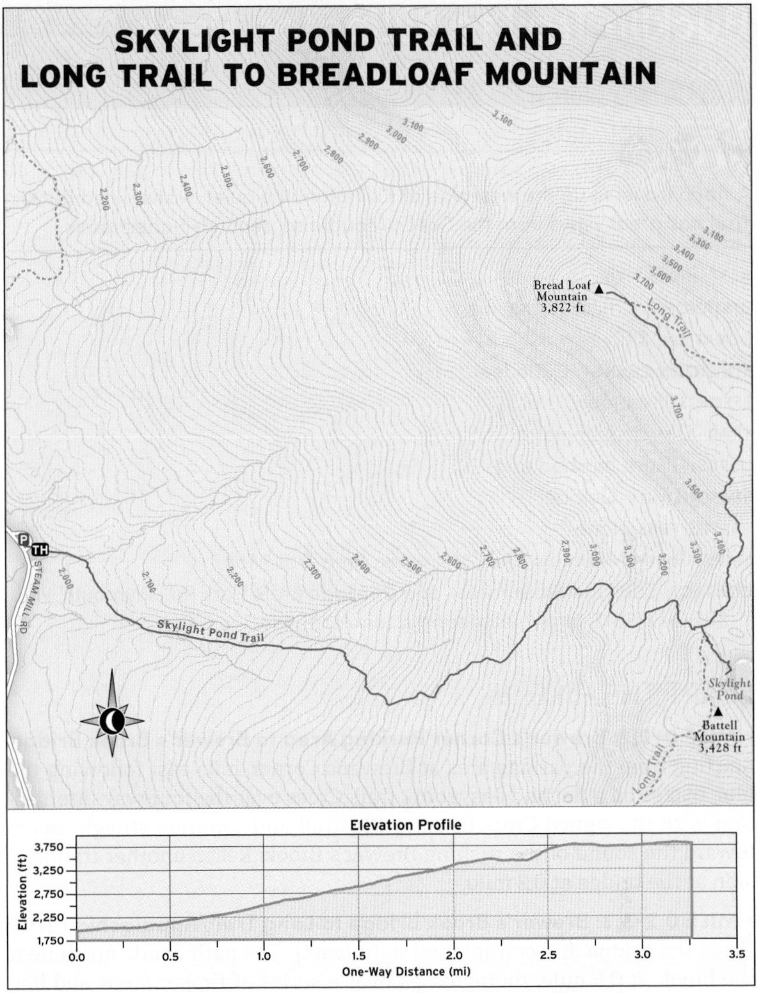

SKYLIGHT POND TRAIL AND LONG TRAIL TO BREADLOAF MOUNTAIN

Bread Loaf Mountain 3,822 ft
Long Trail
Skylight Pond Trail
Steam Mill Rd
P
TH
Skylight Pond
Battell Mountain 3,428 ft

Elevation Profile

Elevation (ft): 1,750 · 2,250 · 2,750 · 3,250 · 3,750

One-Way Distance (mi): 0.0 · 0.5 · 1.0 · 1.5 · 2.0 · 2.5 · 3.0 · 3.5

▲ THE SKYLINE LODGE

5 Bucklin Trail to Killington Peak

COOLIDGE STATE FOREST, MENDON

A steep traverse up the west side of Killington, the quiet, water-lined Bucklin Trail has great views from the Green Mountains' second-highest peak.

BEST: Brew hikes
DISTANCE: 7.4 miles round-trip
DURATION: 4 hours
ELEVATION CHANGE: 2,305 feet
EFFORT: Strenuous
TRAIL: Dirt/rock singletrack
USERS: Hikers, leashed dogs
SEASON: May-October
PASSES/FEES: None
MAPS: Green Mountain Club, "Killington Area Trail Map"
CONTACT: Coolidge State Forest, 855 Coolidge State Park Rd., Plymouth, VT, 802/672-3612, http://vtstateparks.com/coolidge

START THE HIKE

▸ MILE 0-0.2: Brewer's Corner Parking Area to Brewer's Brook Bridge
Starting from the parking area at Brewer's Corner, hike east following the blue blazes on a flat and easygoing trail. Cross over the four-way intersection with the signed Cross Country Ski Trail and continue straight (east) toward the sound of the rushing Brewer's Brook. Reach another trailhead sign at the bridge at 0.2 mile.

▸ MILE 0.2-3.3: Brewer's Brook Bridge to Long Trail/Appalachian Trail
Cross the **bridge** and continue straight (east). The path bends north near the brook at 0.5 mile, then crosses over a series of timber steps and bog bridges lined with lush ferns, grasses, and hobblebush. Follow the trail straight over Brewer's Brook on another large **bridge** at 1.3 miles, and continue over a narrow, rocky doubletrack that climbs above the stream. At 1.9 miles, the trail overlooks a small unnamed **cascade** plunging to meet Brewer's Brook to the left. Shortly after, the trail steepens dramatically, climbing southeast away from the brook for 1.4 miles. Here, it reaches a signed intersection with the **Long Trail/Appalachian Trail.**

▸ MILE 3.3-3.5: Long Trail/Appalachian Trail to Killington Spur Trail
Continue straight (east) at the intersection, on the Long Trail/Appalachian Trail southbound, following the white blazes. Reach the **Cooper Lodge/tent area** and a sign for the **Killington Spur** trail at 3.5 miles.

▸ MILE 3.5-3.7: Killington Spur Trail to Killington Summit
Follow the blue-blazed spur trail straight southeast on a steep, rocky climb toward the summit. Hikers may be required to use their hands on this challenging stretch of rocks, especially if they are slick with rain. Reach

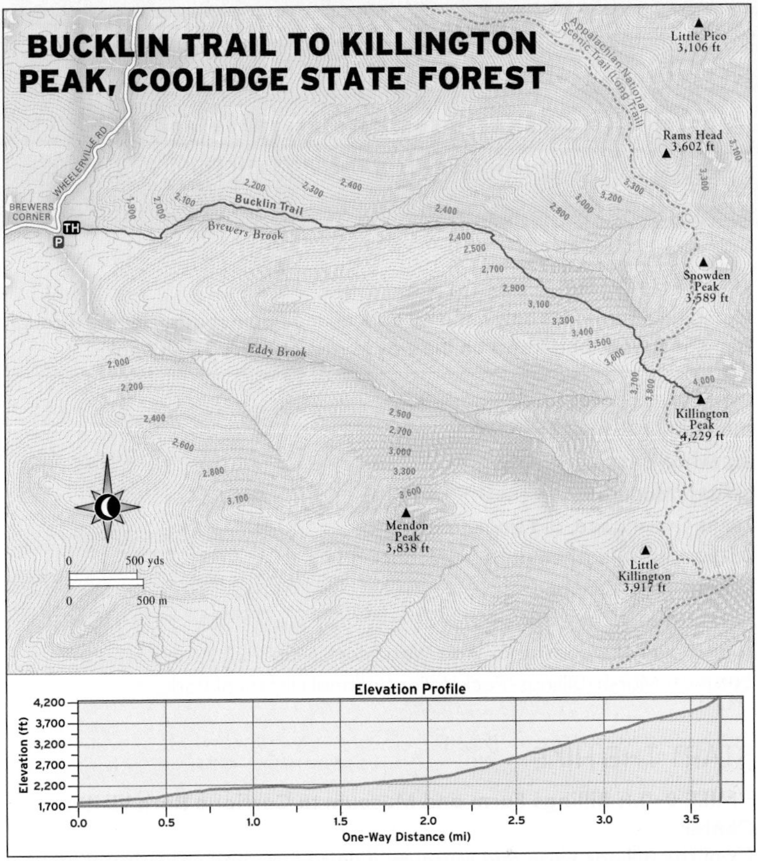

BUCKLIN TRAIL TO KILLINGTON PEAK, COOLIDGE STATE FOREST

the summit, marked with a communication tower, at 3.7 miles. There are 360-degree views of sprawling mountains from the bald granite rocks atop this second-highest peak in Vermont (4,229 feet). Return to the parking area via the same route.

DIRECTIONS

From Rutland, drive east on US-4/Woodstock Avenue. In 5 miles, turn right onto Wheelerville Road. The trailhead and a large parking area are marked with a sign about 4 miles down this dirt road.

GPS COORDINATES: 43°37'09.2"N 72°52'36.8"W

BEST NEARBY BREWS

No hiker should travel through Vermont without visiting **Long Trail Brewing Company** (550 US-4, Bridgewater Corners, 802/672-5011, http://longtrail.com, 10am-6pm Sun.-Thurs., 10am-7pm Fri.-Sat.) for a riverfront beer-tasting and seasonal pub grub. It's 21 miles from the trailhead.

6 Upper Meadow Road, Mountain Road, Mount Tom Road, and Precipice Trail to Mount Tom

MARSH-BILLINGS-ROCKEFELLER NATIONAL HISTORICAL PARK, WOODSTOCK

Experience Vermont's only national park on mountain roads winding through pond, meadow, and forest on the way to Mount Tom's South Peak.

DISTANCE: 3.6 miles round-trip
DURATION: 1.75 hours
ELEVATION CHANGE: 615 feet
EFFORT: Moderate
TRAIL: Gravel road, dirt singletrack
USERS: Hikers, leashed dogs, horseback riders
SEASON: May-October
PASSES/FEES: None
MAPS: Town of Woodstock, "Walk Woodstock Map"
CONTACT: Marsh-Billings-Rockefeller National Historical Park

START THE HIKE

▸ MILE 0-0.1: Billings Farm and Museum to Carriage Barn Visitor Center

From the **Billings Farm and Museum**, a dairy farm and agricultural history museum (April-November daily 10am-5pm, $16 per person per day), follow the walkway alongside the building, straight west across VT-12 and into the park. Turn left (south) up the hill, passing the **Carriage Barn Visitor Center** on your right.

▸ MILE 0.1-1.5: Carriage Barn Visitor Center to Four-Way Intersection

Continue on, passing beautiful gardens and the mansion on your left. Once you reach the Belvedere (the white building on the left 0.2 mile from the parking area), bear right (northwest) up the hill onto a carriage road lined with huge pine trees. Continue along the road, stay straight past the horse barn on the right, and bend right (north) to keep the trail on your right. Climb the trail as it gradually moves uphill to the left (west). When you reach an intersection (marked by a stone birdbath) at 1.2 miles, continue straight (west) onto Mountain Road. You'll catch glimpses of a pasture to your right, and views of another field on the left where the trail flattens. Come to a signed four-way intersection at 1.5 miles. (Optional: Continue straight [west] for a couple of hundred feet to view The Pogue, a beautiful pond lined with wildflowers and featuring reflective mountain views.)

▲ VIEW FROM SOUTH PEAK

▸ MILE 1.5-2.5: Four-Way Intersection to South Peak

Turn left (south) on **Mount Tom Road,** following signs for South Peak. The Mount Tom carriage road skirts the edge of a field, then bends east through a forest. Shortly after emerging from the forest, the path slopes downhill under a series of ledges for about 1 mile in order to reach the **South Peak.** This summit is encircled by a loop trail with multiple vistas. The first vista features a scenic west-facing bench.

▸ MILE 2.5-3.6: South Peak to Mountain Road

Continue around the loop for more views of Woodstock village below, then turn right (east) onto the **Precipice Trail** at 2.6 miles. This adventurous 0.5-mile descent features steep switchbacks with handrail assists to help hikers through a collection of ledges and small caves to a signed intersection with the **North Peak Trail.** Continue straight (east) on the Precipice Trail. Then bear left (east) toward **Mountain Road,** which you will reach after 0.1 mile. Turn right (southeast) onto Mountain Road and retrace your steps 0.4 mile back to the parking lot.

DIRECTIONS

From US-4/Woodstock center, go east and then turn left onto Elm Street. In 0.3 mile, turn right onto VT-12 N. After 0.2 mile, turn right onto Old River Road, then turn right into the large paved parking area for the Billings Farm and Museum. The entrance to the historical park is across VT-12.

GPS COORDINATES: 43°37'58.3"N 72°31'00.3"W

UPPER MEADOW RD, MOUNTAIN RD, MOUNT TOM RD, AND PRECIPICE TRAIL TO MOUNT TOM

Marsh-Billings-Rockefeller National Historical Park
The Pogue
Mountain Road
Mount Tom Road
Mount Tom 1,341 ft
South Peak
Billings Park
Barnard Brook
BILLINGS FARM AND MUSEUM
Ottauquechee River
Woodstock
West Woodstock
ELM ST
RIVER RD
RIVER ST
PLEASANT ST
CENTRAL ST
MOUNTAIN AVE
CHURCH ST
COLLEGE HILL
GOLF AVE
LINDEN HILL
SOUTH ST
PROSPECT ST
FRENCHS RD
ROSE HILL
US HWY 4
THOMAS HILL
0 400 yds
0 400 m

Elevation Profile
Elevation (ft): 675, 825, 975, 1,125, 1,275
Distance (mi): 0.0, 0.5, 1.0, 1.5, 2.0, 2.5, 3.0

▲ TRAIL ART ON MOUNTAIN ROAD

7 Falls of Lana and Rattlesnake Cliffs

GREEN MOUNTAIN NATIONAL FOREST, SALISBURY

This forest hike visits a dramatic multilevel waterfall before ascending to an exposed cliff that offers stellar views of nearby Lake Dunmore and all the way into upstate New York.

BEST: Summer hikes, brew hikes, spots for a swim

DISTANCE: 4.9 miles round-trip

DURATION: 2.5 hours

ELEVATION CHANGE: 1,627 feet

EFFORT: Moderate

TRAIL: Dirt path, rocks, wooden bridges, water crossings on stones

USERS: Hikers, leashed dogs

SEASON: June-October

FEES/PASSES: None

MAPS: Green Mountain and Finger Lakes National Forests website

CONTACT: Green Mountain and Finger Lakes National Forests, 802/747-6700, www.fs.usda.gov/main/gmfl/home

START THE HIKE

▸ MILE 0-0.5: Trail Information Kiosk to Falls of Lana

Begin by the trail information kiosk on the east side of the parking lot for Falls of Lana and Silver Lake. Climb a set of stone stairs into a boulder-strewn forest of spruce and maple trees and follow a brief dirt path to a dirt road. Turn right onto the road and ascend a series of switchbacks before arriving at a clearing. A big black water supply pipe passes through here on stilt-like supports. As you pass underneath the line, you'll hear the churning of water inside the pipe and the brighter crashing of water ahead. The trail dips back into the forest and pops around a curve.

▸ MILE 0.5-0.7: Falls of Lana to Rattlesnake Cliffs Trail

At 0.5 mile, you'll reach a rocky overlook on your left that allows you to gaze down into the frothing torrent and reflective pools of **Falls of Lana.** (You can reach additional pools and cascades by backtracking to the water supply pipe, following the pipe downhill, and then bushwhacking right into the woods.) Be careful around the overlook during wet weather—it gets quite slippery.

From the falls, the trail ascends north at a gentle grade along **Sucker Brook,** which feeds the cascades. At 0.6 mile, you'll reach a junction with the Silver Lake Trail; keep left here and continue to a wooden bridge that crosses the brook. On the other side of the bridge, turn right onto the **Rattlesnake Cliffs Trail,** marked by blue blazes. Stroll alongside the brook past some picnic tables.

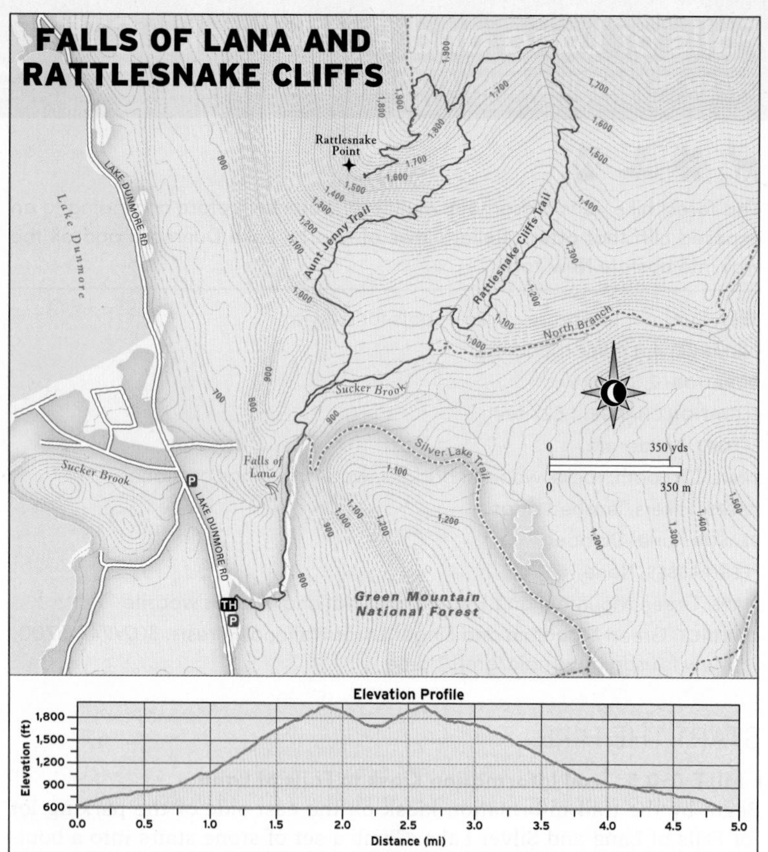

‣ MILE 0.7-1.7: Rattlesnake Cliffs Trail to Aunt Jenny Trail

At 0.7 mile, turn left to pick up the **Aunt Jenny Trail,** which ascends steadily through the forest on a wide path that's swimming with tree roots. A slight curve to the northwest takes you across a ledge-like section of trail that bypasses a very steep and wooded hillside that seems to descend forever. The hemlocks here are spaced enough to offer some partial views of Lake Dunmore.

At 1 mile, the trail swings north again and begins climbing at a steeper grade. As the trail becomes narrower and steeper, winding rock stairs become a recurring feature. Continue north, climbing higher into the forest as the trees start to open up, allowing sunlight and wind to break through. A height of land looms through the trees as the trail scrambles up some darker slabs of rock.

‣ MILE 1.7-2.3: Rattlesnake Cliffs Trail to Rattlesnake Cliffs

At 1.7 miles, you'll reach another junction for the **Rattlesnake Cliffs Trail.** Turn left onto the Rattlesnake Cliffs Trail, which switchbacks up a series of steeper rocky ledges before heading west through a thinner forest that's rich with birdsong (peregrine falcons are known to nest here). You'll pass a junction with Oak Ridge Trail in 0.2 mile; keep left to stay on Rattlesnake Cliffs. After another 0.1 mile, you'll step onto the exposed, rocky majesty of Rattlesnake Cliffs.

▲ ANCIENT ABOVE-GROUND WATER PIPE ALONG THE TRAIL

▸ MILE 2.3–3.5: Rattlesnake Cliffs to North Branch Trail Junction

Return by backtracking down Rattlesnake Cliffs Trail to the Aunt Jenny Trail junction. Turn left to stay on Rattlesnake Cliffs Trail and descend a gently graded dirt path that meanders through thick ferns and vegetation. After crossing several little streams on rocks, the trail begins to descend a steeper dirt path that becomes rockier as the surrounding forest again transitions from deciduous trees to hemlocks.

▸ MILE 3.5–4.0: North Branch Trail Junction to Aunt Jenny Trail Junction

At 3.5 miles, you'll pass a pyre-like rock formation and hear the nearby rippling of Sucker Brook again, which the trail crosses on rocks at 3.8 miles. Continue to hike southwest along the brook into a meadow for 0.2 mile until you reach a junction with the North Branch Trail. Keep right to continue on **Rattlesnake Cliffs Trail,** which heads back into the forest.

▸ MILE 4.0–4.9: Aunt Jenny Trail Junction

At 4.2 miles, you'll arrive at the **Aunt Jenny Trail junction** again. Turn left to stay on Rattlesnake and backtrack over the bridge and past the Falls of Lana to the parking lot to complete your loop hike.

DIRECTIONS

From Burlington, drive south on US-7 S for 25 miles; upon reaching downtown Middlebury, turn left onto Court Square and then right onto US-7 S/Court Street. Continue south for another 7 miles before swinging left onto VT-53. Drive for roughly 4 miles past Lake Dunmore and you'll soon see the hiker parking lot for Falls of Lana and the Silver Lake Trail on your left.

GPS COORDINATES: 43°54'04.2"N 73°03'51.4"W, 43.901165, -73.064266

BEST NEARBY BREWS

Middlebury and Vergennes—not far north from the trailhead—are your best bets for dining. But if you appreciate the science of beer, head south and sample some of the locally beloved suds (especially the IPAs) at **Foley Brothers** (79 Stone Dam Mill Rd., Brandon, 802/465-8413, www.foleybrothersbrewing.com, 11am-5pm Wed.-Sat., 11am-4pm Sun.).

NEARBY CAMPGROUNDS

Dispersed primitive camping and shelters are available within Green Mountain National Forest

NAME	LOCATION	FACILITIES	SEASON	FEE
Allis State Park	284 Allis State Park Rd., Randolph, VT 05060	18 tent sites, 8 lean-to sites; restrooms	late May-early September	$20-27
802/276-3175, http://vtstateparks.com/allis				
Branbury State Park	3570 Lake Dunmore Rd., Brandon, VT 05733	36 tent sites, 7 lean-to sites; restrooms	mid-May-mid-October	$20-27
802/247-5925, http://vtstateparks.com/branbury				
Gifford Woods State Park	34 Gifford Woods Acc., Killington, VT 05751	21 RV/tent sites, 19 lean-to sites, 4 cabins; restrooms	mid-May-mid-October	$20-50
802/775-5354, http://vtstateparks.com/Gifford				
Silver Lake State Park	20 State Park Beach Rd., Barnard, VT 05031	39 RV/tent sites, 7 lean-to sites; restrooms	late-May-early September	$20-27
802/234-9451, http://vtstateparks.com/silver				
Quechee State Park	5800 Woodstock Rd., Hartford, VT 05047	45 RV/tent sites, 7 lean-to sites; restrooms	mid-May-mid-October	$20-27
802/295-2990, http://vtstateparks.com/quechee				
Coolidge State Park	855 Coolidge State Park Rd., Plymouth, VT 05056	26 RV/tent sites, 36 lean-to sites; restrooms	late May-mid-October	$20-27
802/672-3612, http://vtstateparks.com/Coolidge				
Camp Plymouth State Park	2008 Scout Camp Rd., Ludlow, VT 05149	6 lean-to sites, 4 cottages, horse camping area; restrooms	late May-late September	$27-97
802/228-2025, http://vtstateparks.com/Plymouth				

NEARBY CAMPGROUNDS (continued)				
NAME	LOCATION	FACILITIES	SEASON	FEE
Chittenden Brook Campground	Forest Road 45, Chittenden, VT 05737	17 RV/tent sites; vault toilets; no water	late May-mid October	$15
802/767-4261, http://fs.usda.gov				
Moosalamoo Campground	Forest Road 24, Salisbury, VT 05769	19 RV/tent sites; vault toilets; no water	late May-mid-October	$15
802/767-4261, http://fs.usda.gov				
Silver Lake Campground	Silver Lake Rd., Salisbury, VT 05769	15 tent sites; vault toilets; no water	late May-mid-October	$10
Hike-in access only, 802/767-4261, http://fs.usda.gov				

▲ RED EFT (EASTERN NEWT JUVENILE) ON MOUNT ABRAHAM

SOUTHERN GREEN MOUNTAINS

Nestled among the quaint villages and productive farms of southern Vermont, the lower section of the Green Mountain National Forest sprawls over a terrain of granite peaks, peaceful lakes, and some of the most impressive gushing waterfalls in the state. Just outside the national forest, a number of state, town, and independently run parks protect a diversity of geological features, from historic quarries to explorable, stalactite-decorated caves. Whether you peak-bag on the Long Trail or wander the green shires of the state's southwest corner, southern Vermont's trails never fail to delight.

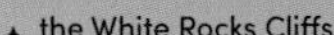
▲ the White Rocks Cliffs

▲ Stratton Pond

◂ LYE BROOK FALLS

1 Lake Trail and Long Trail (Appalachian Trail) to Baker Peak and Griffith Lake
DISTANCE: 8.4 miles round-trip
DURATION: 4.5 hours
EFFORT: Strenuous

2 Old Town Road and Antone Road to Antone Mountain
DISTANCE: 3.2 miles round-trip
DURATION: 1.75 hours
EFFORT: Moderate

3 Colby M. Chester Memorial Trail to Haystack Mountain
DISTANCE: 3.2 miles round-trip
DURATION: 1.75 hours
EFFORT: Moderate

4 Keewaydin Trail and Long Trail (Appalachian Trail) to White Rocks Cliffs
DISTANCE: 3.6 miles round-trip
DURATION: 2.5 hours
EFFORT: Moderate/strenuous

5 Blue Trail to Gettysburg Quarry and Gilbert Lookout
DISTANCE: 2.4 miles round-trip
DURATION: 1.5 hours
EFFORT: Moderate/strenuous

6 Blue Summit Trail to Mount Equinox and Lookout Rock
DISTANCE: 6 miles round-trip
DURATION: 3.25 hours
EFFORT: Strenuous

7 Lye Brook Falls Trail
DISTANCE: 4.4 miles round-trip
DURATION: 2.25 hours
EFFORT: Moderate

8 Stratton Pond Trail
DISTANCE: 7.4 miles round-trip
DURATION: 3.75 hours
EFFORT: Easy/moderate

9 West River Trail and Hamilton Falls Trail
DISTANCE: 5.6 miles round-trip
DURATION: 3 hours
EFFORT: Easy/moderate

10 Weathersfield Trail to Mount Ascutney
DISTANCE: 5.2 miles round-trip
DURATION: 3 hours
EFFORT: Strenuous

11 Everett Path, Halloween Tree, Cave Trail, and Carriage Road to Everett Cave
DISTANCE: 2.7 miles round-trip
DURATION: 1.5 hours
EFFORT: Easy

12 Haystack Mountain Trail
DISTANCE: 4.2 miles round-trip
DURATION: 2 hours
EFFORT: Moderate

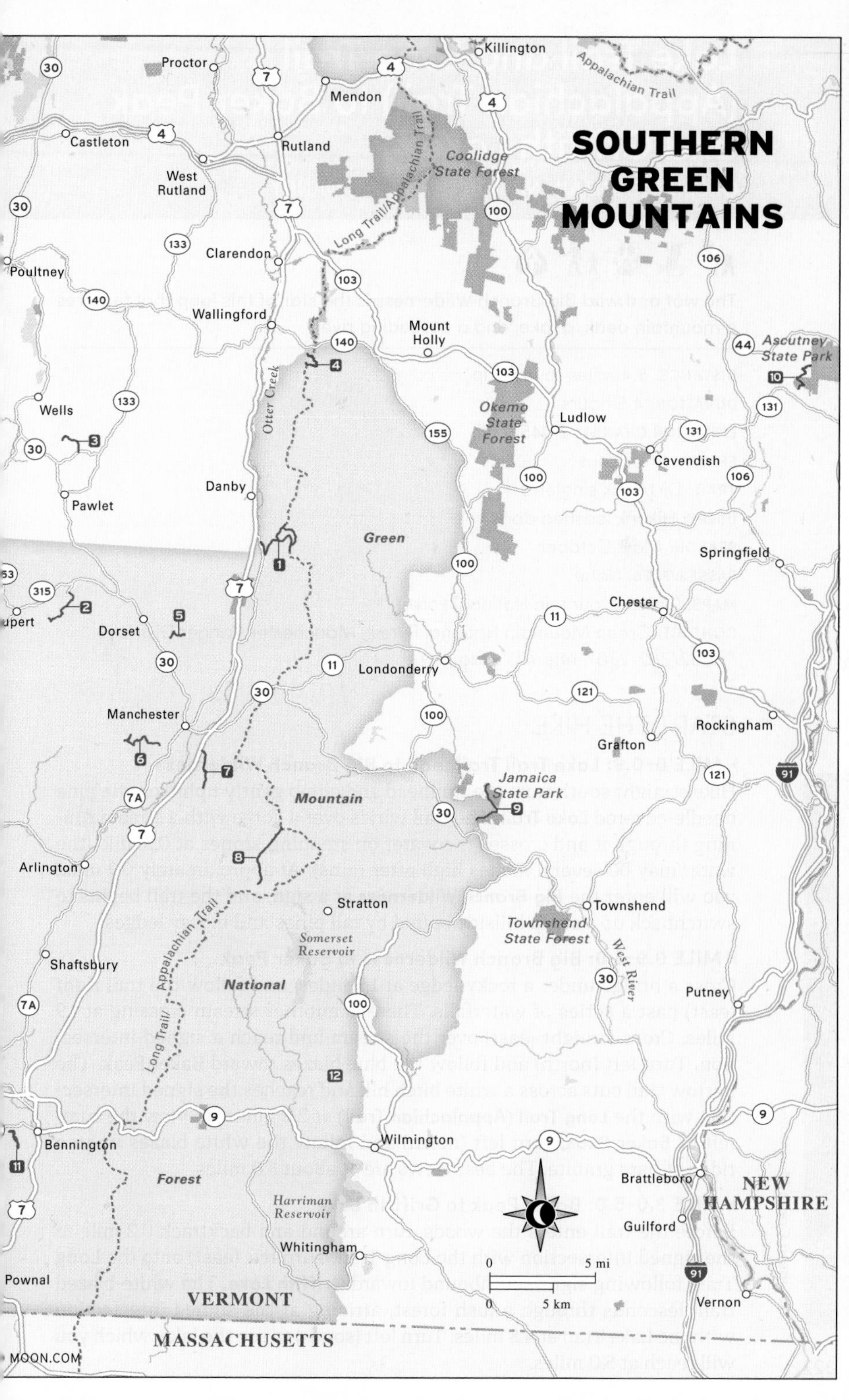

SOUTHERN GREEN MOUNTAINS
Killington
Proctor
Mendon
Appalachian Trail
Castleton
Rutland
West Rutland
Coolidge State Forest
Long Trail/Appalachian Trail
Clarendon
Poultney
Wallingford
Mount Holly
Ascutney State Park
Wells
Otter Creek
Okemo State Forest
Ludlow
Cavendish
Pawlet
Danby
Green
Springfield
Rupert
Dorset
Chester
Londonderry
Manchester
Rockingham
Grafton
Jamaica State Park
Mountain
Arlington
Stratton
Townshend
Townshend State Forest
Somerset Reservoir
Shaftsbury
West River
National
Putney
Bennington
Wilmington
Forest
Brattleboro
NEW HAMPSHIRE
Harriman Reservoir
Guilford
Whitingham
Pownal
Vernon
VERMONT
MASSACHUSETTS
0 5 mi
0 5 km
MOON.COM

1 Lake Trail and Long Trail (Appalachian Trail) to Baker Peak and Griffith Lake

GREEN MOUNTAIN NATIONAL FOREST, DANBY

The wet and wild Big Branch Wilderness is the star of this loop that features a mountain peak, a lake, and a cascading river.

DISTANCE: 8.4 miles round-trip

DURATION: 4.5 hours

ELEVATION CHANGE: 2,045 feet

EFFORT: Strenuous

TRAIL: Dirt/rock singletrack

USERS: Hikers, leashed dogs

SEASON: May-October

PASSES/FEES: None

MAPS: Green Mountain National Forest

CONTACT: Green Mountain National Forest, Manchester Ranger District, 802/362-2307, http://fs.usda.gov

START THE HIKE

▸ MILE 0-0.9: Lake Trail Trailhead to Big Branch Wilderness

Hike straight south from the trailhead and climb gently uphill on the pine needle-covered **Lake Trail.** The trail winds over a gorge with a stream running through it and crosses the water on stepping-stones at 0.3 mile (the water may be several inches high after rains). At approximately 0.9 mile, you will enter the **Big Branch Wilderness** at a sign, and the trail begins to switchback up a steep hillside bound by tall pines and mossy ledges.

▸ MILE 0.9-3.0: Big Branch Wilderness to Baker Peak

Cross a bridge under a rocky ledge at 1.5 miles, and follow the trail right (east) past a series of waterfalls. There is another stream crossing at 1.9 miles. Cross straight (east) over the stream and reach a signed intersection. Turn left (north) and follow the blue blazes toward Baker Peak. The narrow trail cuts across a white birch hill and reaches the signed intersection with the **Long Trail (Appalachian Trail)** at 2.8 miles. To view the summit of **Baker Peak,** turn left (north) and follow the white blazes up to a ridge of bare granite. The best views are at about 3.0 miles.

▸ MILE 3.0-5.0: Baker Peak to Griffith Lake

Before the trail enters the woods, turn around and backtrack 0.2 mile to the signed intersection with the Long Trail. Turn left (east) onto the Long Trail, following signs southbound toward **Griffith Lake.** The white-blazed trail descends through a lush forest, arriving at the signed intersection with the Lake Trail at 4.8 miles. Turn left (south) to see the lake, which you will reach at 5.0 miles.

▲ BIG BRANCH WILDERNESS

▸ MILE 5.0-8.4: Griffith Lake to Lake Trail

After enjoying the secluded mountain lake—a great spot to see wildlife—backtrack 0.2 mile to the intersection with the Lake Trail and bear left (northeast) onto the Lake Trail. This narrow, sometimes muddy path crosses several bubbling streams and arrives at the intersection with the trail to Baker Peak at 6.5 miles. Cross the stream and continue straight (west) down the Lake Trail, which will return to the parking lot in 1.9 miles.

DIRECTIONS

From US-7, turn east onto South End Road (Forest Road 259). The trailhead and parking lot are about 0.5 mile down the road on the left, marked with a Forest Service sign.

GPS COORDINATES: 43°18'45.5"N 72°59'12.9"W

BEST NEARBY BITES

Indulge in fresh comfort food (including great breakfast) at **Pawlet Station** (50 School St., Pawlet, 802/325-2503, http://pawletstation.com, 7am-3pm and 4:30pm-8:30pm Mon.-Tues., 7am-3pm Thurs.-Sat., 7am-2pm Sun.). It's 13 miles from the trailhead.

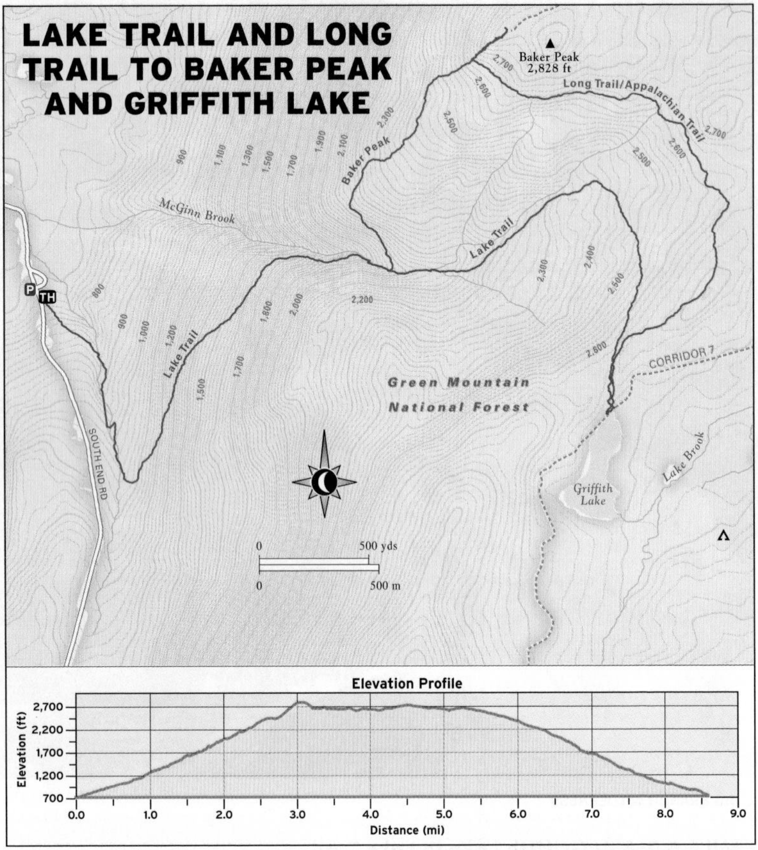
LAKE TRAIL AND LONG TRAIL TO BAKER PEAK AND GRIFFITH LAKE
Baker Peak
2,828 ft
Long Trail/Appalachian Trail
Baker Peak
McGinn Brook
Lake Trail
Lake Trail
P
TH
SOUTH END RD
Green Mountain
National Forest
CORRIDOR 7
Griffith
Lake
Lake Brook
0
500 yds
0
500 m
800
900
1,000
1,100
1,200
1,300
1,500
1,700
1,800
1,900
2,000
2,100
2,200
2,300
2,380
2,400
2,500
2,600
2,700
Elevation Profile
Elevation (ft)
2,700
2,200
1,700
1,200
700
0.0
1.0
2.0
3.0
4.0
5.0
6.0
7.0
8.0
9.0
Distance (mi)

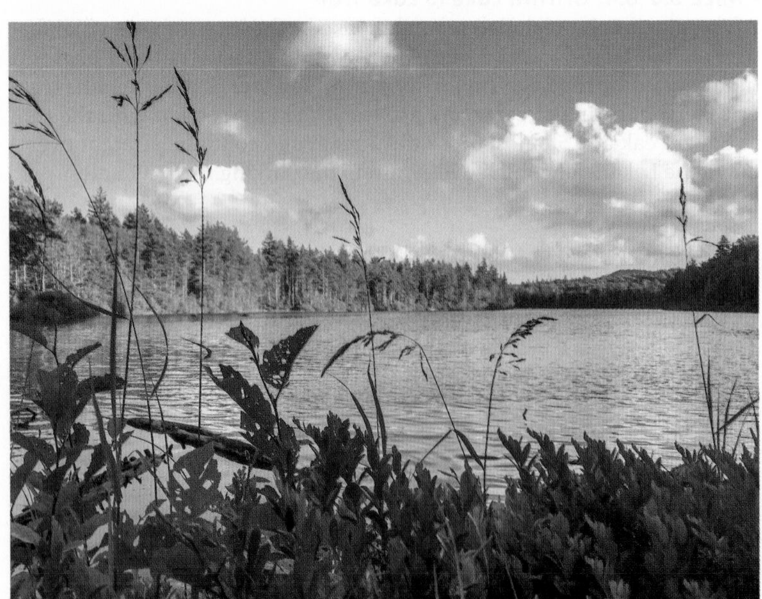

▲ GRIFFITH LAKE

2 Old Town Road and Antone Road to Antone Mountain

MERCK FOREST AND FARMLAND CENTER, RUPERT

Pick raspberries as you walk through a pastoral working farm and catch views from its highest peak.

DISTANCE: 5.2 miles round-trip
DURATION: 2.75 hours
ELEVATION CHANGE: 828 feet
EFFORT: Moderate
TRAIL: Gravel/grass doubletrack
USERS: Hikers, leashed dogs, horseback riders, cross-country skiers
SEASON: Year-round
PASSES/FEES: None
MAPS: Merck Forest and Farmland Center
CONTACT: Merck Forest and Farmland Center, 802/394-7836, http://merckforest.org

START THE HIKE

▸ MILE 0-0.3: Visitors Center to Old Town Road Vista

From the Merck Forest and Farmland visitors center, head southeast on **Old Town Road,** a wide gravel path that travels through the main section of **farm.** At 0.3 mile, bear right (southwest) to stay on Old Town Road. This vista, sometimes bustling with livestock, looks out over the farm to the **Rupert Valley** in the west.

▸ MILE 0.3-1.5: Old Town Road Vista to Antone Road

Heading southwest from the farm, the road enters a mixed hardwood forest and steadily ascends for 0.6 mile. Reach a signed intersection and continue straight (south) on **Antone Road** toward **Antone Mountain.** The grassy doubletrack works its way along a ridgeline for 0.6 mile and into a field where hikers can pick raspberries in the late summer/early fall. At the Clark's Clearing Cabin, follow the sign straight (south) to stay on Antone Road.

▸ MILE 1.5-2.6: Antone Road to Mount Antone Summit

The path narrows and climbs steeply for 0.5 mile. Here, it dips into a flat saddle and reaches another signed intersection. Go straight (west) past the Lookout Trail junction and follow Antone Road to its end at 2.4 miles. Turn right (west) and follow the trail to the **summit of Mount Antone** at 2.6 miles. The best views are looking northeast back over the farm. Descend via the same route to the visitors center.

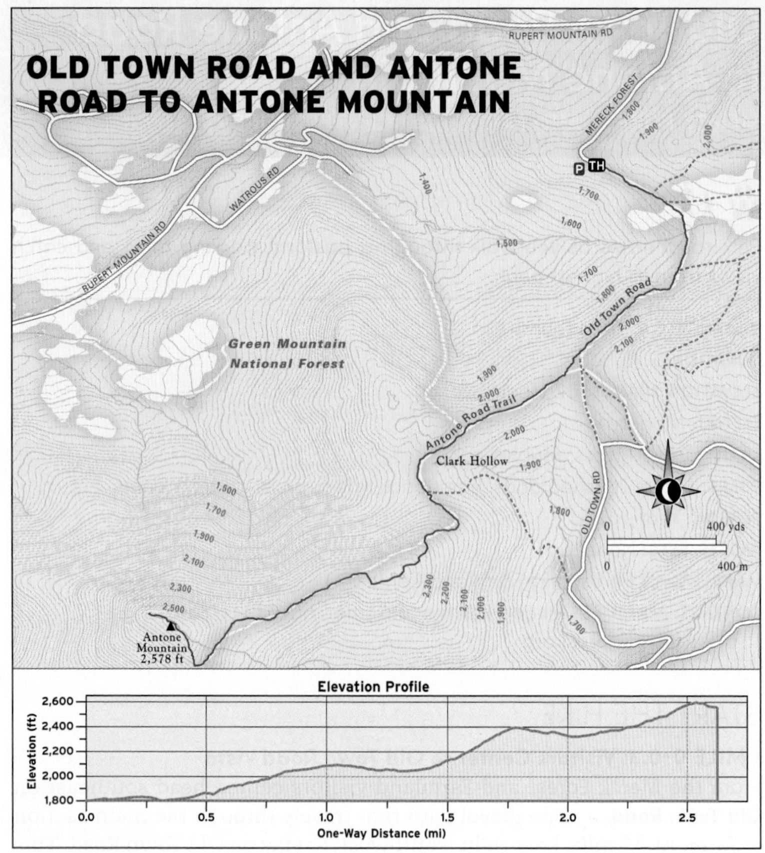

DIRECTIONS

Follow VT-30 N through Manchester and Dorset for about 8 miles to its junction with VT-315. Turn left onto VT-315 and follow it for about 2.6 miles. The main entrance to Merck Forest and Farmland Center is marked with a large sign on the left-hand side.

GPS COORDINATES: 43°16'51.8"N 73°10'08.5"W

BEST NEARBY BITES

Dorset Rising (3239 Route 30, Dorset, 802/867-7021, http://dorsetrising.com, 8am-4pm daily), a cozy eatery with outdoor seating, offers sandwiches, soups, and salads, plus amazing coffee drinks and baked goods. It's 5 miles from the trailhead.

3 Colby M. Chester Memorial Trail to Haystack Mountain

NORTH PAWLET HILLS NATURAL AREA, PAWLET

This off-the-beaten-path mountain climb is tough but quick, and hikers are rewarded with soaring views of the farm-speckled Mettawee Valley.

DISTANCE: 3.2 miles round-trip
DURATION: 1.75 hours
ELEVATION CHANGE: 998 feet
EFFORT: Moderate
TRAIL: Gravel road, dirt/rock singletrack
USERS: Hikers, leashed dogs
SEASON: May-October
PASSES/FEES: None
MAPS: None
CONTACT: The Nature Conservancy, 802/229-4425, http://nature.org

START THE HIKE

▸ MILE 0-0.6: Waite Hill Road to Colby M. Chester Memorial Trail

After parking on Waite Hill Road, follow the gravel side street (Tunket Road) north through fields for 0.2 mile until the road splits at a three-way intersection. Continue straight (north) on the main road as it climbs through woods. Reach a yellow-and-green sign for Haystack Mountain at 0.6 mile and turn left (west) onto the **Colby M. Chester Memorial Trail.**

▸ MILE 0.6-3.2: Colby M. Chester Memorial Trail to Haystack Mountain Summit

This pine needle path veers into the woods for 0.2 mile and dips into a valley where it crosses a bridge. After the bridge, the trail turns to a loose gravel path bound with beech tree roots and steepens for 0.3 mile. The path levels out temporarily for 0.2 mile under exposed rock ledges, then begins a final push to the summit of **Haystack Mountain.** The last 0.3 mile of the trail is quite steep, but the views from the bald ledge of the summit take in a panorama of mountains, farmlands, and expansive sky. The Pawlet Hills and the Mettawee River roll out to the south and west while the upper section of the Green Mountain National Forest unfolds to the north. On a clear day, views reach well into New York. Carefully use the same route to return.

▲ SUMMIT OF HAYSTACK MOUNTAIN

DIRECTIONS

Follow VT-30 north through the center of Pawlet and continue for 1.7 miles. Turn right onto Waite Hill Road and drive east for about 0.4 mile to the intersection with Tunket Road. A small green-and-yellow sign on the left side designates the start of the trail. Park along the left side of Waite Hill Road.

GPS COORDINATES: 43°22'38.2"N 73°09'53.8"W / 43.377278, -73.164956

BEST NEARBY BITES

Grab a sandwich for the trip at the **Wells Country Store** (1450 Route 30, Wells, 802/645-0332, 7am-6pm daily), which also serves beer, ice cream, and hot daily specials. It's 5 miles from the trailhead.

COLBY M. CHESTER MEMORIAL TRAIL TO HAYSTACK MOUNTAIN

Middle Mountain
1,949 ft

Haystack Mountain
1,912 ft

The Fox Cobble
1,627 ft

Edgerton Hill
1,099 ft

Colby M Chester Memorial Trail

TUNKET RD

EDGERTON DR

WAITE HILL RD

TH

0 400 yds

0 400 m

© MOON.COM

Elevation Profile

Elevation (ft): 900, 1,100, 1,300, 1,500, 1,700, 1,900

Distance (mi): 0.0, 0.5, 1.0, 1.5

▲ HAYSTACK MOUNTAIN

4 Keewaydin Trail and Long Trail (Appalachian Trail) to White Rocks Cliffs

WHITE ROCKS NATIONAL RECREATION AREA, WALLINGFORD

Climb to a sheer face of exposed white quartzite on this beautifully forested section of trail.

BEST: Vistas
DISTANCE: 3.6 miles round-trip
DURATION: 2.5 hours
ELEVATION CHANGE: 1,186 feet
EFFORT: Moderate/strenuous
TRAIL: Dirt/rock singletrack
USERS: Hikers, leashed dogs
SEASON: May-October
PASSES/FEES: None
MAPS: Green Mountain National Forest
CONTACT: Green Mountain National Forest, Manchester Ranger District, 802/362-2307, http://fs.usda.gov

START THE HIKE

▸ MILE 0-1.1: Keewaydin Trail to Long Trail (Appalachian Trail)

Find the **Keewaydin Trail** on the east end of the parking area and hike south for 0.2 mile. Bear right along the stream and climb uphill for 0.3 mile on a wide dirt path as it travels above a waterfall. The path gets narrow and rocky as it reaches the signed intersection with the **Long Trail (Appalachian Trail).** Bear right (east) to follow the white blazes southbound toward White Rocks Mountain. Continue steadily uphill to another signed junction at 1.1 miles.

▸ MILE 1.1-3.6: Long Trail (Appalachian Trail) to White Rocks Cliff Trail and Overlook

Turn right (west) to stay on the Long Trail (AT) southbound for 0.5 mile as it edges west around the mountain, crossing several bubbling creeks and mossy slabs of rock amid the shade of tall conifers. Wind through a forest of spruce saplings and reach a sign surrounded by white rock cairns. Turn right (west) to follow the blue blazes of **White Rocks Cliff Trail** toward the **White Rocks Cliff overlook.** After a slight downhill through a pine grove, the trail dead-ends at the sheer, white cliff face, 0.2 mile from the start of the blue blazes. The vista overlooks the white quartzite tumble of an ice bed exposed by glaciers, as wells as the sprawling Taconic and Adirondack Ranges in the distance. Backtrack to the parking area via the same route.

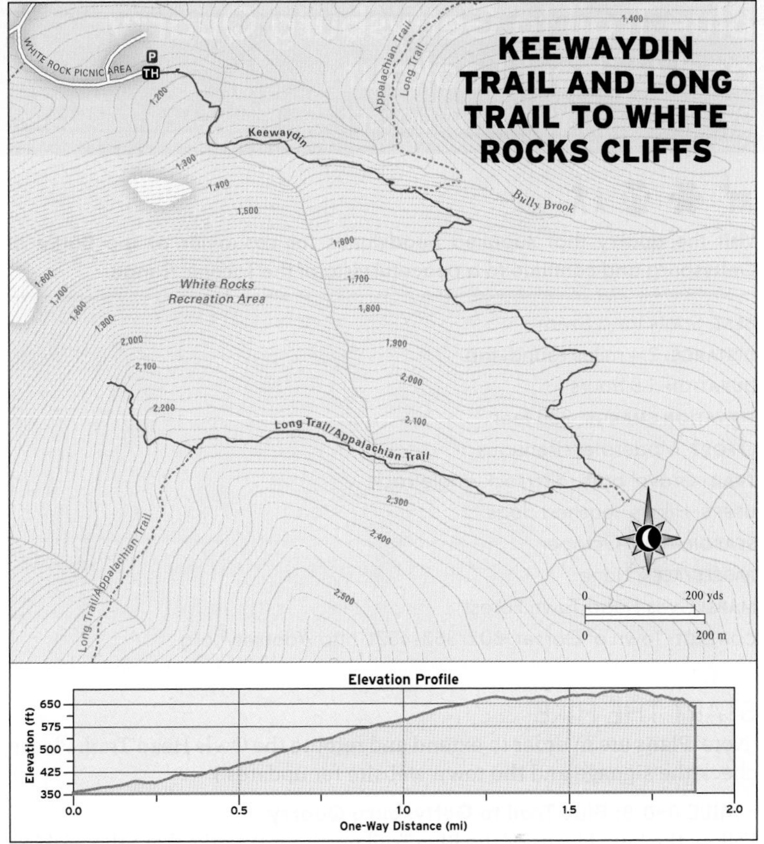

DIRECTIONS

Follow US-7 N to the center of Wallingford and then turn right onto VT-140 E. In 2 miles, bear slightly right onto Russell Road (Sugar Hill Road) and then turn right into the White Rock Picnic Area. There is a large parking lot.

GPS COORDINATES: 43°27'03.4"N 72°56'36.3"W

BEST NEARBY BITES

The Rustic Rooster Restaurant Bar and Grill (5446 Route 103, Cuttingsville, 802/492-3433, http://vtrusticrooster.com, 5pm-9pm Mon., Wed., and Thurs., noon-9pm Fri.-Sat., 10am-9pm Sun.) is a local favorite for lunch, dinner, or Sunday brunch. It is 7 miles from the trailhead.

5 Blue Trail to Gettysburg Quarry and Gilbert Lookout

OWL'S HEAD TOWN FOREST, DORSET

Visit the quarry that supplied headstones for casualties of the Battle of Gettysburg and continue to a peaceful vista of the Taconic Range.

BEST: Spots for a Swim
DISTANCE: 2.4 miles round-trip
DURATION: 1.5 hours
ELEVATION CHANGE: 936 feet
EFFORT: Moderate/strenuous
TRAIL: Gravel path, dirt/rock singletrack
USERS: Hikers, leashed dogs
SEASON: April-October
PASSES/FEES: None
MAPS: Owls Head Town Forest
CONTACT: Town of Dorset, 802/362-4571, http://dorsetvt.org

START THE HIKE

(Note: Plans are in order to extend and reroute the Owls Head Trail. Please check the signage and the town website for updates.)

▸ MILE 0-0.8: Blue Trail to Gettysburg Quarry

Follow the blue blazes of the **Blue Trail** north for 0.4 mile from the parking lot to Gettysburg Quarry. The wide dirt path, lined with a variety of wildflowers, carries straight uphill past an old root cellar and the turnoff for Klondike Quarry. Reach **Gettysburg Quarry,** an enormous former marble quarry, at 0.8 mile. The croak of frogs and sound of water droplets echo in the pools that have formed under the excavated sections of these rock cliffs. To the left (west) hikers can take in views of the Dorset hills and quarries from the knoll of the Art's Bench overlook.

▸ MILE 0.8-1.7: Gettysburg Quarry to Gilbert's Overlook

When you're done here, follow the trail to the right (south) where it continues toward **Owls Head** and Gilbert's Overlook. Walk along the staircases to a small vista of the quarries at 1.1 miles. From here, continue along the trail for 0.3 mile to the shoulder of Owls Head. Flagging and signs mark the trail as it climbs 0.3 mile of switchbacks up a steep, ledgy hill to **Gilbert's Overlook.** This rocky, blueberry-lined perch boasts great views west across the Taconic Range; the hill drops steeply into the green valley below. Follow the same route back to the parking lot. Cool off with a dip in **Norcross-West (Dorset) Quarry** at the end of Black Rock Lane.

▲ GETTYSBURG QUARRY

DIRECTIONS

Take VT-30 to just south of Dorset center and then turn onto Black Rock Lane. At the fork, bear right to stay on Black Rock Lane and then turn right onto Ken Camp Road. The trailhead is marked with a sign at the end of Ken Camp Road.

GPS COORDINATES: 43°14'44.8"N 73°04'50.7"W

BEST NEARBY BITES

Find the **Mio Bistro Mobile food truck** (802/353-2999, http://miobistromobile.com, hours vary) for out-of-this-world pizzas using fresh, healthy, locally sourced ingredients. It's usually parked at the JK Adams Kitchen Store (1430 Route 30, Dorset), 2 miles from the trailhead.

BLUE TRAIL TO GETTYSBURG QUARRY AND GILBERT LOOKOUT

Gettysburg Quarry

P TH

KEN'S CAMP RD

1,300
1,400
1,500
1,600
1,700
1,800
1,900
2,000
2,080
2,200
2,300

Owls Head 2,457 ft

Dorset Memorial Forest

0 250 yds
0 250 m

Elevation Profile

Elevation (ft): 1,200 – 1,450 – 1,700 – 1,950 – 2,200

One-Way Distance (mi): 0.0 – 0.3 – 0.5 – 0.8 – 1.0 – 1.3

▲ THIN LEAF SUNFLOWER ON THE BLUE TRAIL

6 Blue Summit Trail to Mount Equinox and Lookout Rock

EQUINOX PRESERVE, MANCHESTER

While you can drive to the top of this tallest Taconic peak, hiking to its 360-degree views on the long, steep summit trail is much more rewarding.

DISTANCE: 6 miles round-trip
DURATION: 3.25 hours
ELEVATION CHANGE: 2,772 feet
EFFORT: Strenuous
TRAIL: Gravel road, dirt/rock singletrack
USERS: Hikers, leashed dogs
SEASON: May-October
PASSES/FEES: None
MAPS: Equinox Preservation Trust, "Trail Map and Guide"
CONTACT: Equinox Preservation Trust, 802/366-1400, http://equinoxpreservationtrust.org

START THE HIKE

▸ MILE 0-1.6: Trailhead Gate to Blue Trail (and Bench)

Hike north through the gate and past the trailhead sign on the main dirt road surrounded by tall oaks. At the signed intersection at 0.4 mile, bear right (west) for the Blue Summit Trail. Follow the blue blazes west along the road, which inclines steadily to another signed intersection at 0.7 mile. Keep straight (west) to stay on the blue trail. The trail becomes rather strenuous as it climbs through a quiet wood. Reach a bench with a sign at 1.6 miles.

▸ MILE 1.6-2.7: Blue Trail (and Bench) to Visitors Center

Turn right (west) at the bench to follow the blue trail uphill on a steep and rocky trajectory with intermittent mountain views peering out from the mixed hardwood forest. The trail bends north and climbs into a cool and mossy hemlock forest. Reach an intersection at 2.5 miles and go straight (west) at the intersection, following signs for the summit/visitors center. The trail curls north around a communications tower, then turns left (south) to reach the summit and visitors center at 2.7 miles.

▸ MILE 2.7-6.0: Visitors Center to Lookout Rock

The **visitors center's lookouts** and marble benches allow hikers to survey 360-degree views of the Taconic Range and beyond. Inside the visitors center are restrooms, natural and geographic interpretive information, and historical information on the Carthusian Monastery that calls the mountain home. After enjoying the lessons and views, backtrack to the start on the blue-blazed trail, or (optional) follow the **Lookout Rock Spur** trail straight north from the visitors center for 0.5 mile to **Lookout Rock** for a great vista of Manchester below.

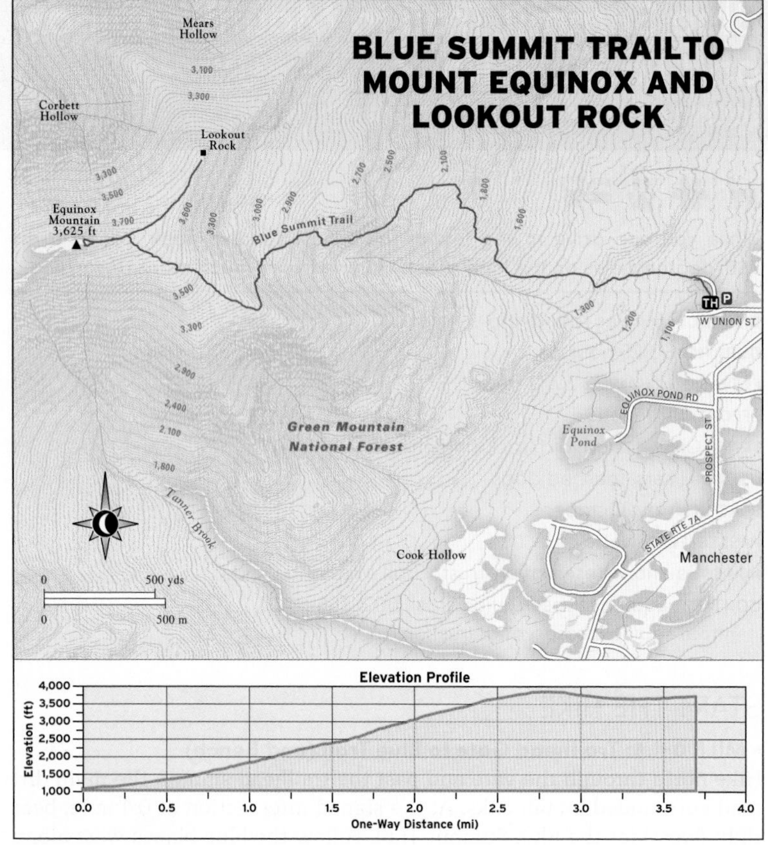

DIRECTIONS

From Main Street in Manchester, go south on VT-7A for about 1.5 miles, then turn right onto Seminary Avenue. Continue onto Prospect Street, then turn right onto West Union Street. The large parking area is marked with a sign on the right side of the road.

GPS COORDINATES: 43°09'48.3"N 73°04'57.7"W

BEST NEARBY BITES

Manchester is full of swanky restaurants, but for an affordable yet totally tasty option, try **Thai Basil** (4950 Main St., Manchester, 802/768-8433, http://thaibasilvt.com, 11:30am-3pm and 5pm-9pm Thurs.-Tues.), renowned for its noodle entrees. It is 2 miles from the trailhead.

7 Lye Brook Falls Trail

GREEN MOUNTAIN NATIONAL FOREST, MANCHESTER

This out-and-back hike to a stunning 160-foot falls follows a relatively easy route over old logging roads.

BEST: Spring hikes

DISTANCE: 4.4 miles round-trip

DURATION: 2.25 hours

ELEVATION CHANGE: 936 feet

EFFORT: Moderate

TRAIL: Dirt singletrack

USERS: Hikers, leashed dogs

SEASON: Year-round

PASSES/FEES: None

MAPS: Green Mountain National Forest

CONTACT: Green Mountain National Forest, Manchester Ranger District, 802/362-2307, http://fs.usda.gov

START THE HIKE

▸ MILE 0-0.4: Lye Brook Falls Trail to Lye Brook Wilderness

Head east on the **Lye Brook Falls Trail,** following the blue blazes for 0.4 mile. The trail wraps south toward the brook on a nice, flat track, to a sign marking the entrance to the **Lye Brook Wilderness.** Hop over two narrow streams that flow across the trail and head downhill into the Lye Brook Wilderness. The trail begins a mild elevation gain 0.6 mile from the Lye Brook Wilderness sign.

▸ MILE 0.4-2.2: Lye Brook Wilderness to Lye Brook Falls

As you make your way up the loose, gravelly trail, listen for the ethereal call of wood thrushes in the canopy of tall, thin hemlocks. Reach a signed fork at approximately 1.8 miles and bear right (west) toward the falls. This section of trail is narrow as it snakes along the edge of a densely vegetated hillside and across a slide of large rocks. The path ends at a rocky cliff near the falls at 2.2 miles. The best views of **Lye Brook Falls** are to the left (east), slightly uphill. You can also view the lower falls from the brook downhill to the right (west). Backtrack along the same route to return to the parking lot.

▲ LYE BROOK FALLS

DIRECTIONS

From Manchester Center, go east on Depot Street and then turn right onto Richville Road. Just past the post office, turn left onto East Manchester Road. Cross under US-7 and turn right onto Glen Road. Bear right onto the Lye Brook Falls Service Road and follow it to the large parking area at the end.

GPS COORDINATES: 43°09'32.9"N 73°02'29.4"W

BEST NEARBY BITES

Choose between the two outposts of local favorite **Zoey's** (http://zoeys.com): enjoy a lunch or dinner of creative American entrees at **Zoey's Double Hex Restaurant** (1568 Depot St., Manchester, 802/362-4600, 11am-9pm Wed.-Mon.), or grab a quick bite at its sister sandwich shop, **Zoey's Deli** (539 Depot St., Manchester, 802/362-0006, 10:30am-3pm daily).

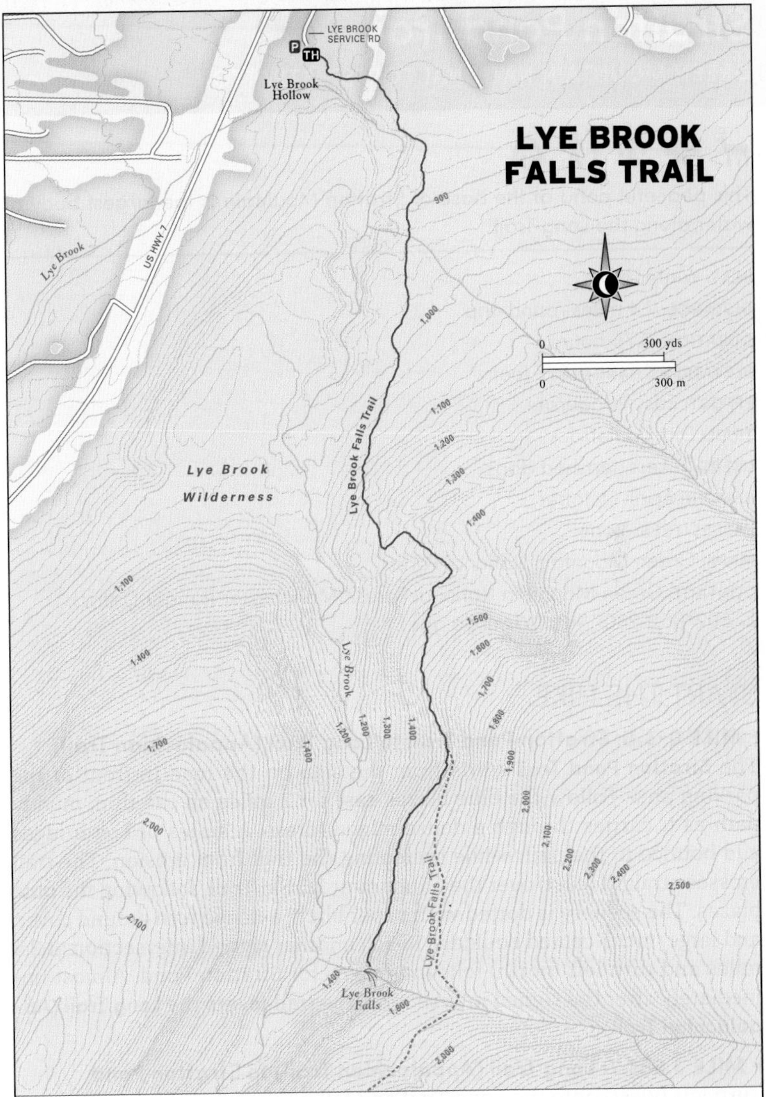

LYE BROOK FALLS TRAIL

LYE BROOK SERVICE RD

P TH

Lye Brook Hollow

Lye Brook

US HWY 7

Lye Brook Wilderness

Lye Brook Falls Trail

Lye Brook

Lye Brook Falls

0 300 yds

0 300 m

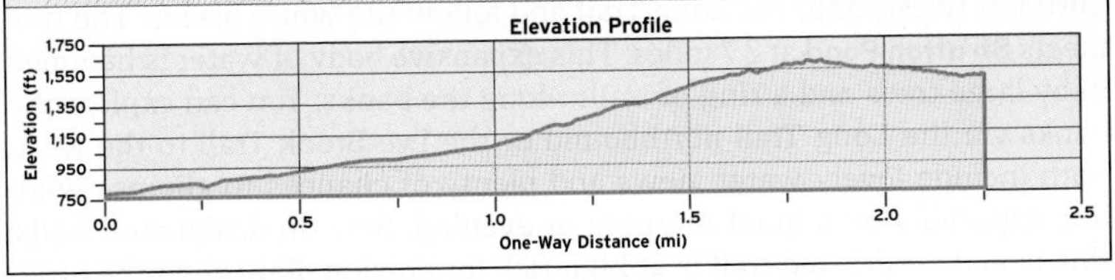

Elevation Profile

Elevation (ft): 750, 950, 1,150, 1,350, 1,550, 1,750

One-Way Distance (mi): 0.0, 0.5, 1.0, 1.5, 2.0, 2.5

8 Stratton Pond Trail

GREEN MOUNTAIN NATIONAL FOREST, STRATTON

This peaceful pond at the base of Stratton Mountain is the largest body of water along the Long Trail.

BEST: Winter hikes

DISTANCE: 7.4 miles round-trip

DURATION: 3.75 hours

ELEVATION CHANGE: 677 feet

EFFORT: Easy/moderate

TRAIL: Dirt singletrack

USERS: Hikers, leashed dogs

SEASON: April-October

PASSES/FEES: None

MAPS: Green Mountain National Forest

CONTACT: Green Mountain National Forest, Manchester Ranger District, 802/362-2307, http://fs.usda.gov

START THE HIKE

▸ MILE 0-3.5: Stratton Pond Trail to Long Trail (Appalachian Trail)

The **Stratton Pond Trail** starts from the sign on the road in front of the parking area. Follow the blue blazes east for 2 miles on the thin, muddy path as it carries through a dense mixed forest. A series of bog bridges add bounce to the path while protecting the trail from erosion. The trail crosses straight (east) over the Catamount XC Ski Trail, following the blue blazes. The scenery is dotted with paper birch, a dense fern ground cover, and large, moss-coated boulders. Reach another signed intersection at 3.5 miles and turn left (north) following signs for Stratton Pond. Almost immediately after the signed intersection, the trail meets the **Long Trail (Appalachian Trail).**

▸ MILE 3.5-3.7: Long Trail (Appalachian Trail) to Stratton Pond

Turn left (west) onto the Long Trail and follow the white blazes. The trail meets **Stratton Pond** at 3.7 miles. This expansive body of water is hemmed in by large trees and a ring of trails along the banks. You can explore the banks via the Long Trail northbound or the Lye Brook Trail to the west. Both include lovely water views and plenty of chances to glimpse wildlife, especially on a quiet morning or evening. Stay on designated trails; this heavily trafficked trail is at high risk for erosion. Return on the Stratton Pond Trail via the same route.

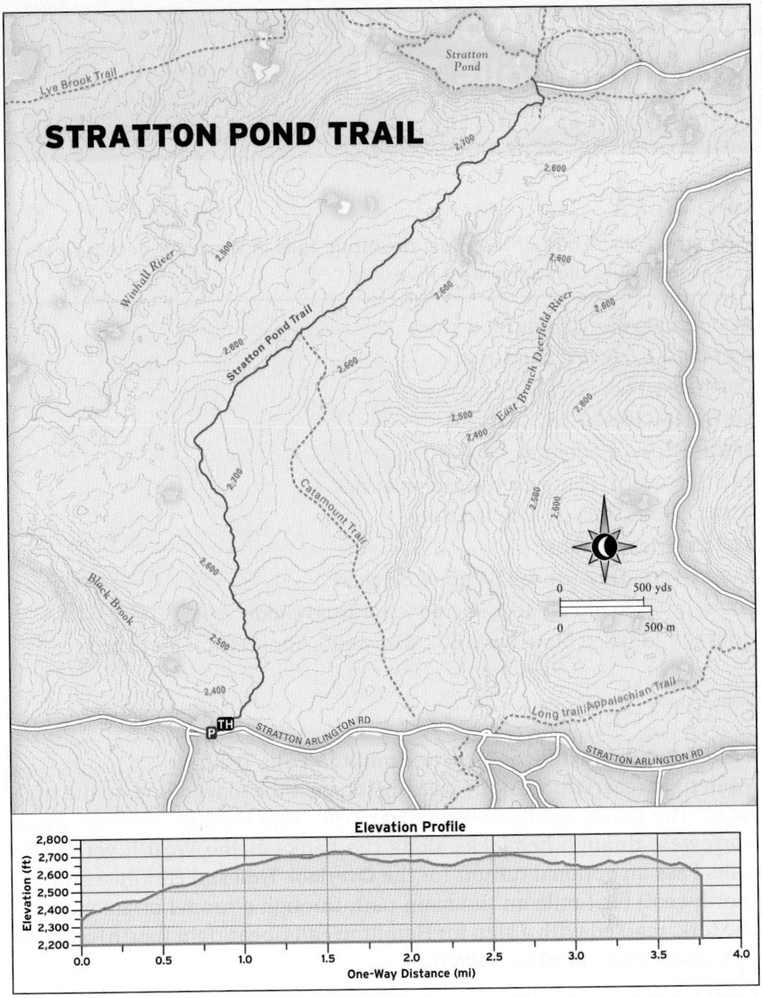

STRATTON POND TRAIL

DIRECTIONS

From VT-100, turn west onto Stratton Arlington Road toward Stratton Village. Continue for 7.7 miles to the Stratton Pond Trailhead sign on the right. Just after the sign is a dirt parking area.

GPS COORDINATES: 43°03'41.7"N 72°59'12.8"W

BEST NEARBY BREWS

Head south to Dover and relax with pub fare creations, beer, and billiards at **Dover Forge/One More Time Billiards Parlor and Tavern** (183 Route 100, Dover, 802/464-5320, http://doverforge.com, 4pm-2am daily). It's 13 miles from the trailhead.

9 West River Trail and Hamilton Falls Trail

JAMAICA STATE PARK, JAMAICA

Hamilton Falls is one of the most dramatic falls in Vermont, accessed via a flat scenic route along the West River.

BEST: Spring hikes, spots for a swim
DISTANCE: 5.6 miles round-trip
DURATION: 3 hours
ELEVATION CHANGE: 697 feet
EFFORT: Easy/moderate
TRAIL: Gravel multiuse path, dirt singletrack
USERS: Hikers, cyclists, leashed dogs
SEASON: May-October
PASSES/FEES: Day-use fee $4 adult, $2 child
MAPS: Jamaica State Park, "Recreational Trails Guide"
CONTACT: Jamaica State Park, 802/874-4600, http://vtstateparks.com

START THE HIKE

▸ MILE 0-1.9: West River Trail to Hamilton Falls Trail

Walk right (east) through the parking lot, past the playground, to the trailhead. The gravel multiuse **West River Trail** (also used for cycling) winds northwest through hemlocks along the banks of the West River for 0.9 mile. Pass an optional turnoff for the **Overlook Trail** and continue straight (northwest) for 1 mile on the main path through a tunnel of greenery. At the fork, marked with a sign for Hamilton Falls, bear right (north) onto the dirt singletrack **Hamilton Falls Trail.**

▸ MILE 1.9-2.8: Hamilton Falls Trail to Hamilton Falls

Continue uphill for 0.4 mile on the rocky blue-blazed path, which climbs high over the Cobb River gorge with small cascades flowing below. The trail, originally an old wagon road, evens out and softens to a smooth dirt surface atop a wooded ridgeline. Reach a sign pointing left (north) to Hamilton Falls at 2.7 miles. Turn left (north) past the sign and descend the wooden stairs. Then, travel right (east) on the sloping dirt path along the hillside to reach the falls at 2.8 miles. Enjoy marveling at this impressive 125-foot cascade, but please resist the urge to go swimming—there have been a number of fatalities here. When you're done admiring the falls, backtrack to the Jamaica State Park parking area via the same route and cool off with a dip in **Salmon Hole,** on the river just left (west) of the parking area.

▲ HAMILTON FALLS

DIRECTIONS

Take VT-30 into the center of Jamaica and turn onto Depot Street. Turn left onto Salmon Hole Lane and follow it to the end, where you'll find the signed entrance to Jamaica State Park. Check in at the station to pay the entrance fee and receive parking directions.

GPS COORDINATES: 43°06'28.3"N 72°46'28.8"W

BEST NEARBY BITES

Visit the renovated **North Country General** (3894 Route 30, Jamaica, 802/444-0269, 4pm-8pm Tues., 11am-9pm Thurs., 8am-9pm Fri.-Sat., 8am-4pm Sun.) for killer breakfasts, sandwiches, and beer on draft. Check its Facebook page for events listings, including live music and farm-to-table dinners. It's 1 mile from the trailhead.

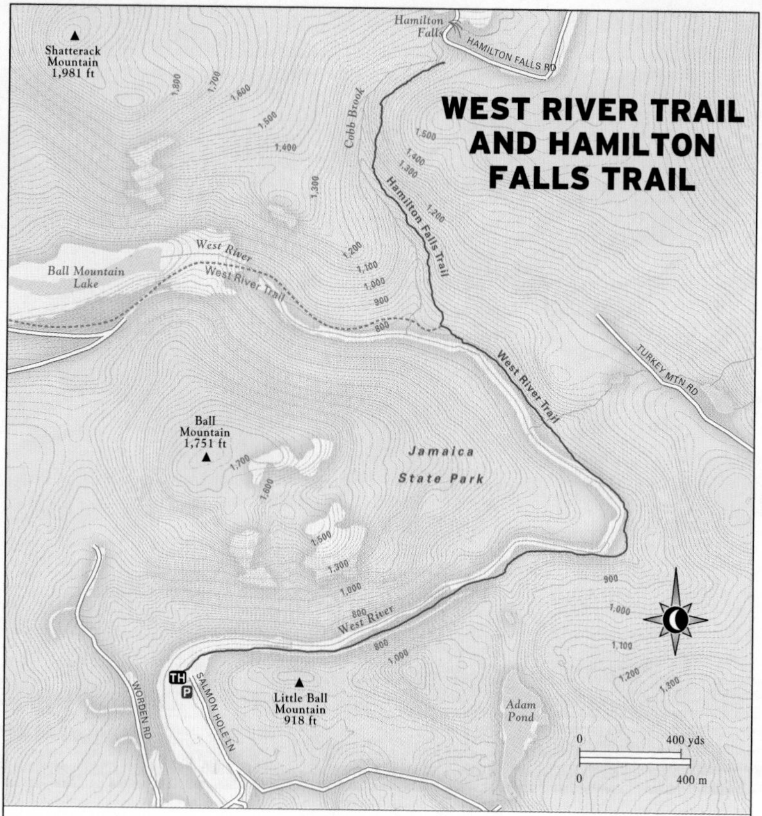

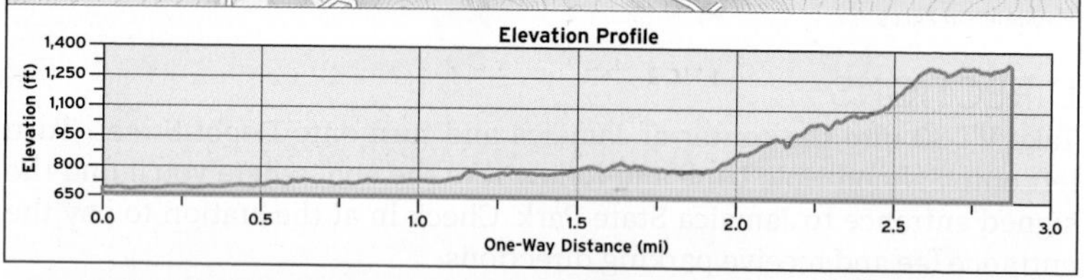

WEST RIVER TRAIL AND HAMILTON FALLS TRAIL

Elevation Profile

▲ THE HAMILTON FALLS TRAIL

10 Weathersfield Trail to Mount Ascutney

MOUNT ASCUTNEY STATE PARK, WEATHERSFIELD

This path to the observation tower on Ascutney's 3,144-foot summit passes two rushing waterfalls and several scenic vistas.

BEST: Brew hikes
DISTANCE: 5.2 miles round-trip
DURATION: 3 hours
ELEVATION CHANGE: 1,766 feet
EFFORT: Strenuous
TRAIL: Dirt/rock path
USERS: Hikers, leashed dogs
SEASON: April-November
PASSES/FEES: None
MAPS: Mount Ascutney State Park, "Recreational Guide"
CONTACT: Mount Ascutney State Park, 802/674-2060, http://vtstateparks.com

START THE HIKE

▸ MILE 0-1.1: Weathersfield Trail to Crystal Cascade Falls

Follow the white blazes of the **Weathersfield Trail** north from the parking area on a slight uphill for 0.4 mile. Cross straight (east) over **Little Cascade Falls** and commence climbing the hill. At the top of the hill, at 0.5 mile, hop over the small stream. Pass under a huge ledge and then climb the ladder to a small rocky vista. Edge along the west side of the hill to reach a signed intersection at 1.0 mile. Continue straight (west) on the Weathersfield Trail toward **Crystal Cascade Falls.** Reach the falls and vista at 1.1 miles.

▸ MILE 1.1-2.1: Crystal Cascade Falls to Gus's Lookout

This sliding cascade drops steeply to the left (west), revealing views of Little Ascutney Mountain along the horizon. Use caution at the top of the falls; the rocks can be very slippery. Turn right (east) to follow the trail. Cross another stream at 1.4 miles and begin a steep climb for 0.7 mile. There is a signed (optional) turnoff right (south) to **Gus's Lookout.** If you choose to take it, rejoin the main trail after the turnoff and continue past a series of huge boulders.

▸ MILE 2.1-2.6: Gus's Lookout to Mount Ascutney and Observation Tower

At 2.3 miles, reach a signed intersection where another optional spur leads left (west) to the vistas of **West Peak.** The Weathersfield Trail continues straight (east) through the intersection and over some steep scrambles. Reach the end of the trail at 2.6 miles. For the best views, turn left (west) to the **observation tower** and climb to the top. This 360-degree view across the Connecticut River and into New York, New Hampshire, and

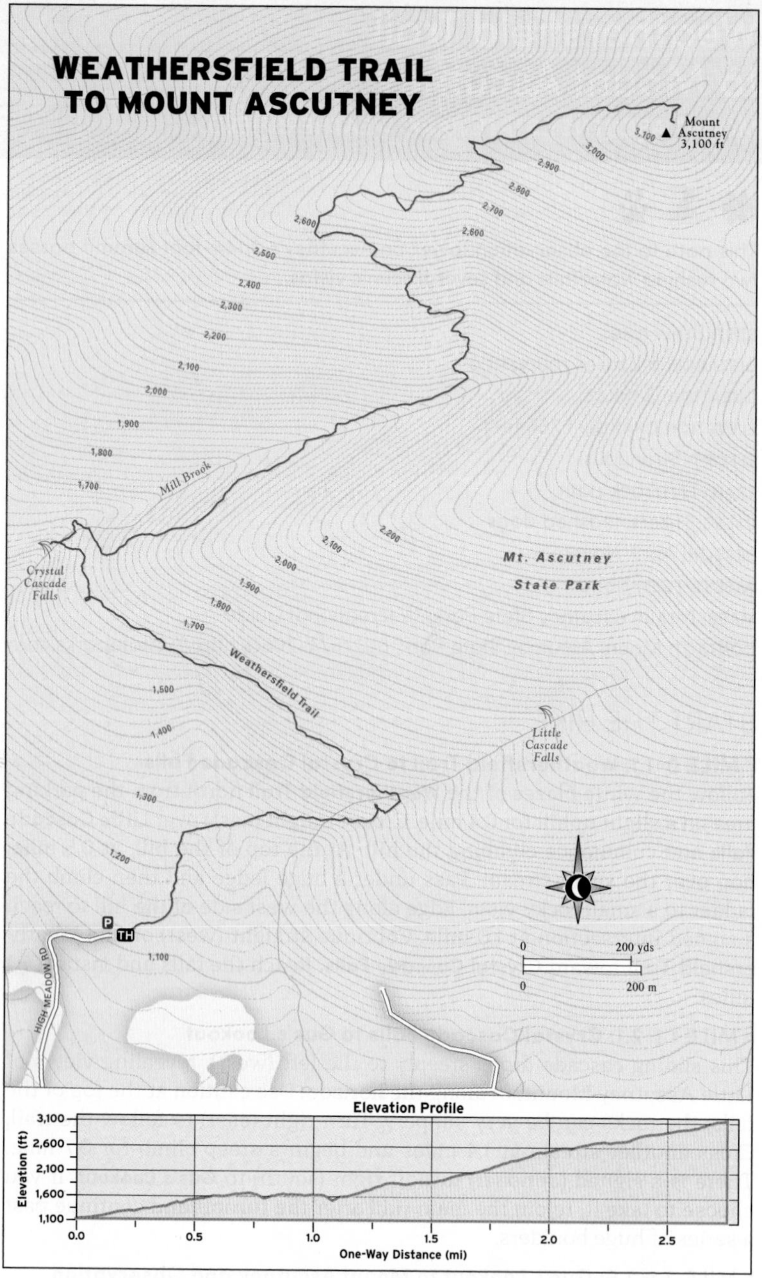

WEATHERSFIELD TRAIL TO MOUNT ASCUTNEY

Mount Ascutney 3,100 ft

Mt. Ascutney State Park

Mill Brook

Crystal Cascade Falls

Weathersfield Trail

Little Cascade Falls

HIGH MEADOW RD

P

TH

0 200 yds

0 200 m

3,100 3,000 2,900 2,800 2,700 2,600 2,600 2,500 2,400 2,300 2,200 2,100 2,000 1,900 1,800 1,700 2,200 2,100 2,000 1,900 1,800 1,700 1,500 1,400 1,300 1,200 1,100

Elevation Profile

Elevation (ft): 1,100 1,600 2,100 2,600 3,100

One-Way Distance (mi): 0.0 0.5 1.0 1.5 2.0 2.5

▲ CRYSTAL CASCADE FALLS

Massachusetts is among the best in southern Vermont on a clear day. Descend the same route on the Weathersfield Trail to reach the trailhead.

DIRECTIONS

From Weathersfield, travel west on VT-131 for 3.2 miles; then turn right onto Weathersfield Trail Road. The parking area/trailhead sign are at the end of the road.

GPS COORDINATES: 43°25'36.7"N 72°27'59.4"W

BEST NEARBY BREWS

Ascutney is just around the corner from Harpoon Brewery's **Riverbend Taps and Beer Garden** (336 Ruth Carney Dr., Windsor, 802/674-5491, http://harpoonbrewery.com, 10am-9pm daily). Take a tour and then enjoy a fresh draft and some maple Sriracha wings in the taproom. The taproom is 13 miles from the trailhead.

11 Everett Path, Halloween Tree, Cave Trail, and Carriage Road to Everett Cave

BENNINGTON AREA TRAILS SYSTEM, BENNINGTON

Hike these quiet trails on the Southern Vermont College campus to Everett Cave, a marble solution cave with high chambers to explore.

DISTANCE: 2.7 miles round-trip
DURATION: 1.5 hours
ELEVATION CHANGE: 252 feet
EFFORT: Easy
TRAIL: Gravel road, dirt singletrack
USERS: Hikers, leashed dogs, mountain bikers
SEASON: April–November
PASSES/FEES: None
MAPS: Bennington Area Trail System, "Trail Map"
CONTACT: Bennington Area Trail System, http://batsvt.org

START THE HIKE

▸ MILE 0–0.3: Trailhead to Halloween Tree Trail

Depart west from the trailhead and then turn right (north) onto **Everett Path,** a wide gravel road with red blazes. Continue past the water tank and the run-down stonework and statues above the **Everett Mansion.** At 0.3 mile, bear left (west) to follow the red blazes onto the **Halloween Tree Trail.**

▸ MILE 0.3–1.8: Halloween Tree Trail to Cave Trail

The path winds through a shady forest on the edge of the Southern Vermont College fields for 0.2 mile, with great views of the Green Mountains across campus. At the intersection with Ursa Way, continue straight (north) for 0.2 mile. Then, reach another intersection with the Lower Beacon Trail. Turn right (northeast) to stay on the Halloween Tree Trail, which winds through a hilly birch forest. After climbing a series of rolling switchbacks for 0.2 mile, the trail meets an unmarked fork at 1.1 miles. Turn left (north) to stay on the Halloween Tree Trail. The path crosses under the power lines and reaches the "**Halloween Tree**" at 1.2 miles. This spooky sugar maple is a sight to behold, with its massive gnarled trunk and weighty branches. From the tree, the trail switchbacks far to the west for 0.3 mile, then doubles back east to meet the yellow-blazed **Cave Trail** at 1.8 miles.

▸ MILE 1.8–2.2: Cave Trail to Everett Cave

Go straight (south) onto the Cave Trail for approximately 0.4 mile, where it meets an intersection with the spur trail to Everett Cave. Turn right (west)

▲ VISTA ON THE CARRIAGE ROAD

onto the spur trail and climb the slope for 210 feet to the mouth of the cave. This mossy, rocky formation may not look like much from the outside, but bring a flashlight and travel west through the narrow opening to arrive in a cool and spacious chamber composed of marble drip formations.

▸ **MILE 2.2–2.7: Everett Cave to Carriage Road and Everett Mansion**
After exploring the cave, backtrack to the intersection with the **Cave Trail** and continue right (south) on the yellow-blazed Carriage Road. This historic cobblestone road leads back to the elegant stone **Everett Mansion** at 2.7 miles. Walk through or around the mansion to arrive back at the parking lot. (Note: the mansion sometimes hosts weddings and other events, so be sure not to crash one in your hiking clothes!)

DIRECTIONS

From Main Street in the center of Bennington, go west for 1 mile and then turn left onto West Road. At the first intersection, turn right onto Monument Ave and continue for 0.5 mile. Then, turn right onto Regwood Road. At the fork, bear left onto Mansion Drive and follow it to the parking lot at the end. Parking for trails is marked with signs at the southwest corner of the lot.

GPS COORDINATES: 42°51'56.9"N 73°13'07.2"W

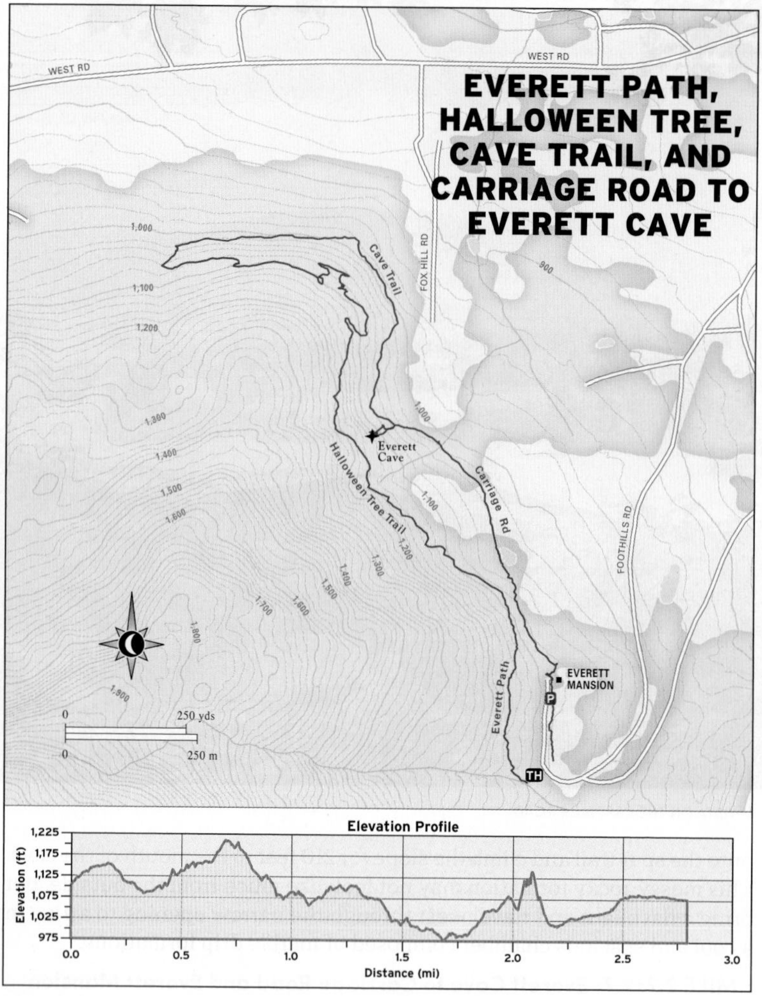

EVERETT PATH, HALLOWEEN TREE, CAVE TRAIL, AND CARRIAGE ROAD TO EVERETT CAVE

WEST RD
FOX HILL RD
FOOTHILLS RD
Cave Trail
Halloween Tree Trail
Carriage Rd
Everett Path
Everett Cave
EVERETT MANSION
P
TH
0 250 yds
0 250 m

Elevation Profile
Elevation (ft): 975, 1,025, 1,075, 1,125, 1,175, 1,225
Distance (mi): 0.0, 0.5, 1.0, 1.5, 2.0, 2.5, 3.0

BEST NEARBY BREWS

Bennington is a little-known foodie gem. Check out local favorite **Madison Brewing Company Pub and Restaurant** (428 Main St., Bennington, 802/442-7397, http://madisonbrewingco.com, 11:30am-9pm Sun.-Thurs., 11:30am-10pm Fri.-Sat.), 2 miles from the trailhead, for hot pub grub and house-made brews and sodas.

12 Haystack Mountain Trail

GREEN MOUNTAIN NATIONAL FOREST, WILMINGTON

The quiet, hemlock-bound Haystack Mountain Trail cuts through a series of ledges to lovely views of Haystack Pond and Mount Snow.

DISTANCE: 4.2 miles round-trip

DURATION: 2 hours

ELEVATION CHANGE: 948 feet

EFFORT: Moderate

TRAIL: Gravel road, dirt/rock singletrack

USERS: Hikers, leashed dogs

SEASON: April-November

PASSES/FEES: None

MAPS: USGS Mount Snow Quad

CONTACT: Green Mountain National Forest, Manchester Ranger District, 802/362-2307, http://fs.usda.gov

START THE HIKE

▸ MILE 0-0.6: Haystack Mountain Trailhead to Deerfield Ridge Trail

Hike north from the trailhead on the wide gravel road for 575 feet as it gradually gains elevation. At the gate, continue straight (north) as the road continues slightly uphill for approximately 0.5 mile. Reach a signed intersection with the **Deerfield Ridge Trail** at the **Binney Brook Ravine.**

▸ MILE 0.6-4.2: Deerfield Ridge Trail to Haystack Summit

Turn left (southwest), following signs for the Haystack Mountain Trail/Deerfield Ridge Trail, toward the Haystack Mountain summit. The rocky trail crosses narrow tributary streams and enters a sprawling wood. After traveling southwest over rolling hills, the trail bends sharply northwest to ascend a rather steep hill. The trail is marked with blue blazes, but they are intermittent. Reach a ridgeline where the trail flattens out and carries through a thick hemlock forest bordered by granite ledges. After winding through the ledges, the trail comes to a signed intersection at 1.8 miles. Turn right (east), following signs for the **Haystack Summit.** Blue arrows mark the way up a sharp, rocky ascent through a thick coniferous forest. Reach the summit at 2.1 miles. Though this peak is partially forested, there are great views of Haystack Pond below, the Harriman Reservoir to the south, and Mount Pisgah (more commonly known as Mount Snow) to the north. Hikers can also catch glimpses of a farm of wind turbines to the southwest on a clear day. Descend via the same track for a round-trip of about 4.2 miles.

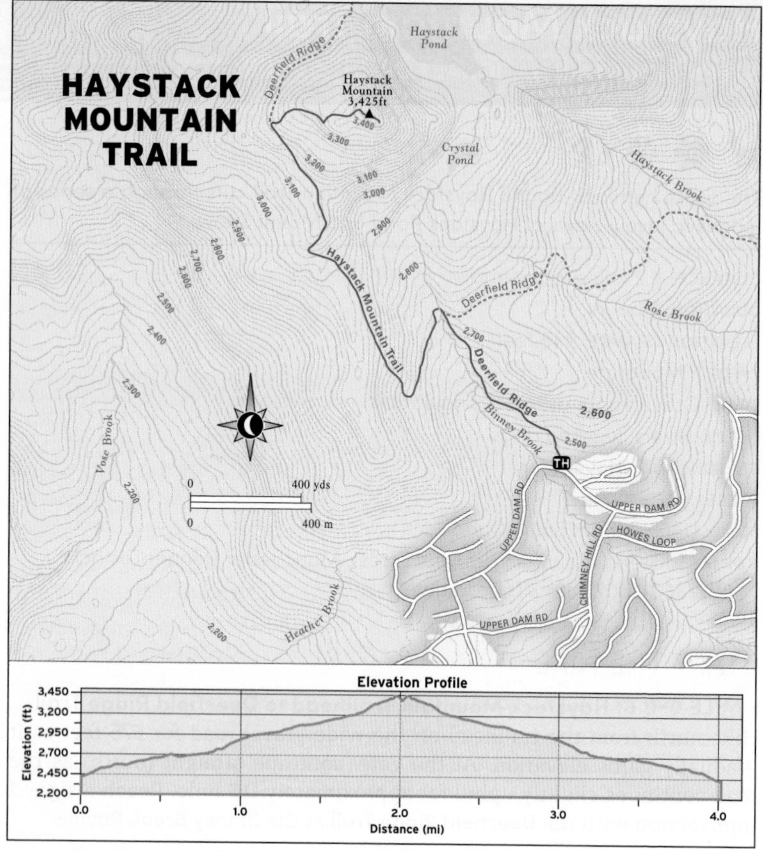

DIRECTIONS

Take VT-9 just west of downtown Wilmington and turn north onto Haystack Road. Follow Haystack Road for about 1 mile, then turn left onto Chimney Hill Road. At the intersection in 1.7 miles, turn left onto Upper Dam Road. The trailhead is on the right in 0.2 mile. There is no lot, but limited roadside parking is available.

GPS COORDINATES: 42°53'58.7"N 72°54'38.9"W / 42.899626, -72.910800

BEST NEARBY BITES

The **Village Roost** (20 W. Main St., Wilmington, 802/464-3344, http://villageroost.com, 8am-4pm Mon.-Thurs., 8am-6pm Fri.-Sun, hours may change seasonally), 4 miles from the trailhead, serves up organic sandwiches, burgers, and excellent fries and coffee in a cozy, low-key environment with plenty of indoor and outdoor seating. Beer, wine, and cider are available.

NEARBY CAMPGROUNDS

Dispersed primitive camping and shelters are available within Green Mountain National Forest

NAME	LOCATION	FACILITIES	SEASON	FEE
Greendale Campground	698 Greendale Rd., Weston, VT 05161	11 RV/tent sites; vault toilets; no water	late May-mid-October	$10
802/362-2307, http://fs.usda.gov				
Grout Pond Recreation Area	Forest Road 263, Stratton, VT 05360	6 RV sites, 11 walk-in tent sites; vault toilets; pump water	year-round	$16
802/362-2307, http://fs.usda.gov				
Hapgood Pond Recreation Area	1615 Hapgood Pond Rd., Peru, VT 05152	28 tent sites; restrooms	late May-mid-October	$20
802/888-1349, http://fs.usda.gov				
Jamaica State Park	48 Salmon Hole Ln., West Townshend, VT 05359	41 RV/tent sites; restrooms	early May-mid-October	$20-27
802/874-4600, http://vtstateparks.com/Jamaica				
Mount Ascutney State Park	1826 Back Mountain Rd., Windsor, VT 05089	38 tent/RV sites, 10 lean-to sites; restrooms	mid-May-mid-October	$20-27
802/674-2060, http://vtstateparks.com/ascutney				
Wilgus State Park	3985 Route 5, Ascutney, VT 05030	15 RV/tent sites, 9 lean-to sites, 4 cabins; restrooms	late-April-mid-October	$20-50
802/674-5422, http://vtstateparks.com/wilgus				
Woodford State Park	142 State Park Rd., Woodford, VT 05201	76 RV/tent sites, 20 lean-to sites, 4 cabins; restrooms	May-mid-October	$20-50
802/447-7169, http://vtstateparks.com/woodford				
Emerald Lake State Park	65 Emerald Lake Ln., East Dorset, VT 05253	66 RV/tent sites, 37 lean-to sites; restrooms	late May-mid-October	$20-27
802/362-1655, http://vtstateparks.com/emerald				

CHAMPLAIN VALLEY AND STOWE

Sweeping green hills. Red farmhouses with cow pastures. Great lumbering mountains that seem to cast shadows over the lush landscape. This is Vermont as many imagine it. The landscape around the Champlain Valley and Stowe is an unlikely mix of soft farmlands and titanic peaks that contain some of the toughest trails in Vermont—many of which offer indelible views of Lake Champlain's deep-blue waters. And thanks to the proximity of growing towns like Burlington, a day in the backcountry here can be complemented by a glass of imperial IPA and a dinner of oyster ssam with local kimchi, followed by a maple creemee. It's almost excessively Vermont! But a little decadence never hurt anyone—especially after a tough hike.

▲ the meadow path to the Chazy Fossil Reef

▲ the craggy summit of Mount Mansfield

◂ ADIRONDACK CHAIRS ON TOP OF MOUNT PHILO

1 Stowe Pinnacle
DISTANCE: 3.4 miles round-trip
DURATION: 2.5 hours
EFFORT: Moderate

2 Sterling Pond
DISTANCE: 2.6 miles round-trip
DURATION: 3 hours
EFFORT: Moderate

3 Mount Mansfield via the Sunset Ridge Trail
DISTANCE: 5.2 miles round-trip
DURATION: 4.5 hours
EFFORT: Strenuous

4 Little River History Hike
DISTANCE: 4 miles round-trip
DURATION: 2 hours
EFFORT: Easy

5 Camel's Hump
DISTANCE: 6.8 miles round-trip
DURATION: 5 hours
EFFORT: Strenuous

6 Mount Philo
DISTANCE: 2.2 miles round-trip
DURATION: 1.5 hours
EFFORT: Moderate

7 Waterbury Trail to Mount Hunger
DISTANCE: 3.9 miles round-trip
DURATION: 3 hours
EFFORT: Strenuous

8 Chazy Fossil Reef
DISTANCE: 1.7 miles round-trip
DURATION: 1 hour
EFFORT: Easy

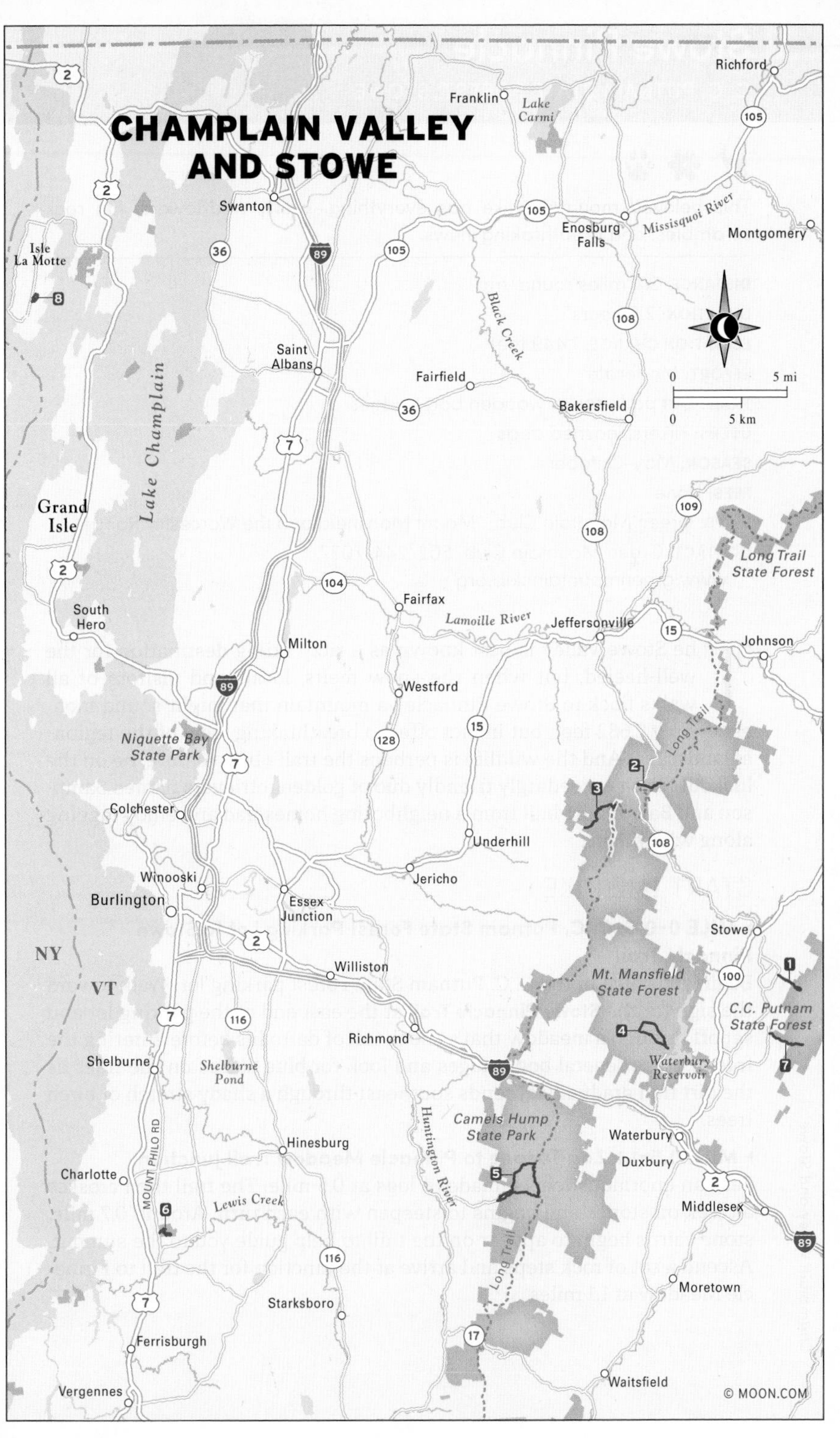
CHAMPLAIN VALLEY AND STOWE
Richford
Franklin
Lake Carmi
Swanton
Enosburg Falls
Missisquoi River
Montgomery
Isle La Motte
Black Creek
Saint Albans
Fairfield
Bakersfield
Lake Champlain
0 5 mi
0 5 km
Grand Isle
Long Trail State Forest
Fairfax
Lamoille River
Jeffersonville
South Hero
Milton
Johnson
Westford
Long Trail
Niquette Bay State Park
Colchester
Underhill
Winooski
Jericho
Burlington
Essex Junction
Stowe
NY
VT
Williston
Mt. Mansfield State Forest
C.C. Putnam State Forest
Richmond
Shelburne
Shelburne Pond
Waterbury Reservoir
Huntington River
Camels Hump State Park
Waterbury
Hinesburg
Duxbury
Charlotte
MOUNT PHILO RD
Lewis Creek
Middlesex
Long Trail
Moretown
Starksboro
Ferrisburgh
Waitsfield
Vergennes
© MOON.COM

1 Stowe Pinnacle

C. C. PUTNAM STATE FOREST, STOWE

This beloved mountain hike has everything—pretty wildflowers, fun rock scrambles, and breathtaking views.

DISTANCE: 3.4 miles round-trip

DURATION: 2.5 hours

ELEVATION CHANGE: 1,449 feet

EFFORT: Moderate

TRAIL: Dirt path, rocks, wooden bog bridges

USERS: Hikers, leashed dogs

SEASON: May-October

FEES: None

MAPS: Green Mountain Club, "Mount Mansfield and the Worcester Range"

CONTACT: Green Mountain Club, 802/244-7037, www.greenmountainclub.org

The Stowe Valley is best known as a ritzy skiing destination for the well-heeled, but when the snow melts, locals and visitors of all walks flock to Stowe Pinnacle—a mountain that might sound modest at only 2,682 feet, but in fact offers a breathtaking view of the regional landscape. And the wildlife is perhaps the trail's best feature; be on the lookout for an exceedingly friendly duo of golden retrievers named Sampson and Baylor who hail from a neighboring homestead and enjoy tagging along with hikers.

START THE HIKE

▸ MILE 0-0.5: C. C. Putnam State Forest Parking Lot to Stowe Pinnacle Trail

Begin your hike in the C. C. Putnam State Forest parking lot. Walk toward the sign for the **Stowe Pinnacle Trail** at the east end of the parking lot and set off through a meadow that's chock full of daffodils before entering the forest. Cross several bog bridges and look for blue blazes on the trees as the dirt trail gradually ascends southeast through a shady stretch of birch trees.

▸ MILE 0.5-1.1: Log Teepee to Pinnacle Meadow Trail Junction

Pass an enormous teepee made of logs at 0.5 mile. The trail then crosses a creek on stones and begins to steepen with each turn. Around 0.7 mile, stone cairns begin to appear on the trail to help guide you to the summit. Ascend a set of rock steps and arrive at the junction for the trail to Pinnacle Meadow at 1.1 miles.

▲ THE EXPOSED SUMMIT OF STOWE PINNACLE

▸ MILE 1.1–1.5: Stowe Pinnacle Meadow Trail Junction to Hogback Mountain Trail Junction

At the junction with Pinnacle Meadow Trail, keep right to stay on Stowe Pinnacle Trail and continue ascending the mountain. Make your way up a steeper series of stone staircases and look for a sign reading "Vista" nailed to a tree at 1.2 miles. This ledge offers partial views of the Stowe Valley. The forest starts to become airier after this point, hinting at your proximity to the top. The trail starts to curve around the cone of the summit and bypasses a couple of wooden stepladders and a few more (smaller) stone staircases.

▸ MILE 1.5–1.7: Hogback Mountain Trail Junction to Stowe Summit

Turn right at the junction for **Hogback Mountain Trail** at 1.5 miles and pass into boreal forest. This final 0.2-mile stretch becomes a fun scramble up several sloped rock faces. There are a few stepladders to aid your passage. You'll reach the summit of **Stowe Pinnacle** at 1.7 miles. (This is where you're most likely to encounter the golden retrievers.)

Once you're ready to return to your car, you can retrace your steps, or you can extend the hike into a loop by backtracking to the junction for Pinnacle Meadows Trail, taking a right onto that trail, and descending through the meadows back to the road. It's not as scenic as it sounds—most of the meadow views are obscured by trees—but it's a useful modification for hikers who want more exercise.

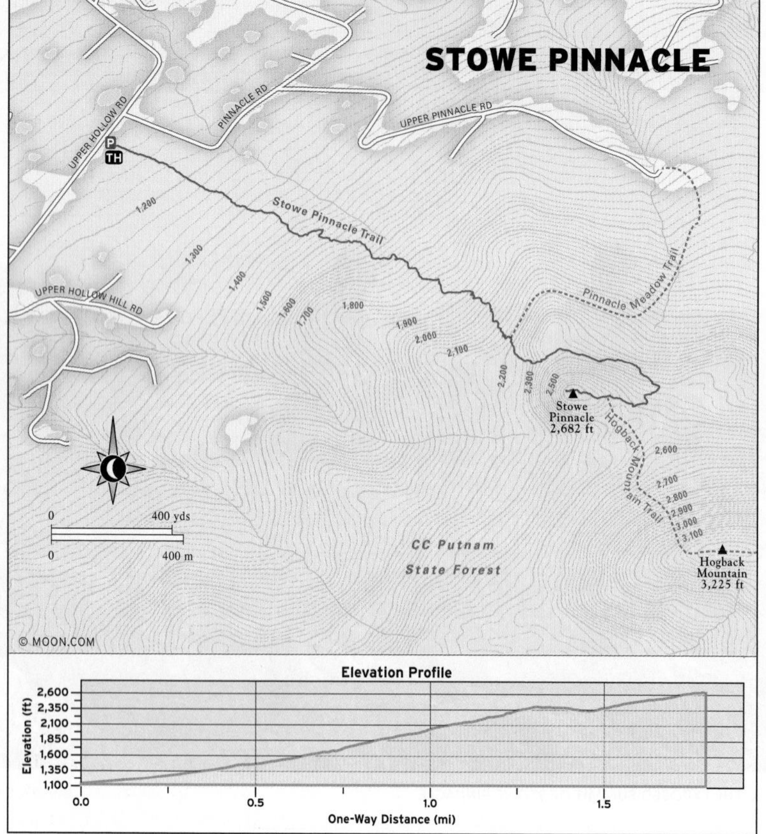

DIRECTIONS

From Burlington, drive southeast on I-89 S and take Exit 10 for VT-100 N toward Stowe. Turn left onto VT-100 N and head north for 8 miles. Take a right turn onto Gold Brook Road, cross the bridge over Gold Brook, and then make an immediate left to stay on Gold Brook Road. Drive east to end of the road, turn right onto Upper Hollow Road, and then make a left turn into the Stowe Pinnacle Trailhead parking lot. If the lot is full, you can park alongside the road near the lot.

GPS COORDINATES: 44°26'19.5"N 72°40'03.9"W, 44.438751, -72.667751

BEST NEARBY BITES

There are few better ways to appreciate Vermont's agricultural scene than by munching on a Mediterranean salad or a veggie-loaded, lemon-infused hummus wrap at Stowe's **Green Goddess Café** (618 S Main St., Stowe, 802/253-5255, www.greengoddessvt.com, 7:30am-3pm Mon.-Fri., 8am-3pm Sat.-Sun.). If it's a post-hike libation you're after, you can't go wrong with a glass of malbec and some charcuterie or tapas at **Cork Wine Bar & Market** (35 School St., Stowe, 802/760-6143, www.corkvt.com, 4pm-9pm Mon.-Sun.).

2 Sterling Pond

SMUGGLERS' NOTCH STATE PARK, JEFFERSONVILLE

This mountain hike gives your calves a solid workout before delivering you to Vermont's highest-elevation trout pond.

BEST: Spring hikes, brew hikes
DISTANCE: 2.6 miles round-trip
DURATION: 3 hours
ELEVATION CHANGE: 1,040 feet
EFFORT: Moderate
TRAIL: Dirt path, rock and wood stairs, wooden bog bridges, water crossings on stones
USERS: Hikers, leashed dogs
SEASON: May-October
PASSES/FEES: None
MAPS: Smugglers' Notch State Park website
CONTACT: Smugglers' Notch State Park, 802/253-4014, www.vtstateparks.com/smugglers.html

Sitting pretty in the northeastern heights of Smugglers' Notch—a wooded cleft between Mount Mansfield and Spruce Peak through which Prohibition-era bootleggers trafficked shipments of hooch—Sterling Pond is one of Vermont's most elegant and tranquil bodies of water. It's also stocked with trout, which makes it a popular hangout for adventurous fly-fishers. The most direct access route is the Sterling Pond Trail, which climbs from the notch floor and merges with Vermont's famous Long Trail (the oldest long-distance backpacking trail in America) to reach the pond.

START THE HIKE

▸ MILE 0-0.2: Smugglers' Notch Visitors Center to Sterling Pond Trail

Begin the hike in the Smugglers' Notch visitors center parking lot on Mountain Road. Walk east across the road and pick up the **Sterling Pond Trail** by the trailhead sign. Blue blazes mark the way forward. Heading east through a forest of birch and maple trees the trail kicks off with a steep and winding staircase of rocks and thick tree roots. The widely spaced trees offer nice views of the road below. You may be surprised by how efficiently the trail gains elevation. The footing here tends to be slippery due to streams that spill alongside the trail and create mud, so be extra mindful when stepping over those tree roots.

▸ MILE 0.2-1.0: Sterling Pond Trail to Long Trail

The trail climbs steadily up the western slopes of Spruce Peak for a solid mile. As the leafy deciduous trees transition into thinner boreal arbors, partial views of Smugglers' Notch and the northward hills of Jeffersonville become a fixture. As the trail gradually curves east and then

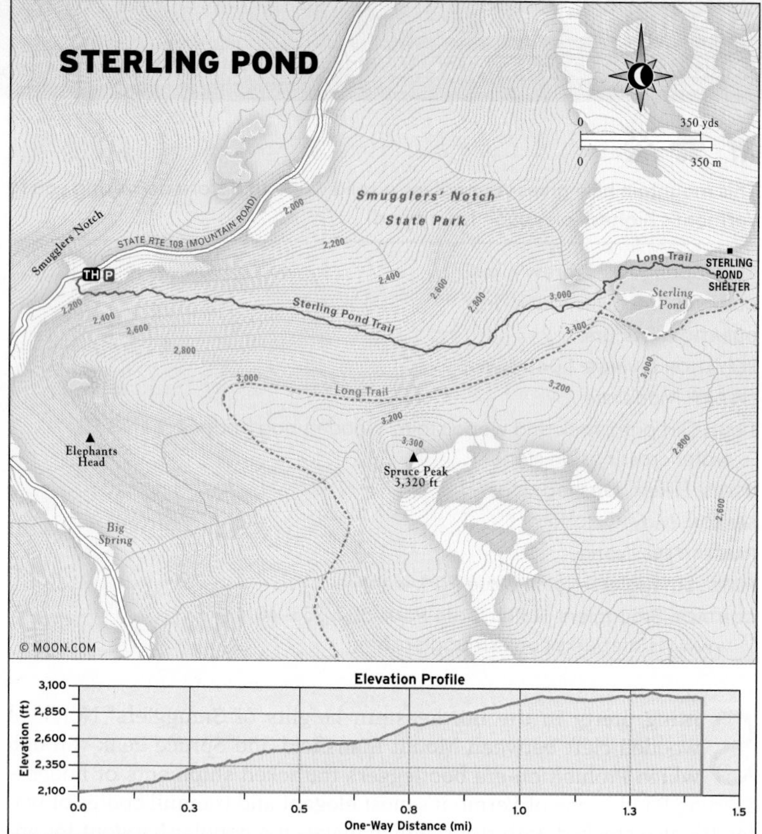

northeast—bypassing some smooth yet perpetually soggy slabs of rock—the grade starts to soften a bit, allowing your calves a reprieve. Weave through the woods over rock and root on a wider stretch of path for the final 0.2 mile of the climb before emerging from the woods on the ridge of Spruce Peak and reaching the **Long Trail** at 1 mile.

▸ MILE 1.0-1.1: Long Trail to Sterling Pond

Turn left to head east down a sun-splashed and rockier path toward the sound of lapping water. After another 0.1 mile, the Long Trail arrives at the boggy western shore of **Sterling Pond.** Hikers can dip their feet in the cool water and sun themselves on several large nearby rocks before continuing to the climactic pond overlook point.

▸ MILE 1.1-1.2: Sterling Pond to Sterling Pond Trail

Hop back onto the Sterling Pond Trail and head east as the trail enters the pondside woods and climbs a steep wooden staircase. As you amble through the forest on the pond's northern shore, keep an eye peeled for falcons, who occasionally dive-bomb the pond for fish.

At 1.2 miles, the trail pops out of the woods again and crosses beneath the towers of Sterling Chairlift—part of the skiing infrastructure at the nearby Smugglers' Notch Resort.

▲ STERLING POND

▸ MILE 1.2-1.3: Sterling Pond Trail to Sterling Pond Shelter

Reenter the forest and ascend a final stretch of rocky ground before reaching the **Sterling Pond Shelter** at 1.3 miles. Here you'll find a scenic pond overlook complete with a cute little log bench for hikers. It's the perfect note on which to conclude the hike.

DIRECTIONS

From Boston, drive north on I-93 through New Hampshire and into northeastern Vermont. Exit onto I-91 N to St. Johnsbury and then take Exit 21 to merge onto US-2 W. Continue driving west and turn right at the junction for VT-15 W. Drive northwest on VT-15 W until you reach the traffic circle with the exit for VT-108. Take the VT-108 exit and drive south toward Smugglers' Notch. (Watch your speed as the road narrows and twists around several large trees and boulders.) The Smugglers' Notch visitor center parking lot will be on your left.

GPS COORDINATES: 44°33'23.8"N 72°47'40.1"W, 44.556599, -72.794469

BEST NEARBY BREWS

It's impossible to talk about Vermont craft beer without describing the pine-scented double IPA known as Heady Topper, which can be procured in glasses and cans at **The Alchemist** (100 Cottage Club Rd., Stowe, 802/882-8165, www.alchemistbeer.com, 11am-7pm Mon.-Sat., 10am-4pm Sun.). Down the road in Stowe, you can kick back with more Vermont brews and an impressive menu of farm-raised comfort food at **Doc Ponds** (294 Mountain Rd., Stowe, 802/760-6066, www.docponds.com, 4pm-midnight Tues.-Thurs., 11am-midnight Fri.-Mon.).

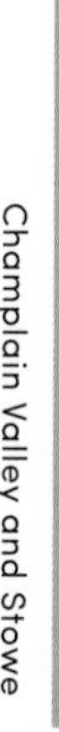

3 Mount Mansfield via the Sunset Ridge Trail

UNDERHILL STATE PARK, UNDERHILL

Scale Vermont's tallest peak—at sunset, ideally—to get an unbeatable panorama of the Champlain Valley.

BEST: Vistas

DISTANCE: 5.2 miles round-trip

DURATION: 4.5 hours

ELEVATION CHANGE: 2,429 feet

EFFORT: Strenuous

TRAIL: Dirt path, rocks, wooden bridges

USERS: Hikers, leashed dogs

SEASON: May-October

FEES/PASSES: Day-use fee $4/adult

MAPS: Underhill State Park website

CONTACT: Mount Mansfield State Forest, 802/793-3432, www.vtstateparks.com/underhill

There are many ways to ascend the highest mountain in Vermont. Hell Brook Trail is made for masochists while the Long Trail offers a more relaxing climb. But the most stunning route is the aptly named Sunset Ridge Trail.

START THE HIKE

‣ MILE 0-0.7: Sunset Ridge Trail Parking Lot to Sunset Ridge Trail

Begin your hike in the Sunset Ridge Trail parking lot and walk uphill to the east end of the lot. Pick up the **Eagle Cut connector trail,** which ascends gently through the deciduous woods for 0.4 mile before ending at a gravel access road. Turn left onto the road and walk northeast for 0.3 mile until you reach the register for the Sunset Ridge Trail. Write your name in the register before stepping into the welcoming shade of the Mansfield woods to begin the **Sunset Ridge Trail,** marked with blue blazes.

‣ MILE 0.7-1.4: Sunset Ridge Trail Parking Lot to Cantilever Rock Junction

The Sunset Ridge Trail crosses a series of streams on wooden bridges and snakes northward through a sun-splashed forest of birch and beech. Upon reaching the junction for the Laura Cowles Trail at 0.8 mile, keep left to stay on Sunset Ridge Trail and climb gradually up a series of wooden staircases and rock steps. As the trail switchbacks, it curves northeast and climbs at a steeper grade, offering occasional views of the valley. After passing some open ledges around 1.4 miles, the trail arrives at the spur cutoff for Cantilever Rock—a long, wafer-shaped rock that's precariously balanced atop a heap of boulders. (It's well worth the 0.2-mile detour.)

▲ THE BEAUTIFUL DESCENT DOWN SUNSET RIDGE

▸ **MILE 1.4–1.9: Cantilever Rock Junction to "The Chin"**

From this junction, veer right and keep climbing to stay on the Sunset Ridge Trail. Feel the adrenaline kick in as the trail ascends some very steep, exposed rock ledges that require hand and foot scrambling. Enjoy the breeze as you emerge onto the base of Sunset Ridge around 1.5 miles. The remainder of your climb is right in front of you, as is your destination: the summit of Mansfield, nicknamed "The Chin." As you ascend the ridge, keep an eye out above for hawks—and below for wet rocks. The smooth and lichen-covered rock slabs up here can be slippery, even in dry conditions. After rain, rivulets of water spill down the ridge from the top.

▸ **MILE 1.9–2.4: "The Chin" to Long Trail**

After roughly 0.5 mile of exposed climbing, the trail reaches a height of land before taking a sharp right through a passage of krummholz. Keep climbing onto the south shoulder of Mansfield for another 0.5 mile before reaching another junction with the Laura Cowles Trail at 2.4 miles. Keep left and enjoy the last 0.2 mile of the Sunset Ridge Trail before you reach a junction with the Long Trail.

▸ **MILE 2.4–2.6: Long Trail to Mount Mansfield Summit**

Turn left onto **Long Trail,** cross a series of bog bridges, and billy-goat your way up one last moderately steep rock slab to reach the summit of Mansfield at 2.6 miles. This summit is an ideal place to catch a sunset, but the perfect view of Lake Champlain's watery expanse is enjoyable at any time of day. Head down the same way you came.

DIRECTIONS

From Burlington, take I-89 S to Exit 11 for US-2 toward Richmond/Bolton/VT-117. Turn left onto US-2 W, then turn right onto VT-117 before taking an immediate right onto Governor Peck Highway. Drive northeast for roughly 2 miles and then turn left onto Browns Trace Road. Continue north into downtown Jericho and then take a left and a right to stay on Browns Trace

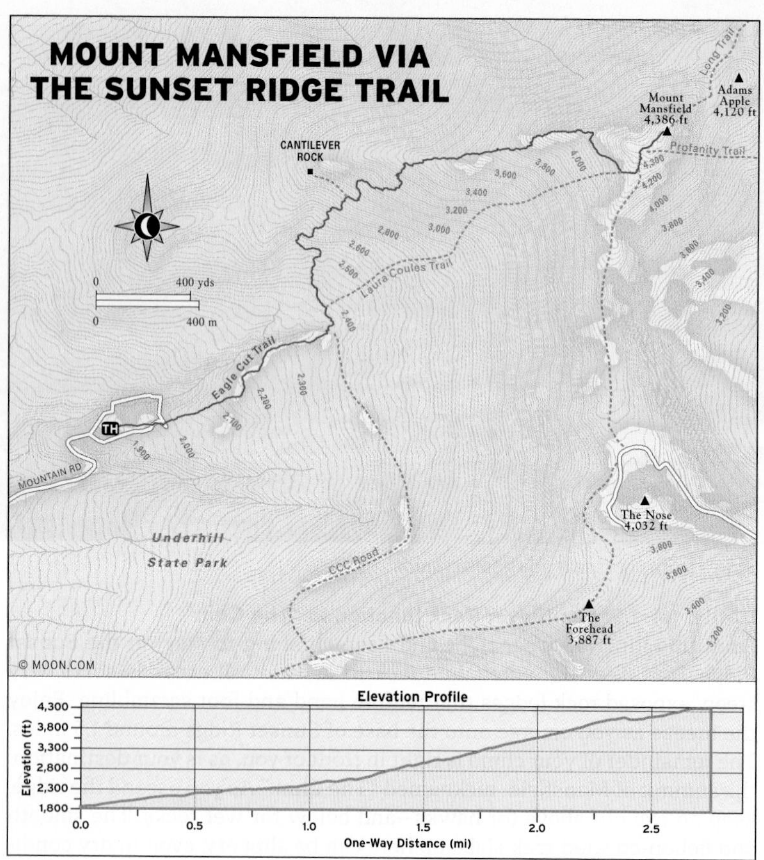

Road. Drive north along Browns Trace Road until you reach its terminus. Veer right onto VT-15 E; at the fork, turn right onto River Road. Drive southeast and then northeast for another 3 miles and then start looking for Mountain Road, which will be on your right. Swing right onto Mountain Road and climb a gravel access road that winds through Mansfield State Forest at a moderately steep grade. After 2.5 miles of car climbing, arrive at the Underhill State Park entrance. The ranger station is on your right and the trail parking lot is straight ahead.

GPS COORDINATES: 44°13'12.0"N 70°59'08.3"W, 44.219999, -70.985643

BEST NEARBY BITES

For a meal with a view, hike south along Mansfield's ridgeline on the Long Trail, turn left onto the Cliff Trail, and then take one more left turn to reach the beautiful **Cliff House Restaurant** (5781 Mountain Rd., Stowe, 802/253-3665, www.gostowe.com, call for hours). If you're famished upon returning to your car, swing by Underhill and purchase a small-batch fruit or cream pie from the self-service shed at the popular **Poorhouse Pies** (23 Park St., Underhill, 802/899-1346, www.poorhousepies.com, 8am-sundown daily).

4 Little River History Hike

LITTLE RIVER STATE PARK, WATERBURY

This hauntingly beautiful forest hike visits the abandoned houses, orchards, and cemeteries built by some of the first European homesteaders who settled in northern Vermont.

DISTANCE: 4 miles round-trip

DURATION: 2 hours

ELEVATION CHANGE: 733 feet

EFFORT: Easy

TRAIL: Dirt path, rocks, wooden bridges

USERS: Hikers, mountain bikers, leashed dogs

SEASON: June-October

FEES/PASSES: Day-use fee $4/adult

MAPS: Little River State Park website

CONTACT: Little River State Park, 802/244-7103, www.vtstateparks.com/littleriver.html

START THE HIKE

▸ MILE 0-1.0: Trail Information Kiosk to Dalley Loop Trail

Begin the hike by the trail information kiosk across the road from the day-use parking lot. Pick up the **Dalley Loop Trail,** a gravel road that climbs north and passes through a red access gate. (This trail is shared by hikers and mountain bikers, so keep your ears open at all times.) Keep left at a Y-junction; the trail leaves the road and ascends steadily through a deciduous hemlock forest. Down a steep hillside to your left, the monotone rush of water from Stevenson Brook lends the woods a pleasant ambience. Cross a few tiny streams on foot. At 0.5 mile, keep right at the Stevenson Brook Cutoff junction to continue north on the Dalley Loop Trail at a gentler grade, passing some small cascades.

▸ MILE 1.0-1.6: Log Bridge Ruins to Sawmill Trail Junction

One mile in, you'll reach the ruins of an old log bridge that's still visible in the woods alongside the trail. From here, the trail emerges into a clearing and arrives at a beautiful **farmhouse** built with local timber by Almeron Goodell. A nearby sign tells the history of the Goodell family and their homesteading tribulations here. Beyond the farmhouse, the trail crosses a wooden bridge over a creek, passing through a lush hollow of ferns, and then by an apple orchard, part of the **Patsy Herbert Farm.** Continue to reach a junction with the Sawmill Trail at 1.6 miles.

▸ MILE 1.6-2.1: Sawmill Trail Junction to Patterson Trail Junction

Turn right to stay on the Dalley Loop Trail, now marked by blue blazes, and amble along crumbling stone walls at a level grade. At 1.7 miles, make another right at the junction and enter the realm of the **Joseph Ricker Farm.**

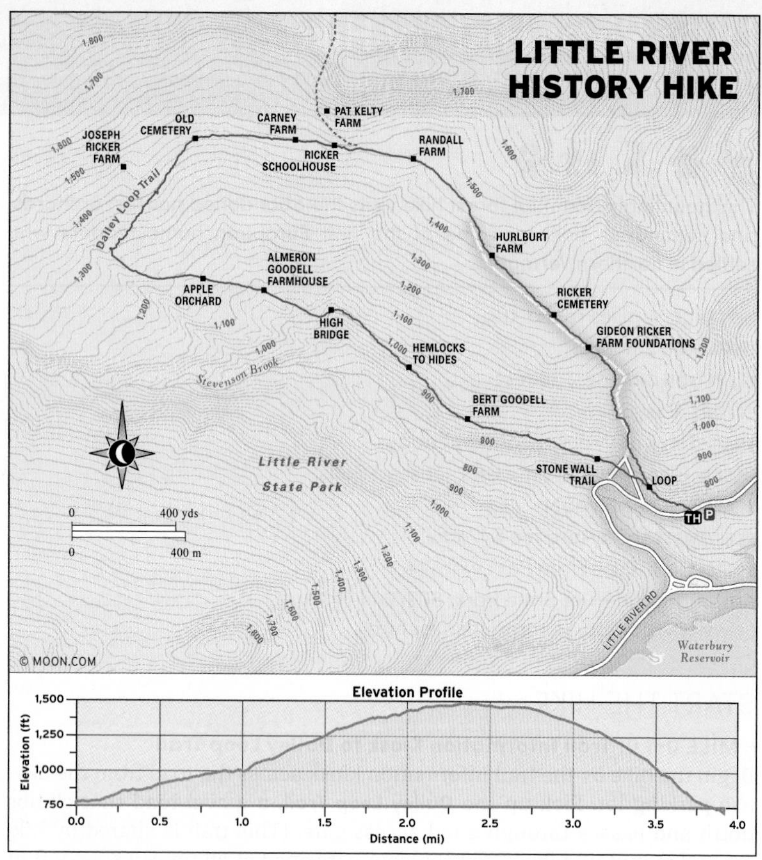

(Ricker was one of the first homesteaders to arrive here—a nearby mountain is named after him.)

As the forest thickens, keep an eye out on your left for the most haunting site yet—the **Upper Cemetery,** where members of the Ricker family are buried. The tombstones here are covered with moss and brush. Take in the beauty of this wooded resting place before continuing along the Dalley Loop Trail to reach the Patterson Trail junction at 2.1 miles.

▸ MILE 2.1–3.3: Patterson Trail to Bear Lane Trail Junction

Make a right to stay on the Dalley Loop Trail; keep right to stay on this trail at the nearby junction with the cutoff for Kelty Corners. A steady descent begins as the trail heads south alongside a bubbling stream and passes through a few sunlit meadows. You'll reach the Ricker Farm Trail junction in 1 mile. Stay to the right to continue on Patterson Trail, which steepens and becomes rockier after this point. On the right, another **cemetery** with graves of members of the Ricker family appears. Continue southwest as the steeper trail becomes more eroded in places before reaching a junction with Bear Lane Trail.

▲ THE UPPER CEMETERY

▸ MILE 3.3-4.0: Bear Lane Trail Junction to Dalley Loop Trail
At 3.3 miles, turn right to stay on the Dalley Loop Trail. A final rocky pitch delivers you back to the Y-junction from which you began your hike. Backtrack to the parking lot to complete the hike.

DIRECTIONS

From Burlington, drive southeast on I-89 S for 24 miles and take Exit 10 for US-2/VT-100 S toward Waterbury. At the end of the off-ramp, turn right onto VT-100 S and then, at the traffic circle ahead, take the first exit onto US-2 W/North Main Street. Drive west along this road for roughly a mile and then make a right onto Little River Road. Continue north for 2 miles and keep left at the fork to stay on Little River Road. The park entrance is another mile ahead. After paying the entrance fee, continue north along the road. The day-use parking lot for hikers and cyclists will be the first pullout on your right just after the road swerves south.

GPS COORDINATES: 44°23'35.9"N 72°45'59.1"W, 44.393315, -72.766429

BEST NEARBY BITES

Little River might be one of Vermont's quieter state parks, but it's a short drive from two of the state's best restaurants. For award-winning, locally sourced New American fare such as hake with roasted bok choy and watercress vinaigrette, book a table at **Hen Of The Wood** (92 Stowe St., Waterbury, 802/244-7300, www.henofthewood.com, 5pm-9pm Tues.-Sat.).

5 Camel's Hump

CAMEL'S HUMP STATE PARK, HUNTINGTON

This classic mountain hike takes hikers on a gorgeous and dramatic climb to the top of Vermont's most peculiarly shaped peak.

DISTANCE: 6.8 miles round-trip

DURATION: 5 hours

ELEVATION CHANGE: 2,583 feet

EFFORT: Strenuous

TRAIL: Dirt path, rocks, wooden bog bridges

USERS: Hikers, leashed dogs

SEASON: June-October

FEES/PASSES: None

MAPS: Vermont State Parks website

CONTACT: Department of Forests, Parks and Recreation Essex Office, 802/879-6565, www.vtstateparks.com/camelshump.html

Camel's Hump is the tallest undeveloped mountain in the Green Mountain State and one of the most popular day hikes in the Champlain Valley region. There are several ways to ascend Camel's Hump, but the most exciting and beautiful option is to take the Forest City Trail up to the Long Trail, which climbs the exposed south face of the "Hump" in a spectacular rocky fashion. From the top, the Burrows Trail offers a gentler descent route that leads back to the Forest City trailhead to make for a highly photogenic loop hike.

START THE HIKE

▸ MILE 0-0.3: Trailhead Parking Lot to Forest City Trail

Begin the hike at the east end of the parking area by the trailhead sign for the **Forest City Trail,** marked by blue blazes. Follow a gravel path through birch and beech woods, cross a wooden bridge, and hike east as the trail follows the stream deeper into the woods. Hike 0.3 miles before reaching the gentle portion of the ascent.

▸ MILE 0.3-2.1: Camel's Hump Ascent to Long Trail

As the path transitions to rocks and dirt around 0.4 mile, the sound of rushing water begins to fade away and the grade steepens. Continue hiking 1.7 miles at a moderate grade through the deciduous woods, which are rich with ferns and vegetation. Stone-and-log stairs become a frequent feature as the forest transitions to boreal trees. Keep climbing east until you reach the junction for the Long Trail at a grassy clearing at 2.1 miles.

▸ MILE 2.1-3.6: Long Trail to Alpine Trail

Having ascended the lower haunches of Camel's Hump, the real climb is about to begin. Turn left onto the **Long Trail,** marked by white blazes,

▲ THE FAMOUS DROMEDARY PROFILE OF CAMEL'S HUMP (LEFT)

and begin climbing a very steep and exposed series of rock faces that are rough enough to offer good natural traction. Continue to the four-way junction with the Dean and Allis Trails at 2.3 miles. Keep left here, and get your camera ready. A **ledge** at 2.4 miles offers a killer view of Mount Ethan Allen to the south. The trail climbs some more exposed rock slabs for 0.2 mile before entering a muddy boreal forest. For another half mile, the trail weaves along the southern flank of Camel's Hump. As the trail swings around to the southeastern face of the "Hump" itself, you'll climb a very steep and winding series of rock stairs for another 0.3 mile before reaching the junction with the Alpine Trail at 3.6 miles.

▸ MILE 3.6–3.7: Alpine Trail to Camel's Hump Summit

Take a left onto the **Alpine Trail;** it's only 0.1 more mile to the tippy-top. The trail ascends a few more stairs before popping out onto the barren and sheer side of the summit. Watch your footing as the trail bypasses some narrow ledges that require a bit of scrambling. Schlep your way up some sloped rock slabs and follow cairns as the trail curves northeast and arrives at the compact and gusty summit of Camel's Hump. Enjoy the panoramic view of the Champlain Valley wilderness, thousands of feet below.

▸ MILE 3.7–6.0: Camel's Hump Summit at Burrow's Trail to Burrows Trail Parking Lot

To return to the valley, pick up the **Burrows Trail** by following blue blazes northwest from the summit. You'll descend a moderately graded stone path that quickly reenters the woods. Hike your way through the boreal trees for 0.2 mile before reaching a clearing; bear left at this junction with the Monroe Trail to continue on Burrows. Hike southwest for another 2 miles. This portion of the trail is a gradual, meandering descent through the forest—surprisingly mellow for a peak as tall and dramatic as Camel's Hump. You'll cross the creek on stones a couple of times.

▸ MILE 6.0–6.8: Burrows Trail Parking Lot to Forest City Parking Lot

Arrive at the Burrows Trail parking lot at 6.0 miles. The final 0.8 mile is a walk back down **Camel's Hump Road,** which passes a few fields and houses. It will give your legs a break before returning to the Forest City parking lot.

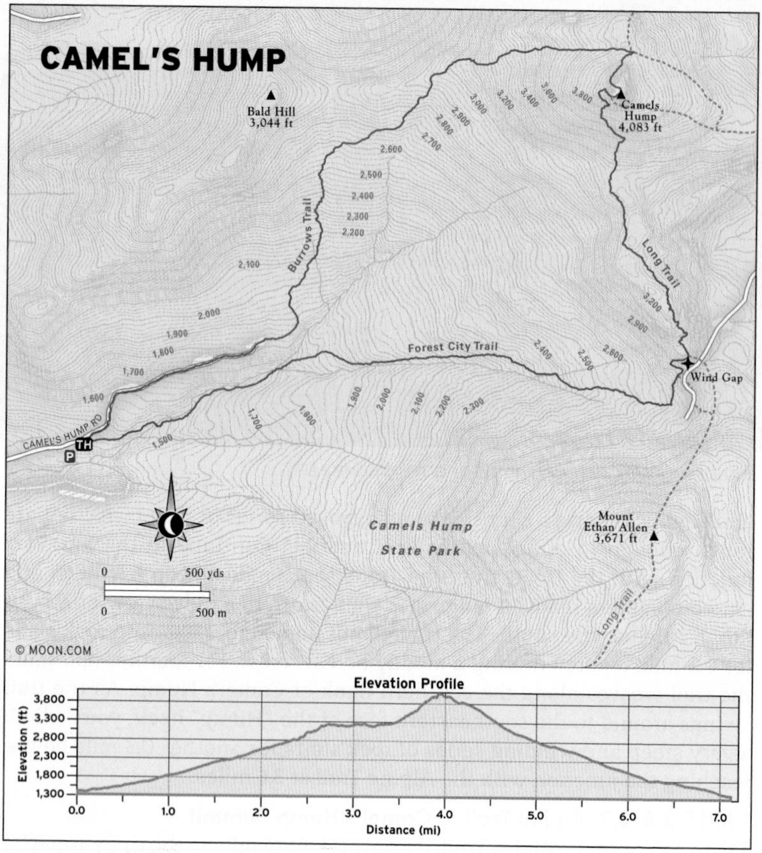

CAMEL'S HUMP

DIRECTIONS

From Burlington, drive east on I-89 S and then take Exit 11 for US-2 toward Richmond/Bolton/VT-117. Turn right onto US-2 at the bottom of the off-ramp. After roughly 1 mile, turn right onto Bridge Street and then take another right onto Huntington Road. Continue south on Huntington Road for 4 miles before making a slight right onto Main Road and heading south for another 2 miles. As you arrive in Huntington Center, turn left onto Camel's Hump Road and take it east as it transitions to dirt. The parking area for the Forest City Trail will be on your right after about 2 miles.

GPS COORDINATES: 44°17'56.4"N 72°55'06.6"W, 44.298992, -72.918499

BEST NEARBY BREWS

After the hike, put Camel's Hump in the rearview mirror, an ice-cold Belgian strong ale or blackberry sour in your glass, and a plateful of fish and shrimp tacos in your belly at **Stone Corral Brewery** (83 Huntington Rd., Richmond, 802/434-5787, www.stonecorral.com, 3pm-10pm Tues.-Thurs., noon-11pm Fri.-Sat., noon-8pm Sun.).

6 Mount Philo

MOUNT PHILO STATE PARK, CHARLOTTE

This mountain hike offers an unbeatable view across the Connecticut River into upstate New York and the Adirondacks, as well as a close-up look at some memorable rock formations.

DISTANCE: 2.2 miles round-trip
DURATION: 1.5 hours
ELEVATION CHANGE: 631 feet
EFFORT: Moderate
TRAIL: Dirt path, rocks, wooden bridges
USERS: Hikers, leashed dogs
SEASON: June-October
FEES/PASSES: Day-use fee $4/adult
MAPS: Vermont State Parks website
CONTACT: Mount Philo State Park, 802/425-2390, www.vtstateparks.com/philo.html

You can drive to the gorgeous, grassy summit of Mount Philo, but the wooden Adirondack chairs waiting at the top are even more rewarding when you choose to hike.

START THE HIKE

▸ MILE 0-0.4: Mount Philo Parking Lot to House Rock Trail

Begin the hike at the south end of the Mount Philo parking lot by the park entrance. Find the sign for the **House Rock Trail,** marked by blue blazes. Hike the dirt path northeast through the forest, climbing some wooden stairs and passing several glacial boulders. As the footing gets rootier, the trail arrives at the trail's namesake: **House Rock,** a massive glacial erratic that could easily crush a bungalow if loosened (Indiana Jones-style). Pass under the boulder's overhang, cross a few bog bridges, and ascend some more stairs to reach the auto road at 0.4 mile.

▸ MILE 0.4-0.7: Auto Road to Mount Philo Summit

Take a right onto the auto road and cross over to the sign for the House Rock Trail, reentering the woods. At a junction with Devil's Chair Trail, keep left to stay on House Rock Trail. The trail steepens considerably with more log stairs before reaching another junction at 0.5 mile; keep left again. Climb a series of rocky switchbacks as the trees start to thin and offer fleeting glimpses of the Charlotte Hills and the Connecticut River. The rock is well worn and slippery in places, even in dry weather, so be careful of your footing. The trail climbs higher before leveling out at 0.6 mile. Pass a small scenic outlook with a chain-link fence as the trail crests the top of Mount Philo before reaching the summit proper at 0.7 mile. Here, hikers have their choice between scrambling up to a rocky height of land with an

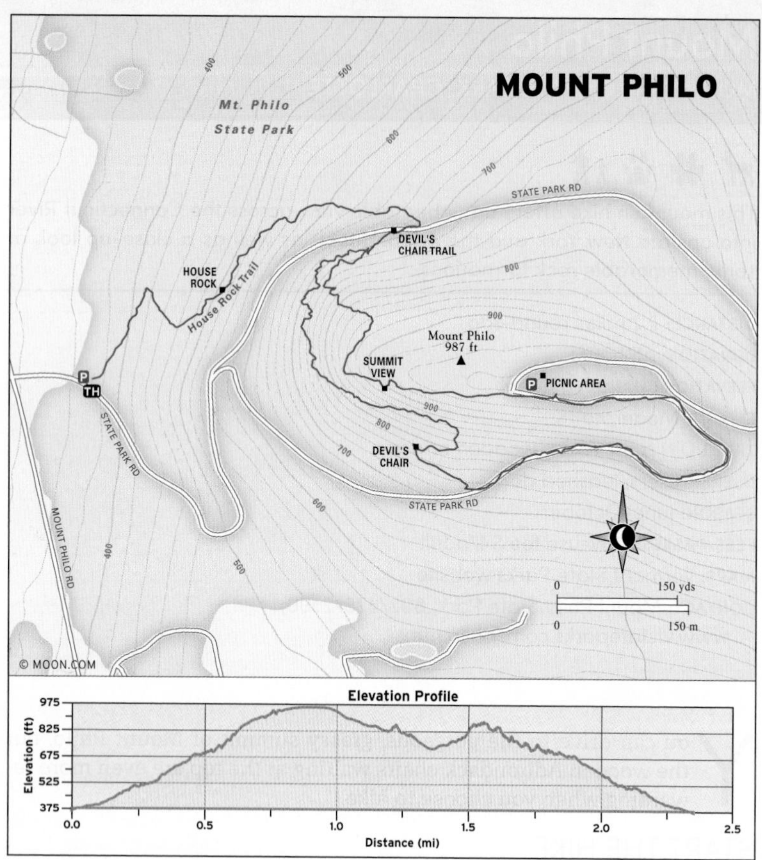

iron safety rail, or taking a seat in one of several Adirondack chairs on a grassy lawn—both of which overlook the epic expanse of Vermont, New York, and the Adirondacks. Take a moment here to prepare for the return journey, which has some unique thrills of its own.

▸ MILE 0.7–2.2: Mount Philo Summit to House Rock Trail

Begin the second half of the hike by walking east past the grassy lawn and across the parking lot for 0.2 mile until you reach the auto road. Walk down the auto road for just over 0.4 mile until you reach the sign for the **Devil's Chair Trail** at 1.4 miles. Turn right here and reenter the forest before arriving at the **Devil's Chair**—a throne-like rock formation that sits on a steep hillside overlooking the woods. The trail zigzags up through the chair and ambles along a series of sheer rock cliffs on somewhat eroded ground. The footing is quite narrow in places and can feel more like a ledge, so go slowly when in doubt.

As the cliffs start to recede, the trail squeezes through a tight jumble of rocks and becomes a more temperate dirt path again before reaching the **House Rock Trail** again at 1.7 miles. Turn left here and backtrack to the parking lot to close the loop at 2.2 miles.

▲ VIEWS OF NEW YORK'S ADIRONDACKS FROM THE SUMMIT OF MOUNT PHILO

DIRECTIONS

From Burlington, drive south along US-7 S. Once you pass through the town of Shelburne, keep an eye out for State Park Road on your left. (You'll see Mount Philo itself shortly before reaching the road.) Turn left onto State Park Road and continue east to the park entrance.

GPS COORDINATES: 44°16'41.4"N 73°13'20.8"W, 44.278177, -73.222446

BEST NEARBY BREWS

Vermont is a strong state for wood-fired pizza, and some of the crispiest and most savory, parmesan-crusted pies in the north country can be devoured at **Folino's** (6305 Shelburne Rd., Shelburne, 802/881-8822, www.folinopizza.com, noon-8pm Sun.-Mon.). Better yet, the pizza parlor is literally connected to the great **Fiddlehead Brewing Company** (6305 Shelburne Rd., Shelburne, 802/399-2994, www.fiddleheadbrewing.com, noon-8pm Sun.-Thurs., noon-9pm Fri., 11am-9pm Sat.).

7 Waterbury Trail to Mount Hunger

C. C. PUTNAM STATE FOREST, WATERBURY

A short but incredibly steep climb, Mount Hunger is a favorite for its sky-high views of the Waterbury-Stowe area and beyond.

DISTANCE: 3.9 miles round-trip
DURATION: 3 hours
ELEVATION CHANGE: 2,158 feet
EFFORT: Strenuous
TRAIL: Dirt/rock singletrack
USERS: Hikers, leashed dogs
SEASON: May-October
PASSES/FEES: None
MAPS: Green Mountain Club, "Mount Mansfield and the Worcester Range"
CONTACT: Vermont Department of Forests, Parks, and Recreation, 802/793-3432, http://fpr.vermont.gov

START THE HIKE

▸ MILE 0.0-1.0: North Trail to Waterfall

Hike east from the parking lot on a wide gravel path that soon turns into dirt singletrack. Follow the blue blazes through a forest punctuated by resting boulders and a thick cover of birch trees. The trail steepens in 0.2 mile; hikers ascend with the help of several stone staircases, but in-between sections may be washed out with exposed roots. At 1.0 mile, arrive at a small **falls.**

▸ MILE 1.0-1.9: Waterfall to White Rocks/Mount Hunger Intersection

The trail bends right (south) over the creek at the top of the falls and then continues to climb. This is a heavily trafficked trail, so it may be muddy during wet weather. At about 0.7 mile from the falls, as the vegetation becomes more coniferous, minor rocky scrambles turn into larger rock walls, and hikers will need to use their hands to climb. At the signed intersection for **White Rocks/Mount Hunger** at 1.9 miles, keep straight (east) toward the Mount Hunger summit.

▸ MILE 1.9-3.9: White Rocks/Mount Hunger Intersection to Mount Hunger Summit

After another 0.2 mile of climbing, the trees part to reveal awesome views of the Worcester Range, Mount Mansfield, and the Waterbury-Stowe valley from a spacious bald granite **summit.** There is plenty of room for hikers to wander the summit, spread out for a picnic, and enjoy the views, but use care to walk only on rocks and not trample delicate alpine vegetation. Keep in mind that this 3,538-foot peak is quite exposed, so wind and cold can be particularly intense above the tree line, and the bald rocks can be slippery in wet weather. Backtrack to the parking area on the Waterbury Trail.

▲ SUMMIT OF MOUNT HUNGER

DIRECTIONS

From VT-100/Waterbury Center, turn onto Howard Avenue. At the end of the road, turn left onto Maple Street. Just after the fire department, turn right onto Loomis Hill Road and go 2 miles, then continue straight onto Sweet Road for another 1.5 miles. The large parking area is marked with a sign for C. C. Putnam State Forest.

GPS COORDINATES: 44°24'08.4"N 72°40'32.3"W, 44.402333, -72.675639

BEST NEARBY BREWS

Get your post-hike fuel at **Prohibition Pig** (23 S. Main St., Waterbury, 802/244-4120, http://prohibitionpig.com, 4pm-10 pm Mon.-Thurs., 11:30am-10pm Fri.-Sun., bar open until 11pm Sun.-Thurs., 11:30pm Fri.-Sat.), a restaurant/brewery with barbecue sandwiches, mac and cheese, poutine, and other comforting classics.

WATERBURY TRAIL TO MOUNT HUNGER

Worcester Mountains

SWEET FARM RD

TH

P

1,300

1,400

1,600

1,800

2,000

2,200

2,400

2,600

2,800

3,000

3,200

3,400

Waterbury Trail

Skyline Trail

White Rocks Trail

Mount Hunger
3,538 ft

CC Putnam
State Forest

White Rock
Mountain
3,166 ft

0 500 yds

0 500 m

Elevation Profile

Elevation (ft)

3,200
2,700
2,200
1,700
1,200

0.0 0.5 1.0 1.5 2.0

One-Way Distance (mi)

▲ SIGNAGE ATOP MOUNT HUNGER

8 Chazy Fossil Reef

GOODSELL RIDGE PRESERVE, ISLE LA MOTTE

This island hike meanders through meadows and forests and across a 480 million-year-old fossilized reef.

BEST: Summer hikes, New England oddities

DISTANCE: 1.5 miles round-trip

DURATION: 1 hour

ELEVATION CHANGE: 46 feet

EFFORT: Easy

TRAIL: Dirt path, rocks

USERS: Hikers

SEASON: June-October

FEES/PASSES: None

MAPS: A basic interactive map is available at Trails.com

CONTACT: Isle La Motte Preservation Trust, 802/238-7040, www.ilmpt.org (The trails can be hiked anytime from June through mid-October; the Goodsell Ridge visitors center barn is open July-August, 1pm-4pm Wed.-Fri., 10am-4pm Sat.-Sun.).

Isle La Motte, an island community on north Lake Champlain, is home to the Chazy Fossil Reef, a black rock formation that contains the fossilized skeletons of Vermont's oldest residents—prehistoric marine creatures. The reef is accessible via a network of trails at the Goodsell Ridge Preserve, a lush oasis of meadows, forests, and wildflowers. The "Walk Through Time Trail" features a series of beautifully rendered paintings that guide hikers through the evolution of life on earth itself. Pair this with the White Trail, which ventures through a boreal spruce forest for a closer look at the reef, and you've got an otherworldly Vermont hike.

START THE HIKE

▸ MILE 0-0.8: Walk Through Time Trail to Visitor Center

Begin the hike outside the **Goodsell Ridge Preserve Visitor Center,** a gorgeous old barn in a grassy clearing. Walk north toward the wooden trailhead sign for the **Walk Through Time Trail.** Turn left onto the trail, keep left at the fork ahead, and pass several flowering ash trees along a mowed grass path. You'll shortly reach the first of the educational paintings, which depicts the origins of Precambrian life. As the trail heads into a lush green meadow filled with daffodils and dandelions, the numerous paintings serve as trail markers.

After circling the meadow for 0.3 mile, the trail heads east toward a boreal spruce and pine forest. Veer left at the fork ahead at 0.4 mile, where the WTT trail briefly merges with the **White Trail** before breaking off just a few yards ahead. (Turn right at this junction to stay on the WTT Trail.) You'll soon come across exposed slabs of black rock in the ground—small

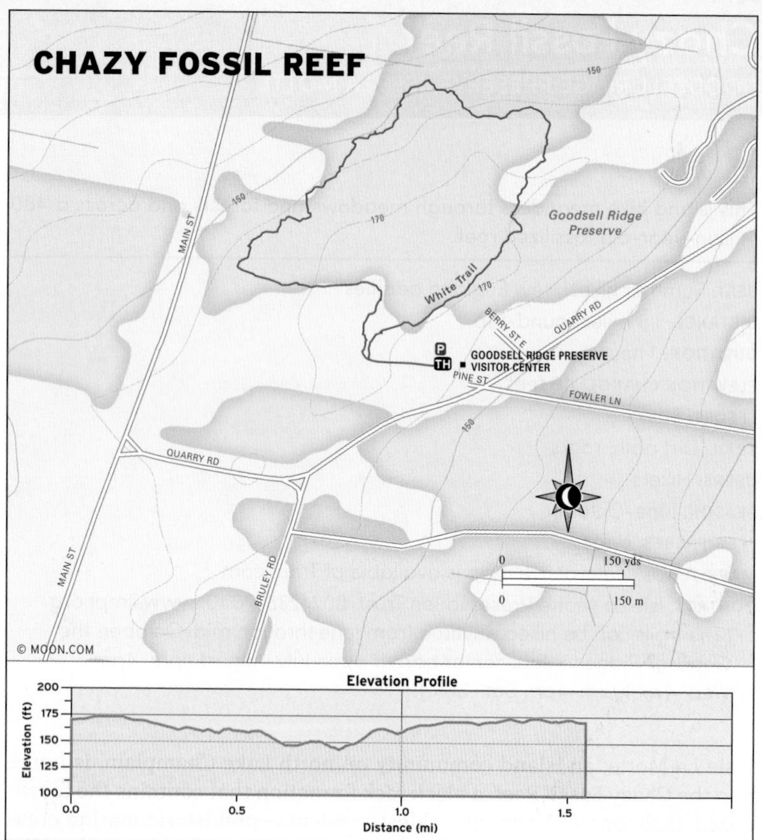

pieces of the **Chazy Fossil Reef.** Look for gastropods and little squid-like cephalopods in the rock slabs. The trail loops through the forest and passes several more sections of reef as the paintings enter the present-day era of mankind.

Merge with the White Trail again at 0.7 mile and then turn left as the WTT Trail branches off once more. The WTT Trail emerges from the woods and into the clearing with the visitors center at 0.8 mile.

▸ MILE 0-0.4: Visitor Centers to White Trail

Now that you're warmed up with a bit of biological history, it's time for a deeper look at the reef. Head back (the 0.4 mile) to the wooden Walk Through Time trailhead sign and turn right onto the **White Trail,** marked by white stakes. Past the portion of the path where the Walk Through Time Trail and White Trail merged, swing left into the woods as the trails split to continue on the White Trail. The footing becomes much rockier as you head north through a corridor of spruce.

▸ MILE 0.4-1.0: White Trail to Chazy Reef

Before you know it, in around 0.2 mile, you're walking along entire sections of the Chazy Reef that are vast enough to fill the space between the trees. (From this point on, look for white blazes on the reef.) The trail curves northeast and then southeast in a circular formation, and the trees become thicker and the ground muddier in places.

▲ THE MEADOW PATH TO THE CHAZY FOSSIL REEF

At 0.5 mile into the Chazy Reef path, you'll emerge into a clearing, where the little spruces bring to mind a Christmas tree farm. Here, the trail reaches a larger chunk of reef with rifts. Hike south over the reef into a zone of mossier hemlock woods. In 0.1 mile, keep right at the fork with the Gray Trail to continue on the White Trail. Ascend a wooded knoll at a gentle grade to arrive at a final large piece of the reef.

▸ MILE 1.0–1.5: Chazy Reef to Walk Through Time Trail

Shortly ahead, the trail enters a familiar-looking meadow and heads southwest to merge with the Walk Through Time Trail once again. This time, when the trails split, keep right to return to the wooden WTT trailhead sign at 0.9 mile.

DIRECTIONS

From Burlington, drive north on I-89 N for 9 miles and take Exit 17 for US-2 toward US-7/Lake Champlain Islands/Milton. At the end of the off-ramp, turn right onto US-2 W and continue along this road for 27 miles as it crosses a bridge onto the Champlain Islands and heads north. Take a left turn onto VT-129 W and drive another 5 miles to reach Isle La Motte. The local highway eventually becomes Main Street. Pull another left onto Quarry Road and continue for roughly 0.25 mile until you see a brown-and-white sign for Goodsell Ridge Preserve on your left. Turn left here onto a driveway and continue to the grass parking area.

GPS COORDINATES: 44°51'11.9"N 73°20'23.8"W, 44.853292, -73.339946

BEST NEARBY BREWS

If you're heading back to Burlington before sundown, swing over to nearby **St. Albans** and try a freshly brewed glass of maple breakfast stout at **14th Star Brewing Co.** (133 N. Main St. #7, St. Albans, 802/528-5988, www.14thstarbrewing.com, 4pm–10pm Tues.–Thurs., 3pm–10pm Fri., 11am–10pm Sat., 11am–4pm Sun.).

NEARBY CAMPGROUNDS

Dispersed primitive camping and shelters are available within Green Mountain National Forest

NAME	LOCATION	FACILITIES	SEASON	FEE
Camp Skyland	398 South St., South Hero, VT 05486	Tent sites, RV sites, cabins, toilets, showers, potable water, laundry	late May-late September	$32-120
802/372-4200				
North Beach Campground	60 Institute Rd., Burlington, VT 05408	Tent sites, lean-tos, RV sites, toilets, showers, potable water, Wi-Fi	May-mid-October	$37-45
802/862-0942, www.enjoyburlington.com				
Shelburne Camping Area	4385 Shelburne Rd., Shelburne, VT 05482	Tent sites, lean-tos, RV sites, RV rentals, cabins, toilets, showers, potable water, laundry, swimming pool, camp store, restaurant, Wi-Fi	April-November	$34-110
802/985-2540, www.shelburnecamping.com				
Mount Philo State Park	5425 Mt Philo Rd., Charlotte, VT 05445	Tent sites, toilets, showers, potable water	late May-mid-October	$18-22
802/425-2390, www.vtstateparks.com				
Maple Hill Campsites	3825 Quaker St., Lincoln, VT 05443	Tent sites, RV sites, toilets, showers, potable water	mid-May-mid-October	$25-30
802/453-3687, www.maplehillcamp.com				
Little River State Park	3444 Little River Rd., Waterbury, VT 05676	Tent sites, lean-tos, RV sites, cabins, toilets, showers, potable water	mid-May-late October	$18-50
802/244-7103, www.vtstateparks.com				

NEARBY CAMPGROUNDS (continued)

NAME	LOCATION	FACILITIES	SEASON	FEE
Brewster River Campground	289 Campground Dr., Jeffersonville, VT 05464	Tent sites, lean-to, RV sites, cabin, loft apartment, toilets, showers, potable water	May-October	$25-80
802/324-9631, www.brewsterrivercampground.com				
Underhill State Park	352 Mountain Rd., Underhill, VT 05489	Tent sites, toilets, potable water,	late May-mid-October	$18-22
802/899-3022, www.vtstateparks.com				
Gold Brook Campground	1900 Waterbury Rd., Stowe, VT 05672	Tent sites, RV sites, toilets, showers, potable water, laundry, Wi-Fi	July-mid-October	$30-49
802/253-7683, www.campvermont.com				

▲ BLOOMING WILDFLOWERS NEAR CHAZY FOSSIL REEF

NORTHEAST KINGDOM

Known for its vibrant displays of fall foliage, and often the first region in New England to "turn" to warm autumnal hues, the Northeast Kingdom of Vermont is a vast and rural landscape that feels untouched by the hands of time. Willoughby State Forest, with its jagged peaks surrounding a lake of the same name, is the hub of adventure in this region, but there are wonderful hidden gems in the wildlife-brimming bogs, sky-high fire towers, and mystical ravines that make up this diverse and wide-ranging patch of New England paradise.

▲ views from Bald Mountain fire tower

▲ the Long Trail

1 **North Trail to Mount Pisgah, Willoughby State Forest**
DISTANCE: 4.3 miles round-trip
DURATION: 2.5 hours
EFFORT: Strenuous

2 **Long Pond Trail to Bald Mountain, Willoughby State Forest**
DISTANCE: 4.2 miles round-trip
DURATION: 2.5 hours
EFFORT: Moderate/strenuous

3 **Long Trail and Babcock Trail to Devil's Gulch, Long Trail State Forest**
DISTANCE: 5.4 miles round-trip
DURATION: 3 hours
EFFORT: Moderate/strenuous

4 **Long Trail: Jay Pass to Jay Peak, Jay State Forest**
DISTANCE: 3.4 miles round-trip
DURATION: 3 hours
EFFORT: Moderate/strenuous

5 **Little Loop and Peacham Bog Trail, Groton State Forest**
DISTANCE: 5.9 miles round-trip
DURATION: 3.5 hours
EFFORT: Moderate

6 **Monadnock Mountain Trail, Monadnock Mountain**
DISTANCE: 4.6 miles round-trip
DURATION: 3.5 hours
ELEVATION CHANGE: 2,062 feet
EFFORT: Strenuous

▲ PITCHER PLANT

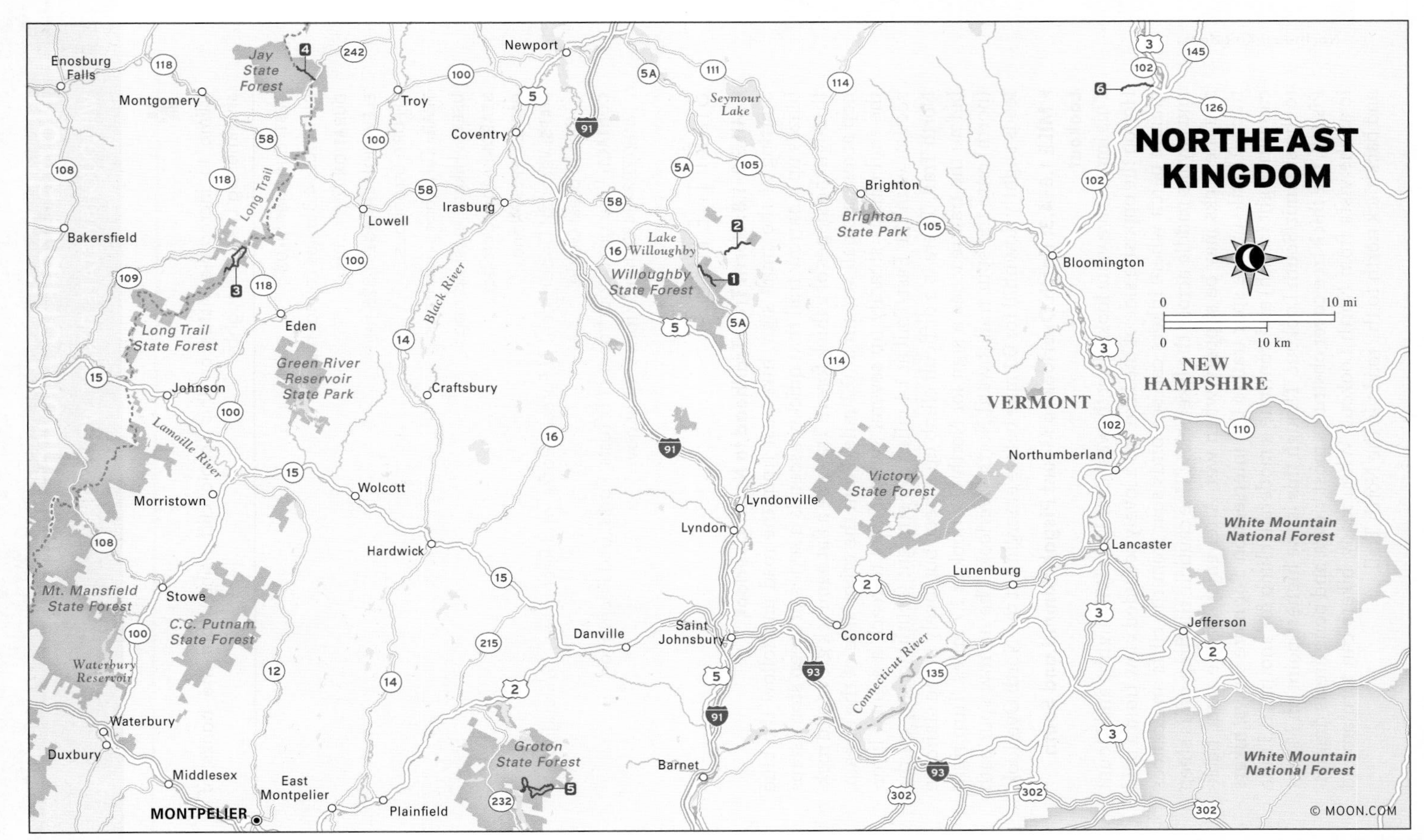
NORTHEAST
KINGDOM
0
10 mi
0
10 km
NEW
HAMPSHIRE
VERMONT
Enosburg
Falls
Montgomery
Jay
State
Forest
Troy
Newport
Coventry
Seymour
Lake
Brighton
Brighton
State Park
Bloomington
Long Trail
Bakersfield
Lowell
Irasburg
Lake
Willoughby
Willoughby
State Forest
Eden
Long Trail
State Forest
Green River
Reservoir
State Park
Black River
Craftsbury
Johnson
Lamoille River
Morristown
Wolcott
Hardwick
Lyndonville
Lyndon
Victory
State Forest
Northumberland
Lancaster
White Mountain
National Forest
Lunenburg
Mt. Mansfield
State Forest
Stowe
C.C. Putnam
State Forest
Waterbury
Reservoir
Danville
Saint
Johnsbury
Concord
Jefferson
Connecticut River
Waterbury
Duxbury
Middlesex
East
Montpelier
MONTPELIER
Plainfield
Groton
State Forest
Barnet
White Mountain
National Forest
© MOON.COM

1 North Trail to Mount Pisgah

WILLOUGHBY STATE FOREST, WESTMORE

Climb to incredible vistas on this scenic cliff rising from the banks of shimmering Lake Willoughby.

BEST: Summer hikes

DISTANCE: 4.3 miles round-trip

DURATION: 2.5 hours

ELEVATION CHANGE: 1,326 feet

EFFORT: Strenuous

TRAIL: Dirt/rock singletrack

USERS: Hikers, leashed dogs

SEASON: May–October

PASSES/FEES: None

MAPS: Vermont Department of Forests, Parks, and Recreation, "Willoughby State Forest Guide"

CONTACT: Vermont Department of Forests, Parks, and Recreation, 802/793-3432, http://fpr.vermont.gov

START THE HIKE

▸ MILE 0–1.8: North Trail Trailhead to North Overlook

Starting at the small sign, hike east from the road and follow the blue blazes up a narrow trail that quickly ascends a series of steep stone steps through the slopes of a thick forest. Traverse a flat hemlock grove and rock-hop across a small stream at 0.2 mile. From the other side of the stream, the trail climbs steadily up several switchbacks to reach a signed intersection with the East Trail at 1.4 miles. Go straight (south) to stay on the North Trail. There is a difficult climb up a steep but lovely stone staircase before the trail reaches a sign for North Overlook at 1.7 miles. Turn right (north) onto the spur trail toward North Overlook. The narrow spur path leads slightly downhill for 0.1 mile before emerging at the North Overlook.

▸ MILE 1.8–4.3: North Overlook to Mount Pisgah Summit and South Lookout

This impressive vista looks directly west over Lake Willoughby and Mount Hor on the opposite side of the lake. It's a lovely secluded view from a bald granite perch where hikers can see birds soar from the cliffs and canoes and kayaks paddle across the lake below. Use caution; the drop-off is steep and the rocks may be slippery when wet. After enjoying the vista, backtrack 0.1 mile up the spur trail to the intersection. For more views, hikers can turn right (south) and continue a moderate climb for another 0.3 mile to the summit/South Lookout. Though this is the highest point on Mount Pisgah, the thick tree cover obstructs most views, and none are as dramatic as the vista from North Lookout. When ready, hikers can turn around and backtrack north to the road via the North Trail.

▲ VIEWS FROM MOUNT PISGAH

DIRECTIONS

From St. Johnsbury/I-91, take exit 23 for US-5 N. In about 8 miles, turn right onto VT-5A N and continue for about 8.5 miles. The trailhead is marked with a very small sign and a street-side parking area on the right.

GPS COORDINATES: 44°44'42.8"N 72°02'55.9"W

BEST NEARBY BREWS

The Burke Publick House (482 VT-114, East Burke, 802/626-1188, www.burkepub.com, 4pm-10pm Tues.-Fri., noon-10pm Sat.-Sun.), 13 miles from the trailhead in east Burke, serves up creative comfort food alongside a great beer and cocktail menu.

NORTH TRAIL TO MOUNT PISGAH, WILLOUGHBY STATE FOREST

STATE RTE 5A
TH P
Hedgehog Mountain 2,175 ft
Willoughby State Forest
North Trail
1,300
1,400
1,500
1,600
1,700
1,600
1,700
1,800
1,900
2,000
2,200
2,400
2,500
2,600
2,700
0 300 yds
0 300 m
Lake Willoughby
STATE RTE 5A
Mount Pisgah 2,755 ft

Elevation Profile

Elevation (ft): 2,700 · 2,325 · 1,950 · 1,575 · 1,200

One-Way Distance (mi): 0.0 · 0.5 · 1.0 · 1.5 · 2.0

▲ NORTH VISTA OF MOUNT PISGAH

2 Long Pond Trail to Bald Mountain

WILLOUGHBY STATE FOREST, WESTMORE

A challenging ascent to the pinnacle of Willoughby State Forest features a fire tower with some of the best views in Vermont.

BEST: Fall hikes, vistas
DISTANCE: 4.2 miles round-trip
DURATION: 2.5 hours
ELEVATION CHANGE: 1,233 feet
EFFORT: Moderate/strenuous
TRAIL: Gravel fire road, dirt/rock singletrack
USERS: Hikers, leashed dogs
SEASON: May-October
PASSES/FEES: None
MAPS: Vermont Department of Forests, Parks, and Recreation, "Willoughby State Forest Guide"
CONTACT: Vermont Department of Forests, Parks, and Recreation, 802/793-3432, http://fpr.vermont.gov

START THE HIKE

▸ MILE 0-0.6: Long Pond Trail Parking Lot to Bald Mountain/Long Pond Trail

Hike north from the parking area, passing through the gate and onto the **gravel logging road.** Where the **road forks** at 0.2 mile, bear right (east). The wide road climbs gradually, reaching a **meadow** at 0.6 mile. Although the meadow is technically a log landing used for forestry, it is a great spot to catch glimpses of wildlife on a quiet day, as well as wildflowers in season and some nice views of rolling hills to the south. Walk straight (east) through the field until you reach a **sign** marked "Trail," and then turn right (south) onto a singletrack path. Shortly after, turn left (east) at the trail sign for **Bald Mountain/Long Pond Trail.**

▸ MILE 0.6-4.2: Bald Mountain/Long Pond Trail to Bald Mountain Summit

From this point, the trail is marked with blue blazes. Follow the blue blazes along a series of creeks. There are some steep, rooty sections, and a few sets of timber steps to help hikers over hills. The trail climbs 0.7 mile to an area of cool, mossy caves and rock formations that can be observed from the trail. Continue climbing straight west through this rocky subalpine spruce-fir forest, being mindful of slick terrain. This section of trail is quite strenuous as it leads straight up to the peak of Bald Mountain.

The trail emerges on the summit in 0.8 mile. There is a small **cabin** on the summit, which is a newly restored relic of the 1920s effort to create a fire lookout system across the state of Vermont. Inside, there is a woodstove and a few bunks where hikers can spend the night in the company of northern Vermont wildlife such as snowshoe hares. The lookout's

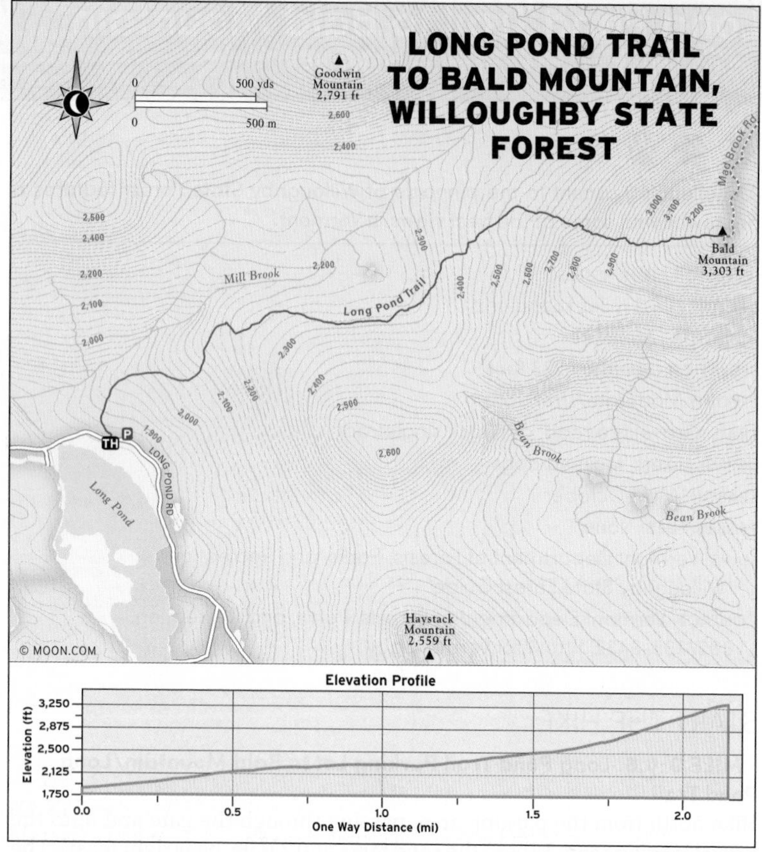

companion **fire tower** is still standing strong, and hikers can climb the steps to the top for 360-degree views stretching across the Northeast Kingdom to New Hampshire's White Mountains. The hike to this 3,314-foot summit may be tough, but locals agree these are some of the most spectacular views in Vermont. When finished drinking in the sights, back-track on the Long Pond Trail back to the parking lot.

DIRECTIONS

From St. Johnsbury/I-91, take exit 23 for US-5 N. In about 8 miles, turn right onto VT-5A N. At the Willoughby Lake Store, turn right onto Long Pond Road. The parking area for the trailhead is about 2.2 miles up the road on the left, just past the fishing access area. A small sign marks the start of the Long Pond Trail at the end of a gated logging road.

GPS COORDINATES: 44°45'23.6"N 72°01'04.7"W

3 Long Trail and Babcock Trail to Devil's Gulch

LONG TRAIL STATE FOREST, EDEN

Visit a unique section of the Long Trail with this moderate hike through a ravine complete with caves, cascades, and climbing ladders.

DISTANCE: 5.4 miles round-trip
DURATION: 3 hours
ELEVATION CHANGE: 1,387 feet
EFFORT: Moderate/strenuous
TRAIL: Dirt/rock singletrack
USERS: Hikers, leashed dogs
SEASON: May–October
PASSES/FEES: None
MAPS: Green Mountain Club "Vermont's Long Trail"
CONTACT: Vermont Department of Forests, Parks, and Recreation, 802/793-3432, http://fpr.vermont.gov

START THE HIKE

▸ MILE 0–1.3: Long Trail Trailhead to Ritterbush Overlook

Hike south on the **Long Trail** and follow the white blazes across VT-118, being mindful of traffic. The trail traverses a hillside, then winds away from the road and over a series of rolling hills and valleys in an increasingly wild forest. At 1.3 miles, the trail arrives at the **Ritterbush Overlook,** where hikers can take in views of a scenic mountain pond.

▸ MILE 1.3–1.7: Ritterbush Overlook to Babcock Trail Intersection

From here, the trail drops in elevation, switchbacking north down the hill and descending a steep stone staircase. Cross over a small stream, using rocks for stepping-stones, and reach the intersection with the **Babcock Trail** at 1.7 miles.

▸ MILE 1.7–2.3: Babcock Trail Intersection to Devil's Perch Outlook

Continue straight (west) on the **Long Trail,** following signs for Devil's Gulch. Reach a **cascade** at 2.0 miles, where the trail turns right (west) and climbs a six-foot wooden ladder. Shortly after, a sign marks the beginning of **Devil's Gulch,** and the path winds through a vibrant ravine with caves, bridges, and rocky scrambles for about 0.2 mile. Continue on the Long Trail until you reach the signed intersection for **Spruce Ledge Camp.** Turn left (east) across the brook and follow the blue blazes up the stone staircase to the **Devil's Perch Outlook** for great views of the pond and Belvidere Mountain and its abandoned asbestos mine.

▲ CASCADE AT DEVIL'S GULCH

▸ **MILE 2.3–5.4: Devil's Perch Outlook to Babcock Trail**

When ready, backtrack 1 mile through the gulch to the intersection with the **Babcock Trail.** Turn left (north) onto the Babcock Trail and follow the blue blazes up the hillside. The trail arrives on the banks of **Big Muddy Pond** at 3.7 miles, then rolls gently downhill. Arrive at VT-118 in 1 mile and cross the road straight (north) onto the **Babcock Extension Trail.** Turn right (east) onto the gravel road at the end of the path at 3.9 miles, then turn right (east) again at the sign where the blue blazes enter the woods. After crossing a series of bog bridges, the trail returns to the parking lot in 0.5 mile.

DIRECTIONS

From VT-100, take VT-118 N from the center of Eden. Long Trail State Forest is marked with a large sign on the right after about 5 miles. The parking lot/trailhead is at the end of the long gravel driveway.

GPS COORDINATES: 44°45'49.5"N 72°35'16.1"W

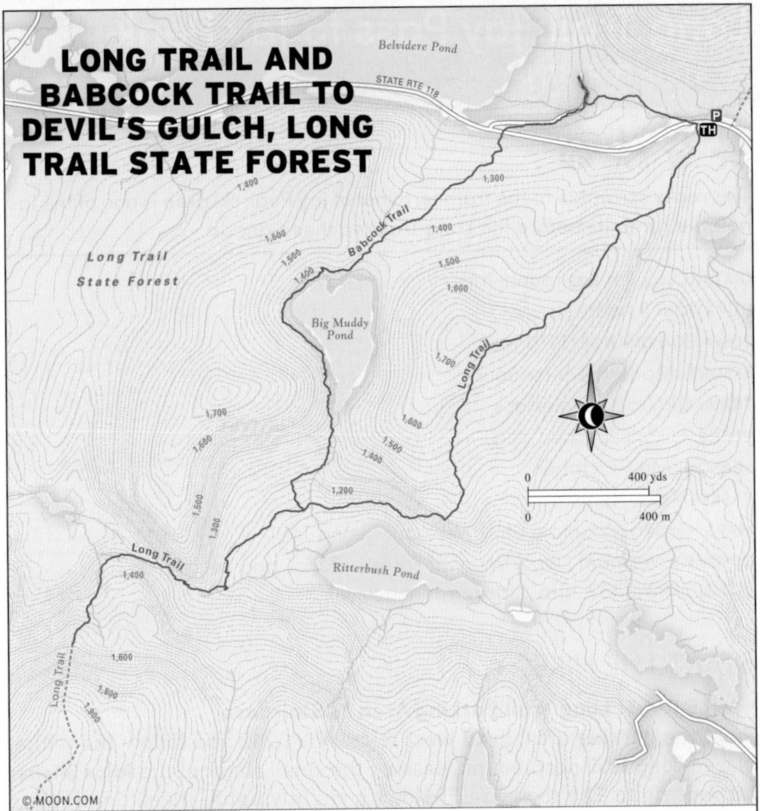

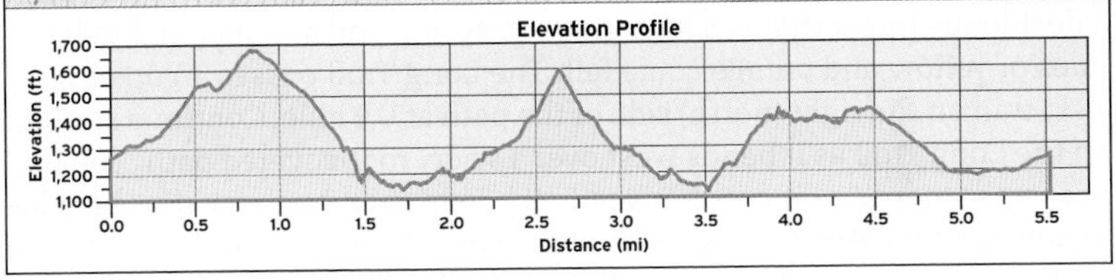

LONG TRAIL AND BABCOCK TRAIL TO DEVIL'S GULCH, LONG TRAIL STATE FOREST

Elevation Profile

BEST NEARBY BREWS

Kingdom Brewing (353 Coburn Hill Rd., Newport, 802/334-7096, http://kingdombrewingvt.com, 3pm-9pm Thurs.-Sat.) is a popular name in Vermont beer, and its taproom in Newport, 18 miles from the trailhead, is beloved for its ski lodge atmosphere, great live music, and its snack bar.

4 Long Trail: Jay Pass to Jay Peak

JAY STATE FOREST, JAY

This rocky scramble to the tram terminal of Jay Peak ski area is one of the last notable summits before the Long Trail reaches Canada.

DISTANCE: 3.4 miles round-trip
DURATION: 3 hours
ELEVATION CHANGE: 1,521 feet
EFFORT: Moderate/strenuous
TRAIL: Dirt/rock singletrack
USERS: Hikers, leashed dogs
SEASON: May-October
PASSES/FEES: None
MAPS: Green Mountain Club "Vermont's Long Trail"
CONTACT: Vermont Department of Forests, Parks, and Recreation, 802/793-3432, http://fpr.vermont.gov

START THE HIKE

▸ MILE 0-1.5: Long Trail Parking Area to Staircase

From the parking area, head west to cross VT-242 and follow the white-blazed **Long Trail** northbound, passing the small shack of the **Atlas Shelter** on your right. The rocky trail follows a slightly uphill trajectory through a deciduous forest that is a lush green in spring and summer and radiates hues of yellow and orange come fall. The Long Trail passes an opening to a ski trail on the right (north) side of the path at 0.9 mile. Continue straight on the Long Trail as it bends west over a wide, root-covered path. The trail becomes steeper as it cuts between rock ledges and narrow passages between conifers. Ascend a wooden staircase at 1.5 miles and then continue north, crossing straight over another **ski trail.**

▸ MILE 1.5-3.4: Staircase to Jay Peak Summit

From here, the remainder of the 0.2-mile climb is a steep, rocky scramble to the northwest, where the Long Trail meets the top of the summit **tram** line. Great views extend across Vermont and Canada on a clear day, but locals say the peak is frequently shrouded in "the Jay Cloud," a somewhat mystical and precipitous weather system caused by the mountain's unique orientation, elevation, and location; some claim it is responsible for the peak's epic ski conditions. To return to the parking area, backtrack down the Long Trail.

DIRECTIONS

From VT-100, drive to the center of Troy and turn right onto VT-101 N. In 3 miles, turn left onto VT-242 W and drive through the ski area for about 6.5 miles. The trailhead is a large parking turnoff on the left, and the route begins across the street.

GPS COORDINATES: 44°54'46.1"N 72°30'13.6"W

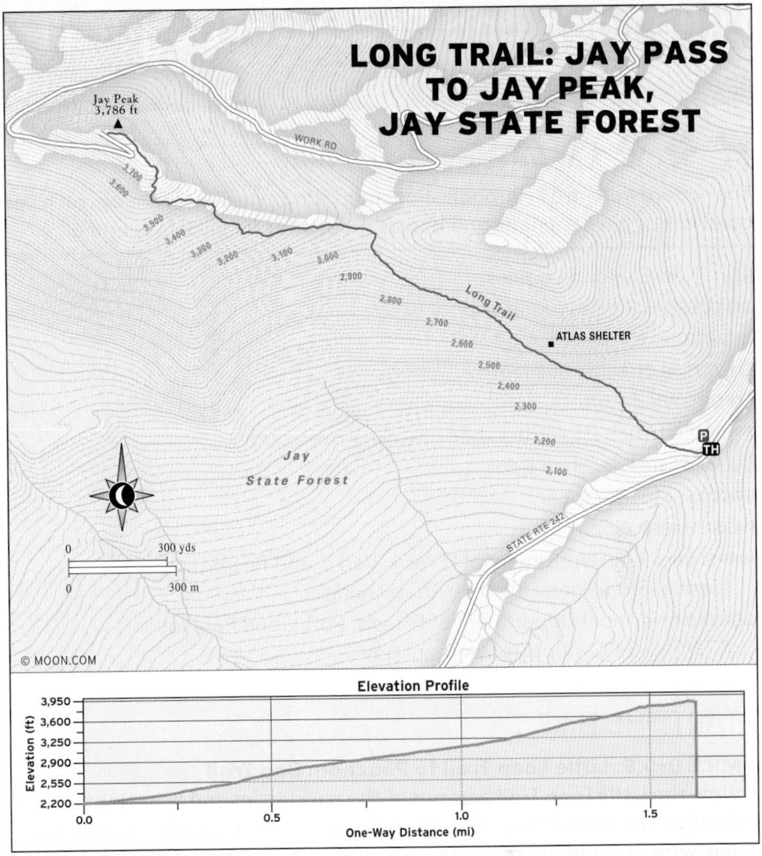

LONG TRAIL: JAY PASS TO JAY PEAK, JAY STATE FOREST

Jay Peak
3,786 ft

WORK RD

Long Trail

ATLAS SHELTER

P
TH

Jay
State Forest

STATE RTE 242

0 300 yds
0 300 m

Elevation Profile

Elevation (ft)
3,950
3,600
3,250
2,900
2,550
2,200

0.0 0.5 1.0 1.5
One-Way Distance (mi)

▲ THE LONG TRAIL

5 Little Loop and Peacham Bog Trail

GROTON STATE FOREST, GROTON

The boardwalk trail through Peacham Bog includes rarities such as carnivorous pitcher plants and boasts great odds for wildlife spotting.

BEST: New England oddities

DISTANCE: 5.9 miles round-trip

DURATION: 3.5 hours

ELEVATION CHANGE: 662 feet

EFFORT: Moderate

TRAIL: Dirt/rock singletrack, boardwalk, gravel road

USERS: Hikers, leashed dogs

SEASON: May-October

PASSES/FEES: None

MAPS: Vermont Department of Forests, Parks, and Recreation "Groton State Forest Summer Trails Guide"

CONTACT: Vermont Department of Forests, Parks, and Recreation, 802/793-3432, http://fpr.vermont.gov

START THE HIKE

▸ MILE 0-0.6: Little Loop Trail to Peacham Bog Trail

Follow the **Little Loop Trail** east out of the parking lot and bear right (south) just after the bridge. The blue-blazed trail winds through a forest decorated with large boulders, then climbs to a ridge above the stream. Pass a **bench** looking out over the marsh at 0.4 mile and follow the trail as it bends left (west). Reach a signed intersection with the **Peacham Bog Trail** at 0.6 mile and turn right (north) onto the Peacham Bog Trail.

▸ MILE 0.6-2.4: Peacham Bog Trail to Viewpoint

Cross straight over Coldwater Brook Road at 0.9 mile and continue on the blue-and-yellow-blazed trail. The mossy path winds east over rolling hills and small creeks, entering the **Peacham Bog Natural Area** at 1.8 miles. In another 0.6 mile, the trail emerges from a pine-scented thicket onto a boardwalk that carries hikers into the heart of the bog. Bear left at the fork and hike approximately 25 feet to the scenic **viewing platform.**

▸ MILE 2.4-3.6: Viewpoint to Coldwater Road

After enjoying the view at the platform, backtrack to the fork and continue straight (south) through the remainder of the bog. Reach an **intersection** at 2.8 miles and turn right (west), then turn right again at the intersection at 3.0 miles, following signs for the **Peacham Bog Trail.** A wide, leafy corridor leads downhill and reaches another sign for Peacham Bog at 3.3 miles. Bear left (south) downhill to reach **Coldwater Road** at 3.6 miles.

▲ THE PEACHAM BOG BOARDWALK

▸ MILE 3.6–5.9: Coldwater Road to Little Loop Trail/Peacham Bog Trail
Turn right (north) onto the gravel road and go through a clearing with great views to the west. At the intersection with the Little Loop Trail at 5.3 miles, turn left (west) onto the Little Loop Trail. Cross the **bridge** and carry on straight (south) for 0.3 mile. Pass straight (south) through the signed intersection of the **Little Loop Trail/Peacham Bog Trail** to return to the parking area in 0.3 mile.

DIRECTIONS

From VT-302/Groton, take VT-232 N for about 5 miles, then turn right onto Boulder Beach Road. Park at the Groton Nature Center, which is marked with a sign about 1.5 miles down the road on the left.

GPS COORDINATES: 44°17'08.3"N 72°15'55.2"W

BEST NEARBY BITES

For a quick and friendly meal made with lots of local ingredients, grab a craft beer and a homemade thin-crust specialty pizza at **Mountain Man Pizza** (1261 Scott Hwy., Groton, 802/584-9900, 11 am-7pm Sun. and Tues.-Thurs., 11am-9pm Fri.-Sat.) in downtown Groton. Try the "Mountain Goat," topped with goat cheese and caramelized onion. Mountain Man is 9 miles from the trailhead.

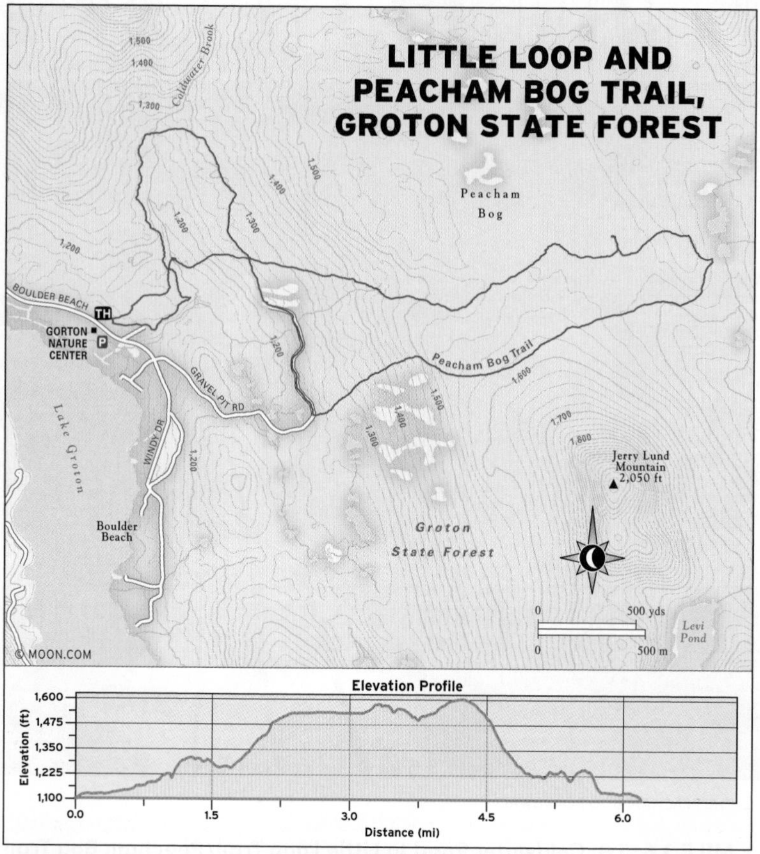

LITTLE LOOP AND PEACHAM BOG TRAIL, GROTON STATE FOREST

Coldwater Brook
Peacham Bog
Peacham Bog Trail
BOULDER BEACH
TH
GORTON NATURE CENTER
P
GRAVEL PIT RD
WINDY DR
Lake Groton
Boulder Beach
Groton State Forest
Jerry Lund Mountain 2,050 ft
Levi Pond
0 500 yds
0 500 m
1,200
1,300
1,400
1,500
1,600
1,700
1,800
© MOON.COM

Elevation Profile
Elevation (ft): 1,100 / 1,225 / 1,350 / 1,475 / 1,600
Distance (mi): 0.0 / 1.5 / 3.0 / 4.5 / 6.0

▲ BLACKBERRIES ALONG THE PEACHAM BOG TRAIL

6 Monadnock Mountain Trail

MONADNOCK MOUNTAIN, LEMINGTON

A lesser-known, diamond-in-the-rough path features a steep, heavily forested climb culminating in stunning fire tower views of the Northeast Kingdom.

DISTANCE: 4.6 miles round-trip

DURATION: 3.5 hours

ELEVATION CHANGE: 2,062 feet

EFFORT: Strenuous

TRAIL: Gravel fire road, dirt doubletrack, dirt/rock singletrack

USERS: Hikers, leashed dogs

SEASON: May-October

PASSES/FEES: None

MAPS: None

CONTACT: None (private conserved land)

START THE HIKE

▸ MILE 0-0.6: Monadnock Mountain Trail Parking Lot to Cascade

Take the **fire road** west from the parking area. The **trailhead** is marked with a sign about 345 feet up the road on the left. Hike south through the fields and into a hemlock forest. Follow the yellow blazes along the stream and bend around a high hanging ledge. There is a small cascade that can be viewed to the left (south) of the trail at 0.6 mile.

▸ MILE 0.6-1.0: Cascade to Bridge

At the cairn at 0.7 mile, turn right (west) onto a grassy doubletrack path that makes a steep, rocky ascent along the stream. This section of trail is quite strenuous, but has a quiet, remote feel. Reach a **bridge** at 1.0 mile and follow it right (north) over the stream.

▸ MILE 1.0-2.3: Bridge to Monadnock Mountain Summit

The path narrows and climbs sharply from this point. At about 2 miles, the path forks and becomes even more narrow and rocky. Bear right (west) at the fork and climb another 0.3 mile to the summit. The summit is a thick forest of massive balsam firs, so hikers will have to climb the **fire tower** for views. This 360-degree viewpoint does not disappoint—not only are there vistas of the Connecticut River below, but this mountain's "standalone" location affords expansive panoramas ranging into Canada and New Hampshire on a clear day. Descend the steps of the fire tower and return on the same path back to the parking lot.

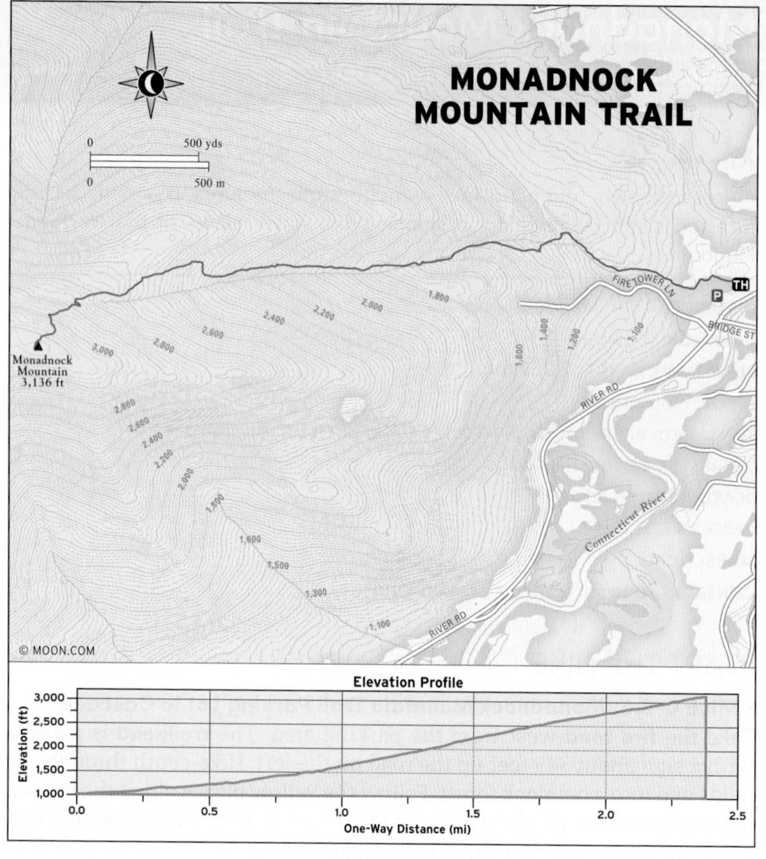

DIRECTIONS

Take VT-102 N through Lennington. Just after the bridge leading to Route 26, turn left into the large gravel lot. The area is an active quarry, but there is free public parking for Monadnock Mountain (marked with a small sign) on the far left side at the end of the fire road.

GPS COORDINATES: 44°53'57.7"N 71°30'30.3"W

BEST NEARBY BITES

Hop the border to Colebrook, New Hampshire, for a sandwich, beer, or coffee drink at **Moose Muck Coffee House** (25 Parsons St., Colebrook, NH, 603/237-4677, 10:30am-5:30pm daily), just 1 mile from the trailhead. Friendly staff and a cozy cabin vibe are a plus.

MASSACHUSETTS

GREATER BOSTON, NORTH AND SOUTH SHORE

Boston may look like natureless concrete sprawl, but an abundance of spectacular hikes lies within roughly an hour's drive from the city, including some of the best coastal scenery New England has to offer. The Boston metropolitan area includes the coast to the north of the city, known as the North Shore, and its southern equivalent, the South Shore. Along these coasts, sandy dunes and salt marshes cling to the skirts of the sea while fishing boats bob in the distance. In a crescent around the city, several hills rise up from the coastal plain as sentinels, where one can survey the city skyline against the sparkle of the Atlantic Ocean. The trails in this region prove that even in New England's largest city, a great hike is never far away.

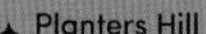

▲ Planters Hill

▲ Crane Beach

1 **Skyline Trail to Great Blue Hill**
DISTANCE: 5.7 miles round-trip
DURATION: 3 hours
EFFORT: Moderate/strenuous

2 **Carriage Paths**
DISTANCE: 4.1 miles round-trip (with optional additions)
DURATION: 2 hours
EFFORT: Easy

3 **Alternate Pond Loop and Emerson's Cliff**
DISTANCE: 2.2 miles round-trip
DURATION: 1.5 hours
EFFORT: Easy

4 **Castle Neck Loop, Crane Beach**
DISTANCE: 5.6 miles round-trip
DURATION: 3.5 hours
EFFORT: Moderate

5 **Midstate Trail to Mount Wachusett**
DISTANCE: 3.9 miles round-trip
DURATION: 2 hours
EFFORT: Moderate

6 **Wapack Trail, Mount Watatic**
DISTANCE: 3 miles round-trip
DURATION: 2 hours
EFFORT: Moderate

▲ BLACK CHERRY

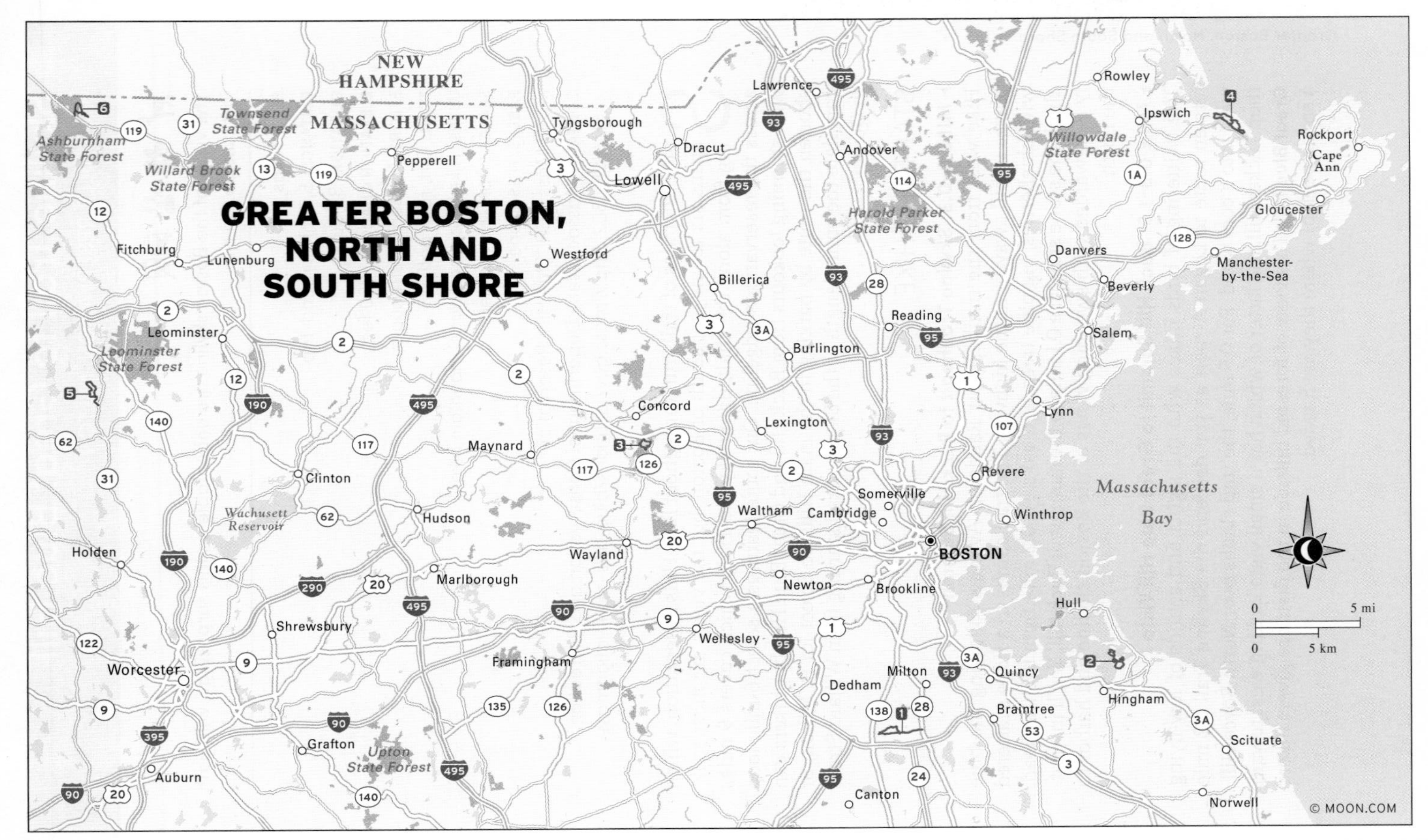
GREATER BOSTON, NORTH AND SOUTH SHORE
NEW HAMPSHIRE
MASSACHUSETTS
Ashburnham State Forest
Townsend State Forest
Willard Brook State Forest
Leominster State Forest
Wachusett Reservoir
Harold Parker State Forest
Willowdale State Forest
Upton State Forest
Massachusetts Bay
Fitchburg
Lunenburg
Leominster
Pepperell
Tyngsborough
Dracut
Lowell
Westford
Lawrence
Andover
Rowley
Ipswich
Rockport
Cape Ann
Gloucester
Danvers
Beverly
Manchester-by-the-Sea
Salem
Lynn
Billerica
Burlington
Reading
Concord
Lexington
Maynard
Clinton
Hudson
Holden
Wayland
Marlborough
Shrewsbury
Worcester
Framingham
Wellesley
Waltham
Cambridge
Somerville
Revere
Winthrop
BOSTON
Newton
Brookline
Hull
Milton
Quincy
Dedham
Braintree
Hingham
Scituate
Norwell
Canton
Grafton
Auburn
0 5 mi
0 5 km
© MOON.COM

1 Skyline Trail to Great Blue Hill

BLUE HILLS RESERVATION, MILTON

The views of the Boston skyline are unbeatable on this surprisingly wild path just outside the city.

BEST: Vistas

DISTANCE: 5.7 miles round-trip

DURATION: 3 hours

ELEVATION CHANGE: 1,260 feet

EFFORT: Moderate/strenuous

TRAIL: Dirt, rock path

USERS: Hikers, leashed dogs, mountain bikers

SEASON: April-November

PASSES/FEES: None

MAPS: Mass DCR "Blue Hills Reservation"

CONTACT: Massachusetts Department of Conservation and Recreation, 617/698-1802, http://mass.gov/locations/blue-hills-reservationmass

Some 125 miles of trails run throughout Blue Hills Reservation, which spans six towns just south of Boston, but the views are most striking from along the challenging Skyline Trail, which covers 9 miles across the reservation's ridgeline. Our route features a select 6-mile loop with stunning lookouts from Buck Hill and Great Blue Hill, but hikers can shorten the route by parking in the main Hillside Street lot in Milton, or complete the entire length of the Skyline Trail starting from Willard Street in Quincy.

START THE HIKE

▸ MILE 0-0.3: Skyline Trailhead to Buck Hill Summit

Hike west from the trailhead off Randolph Avenue, following the blue blazes uphill away from the highway. The trail climbs to a ridge scattered with blueberries, big pine trees, and oaks. At 0.2 mile from the trailhead, climb the stone staircase 0.1 mile to the summit of **Buck Hill.** You'll instantly be rewarded with sweeping views of the Boston skyline and harbor to the north.

▸ MILE 0.3-1.0: Buck Hill Summit to Great Blue Hill Vista

The twittering of birds mixes with the sights and sounds of low-flying jets en route to Logan Airport as you descend the Skyline Trail 0.2 mile west into a cool wood. For 0.5 mile, the trail climbs over North Boyce Hill, then Tucker Hill, the latter of which has a small vista looking west toward **Great Blue Hill.** This view of forested hillside in the distance givers hikers a sneak peek of where they are headed.

▲ SUNSET FROM BUCK HILL SUMMIT

▸ MILE 1.0–1.8: Great Blue Hill Vista to Hancock Hill

From the vista, continue straight (west) for 0.3 mile and then turn right (north) onto the gravel road, which reaches the **Blue Hills Reservation Headquarters** at 1.4 miles. Cross Hillside Street into the headquarters parking lot and find the sign for the continuation of the **North Skyline Trail** to the left of the information center. Turn right (north) up the stone steps, following the blue blazes and signs for the Skyline Trail and Great Blue Hill. This rooty path takes on a challenging ascent of rock slabs leading to **Hancock Hill** at 1.8 miles, then descends.

▸ MILE 1.8–2.9: Hancock Hill to Great Blue Hill Summit and Eliot Tower

A half mile from the peak of Hancock Hill, continue straight (west) across the intersection on the rock-strewn but mellow trail over Hemenway and Wolcott Hills. In spite of dense vegetation and some low-hanging trees, views peek out from these exposed summits in all directions. In 0.4 mile, the trail climbs a stone staircase and begins a steady 0.2-mile ascent to the peak of **Great Blue Hill** at 2.9 miles. At the summit, the **Eliot Tower,** a stone building with a climbable staircase, offers more great views of the **Boston skyline** and beyond.

▸ MILE 2.9–5.7: Great Blue Hill Summit and Eliot Tower to Skyline Trail

To continue on the south branch of the Skyline Trail, go south from the Eliot Tower across the stone bridge and take a left (east) onto the trail at the sign in 0.1 mile. The trail makes a tough plunge downhill, but the views remain incredible along the way. In 0.3 mile, turn right (south) onto the smooth gravel path where the blue blazes of the **Skyline Trail** continue along a much easier route downhill, then switchback left (north) in 0.2 mile. From there, the trail flows along a rolling track for 0.4 mile to the top

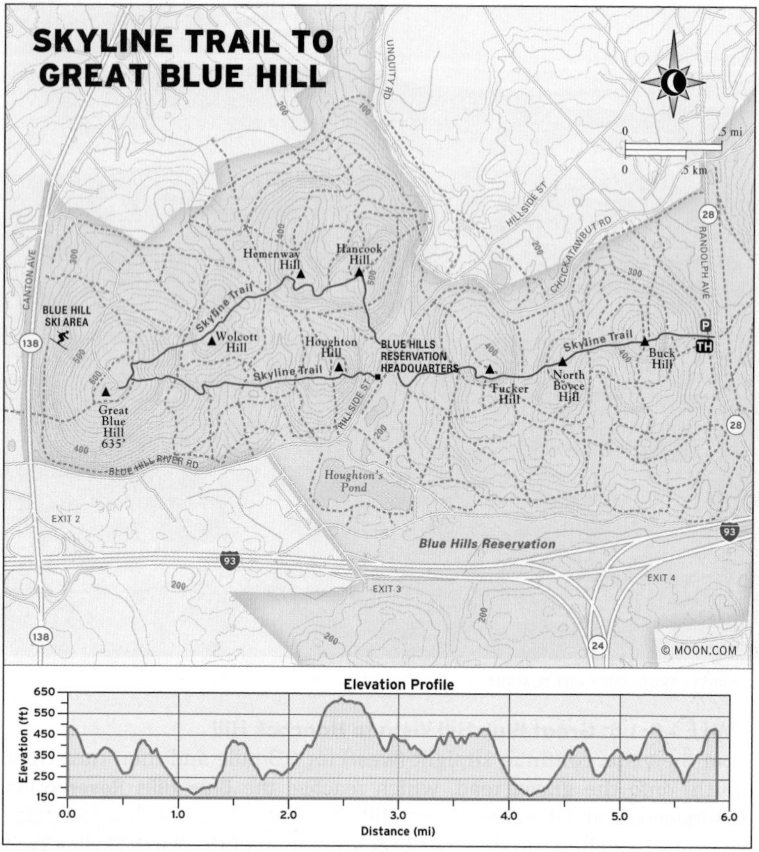

SKYLINE TRAIL TO GREAT BLUE HILL

Elevation Profile

of Houghton Hill, then gradually descends to Hillside Street in 0.2 mile. Take a left (north) up the street, use the crosswalk, and head south 0.2 mile on the gravel road to the eastern end of the Skyline Trail. Backtrack 1.4 miles over Tucker, North Boyce, and Buck Hills to return to the start.

DIRECTIONS

From I-93, take the exit for MA-28 to Milton. Parking is on the west side of MA-28 (Randolph Avenue) in Milton. The turnout off this busy street is small and marked only with a trailhead map.

GPS COORDINATES: 42°12'51.2"N 71°04'11.6"W

BEST NEARBY BREWS

Trillium Brewing Company (110 Shawmut Rd., Canton, 781/562-0073, www.trilliumbrewing.com/trillium-brewing-canton-location, 11am-7:30pm Mon.-Wed., 11am-9pm Thurs., 11am-10pm Fri.-Sat., noon-8pm Sun.), 8 miles from the trailhead, serves up what many consider to be the best beer around, and usually hosts food trucks on weekends.

2 Carriage Paths

WORLDS END RESERVATION, HINGHAM

This Frederick Law Olmsted-designed park boasts remarkable trees, scenic coastline, and fantastic views of the Boston skyline from its rolling carriage paths.

BEST: Winter hikes
DISTANCE: 3.8 miles round-trip
DURATION: 2 hours
ELEVATION CHANGE: 538 feet
EFFORT: Easy
TRAIL: Dirt path
USERS: Hikers, leashed dogs
SEASON: Year-round
PASSES/FEES: $6 ($8 on weekends and holidays) or free with a Trustees membership.
MAPS: The Trustees of Reservations "Worlds End Reservation"
CONTACT: The Trustees of Reservations, 781/740-7233, www.thetrustees.org/places-to-visit/south-shore/worlds-end.html

START THE HIKE

▸ MILE 0-0.7: Planters Hill Carriage Path to Planters Hill Summit

Walk west from the parking lot, past the restrooms and toward the entrance kiosk. Turn right (northwest) over the bridge and follow the **Planters Hill carriage path** straight (north) for 0.4 mile. At the fork with **Barnes Road,** bear right to continue straight (north) up the Planters Hill carriage path. As you ascend the hill, you'll catch intermittent views of the **Boston skyline** to your left (west) and boats bobbing in **Hull Harbor** to your right (east). From the east-facing bench of the Hull Harbor vista, the path curls west, offering great views from the summit of **Planters Hill** (also known as Brewers Grove) at 0.7 mile.

▸ MILE 0.7-0.9: Planters Hill Summit to Brewer Road Carriage Path

This is a great spot to lounge in the grass under the shade of massive oaks and drink in the view. Continue on the Planters Hill path as it turns south; at 0.9 mile, turn sharply right (north) onto the **Brewer Road carriage path.**

▸ MILE 0.9-2.7: Brewer Road Carriage Path to Barnes Road Carriage Path

In 0.3 mile, the path cuts through **"The Bar,"** a low and narrow spit between the bays of Hingham Harbor and the Weir River where hikers may spot waterfowl floating on the water. From The Bar, the path continues north. Turn left (west) where the trail branches off in 0.1 mile. Stay west on the tree-lined path, which cuts inland to a forested **valley** in 0.5 mile. It's common to catch deer grazing on acorns and other vegetation in these shady lowlands. At the valley, turn left (west) on a slight uphill

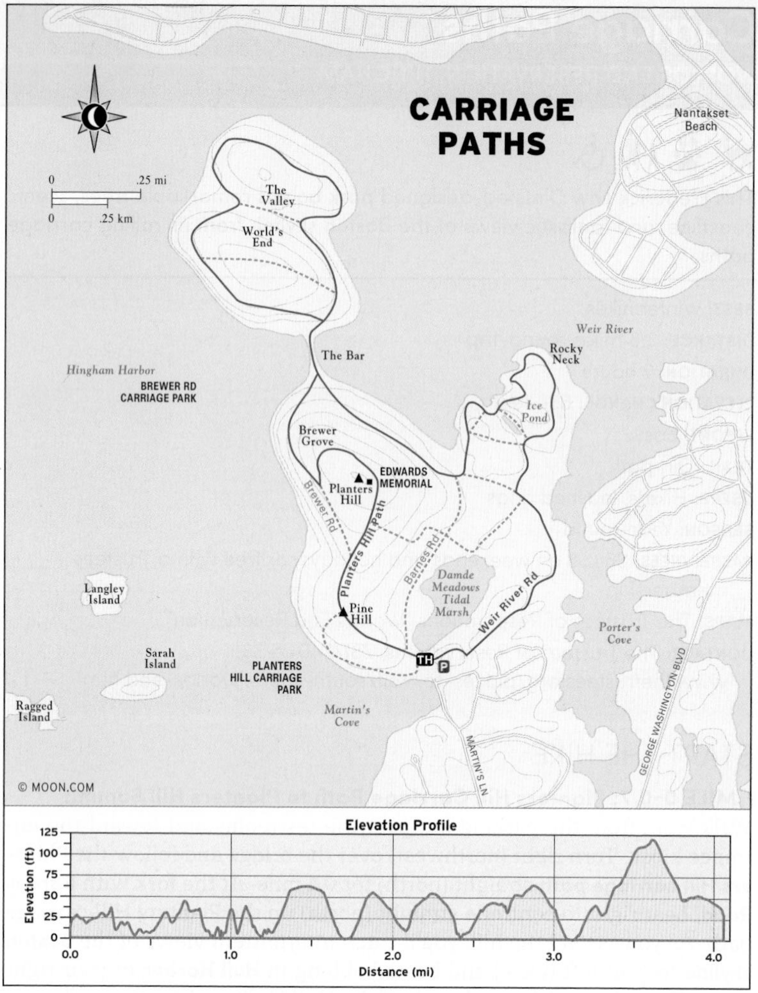

CARRIAGE PATHS

Nantakset Beach
0 .25 mi
0 .25 km
The Valley
World's End
The Bar
Weir River
Rocky Neck
Hingham Harbor
BREWER RD CARRIAGE PARK
Ice Pond
Brewer Grove
EDWARDS MEMORIAL
Planters Hill
Brewer Rd
Planters Hill Path
Barnes Rd
Damde Meadows Tidal Marsh
Weir River Rd
Langley Island
Pine Hill
Porter's Cove
Sarah Island
PLANTERS HILL CARRIAGE PARK
TH
P
GEORGE WASHINGTON BLVD
Ragged Island
Martin's Cove
MARTIN'S LN
© MOON.COM

Elevation Profile
Elevation (ft)
125
100
75
50
25
0
0.0
1.0
2.0
3.0
4.0
Distance (mi)

trail through thick, green vegetation. The path rounds the northern tip of Worlds End, emerging at water views and the sound of waves before curving south back into the valley in 0.5 mile. Keep left in the valley to follow the eastern path 0.1 mile back to The Bar. Pass back through The Bar, turn left onto the **Barnes Road carriage path,** and follow it 0.3 mile.

▸ MILE 2.7-3.8: Barnes Road Carriage Path to Damde Meadows Tidal Marsh and Observation Deck

Here, hikers can turn left (north) onto the narrow trail around **Rocky Neck.** This slightly more rugged section of trail traverses the coastline jutting into the **Weir River,** and is a lovely spot to sit by the water in solitude even when the park is busy. The Rocky Neck trail loops back to the **Weir River Road carriage path** in 0.6 mile. Turn left (southeast) onto Weir River Road, which wraps around **Damde Meadows tidal marsh.** An observation deck here offers a chance to glimpse coastal birds and other tidal flora and fauna. The trail continues south back to the east side of the parking lot in 0.5 mile.

▲ THE CARRIAGE PATHS

DIRECTIONS

From MA-3, take Exit 14 onto MA-228 N and travel 6.5 miles. Turn left onto MA-3A and go 0.7 mile. Turn right onto Summer Street; at the Rockland Street intersection, continue straight across onto Martin's Lane. The parking area, marked with a Trustees of Reservations sign, is 0.7 mile ahead at the end of the road.

GPS COORDINATES: 42°15'30.4"N 70°52'25.1"W

BEST NEARBY BITES

Toast your adventure with a flight of microbrews at **Stars on Hingham Harbor** (3 Otis St., Hingham, 781/749-3200, www.starshingham.com, 7am-1am daily), which also serves apps and entrees and hosts live music. It's 1.5 miles from the trailhead.

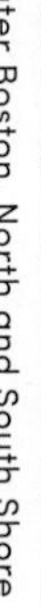

3 Alternate Pond Loop and Emerson's Cliff

WALDEN POND STATE RESERVATION, CONCORD

Historic Walden is well loved for its crystalline swimming water and trails near the former house site of Henry David Thoreau.

BEST: Spots for a swim
DISTANCE: 2.2 miles round-trip
DURATION: 1.5 hours
ELEVATION CHANGE: 251 feet
EFFORT: Easy
TRAIL: Dirt and sand path
USERS: Hikers only
SEASON: Year-round
PASSES/FEES: Parking fee $8 MA residents, $15 nonresidents
MAPS: Mass DCR "Walden Pond State Reservation," Appalachian Mountain Club "Bay Circuit Trail"
CONTACT: Massachusetts Department of Conservation and Recreation, 978/369-3254, www.mass.gov/locations/walden-pond-state-reservation

Hikes don't get much more historic than Walden Pond, where the transcendentalist writer Henry David Thoreau conducted his famous experiment in living simply and deliberately upon the land from 1845 to 1847. The trails in this current-day state park (which is part of the Bay Circuit Trail system) remain inspiring, if a little overcrowded. This route takes hikers to sites on some of the less-traveled park paths, including the Alternate Pond Loop's water views, the scenic bog of Heywood's Meadow, and the peaceful vista of Emerson's Cliff.

START THE HIKE

▸ MILE 0-0.5: Visitors Center to Thoreau's Cove

From the main parking lot near the visitors center, walk southwest across Walden Street and follow the paved ramp toward the beach. In 435 feet, take a sharp right onto the **Sherwood Trail,** following signs for the **Alternate Pond Loop.** In 0.2 mile, continue straight west on the **Ridge Path,** which treks above the pond for great views to the south. The Alternate Pond Loop continues straight west on the Wyman Path in 0.1 mile, curving northwest over Wyman Meadow. Turn left (south) where the path branches off in 0.2 mile. The trail bends right (west) into **Thoreau's Cove,** where there is a monument to the author's original **cabin site.** The original cabin no longer exists, but you can walk through a replica of Thoreau's "tiny house" back at the visitors center.

▲ WALDEN POND

▸ MILE 0.5–1.3: Thoreau's Cove to Esker Trail

Continue south from the cabin site on the Alternate Pond Loop, which merges with the main pond loop (Bay Circuit Trail) at Ice Fort Cove in 0.3 mile. The trail passes between the beach on the left (east) and the MBTA Commuter Rail tracks on the right (west). At 1.1 miles, go south up the steps and turn left (east) onto the **Esker Trail.** Bear right (southeast) onto the unmarked Esker Trail loop at 1.3 miles.

▸ MILE 1.3–1.6: Esker Trail to Emerson's Cliff Vista

When you reach the next intersection at 1.4 miles, take a sharp right (southeast) downhill onto the **Heywood's Meadow Path.** This quiet area of the park is less traveled, and features a colorful bog scattered with lily pads. Walk southeast, around the bog's banks, for 0.2 mile, then turn left (north) onto the **Emerson's Cliff Trail** at the sign. This short, steep path climbs around some large boulders to a small south-facing vista. Thoreau named this ridge for fellow transcendentalist writer Ralph Waldo Emerson, who once considered building his own rural cabin at this site.

▸ MILE 1.6–2.2: Emerson's Cliff Vista to Esker Trail and Beach

Continue north across the ridge, then descend back to the **Esker Trail** in 0.3 mile. Turn right (east) onto the Esker Trail and follow it for 0.1 mile before bearing left (northeast) in the direction of the pond. From the boat launch, use the beach to walk north the remaining 0.2 mile to the starting point.

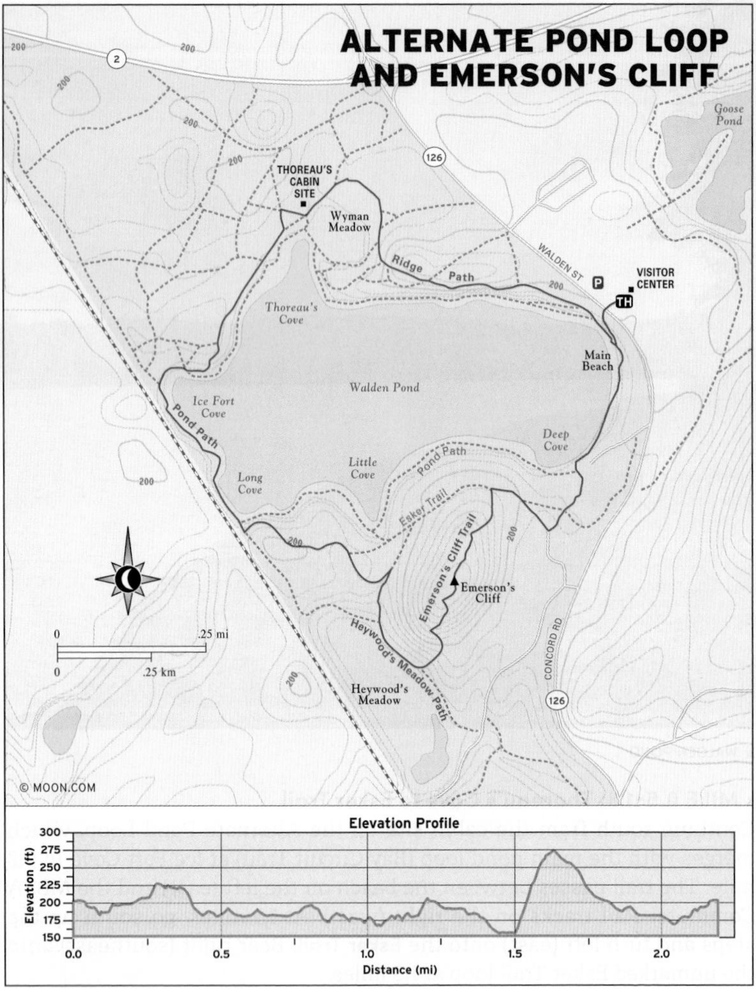

ALTERNATE POND LOOP AND EMERSON'S CLIFF

© MOON.COM

DIRECTIONS

From MA-2, take MA-126 (Walden Street) south. The large parking area is well marked on the left side of the street. There is a parking fee, and parking is not permitted anywhere along the street.

GPS COORDINATES: 42°26'26.0"N 71°20'05.9"W

BEST NEARBY BITES

Trail's End Café (97 Lowell Rd., 978/610-6633, www.thetrailsendcafe.com, 7am-9pm Sun., Tues., Wed.), 2 miles from trailhead, is a relaxed hangout for coffee, baked goods, and creative American fare.

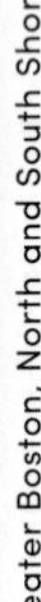

4 Castle Neck Trails

CRANE BEACH, IPSWICH

Tucked between the Essex River and the Atlantic Ocean, the dunes, forests, and vernal pools of Crane Beach make up one of the most diverse—and beautiful—coastal habitats in southern New England.

BEST: Summer hikes, spots for a swim

DISTANCE: 5.6 miles round-trip

DURATION: 3.5 hours

ELEVATION CHANGE: 100 feet

EFFORT: Moderate

TRAIL: Sand path

USERS: Hikers only (leashed dogs permitted with a small fee between October and March)

SEASON: Year-round

PASSES/FEES: Summer: $25, $30 weekends and holidays. Extended season: $10, $20 weekends and holidays. Off-season: $10. Discounts available with Trustees membership and parking sticker.

MAPS: Trustees of Reservations "Crane Estate"

CONTACT: The Trustees of Reservations, 978/356-4354, www.thetrustees.org/places-to-visit/north-shore/crane-beach-admission-prices.html

Trekking through the soft sand of the Castle Neck trails on Crane Beach can be tiring, but the chance to get up close and personal with these scenic dune trails is not to be missed. Hikers will wind through pine forests and salt marshes, over sweeping hills and along gentle coastline, to reach stunning vistas of the Essex and Ipswich Bays. Crane Beach is considered a top birding habitat, especially for threatened shorebirds such as the piping plover, and the beach here is widely regarded as one of the prettiest in the Northeast. Take advantage of all Crane has to offer and top off your hike with a refreshing plunge into the Atlantic!

START THE HIKE

▶ MILE 0–1.3: Castle Neck Trails Trailhead to Wigwam Hill

Find the trailhead at the far east end of the beach parking lot and head southeast on the sand-and-boardwalk trail through overhanging scrub oak. In 0.1 mile, turn right (south) onto the **Green Trail.** Make sure to hike within the fencing to protect delicate wildlife and vegetation along the trail. The sand path wraps south, then east, along the border of a pine swamp for 0.7 mile before it intersects with the **Red Trail.** Bear right (east) on the Red Trail, which climbs 0.5 mile over the crest of **Wigwam Hill,** a massive dune with sweeping views of the Essex Bay and Choate Island; the 1996 movie The Crucible was filmed here.

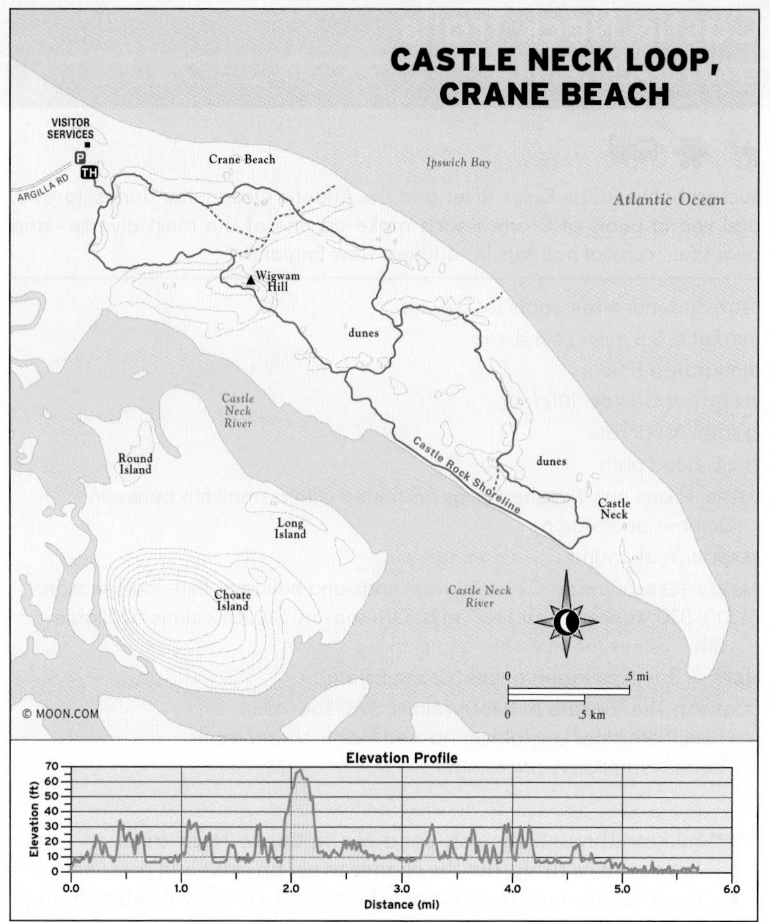

▸ MILE 1.3-3.4: Wigwam Hill to Essex Bay Beach

From Wigwam Hill, the trail descends steeply into marshland and reaches an intersection in 0.4 mile. Turn left (east) to stay on the **Red Trail.** Reach the **Blue Trail** in 0.3 mile and turn right (northeast) onto the Blue Trail. The path ascends to a dune-top ridge with great views of Ipswich Bay. Follow the path southeast for 0.3 mile to where it meets the **Yellow Trail.** Continue southeast on the Yellow Trail for 0.8 mile, then turn left (east) onto the **Black Trail.** This path will deliver you to the beach on the Essex Bay side of the property—a great spot for a picnic or swimming break—in 0.3 mile.

▸ MILE 3.4-4.3: Essex Bay Beach to Red Trail

Turn right (northwest) onto the beach and follow the shoreline along the **Castle Neck River.** In 0.9 mile, cut right (northeast) inland on a white-marked trail through high dune grass, which will return you to the Red Trail. Follow the Red Trail back to the Blue Trail intersection, but this time, turn left (north) to stay on the Red Trail.

▲ THE CASTLE NECK RIVER FROM WIGWAM HILL

▸ MILE 4.3-5.6: Red Trail to Green Trail

Follow the Red Trail west along the dunes for 0.7 mile, then keep straight west on the **Orange Trail.** This dune-side path skirts a series of vernal pools and cranberry bogs, then wraps back into the pines to meet the Green Trail in 0.3 mile. Take a right (north) onto the Green Trail, which carries on over a boardwalk and back into the dunes. In 0.2 mile, turn right (east) to follow the Green Trail spur 0.1 mile back to the parking area.

DIRECTIONS

From MA-128 N, take exit 20A to MA-1A N and continue 8 miles to Ipswich. Turn right onto MA-133 E; follow it for 1.5 miles and then turn left onto Northgate Road. In 0.5 mile, turn right onto Argilla Road. The well-marked parking area is in 2.5 miles at the end of road, through the gatehouse.

GPS COORDINATES: 42°40'58.1"N 70°46'14.8"W

BEST NEARBY BITES

Using only the simplest ingredients, **Riverview Restaurant** (20 Estes St., Ipswich, 978/356-0500, 4pm-11pm Tues.-Sun.) serves up the perfect post-hike personal pizza, with classic toppings as well as local favorites such as kielbasa, in a hometown diner-like atmosphere with a bar. It's 5 miles from the trailhead.

5 Midstate Trail to Mount Wachusett

WACHUSETT MOUNTAIN STATE RESERVATION, PRINCETON

Explore the only known old-growth forest east of the Connecticut River on this scenic tour of Wachusett Mountain's western slopes.

DISTANCE: 3.9 miles round-trip

DURATION: 2 hours

ELEVATION CHANGE: 1,122 feet

EFFORT: Moderate

TRAIL: Dirt and rock path

USERS: Hikers, leashed dogs

SEASON: April-November

PASSES/FEES: No fee at Echo Lake lot. Parking fee ($5 MA residents, $10 nonresidents) charged in main lot.

MAPS: Mass DCR "Wachusett Mountain State Reservation," Massachusetts Midstate Trail Guidebook

CONTACT: Massachusetts Department of Conservation and Recreation, 978/464-2987, www.mass.gov/locations/wachusett-mountain-state-reservation

Wachusett Mountain is best known as a ski area, but this route around the west side of the state reservation will take hikers through the undeveloped splendor of granite slopes, blossoming meadows, a sprawling old-growth forest, and vistas galore. The hike begins on the quiet, less-traveled trails near Echo Lake and winds its way to the 2,006-foot summit using a prized section of the Midstate Trail. From there, views of mountains and lakes stretch from Boston to the Berkshires, and north into New Hampshire and Vermont.

START THE HIKE

▸ MILE 0-0.6: Echo Lake Road to Jack Frost Trail

Enter the gate straight ahead of the parking area and hike straight (west) on the flat, dirt-surface **Echo Lake Road** for 0.3 mile. At the **Echo Lake picnic area,** turn right (northeast) onto the **High Meadow Trail.** This sometimes-muddy section may require some rock-hopping, but the path is more reliably dry as it ascends the hill. In 0.2 mile, the trail winds through the apple tree-dotted **High Meadow,** where a bench looks out over grasslands to an east-facing vista of a flat valley stretching toward Boston. Continue straight (north) past the bench on the rocky High Meadow Trail for 0.1 mile and reach the intersection with the **Jack Frost Trail.**

▸ MILE 0.6-2.0: Jack Frost Trail to West Side (Midstate) Trail

Take a left (west) onto Jack Frost Trail, where you will descend again on a path through pines and granite boulders. In 0.3 mile, turn right (north) on the **Lower Link Trail,** which intersects with the **Harrington (Midstate) Trail** in 0.3 mile. Turn right (east) onto the red-blazed Harrington Trail and

▲ THE OLD INDIAN TRAIL

climb it for 0.2 mile. Then, turn left (north) onto the **Semuhenna (Midstate) Trail.** The blue-blazed Semuhenna Trail is mostly flat granite. Follow it north for 0.6 mile to reach the **West Side (Midstate) Trail** at 2.0 miles.

▸ MILE 2.0–2.6: West Side (Midstate) Trail to Mount Wachusett Summit and Lookout Tower

Turn right (east) onto the West Side Trail, which connects with the **Old Indian Trail** in 0.2 mile. Follow signs for the Midstate Trail right (south) and climb the ledges of the Old Indian Trail up through this spectacular section of old-growth forest where sunlight dapples tall, gnarled hardwoods. Reach the summit in 0.4 mile and enjoy 360-degree views from the **lookout tower.**

▸ MILE 2.6–3.9: Mount Wachusett Summit and Lookout Tower to Echo Lake Road

Descend to the south via the Mountain House (Midstate) Trail. In 0.3 mile, bear right for the Jack Frost Trail and follow it through a hemlock forest for 0.3 mile back to the intersection with the High Meadow Trail. Descend via the High Meadow Trail and Echo Lake Road for a round-trip of 3.9 miles.

DIRECTIONS

From MA-2, take the exit for MA-140 and follow it south to Park Road. Turn right onto Park Road, then bear left onto Mountain Road and follow it for 2 miles to Echo Lake Road, on the right. The small lot is marked only with a trailhead map.

GPS COORDINATES: 42°28'29.8"N 71°53'00.7"W

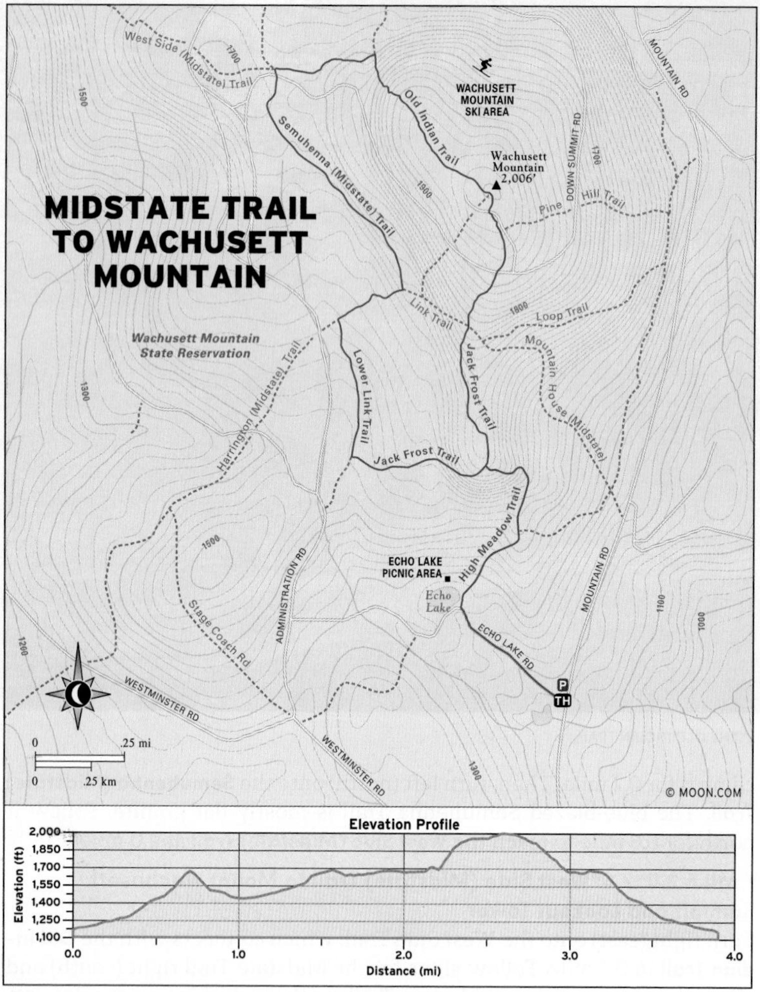

MIDSTATE TRAIL TO WACHUSETT MOUNTAIN

© MOON.COM

BEST NEARBY BREWS

Visit **Wachusett Brewing Company** (175 State Rd. E., Westminster, 978/874-9965, www.wachusettbrewingcompany.com, noon-8pm Sun.-Thurs., noon-10pm Fri.-Sat.) and the "Brew Yard" for beer served from an Airstream trailer, outdoor seating, live music, and apps and sandwiches. It's 7 miles from the trailhead.

6 Wapack Trail to Mount Watatic

MOUNT WATATIC STATE RESERVATION, ASHBURNHAM

The starting point of the Wapack Trail, and the only section in Massachusetts, 1,830-foot Mount Watatic is known for its spectacular views and blueberry picking.

DISTANCE: 3 miles round-trip
DURATION: 2 hours
ELEVATION CHANGE: 650 feet
EFFORT: Moderate
TRAIL: Dirt and rock path
USERS: Hikers, leashed dogs
SEASON: April-November
PASSES/FEES: None
MAPS: Friends of the Wapack "The Wapack Trail"
CONTACT: Friends of the Wapack, www.wapack.org/the-friends/contat-us/

Mount Watatic is off the beaten path, but locals cherish this gem for its scenic views of Ashburnham's many lakes and its abundance of blueberries. It also offers great views of nearby Mount Monadnock, and, on a clear day, the Boston skyline. This moderate loop takes hikers over Nutting Hill to the summit of Watatic on the first section of the Wapack Trail, which is also the final section of the Midstate Trail. For more great hiking, continue on the Wapack over the New Hampshire state line.

START THE HIKE

▸ MILE 0-0.9: Parking Lot to Nutting Hill

Hike north from the parking lot, following the yellow Wapack Trail markers through the gate and over a series of bridges along the bog. In 0.2 mile, you will see signs for the Wapack Trail and **Watatic Summit** pointing right (these indicate the "shortcut" to the summit). Pass the signs and continue straight north on the wide dirt path. This trail follows a gradual rocky incline to another intersection with the Wapack Trail in 0.5 mile. Turn right (southeast) onto the Wapack Trail at this intersection and follow the yellow markers 0.2 mile to the grass-and-granite slopes of **Nutting Hill,** a lovely bald top with views and bountiful blueberries that looks upon the summit of Watatic to the south.

▸ MILE 0.9-1.7: Nutting Hill to Mount Watatic Summit

Follow the cairns south 0.1 mile as you descend Nutting Hill back into the woods. The path levels out along a stone wall, then bends slightly east through a fern-covered forest floor. In 0.5 mile, the trail begins its gradual ascent to the **Watatic summit.** Cross the gravel access road straight east in 0.1 mile and climb the final section to the blueberry-speckled summit. The views are even more dramatic from Watatic's false summit, 0.1 mile to

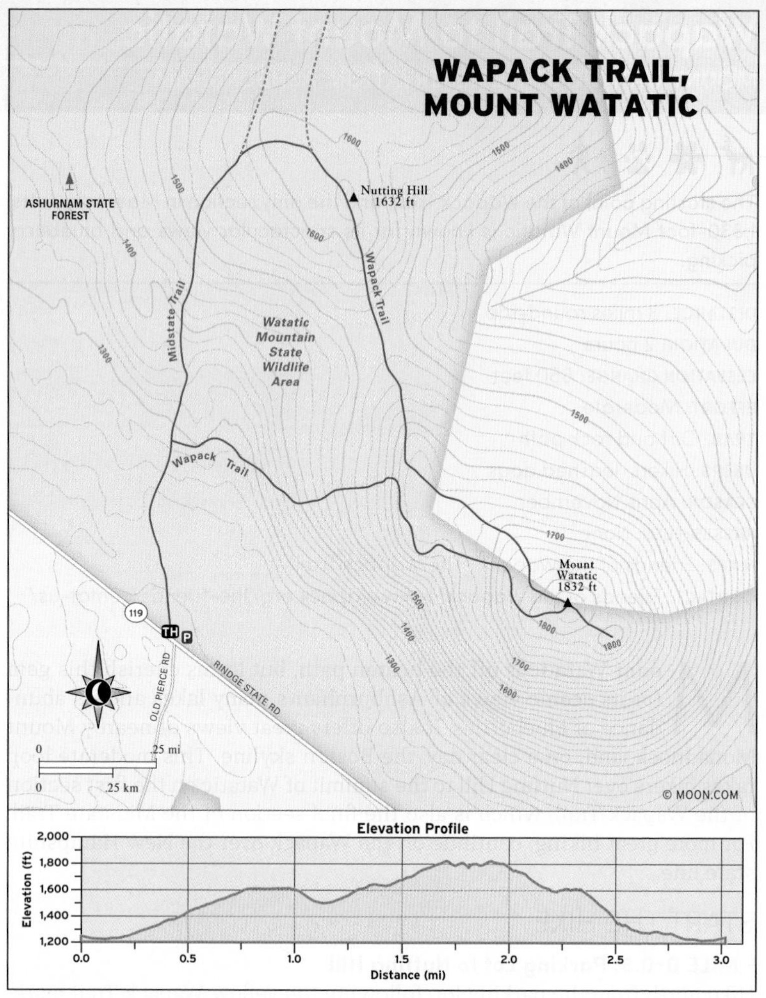

the west down a rocky corridor, where hikers can view Mount Wachusett, Mount Monadnock, and even the Boston skyline on a clear day.

▸ MILE 1.7-3.0: Mount Watatic Summit to Wapack Trail

Backtrack 0.1 mile to the main summit and find the south Wapack Trail to the west. This steep trail descends through granite tumbles and hemlocks, offering another nice west-facing vista in 0.4 mile. From there, the path descends 0.5 mile, winding between two large boulders and crossing a small stream before leveling to meet the main path in 0.1 mile. Turn left (south) to return 0.2 mile to the parking lot.

DIRECTIONS

Off MA-119 in Ashburnham, the Mount Watatic parking area is marked with a sign across from Old Pierce Road. If the lot is full, parking along the side of 119 is permissible.

GPS COORDINATES: 42°41'46.0"N 71°54'14.8"W

▲ MOUNT WATATIC FROM NUTTING HILL

BEST NEARBY BREWS

While there aren't many commercial businesses in this rural area, a quick trip over the state line to Jaffrey, New Hampshire, takes you to the **Lab 'N Lager** (4 Stratton Rd., Jaffrey, NH, 603/532-1195, www.lab-nlager.com, 3pm-11pm Mon.-Thurs., 11:30am-1am Fri.-Sat., 11:30am-11pm Sun.) for great burgers, sweet potato fries, beer, and pool. It's 12 miles from the trailhead.

NEARBY CAMPGROUNDS

NAME	LOCATION	FACILITIES	SEASON	FEE
Boston Harbor Islands	191w Atlantic Ave., Boston, MA 02110	33 tent sites, 6 yurts; compositing toilets; no water	June-September	$10-60
617/223-8666, www.bostonharborislands.org/campground-reservations				
Myles Standish State Forest	194 Cranberry Rd., Carver, MA 02330	400 RV/tent sites; restrooms	mid-May-mid-October	$27
508/866-2526, www.mass.gov/locations/myles-standish-state-forest				
Blue Hills Reservation, Ponkapoag	695 Hillside St., Milton, MA 02186	20 cabins, 2 tent sites; outhouses; no water	year-round	$45-75
617/698-1802, www.outdoors.org/lodging-camping/camps-cabins/ponkapoag				
Harold Parker State Forest	305 Middleton Rd., North Andover, MA 01845	84 RV/tent sites; restrooms	early May-mid-October	$27
978/686-3391, www.mass.gov/locations/harold-parker-state-forest				
Lake Dennison Recreation Area	747 Alger St., Winchendon, MA 01475	151 RV/tent sites; restrooms	mid-May-early September	$27
978/297-1609, www.mass.gov/locations/lake-dennison-recreation-area				
Pearl Hill State Park	105 New Fitchburg Rd., Townsend, MA 01474	50 RV/tent sites; restrooms	mid-May-mid-October	$27
978/597-8802, www.mass.gov/locations/pearl-hill-state-park				
Willard Brook State Forest	10 Townsend Rd., Ashby, MA 01431	19 RV/tent sites, 1 group yurt; restrooms	mid-May-early September	$20-115
978/597-8802, www.mass.gov/locations/willard-brook-state-forest				
Wompatuck State Park	204 Union St., Hingham, MA 02043	260 RV/tent sites; restrooms	mid-May-mid-October	$27
781/749-7160, www.mass.gov/locations/wompatuck-state-park				

CAPE COD AND THE ISLANDS

Quaint, colorful Cape Cod is a land of flowing dunes and windswept grasses, where plovers tuck away their fragile nests and summer tourists flock to the expansive, pastel-hued beaches. It's also the launching point for the offshore islands of Martha's Vineyard and Nantucket, revered for their beauty by both A-list celebrities and lifelong fishermen. Though many of the shores here are occupied by grandiose mansions and humble beach cottages, a remarkable amount of conservation land has been set aside as the Cape Cod National Seashore, in town preserves, and in land-bank systems on both of the islands. As a result, miles of coastal trails wind through the goldenrod and beach plum, offering seaside vistas that are sure to inspire even the saltiest hearts.

▲ Cape Cod National Seashore

▲ Sanford Farm

1 **Prospect Hill and the Great Sand Bank**
DISTANCE: 3.1 miles round-trip
DURATION: 2 hours
EFFORT: Easy/moderate

2 **Ocean Walk, Sanford Farm, Ram Pasture, and The Woods**
DISTANCE: 5.7 miles round-trip
DURATION: 2.5 hours
EFFORT: Easy

3 **Great Island Trail, Cape Cod National Seashore**
DISTANCE: 5.6 miles (with longer options at low tide)
DURATION: 3 hours
EFFORT: Moderate

4 **Marsh Trail, Sandy Neck Beach Park**
DISTANCE: 7.9 miles round-trip
DURATION: 4 hours
EFFORT: Moderate

▲ SUNSET AT SANDY NECK BEACH PARK

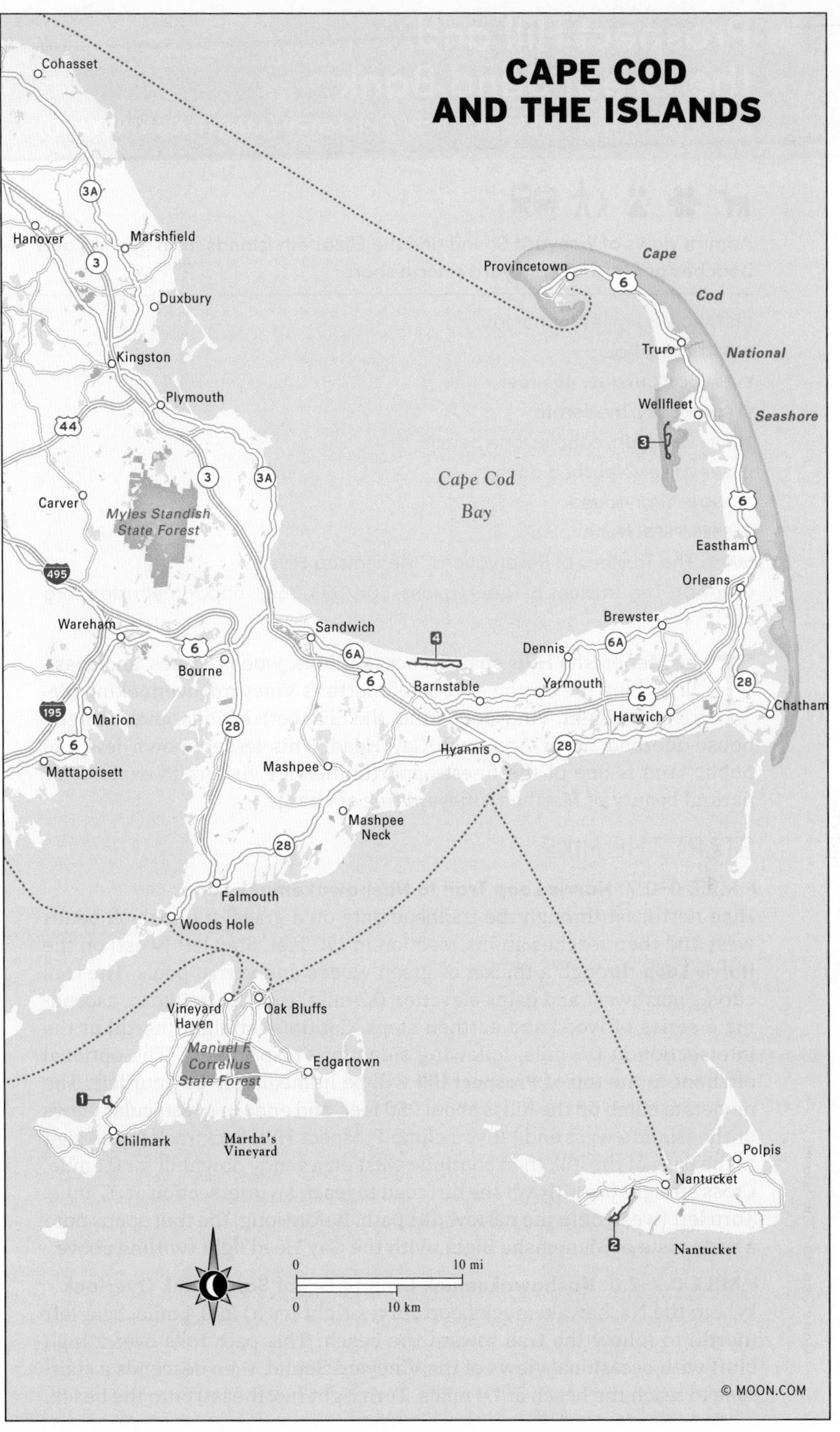
CAPE COD
AND THE ISLANDS
Cohasset
Hanover
Marshfield
Duxbury
Kingston
Plymouth
Carver
Myles Standish
State Forest
Wareham
Bourne
Marion
Mattapoisett
Sandwich
Barnstable
Dennis
Yarmouth
Brewster
Orleans
Eastham
Wellfleet
Truro
Provincetown
Cape
Cod
National
Seashore
Cape Cod
Bay
Harwich
Chatham
Hyannis
Mashpee
Mashpee
Neck
Falmouth
Woods Hole
Vineyard
Haven
Oak Bluffs
Manuel F.
Correllus
State Forest
Edgartown
Chilmark
Martha's
Vineyard
Nantucket
Polpis
Nantucket
0
10 mi
0
10 km
© MOON.COM

1 Prospect Hill and the Great Sand Bank

MENEMSHA HILLS RESERVATION, CHILMARK (MARTHA'S VINEYARD)

Admire views of Vineyard Sound and the Elizabeth Islands from the hills and beaches of Martha's Vineyard's north shore.

DISTANCE: 3.1 miles round-trip
DURATION: 2 hours
ELEVATION CHANGE: 468 feet
EFFORT: Easy/moderate
TRAIL: Dirt path, cobblestone beach
USERS: Hikers, leashed dogs
SEASON: Year-round
PASSES/FEES: None
MAPS: The Trustees of Reservations "Menemsha Hills"
CONTACT: The Trustees of Reservations, 508/693-3678, http:// thetrustees.org

The Menemsha Hills span 211 acres of hills, woods, dunes, and coastline along the northwest end of Martha's Vineyard, overlooking Menemsha Bight, Vineyard Sound, the Elizabeth Islands, and the lighthouse-adorned tip of Aquinnah/Gay Head. This lesser-known jewel of public land is one of the finest opportunities for visitors to explore the natural beauty of Martha's Vineyard free of charge.

START THE HIKE

▸ MILE 0-0.7: Harris Loop Trail to Nashawakemuck Loop

Hike northeast through the trailhead gate on a gravel trail, which bends west and then reaches an intersection in 150 feet. Stay left (west) on the **Harris Loop** through a thicket of green woods and vernal pools. The trail curves northwest and gains elevation 0.2 mile from the trailhead, ascending a series of wood and earthen steps. Continue straight (north) at the intersection at 0.5 mile, following signs for Prospect Hill. (The optional offshoot to the top of **Prospect Hill** will be immediately on your left. The moderate climb up the hill is about 250 feet, and ends in spectacular views of the island's west end.) If you climb Prospect Hill, backtrack to the sign at the base of the hill, then continue west on a sandy downhill for 0.1 mile. Cross straight (north) over the dirt road to reach an intersection at 0.7 mile. Turn left (west) onto the narrow dirt path. Before long, the trail opens onto a wide vista of Menemsha Bight, with the Gay Head light twirling above.

▸ MILE 0.7-2.0: Nashawakemuck Loop to Great Sand Bank Overlook

Where the Nashawakemuck Loop curves right (east) in 0.4 mile, bear left (north) to follow the trail toward the beach. This path rolls over a high bluff with occasional views of the Vineyard Sound, then descends a staircase to reach the beach at 1.4 miles. Turn right (northeast) onto the beach,

▲ THE COBBLESTONE BEACH AT MENEMSHA HILLS RESERVATION

stepping with care across the cobblestone shoreline. At a collection of wave-beaten boulders at 1.7 miles, another staircase heads right (southeast) into the dunes. Ascend the staircase and continue on the somewhat steep path as it climbs to the top of the Great Sand Bank. At the intersection on the hilltop at 2.0 miles, there is a 150-foot spur to the left (northwest) that leads to the **Great Sand Bank Overlook.**

▸ MILE 2.0-3.1: Great Sand Bank Overlook to Trailhead

After enjoying the overlook, turn around and continue straight (south). The trail leads back to the **Nashawakemuck Loop** at 2.1 miles. Continue straight (south) on the Nashawakemuck Loop for 0.5 mile. At the intersection, turn left (south), then cross back over the dirt road and continue straight (southeast) to reach the parking lot in another 0.5 mile.

DIRECTIONS

Follow State Road into West Tisbury and turn right onto North Road. Continue west for 4.7 miles, then turn right onto Trustees Lane at the Trustees of Reservations sign. The large parking area is on the right.

GPS COORDINATES: 41°21'53.7"N 70°44'33.2"W

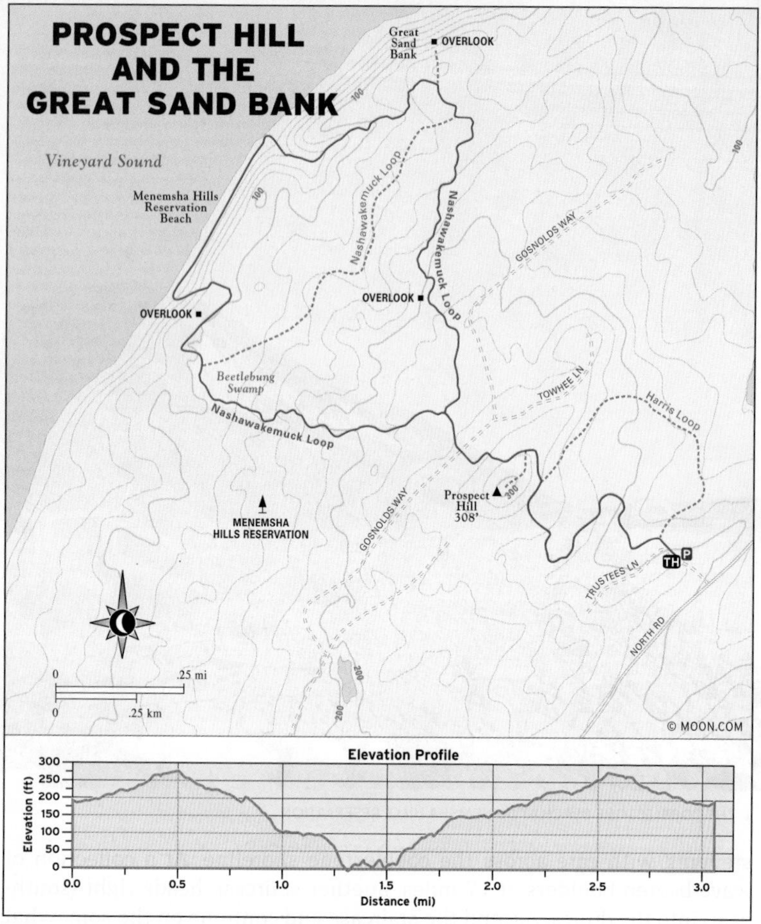

BEST NEARBY BREWS

Grab a local Offshore Ale and BYOB to **Menemsha Beach,** where you can watch the sun set with some food or ice cream from **The Galley** (515 North Road, 508/645-9819, www.menemshagalley.com, 11am–8pm daily, hours vary seasonally, call ahead), 2 miles from trailhead.

2 Ocean Walk

SANFORD FARM, RAM PASTURE, AND THE WOODS, NANTUCKET

Wind your way to the ocean on this quaint path through historic farmland, exploring sand plains, heaths, and ponds.

BEST: Brew hikes, spots for a swim
DISTANCE: 5.7 miles round-trip
DURATION: 2.5 hours
ELEVATION CHANGE: 74 feet
EFFORT: Easy
TRAIL: Grass/sand path
USERS: Hikers, leashed dogs, bicyclists
SEASON: Year-round
PASSES/FEES: None
MAPS: Nantucket Conservation Foundation "A Trail Guide to Sanford Farm, Ram Pasture, and The Woods"
CONTACT: Nantucket Conservation Foundation, 508/228-2884, http://nantucketconservation.org

This easy but lengthy stroll across Nantucket is a tour of all the island's natural delights: grassy pastures, kettle ponds, unspoiled sandy shoreline. The roughly 6-mile Ocean Walk takes hikers through three key sections of conservation land, starting with Sanford Farm and then traveling through The Woods and Ram Pasture to reach a wide-open sand plain abutting the ocean. Aside from fantastic water views, be on the lookout for deer, osprey, and a variety of unique plant life.

START THE HIKE

▸ MILE 0-1.6: Sanford Farm Parking Area to Historic Barn

From the **Sanford Farm** parking area, find the trail through the turnstile to the south. The wide sand-and-crushed stone path carries hikers over rolling hills, with grasslands to the right and views of the **Waqutaquaib kettle pond** to the left. The scenic corridor emerges at a historic **barn** atop a hill in about 1.6 miles, with great views stretching across North Head and Hummock Pond to the Atlantic Ocean.

▸ MILE 1.6-2.9: Historic Barn to Beach

Continue straight (south) down the hill through **The Woods,** where hawthorn, shadbush, and black cherry form a dense thicket around the path. Reach a fork at 2.0 miles. Bear left (south) skirting the edge of **Ram Pasture,** a vast sand plain where birds and insects flitter among colorful grasses. You may even catch a glimpse of an osprey perched atop the nesting pole here. The sound of the ocean draws nearer as the trail wraps west along the coast. There is an optional side path to the left (south) at 2.9 miles that leads to the **beach.**

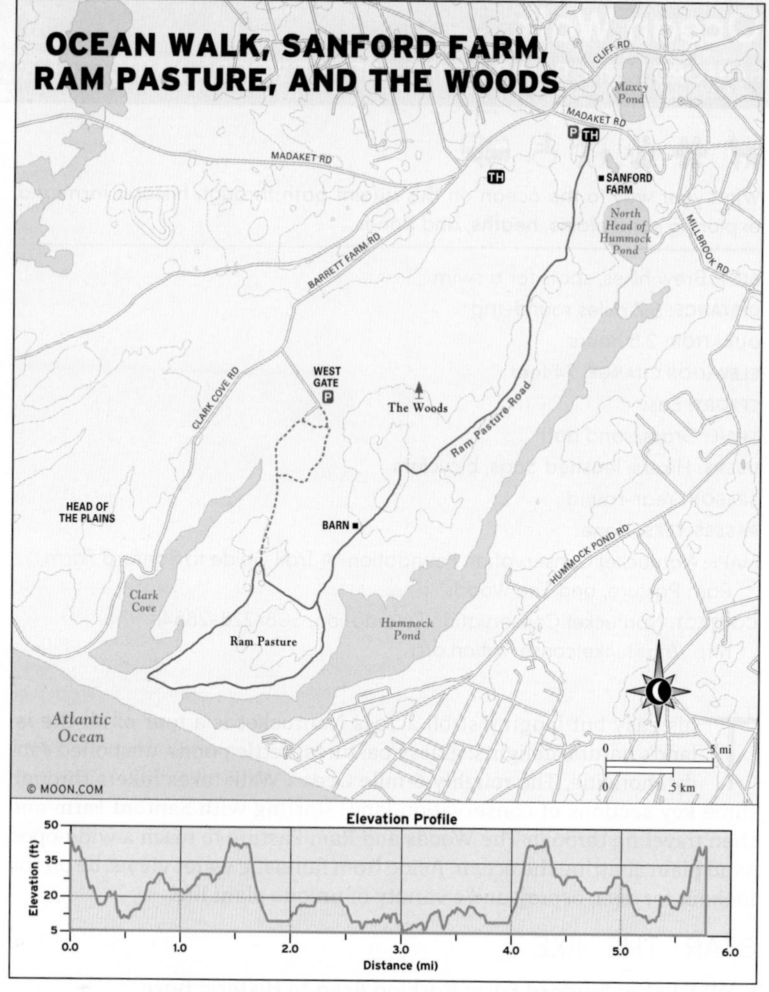

▸ MILE 2.9-5.7: Beach to Sanford Farm

The main path turns northeast here, tracing the north edge of Ram Pasture for 0.6 mile. When you reach the next intersection, turn right (south) to follow the trail east for 0.3 mile to the main path. Take a left (north) to backtrack 1.9 miles through The Woods to the Sanford Farm lot.

DIRECTIONS

From the center of town, follow Madaket Road west for approximately 1.5 miles. The large parking lot and marked trailhead are on the left, across from 121 Madaket Road.

GPS COORDINATES: 41°17'01.5"N 70°08'12.6"W

▲ THE PATH THROUGH SANFORD FARM

BEST NEARBY BREWS

Stop by **Cisco Brewers** (5 Bartlett Farm Rd., 508/325-5929, www.ciscobrewers.com, 11am-7pm Mon.-Sat., noon-6pm Sun.) for a fresh local pint and a happening scene that includes food trucks, live music, art, and shopping. It's 4 miles from the trailhead.

3 Great Island Trail

CAPE COD NATIONAL SEASHORE, WELLFLEET

Traverse pitch pine forests, dunes, and undeveloped beaches with this long hike through the bay side of Cape Cod National Seashore.

BEST: Summer hikes, spots for a swim
DISTANCE: 5.6 miles (with longer options at low tide)
DURATION: 3 hours
ELEVATION CHANGE: 153 feet
EFFORT: Moderate
TRAIL: Sand, dirt path
USERS: Hikers, leashed dogs
SEASON: Year-round
PASSES/FEES: None
MAPS: National Park Service "Cape Cod National Seashore"
CONTACT: National Park Service, 508/771-2144, http://nps.gov/caco

The 8-plus-mile Great Island Trail begins along a coastal salt marsh, then alternates between sandy dune paths and pitch pine-lined hills before arriving on the shores of a beautiful beach. At low tide (the best time to hike this trail), hikers can put in extra mileage on the way to Jeremy's Point, a vast expanse of sand that emerges above the waterline to jut into Cape Cod Bay. This pristine shoreline, with its abundant wildlife and magical sunsets, captures the heart and soul of the Cape Cod National Seashore.

START THE HIKE

▸ MILE 0-1.2: Great Island Trail Parking Lot to Marsh

Follow the gravel trail east from the parking lot and down a series of steps to reach the marsh at 0.2 mile. Turn right (west) onto the **Great Island Trail,** which wraps around the west side of the marsh. At high tide, the marsh section of the trail may be submerged. Follow the grassy west perimeter of the marsh for approximately 1 mile.

▸ MILE 1.2-1.4: Marsh to William Bradford Monument and Vista

Here, the trail cuts right (south) into a forest of scrub oak and pitch pine, on a springy pine needle path. (In 0.3 mile, there is an optional spur to the left that leads to the former site of the **Great Island Tavern.**) Continue straight (south) on the main trail, passing a **monument** to William Bradford, a Pilgrim on the Mayflower and the first governor of the Massachusetts Bay Colony. Descend the hill for 0.2 mile, where the path widens into a vista of the marsh and the dunes beyond.

▲ THE MARSH AT GREAT ISLAND

▸ MILE 1.4–2.6: William Bradford Monument and Vista to Beach

At the opening, the trail continues to the right (west) back along the edge of the marsh. Again, depending on the tide, the trail may be wet here. The trail returns to sand in 0.5 mile, climbing over a high dune before winding back into another forest. This section of trail climbs over **Great Beach Hill,** then bends west to reach the beach in 0.7 mile.

▸ MILE 2.6–5.6: Beach to Great Island Trail Parking Lot

To return, turn right (north) and follow the beach for 1.8 miles to "The Gut," where it intersects with the 1.2-mile trail back to the parking lot. (Optional: At low tide, hikers can continue south on the beach for 1.6 miles to Jeremy's Point and the long sandbar that emerges to the south. Be sure to consult a tide chart before your hike.)

DIRECTIONS

From US-6 E, turn left onto Main Street and follow signs to Wellfleet Center. In 0.7 mile, turn left onto Holbrook Avenue and then turn right onto Chequessett Neck Road. The large parking area is marked with a National Park Service sign on the left.

GPS COORDINATES: 41°55'58.2"N 70°04'08.2"W

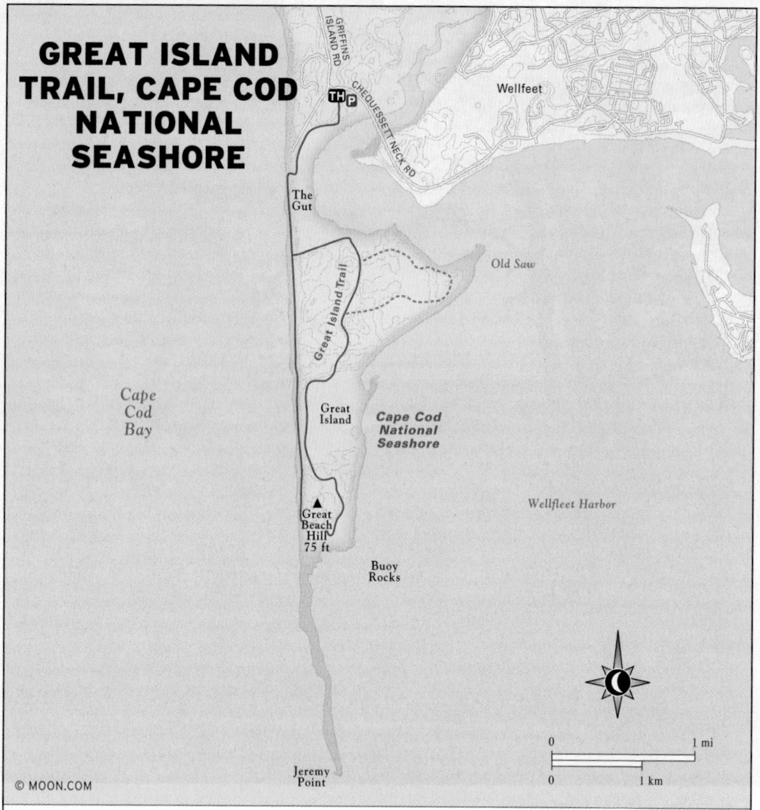

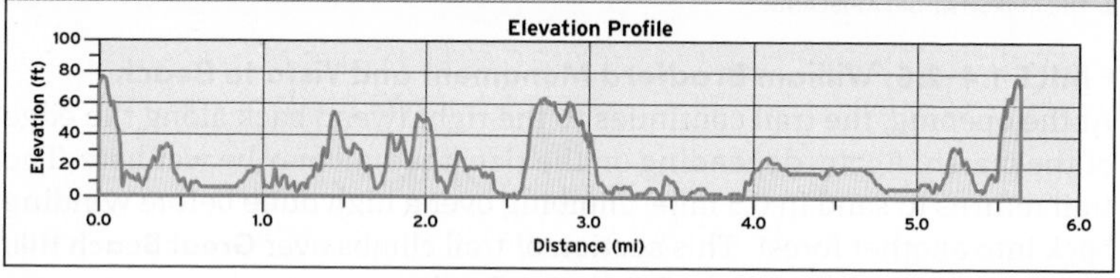

GREAT ISLAND TRAIL, CAPE COD NATIONAL SEASHORE

GRIFFINS ISLAND RD
CHEQUESSETT NECK RD
Wellfeet
The Gut
Great Island Trail
Old Saw
Cape Cod Bay
Great Island
Cape Cod National Seashore
Wellfleet Harbor
Great Beach Hill 75 ft
Buoy Rocks
Jeremy Point
0 1 mi
0 1 km

Elevation Profile

Elevation (ft)
Distance (mi)

BEST NEARBY BREWS

Catch a bite and a live performance at **The Beachcomber** (1120 Cahoon Hollow Rd., Wellfleet, 508/349-6055, www.thebeachcomber.com, 11:30am-1am daily, hours vary seasonally, call ahead), a lively beachfront bar with great summertime vibes. It's 6 miles from the trailhead.

Marsh Trail

SANDY NECK BEACH PARK, BARNSTABLE

The expansive marshes and high dunes of this long spit of barrier beach are home to a variety of rare wildlife species.

DISTANCE: 7.9 miles round-trip
DURATION: 4 hours
ELEVATION CHANGE: 214 feet
EFFORT: Moderate
TRAIL: Sand
USERS: Hikers, leashed dogs, horseback riders, fat-tire bikes
SEASON: Year-round
PASSES/FEES: Day pass $20
MAPS: Town of Barnstable "Sandy Neck"
CONTACT: Town of Barnstable, 508/362-8300, http://town.barnstable.ma.us/sandyneckpark

The mid-Cape town of Barnstable is home to one of the most interesting conservation properties on Cape Cod: the 6-mile-long barrier beach of Sandy Neck, which reaches out between the Barnstable Great Marsh and Cape Cod Bay. The trail through this town park skirts the edge of the marsh, then cuts across a divider of white sand dunes to the shores of scenic Sandy Neck Beach, offering excellent opportunities to spot rare wildlife from diamondback terrapins to river otters. Break up your hike with a one-of-a-kind camping experience at the hike-in tent site among the dunes.

START THE HIKE

▸ MILE 0-3.8: Visitors Kiosk and Marsh Trail to Trail 4

The **Marsh Trail** begins across from the visitors kiosk and travels east through the gate on a crushed-rock path. Hikers will be rewarded immediately with views of the **Great Marsh** to their right (south) and views of large dunes, gnarled cedar, and scrub oak to their left (north). The path turns to deep sand and walking becomes more strenuous after 0.2 mile. At the signed intersection with Trail 1, 0.5 mile from the start, keep right on the Marsh Trail. Hikers will notice a few fishing cottages along the trail, which doubles as an over-sand road for local residents. Keep an eye out for unique birds among the many birdhouses and osprey nesting poles in the marsh. Pass the marked left turn for Trail 2 in 1.3 miles (Trail 3 is no longer open). Reach the sign for **Trail 4** at 3.8 miles.

▸ MILE 3.8-4.5: Trail 4 to Beach

Turn left (north) on Trail 4, climbing through the dunes and following signs for the campsite. Bear left at the fork at 4.0 miles and hike through the campsite. Trail 4 continues north through a pitch pine forest and over the dunes to reach the beach at 4.5 miles.

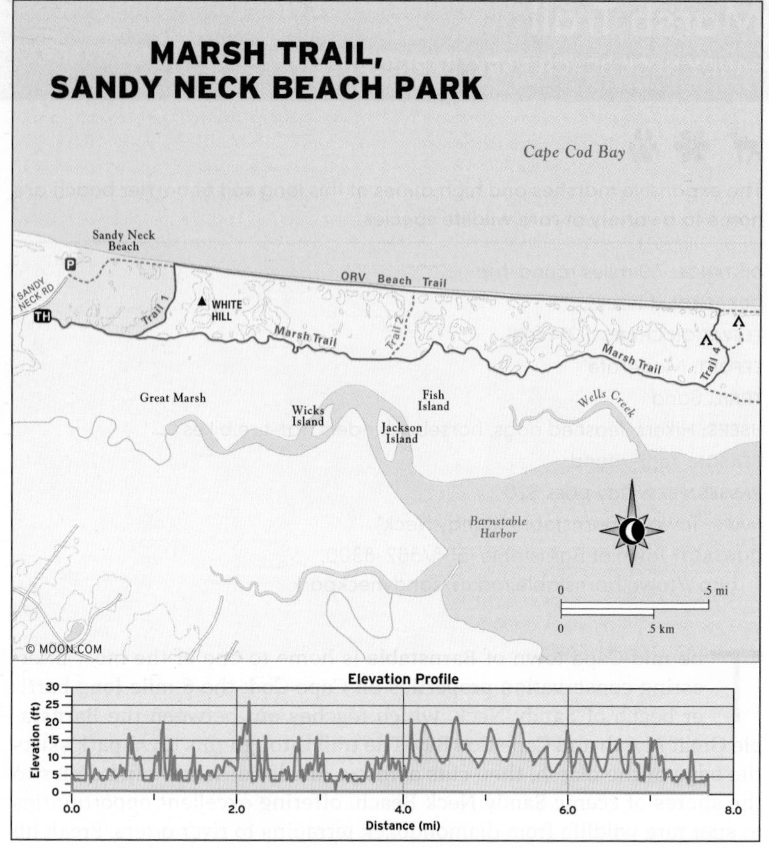

▸ **MILE 4.5-7.9: Beach to White Hill Vista and Marsh Trail Trailhead**

Turn left (west) onto the beach and follow the shore on the ORV Beach Trail for 2.5 miles until the intersection with Trail 1, then turn left (south) onto Trail 1. Climb south over the dunes of White Hill for a lovely seaside vista, then reach the Marsh Trail again at 7.4 miles. Turn right (west) on the Marsh Trail to return 0.5 mile to the lot.

DIRECTIONS

From US-6 East, take Exit 4 to Chase Road. Follow Chase Road to where it turns into Old County Road and then take a left onto Jones Lane. In 0.5 mile, turn right onto Old King's Highway (MA-6A), and then turn left onto Sandy Neck Road. The gatehouse is about 0.5 mile down the road. Consult an attendant for fees and parking directions.

GPS COORDINATES: 41°44'06.6"N 70°23'05.7"W

▲ THE MARSH TRAIL

BEST NEARBY BITES

In downtown Hyannis **emBargo** (453 Main St., Hyannis, 508/771-9700, www.embargorestaurant.com, 4:30pm-1am daily) is a choice spot for cocktails and tapas, with dancing and live entertainment most nights. It's 9 miles from the trailhead.

NEARBY CAMPGROUNDS

NAME	LOCATION	FACILITIES	SEASON	FEE
Sandy Neck Beach Park	425 Sandy Neck Rd., West Barnstable, MA 02668	self-contained RVs and 5 primitive tent sites; no restrooms	Memorial Day-Labor Day	$20
508/362-8300, www.town.barnstable.ma.us/SandyNeckPark/				
Nickerson State Park	3488 Main St., Brewster, MA 02631	372 RV/tent sites, 6 yurts; restrooms	May-October	$35-70
508/896-3491, www.mass.gov/locations/nickerson-state-park				
Shawme Crowell State Forest	42 Main St., Sandwich, MA 02563	230 RV/tent sites, 6 yurts; restrooms	May-October	$60-70
508/888-0351, www.mass.gov/locations/shawme-crowell-state-forest				
Dunes' Edge Campground	386 US-6, Provincetown, MA 02657	85 tent sites, 15 RV sites; restrooms	mid-May-September	$49-61
508/487-9815, www.thetrustees.org/places-to-visit/places-to-stay/dunes-edge-campground/				
Scusset Beach State Reservation	20 Scusset Beach Rd., Sagamore Beach, MA 02562	98 RV sites, 5 tent sites; restrooms	mid-April-late October; off-season RV camping available	$35
508/888-0859, www.mass.gov/locations/scusset-beach-state-reservation				

▲ PAINTED TURTLE

THE BERKSHIRES

The Berkshires are perhaps the most popular hiking destination in Massachusetts, and for good reason. Not only do they boast the highest peaks in the state—most notably, Mount Greylock—they emanate a quintessential New England feel, with small artsy towns, rolling farmland, and lush green forests where secluded waterfalls patter out their perpetual rhythms in solitude. Though the region is commonly referred to as the Berkshire Hills, the highlands of western Massachusetts are actually the amalgamation of several mountain ranges, including the southern Green Mountains and the eastern Taconic Mountains. These peaks are your best bet for elevation in southern New England, with sweeping views that reach across state lines to Vermont, Connecticut, New York, and beyond.

▲ cottonwood tree on the Spero Trail

▲ Spruce Hill

1 **Indian Monument, Squaw Peak, and Hickey Trails to Monument Mountain**
DISTANCE: 2.4 miles round-trip
DURATION: 1.25 hours
EFFORT: Moderate

2 **Loop Trail, Jug End State Reservation and Wildlife Area**
DISTANCE: 4.4 miles round-trip
DURATION: 2 hours
EFFORT: Easy/moderate

3 **Pine Cobble, Appalachian, and Class of '98 Trails**
DISTANCE: 4.9 miles round-trip
DURATION: 2.45 hours
EFFORT: Moderate

4 **Hoosac Range Trail to Spruce Hill**
DISTANCE: 5.4 miles round-trip
DURATION: 2.75 hours
EFFORT: Moderate

5 **Money Brook, Appalachian, Hopper, Sperry Road, and Haley Farm Trails to Mount Greylock**
DISTANCE: 11.8 miles round-trip
DURATION: 6 hours
EFFORT: Strenuous

6 **Mahican-Mohawk and Indian Trails to Todd Mountain**
DISTANCE: 5 miles round-trip
DURATION: 2.5 hours
EFFORT: Strenuous

7 **Alander Mountain Trail, Mount Washington State Forest**
DISTANCE: 6 miles round-trip
DURATION: 3.5 hours
EFFORT: Moderate

8 **Race Brook Falls and Appalachian Trail to Race Mountain**
DISTANCE: 5.8 miles round-trip
DURATION: 4 hours
EFFORT: Strenuous

9 **Ledges, Bailey, Spero, Tulip Tree, and Tractor Path Trails, Bartholomew's Cobble Reservation**
DISTANCE: 3.2 miles round-trip
DURATION: 1.75 hours
EFFORT: Easy/moderate

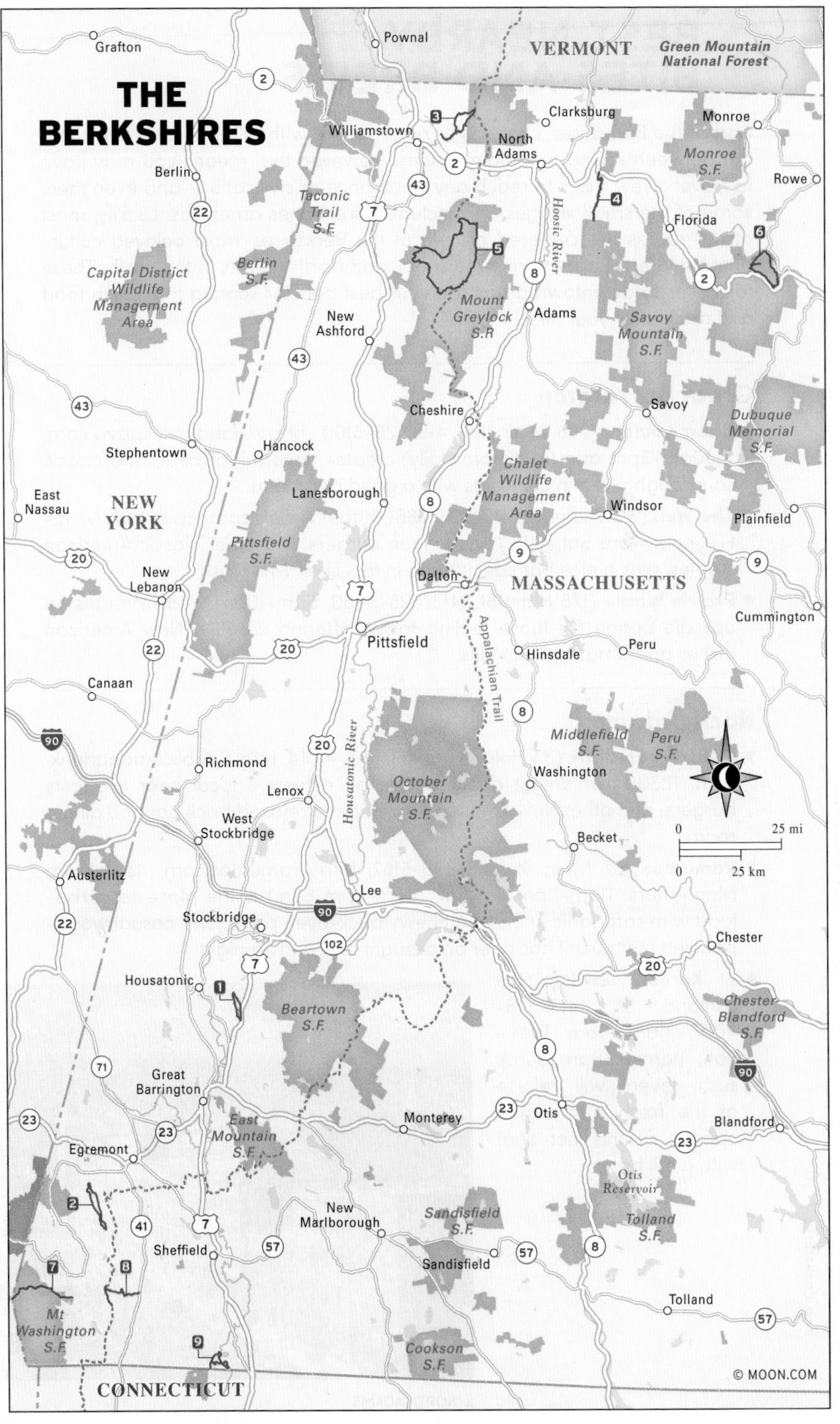
THE BERKSHIRES
VERMONT
Green Mountain National Forest
NEW YORK
MASSACHUSETTS
CONNECTICUT
Grafton
Pownal
Clarksburg
Monroe
Williamstown
North Adams
Monroe S.F.
Rowe
Berlin
Taconic Trail S.F.
Hoosic River
Florida
Berlin S.F.
Capital District Wildlife Management Area
Mount Greylock S.R.
Adams
Savoy Mountain S.F.
New Ashford
Cheshire
Savoy
Dubuque Memorial S.F.
Stephentown
Hancock
Chalet Wildlife Management Area
East Nassau
Lanesborough
Windsor
Plainfield
Pittsfield S.F.
New Lebanon
Dalton
Cummington
Pittsfield
Appalachian Trail
Hinsdale
Peru
Canaan
Middlefield S.F.
Peru S.F.
Richmond
Housatonic River
Washington
Lenox
October Mountain S.F.
West Stockbridge
Becket
Austerlitz
Lee
Stockbridge
Chester
Housatonic
Chester-Blandford S.F.
Beartown S.F.
Great Barrington
Monterey
Otis
Blandford
East Mountain S.F.
Egremont
Otis Reservoir
New Marlborough
Sandisfield S.F.
Tolland S.F.
Sheffield
Sandisfield
Tolland
Mt Washington S.F.
Cookson S.F.
0 25 mi
0 25 km
© MOON.COM

BEST NEARBY BITES AND BREWS

Part of the Berkshires' charm is its rural nature, with miles of farm stretching out between rolling mountain ranges. However, that means you may have to travel a few miles to reach any semblance of civilization—and even then, some of the small villages only include bare-bones amenities. Luckily, most of our routes are centered on two of the Berkshires' most beloved cultural hubs: Great Barrington in the south, and North Adams in the north. These towns' artsy downtown areas are your best bets for scoring top-notch food and drink after your hike.

Great Barrington

- **Baba Louie's** (286 Main St., 413/528-8100, http://babalouiespizza.com, 11:30am-3pm and 5pm-9pm daily) creates flavorful, offbeat, and classic sourdough pizza in cozy digs with a good bar menu.
- **The Well** (312 Main St., 413/528-3651, http://wellgb.com, 3pm-1am Mon.-Fri., noon-1am Sat.-Sun.) has unique burgers and other classic American staples, plus a nice bar specializing in top-shelf whiskeys.
- **Prairie Whale** (178 Main St., 413/528-5050, 5pm-10pm Wed.-Mon.) is an upscale option for those feeling fancy, offering creative New American dishes and amazing cocktails.

North Adams

- **PUBLIC eat+drink** (34 Holden St., 413/664-4444, http://publiceatanddrink.com, 11:30am-midnight daily) boasts an extensive local beer list, tasty burgers, and other New American options in a relaxed brick bar and dining room.
- **Ramuntos** (67 Main St., 413/398-5152, http://ramuntos.com, 11am-10pm Mon.-Thurs. 11am-11pm Fri.-Sat., 11am-9pm Sun.) is the place to carbo-load with soft garlic knots and chewy brick-oven pizza. This casual wood-paneled restaurant has beer on draught and a trivia night.
- At **Korean Garden** (139 Ashland St., 413/346-4097, 11am-10pm Tues.-Sat., 11am-9:30pm Sun.), sushi lovers will rejoice at the fresh and varied options at this hot spot with a full bar.

▲ NORTH ADAMS

1 Indian Monument, Squaw Peak, and Hickey Trails to Monument Mountain

MONUMENT MOUNTAIN RESERVATION, GREAT BARRINGTON

The pale quartz vistas of Monument Mountain offer inspiring views of the Berkshires, Taconics, and Catskills in exchange for a short climb.

DISTANCE: 2.4 miles round-trip
DURATION: 1.25 hours
ELEVATION CHANGE: 601 feet
EFFORT: Moderate
TRAIL: Dirt/rock path
USERS: Hikers, leashed dogs
SEASON: April-November
PASSES/FEES: $5 per vehicle parking fee (pay at kiosk)
MAPS: The Trustees of Reservations, "Monument Mountain"
CONTACT: The Trustees of Reservations, 413/298-3239, http://thetrustees.org

Monument Mountain is an extremely popular hike for its ease of access, but don't be fooled—this quick climb boasts some of the most spectacular views around and some surprisingly steep rock scrambles. Begin on the Indian Monument Trail, climb up to the scenic Devil's Pulpit and Squaw Peak overlooks via the Squaw Peak Trail, and return via the Hickey Trail.

START THE HIKE

▸ MILE 0-0.9: Indian Monument Trail to Squaw Peak Trail

Hike south on the **Indian Monument Trail,** following the blue blazes from the left (south) side of the parking lot. The rocky path winds through boulders and hemlock forest, skirting the road for about 0.2 mile. Traffic noise dissipates as the trail bends north away from the road. Here, the wide path gains elevation at a gentle grade. At 0.6 mile, turn sharply right (east) onto the red-blazed **Squaw Peak Trail.** The trail heads uphill through tangles of roots followed by a jagged quartz ridge. At 0.9 mile, it bends west to reach a series of south-facing viewpoints over the Housatonic River valley.

▸ MILE 0.9-1.0: Squaw Peak Trail to Devil's Pulpit

At 1.0 mile, continue straight through the intersection and climb the stone steps toward **Devil's Pulpit**—a rocky perch with views of hoodoo-like quartzite cliffs across a steep drop-off. Enjoy the views, then backtrack on the Squaw Peak Trail to the intersection.

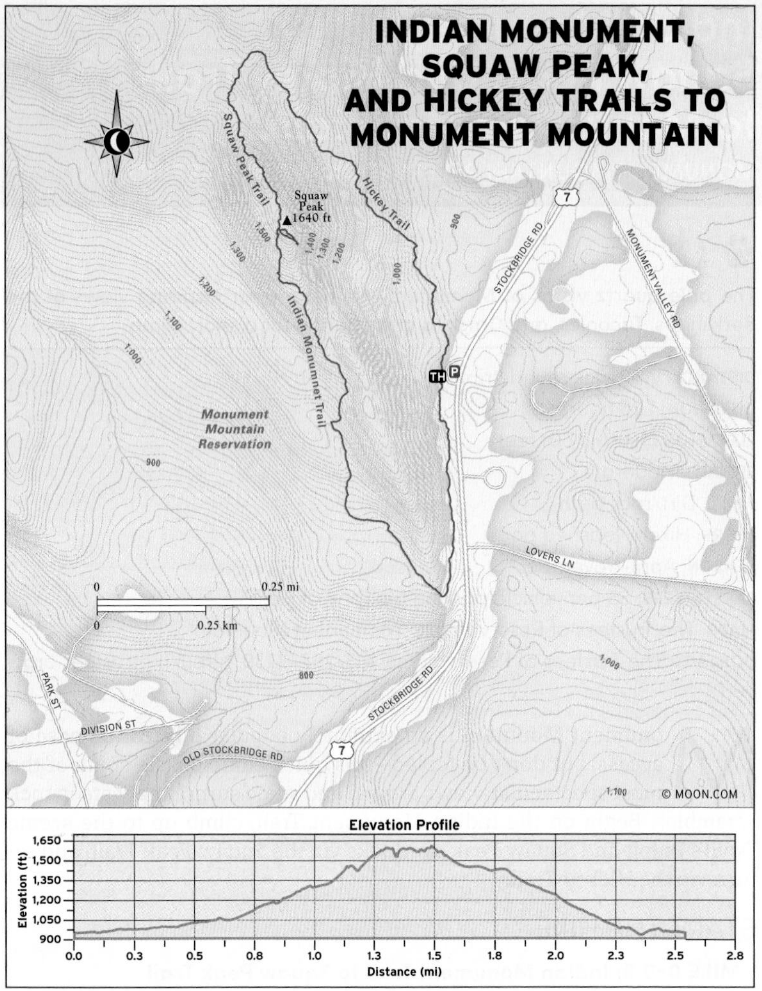

▸ **MILE 1.0–1.2: Devil's Pulpit to Squaw Peak Summit**

Turn right (north) at the intersection and follow the Squaw Peak Trail for 0.2 mile toward the summit of **Squaw Peak.** The massive quartz formations of the summit provide views in all directions, most notably of Mount Greylock to the north, the Catskill Range to the west, and the Housatonic River just below. Use caution following the trail along the summit, especially in wet weather; the trail surface can be slippery.

▸ **MILE 1.2–2.4: Squaw Peak Summit to Hickey Trail**

After 0.2 mile across the summit, the trail begins to descend. Reach the "**Inscription Rock,**" dedicating the reservation to the people of the Berkshires, at 1.5 miles. Then, turn right (north) onto the yellow-blazed **Hickey Trail.** At 1.7 miles, the trail switchbacks south and steadily declines through boulder fields and hemlock forest to return to the parking lot in 2.4 miles.

▲ SQUAW PEAK

DIRECTIONS

From Great Barrington center, follow US-7 north for 4 miles. From other points, use MA-102 E to connect to US-7 S, then follow the latter for 3 miles. The large parking area is marked with a Trustees of Reservations sign. Pay at the kiosk.

GPS COORDINATES: 42°14'35.1"N 73°20'07.2"W

2 Loop Trail

JUG END STATE RESERVATION AND WILDLIFE AREA, EGREMONT

The high, open meadows of Jug End Reservation offer some of the most distinctive and secluded hiking in the Berkshires.

DISTANCE: 4.4 miles round-trip
DURATION: 2 hours
ELEVATION CHANGE: 508 feet
EFFORT: Easy/moderate
TRAIL: Dirt/grass path
USERS: Hikers, leashed dogs
SEASON: Year-round
PASSES/FEES: None
MAPS: MA DCR "Mt. Washington State Forest"
CONTACT: MA DCR Mount Washington State Forest, 413/528-0330, http://mass.gov/orgs/department-of-conservation-recreation

Jug End is a beloved vista of the famously beautiful Riga Plateau section of the Appalachian Trail, but the other features of this gorgeous ridgeline are front and center at Jug End State Reservation. The park's Loop Trail winds along Fenton Brook and climbs through an enchanting forest to an old stone chimney. From there, the east end of the loop winds through a series of wide, open meadows brimming with butterflies and wildflowers. Though it's widely regarded as one of the Berkshires' most kid-friendly hikes, Jug End is a treat for all ages.

START THE HIKE

▸ MILE 0-0.3: Loop Trail to Fenton Brook

Head west on the **Loop Trail,** cross the bridge, and turn left (south) into the woods. The grassy path, shaded by large trees, follows bubbling **Fenton Brook** for 0.2 mile with views of the ridgeline ahead. Where the path branches, stay left (south) along Fenton Brook.

▸ MILE 0.3-1.7: Fenton Brook to Upper Loop/Main Loop

The trail winds in and out of an open field for 0.5 mile until reaching another fork. Turn right (south) and begin a gradual ascent through a shady mixed hardwood forest, following the blue blazes. The wide track gains elevation for 0.9 mile above the Fenton Brook valley before narrowing into a flat path. Shortly after the path narrows and becomes noticeably flat, you'll reach the **Upper Loop/Main Loop** intersection where an abandoned **stone chimney** remains from Jug End's days as a ski resort just off the trail.

▲ STONE CHIMNEY AT JUG END

▸ MILE 1.7–4.4: Upper Loop/Main Loop to Ridgeline

Continue straight south onto t**he Upper Loop,** a narrow track that carries uphill through fern and jewelweed to a hemlock forest. The path curls east in 0.6 mile, then back north for 0.6 mile to the **Main Loop.** From there, the east end of the loop enters a grassy meadow with excellent views of wildflowers and the ridgeline of Whitbeck, Sterling, and Darby peaks. After winding in and out of several of these meadows for 0.7 mile, the path descends through a patch of apple trees to return to the parking lot at 4.4 miles.

DIRECTIONS

From Great Barrington/US-7, turn right onto MA-41 S and follow it for 4.4 miles through Egremont, then turn left to stay on MA-41. Just after the turn, make a right onto Mount Washington Road. After 1.7 miles, turn left onto Jug End Road. The trailhead and large parking area are marked with a large sign 0.5 mile down the road on the right.

GPS COORDINATES: 42°08'53.5"N 73°27'00.4"W

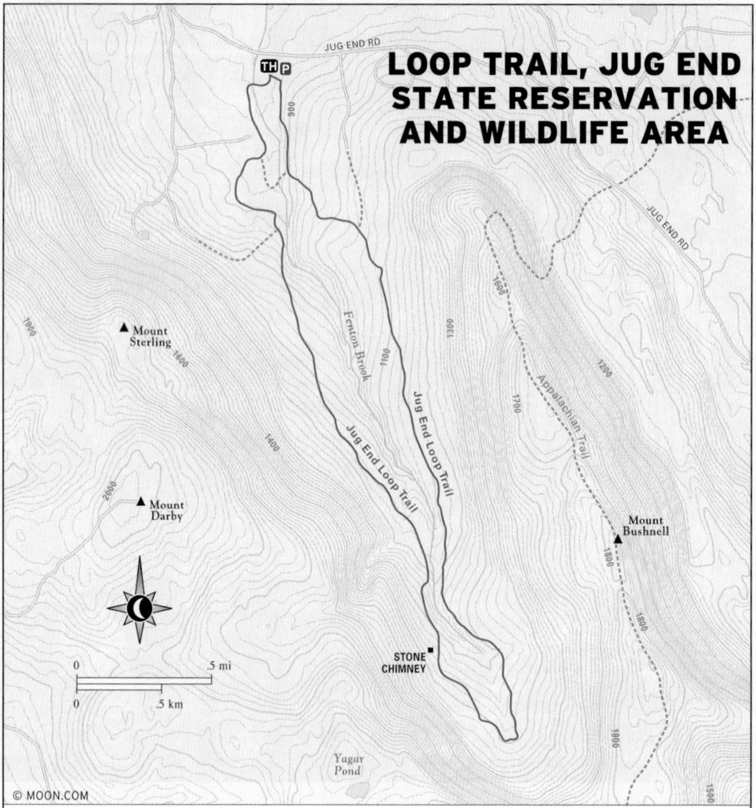
LOOP TRAIL, JUG END STATE RESERVATION AND WILDLIFE AREA
JUG END RD
TH
P
900
JUG END RD
1600
1900
Mount Sterling
1600
Fenton Brook
1100
1300
1200
1700
Appalachian Trail
Jug End Loop Trail
Jug End Loop Trail
1400
2000
Mount Darby
Mount Bushnell
1800
1800
STONE CHIMNEY
0
.5 mi
0
.5 km
1800
Yagar Pond
1500
© MOON.COM

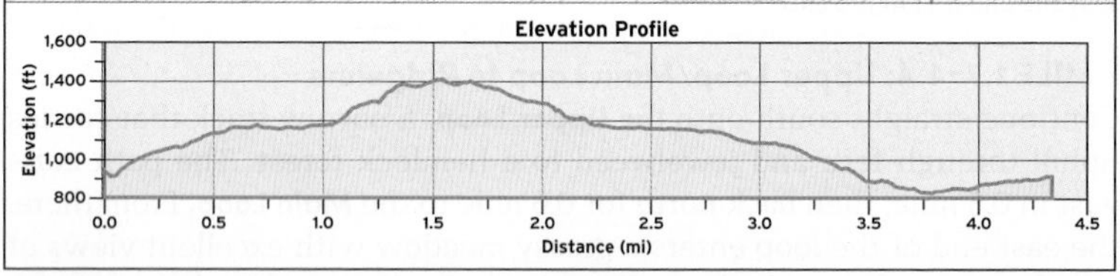
Elevation Profile
Elevation (ft)
1,600
1,400
1,200
1,000
800
0.0
0.5
1.0
1.5
2.0
2.5
3.0
3.5
4.0
4.5
Distance (mi)

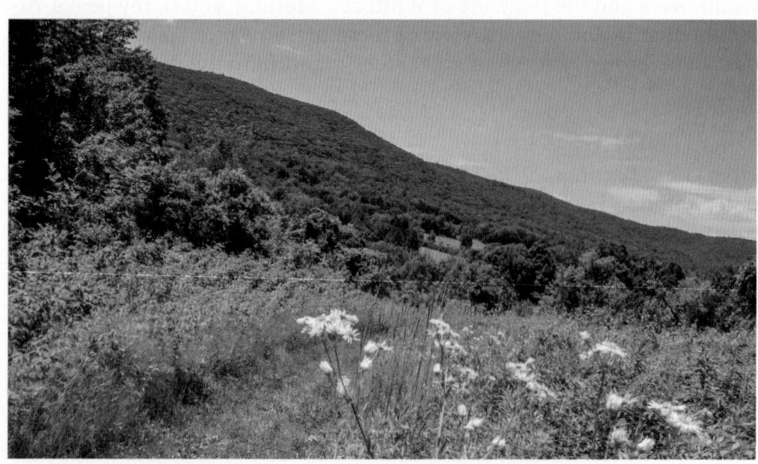

▲ THE MEADOW AT JUG END

3 Pine Cobble, Appalachian, and Class of '98 Trails

PINE COBBLE PRESERVE/CLARKSBURG STATE FOREST, WILLIAMSTOWN

The short but tough climb up to Pine Cobble rewards with several vistas of the northern Berkshires.

DISTANCE: 4.9 miles round-trip
DURATION: 2.45 hours
ELEVATION CHANGE: 1,427 feet
EFFORT: Moderate
TRAIL: Dirt/rock path
USERS: Hikers, leashed dogs
SEASON: April-November
PASSES/FEES: None
MAPS: None
CONTACT: Williamstown Rural Lands Foundation, 413/458-2494, http://wrlf.org

This hike begins in Pine Cobble Preserve, making a steep 1.6-mile ascent through an oak forest to two quartzite outcroppings where hikers can enjoy vistas toward both North Adams and Williamstown. From there, the trail climbs to the summit of East Mountain for another vista before meeting the Appalachian Trail. Hikers will walk across a beautiful section of forest before descending on the rocky slopes of the Class of '98 Trail.

START THE HIKE

▸ MILE 0-1.5: Trailhead to Pine Cobble Signage

Find the trailhead just north from the parking area on the right side of the road. The blue-blazed trail winds up and away from the road and steepens quickly after 0.2 mile. Several switchbacks and staircases carry hikers up through a forest with multiple species of oak for 0.5 mile. The path flattens for 0.2 mile and passes the intersection with the Class of '98 Trail. Continue straight west. The path becomes quite rocky as it makes its final 0.6-mile climb to a sign for Pine Cobble at 1.5 miles.

▸ MILE 1.5-1.6: Pine Cobble Signage to Pine Cobble Vista

Turn right (south) at the sign and reach the **Pine Cobble** vistas at 1.6 miles. One vista faces west toward the old-timey village of Williamstown and into the green hills of Vermont, while another faces east toward Mount Greylock and the church steeples of North Adams.

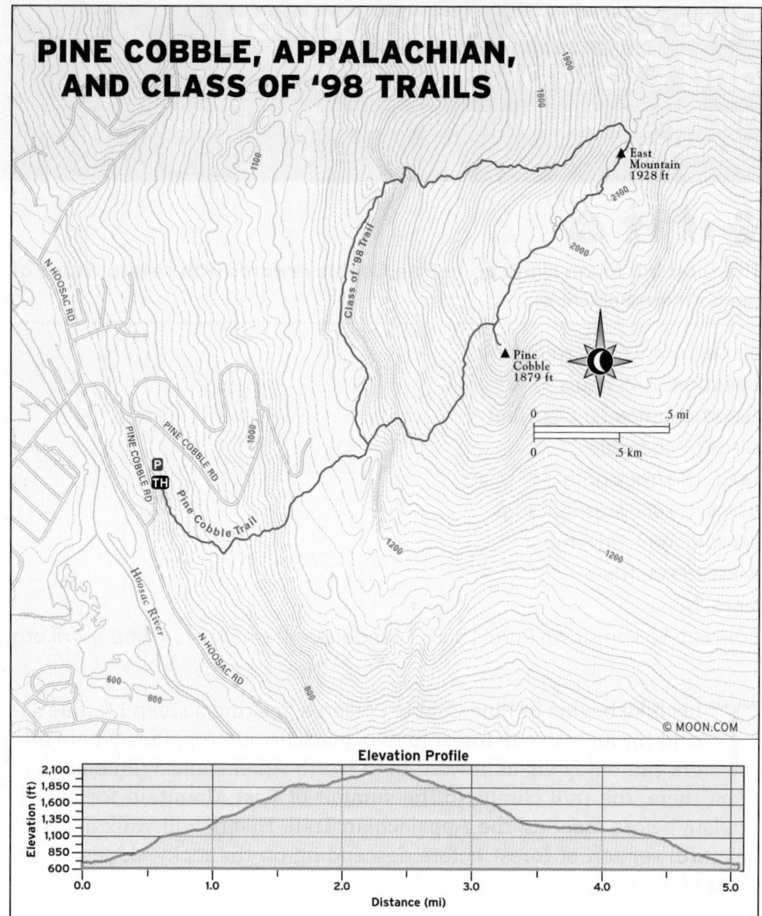

▸ MILE 1.6–2.1: Pine Cobble Vista to East Mountain Summit

After enjoying the views, backtrack to the sign for Pine Cobble and continue straight north. The narrow path continues uphill for 0.5 mile through forest and quartz tumbles to reach the summit of **East Mountain,** marked with cairns.

▸ MILE 2.1–2.4: East Mountain Summit to Class of '98 Trail

One-tenth of a mile west of the summit, the Pine Cobble Trail reaches an intersection with the **Appalachian Trail (AT).** Turn left (north) onto the white-blazed AT and follow it for 0.2 mile. Look out for the sign for the **Class of '98 Trail** on the left side of the path at 2.4 miles—it may be slightly overgrown.

▸ MILE 2.4–4.9: Class of '98 Trail to Pine Cobble Trail

Turn left (west) onto the Class of '98 Trail and follow the narrow track steadily downhill. Use caution on the very steep and rocky 315-foot section at 3.2 miles. At the bottom of the rock slope, the trail enters a sapling forest, passes an intersection with the Chestnut Trail, and meets the Pine Cobble Trail at 4.0 miles. Turn right (west) to follow the Pine Cobble Trail 0.9 mile back to the trailhead.

▲ EAST MOUNTAIN

DIRECTIONS

From North Adams/MA-2, turn right (north) onto Eagle Street and cross the bridge. At the lights, turn left onto River Street, which turns into Massachusetts Avenue, then North Hoosac Road, and follow it for 5 miles. Then, turn right onto Pine Cobble Road. The parking area is marked with a sign 0.1 mile north on the left. The trailhead is across the street.

GPS COORDINATES: 42°42'58.9"N 73°11'06.5"W

4 Hoosac Range Trail to Spruce Hill

HOOSAC RANGE RESERVE AND SAVOY MOUNTAIN STATE FOREST, NORTH ADAMS

Reach stunning views at the summit of Spruce Hill with very little climbing on this pleasant ridgeline hike.

DISTANCE: 5.4 miles round-trip

DURATION: 2.75 hours

ELEVATION CHANGE: 823 feet

EFFORT: Moderate

TRAIL: Dirt/rock trail

USERS: Hikers, leashed dogs

SEASON: April-November

PASSES/FEES: None

MAPS: Berkshire Natural Resources Council "Hoosac Range Reserve"

CONTACT: Berkshire Natural Resources Council, 413-499-0596, http://bnrc.org

Just before MA-2 W plummets down a hairpin turn into North Adams, hikers have the opportunity to hop on the Hoosac Range Trail across the Western Summit. This 5.4-mile out-and-back carries hikers across a scenic ridgeline from the west-facing Sunset Rock to the expansive panorama of Savoy Mountain State Forest's Spruce Hill. Visitors don't have to work too hard for the reward—the valley floor simply drops down from the trailhead, leaving nothing but views.

START THE HIKE

▸ MILE 0-0.7: Trailhead to Sunset Rock Vista

Go south through the fence at the trailhead. The trail heads through maple, beech, and hobblebush, following the red and white blazes. Gain elevation climbing several switchbacks and reach a posted intersection at 0.4 mile. Turn left (north) to visit **Sunset Rock.** The narrow path through grass and fern reaches the vista at 0.7 mile, with great views of **North Adams** tucked between the **Greylock Range** and the Hoosic River. As the name suggests, it's a wonderful place to watch the sun lower itself behind Mount Greylock.

▸ MILE 0.7-2.1: Sunset Rock Vista to Schist Rock Ledge

Continue south from Sunset Rock and reach another posted intersection. Turn left (east) toward Spruce Hill. This fun, winding path snakes between boulders and birch forest for 1.3 miles, with hints of a view in both directions, before reaching a sign pointing to another vista at 2.1 miles. Follow the sign left (east) for a 0.1 mile (round-trip) side trip, which leads to a **schist rock ledge** offering great views of Flat Rock Hill and the Cold River.

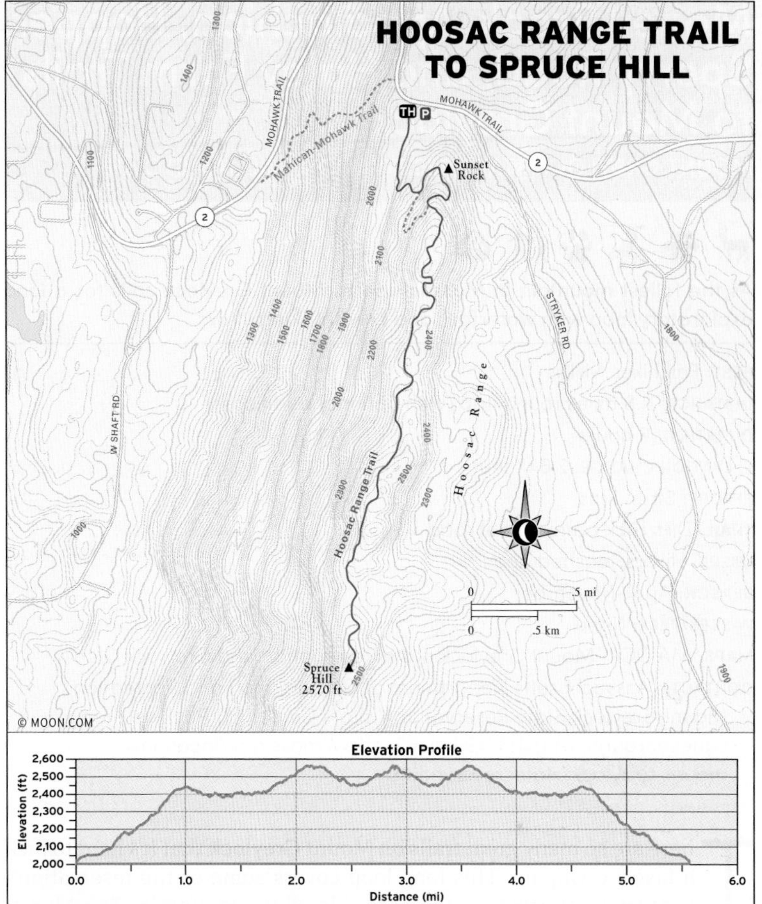

MILE 2.1–2.7: Schist Rock Ledge to Spruce Hill

Backtrack from the ledge to the main path and continue straight south for 0.3 mile, skirting the edge of a hill, passing grass-covered rock formations and vernal pools, and traveling under a set of power lines. At 2.6 miles, when the blazes turn to light blue, follow the side trail right (west) over the rock slabs and up the steps. Reach the summit of **Spruce Hill** at 2.7 miles, with panoramic views looking across the **Hoosic River Valley** to **Mount Greylock.** It's a great place to take in the beauty of the **Berkshires** and look for migrating raptors before returning to the parking lot along the same route.

DIRECTIONS

Follow MA-2 W through the town of Florida and continue for 4 miles. The parking lot is on the left just after Stryker Road and before the hairpin turn where the road descends into North Adams.

GPS COORDINATES: 42°41'48.1"N 73°03'54.1"W / 42.696685, -73.065037

5 Money Brook, Appalachian, Hopper, Sperry Road, and Haley Farm Trails to Mount Greylock

MOUNT GREYLOCK STATE RESERVATION, WILLIAMSTOWN

As the tallest mountain in Massachusetts, Mount Greylock calls for a long exploratory loop with waterfalls and breathtaking views.

BEST: Fall hikes, vistas

DISTANCE: 11.8 miles round-trip (with optional additions)

DURATION: 6 hours

ELEVATION CHANGE: 2,647 feet

EFFORT: Strenuous

TRAIL: Dirt/rock path, gravel road

USERS: Hikers, leashed dogs

SEASON: April-November

PASSES/FEES: None

MAPS: MA DCR "Mount Greylock State Reservation and Greylock Glen"

CONTACT: Massachusetts Department of Conservation and Recreation, Mount Greylock State Reservation Visitors Center, 30 Rockwell Road, Lanesborough, MA, 413/499-4262, http://mass.gov/locations/mount-greylock-state-reservation

There are so many great trails on Mount Greylock that it's hard to pick a favorite way up. This long loop covers some of the reservation's best trails, starting on the east side of the mountain. The Money Brook Trail meanders along its namesake waterway to a stunning falls, then climbs to the Appalachian Trail where it traverses the scenic Greylock Range ridgeline to the 3,488-foot summit. Descend via the Hopper Trail, Sperry Road, and the Haley Farm Trail, hitting March Cataract Falls and the pristine vista of Stony Ledge along the way.

START THE HIKE

▸ MILE 0-2.8: Hopper Trail to Money Brook Falls

Hike east from the parking lot on the Hopper Trail and pass through the gate into the Hopper Natural Area. Reach an intersection in 0.3 mile and continue straight on the **Money Brook Trail.** Follow the light blue blazes for 2.5 miles through the forest, along a bubbling brook, over several bridges, and then up a steep ascent over the valley. At 2.8 miles, reach a sign that reads "Money Brook Falls 100 yards ahead" at the top of the ascent. **Money Brook Falls,** just to the east of the sign, is a remarkable 80-foot cascade.

▸ MILE 2.8-3.5: Money Brook Falls to Appalachian Trail

When you're finished admiring the falls, head back to the sign, then hike west for 0.3 mile on a steep uphill toward Notch Road. Reach another

▲ STONY LEDGE

posted intersection and turn left (north) toward **Wilbur's Clearing.** This flat section of trail passes the Wilbur's Clearing camping area and meets the **Appalachian Trail (AT)** at a junction of bog bridges at 3.5 miles.

▸ MILE 3.5-4.6: Appalachian Trail to Mount Williams Summit

Turn right (north) on the AT southbound, following the white blazes toward **Notch Road.** The AT crosses the paved road at 3.8 miles and then begins a steep, rocky ascent to the summit of **Mount Williams.** Reach the north-facing vista at 4.6 miles, then continue east on the southbound AT.

▸ MILE 4.6-7.0: Mount Williams Summit to Greylock Summit

From here, the trail traverses the ridgeline of Mount Fitch, dropping into the only boreal forest in Massachusetts. Follow the trail for 1.9 miles to the intersection with the **Bellows Pipe Trail.** Turn right (south) to continue on the AT, which climbs a steep, rocky path for 0.4 mile to meet Notch Road again. Cross straight (south) over Notch Road and continue on the asphalt path for 0.1 mile to the **Veterans War Memorial** tower at **Greylock's summit.** This 93-foot stone tower, topped with a light globe, honors Massachusetts casualties of World War I. The best views from the summit are facing east toward the town of Adams.

▸ MILE 7.0-8.7: Greylock Summit to Sperry Road

To descend from the summit, head west and rejoin the southbound AT, passing the **Bascom Lodge** and following signs for the **Hopper Trail.** Where the rocky downhill trail meets the road at 7.5 miles, cross the road and turn right (north) onto the Hopper Trail. Pass a pond and reach another intersection at 7.6 miles. Bear right (north) to remain on the Hopper Trail. At the signed intersection with the Overlook Trail at 7.9 miles, bear left (west). The wide rock-and-gravel path reaches a sign pointing toward Sperry Road at 8.5 miles. Turn right (west) and reach the gravel track of Sperry Road at 8.7 miles. Turn right (north) on **Sperry Road.** (Optional: Turn right [north] at the sign in 0.1 mile for a 1.6-mile out-and-back detour to **March Cataract Falls**).

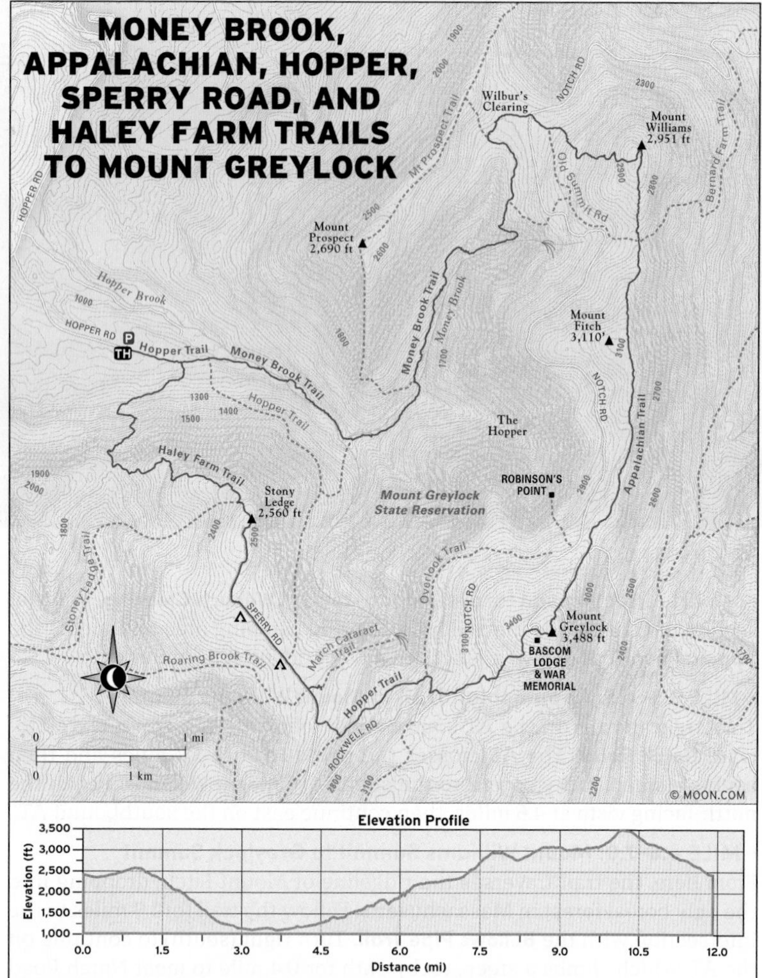

▸ **MILE 8.7-9.7: Sperry Road to Stony Ledge Vista**

Follow Sperry Road north through the campground to its terminus at the **Stony Ledge vista** at 11.4 miles. Many consider this peak to be the best view in Greylock, looking out over the Hopper and the ridgeline you've just crossed.

▸ **MILE 9.7-11.8: Stony Ledge Vista to Hopper Trail**

Descend to the left (north) on the Haley Farm Trail, which drops 1.9 miles through a gorgeous hardwood forest to the Hopper Trail. Turn left (west) onto the Hopper Trail and continue 0.2 mile to return to the parking lot.

DIRECTIONS

Follow US-7 to its intersection with MA-43 and take MA-43 N (Green River Road) for 2.3 miles. Turn right onto Hopper Road and follow it until the end. The trailhead is marked with a sign in a dirt parking lot on the right side of the road.

GPS COORDINATES: 42°39'19.1"N 73°12'15.4"W

6 Mahican-Mohawk and Indian Trails to Todd Mountain

MOHAWK STATE FOREST, CHARLEMONT

Follow in the footsteps of the Berkshires' native peoples on this section of the Mahican-Mohawk trail along the Deerfield River and up Todd Mountain.

DISTANCE: 5 miles round-trip
DURATION: 2.5 hours
ELEVATION CHANGE: 1,158 feet
EFFORT: Strenuous
TRAIL: Dirt doubletrack, dirt/rock path
USERS: Hikers, leashed dogs
SEASON: April–November
PASSES/FEES: $5 MA resident, $10 nonresident
MAPS: MA DCR "Mohawk Trail State Forest"
CONTACT: Mohawk Trail State Forest, 413/339-5504, http://mass.gov

The 40-mile-long Mahican-Mohawk Trail, which traverses railroad beds, riverways, and footpaths across the Deerfield River Valley, is a nod to the ancient routes first traveled by the Mohawk and neighboring tribes. The oldest documented section of this trail is this path over the summit of Todd Mountain. This steep hike includes grassy fields and views along the banks of the Deerfield and Cold Rivers.

START THE HIKE

▸ MILE 0–0.5: Mahican-Mohawk Parking Area to Mahican-Mohawk Trail

Walk southeast 0.2 mile from the parking area, back toward the bridge at the entrance of the park. Pass through the gate onto a gravel doubletrack, marked with a sign for the **Mahican-Mohawk Trail.** Continue southeast along the **Cold River** for 0.3 mile, where you reach another sign for the Mahican-Mohawk trail on the left. Turn left (northeast) into the woods on the Mahican-Mohawk Trail and follow the white blazes through a shady pine forest.

▸ MILE 0.5–2.2: Mahican-Mohawk Trail to Large Boulders

Keep straight (north) past the **Thumper Mountain** spur following signs toward the **Todd Lookout.** The trail reaches an intersection at the bank high above the Deerfield River at 1.1 miles. Follow signs for the Mahican-Mohawk Trail left (west) on another wide doubletrack path. At the fork at 1.3 miles, bear left (northwest). Follow signs at 1.4 miles where the trail turns right (north) back onto a narrow forested track. Pass through an opening in the stone walls of a 1700s **sheep range** into a grassy clearing with Todd Mountain rising above it. Continue straight (west) on the trail for 0.3 mile

▲ TODD MOUNTAIN

as it plunges back into a pine grove. Follow the path another 0.5 mile past large boulders as it skirts the hillside.

▸ MILE 2.2-3.4: Elder Grove Trail Junction to Todd Mountain Summit

At the signed connection for the **Elder Grove Trail,** turn left (south) to stay on the Mahican-Mohawk Trail. The narrow trail soon becomes very steep as it edges up the slopes of Todd Mountain. Reach a sign for the Indian Trail at the top of a ridgeline at 3.0 miles. Turn left (east) to follow the blue-blazed Indian Trail to the summit of Todd Mountain. The actual summit is in 0.4 miles, but the best views are to the right (south) at the clearing in 0.2 miles.

▸ MILE 3.4-5.0: Todd Mountain Summit to Indian Trail

Backtrack 0.4 mile to the intersection with the Mahican-Mohawk Trail and turn left (south) down the hill on the Indian Trail, following signs for the campground. The trail descends on a steep slope through laurel. Reach the bottom of the hill in 0.4 mile and turn left (east) through the gate to the paved road. Follow the road southeast through the campground for 0.8 mile to return to the parking area.

DIRECTIONS

Follow MA-2 west through the town of Charlemont and continue for 4.2 miles. Just after a dirt turnoff on the highway, turn right onto Cold River Road, which is marked with a large Mohawk Trail State Forest sign. Cross the bridge and turn left toward the check-in station. After checking in at the gate, day-hiker parking is located to the left.

GPS COORDINATES: 42°38'14.3"N 72°56'06.2"W

MAHICAN-MOHAWK AND INDIAN TRAILS TO TODD MOUNTAIN

Deerfield River
Elder Grove Trail
Mahican-Mohawk Trail
Indian Trail
Todd Mountain
Mohawk Trail State Forest
Elder Grove Trail
Mahican-Mohawk Trail
Deerfield River
MOHAWK TRAIL
Cold River
Thumper Mountain
COLD RIVER RD
Totem Trail
Mahican-Mohawk Trail
2
0 .5 mi
0 .5 km
© MOON.COM

Elevation Profile
Elevation (ft): 1,000 – 1,500 – 2,000 – 2,500 – 3,000 – 3,500
Distance (mi): 0.0 – 1.0 – 2.0 – 3.0 – 4.0 – 5.0

▲ THE COLD RIVER

7 Alander Mountain Trail

MOUNT WASHINGTON STATE FOREST, MOUNT WASHINGTON

This hike is a favorite for its trail along a bubbling brook and long tristate views from the Alander Mountain summit.

BEST: Vistas

DISTANCE: 6 miles round-trip

DURATION: 3.5 hours

ELEVATION CHANGE: 1,012 feet

EFFORT: Moderate

TRAIL: Dirt/rock path

USERS: Hikers, leashed dogs, horseback riders

SEASON: April–November

PASSES/FEES: None

MAPS: MA DCR "Mount Washington State Forest."

CONTACT: Massachusetts Department of Conservation and Recreation, Mt. Washington State Forest, 413/528-0330, http://mass.gov

Located in the very southwest corner of Massachusetts, the spacious summit of Alander Mountain offers some of the best views in the state—stretching far into New York and Connecticut. This out-and-back hike to the viewpoint is just as pleasant, climbing through a serene forest along Ashley Hill Brook. There is a primitive campground along the way for those who want to extend their trip into an overnight. (Note: A second Massachusetts access point to Alander Mountain, via a connector trail to the South Taconic Trail at Bash Bish Falls State Park, is now closed. The South Taconic Trail can be accessed at Taconic State Park in New York.)

START THE HIKE

▸ MILE 0–0.7: Alander Mountain Trail to Ashley Hill Trail Junction

Go west from the trailhead sign and hike through a grassy field, following signs for the **Alander Mountain Trail.** When the trail enters a pine forest, the wide, flat path is marked with blue blazes. Reach a sign at 0.3 mile and bear left (west) on the Alander Mountain Trail. The dirt trail crosses a wooden bridge at 0.5 mile and bends right (west) along the brook. A sign at 0.7 mile marks the intersection with the **Ashley Hill Trail.**

▸ MILE 0.7–2.8: Ashley Hill Trail Junction to Shelter Cabin

Turn right (north) to stay on the Alander Mountain Trail, heading toward the **camping area**. After crossing another bridge, the trail hugs the bank of **Ashley Brook** where there is a small (approximately 3-foot) cascade. Reach a sign pointing to the camping area at 1.6 miles and continue straight (west), following signs for **Alander Summit.** The trail narrows into a loose rock and gravel path through a corridor of laurel, passing a mossy

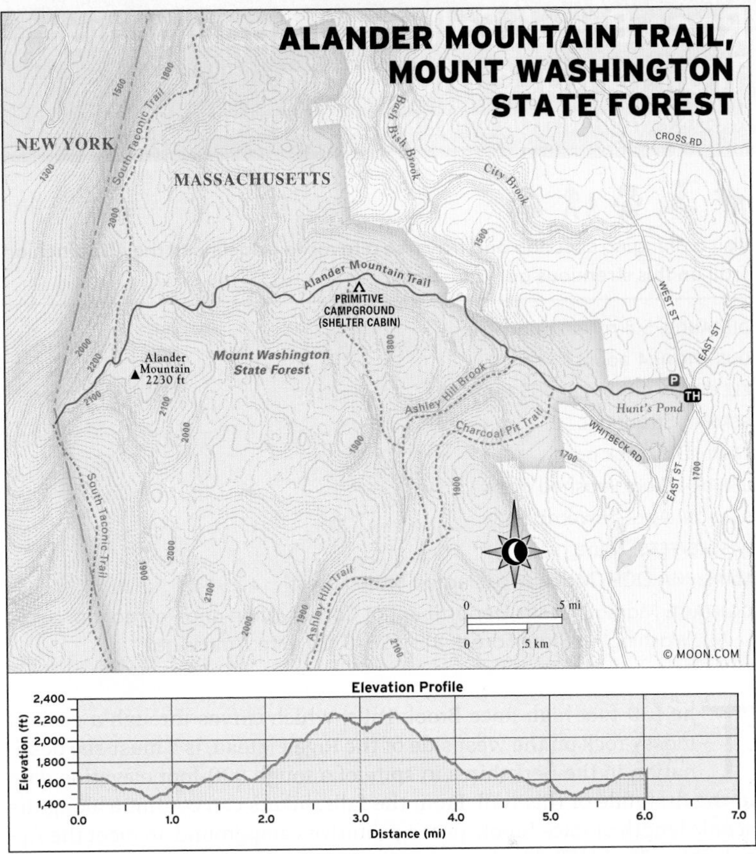

tributary of the brook. Arrive at a fork in front of a rugged shelter **cabin** 1.2 miles from the campground trail.

‣ MILE 2.8-3.0: Shelter Cabin to Alander Mountain Summit

Follow signs to the right (west) toward the Alander Summit, ascending a steep rock face. At the cairn atop the rock face, go left (south), following the narrow path through blueberry bushes. The trail reaches the summit at 3.0 miles. For a variety of vantage points, hikers can wander along the long summit ridge on the South Taconic Trail. After enjoying the broad tri-state views, backtrack to the parking area via the Alander Mountain Trail.

DIRECTIONS

From Great Barrington/US-7 South, turn right onto MA-41 S; follow it for 4.4 miles through Egremont and then turn left to stay on US-41. Make an immediate right onto Mount Washington Road and follow it for 4.4 miles. Turn left onto East Street; in 1 mile, turn left to stay on East Street. In 3.6 miles, Mount Washington State Forest Headquarters is marked with a sign on the right. Turn right, pass the headquarters building, and find the parking area/trailhead to the left.

GPS COORDINATES: 42°05'10.7"N 73°27'43.6"W

8 Race Brook Falls and Appalachian Trail to Race Mountain

MOUNT WASHINGTON STATE FOREST, SHEFFIELD

Visit a plunging cascade and traverse a favorite ridgeline of the Appalachian Trail on this strenuous out-and-back.

DISTANCE: 5.8 miles round-trip
DURATION: 4 hours
ELEVATION CHANGE: 1,455 feet
EFFORT: Strenuous
TRAIL: Dirt/rock path
USERS: Hikers, leashed dogs
SEASON: April–November
PASSES/FEES: None
MAPS: MA DCR "Mount Washington State Forest"
CONTACT: Massachusetts Department of Conservation and Recreation, Mt. Washington State Forest, 413/528-0330, http://mass.gov

The 100-foot-high Race Brook Falls, which carves through a gash of mossy rock on the west side of the Riga Plateau, is a must-see destination in the Berkshires in spite of a tough 900-foot elevation gain in the first mile of this trail. From the falls, hikers can continue along the scenic length of Race Brook, past a primitive campground, to meet the Appalachian Trail (AT). The best views are on the southbound stretch of the AT, looking out from the summit of Race Mountain.

START THE HIKE

▸ MILE 0–0.9: Race Brook Falls Trail to Upper Race Brook Falls

Hike south on the Race Brook Falls Trail, following the blue blazes over a dry creek bed and through a meadow. At the signed fork at 0.3 mile, turn left (southwest) toward Upper Falls/Campsite/AT. The trail goes along the brook, then hops along rocks to cross the water to the left (south) at 0.4 mile. From here, the path begins climbing above the gorge, becoming very rocky and steep. Reach the base of **Upper Race Brook Falls** at 0.9 mile.

▸ MILE 0.9–2.0: Upper Race Brook Falls to Appalachian Trail

From the falls, the trail continues north across the brook, and the narrow, rocky path works its way up to a ridgeline at 1.2 miles where there is a small vista to the east. Shortly after, reach the brook again and turn right (west) upstream. This more level section of trail wanders along the lush plain of the brook, reaching the **primitive campsite** at 1.6 miles. Follow the blue blazes through the campground, continuing west toward the Appalachian Trail (AT). Reach the intersection with the AT at 2.0 miles and turn left (south) onto the AT southbound toward Laurel Ridge.

▲ RACE BROOK

▸ MILE 2.0–2.9: Appalachian Trail to Race Mountain Summit

The trail heads over a slight incline to a rocky ridgeline. You may need to use your hands at times to navigate over steep rocks. Arrive at the summit of **Race Mountain** at 2.9 miles. Though the ridge is grown in with oak, pine, and blueberry, there are 360-degree views of the **Housatonic River valley** stretching into Connecticut and New York. Backtrack to the parking area via the AT northbound and the Race Brook Falls Trail.

DIRECTIONS

From Great Barrington/US-7 South, turn right onto MA-41 S. Follow it for 4.4 miles through Egremont and then turn left to stay on MA-41. The paved parking turnoff is marked with a small sign on the right side of MA-41 in 5 miles.

GPS COORDINATES: 42°05'23.3"N 73°24'40.2"W

RACE BROOK FALLS AND APPALACHIAN TRAIL TO MOUNT RACE

Mount Everett State Reservation
PRIMITIVE CAMPGROUND
Race Brook Trail
Race Brook Falls
Appalachian Trail
Mount Race 2365 ft
S UNDERMOUNTAIN RD
41
P
TH
SALISBURY RD
Race Brook
0 .5 mi
0 .5 km
© MOON.COM

Elevation Profile
Elevation (ft): 2,300; 1,900; 1,500; 1,100; 700
Distance (mi): 0.0; 1.5; 3.0; 4.5; 6.0

▲ VIEWS OF MOUNT EVERETT FROM RACE MOUNTAIN

9 Ledges, Bailey, Spero, Tulip Tree, and Tractor Path Trails

BARTHOLOMEW'S COBBLE RESERVATION, SHEFFIELD

This amazingly diverse property includes rock formations, sections along the Housatonic River, and views of the Berkshire-Taconic Range from Hurlburt's Hill.

BEST: Fall hikes, New England oddities

DISTANCE: 3.2 miles round-trip

DURATION: 1.75 hours

ELEVATION CHANGE: 400 feet

EFFORT: Easy/moderate

TRAIL: Dirt path, grass/dirt doubletrack

USERS: Hikers only

SEASON: Year-round

PASSES/FEES: $5 donation

MAPS: The Trustees of Reservations, "Bartholomew's Cobble"

CONTACT: The Trustees of Reservations, 413/229-8600, http://thetrustees.org

Bartholomew's Cobble is a popular hike for families with kids due to its fairly easy terrain, explorable rock features, and frolic-friendly fields. However, this National Natural Landmark is also a favorite among naturalists for its fascinating ecology. As hikers visit riverbanks, forests, and meadows, they can appreciate a number of plant species, including one of the largest cottonwood trees in the state and one of the greatest diversities of ferns in North America. To top it off, the captivating view from Hurlburt's Hill is a picture-perfect Berkshires scene.

START THE HIKE

▸ MILE 0-0.4: Visitors Center to Bailey Trail

Follow the trail east behind the visitors center for 200 feet and then turn left (northeast) onto the **Ledges Trail.** This flat, pine needle-covered path cuts through ledges and boulders, winding along a section of the **Housatonic River.** At 0.4 mile, the trail reaches a grassy clearing with a sign for the **Bailey Trail.**

▸ MILE 0.4-1.6: Bailey Trail to Spero Loop Trail

Turn left (east) onto the Bailey Trail, which crosses over several bridges, following the length of the river for 0.3 mile. At the intersection, turn left (east) on the Spero Trail. Follow the yellow blazes through a forest of huge pines for approximately 0.1 mile, then turn left (north) onto the **Spero Loop Trail.** This grassy path winds from the **Half River Oxbow** through a silver maple floodplain forest that offers great views of the Housatonic. After passing through a field, the trail doubles back through a hemlock grove,

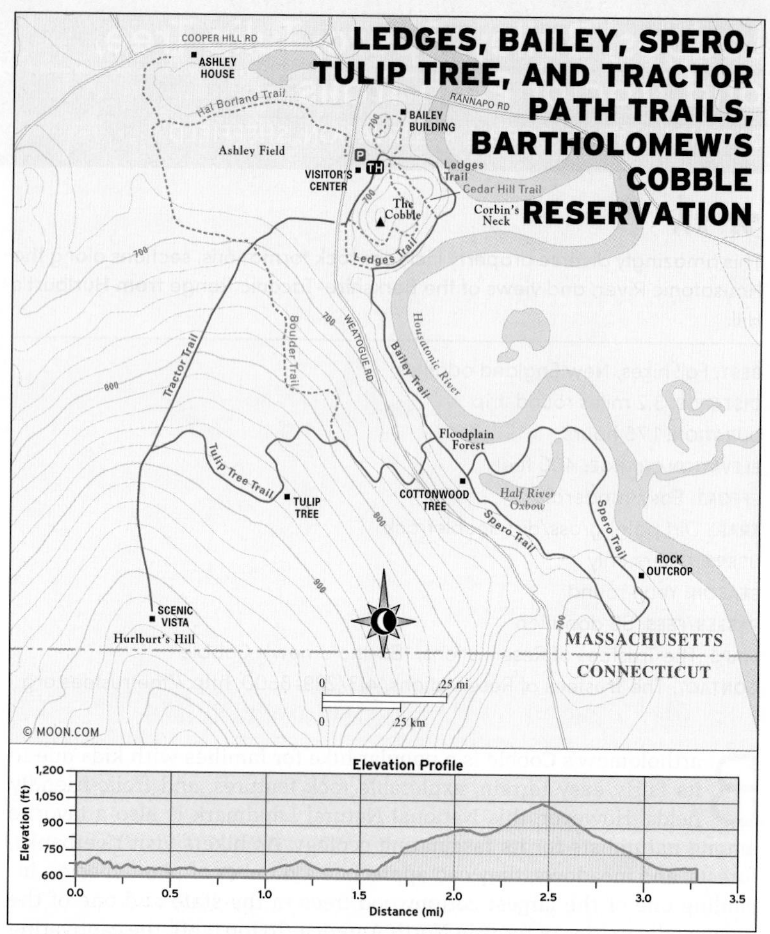

returning to the end of the loop at 1.6 miles. Note the huge **cottonwood** to the left (west) here—it's one of the largest in the state.

‣ MILE 1.6-1.7: Spero Loop Trail to Tulip Tree Trail

Continue straight west toward the Tulip Tree Trail for 0.1 mile and then turn left (west) up the hill on the white-blazed **Tulip Tree Trail.** At the top of the hill, the trail crosses straight (west) over a dirt road, after which it meanders through a forest of rare and varied ferns.

‣ MILE 1.7-2.5: Tulip Tree Trail to Hurlburt's Hill Summit

At the signed intersection with the Boulder Trail at 1.9 miles, turn left (west) to stay on the Tulip Tree Trail. After a wildflower meadow and a series of bridges and stepping-stones, the path meets the **Tractor Path** at 2.3 miles. Turn left (south) onto the Tractor Path, following signs for the **Hurlburt's Hill summit.** The grassy path heads uphill through a birdhouse-lined meadow for 0.2 mile, where it ends at a series of benches overlooking an incredible vista of the **Housatonic River valley,** the Riga Plateau, and the many farms and peaks beyond.

▲ HURLBURT'S HILL

▸ MILE 2.5–3.2: Hurlburt's Hill Summit to Visitors Center

Descend north for 0.7 mile on the wide tractor path through forests and meadows until it ends at the dirt road. Cross the road straight (east) through the fence then turn immediately left (north) onto the short leg of the Ledges Trail that returns to the visitors center.

DIRECTIONS

From Great Barrington/US-7, follow US-7 south 8 miles through Sheffield, then keep right onto MA-7A. In 0.5 mile, turn right onto Rannapo Road. In 1.5 miles, turn right again onto Weatogue Road. The visitors center and parking area are marked with a Trustees of Reservations sign on the left in 0.1 mile.

GPS COORDINATES: 42°03'27.4"N 73°21'03.6"W

NEARBY CAMPGROUNDS

NAME	LOCATION	FACILITIES	SEASON	FEE
Clarksburg State Park	1199 Middle Rd., Clarksburg, MA 01247	45 RV/tent sites; restrooms	mid-May-mid-October	$27
413/664-8345, www.mass.gov/locations/clarksburg-state-park				
Savoy Mountain State Forest	260 Central Shaft Rd., Florida, MA 01247	45 RV/tent sites, 4 cabins; restrooms	mid-May-mid-October	$27-75
413/663-8469, www.mass.gov/locations/savoy-mountain-state-forest				
Mohawk Trail State Forest	Cold River Rd., Charlemont, MA 01339	50 RV/tent sites, 6 cabins; restrooms	early May-mid-October	$27-85
413/339-5504, www.mass.gov/locations/mohawk-trail-state-forest				
Pittsfield State Forest	1041 Cascade St., Pittsfield, MA 01201	40 RV/tent sites; restrooms	mid-May-mid-October	$20-27
413/442-8992, www.mass.gov/locations/pittsfield-state-forest				
October Mountain State Forest	317 Woodland Rd., Lee, MA 01238	43 RV/tent sites, 3 yurts; restrooms	early May-mid-October	$27-70
413/243-1778, www.mass.gov/locations/october-mountain-state-forest				
Beartown State Forest	69 Blue Hill Rd., Monterey, MA 01245	12 RV/tent sites; composting toilets	early May-mid-October; off-season camping available	$20
413/528-0904, www.mass.gov/locations/beartown-state-forest				
Tolland State Forest	410 Tolland Rd., East Otis, MA 01029	92 RV/tent sites; restrooms	mid-May-mid-October	$27
413/269-6002, www.mass.gov/locations/tolland-state-forest				

THE PIONEER VALLEY AND NORTH QUABBIN

The Pioneer Valley occupies the fertile rift where the Connecticut River flows through Massachusetts, separating the eastern hills from the Berkshire Range to the west. This central section of the state is known as a patchwork of farmlands and college towns, but it's also one of the most geologically significant areas of New England. The Metacomet Ridge stretches up the river from Connecticut, forming a roller coaster of teardrop-shaped mountains over which runs the Metacomet-Monadnock section of the New England National Scenic Trail. To the east of the valley, the 38.6-square-mile Quabbin Reservoir—created as the water supply for Boston—is surrounded by beautiful forestland where waterfalls plunge toward the Tully and Millers Rivers. Hikers in this region can take in dramatic views from high cliff faces, or explore waterways in the valleys below.

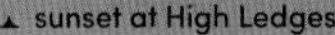

▲ sunset at High Ledges

▲ Roaring Brook Falls

1 **Robert Frost Trail to Mount Toby**

DISTANCE: 4.3 miles round-trip (with optional additions)
DURATION: 3 hours
EFFORT: Moderate

2 **Metacomet Monadnock Trail to Norwottuck Horse Caves and Rattlesnake Knob**

DISTANCE: 3.9 miles round-trip
DURATION: 3 hours
EFFORT: Moderate

3 **Metacomet Monadnock Trail to Mount Tom**

DISTANCE: 6.6 miles round-trip
DURATION: 3 hours
EFFORT: Moderate

4 **Tully Trail to Doane's Falls**

DISTANCE: 6 miles round-trip (with optional additions)
DURATION: 4 hours
EFFORT: Easy/moderate

5 **Metacomet Monadnock Trail to Hermit's Castle**

DISTANCE: 5.7 miles round-trip
DURATION: 4 hours
EFFORT: Moderate

6 **Sanctuary Road Loop to High Ledges**

DISTANCE: 3.3 miles round-trip (with optional additions)
DURATION: 2 hours
EFFORT: Easy

▲ TRAPROCK CLIFFS

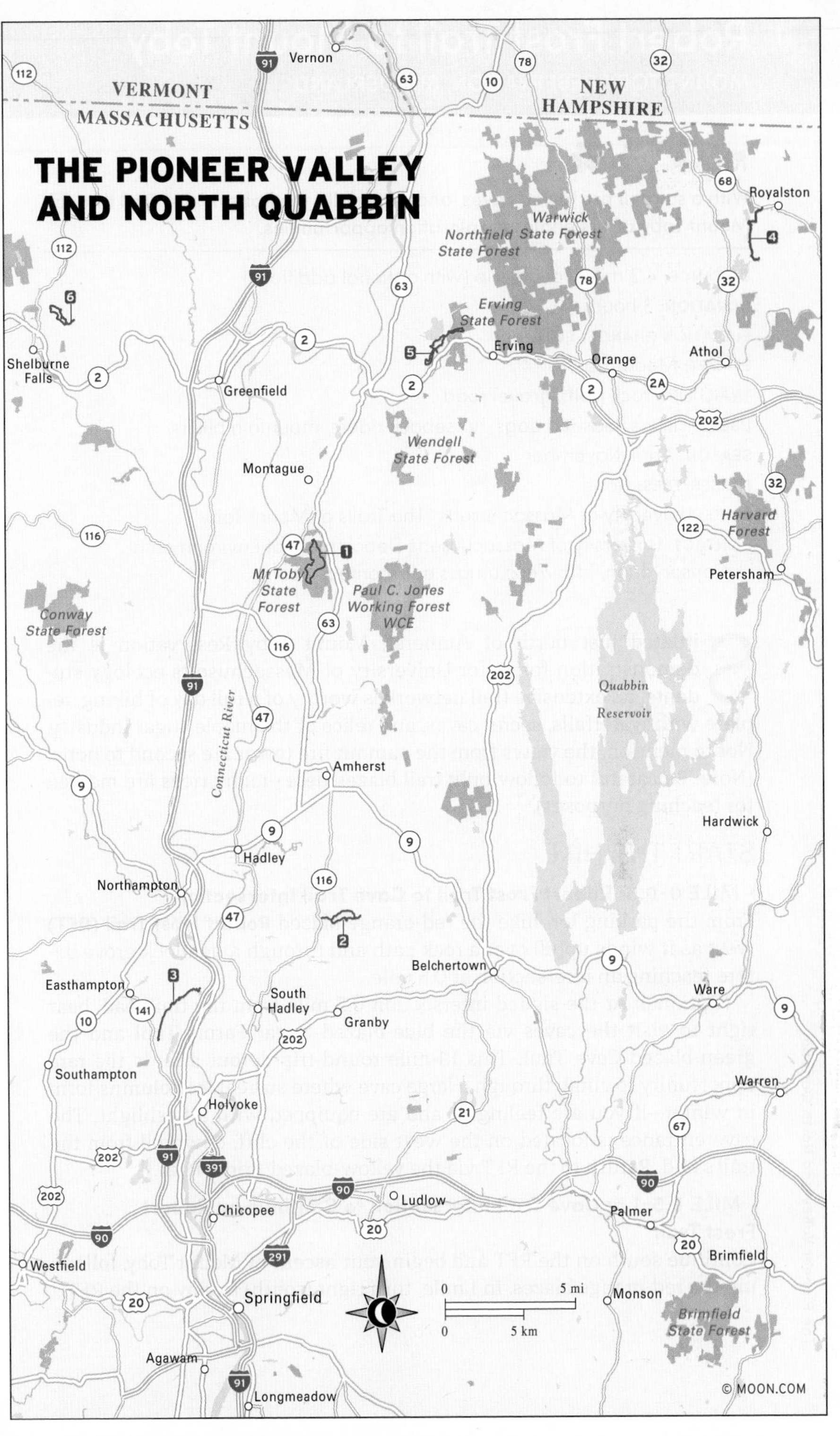
THE PIONEER VALLEY
AND NORTH QUABBIN
VERMONT
MASSACHUSETTS
NEW
HAMPSHIRE
Vernon
Royalston
Warwick
Northfield State Forest
Northfield
State Forest
Erving
State Forest
Erving
Orange
Athol
Shelburne
Falls
Greenfield
Wendell
State Forest
Montague
Harvard
Forest
Petersham
Mt Toby
State
Forest
Paul C. Jones
Working Forest
WCE
Conway
State Forest
Quabbin
Reservoir
Connecticut River
Amherst
Hardwick
Hadley
Northampton
Belchertown
Easthampton
South
Hadley
Granby
Ware
Southampton
Warren
Holyoke
Chicopee
Ludlow
Palmer
Brimfield
Westfield
Springfield
Monson
Brimfield
State Forest
Agawam
Longmeadow
0
5 mi
0
5 km
© MOON.COM

1 Robert Frost Trail to Mount Toby

MOUNT TOBY RESERVATION, SUNDERLAND

With a summit fire tower, caves, and waterfalls, the Robert Frost Trail through Mount Toby offers endless exploration opportunities.

DISTANCE: 4.3 miles round-trip (with optional additions)
DURATION: 3 hours
ELEVATION CHANGE: 1,017 feet
EFFORT: Moderate
TRAIL: Dirt/rock path, gravel road
USERS: Hikers, leashed dogs, horseback riders, mountain bikers
SEASON: April-November
PASSES/FEES: None
MAPS: University of Massachusetts "The Trails of Mount Toby"
CONTACT: University of Massachusetts Department of Environmental Conservation, http://eco.umass.edu/contact-eco

Situated just north of Amherst, Mount Toby Reservation is the demonstration forest for University of Massachusetts ecology students. Its extensive trail network is worthy of a full day of hiking, replete with waterfalls, secret caves, and relics of the maple sugar industry. Not to mention, the views from the summit fire tower are second to none. (Note: Be careful to follow only trail blazes here—many trees are marked for teaching purposes).

START THE HIKE

▸ MILE 0-0.5: Robert Frost Trail to Cave Trail Intersection

From the parking lot, hike the red-orange blazed **Robert Frost Trail (RFT)** west as it winds uphill over a rock path and through a hemlock grove before reaching an intersection at 0.5 mile.

(Optional: At the signed intersection 0.5 mile from the trailhead, bear right to visit the caves via the blue-blazed Sugar Farms Trail and the green-blazed Cave Trail. This 1.1-mile round-trip detour affords the rare opportunity to climb through a large cave where surreal ice columns form in winter—if you are feeling fit and are equipped with a flashlight. The cave entrance is located on the west side of the cliff, downhill from the trail's end. Return to the RFT via the yellow-blazed Bridle Path.)

▸ MILE 0.5-1.5: Cave Trail Intersection to Continue on Robert Frost Trail

Continue south on the RFT and begin your ascent of Mount Toby, following the red-orange blazes. In 1 mile, turn right (south) to stay on the RFT.

▲ ALONG THE CAVE TRAIL

▸ MILE 1.5–2.2: Robert Frost Trail to Mount Toby Summit

Here, the trail steepens and joins the corridor of the phone lines. At the intersection with the Upper Link Trail at 1.2 miles, turn right (west) to continue uphill on the RFT. Reach the summit after a tough 0.5-mile climb. For the best views, climb to the top of the fire tower. This 360-degree panorama includes stunning views of the Connecticut River and surrounding peaks.

▸ MILE 2.2–4.3: Mount Toby Summit and Fire Tower to Tower Road

When you're ready, descend to the east via the **RFT/Tower Road,** a long gravel doubletrack that sweeps down the eastern slope of the mountain following Roaring Brook. Where the RFT diverges east at 1 mile, continue straight north on Tower Road. (Optional: 0.6 mile from where the RFT diverges, take a right [east] and follow the blue blazes 440 feet downhill to reach **Roaring Brook Falls.**) The parking lot is 1.1 miles north on Tower Road from the falls intersection.

DIRECTIONS

From the intersection of MA-116 and MA-47 in Sunderland, follow MA-47 north to the Montague town line. Just after the town sign, turn right onto Reservation Road. The parking area and trailhead are about 0.5 mile down on the right. When you park, take care not to block the access road or the school bus turnaround. Parking is free.

GPS COORDINATES: 42°30'13.5"N 72°31'48.2"W / 42.503750, -72.530067

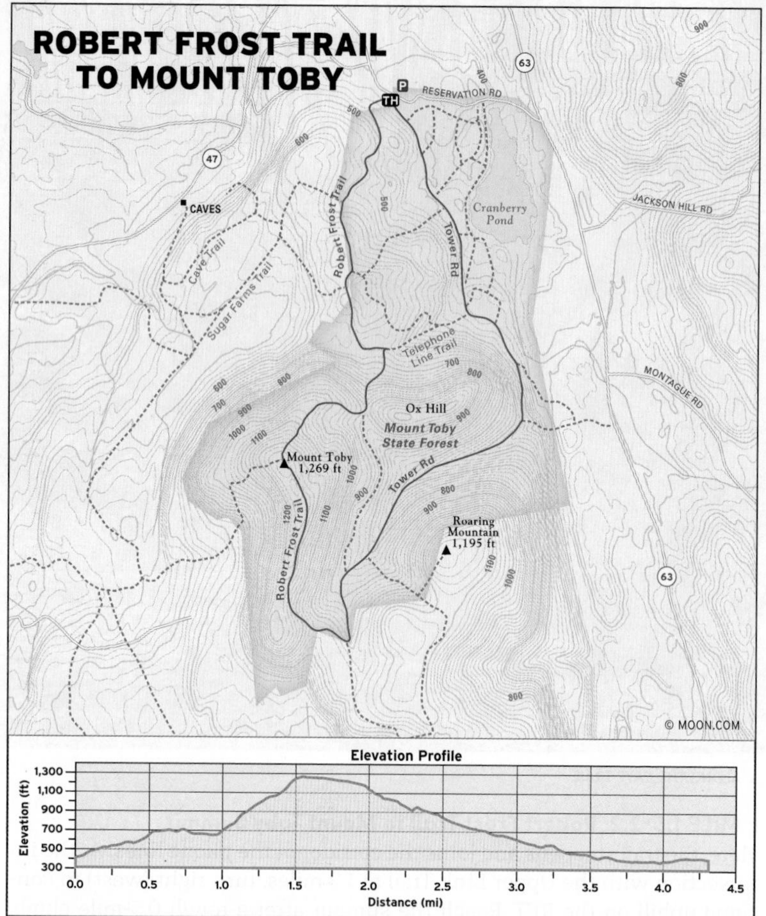

BEST NEARBY BITES

Peruse the shelves of the **Montague Book Mill** (440 Greenfield Rd., Montague, 413/367-9206, http://montaguebookmill.com, 10am-6pm daily), which serves beer, coffee, and more from its Lady Killigrew Café (8am-9pm daily). For finer dining, head to the **Alvah Stone downstairs** (lunch noon-2pm, dinner from 5pm). The Book Mill is 3 miles from the trailhead.

2 Metacomet-Monadnock Trail to Norwottuck Horse Caves and Rattlesnake Knob

MOUNT HOLYOKE RANGE STATE PARK, AMHERST

The overhanging rock ledges of the Norwottuck Horse Caves and the secluded bald vistas overlooking the Connecticut River valley are iconic features of the Metacomet-Monadnock Trail as it winds through Mount Holyoke Range State Park.

DISTANCE: 3.9 miles round-trip
DURATION: 3 hours
ELEVATION CHANGE: 875 feet
EFFORT: Moderate
TRAIL: Dirt/rock path
USERS: Hikers, leashed dogs
SEASON: April-November
PASSES/FEES: None
MAPS: Massachusetts DCR "Joseph Allen Skinner and Mt. Holyoke Range State Parks," Appalachian Mountain Club "Massachusetts Trail Map #4 and #5"
CONTACT: Massachusetts DCR, 413/253-2883, http://mass.gov/locations/mount-holyoke-range-state-park

START THE HIKE

▸ MILE 0-0.5: Notch Visitor Center to Metacomet-Monadnock Trail

Starting from the **Notch Visitor Center** parking lot, find the trailhead behind the building to the southeast. Follow the red, white, and blue blazes, which designate the **Robert Frost Trail** (red), **Metacomet-Monadnock Trail** (white), and **Ken Cuddebank Trail** (blue). The trail reaches a set of power lines where it turns right (east) and then descends to an intersection. Continue straight east on the gravel doubletrack past the quarry, following the red and white blazes. (Note: You may hear gunfire from a nearby private shooting range, but the trail eventually moves out of earshot.) Turn right (south) onto the **Metacomet-Monadnock Trail** at 0.5 mile, following the white blazes.

▸ MILE 0.5-1.0: Metacomet-Monadnock Trail to Mount Norwottuck Summit

This moderate section of trail climbs steeply and steadily through a mixed oak and hickory forest, gaining over 500 feet of altitude. The white blazes are sparse along this section of the ridge, but the path is clear as it levels out, dips, and then ascends a brief section of steep scree. Reach the summit of **Mount Norwottuck** at 1.0 mile and enjoy nearly 360-degree views of the valley below from atop a grassy knob.

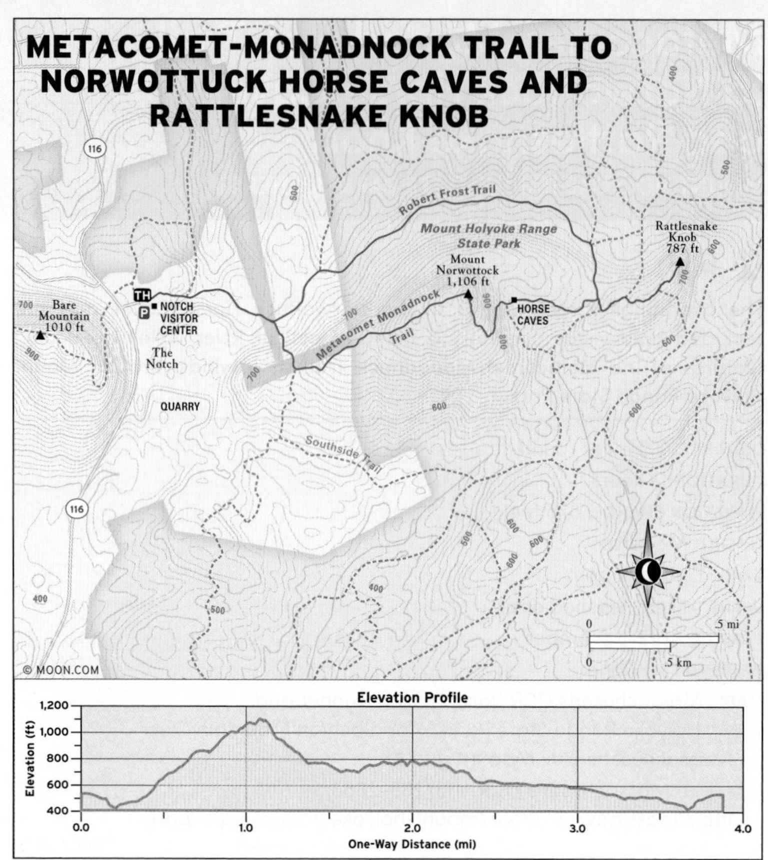

▸ **MILE 1.0–1.2: Mount Norwottuck Summit to Norwottuck Horse Caves**

Descend via the Metacomet-Monadnock Trail to the north. Be mindful of loose rock as you step down the cliffside. The trail winds through a large boulder field and cuts through a narrow crack between two rocks at 1.2 miles. On the east side of the rocks, directly off the trail, are the imposing Norwottuck Horse Caves, a series of wide, overhanging ledges that invite exploration.

▸ **MILE 1.2–2.0: Norwottuck Horse Caves to Rattlesnake Knob**

The Metacomet-Monadnock Trail descends to the base of the caves and continues on a bog bridge over a creek. The way is relatively flat from here on out. The trail intersects with the red-blazed **Robert Frost Trail** again about 0.5 mile from the caves. Take a right (east) up the short, steep hill following the red and white blazes. Pass a town line marker separating Amherst and Granby. Shortly after, the **Ken Cuddebank Trail** rejoins the path and the blazes return to red, white, and blue. Where the Robert Frost and Metacomet-Monadnock Trail diverge after 0.3 mile, follow the Cuddebank Trail (blue blazes) straight (east) for 260 feet. The trail ends at **Rattlesnake Knob,** a beautiful series of vistas.

▲ THE NORWOTTUCK HORSE CAVES

▸ MILE 2.0-3.9: Rattlesnake Knob to Robert Frost Trail

To the northwest, hikers can look over the town of Amherst, while to the northeast, there is a striking view of Long Mountain and the surrounding valley. To bypass the steps of Mount Norwottuck on the return, descend west via the Robert Frost Trail, which rounds the base of the mountain back to the parking area in 1.9 miles.

DIRECTIONS

From Atkin's Corner (the intersection of Bay Road and MA-116 in Amherst), follow MA-116 one mile south to the Notch Visitor Center. There is a large parking area.

GPS COORDINATES: 42°18'18.2"N 72°31'42.3"W / 42.305061, -72.528410

BEST NEARBY BREWS

Visit the brew aficionados at **The Moan & Dove** (460 West St., Amherst, 413/256-1710, http://moananddovebar.com, 3pm-1am daily), 3 miles from trailhead in Amherst, for a recommendation from their extensive beer list.

3 Metacomet-Monadnock (New England) Trail

MOUNT TOM STATE RESERVATION, HOLYOKE

This trail traverses a series of sheer cliffs that are some of the best birdwatching perches in the state, especially for raptor species such as broadwinged hawks.

BEST: Brew hikes
DISTANCE: 6.6 miles round-trip
DURATION: 3 hours
ELEVATION CHANGE: 1,246 feet
EFFORT: Moderate
TRAIL: Dirt/rock path
USERS: Hikers, leashed dogs, cross-country skiers
SEASON: April-November
PASSES/FEES: $5 MA residents, $10 nonresidents (in-season)
MAPS: Massachusetts DCR "Mount Tom State Reservation," Appalachian Mountain Club "Massachusetts Trail Map #4 and #5"
CONTACT: Massachusetts DCR, 413/534-1186, http://mass.gov/locations/mount-tom-state-reservation

This hike ascends the eastern side of the Mount Tom Range and then follows a section of the Metacomet-Monadnock Trail along a vast stretch of cliffs with spectacular views to the west. Hikers have a good chance of spotting hawks soaring from the high traprock faces. The hike culminates at the teardrop-shaped summit of Mount Tom, purportedly the inspiration for Mount Crumpit in Dr. Seuss's How the Grinch Stole Christmas.

START THE HIKE

▸ MILE 0-0.2: Universal Access Trail to Kay Bee Trail

Begin on the **Universal Access Trail,** a wide gravel path that wraps west around **Lake Bray.** Turn right (north) onto the blue-blazed **Kay Bee Trail** at the intersection at 0.2 mile. The trail immediately ascends several switchbacks rolling over a traprock bed and through a hemlock forest.

▸ MILE 0.2-2.0: Kay Bee Trail to Metacomet-Monadnock Trail

After 0.5 mile, arrive at a four-way intersection. Continue straight (west) to stay on the Kay Bee Trail. Commence climbing 0.4 mile to reach another intersection. Continue straight (west) onto the **Keystone Extension Trail,** following the orange blazes. The Keystone Extension winds around a series of small hills until it descends into a valley with a creek flowing through it. Cross the footbridge and continue straight (west) onto the **D.O.C Trail** (red blazes). The D.O.C. gains moderate elevation, offering great views to the south in winter and spring when there are no leaves on the

▲ THE VISTA AT MOUNT TOM

trees. The trail arrives at the top of the ridgeline and meets the white-blazed **Metacomet-Monadnock Trail** at 2.0 miles.

▸ MILE 2.0–3.3: Metacomet-Monadnock Trail to Mount Tom Summit
Turn left (south) on the **Metacomet-Monadnock Trail** toward Mount Tom. The views from here on out are spectacular as the trail skirts Deadtop, the rugged traprock ridge between Whiting Peak and Mount Tom. Keep an eye out for raptor species riding currents from the steep cliffs, but use caution in wet weather—the bare rock can be slick. The trail extends straight (south) with a series of vistas and some rocky scrambles. You may need to use your hands to climb up and down. After 1.3 miles on the Metacomet-Monadnock Trail, reach the summit of Mount Tom, punctuated by various communication towers, graffiti, and remnants of a former ski area. While the trail here is not as unspoiled as the ridgeline to the north, it is the highest point of the Mount Tom Range at 1,202 feet, and the views facing west on a clear day reach from Easthampton Village to the Berkshires.

DIRECTIONS

From I-91, take exit 18 to MA-5 south (Mount Tom Road). Turn right onto Reservation Road. The parking lot for this route is at the end of Reservation Road, on the east side of the reservation. There may be an entrance fee in season. (Note: The gates close and lock promptly at the posted time. Be sure to return to your car before closing hours, which vary seasonally).

GPS COORDINATES: 42°16'07.9"N 72°36'59.8"W / 42.268857, -72.616605

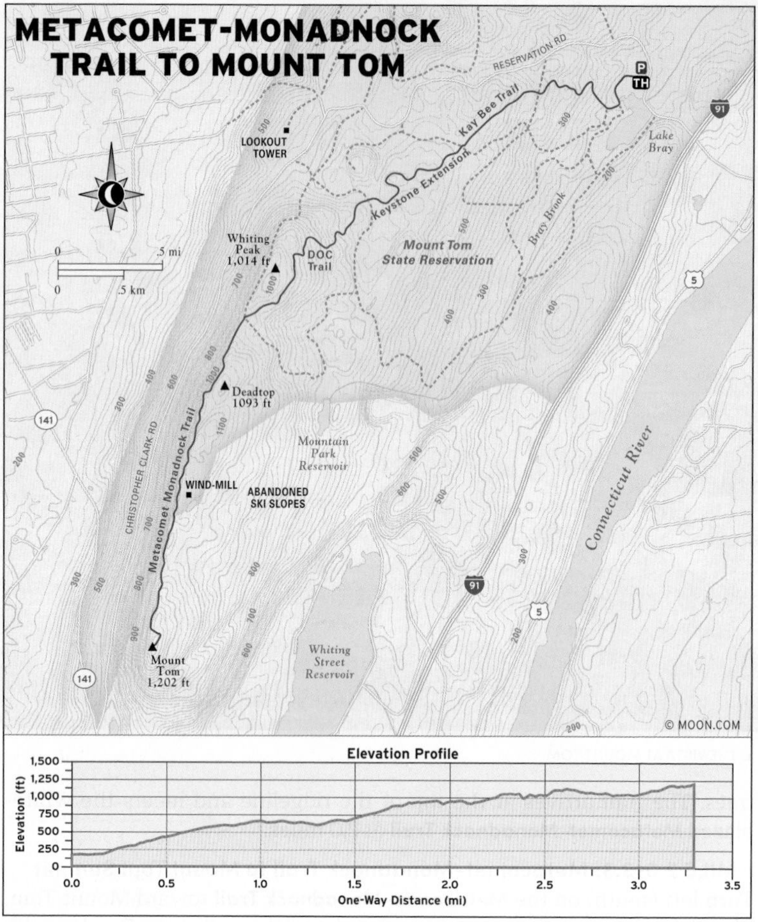

METACOMET-MONADNOCK TRAIL TO MOUNT TOM

Elevation Profile

BEST NEARBY BREWS

Enjoy views of Mount Tom and live music at the taproom of **Fort Hill Brewery** (30 Fort Hill Rd., Easthampton, 413/203-5754, http://forthill-brewery.com, 4pm-7pm Thurs.-Fri., 2pm-8pm Sat., 2pm-6pm Sun.), 4 miles from the trailhead.

4 Tully Trail to Doane's Falls

JACOBS HILL AND DOANE'S FALLS RESERVATIONS, ROYALSTON

Meander along the peaceful shores of the Tully River and hike from waterfall to waterfall on this prized section of the Tully Trail.

BEST: Winter hikes
DISTANCE: 6 miles round-trip (with optional additions)
DURATION: 4 hours
ELEVATION CHANGE: 849 feet
EFFORT: Easy/moderate
TRAIL: Dirt/rock path, gravel road
USERS: Hikers, leashed dogs, mountain bikers
SEASON: Year-round
PASSES/FEES: None
MAPS: Trustees of Reservations "Tully Trail Map"
CONTACT: Trustees of Reservations, 978/249-4947, http://thetrustees.org

START THE HIKE

▸ MILE 0-0.8: Metacomet-Monadnock Trail to Little Pond Stream

Hike south from the parking lot following the white blazes. The trail winds under the power lines and into a shady coniferous forest, where it bends right to the west. Reach an unsigned intersection with the yellow-blazed Jacobs Hill Trail after 0.3 mile. The **Jacobs Hill lookout** is about 300 feet to the right (north) and features great views of Long Pond and Tully Mountain. The trail continues to the left (south) along the ridgeline for 0.4 mile, where it descends to meet the rushing stream flowing from Little Pond.

(Optional: Cross the stream and follow the white blazes straight (south) for 0.5 mile to **The Ledges overlook** (marked with a granite bench) for great views of Tully Lake and beyond.)

▸ MILE 0.8-1.0: Little Pond Stream to Tully Trail

From the stream, turn right (west) downstream and begin a steep, rocky descent to **Spirit Falls,** following the yellow blazes. Continue 0.2 mile west toward the **Tully River,** passing a dramatic section of the falls. Cross the bridge over the stream and turn left (south) on the red-blazed Tully Trail. This section is flat and peaceful, with lovely views from the blueberry-lined banks of **Long Pond** and the Tully River, plus plenty of opportunities for swimming.

▸ MILE 1.0-2.7: Tully Trail to Doane's Falls

The trail passes the ranger station after 1.2 miles and joins the wide doubletrack **Mountain Bike Trail** for 0.3 mile to the intersection with Doane Hill Road. Cross the road and turn left (east) to find the **Doane's Falls** trailhead. This accessible gravel trail heads southeast for 0.2 mile before reaching the first section of the falls.

TULLY TRAIL TO DOANE'S FALLS

© MOON.COM

▸ MILE 2.7-3.0: Doane's Falls to Jacobs Hill

Continue another 0.3 mile up a singletrack trail for more views of the Lawrence Brook in its frenzied tumble downstream. At the intersection with Athol Road, turn around and backtrack to Jacobs Hill.

DIRECTIONS

From MA-2, take Exit 19 and follow MA-2A into Athol. At the intersection of MA-2A and MA-32 in Athol, cross Millers River Bridge and bear right onto Chestnut Hill Road (which becomes Athol Road) north toward Royalston. Continue on MA-68 North (Warwick Road) to Jacobs Hill Reservation. There is a Trustees of Reservation sign and trailhead on the left side of the road. The parking lot is small and can fill quickly, so arrive early and park courteously.

GPS COORDINATES: 42°40'34.9"N 72°11'58.4"W / 42.676371, -72.199541

BEST NEARBY BREWS

The Blind Pig (98 Exchange St., Athol, 978/249-2795, 11:30am-11pm Mon.-Thurs.), 9 miles from the trailhead in Athol, is known for a great cocktail, beer, and craft cider list. It also serves American pub grub.

5 Metacomet-Monadnock Trail to Hermit's Castle

FARLEY LEDGES, ERVING

This playground of boulders and precipitous ledges is a favorite of New England rock climbers, but hikers can enjoy exploring waterfalls, caves, and vistas of the Millers River.

BEST: New England oddities
DISTANCE: 5.7 miles round-trip
DURATION: 4 hours
ELEVATION CHANGE: 1,158 feet
EFFORT: Moderate
TRAIL: Dirt/rock path
USERS: Hikers, leashed dogs, rock climbers
SEASON: April-November
PASSES/FEES: None
MAPS: Appalachian Mountain Club "Massachusetts Trail Map #4 and #5"
CONTACT: Western Massachusetts Climbers Coalition, http://climbgneiss.org/contact-us/

Combined with the tough Red Trail circling Rattlesnake Mountain and the Farley Ledges, this route follows the Metacomet-Monadnock Trail past a scenic overlook of the Millers River and arrives at the Hermit's Castle rock formation, where Scottish recluse John Smith lived from 1867 to 1899. Other highlights include the tumbling waters of Briggs Brook Falls and the chance to watch climbers spidering up the gneiss.

START THE HIKE

MILE 0-0.7: Metacomet-Monadnock Trail to Farley Ledges

Follow the red and white blazes for the **Metacomet-Monadnock Trail** heading straight (north). The narrow path winds along Briggs Brook and arrives at **Briggs Brook Falls** at 0.2 mile. At the falls, turn left (south) and follow the red blazes toward **Farley Ledges.** The trail becomes increasingly rocky as it travels south into an enormous boulder field at the base of the cliffs, where huge slabs of granite rest in the shade of oak and grapevine. Pass a series of wooden signs that designate popular rock-climbing routes.

MILE 0.7-1.3: Farley Ledges to Rattlesnake Mountain Summit

The trail gets steep straight west of the ledges at 0.8 mile. A series of rope holds tied to trees are available to assist hikers with this strenuous section. At the top of the ropes, the trail bears left, wrapping northwest around the ledges into a tangle of mountain laurel and hemlock. Reach the summit of **Rattlesnake Mountain** at 1.3 miles, where a south-facing vista looks out over the Millers River.

▲ FARLEY LEDGES

▸ MILE 1.3–1.8: Rattlesnake Mountain Summit to Red Trail

From the lookout, continue straight north to stay on the Red Trail, which traverses the Rattlesnake ridgeline. This descent involves lowering yourself over rocks. The trail crosses Briggs Brook at the top of the falls in 0.5 mile.

▸ MILE 1.8–2.1: Red Trail to Metacomet-Monadnock Trail

Just after the crossing, turn left to follow the white blazes of the **Metacomet-Monadnock Trail.** The path leads 0.2 mile upstream, crisscrossing the brook. At the third crossing, follow the white blazes right (east) at the sign for Hermit's Castle. Here, the trail is less scenic as it follows the embankment along the Northfield Mountain Reservoir.

▸ MILE 2.1–3.4: Metacomet-Monadnock Trail to M&M North Overlook

After 0.8 mile, cross the bridge over the creek and, after a slight uphill, reach the Hermit's Castle intersection. Take the second right (east), following the white blazes toward the **M&M North overlook.** The overlook, 0.4 mile up the path, provides more great views of the Millers River to the south.

▸ MILE 3.4–4.1: M&M North Overlook to Hermit's Castle

Continue (east) 0.2 mile, then turn right (south) at the blue-blazed sign for the Castle. The trail switchbacks 0.4 mile down a steep hill and then curls right (west) to the caves of **Hermit's Castle.**

▸ MILE 4.1–5.7: Hermit's Castle to Metacomet-Monadnock Trail and Briggs Brook Falls

In 0.5 mile, follow the trail straight (west) to rejoin the **Metacomet-Monadnock Trail** heading south. Just past the bridge in 0.2 mile, turn left (south) onto the **Gold Dot Trail.** The blazes are small and somewhat faint, but the path is obvious. It rolls steadily downhill and over several small

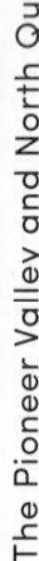

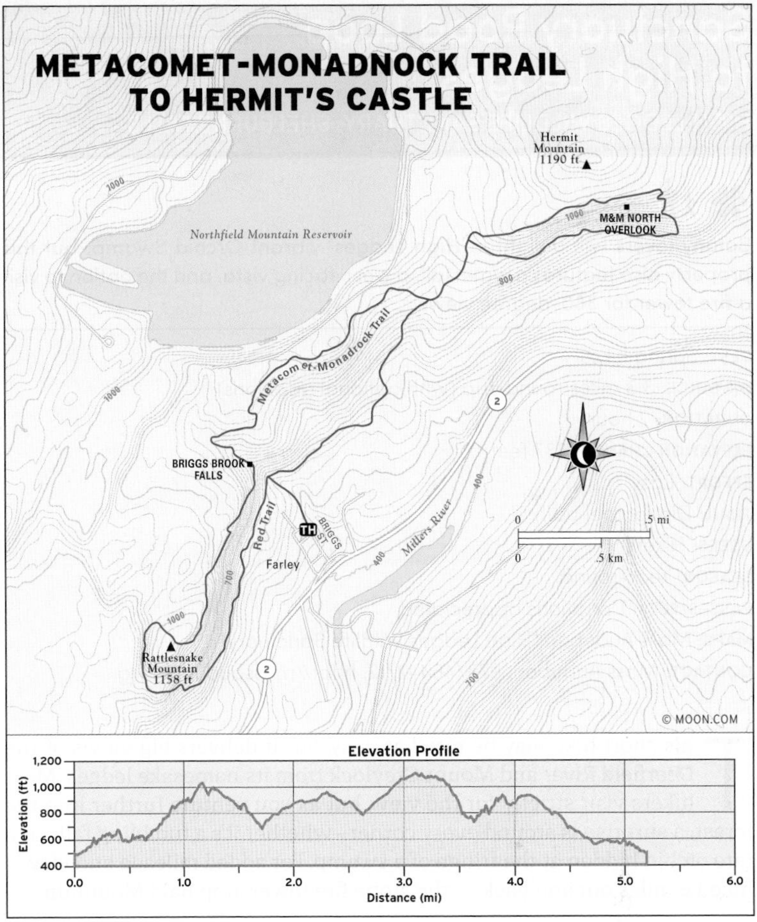

METACOMET-MONADNOCK TRAIL TO HERMIT'S CASTLE

Hermit Mountain 1190 ft
M&M NORTH OVERLOOK
Northfield Mountain Reservoir
Metacomet-Monadnock Trail
BRIGGS BROOK FALLS
Red Trail
TH
BRIGGS ST
Farley
Millers River
Rattlesnake Mountain 1158 ft
0 .5 mi
0 .5 km
© MOON.COM

Elevation Profile
Elevation (ft)
Distance (mi)

brooks for 0.7 mile before emerging on the Metacomet-Monadnock Trail at the base of Briggs Brook Falls. Take a left (east) after the falls bridge and continue 0.2 mile to return to the parking lot.

DIRECTIONS

From MA-2, turn onto Holmes Avenue and follow Briggs Street north to Cross Street. Parking for this route is located off Cross Street. The trailhead is to the east of the parking area, at the end of Briggs Street. The parking lot is small and fills quickly, so arrive early and park courteously.

GPS COORDINATES: 42°36'04.8"N 72°26'24.4"W / 42.601343, -72.440107

BEST NEARBY BREWS

Element Brewing Company (16 Bridge St., Millers Falls, 413/835-6340, http://elementbeer.com, noon-6pm Sun.-Thurs., noon-9pm Fri.-Sat.), 4 miles from the trailhead, has a great selection of craft brews, a game room, and a food truck (Fri.-Sun.).

6 Sanctuary Road Loop to High Ledges

HIGH LEDGES WILDLIFE SANCTUARY, SHELBURNE FALLS

Botany lovers will delight in High Ledges' vibrant Orchid Swamp, but this property also features a waterfall, a west-facing vista, and the option to visit a fire tower for 360-degree views.

BEST: Spring hikes

DISTANCE: 3.3 miles round-trip (with optional additions)

DURATION: 2 hours

ELEVATION CHANGE: 637 feet

EFFORT: Easy

TRAIL: Dirt/gravel path

USERS: Hikers

SEASON: Year-round

PASSES/FEES: Donations appreciated

MAPS: Mass Audubon "High Ledges Wildlife Sanctuary"

CONTACT: Mass Audubon, 978/464-2712, http://massaudubon.org

This short hike may be rated as easy, but it delivers big views of the Deerfield River and Mount Greylock from its namesake ledges. Most hikers visit strictly for the view, but as you venture further into the forest, a surprise is around every corner—whether it's a tumbling falls or a rare orchid hidden at the fringe of a swamp. For added mileage and views, hike 1.6 miles out and back to the stone fire tower atop Bald Mountain.

START THE HIKE

▸ MILE 0-0.5: Sanctuary Road to Optional Shelburne Fire Tower Detour

Head southwest down **Sanctuary Road** for 525 feet and continue straight through the gate. The path curls slightly uphill on a gravel doubletrack surface. Reach an intersection in 0.2 mile. Stay straight (west) (do not follow the orange arrows) and arrive at a clearing at 0.5 mile. Continue straight (west) to remain on Sanctuary Road. (Optional: Turn left, south, and follow the Shelburne Trails signs for 0.8 mile to the stone **Shelburne Fire Tower** on Bald Mountain for great 360-degree views of the valley.)

▸ MILE 0.5-0.8: Sanctuary Road to High Ledges Lookout

Sanctuary Road continues straight (west) through another gate and down a smooth gravel path, passing a vernal pool. At 0.8 miles, turn left (west) to find the **High Ledges lookout,** an incredible vista with views of the Deerfield River stretching toward Mount Greylock in the distance.

▲ THE VISTA AT HIGH LEDGES

‣ MILE 0.8–2.0: High Ledges Lookout to Wolf's Den Loop Trail

From the lookout, the blue-blazed Dutch and Mary Bernard Trail begins to the right (north) of the High Ledges. Follow this thin, rocky path as it drops into a valley to meet a stream in 0.2 mile. Take a left (west) on the **North Trail,** which follows the brook downstream and then parallels a stone wall. The path crosses over a spring and descends to meet a minor **waterfall** at 1.5 mile. The trail crosses the water and heads downstream for 0.1 mile. Here, turn right (east) up over the ledges. This section is steep, but short, and the blazes change from blue to yellow. Reach the intersection with the **Wolf's Den Loop Trail** at 2 miles, and stay left (northeast). The Wolf's Den loop stretches under a series of ledges with some small caves and pockets to explore.

‣ MILE 2.0–3.3: Wolf's Den Loop Trail to Waterthrush Trail

Continue on the Wolf's Den loop for 0.3 mile to an intersection with the **Dutch and Mary Barnard Trail.** Turn left (south) to follow the yellow blazes of the Barnard Trail. The trail bends through a maze of laurel for 0.3 mile until it reaches **Spring Swamp.** Follow the trail (west) around the swamp, cross the bridge, and turn left (east) onto the **Waterthrush Trail.** Be on the lookout for wildflowers where the trail borders **Orchid Swamp,** an ideal habitat for these delicate blossoms. The Waterthrush Trail returns to Sanctuary Road in 0.5 mile. Take a left (east) to return 0.2 mile to the parking area.

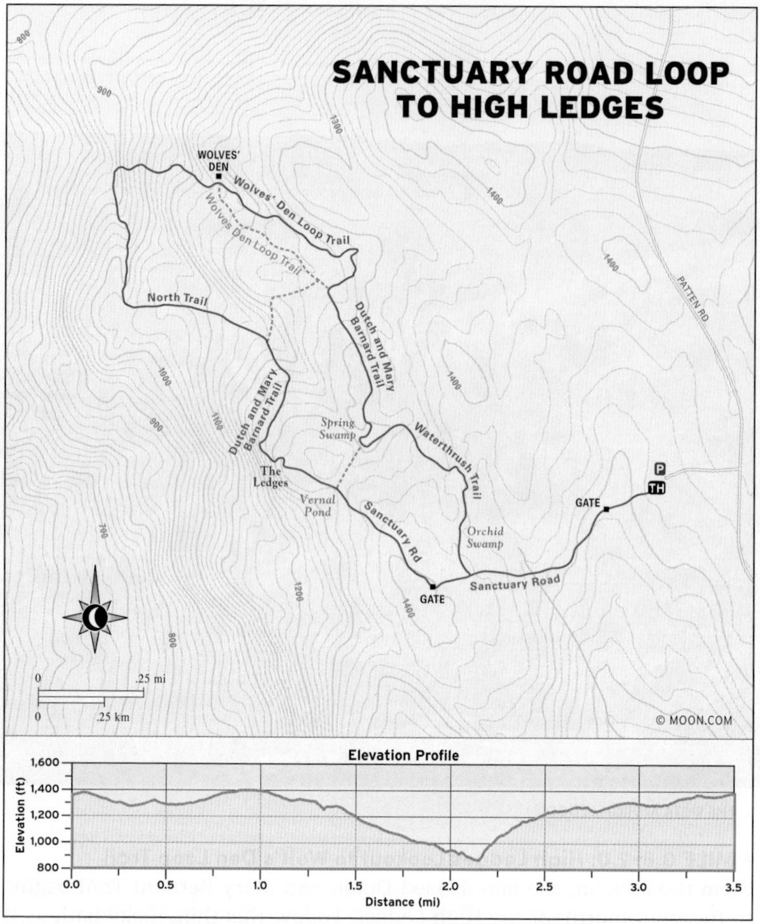

SANCTUARY ROAD LOOP TO HIGH LEDGES

DIRECTIONS

From MA-2, take Frank Williams Road to Little Mohawk Road, then take a left onto Patten Road. The parking lot is about a mile down Patten Road on the left, and is marked with a Mass Audubon sign.

GPS COORDINATES: 42°37'12.2"N 72°42'20.2"W / 42.620051, -72.705606

BEST NEARBY BREWS

Grab a beer flight and some New American fare at **The Blue Rock Restaurant and Bar** (1 Ashfield St., 413/625-8133, http://thebluerock-restaurant.com) in Shelburne Falls, 7 miles from the trailhead.

NEARBY CAMPGROUNDS				
NAME	**LOCATION**	**FACILITIES**	**SEASON**	**FEE**
Tully Lake Campground	25 Doane Hill Rd., Royalston, MA 01368	33 tent sites; restrooms	May-October	$30-75
978/249-4957, www.thetrustees.org/places-to-visit/places-to-stay/tully-lake-campground/				
D.A.R. State Forest	78 Cape St., Goshen, MA 01032	50 RV/tent sites; restrooms	mid-May-mid-October	$27
413/268-7098, www.mass.gov/locations/daughters-of-the-american-revolution-dar-state-forest				
Erving State Forest	1 Laurel Lake Rd., Erving, MA 01344	27 RV/tent sites; restrooms	mid-May-early September	$27
978/544-7745, www.mass.gov/locations/erving-state-forest				
Otter River State Forest	219 Baldwinville State Rd., Winchendon, MA 01475	73 RV/tent sites, 4 yurts; restrooms	early May-mid-October	$27-70
978/939-8962, www.mass.gov/locations/otter-river-state-forest				

▲ THE LEDGES OVERLOOK

▲ THE GREAT CHAUGHAM LOOKOUT IN THE PEOPLE'S STATE FOREST

CONNECTICUT

LITCHFIELD HILLS

Geologically speaking, the Litchfield Hills are the southern continuation of the Berkshires, and they offer many of same spectacular interstate views, high rocky peaks, and abundant farmland fed by the flow of the Housatonic River. This rolling, rural landscape is a respite from the suburban feel that dominates much of Connecticut, and therefore a popular destination for vacationers and second-home owners. Those seeking outdoor adventure flock to the northernmost hills to ascend the highest peaks in the state, while the wide watershed of the Housatonic provides plenty of waterfront scenery at lower elevations. From the trusty corridor of the Appalachian Trail to the isolated lowland forests, there is a trail in northwestern Connecticut to suit every inclination.

▲ along the Pine Knob Loop

▲ Bear Mountain summit

◂ SUNRISE ON MACEDONIA RIDGE

1 **Robert Ross and Agnes Bowman Trails**
DISTANCE: 6.4 miles round-trip
DURATION: 3.5 hours
EFFORT: Moderate

2 **Appalachian Trail: Housatonic River Walk**
DISTANCE: 7.6 miles round-trip
DURATION: 3.5 hours
EFFORT: Easy

3 **Pine Knob Loop**
DISTANCE: 2.5 miles round-trip
DURATION: 2 hours
EFFORT: Moderate

4 **Appalachian Trail: Prospect Mountain and Rand's View**
DISTANCE: 5.2 miles round-trip
DURATION: 2.5 hours
EFFORT: Moderate

5 **Macedonia Ridge Trail**
DISTANCE: 6.4 miles round-trip
DURATION: 3.5 hours
EFFORT: Moderate/strenuous

6 **Steep Rock Loop**
DISTANCE: 4.1 miles round-trip
DURATION: 2 hours
EFFORT: Moderate

7 **Mattatuck and Little Pond Loop "Boardwalk" Trail**
DISTANCE: 3.2 miles round-trip
DURATION: 1.75 hours
EFFORT: Easy

8 **Donkey Trail and Hodge Road Loop**
DISTANCE: 3.3 miles round-trip
DURATION: 2.75 hours
EFFORT: Moderate

9 **Undermountain Trail, Appalachian Trail, and Paradise Lane Trail to Bear Mountain**
DISTANCE: 6.1 miles round-trip
DURATION: 3 hours
EFFORT: Strenuous

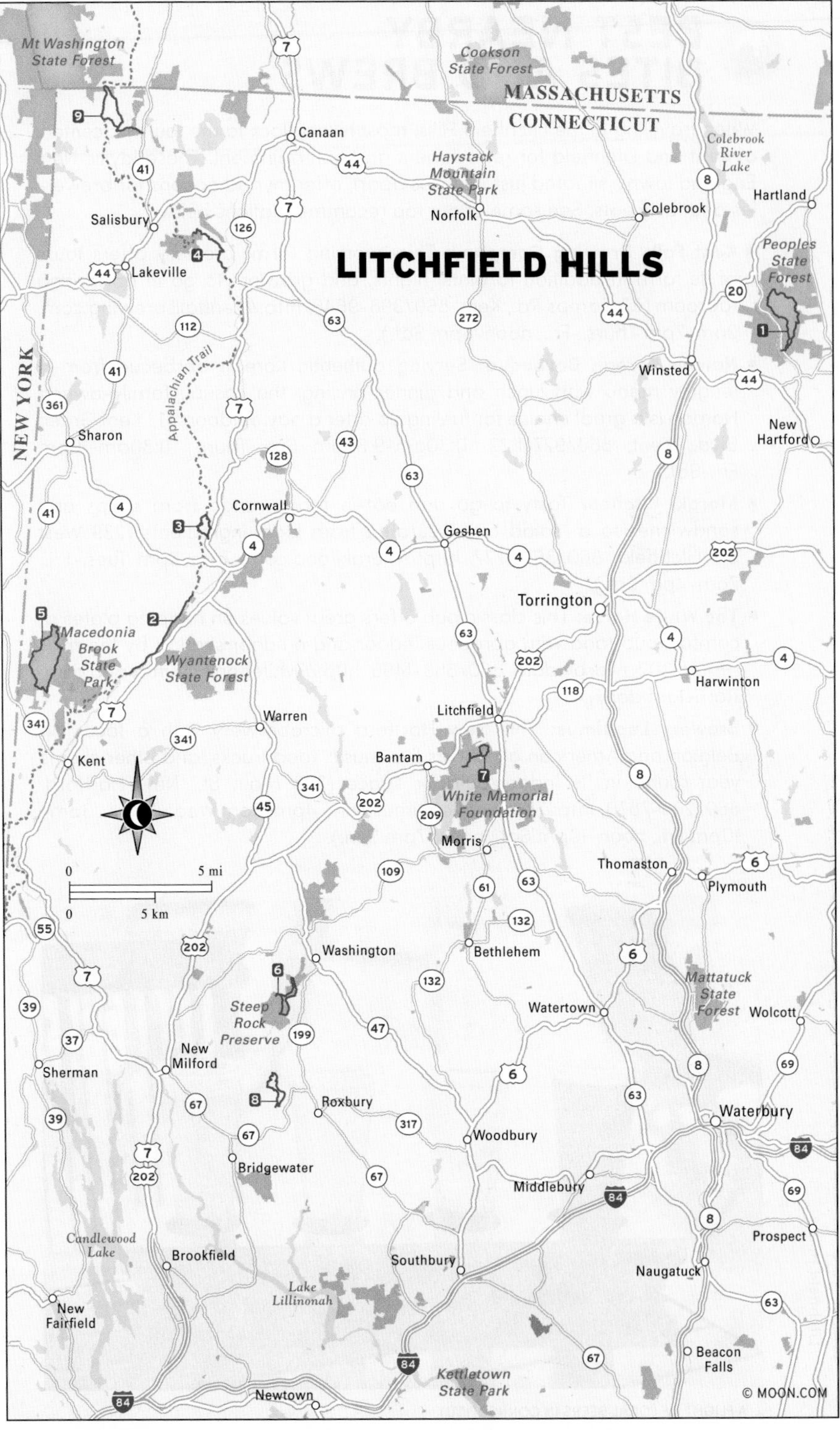

LITCHFIELD HILLS
Mt Washington State Forest
Cookson State Forest
MASSACHUSETTS
CONNECTICUT
NEW YORK
Canaan
Haystack Mountain State Park
Colebrook River Lake
Hartland
Norfolk
Colebrook
Salisbury
Lakeville
Peoples State Forest
Appalachian Trail
Winsted
Sharon
New Hartford
Cornwall
Goshen
Torrington
Macedonia Brook State Park
Wyantenock State Forest
Harwinton
Warren
Litchfield
Kent
Bantam
White Memorial Foundation
Morris
Thomaston
Plymouth
0
5 mi
0
5 km
Washington
Bethlehem
Mattatuck State Forest
Steep Rock Preserve
Watertown
Wolcott
Sherman
New Milford
Roxbury
Waterbury
Woodbury
Bridgewater
Middlebury
Candlewood Lake
Brookfield
Southbury
Prospect
Naugatuck
New Fairfield
Lake Lillinonah
Beacon Falls
Kettletown State Park
Newtown
© MOON.COM

BEST NEARBY BITES AND BREWS

When traveling in the Litchfield Hills, most hikers flock to the touristic centers of Kent and Litchfield for refreshment and entertainment. These idyllic New England towns, situated just 20 miles apart, offer myriad options for breweries and tasty eats. See some of our top recommendations below.

- **Kent Falls Brewing Company:** This "working farm" brewery offers tours of its farm in addition to pints, flights, and growlers to go in an inviting taproom (33 Camps Rd., Kent, 860/398-9645, http://kentfallsbrewing.com, 2pm-7pm Thurs.-Fri., noon-5pm Sat.).
- **Namoo Korean Barbeque:** Serving authentic Korean barbecue from a lengthy menu with lunch and dinner pricing, the casual, family-owned Namoo is a great choice for fueling up after a day outdoors (12 Kent Green Blvd., Kent, 860/927-1122, 11:30am-9:30pm Sun.-Thurs., 11:30am-10pm Fri.-Sat.).
- **Meraki Kitchen:** Tasty to-go and eat-in foods range from soups and sandwiches to a "salad case" curated from local ingredients (239 West St., Litchfield, 860/361-9777, http://merakifood.com, 7am-6pm Tues.-Fri., 7am-4pm Sat.).
- **The White Horse:** This classic pub offers great values on heaping plates of comfort pub food with gorgeous indoor and outdoor seating by the river (Route 202, Marbledale, 860/868-1496, http://whitehorsecountrypub.com, 11am-1am daily).
- **Brewery Legitimus:** This New Hartford microbrewery with a focus on Belgian and American ales hosts live music, food trucks, and other events year-round in its indoor/outdoor space (283 Main St., New Hartford, 860/238-7870, http://brewerylegitimus.com, 4pm-9pm Wed.-Thurs., 3pm-10pm Fri., noon-10pm Sat., noon-7pm Sun.).

▲ A FLIGHT OF LOCAL BEERS IN CONNECTICUT

1 Robert Ross and Agnes Bowman Trails

PEOPLE'S STATE FOREST, BARKHAMSTED

This beautiful hike through pristine forest and over bubbling brooks delivers big views from its overlooks with very little effort.

BEST: Brew hikes
DISTANCE: 6.4 miles round-trip
DURATION: 3.5 hours
ELEVATION CHANGE: 1,019 feet
EFFORT: Moderate
TRAIL: Dirt/rock singletrack
USERS: Hikers, leashed dogs
SEASON: May-November
PASSES/FEES: $15 for nonresidents on weekends and holidays. No charge for CT residents; no charge on weekdays.
MAPS: Friends of American Legion and People's State Forest, "American Legion and People's State Forest Trail Map."
CONTACT: Connecticut DEEP State Parks, 860/526-2336

START THE HIKE

▸ MILE 0-0.3: Mathias Grove Parking Area to Robert Ross Trail

From the Mathias Grove parking area and trailhead, follow signs toward the **Nature Museum,** an educational facility built by the Civilian Conservation Corps in 1935. Reach the museum at 0.2 mile and turn left (north) toward the **Agnes Bowen and Robert Ross Trail** signs, following the blue and orange-blue blazes. At 0.3 mile, bear left on the blue-blazed **Robert Ross Trail.**

▸ MILE 0.3-2.2: Robert Ross Trail to Jessie Gerard Trail

The route chugs steadily uphill through an eclectic mix of trees and shrubs. At 1.0 mile from the trailhead, the trail widens and arrives at the **King Road** intersection. Turn left (northwest) to stay on the Robert Ross Trail. The path rolls downhill until intersecting the **Agnes Bowen Trail** again at 1.5 mile. Turn right (north) and then bear left (west) to continue on the **Robert Ross Trail,** which winds through a clearing and over a creek where a glacial erratic boulder keeps sentinel. There are some views to the west as the trail climbs uphill and wraps around a series of ledges. At 1.9 miles, reach the intersection with the Jessie Gerard Trail. Stay right on Robert Ross to reach the bridge and the intersection with Falls Cutoff at 2.0 miles. Check out the falls to the left (west) before following the Robert Ross Trail straight through the intersection on a rocky uphill path. At 2.2 miles, reach Warner Road and take the blue-and-yellow-blazed Jessie Gerard Trail straight north.

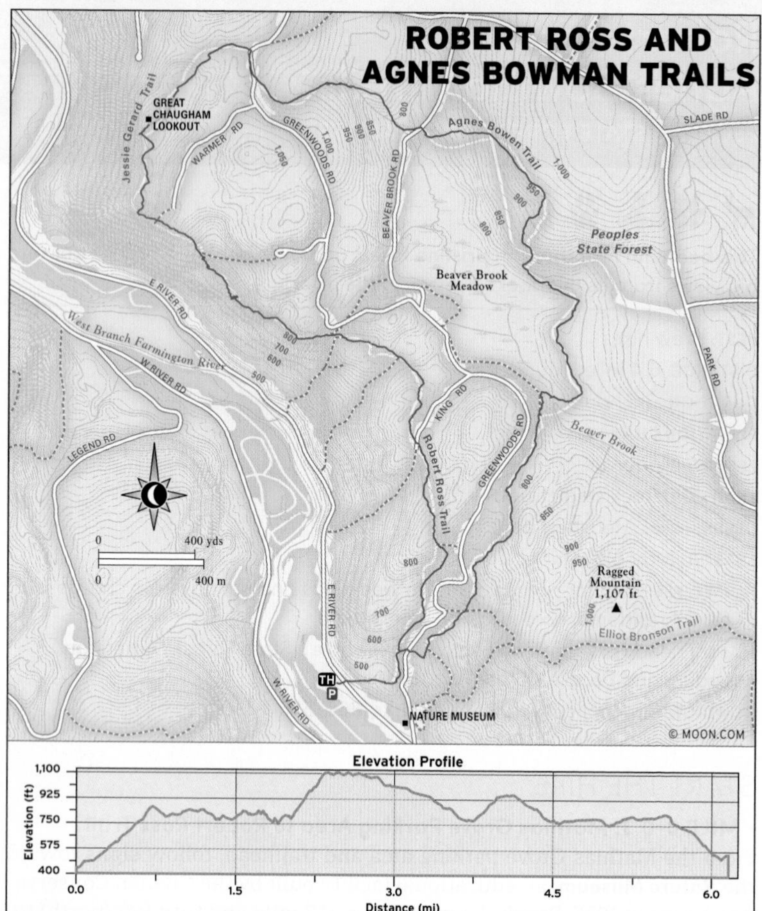

‣ MILE 2.2-2.7: Jessie Gerard Trail to Big Spring Area

At this steepest point in the hike, hundreds of stone steps lead uphill to the Great Chaugham Lookout. The vista offers excellent views of the Farmington River disappearing into a horizon of hills. At 2.4 miles from the trailhead, reach the second lookout, which faces northwest toward the river and Robertsville. As the trail navigates away from the lookouts and back into the woods, pass two more enormous erratics, known as the Veeder Boulders. From here, the path descends to an intersection at the Big Spring area at 2.7 miles.

‣ MILE 2.7-3.7: Big Spring Area to Beaver Brook Recreation Area

Take a right (east) at the Big Spring area intersection to stay on the Jessie Gerard Trail, then take a right (south) on Greenwoods Road. Follow the road through the group camping area, then turn onto the blue-and-yellow-blazed Charles Pack Trail on the left (east). At 2.8 miles, the trail crosses a wet area on a mossy patchwork of stones, crosses a gurgling creek, and descends on a soft pine needle trail. Reach Beaver Brook Road and turn left (north) over the bridge and into the Beaver Brook Recreation Area on your right (east).

▲ GREAT CHAUGHAM LOOKOUT

▸ MILE 3.7–4.8: Beaver Brook Recreation Area to Agnes Bowman Trail

At 3.7 miles, the trail continues past the picnic tables and crosses Pack Grove Road twice before descending through a stand of huge pines toward a bog. This section of the trail is great for spotting wildflowers in spring. At 4.8 miles in, cross another bridge over Beaver Brook and take a left (south) onto the red-and-blue-blazed Agnes Bowman Trail.

▸ MILE 4.8–6.4: Agnes Bowman Trail to Nature Museum

At 5.8 miles, pass a camping area, continue downhill with the stream on your right (west), and then cross a road before meeting the Robert Ross Trail again. Take a left (south) to arrive back at the Nature Museum. Turn right (west) to return to the parking lot, completing the 6.4-mile hike.

DIRECTIONS

From US-44, turn onto CT-318 in Barkhamsted. Cross the bridge and immediately turn left onto East River Road. The park entrance is on the left after 1 mile.

GPS COORDINATES: 41°55'32.0"N 72°59'57.8"W

2 Appalachian Trail: Housatonic River Walk

APPALACHIAN NATIONAL SCENIC TRAIL, KENT

This easygoing meander along the Housatonic River comprises a favorite flat section of the Appalachian Trail.

BEST: Winter hikes, brew hikes

DISTANCE: 7.6 miles round-trip

DURATION: 3.5 hours

ELEVATION CHANGE: 122 feet

EFFORT: Easy

TRAIL: Dirt singletrack

USERS: Hikers, leashed dogs

SEASON: Year-round

PASSES/FEES: None

MAPS: Appalachian Trail Conservancy, "Appalachian Trail," Massachusetts-Connecticut

CONTACT: Appalachian Trail Conservancy, 304/535-633, http://appalachiantrail.org

START THE HIKE

▸ MILE 0-1.3: Appalachian Trailhead to Stewart Hollow Brook Bridge

Hike north from the parking area, following the white blazes upstream on a wide, flat gravel path. The partially shaded trail follows a stone wall lined with a number of large maples, then crosses over North Kent Brook, a fairly wide stream. There is no bridge, so hikers may have to leap to make it over without getting wet. At 0.5 mile from the trailhead, the trail narrows and enters a stand of tall, skinny beech trees, which are particularly beautiful in fall when draped in yellow leaves. At 0.9 mile the trail returns to hug the west bank of the Housatonic River. Cross over the Stewart Hollow Brook on a **wooden bridge** at 1.3 miles, and pass the turnoffs to the **Stewart Hollow** campsite and group area.

▸ MILE 1.3-3.4: Stewart Hollow Brook Bridge to Housatonic Riverbank

The area includes a privy and a lean-to shelter that is a nice spot for a break. Continue to where the path diverts west away from the river and through a grassy open **field** with great views of the tree-covered Kent hillside rising up to the west, 2.9 miles in. At 3.4 miles, the path winds through bramble back to the water's edge. This unique ecosystem is a popular place to spot rare bird species.

▲ BRIDGE ON THE APPALACHIAN TRAIL

▸ MILE 3.4–7.6: Housatonic Riverbank to Gravel Road and Trailhead
When the trail reaches an intersection with a gravel road at 3.8 miles, turn around and backtrack to the trailhead to complete the 7.6-mile loop.

DIRECTIONS

From downtown Kent, take CT-341 west for about 0.2 mile, then turn right onto Skiff Mountain Road. At the fork in 1 mile, bear right onto River Road. The parking area and trailhead is at the end of the road in about 2.5 miles.

GPS COORDINATES: 41°46'06.5"N 73°26'06.8"W

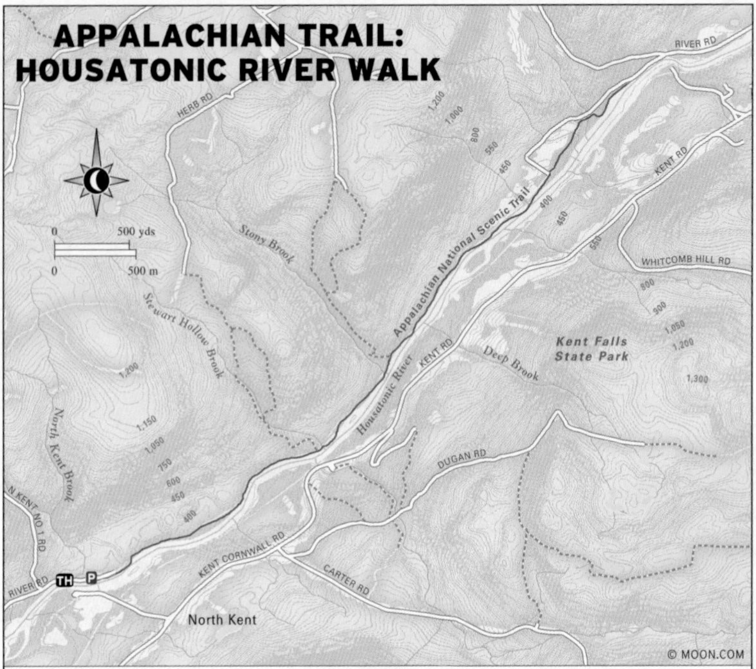

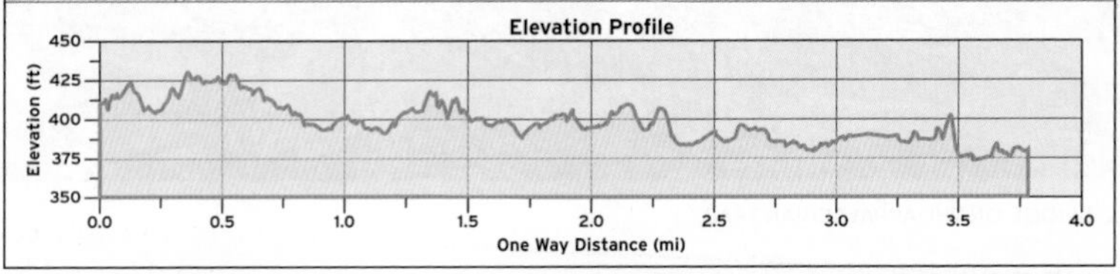

APPALACHIAN TRAIL: HOUSATONIC RIVER WALK

RIVER RD
HERB RD
KENT RD
WHITCOMB HILL RD
Stony Brook
Appalachian National Scenic Trail
Stewart Hollow Brook
Kent Falls State Park
Deep Brook
Housatonic River
North Kent Brook
DUGAN RD
N KENT NO 1 RD
KENT CORNWALL RD
CARTER RD
RIVER RD
TH
P
North Kent
0 500 yds
0 500 m
© MOON.COM

Elevation Profile

Elevation (ft)

One Way Distance (mi)

▲ HOUSATONIC RIVER

3 Pine Knob Loop

HOUSATONIC MEADOWS STATE PARK, SHARON

A quick hike along rolling cascades up to the Pine Knob lookouts results in lovely views of the Litchfield Hills.

DISTANCE: 2.5 miles round-trip

DURATION: 2 hours

ELEVATION CHANGE: 765 feet

EFFORT: Moderate

TRAIL: Dirt/rock singletrack

USERS: Hikers, leashed dogs

SEASON: May–November

PASSES/FEES: None

MAPS: Connecticut Forest and Park Association, "Blue Blazed Hiking Trail System/Connecticut Walk Book"

CONTACT: Connecticut Forest and Park Association, 860/346-8733, http://ctwoodlands.org

START THE HIKE

▸ MILE 0–0.4: Pine Knob Loop Parking Area to Housatonic Meadows State Park Campground

Follow the blue blazes west from the parking area, cross over **Hatch Brook** on foot, and then reach a stone wall where a sign marks the merger of the ends of the Pine Knob Loop in 400 feet. For this counterclockwise route, turn right (north) along the stone wall. The flat trail winds over several creeks, passing the spur to the **Housatonic Meadows State Park Campground** in 0.4 mile.

▸ MILE 0.4–1.0: Housatonic Meadows State Park Campground to First Vista

From the spur, the path climbs switchbacks to meet a small **waterfall** at 0.6 mile. Continue past the waterfall and climb a rocky ridgeline with some scrambling to reach the **first vista** at 1.0 mile. This east-facing lookout peers over nearby conifers for fantastic views of the Litchfield Hills and the Housatonic River valley on a clear day. Fog coming off the river below can add an enchanted quality to the forested vista on a cool morning.

▸ MILE 1.0–1.6: First Vista to Second Vista

Cross over the hilltop northwest of the vista, descend, and reach a sign marking the intersection with the Appalachian Trail (AT) at 1.1 mile. Turn left (west) onto the AT southbound to continue the Pine Knob Loop. The blazes become white and blue when the Pine Knob Trail and the AT merge. The trail traverses the flat saddle between Pine Knob's two peaks. Reach the narrow, **east-facing vista** atop the second peak at about 1.6 miles.

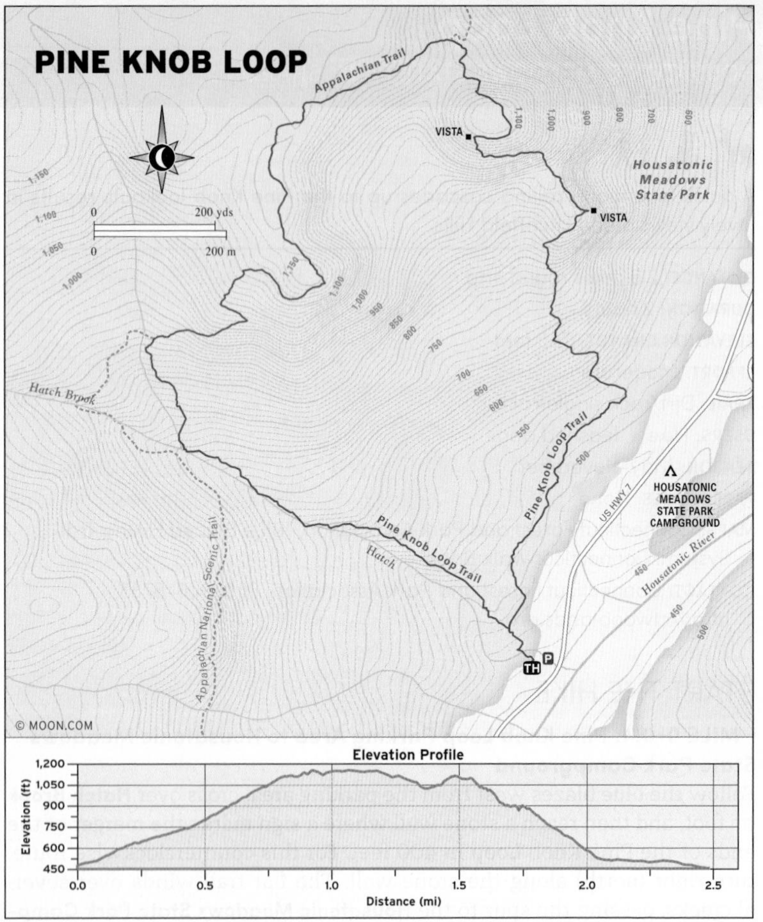

‣ MILE 1.6–2.5: Pine Knob Peaks to Hatch Brook

After taking in the vista, continue to 1.9 miles, where the Pine Knob Loop departs the Appalachian Trail at a marked intersection and the white-and-blue blazes end. Turn left (south) following only the blue blazes, which continue downstream along Hatch Brook. Hikers will pass large boulders and a series of cascades. Return to close the loop at 2.5 miles and turn right (south) to cross the brook and return to the parking area.

DIRECTIONS

The parking area for the Pine Knob Loop is marked with a blue sign on the west side of US-7, approximately 1 mile north of Cornwall Bridge.

GPS COORDINATES: 41°49'59.6"N 73°22'59.8"W

4 Appalachian Trail: Prospect Mountain and Rand's View

APPALACHIAN NATIONAL SCENIC TRAIL, FALLS VILLAGE

Wander over the summit of Mount Prospect to the sprawling fields of Rand's View, tucked underneath the peaks of the Berkshire hills.

BEST: Spring hikes, vistas
DISTANCE: 5.2 miles round-trip
DURATION: 2.5 hours
ELEVATION CHANGE: 979 feet
EFFORT: Moderate
TRAIL: Dirt/rock singletrack
USERS: Hikers, leashed dogs
SEASON: May-November
PASSES/FEES: None
MAPS: Appalachian Trail Conservancy, "Appalachian Trail," Massachusetts-Connecticut Map 3
CONTACT: Appalachian Trail Conservancy, 304/535-633, http://appalachiantrail.org

START THE HIKE

▸ MILE 0-0.2: Prospect Mountain Trailhead Parking Lot to Meadow

From the gated parking area at the falls, cross Housatonic River Road and hike west, following the white blazes uphill for 0.2 mile. The trail winds past a large boulder and enters a meadow, a great spot to glimpse deer and other wildlife feeding in the morning and evening.

▸ MILE 0.2-1.6: Meadow to Prospect Mountain Summit

Travel through an airy beech and maple forest for another 0.2 mile, then dip alongside a stream on the right (east) side of the trail. Cross the stream on foot heading straight (north) and follow the path over several rolling hills for 0.5 mile until the trail bends sharply left (northwest). Begin the 0.7-mile ascent to the rocky ridgeline of **Prospect Mountain.** The trail eases into a soft dirt track leading to the summit of Prospect at 1.6 miles. A narrow but pretty vista looks west toward the Housatonic River and a series of marshes bordered by green hills.

▸ MILE 1.6-2.6: Prospect Mountain Summit to Rand's View

The trail continues straight (west) along the summit. Cross a stone wall and then descend a hill to the signed intersection with the **Limestone Shelter** spur at 2.5 miles. Turn right (west) to stay on the **Appalachian Trail.** In 0.1 mile, the trail arrives at **Rand's View,** a grassy, wide-open clearing with wildflowers and fantastic views of the Berkshire Range.

▲ RAND'S VIEW

▸ MILE 2.6–5.2: Rand's View to Housatonic River Road
After enjoying the view, turn around and backtrack the same route across Prospect Mountain and down the ridgeline to Housatonic River Road.

DIRECTIONS

Take US-7 to the intersection with CT-126 in Falls Village and go west on CT-126. Pass through the center of town, turn left onto Water Street, and pass under a railroad bridge. Shortly after, cross an iron bridge and take the first right onto Housatonic River Road. There is a large gated gravel parking area at the falls in 0.4 mile.

GPS COORDINATES: 41°57'47.8"N 73°22'22.9"W

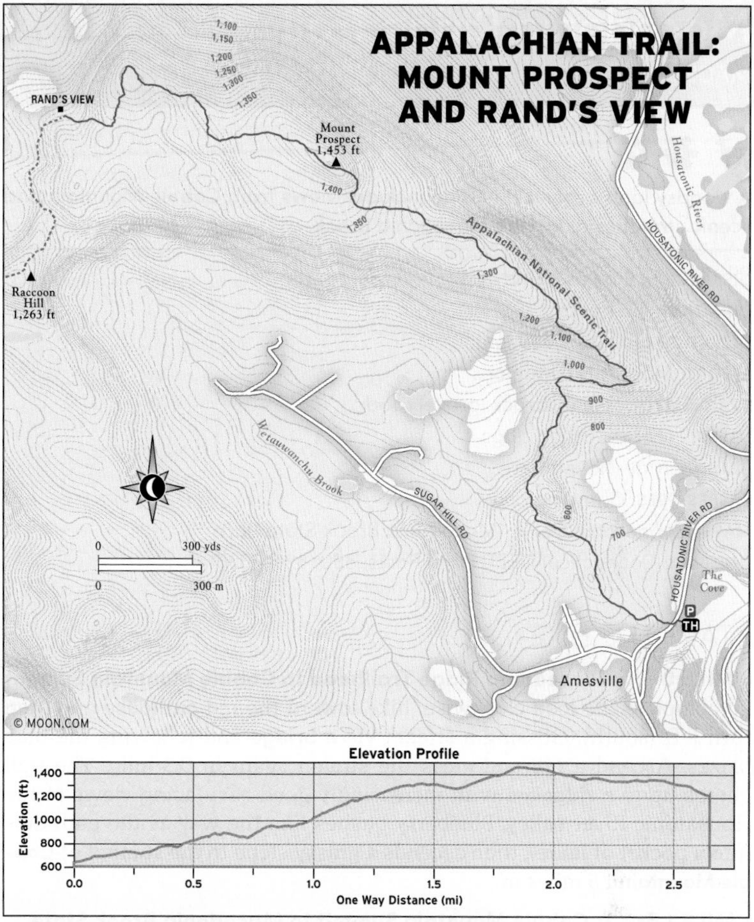

APPALACHIAN TRAIL: MOUNT PROSPECT AND RAND'S VIEW

RAND'S VIEW
Mount Prospect 1,453 ft
Raccoon Hill 1,263 ft
Appalachian National Scenic Trail
Housatonic River
HOUSATONIC RIVER RD
Wetauwanchu Brook
SUGAR HILL RD
The Cove
Amesville
P
TH
1,100
1,150
1,200
1,250
1,300
1,350
1,400
1,350
1,300
1,200
1,100
1,000
900
800
800
700
0 300 yds
0 300 m
© MOON.COM

Elevation Profile
Elevation (ft)
1,400
1,200
1,000
800
600
0.0
0.5
1.0
1.5
2.0
2.5
One Way Distance (mi)

▲ MUSHROOMS ON THE APPALACHIAN TRAIL

5 Macedonia Ridge Trail

MACEDONIA BROOK STATE PARK, KENT

A woodsy loop around a hillside includes views from Cobble Mountain and scenic stretches along the Macedonia Brook.

DISTANCE: 6.4 miles round-trip
DURATION: 3.5 hours
ELEVATION CHANGE: 1,429 feet
EFFORT: Moderate/strenuous
TRAIL: Dirt/rock singletrack, gravel road
USERS: Hikers, leashed dogs
SEASON: May-November
PASSES/FEES: Camping only
MAPS: Connecticut DEEP, "Macedonia Brook State Park"
CONTACT: Connecticut DEEP State Parks, 860/526-2336

START THE HIKE

▸ MILE 0-1.5: Macedonia Ridge Trailhead to Cobble Mountain Summit

To complete the loop clockwise, hike toward the red outhouse and then turn left (south), crossing a stream via a **bridge** and following the blue blazes. Ascend a hill and cross the stream again in 0.3 mile. The trail climbs up to a **ridgeline** with increasingly good east-facing views of the Housatonic River valley. Blueberry bushes line the way as the path dips into a pocket of laurel, then ascends a grassy slope to the summit of **Cobble Mountain** 1.5 miles in.

▸ MILE 1.5-2.7: Cobble Mountain Summit to Macedonia Brook State Park

Follow the blue-and-white blazes north across the summit. There are great vistas facing east over the Macedonia Brook valley and west into New York and the Taconic Range. From Cobble Mountain, the trail descends through ledges for 0.8 mile; hikers may need to use their hands to lower themselves. At the end of the descent, the trail meets a wide gravel road. Turn left (north) and follow the gravel road straight across the paved street and through the gate on the other side. The route travels along a rock wall and meets another gate at the wooden **Macedonia Brook State Park** sign at 2.7 miles.

▸ MILE 2.7-3.6: Macedonia Brook State Park to Macedonia Brook Bridge

Cross the street, and walk left (north) for about 100 feet to a trail sign. At the trail sign, turn right (east) into the woods. There are glimpses of **Hilltop Pond** to the left (east) as the trail winds up a hillside of hemlock for 0.3 mile. Cross through an opening in a stone wall and past a meadow and bog for another 0.3 mile. The trail bends alongside **Macedonia Brook** for 0.2 mile, then crosses over the brook and Keeler Road on a bridge at 3.6 miles.

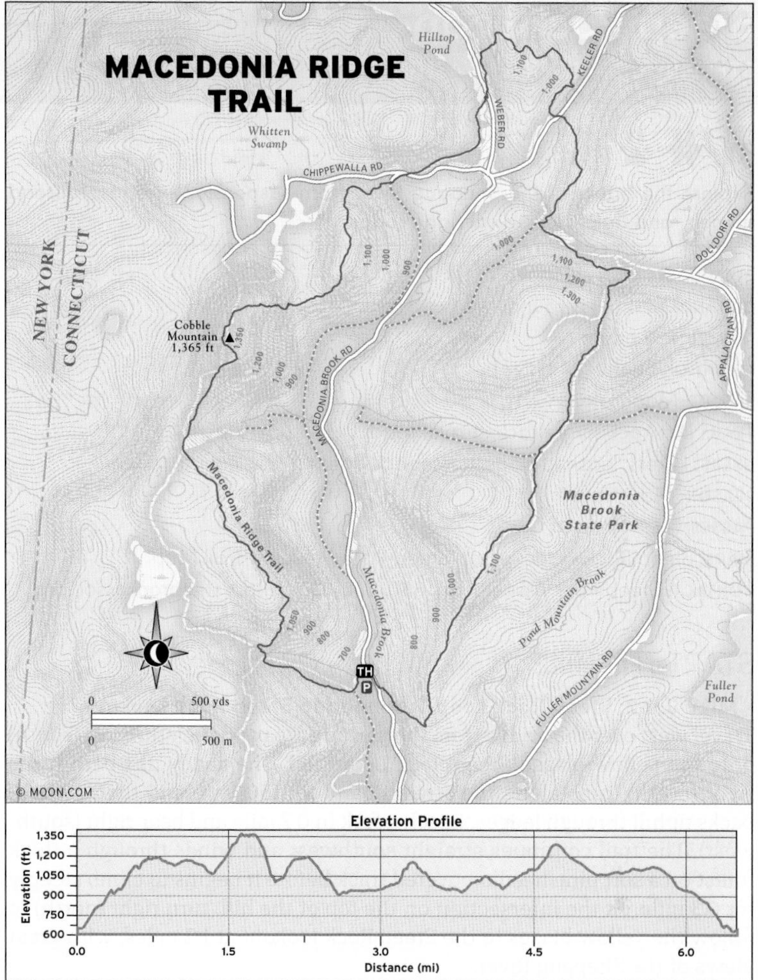

‣ MILE 3.6-6.4: Macedonia Brook Bridge to Macedonia Brook Road

At 4.2 miles, the trail crosses another narrow stream and then bends south. Travel through a rolling beech and maple forest lined with stone walls, and reach the intersection with the green-blazed trail at 4.9 miles. Keep straight (south) through the woods until the trail meets **Macedonia Brook Road** in 1.3 mile. Cross the road and turn right (northwest) to return to the parking area.

DIRECTIONS

From downtown Kent, take CT-341 west for 1.6 miles and then turn right onto Macedonia Brook Road. Follow the road into Macedonia Ridge State Park. The parking area is marked with a small blue-blazed post labeled "Trail" on the left side of the road in about 1.3 miles.

GPS COORDINATES: 41°45'39.4"N 73°29'37.8"W

6 Steep Rock Loop

STEEP ROCK PRESERVE, WASHINGTON

Explore the banks of the Shepaug River from suspension bridges, railroad tunnels, and flat, forested carriage roads.

BEST: Spots for a swim

DISTANCE: 4.4 miles round-trip (with optional detour)

DURATION: 2 hours

ELEVATION CHANGE: 482 feet

EFFORT: Moderate

TRAIL: Dirt/rock singletrack, gravel road

USERS: Hikers, leashed dogs, horseback riders, cross-country skiers

SEASON: May-November

PASSES/FEES: None

MAPS: Steep Rock Association, "Steep Rock Preserve Trail Map"

CONTACT: Steep Rock Association, 860/868-9131, http://steeprockassoc.org

START THE HIKE

▸ MILE 0-1.2: Steep Rock Loop Trailhead to Steep Rock Lookout

Travel west over the bridge from the parking area and then turn left (south) onto the yellow-blazed Steep Rock Loop trail. The shady dirt path turns right (north), runs along the stream bank for 150 feet, and then switchbacks uphill through ledges. Reach a fork in 0.7 mile and bear right (southwest). The trail continues straight southwest and winds through a thick forest on a soft pine needle-covered track before it begins to climb steeply for 0.3 mile. At the intersection on the top of the hill, turn right (north) to follow the yellow blazes to the Steep Rock lookout at 1.2 miles, with great views of the Shepaug River.

▸ MILE 1.2-2.2: Steep Rock Lookout to Suspension Bridge

After enjoying the view, backtrack 0.2 mile east to the intersection and continue straight (south). The trail descends a hill and then bends right (west), following both yellow and green blazes for 0.8 mile along a wide carriage road overlooking the river. Drop into a forest of massive pines and arrive at a suspension bridge over the river at 2.2 miles.

▸ MILE 2.2-4.4: Suspension Bridge to Tunnel Road

Cross the bridge and then turn right (west) to follow the yellow blazes 0.1 mile to a gravel road. (Optional: Follow the blue trail west for 0.3 mile to hike through the 235-foot-long rock railroad tunnel, a photogenic underpass originally constructed as part of the Shepaug Valley Railroad.) Continue east on the wide gravel Tunnel Road, following the yellow blazes upstream directly alongside the river. The road arrives back at the parking area in 1.8 miles.

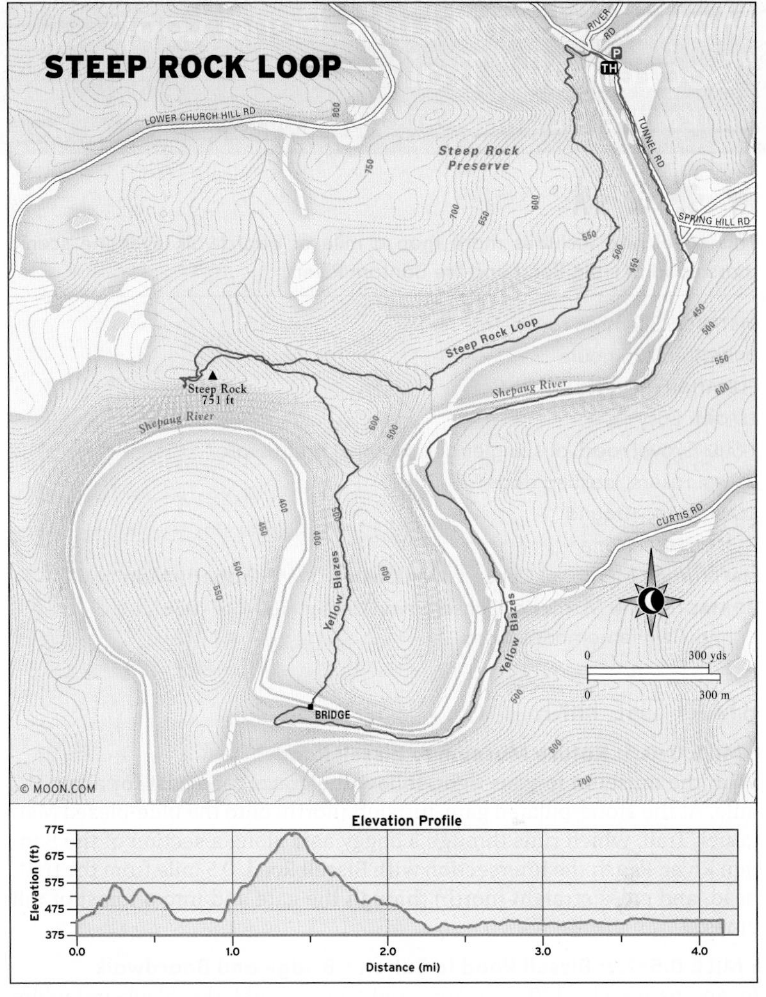

DIRECTIONS

Take CT-47 into Washington Depot and turn right onto River Road. In 1.4 miles, turn left onto Tunnel Road. The large gravel parking area is just after the bridge.

GPS COORDINATES: 41°37'17.5"N 73°19'30.6"W

7 Mattatuck and Little Pond Loop "Boardwalk" Trail

WHITE MEMORIAL CONSERVATION CENTER, LITCHFIELD

This novel hike includes more than a mile of boardwalk over the scenic marshland of Little Pond and the Bantam River.

DISTANCE: 3.2 miles round-trip

DURATION: 1.75 hours

ELEVATION CHANGE: 139 feet

EFFORT: Easy

TRAIL: Gravel road, dirt singletrack, wooden boardwalk

USERS: Hikers, leashed dogs

SEASON: Year-round

PASSES/FEES: None

MAPS: White Memorial Conservation Center, "WMF Property Map"

CONTACT: White Memorial Conservation Center, 860/567-0857, http://whitememorialcc.org

START THE HIKE

▸ MILE 0-0.5: Nature Museum to Bissell Road

With the museum to your right, follow the gravel road east for about 0.2 mile. At the stone-pillared gate, turn left (north) onto the blue-blazed Mattatuck Trail, which runs through a boggy area along a section of the Bantam River. Reach the intersection with Bissell Road, 0.5 mile from the trailhead, and cross straight (north) through the gate and into a forest of tall pines.

▸ MILE 0.5-2.2: Bissell Road to Sutton's Bridge and Boardwalk

In approximately 400 feet, turn right (east) onto the black-and-white blazed Little Pond Loop Trail. After crossing Whites Woods Road, the trail continues east down a grassy path. At the intersection at 1 mile, turn right (south) to complete the boardwalk circuit counterclockwise. The boardwalk winds over the Bantam River and around the surrounding marsh for 1.2 miles. Sutton's Bridge, a high wooden arch bridge at the beginning of the boardwalk, is a particularly scenic perch to look out over the river and the high cattails and colorful grasses that envelop the trail. Hikers with keen eyes may spot waterfowl, beavers, and a variety of wildflowers in the spring and early summer.

▸ MILE 2.2-3.2: Boardwalk to Little Pond Loop Trail

Continue counterclockwise around the boardwalk, which splits in 0.8 mile. Keep left to stay on the Little Pond Loop Trail, which ends at the intersection in 0.4 mile. Turn right (west) at the intersection to backtrack 1 mile to the museum and parking area.

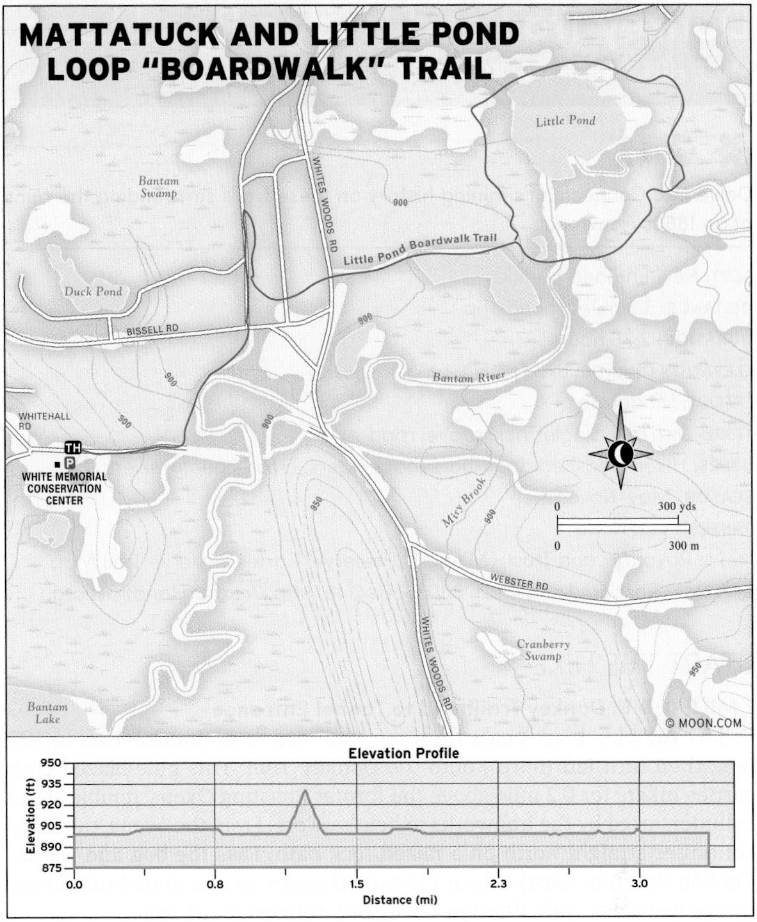

MATTATUCK AND LITTLE POND LOOP "BOARDWALK" TRAIL

Little Pond
Bantam Swamp
WHITES WOODS RD
Little Pond Boardwalk Trail
Duck Pond
BISSELL RD
Bantam River
WHITEHALL RD
TH
P
WHITE MEMORIAL CONSERVATION CENTER
Miry Brook
0 300 yds
0 300 m
WEBSTER RD
Cranberry Swamp
Bantam Lake
© MOON.COM

Elevation Profile
Elevation (ft): 950, 935, 920, 905, 890, 875
Distance (mi): 0.0, 0.8, 1.5, 2.3, 3.0

DIRECTIONS

From Litchfield Center, take US-202 west for 2 miles, then turn left onto Bissell Road. In 100 feet, turn right onto Whitehall Road. There is a large parking area and a trail sign at the visitors center and museum.

GPS COORDINATES: 41°43'27.3"N 73°12'46.5"W

▲ LITTLE POND LOOP "BOARDWALK" TRAIL

8 Donkey Trail and Hodge Road Loop

MINE HILL PRESERVE, ROXBURY

Delve into Connecticut's mining history on these trails surrounding the ruins of an 1860s ironworks.

BEST: New England oddities
DISTANCE: 3.3 miles round-trip
DURATION: 2.75 hours
ELEVATION CHANGE: 675 feet
EFFORT: Moderate
TRAIL: Dirt/rock singletrack, gravel road
USERS: Hikers, leashed dogs, horseback riders, cross-country skiers
SEASON: May-November
PASSES/FEES: None
MAPS: Roxbury Land Trust, "Mine Hill Preserve/Carter Preserve Trail Map"
CONTACT: Roxbury Land Trust, 860/350-4148, http://roxburylandtrust.org

START THE HIKE

▸ MILE 0-0.6: Donkey Trailhead to Tunnel Entrance

Follow the blue blazes east from the trailhead to an intersection in 390 feet, then turn left (north) onto the Donkey Trail. This blue-blazed path carries hikers for 0.2 mile above the former Roasting Ovens, double stone cylinders used by the ironworks to heat raw ore. From the ovens, the route continues straight north on a raised rock path. Pass the bog and Nature Trail on the right (east) side of the trail, then arrive at a grated tunnel entrance (you can't walk through it) on the left (west) at 0.6 mile.

▸ MILE 0.6-1.7: Tunnel Entrance to Hodge Road Trail

Follow the trail left (west) uphill past the tunnel for 0.1 mile to the grated "bat cages," which protect the entrances to several bat hibernacula. At 1.0 mile, reach a signed intersection where the Donkey Trail bends right (north) to wander through laurel and ledges. At the cliff and the small granite quarry bridge at 1.7 miles, turn right (west) onto the Hodge Road Trail.

▸ MILE 1.7-3.3: Hodge Road Trail to Donkey Trailhead and Parking Area

This wide path follows the stream downhill for 0.5 mile and delves into a spacious forest where the terrain flattens into a field. Reach a sign at the edge of the field and follow Hodge Road to the right (south). This gravel road parallels the Shepaug River for about 1 mile before reaching the enormous stone cold-blast furnace, brick chimney, and other remnants of the 19th-century ironworks. This is a good spot to stop, explore, and read the interpretive signs before heading southwest on the trail 0.3 mile back to the parking area.

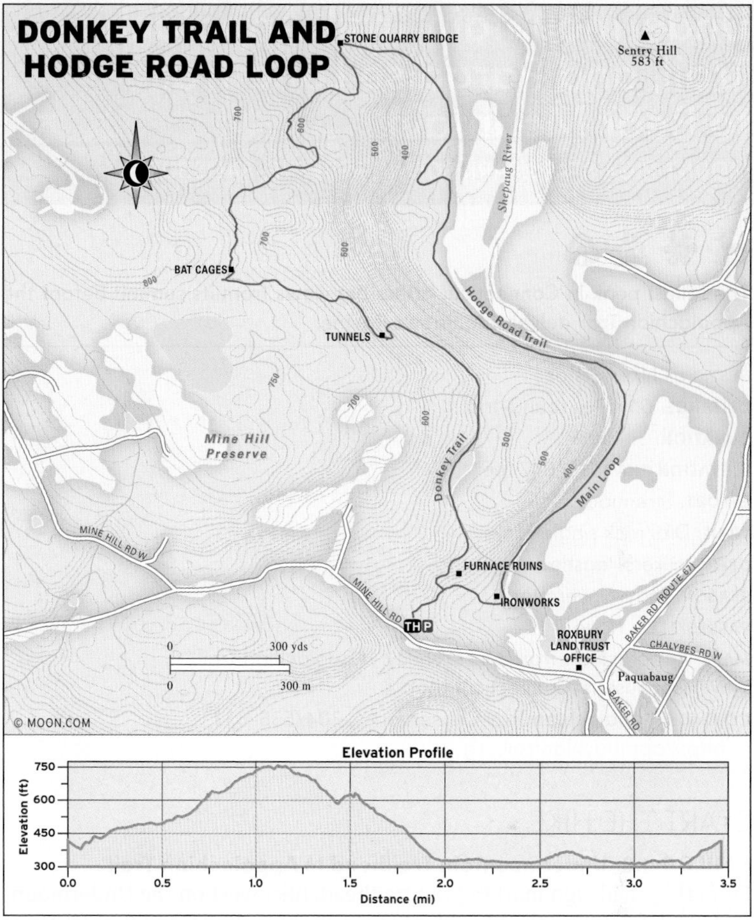

DONKEY TRAIL AND HODGE ROAD LOOP

STONE QUARRY BRIDGE
Sentry Hill
583 ft
Shepaug River
BAT CAGES
TUNNELS
Hodge Road Trail
Mine Hill
Preserve
Donkey Trail
Main Loop
MINE HILL RD W
FURNACE RUINS
IRONWORKS
MINE HILL RD
TH P
ROXBURY
LAND TRUST
OFFICE
BAKER RD (ROUTE 67)
CHALYBES RD W
Paquabaug
BAKER RD
0 300 yds
0 300 m

Elevation Profile
Elevation (ft): 300, 450, 600, 750
Distance (mi): 0.0, 0.5, 1.0, 1.5, 2.0, 2.5, 3.0, 3.5

DIRECTIONS

Take CT-67 west from Roxbury for 2.3 miles, then turn right onto Mine Hill Road. The parking area is marked with a large sign on the right-hand side.

GPS COORDINATES: 41°33'35.1"N 73°20'17.9"W

▲ DONKEY TRAIL

9 Undermountain Trail, Appalachian Trail, and Paradise Lane Trail to Bear Mountain

MOUNT RIGA STATE PARK SCENIC RESERVE, SALISBURY

The tallest peak in Connecticut offers big views from its summit before the Appalachian Trail delves into Sage's Ravine.

BEST: Fall hikes, vistas

DISTANCE: 6.1 miles round-trip

DURATION: 3 hours

ELEVATION CHANGE: 1,547 feet

EFFORT: Strenuous

TRAIL: Dirt/rock singletrack

USERS: Hikers, leashed dogs

SEASON: May-November

PASSES/FEES: None

MAPS: Appalachian Trail Conservancy, "Appalachian Trail," Massachusetts-Connecticut Map 4

CONTACT: Appalachian Trail Conservancy, 304/535-633, http://appalachiantrail.org

START THE HIKE

▸ MILE 0-1.9: Undermountain Trailhead to Appalachian Trail

From the small sign marking the trailhead, hike west on the Undermountain Trail, following the blue blazes up a slight incline through thickets of laurel. Around 0.6 mile in, the path gets steeper, winding up the hillside to meet a ravine. At the signed intersection with the Paradise Lane Trail at 1.2 miles, bear left (west) toward the Appalachian Trail (AT)/Bear Mountain, then bear left again at the next sign in 200 feet. The trail winds over several bog bridges and up a set of timber steps to reach a large sign at the Riga Junction at 1.9 miles. Turn right (north) onto the Appalachian Trail northbound toward Bear Mountain.

▸ MILE 1.9-2.6: Appalachian Trail to Bear Mountain Summit

Follow the white-blazed trail to a fork at 2.0 miles, and bear right (northeast). From here, a set of stone steps begins an ascent to the bare, rocky peak. Vistas improve the higher hikers climb, but the crown jewel is the rock tower atop the summit at 2.6 miles. The best views stretch northwest toward Mount Everett and Mount Race in Massachusetts and northeast toward the "twin lakes" of Salisbury.

▸ MILE 2.6-3.1: Bear Mountain Summit to Paradise Lane Trail

Continue north on the AT, descending a steep, rocky slope. Use caution through this section, especially during wet weather. The trail flattens in 0.5 mile and briefly enters Massachusetts, where hikers will reach a large

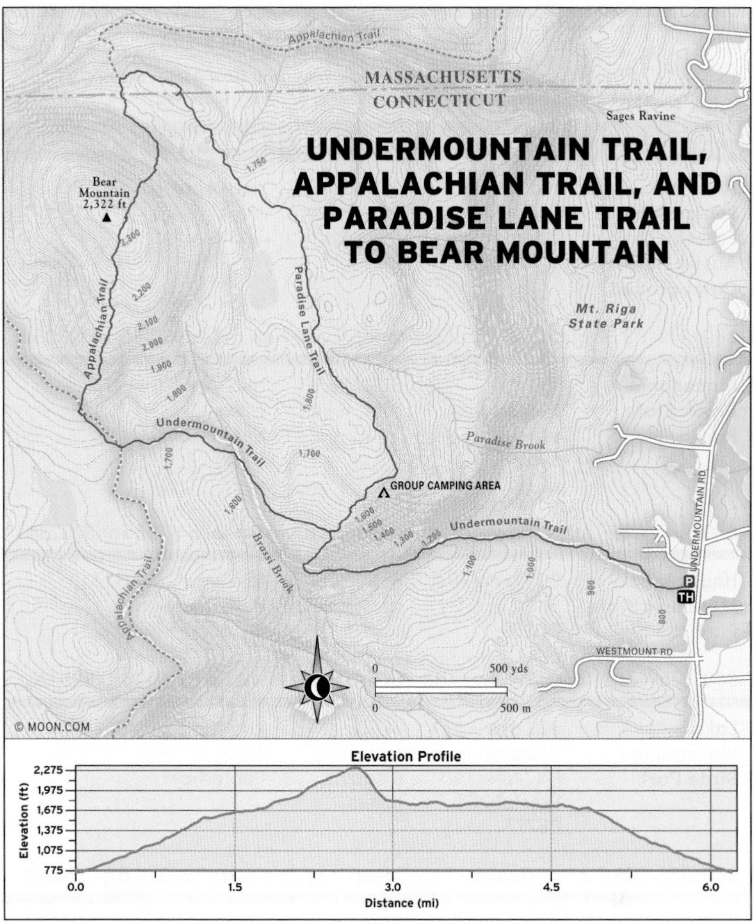

sign for Sage's Ravine at 3.1 miles. Turn right (east) onto the blue-blazed Paradise Lane Trail, which continues uphill through a hemlock forest. Through the trees, there are great views of Bear Mountain overlooking the bog to the right (west) of the trail.

MILE 3.1-6.1: Paradise Lane Trail to Undermountain Trailhead

At 4.6 miles in, pass the group camping area (a privy is available here). Continue for 0.3 mile to return to an intersection with the Undermountain Trail. Turn left (south) to follow the Undermountain Trail 1.2 miles back to the parking lot.

DIRECTIONS

Take CT-41 north from the center of Salisbury. In 3.3 miles, a small blue sign for the Undermountain Trail marks the small free parking area on the left side.

GPS COORDINATES: 42°01'43.6"N 73°25'43.4"W

NEARBY CAMPGROUNDS

The Housatonic River Walk, Rand's View, and Bear Mountain hikes have primitive campsites on or near the routes.

NAME	LOCATION	FACILITIES	SEASON	FEE
American Legion State Forest, Austin Hawes Campground	198 W River Rd., Barkhamsted, CT 06063	30 RV/ tent sites, 6 cabins; toilets	mid-April-early September	$27-60
860/379-0922, https://www.ct.gov/deep/cwp/view.asp?a=2716&q=325054				
Macedonia Brook State Park	159 Macedonia Brook Rd., Kent, CT 06757	51 RV/tent sites; toilets	mid-April-early September	$24
860/927-4100, https://www.ct.gov/deep/cwp/view.asp?a=2716&q=325234				
Housatonic Meadows State Park	90 Route 7, Sharon, CT 06069	61 RV/tent sites; toilets	late May-early October	$27
860/672-6772, https://www.ct.gov/deep/cwp/view.asp?a=2716&q=325220				
Lake Waramaug State Park	30 Lake Waramaug Rd., New Preston, CT 06777	76 RV/ tent sites, 6 cabins; toilets	late May-early September	$27-60
860/868-0220, https://www.ct.gov/deep/cwp/view.asp?a=2716&q=325232				
White Memorial Family Campground	N Shore Rd., Bantam, CT 06750	65 RV/tent sites; toilets	early May-mid-October	$9.50 wooded sites, $14.50 waterfront, $19.50 RV
860/567-0857, http://www.whitememorialcc.org/family-camping				
Steep Rock Preserve	2 Tunnel Rd., Washington Depot, CT 06794	3 tent sites; toilets	mid-April-mid-November	$35
860/868-9131, http://www.steeprockassoc.org/explore/camping/				

METACOMET RIDGE

The Metacomet Range is the fault block ridge that winds its way up from Long Island Sound, through central Connecticut, and well into central Massachusetts alongside the Connecticut River. The steep and narrow ridge is home to miles of hiking trails that creep along traprock cliff faces and descend through bubbling stream corridors and vividly hued swamps. As the only high ground within miles of farmland and the sprawling metropolitan area of Hartford, the ridge is a popular destination for outdoor recreation. Its trails include the southern section of the 114-mile Metacomet-Monadnock Trail, as well as several local and state parks that are the pride and joy of Connecticut.

▲ the pet-friendly Blue Trail

▲ Bradley Hubbard Reservoir from Chauncey Peak

1 **Preserve and Metacomet Trails to Ragged Mountain**
DISTANCE: 5.3 miles round-trip
DURATION: 2 hours
EFFORT: Easy

2 **Mattabesett Trail to Mount Lamentation and Chauncey Peak**
DISTANCE: 3.8 miles round-trip
DURATION: 2 hours
EFFORT: Moderate

3 **Vista Trail, Devil's Hopyard State Park**
DISTANCE: 2.4 miles round-trip
DURATION: 1.5 hours
EFFORT: Easy

4 **Blue and Violet Trails**
DISTANCE: 4.6 miles round-trip
DURATION: 3 hours
EFFORT: Strenuous

5 **Talcott Mountain Trail to Heublein Tower**
DISTANCE: 2.4 miles round-trip
DURATION: 1 hour
EFFORT: Easy/moderate

6 **Blue Trail to Wolf Den and Indian Chair**
DISTANCE: 4.4 miles round-trip
DURATION: 2.5 hours
EFFORT: Easy/moderate

▲ COVERED BRIDGE IN DEVIL'S HOPYARD STATE PARK

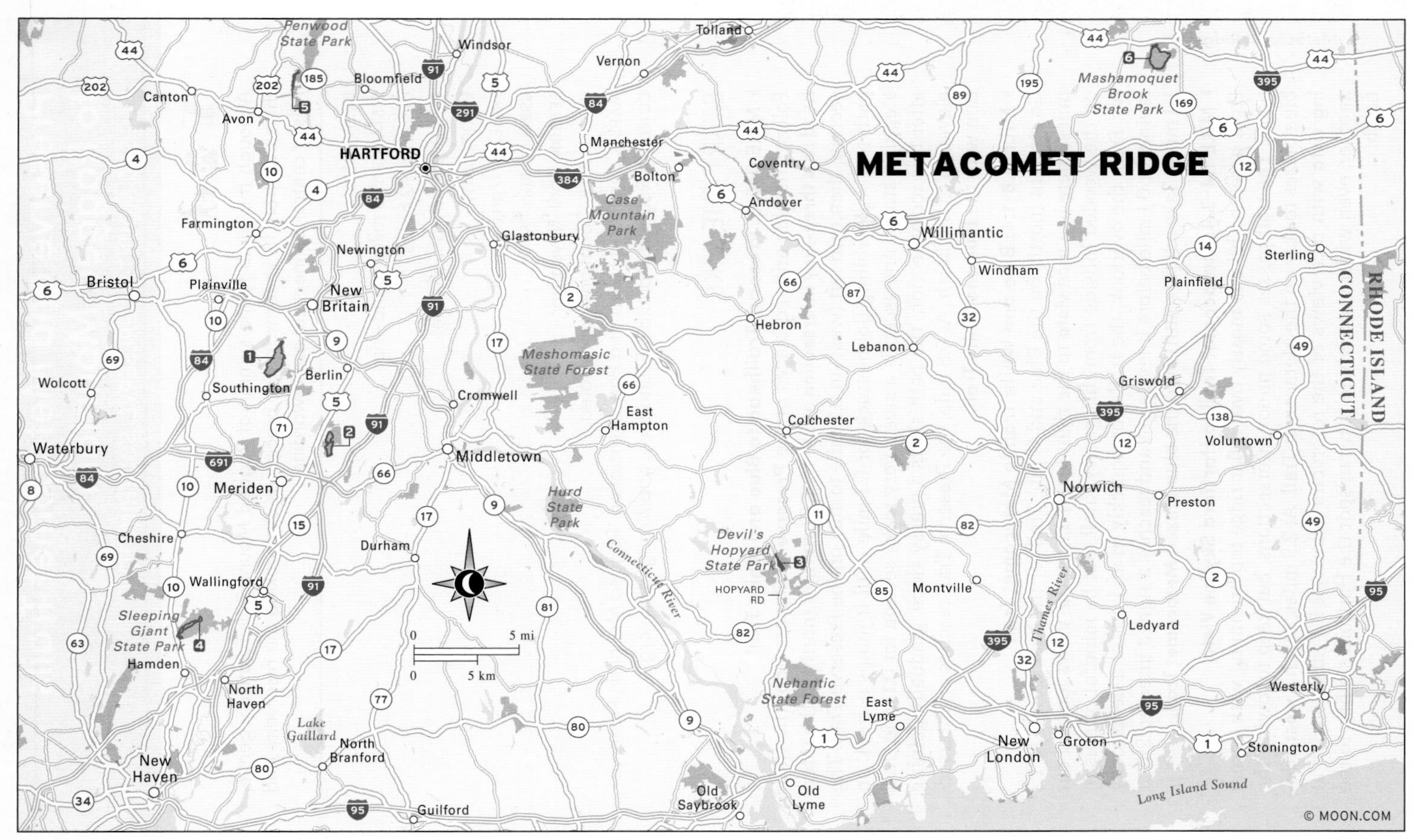
METACOMET RIDGE
HARTFORD
Penwood State Park
Windsor
Bloomfield
Canton
Avon
Vernon
Tolland
Manchester
Bolton
Coventry
Andover
Case Mountain Park
Glastonbury
Farmington
Newington
Bristol
Plainville
New Britain
Willimantic
Windham
Mashamoquet Brook State Park
Sterling
Plainfield
Hebron
Lebanon
Meshomasic State Forest
Wolcott
Southington
Berlin
Cromwell
East Hampton
Colchester
Griswold
Voluntown
Waterbury
Middletown
Meriden
Hurd State Park
Connecticut River
Cheshire
Durham
Devil's Hopyard State Park
HOPYARD RD
Norwich
Preston
Wallingford
Montville
Thames River
Ledyard
Sleeping Giant State Park
Hamden
North Haven
Nehantic State Forest
East Lyme
Westerly
Lake Gaillard
North Branford
New Haven
Guilford
Old Saybrook
Old Lyme
New London
Groton
Stonington
Long Island Sound
CONNECTICUT
RHODE ISLAND
0 5 mi
0 5 km
© MOON.COM

1 Preserve and Metacomet Trails to Ragged Mountain

RAGGED MOUNTAIN PRESERVE, SOUTHINGTON

Although the climb to the summit of Ragged Mountain is relatively gentle, the views from its sheer traprock precipices overlooking the reservoirs and hills of central Connecticut are rewarding.

BEST: Vistas
DISTANCE: 5.3 miles round-trip
DURATION: 2 hours
ELEVATION CHANGE: 637 feet
EFFORT: Easy
TRAIL: Dirt/gravel path
USERS: Hikers
SEASON: April-November
PASSES/FEES: Donations appreciated
MAPS: Connecticut Forest and Park Association "Ragged Mountain Preserve"
CONTACT: Ragged Mountain Foundation, http://raggedmtn.org

START THE HIKE

▸ MILE 0-0.8: Preserve Trailhead to Blue and White Trail

Follow the blue and red blazes of the **Preserve Trail** west from the trailhead to **a three-way intersection** at 215 feet. Turn right (north) at the intersection, then turn left (west) in 0.2 mile to stay on the Preserve Trail. The path is a wide, rolling doubletrack for 0.1 mile until it jumps a creek on stepping-stones and ascends a steep, very rocky section for 0.1 mile. Just after this rocky section, the path skirts a grassy slope, gradually gaining elevation to the north. At 0.8 mile, the Preserve Trail reaches an intersection with the **Blue and White Trail.**

▸ MILE 0.8-1.4: Blue and White Trail to Metacomet Trail

Go straight (north) on the Blue and White Trail for the best views. At 1.2 miles, there is a nice **vista** to the right (east). Enjoy the views looking out on the wooded hillside from this grassy knoll, but be mindful of poison ivy. From the overlook, the trail drops quickly in and out of a deep rocky ravine for 0.1 mile before it levels out and reaches a signed intersection at 1.4 miles. Take a left (south) onto the blue-blazed **Metacomet Trail.**

▸ MILE 1.4-3.4: Metacomet Trail to Hartford Skyline Vista

From here, the hike is mostly over a flat ridge top brimming with vernal pools. The trail passes some minor intersections, but keep following the blue blazes to stay on the Metacomet Trail. At 2.9 miles, reach a **west-facing vista** with nice views of the reservoirs below. At 3.4 miles, arrive at another, even wider **vista** where you can spot the Hartford skyline to the north.

▲ VIEW FROM RAGGED MOUNTAIN

▸ **MILE 3.4–3.8: Hartford Skyline Vista to Ragged Mountain Summit**
From here, the trail snakes back into the woods, descends a ledge, and rolls over some rooty ups and downs. Arrive at the **summit** at 3.8 miles, with views facing primarily south toward Short Mountain.

▸ **MILE 3.8–5.3: Ragged Mountain Summit to Preserve Trailhead**
Descend via the **Red and Blue Trail,** which serves up views of the Hart Ponds to the east from various lookouts along the way. The traprock trail is rugged as it passes this vista, but it smooths out about 1 mile from the summit. From here, the trail widens and continues north 0.5 mile to the trailhead.

DIRECTIONS

From New Britain, turn left (south) onto Kensington Avenue, which becomes High Road. In 1.8 miles, turn right onto West Lane. The roadside parking area is marked with a sign on the right in about 0.8 mile.

GPS COORDINATES: 41°37'41.8"N 72°48'13.6"W

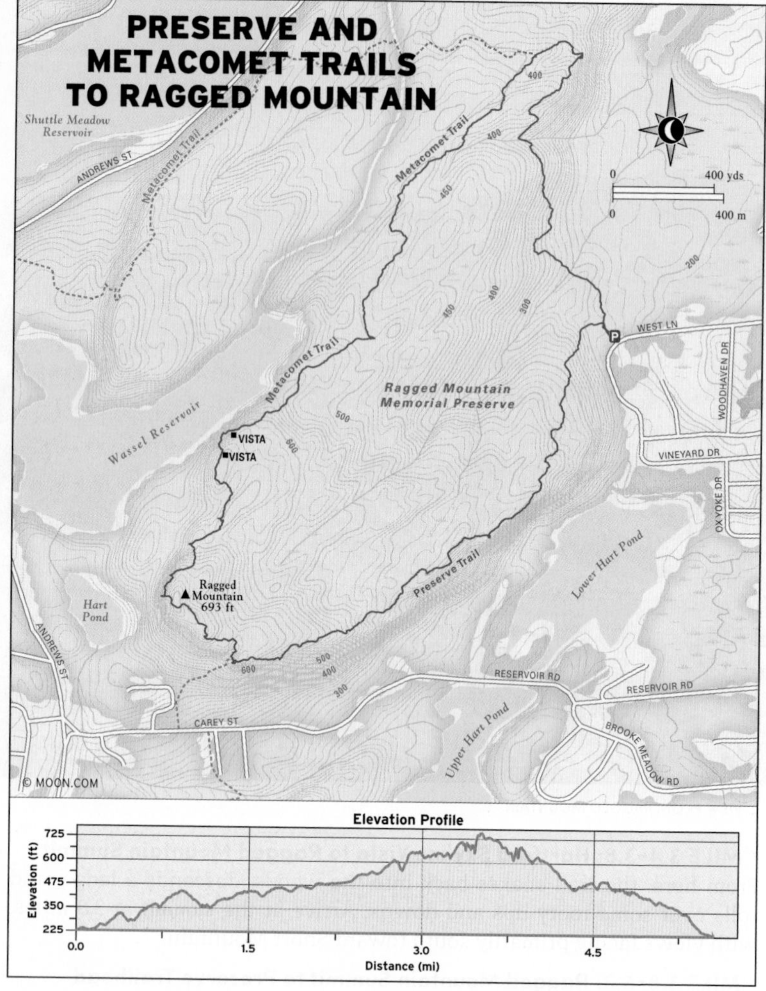

BEST NEARBY BITES

A sushi lover's dream, **Sweet Mango** (692 West St., Southington, 860/276-5888, http://sweet-mango.com, 11am-10pm Mon.-Sat., noon-10pm Sun.) also serves Japanese and Thai entrees and hibachi in a festive setting with a full bar. It's 8 miles from the trailhead.

2 Mattabesett Trail to Lamentation Mountain and Chauncey Peak

GIUFFRIDA PARK, MERIDEN

This little gem of a park right outside the city of Meriden includes a quick climb to the ledges of Lamentation Mountain and Chauncey Peak, with placid views over Crescent Lake.

DISTANCE: 3.8 miles round-trip
DURATION: 2 hours
ELEVATION CHANGE: 598 feet
EFFORT: Moderate
TRAIL: Dirt/rock singletrack, gravel road
USERS: Hikers, leashed dogs
SEASON: April-November
PASSES/FEES: None
MAPS: Meriden Land Trust, "Giuffrida Park"
CONTACT: Meriden Land Trust, 203/630-4259, http://meridenlandtrust.com

START THE HIKE

▸ MILE 0-1.2: Mattabesett Trailhead to Mount Lamentation Summit

Hike north from the parking lot, following the blue-blazed Mattabesett Trail along the wide, pine needle-lined shores of Crescent Lake to your right (east). In 0.3 mile, the Mattabesett Trail turns left (west) away from the water, crosses a paved street, and then turns right (north) onto a gravel access road in 160 feet. Follow the gravel road north along the power lines for about 100 feet, then continue right (north) on the Mattabesett Trail where it retreats into the woods. There is a quick, taxing uphill hike for 0.1 mile to a lower ridge with intermittent views of Chauncey Peak through the trees. In 0.1 mile, reach an intersection and continue straight (north) following the blue blazes. Reach another intersection in 0.4 mile and turn left (west), following the blue blazes again. In 0.3 mile, the trail climbs to the summit of Mount Lamentation.

▸ MILE 1.2-2.9: Mount Lamentation Summit to Chauncey Peak

There are several west-facing vistas along this narrow, grassy, cliff-top path, from which you can spot the Hartford skyline as well as soaring turkey vultures. At the intersection with the yellow-blazed trail at 1.8 miles, turn right (west) to follow the yellow-blazed trail, which descends from the summit on a rocky path. At the intersection at 2.5 miles, turn left (north) onto the red-blazed trail, which descends east toward Crescent Lake. In 0.2 mile, it rejoins with the blue-blazed Mattabesett Trail. Turn right (south) to follow the blue blazes on the wide crushed-stone path along the deep water-filled ravine to your left (east). Cross left (east) over the ravine on the small wooden bridge in 210 feet. The blue-blazed

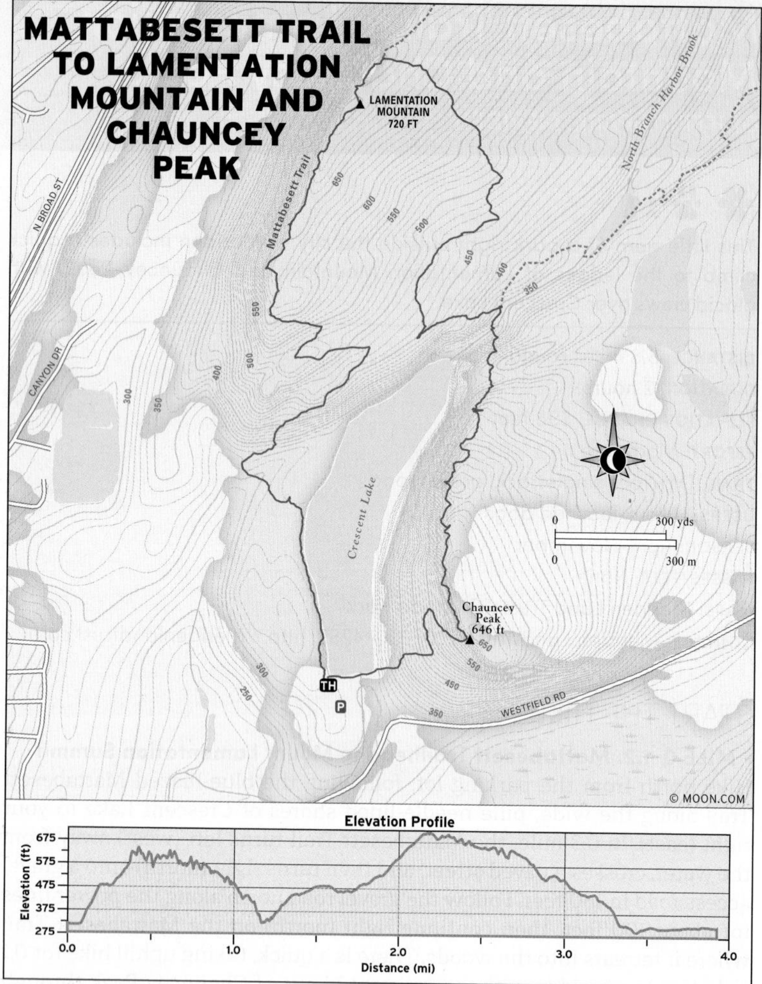

trail then ascends the north side of Chauncey Peak with some steep but short climbs. At 2.9 miles, reach the first of many vistas along the summit of Chauncey Peak.

‣ MILE 2.9–3.8: Chauncey Peak to Mattabessett Trailhead

These sheer traprock cliffs offer great views of Crescent Lake and Mount Lamentation, and their west-facing orientation makes them great for watching a sunset. Continue straight (south) along the ridge. At the signed intersection at 3.4 miles, turn right (west) to descend the south side of the peak on the Mattabessett Trail. This 0.4-mile return to the parking lot is a combination of steep staircases and loose traprock, so descend with care!

▲ VIEW FROM CHAUNCEY PEAK

DIRECTIONS

From Meriden, take I-691 E and then take exit 8 for US-5. Turn right onto US-5 N, then turn right onto Westfield Road in 0.5 mile. At the intersection in 1 mile, turn left to stay on Westfield Road. A large sign on the left marks the entrance to the park in 0.4 mile.

GPS COORDINATES: 41°33'22.8"N 72°45'50.5"W

BEST NEARBY BITES

The Little Rendezvous (256 Pratt St., Meriden, 203/235-0110, http://thelittlevous.com, 1pm-10pm Wed.-Thurs., 11am-10pm Fri.-Sat., 1pm-9pm Sun.), a cash-only pizza joint, attracts big crowds on weekends for its straightforward but delectable coal-fired brick oven pies. It's 2 miles from the trailhead.

3 Vista Trail

DEVIL'S HOPYARD STATE PARK, EAST HADDAM

Start your hike with an enormous cascade and wander along the banks of the Eight Mile River out to an impressive vista.

BEST: Spring hikes
DISTANCE: 2.4 miles round-trip
DURATION: 1.5 hours
ELEVATION CHANGE: 506 feet
EFFORT: Easy
TRAIL: Dirt path
USERS: Hikers, leashed dogs
SEASON: Year-round
PASSES/FEES: None
MAPS: Connecticut DEEP "Devil's Hopyard State Park"
CONTACT: Connecticut DEEP State Parks, 860/526-2336

START THE HIKE:

▸ MILE 0-0.2: Vista Trail Parking Area to Picnic Area and Covered Bridge

From the parking area, cross Foxtown Road and head straight south toward **Chapman Falls.** The best viewing area for the majestic falls is about 425 feet down the unblazed trail on the left (east). Use caution along the river at the end of the trail, as the rocks can be slick. Backtrack from the viewing area to the main trail, which continues 0.2 mile south into the picnic area, where you'll find a covered bridge over the river.

▸ MILE 0.2-0.6: Picnic Area and Covered Bridge to Devil's Oven

Cross left (east) over the **covered bridge** and continue straight east on the wide, flat dirt path through low-hanging vegetation. In 0.2 mile, the trail enters a clearing where the sights and sounds of the **Eight Mile River** pour through huge pine trees. The orange-blazed Vista Trail branches out to both the southeast and southwest. Bear right (southwest) to stay on the west end of the Vista Trail, keeping the river to your right (west). At 0.6 mile, reach an intersection with the side trail for **Devil's Oven.**

(Optional: Turn left [east] for a taxing 400-foot climb up to some interesting rock formations, including the Devil's Oven, a stove-shaped hole in the cliff. Backtrack to the intersection on the same path).

▸ MILE 0.6-1.0: Devil's Oven to Vista Lookout Point

From the Devil's Oven intersection, the orange-blazed Vista Trail continues straight (south), and then bends left (east) away from the river. After a couple of wildflower-dotted stream crossings on log bridges, the path begins to gain elevation. At 0.9 mile, arrive at a hilltop clearing where hikers have built a vast collection of cairns. Continue straight (south) for 0.1 mile

▲ DEVIL'S OVEN VISTA

to the vista, which looks south into the river valley and takes in the surrounding hills.

▸ MILE 1.0–1.6: Vista Lookout Point to Vista Trail Intersection

After enjoying the view, backtrack 0.1 mile to the cairns. Here, turn right (east) onto the east end of the Vista Trail to continue the loop. Follow the orange blazes east, then north, on the fern-lined trail as it crosses back over the bubbling streams flowing toward the river. There are some nice ridge views looking over the river along the way. At the intersection at 1.6 miles, turn left (west) to stay on the east end of the Vista Trail.

▸ MILE 1.6–2.4: Vista Trail Intersection to Chapman Falls and Vista Trailhead

The path descends another 0.3 mile before it reaches the intersection where the east and west ends of the Vista Trail meet. Continue straight north to backtrack the final 0.4 mile to Chapman Falls and the parking area.

DIRECTIONS

From CT-82, turn onto CT-434 and continue north for 3.5 miles. Then, turn right onto Foxtown Road. A large parking/picnic area marked with a sign for Chapman Falls is on the left in 135 feet.

GPS COORDINATES: 41°29'03.6"N 72°20'31.3"W

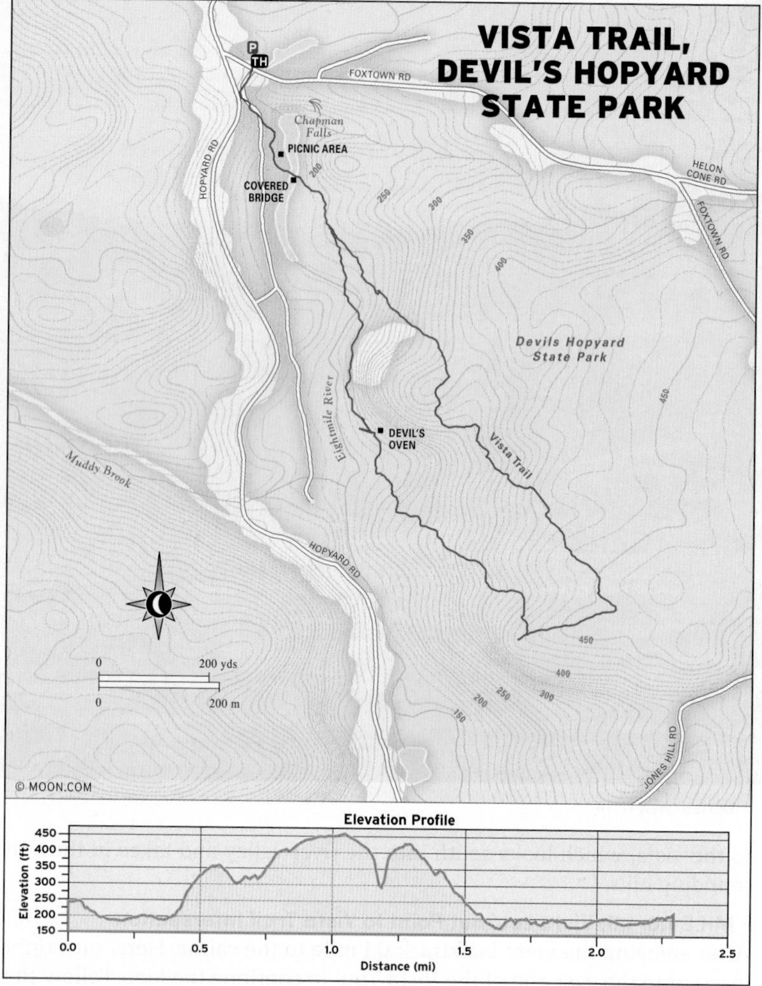

BEST NEARBY BITES

Stop in for coffee, breakfast, lunch, or ice cream at **Two Wrasslin' Cats** (374 Town St., 860/891-8466, 7am-5pm daily), 7 miles from the trailhead in East Haddam. The staff at this quirky cat-themed café will treat you like family.

4 Blue and Violet Trails

SLEEPING GIANT STATE PARK, HAMDEN

Climb across a long ridgeline resembling a giant in repose and enjoy stunning views from its summit tower and traprock cliffs.

BEST: Fall hikes
DISTANCE: 4.6 miles round-trip
DURATION: 3 hours
ELEVATION CHANGE: 1,215 feet
EFFORT: Strenuous
TRAIL: Dirt/rock singletrack
USERS: Hikers, leashed dogs
SEASON: April–November
PASSES/FEES: $15 for nonresidents ($7 after 4 pm) on weekends and holidays only.
MAPS: Connecticut DEEP "Sleeping Giant State Park"
CONTACT: Connecticut DEEP State Parks, 860/526-2336

START THE HIKE

▸ MILE 0–0.1: Blue Trailhead to Mill River Intersection and Bridge

Follow the paved road northwest from the parking area to the north end of the **picnic area** loop. From the top of the picnic area loop, follow the blue blazes downhill west for 0.1 mile to the intersection at the Mill River.

▸ MILE 0.1–0.6: Mill River Intersection and Bridge to Quinnipiac and New Haven Vista

Turn right (north) over the small wooden bridge and continue straight (north) on the **blue trail.** Ascend the hill and reach the first of many vistas in 0.2 mile. Descend, merging with the red trail for about 100 feet, then turn right (east) up the hill, continuing to follow the blue blazes. The way becomes incredibly steep—almost sheer at times—and hikers may need to use their hands to scramble up for 0.3 mile. At the top of the scramble, there are great vistas looking back to the south and west, taking in Quinnipiac and New Haven.

▸ MILE 0.6–1.3: Quinnipiac and New Haven Vista to Summit Castle

The path descends for 0.2 mile, first crossing straight east over the red trail, then crossing straight southeast over the **Tower Trail.** Continue straight (east) uphill on the Blue Trail, cross the red trail and the Tower Trail again in 0.3 mile, then hike 0.2 mile more to reach the **stone summit castle,** which boosts hikers to incredible views of the valley below. Hikers can see miles of farmland rolling out in all directions below the mountain, as well as Long Island Sound meeting the horizon to the south. There are also restrooms at the summit tower.

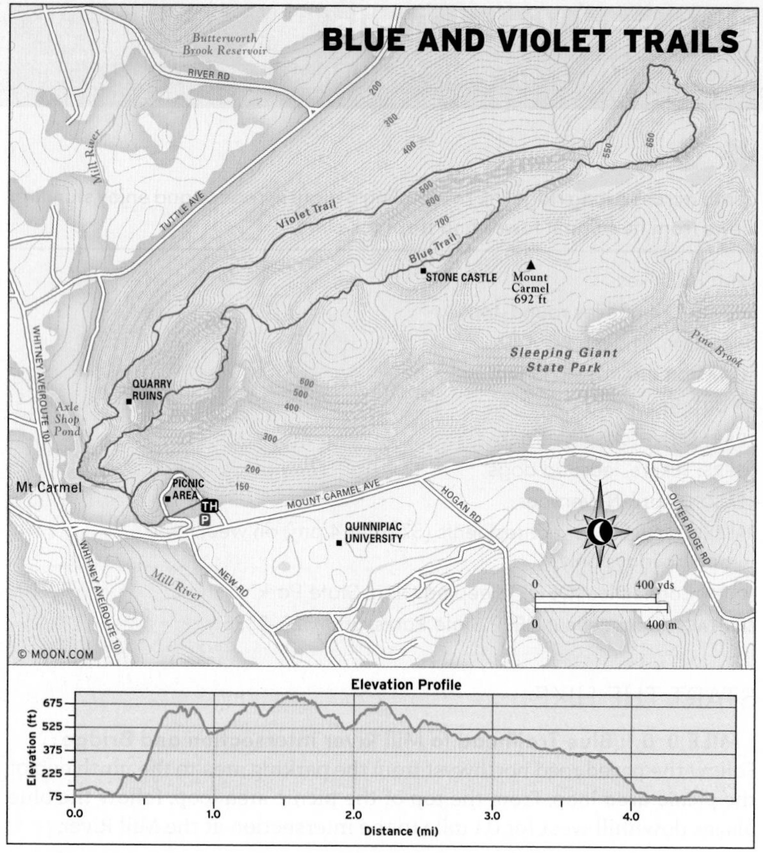

▸ **MILE 1.3-2.2: Summit Castle to Violet Trail**

From the summit, continue northeast on the **Blue Trail** for 0.4 mile, then cross straight (east) over the red trail. At the next intersection in 0.4 mile, turn left (northwest) onto the **Blue/Violet Connector** trail. At the intersection in 0.1 mile, turn left (south) onto the violet-blazed **Violet Trail.**

▸ **MILE 2.2-4.6: Violet Trail to Picnic Area Loop (and Return to Parking Area)**

The Violet Trail bends around the north flank of the Giant, crossing over the red trail four times and passing an old **quarry** before it meets the edge of the **Mill River** in 1.8 miles. Follow the violet blazes southeast along the river for 0.3 mile until you reach the paved picnic area loop. Continue straight east on the paved loop to return to the parking area in 0.2 mile.

Note: Sleeping Giant State Park was devastated by a tornado in 2018. The park and trails are undergoing maintenance and specific trail directions may have changed since the time of this writing.

▲ VIOLETS ALONG THE BLUE TRAIL

DIRECTIONS

From Hamden, take CT-10 N for 2.6 miles and then turn right onto Mount Carmel Avenue. The park entrance/parking lot is marked with a large sign on the left in 0.3 mile.

GPS COORDINATES: 41°25'21.4"N 72°54'02.4"W

BEST NEARBY BREWS

Come for the varied small plates and excellent selection of craft beers, stay for the cozy-yet-classy atmosphere at **Mikro Beer Bar** (0 Depot Ave., Hamden, 203/553-7676, http://microdepot.com, 4pm-9pm Mon., 4pm-10pm Tues.-Thurs., 11:30am-11pm Fri.-Sat., 11:30am-9pm Sun.), a unique gastropub that also serves brunch. It's just 1 mile from the trailhead.

5 Talcott Mountain Trail to Heublein Tower

TALCOTT MOUNTAIN STATE PARK, SIMSBURY

Hike a popular gravel trail to great views from the Heublein Tower and the surrounding traprock cliffs.

DISTANCE: 2.4 miles round-trip

DURATION: 1 hour

ELEVATION CHANGE: 403 feet

EFFORT: Easy/moderate

TRAIL: Gravel road, dirt/rock singletrack

USERS: Hikers, leashed dogs

SEASON: April-November

PASSES/FEES: None

MAPS: Connecticut DEEP, "Talcott Mountain State Park"

CONTACT: Connecticut DEEP State Parks, 860/526-2336

START THE HIKE

▸ MILE 0-1.1: Heublein Tower Trailhead Parking Lot to Metacomet Trail

Follow "tower" signs from the parking lot onto a wide gravel path with yellow blazes. The route winds steadily uphill, passing several benches available for rest breaks. Arrive at the edge of a traprock **ridgeline** in 0.4 mile and turn left (south) for views of the river cutting through the fields below. Continue straight (south) onto the main yellow-blazed path for 0.6 mile as it swoops away from the ridgeline and into a shady corridor of large oaks. Pass under a ledge in 0.1 mile, shortly after which the path merges with the **Metacomet Trail.**

▸ MILE 1.1-1.3: Metacomet Trail to Heublein Tower and Summit

Turn right (south) to follow the blue and yellow blazes. At the **sign for the tower** in 0.1 mile, turn right (south) up the hill on the blue-and-yellow-blazed path. Follow a set of stone steps between the gate and the ledges, and reach the **Heublein Tower** and **picnic area** in 0.1 mile. This Bavarian-inspired former summer home of a food and drink magnate provides panoramic views of the Hartford skyline and the Farmington River. Due to the easy access and stunning scenery, the summit can be quite crowded during peak hours. Those in search of solitude can return via the **Metacomet Trail.**

▸ MILE 1.3-1.5: Heublein Tower and Summit to Metacomet Trail

Backtrack north for 0.2 mile following the blue and yellow blazes to the intersection where the yellow trail and the Metacomet Trail split. Bear right (northeast) onto the Metacomet Trail.

▲ TALCOTT MOUNTAIN RIDGELINE

▸ MILE 1.5–2.4: Metacomet Trail to Heublein Tower Trailhead Parking Lot

Carry along a hemlock-lined ridge for 0.2 mile to arrive at a secluded **grassy knoll.** This ridge, with great views looking west over the river valley, is covered in violets in spring and blueberries in summer. Descend following the blue blazes until you reach the **intersection** with the main yellow-blazed trail in 0.4 mile. Turn right (east) to follow the main trail 0.3 mile back to the parking area.

DIRECTIONS

From Simsbury/US-202, go south then turn left onto CT-185 East/Hartford Road. In 1.5 miles, turn right onto Summit Ridge Drive at the signs for Talcott Mountain State Park. Free parking for the trailhead is marked with trail signs for the tower in 80 feet.

GPS COORDINATES: 41°50'17.8"N 72°47'26.4"W

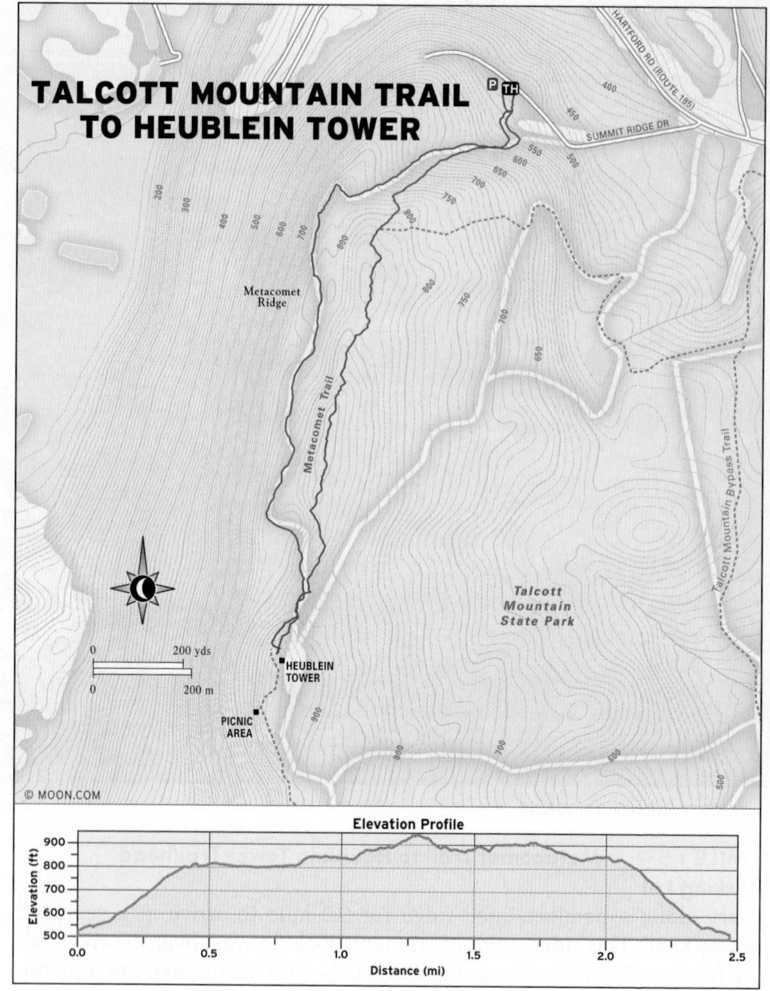

BEST NEARBY BITES

Burgers, beer, and bourbon? What more could a famished and parched hiker ask for? Three miles from the trailhead, stop in to the warm, brick-laced dining room of **Plan B Burger Bar** (4 Railroad St., Simsbury, 860/658-4477, http://burgersbeerbourbon.com, 11:30am-1am Sun.-Thurs., 11:30am-2am Fri.-Sat.) for a good sampling of craft drinks and unique burgers.

6 Blue Trail to Wolf Den and Indian Chair

MASHAMOQUET BROOK STATE PARK, POMFRET

Amble around a bubbling brook to several interesting rock formations including a legendary wolf's den and a natural granite "chair."

BEST: Spots for a swim, New England oddities
DISTANCE: 4.4 miles round-trip
DURATION: 2.5 hours
ELEVATION CHANGE: 650 feet
EFFORT: Easy/moderate
TRAIL: Dirt/rock singletrack
USERS: Hikers, leashed dogs, horseback riders
SEASON: April-November
PASSES/FEES: None
MAPS: Connecticut DEEP, "Mashamoquet State Park"
CONTACT: Connecticut DEEP State Parks, 860/526-2336

START THE HIKE

▸ MILE 0-0.7: Mashamoquet Brook Bridge to Meadow

Cross the Mashamoquet Brook on the wooden **bridge** just to the west of the parking area and bear left (southwest) following signs for "Hiking Trails." Follow the yellow blazes upslope and meet the **blue trail** in 0.2 mile. Turn right (south) onto the blue trail, which crosses a bridge over another brook in 0.1 mile. Wind through a green forest of deciduous trees and lush ferns for 0.4 mile and arrive on the left (west) side of a **meadow** dotted with wildflowers—a great spot for bird-watching.

▸ MILE 0.7-1.7: Meadow to Wolf Den

From here, the trail cuts through a stand of mountain laurel. Arrive at a dirt road in 0.7 mile. Continue across and to the right (west) toward the "Wolf Den Entrance" sign. Follow the dirt road north through the parking and picnic area for 0.2 mile, after which the singletrack trail resumes. Bear right (south) toward signs for "Wolf Den/Indian Chair" and follow the red and blue blazes. The trail continues downhill on a series of stone steps and arrives at the Wolf Den—a narrow cave where Connecticut's last wolf lived and was killed—in 0.1 mile.

▸ MILE 1.7-2.1: Wolf Den to Indian Chair

From here, the trail descends in and out of ledges and then crosses a footbridge over a stream. At the intersection in 0.4 mile, continue straight (east) on the blue trail. Shortly after, the trail arrives at the **Indian Chair,** a bench-like granite structure overlooking the forest floor from atop a ledge. The boulder's perfect positioning is a coincidence caused by glacial movements, but it is a great spot to stop for a snack and enjoy the views.

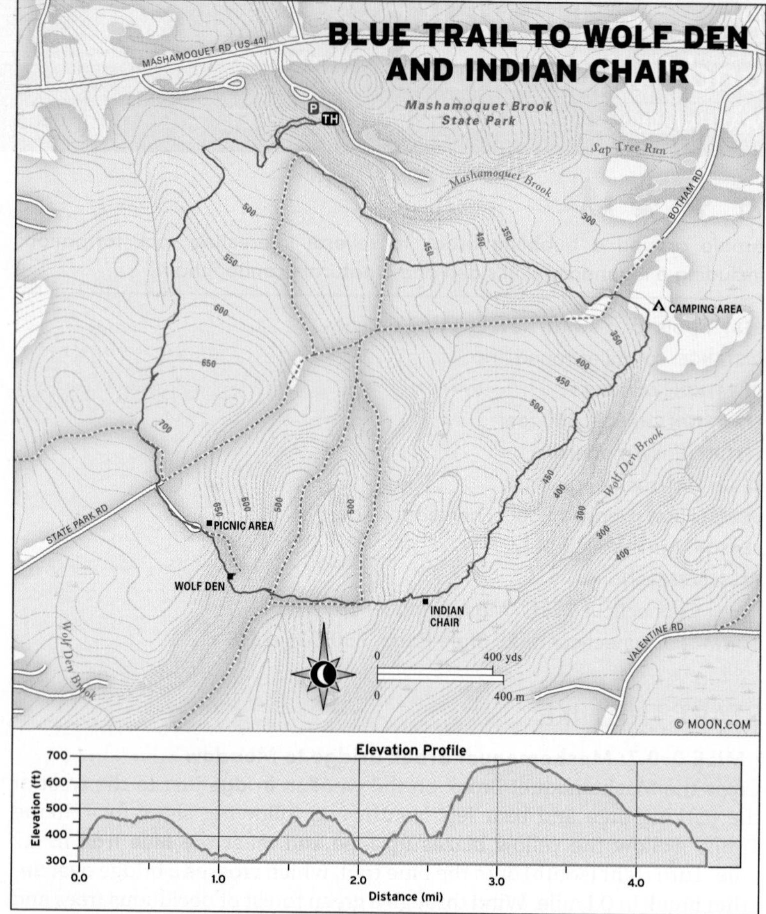

▸ **MILE 2.1–3.1: Indian Chair to Wolf Den Camping Area**

From the Indian Chair, the trail descends through a swampy area, crosses a wooden **bridge,** and then wanders up to a ridgeline crisscrossed with stone walls. In about 1 mile, the trail meets the road to the **Wolf Den camping area,** surrounded by field and meadow. There are also restroom facilities.

▸ **MILE 3.1–4.4: Wolf Den Camping Area to Blue Trail Parking Lot**

Turn left (west) onto the road, exit the gate, and then cross the paved road onto the trail in 0.1 mile. This flat section of trail curls around stone walls and streams on all sides. At the **intersection** in 0.5 mile, turn right (north) to follow the red and blue blazes for 0.4 mile. Bear right (northwest) again to follow the blue blazes for 0.1 mile, then meet the **yellow trail.** Turn right (north) to follow the yellow trail 0.2 mile back to the parking area.

▲ WOLF DEN

DIRECTIONS

Take US-44 though Pomfret and continue west; 3.5 miles from town, a large sign on the left marks the entrance to the state park. Continue straight for 0.2 mile to reach the trailhead parking area near the bridge.

GPS COORDINATES: 41°51'28.7"N 71°58'50.0"W

BEST NEARBY BITES

In addition to fresh comfort food made with local ingredients, the **Vanilla Bean Café** (450 Deerfield Rd., Pomfret, 860/928-1562, http://thevanillabeancafe.com, 7am-3pm Mon.-Tues., 7am-8pm Wed.-Thurs., 7am-9pm Fri., 8am-9pm Sat., 8am-8pm Sun.) hosts live music events throughout the year. It's 4 miles from the trailhead.

▲ CHAPMAN FALLS

▲ RED-TAILED HAWK

NEARBY CAMPGROUNDS				
NAME	**LOCATION**	**FACILITIES**	**SEASON**	**FEE**
Devil's Hopyard State Park	366 Hopyard Rd., East Haddam, CT 06423	21 RV/tent sites; restrooms	mid-April-early September	$24
860/526-2336, https://www.ct.gov/deep/cwp/view.asp?a=2716&q=325188				
Black Rock State Park	2065 Thomaston Rd., Watertown, CT 06795	78 RV/tent sites, 4 cabins; restrooms	late May-early September	$17-60
860/283-8088, https://www.ct.gov/deep/cwp/view.asp?a=2716&q=325176#directions				
Kettletown State Park	1400 Georges Hill Rd., Southbury, CT 06488	61 RV/tent sites, 6 cabins; restrooms	late-May-early September	$27-60
203/264-5678, https://www.ct.gov/deep/cwp/view.asp?a=2716&q=325034&deepNav_GID=1621#kettletown				
Mashamoquet Brook State Park	276 Mashamoquet Rd., Pomfret Center, CT 06259	53 RV/tent sites; restrooms	late May-early September	$24
860/928-6121, https://www.ct.gov/deep/cwp/view.asp?a=2716&q=325238				

▲ OCEAN VIEW LOOP

RHODE ISLAND

RHODE ISLAND

From offshore Block Island to the Narragansett Bay, Rhode Island's vast sandy beaches, imposing clay cliffs, and swaying grasses are a dream for boaters, birders, and hikers. Inland, the state's kettle ponds, erratic rocks, and vibrant plant life are just as alluring. The hikes here are not particularly steep or challenging, but the scenery along these trails is key to understanding the diversity of New England's southeastern landscape, which can fluctuate from gentle and subdued to jagged and dramatic with the turn of a corner. Nowhere is this more true than tiny, watery Rhode Island, which is guaranteed to enchant in spite of its size.

▲ Stepstone Falls

▲ pond on the Grassy Point Trail

◂ VIEWS FROM THE CLAY HEAD BLUFF

1 **North South Trail to Stepstone Falls, Arcadia Management Area**
DISTANCE: 5.6 miles round-trip
DURATION: 3.7 hours
EFFORT: Easy

2 **Coventry and Foster Loops, George B. Parker Woodland Wildlife Refuge**
DISTANCE: 6 miles round-trip
DURATION: 4 hours
EFFORT: Easy

3 **Foster Cove, Cross Refuge, and Grassy Point Trails, Ninigret National Wildlife Refuge**
DISTANCE: 4.5 miles round-trip
DURATION: 2 hours
EFFORT: Easy

4 **Long and Ell Pond Trail, Rockville Management Area**
DISTANCE: 4.4 miles round-trip
DURATION: 2.5 hours
EFFORT: Easy/moderate

5 **Walkabout Trail, George Washington Management Area**
DISTANCE: 7.8 miles round-trip
DURATION: 3.75 hours
EFFORT: Easy/moderate

6 **Flint Point and Ocean View Loops, Sachuest Point National Wildlife Refuge**
DISTANCE: 2.5 miles round-trip
DURATION: 1.25 hours
EFFORT: Easy

7 **Nelson Pond Trail, Norman Bird Sanctuary**
DISTANCE: 2.8 miles round-trip
DURATION: 1.5 hours
EFFORT: Easy/moderate

8 **Pond, Coney Brook, and Flintlock Loops, Tillinghast Pond Management Area**
DISTANCE: 5.4 miles round-trip
DURATION: 2.75 hours
EFFORT: Easy

9 **Grassland, Moraine, and Old Pasture Loops, Francis C. Carter Memorial Preserve**
DISTANCE: 4.4 miles round-trip
DURATION: 2 hours
EFFORT: Easy

10 **Clay Head and The Maze Trails, Clay Head Preserve**
DISTANCE: 2.9 miles round-trip
DURATION: 2 hours
EFFORT: Easy

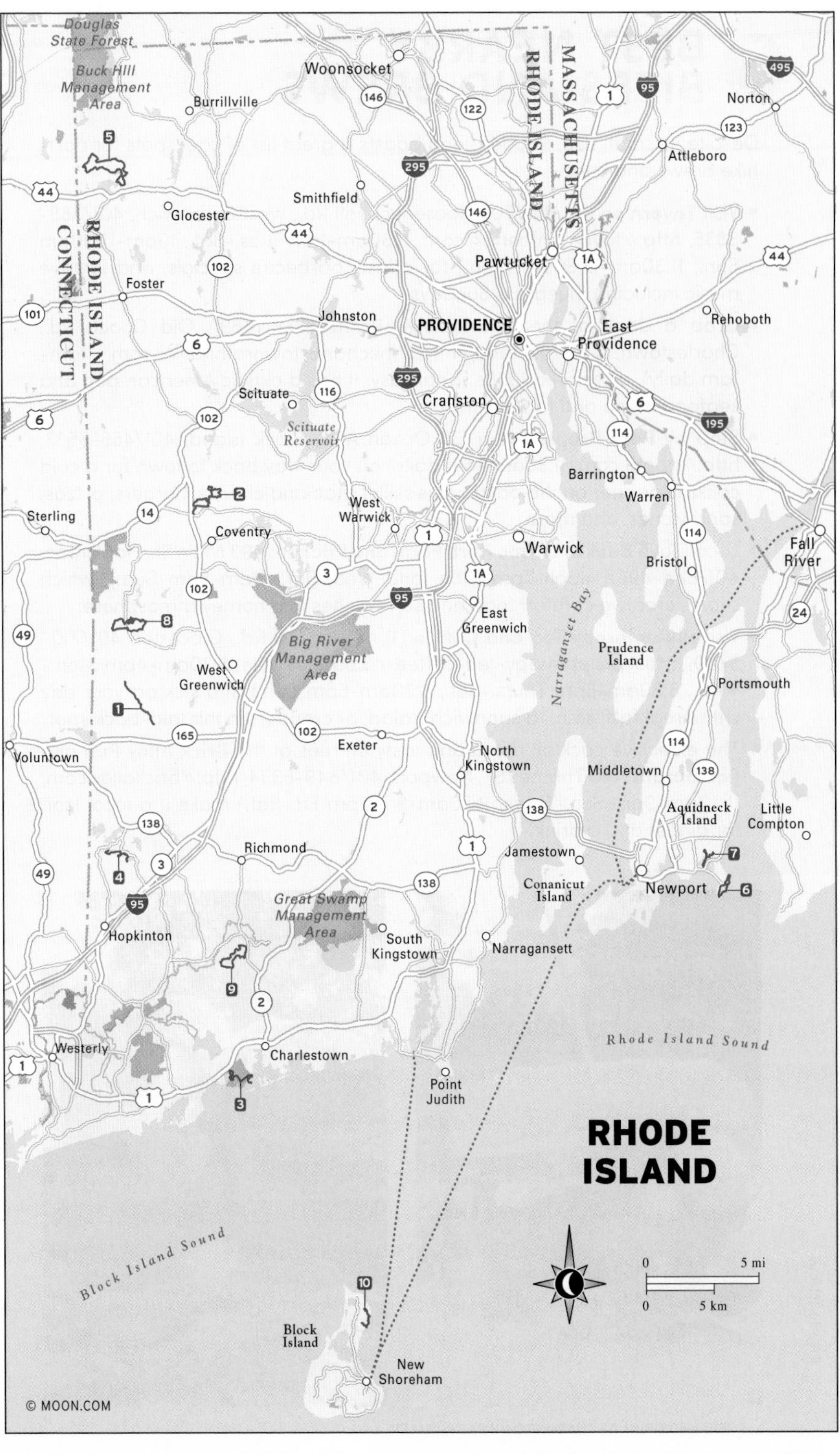

RHODE ISLAND
Douglas State Forest
Buck Hill Management Area
Woonsocket
Burrillville
MASSACHUSETTS
RHODE ISLAND
Norton
Attleboro
Smithfield
Glocester
Pawtucket
Foster
Johnston
PROVIDENCE
East Providence
Rehoboth
RHODE ISLAND
CONNECTICUT
Scituate
Scituate Reservoir
Cranston
Barrington
Warren
Sterling
West Warwick
Coventry
Warwick
Bristol
Fall River
East Greenwich
Narragansett Bay
Prudence Island
Big River Management Area
West Greenwich
Portsmouth
Exeter
Voluntown
North Kingstown
Middletown
Aquidneck Island
Little Compton
Richmond
Jamestown
Conanicut Island
Newport
Great Swamp Management Area
Hopkinton
South Kingstown
Narragansett
Westerly
Charlestown
Rhode Island Sound
Point Judith
Block Island Sound
Block Island
New Shoreham
0
5 mi
0
5 km
© MOON.COM

BEST NEARBY BITES AND BREWS

Despite its small size, Rhode Island boasts a great list of cool spots for post-hike brews and bites:

- Visit **Tavern on the Hill** (809 Nooseneck Hill Rd., West Greenwich, 401/385-3835, http://tavernonthehillri.com, 11:30am-1am Tues.-Sat., 10am-12:30am Sun., 11:30am-12:30am Mon.) for drinks, barbecue specials, and fun live music including Bluegrass Sundays.
- Grab a drink at the **Charlestown Rathskeller** (489A Old Coach Rd., Charlestown, 401/792-1000, http://thecharlestownrathskeller.com, 11am-1am daily), a restored 1930s speakeasy. It has a classic American pub and seafood menu and famous fries.
- Stop by **Poor People's Pub** (33 Ocean Ave., Block Island, 401/466-8533, http://pppbi.com, 11:30am-1am daily) on your way back to town for a cold cocktail or beer on the porch, plus skillet mac and cheese, burgers, pizzas, sandwiches, and more.
- Locals love **Back in Thyme Herb Farm and Kitchen** (493 Main St., Hopkinton, 401/644-4967, noon-7pm Mon. and Wed.-Sat., 11am-5pm Sun.), which serves creative comfort food and sandwiches in a homey atmosphere.
- Visit **Philanthropy Tea and Coffee** (11 Money Hill Rd., Glocester, 401/710-9780, http://philanthropy-tea-coffee-co.business.site, 8:30am-4pm Mon.-Wed., 8:30am-8pm Thurs.-Sat., 8:30am-6pm Sun.) and kick off your day with breakfast, soup, a sandwich, salad, or crepe from this laid-back spot.
- The extensive cocktail menu and tasty entrees at the **Brick Alley Pub and Restaurant** (140 Thames St., Newport, 401/849-6334, http://brickalley.com, 11:30am-9pm Sun.-Thurs, 11:30am-9:30 pm Fri.-Sat.) make it a local icon for dinner and a drink.

▲ FOOD AND DRINK AT CHARLESTOWN RATHSKELLER

1 North South Trail to Stepstone Falls

ARCADIA MANAGEMENT AREA, EXETER

This hidden gem in the Arcadia Management Area features a waterfall and a pleasant walk along the banks of the Falls River, where a variety of rare wildflowers grow.

BEST: Spring hikes, brew hikes
DISTANCE: 5.6 miles round-trip
DURATION: 3.7 hours
ELEVATION CHANGE: 312 feet
EFFORT: Easy
TRAIL: Dirt path
USERS: Hikers, leashed dogs (horseback riders, mountain bikers permitted on some sections)
SEASON: Year-round
PASSES/FEES: Free
MAPS: RI Department of Environmental Management, "Arcadia Management Area North—Rt. 165."
CONTACT: RI Division of Parks and Recreation, 401/539-2356

Rhode Island's North South Trail stretches 78 miles across the state, and this segment through the Arcadia Management Area is one of the most scenic and unspoiled sections, traveling on secluded footpaths through the heart of the park. It's a gentle trail, but rare plant life, a rushing river, and a series of uniquely shaped falls make this hike feel truly wild.

START THE HIKE

▸ MILE 0-1.2: North South Trailhead to Austin Farm Road

Heading right (east) from the trailhead, follow the blue-blazed **North South Trail** from where it splits from Barber Road. From the marshy meadow off Barber Road, the narrow trail bends into a secluded pine grove on a flat, winding track. Boardwalks assist hikers through muddy portions, and blueberries are prevalent along the trailside. Pass the **Spur Trail,** the **Sand Hill Trail,** and the **Escoheag Trail,** keeping right to stay on the well-marked North South Trail. Arrive at **Austin Farm Road** at 1.2 miles.

▸ MILE 1.2-2.4: Austin Farm Road to Wooden Bridge

Cross to the right (east) side of the road, then take a left (north) just before the bridge. Here, the North South Trail merges with the yellow-blazed **Ben Utter Trail** and heads north upstream along the river. (The following length of trail, approximately 1 mile, is truly spectacular, with crafted footbridges, rushing water, and blossoms of rare wildflowers, such as pink lady's slippers and azaleas along the riverbanks.)

At 0.5 mile from the start of the Ben Utter Trail, reach a dirt road and turn right (east) to stay on the blue-blazed trail. At the fork in 0.6 mile, bear

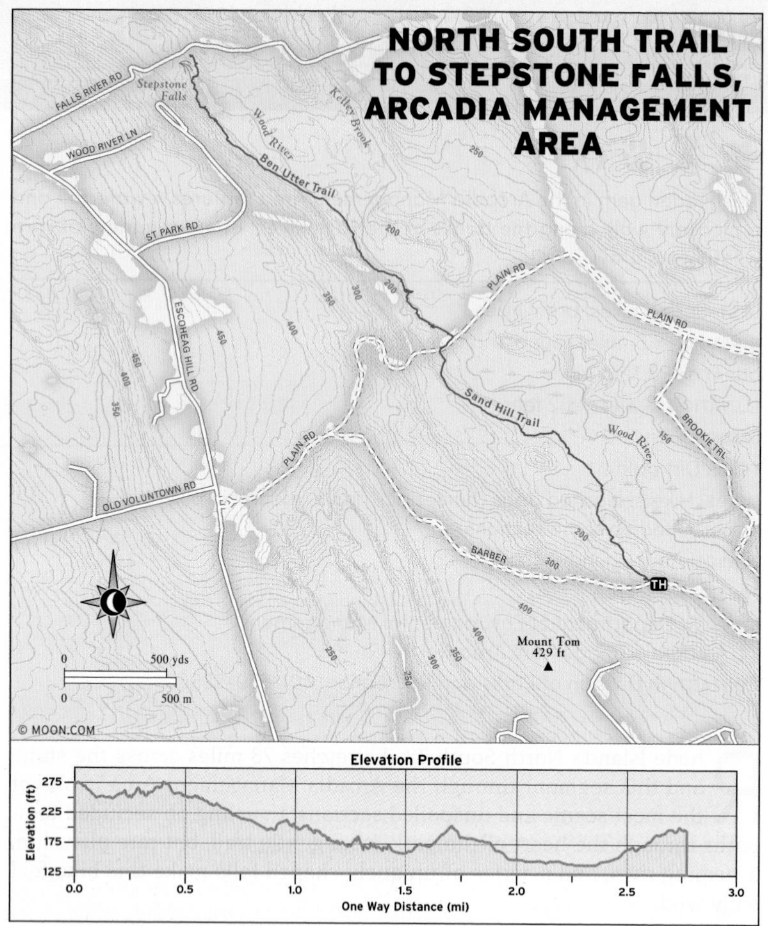

right (east) again to stay on the North South trail. The trail becomes rocky as the river widens through swampland. Arrive at a wooden bridge across the river at 2.4 miles.

▸ MILE 2.4-5.6: Wooden Bridge to Stepstone Falls

Turn right (east) onto the bridge, then turn immediately left (north) to follow the river upstream. In 0.2 mile, reach **Stepstone Falls,** a cascade over a series of square-shaped boulders. Backtrack from the falls for a 5.6-mile round-trip.

DIRECTIONS

From RI-3 or I-95, take RI-165 W (Ten Rod Road). Turn right into the Midway parking area and continue north on the dirt road, following the blue blazes of the North South Trail. In 0.5 mile, turn left over the bridge onto Barber Road and follow it for 0.9 mile. Park at the turnoff where the North South Trail splits into the woods on the right.

GPS COORDINATES: 41°35'07.9"N 71°44'02.5"W

2 Coventry and Foster Loops

GEORGE B. PARKER WOODLAND WILDLIFE REFUGE, COVENTRY

With stone walls, historic sites, and enormous glacial erratic rocks, this hike in and around a bubbling brook is a pleasant setting for birding and wildlife viewing.

DISTANCE: 6 miles round-trip

DURATION: 4 hours

ELEVATION CHANGE: 611 feet

EFFORT: Easy

TRAIL: Dirt path, boardwalk

USERS: Hikers only

SEASON: Year-round

PASSES/FEES: Free

MAPS: Audubon Society of Rhode Island "George B. Parker Woodland Wildlife Refuge"

CONTACT: Audubon Society of Rhode Island, 401/295-8283, http://asri.org

START THE HIKE

▸ MILE 0-0.5: Trailhead Parking Lot to Coventry Loop

Hikers can enjoy the warbles and twitters of birds in the greenery while traversing long boardwalks through wetlands, exploring gigantic boulders along a brook, or seeking out deer on the edge of a pastoral meadow. The trail heads north out of the parking lot. Take a left (west) toward the meadow at the sign and follow the path through a grassy field, a great spot for wildlife viewing when quiet. Continue along the orange-blazed trail as it enters the woods and reaches an intersection at 0.2 mile. Stay straight (north) on the orange trail, which bounds over a series of long boardwalks and bog bridges. Reach the intersection with the blue-blazed Coventry Loop in 0.3 mile.

▸ MILE 0.5-0.8: Coventry Loop to Foster Loop

Turn left (west) onto the Coventry Loop to complete the circuit clockwise. The path winds along stone walls, through a beech and oak forest, and passes the historic **Vaughn Farm site.** After descending past several overhanging ledges, the rolling trail arrives at a massive boulder at 0.8 mile, where a sign marks the yellow-blazed connector trail leading toward the **Foster Loop.**

▸ MILE 0.8-1.6: Foster Loop to Milton A. Gowdey Memorial Trail

Turn left (northeast) and follow the yellow blazes, which trek through a boulder field and along the stream. The yellow connector trail reaches the **Milton A. Gowdey Memorial Trail/Foster Loop** (marked with blue blazes) at 1.6 miles.

▲ BOULDER AT THE COVENTRY LOOP AND FOSTER LOOP INTERSECTION

▸ MILE 1.6–4.2: Milton A. Gowdey Memorial Trail to Coventry Loop
Turn left (north) onto this blue-blazed loop, which rolls through an enormous field of blueberries, descends in and out of a brook valley, and passes the flat granite slab known as **Table Rock.** The trail crosses a dirt road and goes through a gate in 2 miles; it returns to the junction with the connector trail 0.2 mile later. Take a left (west) and follow the yellow-blazed trail 0.4 mile back to the intersection with the large boulder.

▸ MILE 4.2–6.0: Coventry Loop to Trailhead Parking Lot
Turn left (south) around the boulder to join with the other end of the blue-blazed Coventry Loop. This section of trail travels along the brook banks for about 1 mile before reaching an intersection with the path toward Parking Lot 2. Stay straight on the blue-blazed trail toward Parking Lot 1, which passes a collection of more than 100 historic **stone cairns.** Reach the intersection with the orange trail in another 0.3 mile, and turn left (south) onto the orange trail back toward the lot.

DIRECTIONS

From West Greenwich, head north on RI-102 (Victory Highway) for 6.5 miles, then turn right onto Maple Valley Road. The well-marked gated parking area is 0.1 mile down the road on the left.

GPS COORDINATES: 41°43'00.1"N 71°41'53.0"W

COVENTRY AND FOSTER LOOPS, GEORGE B. PARKER WOODLAND WILDLIFE REFUGE

TABLE ROCK
Milton A Gowdey Memorial Trail
Biscuit Hill
Pine Swamp Brook
BISCUIT HILL RD
Foster Trail
Coventry Loop
FARM SITE
PIG HILL RD
Flat River
RIDGEWOOD TR
VICTORY HWY (ROUTE 102)
MAPLE VALLEY RD
GAREAU DR
TH P
0 400 yds
0 400 m
© MOON.COM

Elevation Profile
Elevation (ft)
Distance (mi)

▲ BOG BRIDGE

3 Foster Cove, Cross Refuge, and Grassy Point Trails

NINIGRET NATIONAL WILDLIFE REFUGE, CHARLESTOWN

Hike on this gentle grass and gravel track to a scenic barrier beach where shorebirds and wildflowers flourish.

BEST: New England oddities, brew hikes
DISTANCE: 4.5 miles round-trip
DURATION: 2 hours
ELEVATION CHANGE: 22 feet
EFFORT: Easy
TRAIL: Grass/gravel path
USERS: Hikers, bikers
SEASON: Year-round
PASSES/FEES: None
MAPS: U.S. Fish and Wildlife Service, "Ninigret National Wildlife Refuge Salt Pond Unit"
CONTACT: U.S. Fish and Wildlife Service Ninigret Refuge Headquarters, 401/364-9124, http://fws.gov/refuge/Ninigret

START THE HIKE

▸ MILE 0-0.5: Trailhead to Cross Refuge Trail

From the trailhead sign, go right (west) onto the **Foster Cove Loop,** a wide grass and gravel track surrounded by thick vegetation and perfumed with honeysuckle. The flat and easy trail arrives at water views of Foster Cove in 0.2 mile. Reach an intersection 0.3 mile farther on the trail.

▸ MILE 0.5-1.6: Cross Refuge Trail to Auxiliary Air Station Runway

Stay straight (south) for the **Cross Refuge Trail,** which crosses over a strip of pavement and returns to a gravel surface. The trail slips between two lily pad-laden bogs. At the gated intersection at 1.3 miles, bear left (east). The vegetation opens into a spacious, grassy habitat where wildflowers and birds abound. Reach the parking area at 1.6 miles, and walk right (east) through the lot to the site of an old **runway** from Ninigret's days as Naval Auxiliary Air Station Charlestown.

▸ MILE 1.6-1.8: Auxiliary Air Station Runway to Grassy Point Trail

The trail continues on the far east side of the runway. Turn left (northwest) onto the **Grassy Point Trail,** which passes into the woods and then hugs the edge of Ninigret Pond, with great water views. After 0.2 mile, cross the bridge and then turn left (south) to follow the grassy trail to the end of the point.

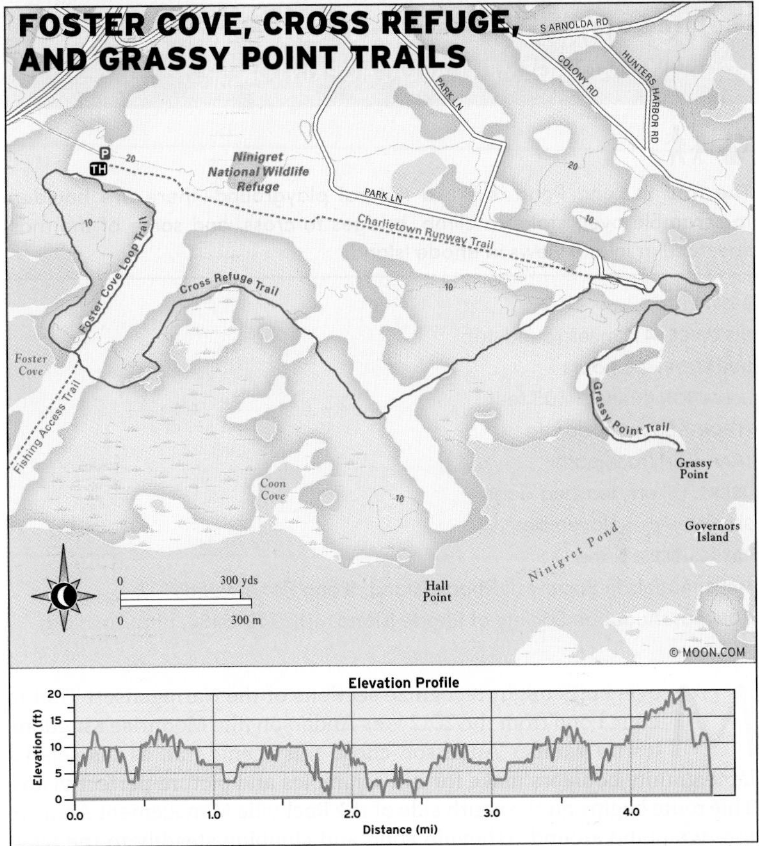

‣ MILE 1.8–2.6: Grassy Point Trail to Cross Refuge Trail

At the trail's terminus in 0.5 mile, you can enjoy more water views and wildlife from the **observation deck.** Backtrack 0.3 mile to the intersection and turn left (west), following signs for the **Cross Refuge Trail.**

‣ MILE 2.6–4.5: Cross Refuge Trail to Foster Cove Loop

Turn left (southwest) again onto the **Cross Refuge Trail** at 2.8 miles, and backtrack to the **Foster Cove Loop** in 1.1 miles. For variety, you can turn right onto the eastern side of the Foster Cove Loop and hike 0.6 mile to return to the lot.

DIRECTIONS

From US-1, use the large brown signs to navigate to the West Entrance of the refuge, which is directly off the highway. Those coming from the north should pass the entrance and then double back onto US-1 N at Wildflower Road. There is a large parking lot at the trailhead.

GPS COORDINATES: 41°22'05.9"N 71°40'19.6"W

4 Long and Ell Pond Trail

ROCKVILLE MANAGEMENT AREA, HOPKINTON

The trail to Long Pond is like a natural playground—there are boulders to scramble over, stairs to climb, bridges to cross, and some of the most spectacular inland views in Rhode Island.

BEST: Vistas
DISTANCE: 4.4 miles round-trip
DURATION: 2.5 hours
ELEVATION CHANGE: 405 feet
EFFORT: Easy/moderate
TRAIL: Dirt/rock path
USERS: Hikers, leashed dogs
SEASON: April–November
PASSES/FEES: None
MAPS: Audubon Society of Rhode Island, "Long Pond Woods"
CONTACT: Audubon Society of Rhode Island, 401/949-5454, http://asri.org

Movie buffs might recognize sections of the Narragansett Trail to Long Pond from the 2012 Wes Anderson film Moonrise Kingdom. It's no wonder Anderson chose this scenic trail as his set—its large granite boulders make for fun scrambles and picture-perfect vistas. This route begins on the south side of the Rockville Management Area before wrapping around Asheville Pond and climbing steadily to the overlook above Long Pond.

START THE HIKE

▸ MILE 0–0.5: Trailhead to Canonchet Road Parking Area

Hike north from the trailhead toward **Asheville Pond.** The dirt trail winds along the west edge of the pond and continues north for 0.5 mile. Here the trail bends sharply right (east), then wraps to the west, and then switchbacks east again through a tunnel of giant laurel bushes.

▸ MILE 0.5–1.5: Canonchet Road Parking Area to Valley

Pass the **Canonchet Road parking area** at 1.2 miles and turn left (west). The trail gains elevation along a rock ridge, passes a pair of huge boulders, and follows a stone wall west for about 0.3 mile. As the trail reaches the top of a hill, the waters of Long Pond peek out from beyond the trees. The trail then leads hikers down through a pile of boulders and into a green valley.

▸ MILE 1.5–1.9: Green Valley to Long Pond Overlook

Past the valley, make a steep ascent to the top of a ridge. The trail continues to ascend and descend for 0.3 mile before skirting the east edge of a root-bound hill. At the bottom of the hill, go down the stairs and cross the long wooden bridge through a cedar bog. At the other end of the bridge,

▲ CLIFFS AT LONG POND

climb through a final steep corridor of rock to arrive at an intersection at 1.9 miles. Go straight (north) through the intersection for the trail leading to **Long Pond overlook.**

▸ MILE 1.9–2.2: Long Pond Overlook to Summit

The path passes several rock outcroppings and then descends a hill. It reaches a towering rock formation at 2.1 miles. Follow the trail around to the north side of the rocks. At the "End of Trail" sign, ascend to the right, up the east side of the formation. Reach the "summit" of the rocks at 2.2 miles for vast views of Long Pond below. Backtrack on the same trail to return to the lot.

DIRECTIONS

From RI-3, turn north onto Canonchet Road. Then turn left onto Stubtown Road. The Asheville Pond parking area is marked with a Rockville Management Area sign.

GPS COORDINATES: 41°29'59.4"N 71°45'37.4"W

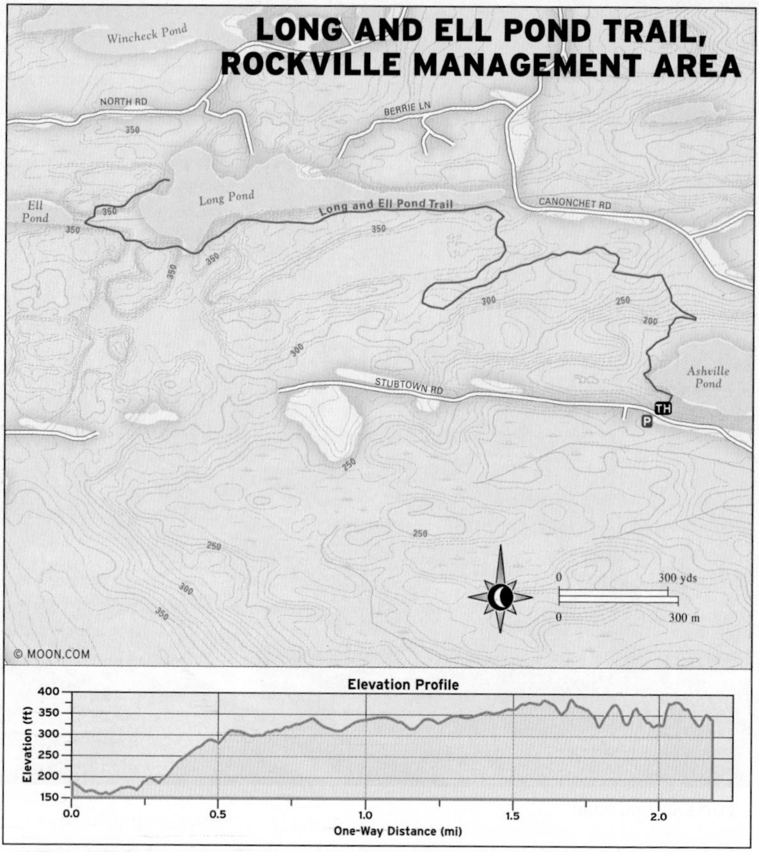

LONG AND ELL POND TRAIL, ROCKVILLE MANAGEMENT AREA

Wincheck Pond
NORTH RD
BERRIE LN
350
Long Pond
Ell Pond
Long and Ell Pond Trail
CANONCHET RD
350
300
250
200
Ashville Pond
STUBTOWN RD
TH
P
250
250
250
300
350
0 300 yds
0 300 m
© MOON.COM

Elevation Profile

Elevation (ft): 400, 350, 300, 250, 200, 150
One-Way Distance (mi): 0.0, 0.5, 1.0, 1.5, 2.0

▲ LONG POND

5 Walkabout Trail

GEORGE WASHINGTON MANAGEMENT AREA, CHEPACHET

Built by a group of Australian sailors in 1965, the Walkabout Trail is a secluded loop through woods and around sparkling lakes.

BEST: Spots for a swim, New England oddities

DISTANCE: 7.8 miles round-trip

DURATION: 3.75 hours

ELEVATION CHANGE: 375 feet

EFFORT: Easy/moderate

TRAIL: Dirt/rock path

USERS: Hikers, leashed dogs, horseback riders

SEASON: Year-round

PASSES/FEES: $2 per vehicle daily visitors pass

MAPS: Rhode Island Division of Parks and Recreation, "George Washington/ Pulaski Wildlife Management Area"

CONTACT: Rhode Island Division of Parks and Recreation, 401/568-2085, http://riparks.com

START THE HIKE

▸ MILE 0-3.3: Bowdish Reservoir Beach to Pulaski Management Area

Start at the Bowdish Reservoir beach and hike north, following the trail with orange, red, and blue blazes into the woods. The muddy path traces the edge of the lake, highlighting unspoiled waterfront and enormous granite boulders. The trail bends east toward **Wilbur Pond** in 0.4 mile. Cross the road and continue straight east in 0.3 mile. The blue trail branches off to the east at 0.8 mile. Turn left (north) to follow the orange and red blazes around Wilbur Pond. At the next intersection at 2.0 miles, turn left (west) to follow only the orange blazes. The trail crosses straight across several dirt roads and through a hemlock grove. At the intersection at 3.3 miles, follow the orange blazes straight (north) downhill. Cross a long wooden footbridge and enter **Pulaski Management Area.**

▸ MILE 3.3-4.5: Pulaski Management Area to Pulaski Wildlife Marsh

Just after the sign, turn right (northeast) and continue to follow the orange blazes through a wetland area along a stream. At 4.5 miles, the trail crosses another dirt road and arrives at the **Pulaski Wildlife Marsh.**

▸ MILE 4.5-7.8: Pulaski Wildlife Marsh to North South Trail

Continue south along the edge of the marsh. At the southwest edge of the marsh, turn left (east) and follow signs for the **North South Trail** across the levee bridges and into the woods. Turn left again to stay on the orange-blazed North South Trail heading north. The trail winds through a swamp, merging with the red trail at 5.1 miles. Follow the orange and red blazes east through a muddy cedar swamp with plenty of interesting log bridges to help your footing. The path joins the blue trail in 1.5 miles. Keep

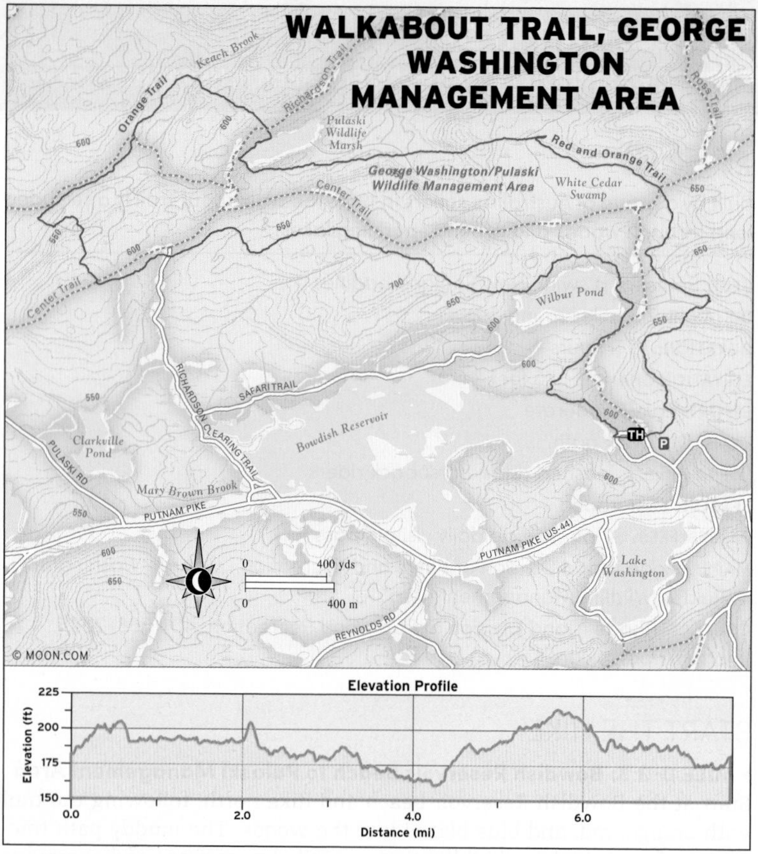

WALKABOUT TRAIL, GEORGE WASHINGTON MANAGEMENT AREA

Elevation Profile

straight, following the red, orange, and blue blazes south for 1.2 miles back to the beach.

DIRECTIONS

From Glocester, take US-44 (Putnam Pike) west and turn right (north) into the well-signed George Washington State Campground and Management Area. After checking in at the gate, continue north to the parking area/restrooms near the Bowdish Reservoir beach.

GPS COORDINATES: 41°55'11.4"N 71°45'17.9"W

▲ BOWDISH RESERVOIR BEACH

6 Flint Point and Ocean View Loops

SACHUEST POINT NATIONAL WILDLIFE REFUGE, MIDDLETOWN

Enjoy miles of waterfront views on this easy trail that winds between golden fields and a rocky peninsula jutting into the Atlantic Ocean.

BEST: Summer hikes, brew hikes

DISTANCE: 2.5 miles round-trip

DURATION: 1.25 hours

ELEVATION CHANGE: 53 feet

EFFORT: Easy

TRAIL: Gravel path

USERS: Hikers

SEASON: Year-round

PASSES/FEES: None

MAPS: U.S. Fish and Wildlife Service, "Sachuest Point National Wildlife Refuge"

CONTACT: U.S. Fish and Wildlife Service, 401/619-2680, http://fws.gov

Situated on a peninsula just east of Newport, the 242-acre Sachuest Point refuge is both a destination for migratory shorebirds and a prized fishing area. Our route follows the park's two main trails—Flint Point and Ocean View—which follow the coastline on an easy gravel track featuring observation platforms, grassy bird habitat, and a hypnotizing jagged shoreline.

START THE HIKE

▸ MILE 0-0.6: Trailhead to Flint Point Observation Deck

Find the trailhead in the northeast corner of the parking area and head straight east toward the Flint Point Loop on the wide gravel path. In 600 feet, bear left (north) on the **Flint Point Loop,** which winds through grassland and thick vine before arriving at ocean views. Reach the **Flint Point observation deck** at 0.6 mile, where you can view boats bobbing in the Sakonnet River to the north and east.

▸ MILE 0.6-1.2: Flint Point Observation Deck to Price Neck Overlook

From here, the path bends east along the coast through wild beach rose and honeysuckle. Shoreline views of sunbathing cormorants and sailboats persist to the east. Reach another **observation deck** at 1.0 mile. Then, continue straight south onto the **Ocean View Loop.** Bear right (west) up the stairs at 1.2 miles toward the **Price Neck Overlook.** This rocky ledge affords panoramic views of the shoreline below.

▲ SACHUEST POINT

▸ MILE 1.2–2.5: Price Neck Overlook to Sachuest Point

The Price Neck path drops back down to the Ocean View Loop at 1.4 miles. Hike right (south), with vast fields to one side and the increasingly dramatic coastline to the other. Reach the tip of **Sachuest Point** at 1.8 miles. Here, you may want to take some time to explore the rocks before continuing the 0.7 mile on the path north back to the visitors center and parking area.

DIRECTIONS

From US-1, take RI-138 E over the Newport Bridge. Take the Newport exit and pass through downtown Newport on RI-138A. After First Beach, take a right onto Purgatory Road. Then turn right onto Sachuest Point Drive and follow it to Sachuest Point Visitors Center at the very end of the road.

GPS COORDINATES: 41°28'47.4"N 71°14'38.0"W

FLINT POINT AND OCEAN VIEW LOOPS, SACHUEST POINT NATIONAL WILDLIFE REFUGE

Flint Point
Sachuest Point National Wildlife Refuge
Flint Point Loop
SACHUEST POINT RD
Island Rocks
Flint Rock
Sakonnet River
TH P
0 200 yds
0 200 m
PRICE NECK OVERLOOK
Ocean View Loop
Sachuest Bay
Sachuest Point
Atlantic Ocean
© MOON.COM

Elevation Profile
Elevation (ft): 50, 35, 20, 5
Distance (mi): 0.0, 0.5, 1.0, 1.5, 2.0, 2.5

7 Nelson Pond Trail

NORMAN BIRD SANCTUARY, MIDDLETOWN

Bird lovers will delight at the diverse collection of fields, woods, ponds, and ledges at Norman Bird Sanctuary, which attracts a variety of species.

BEST: Vistas

DISTANCE: 2.8 miles round-trip

DURATION: 1.5 hours

ELEVATION CHANGE: 188 feet

EFFORT: Easy/moderate

TRAIL: Dirt/rock path, boardwalk

USERS: Hikers

SEASON: Year-round

PASSES/FEES: $7 adult, $6 senior/military, $3 student/child

MAPS: Norman Bird Sanctuary, "Norman Bird Sanctuary Trail Map"

CONTACT: Norman Bird Sanctuary, 401/846-2577, http://normanbirdsanctuary.org

The many trails of Norman Bird Sanctuary offer myriad habitats, but hikers are often most attracted to the park's "Ridge Trails"—long pudding stone fingers that reach out toward the Atlantic Ocean. To access the ridges, our route follows the main Universal Trail through field, shrub, and forest, and then forms a loop on the Red Fox, Nelson Pond, and Gray Craig Trails.

START THE HIKE

▸ MILE 0-0.4: Visitors Center to Red Maple Pond

Check in at the visitors center and then walk north on the **Universal Trail** through fields and around the garden. Reach an intersection at 0.2 mile and keep right (west) on the gravel path. The trail ventures into shady woods and along a stone wall to reach another intersection at 0.4 mile. Turn left (south) and hike along the long boardwalk, which ends at the observation deck on **Red Maple Pond.**

▸ MILE 0.4-0.7: Red Maple Pond to Red Fox Trail

Turn right to head west around the pond and over the bridge. Follow the stone steps for 0.1 mile and then turn left (south). Almost immediately, turn right (west) onto another boardwalk, following signs toward Nelson Pond. Continue to bear right following signs for the **Red Fox Trail.** Then, at 0.7 mile, bear left (south) onto the Red Fox Trail.

▸ MILE 0.7-1.1: Red Fox Trail to Red Fox Ridge

The path enters a cool forest protected by massive beech trees and climbs slightly uphill over a series of ledges, with deep green valleys on either side. Reach the end of the Red Fox ridge at 1.1 miles, with great views looking east toward **Hanging Rock** and south to the ocean.

▲ NELSON POND

▸ MILE 1.1–1.7: Red Fox Ridge to Gray Craig Trail
Descend straight to the south and follow the low, grassy trail for 0.1 mile. Turn left (west) onto the boardwalk then follow the trail left (west) as it climbs the ledges to more great views. The trail continues north on easy terrain, reaching a rocky viewpoint of **Nelson Pond** at 1.5 miles. Follow the viewpoint trail to the left (west); it descends to the main path at 1.5 miles. At the signed intersection at 1.7 miles, bear left (north) onto the **Gray Craig Trail.**

▸ MILE 1.7–2.8: Gray Craig Trail to Universal Trail and Visitors Center
Follow the path through the woods and over another boardwalk, which crosses a marsh brimming with plant life. At 2.1 miles, the trail climbs uphill to another ledge—a great, secluded spot for bird-watching. The narrow path then descends and loops back to its start at 2.3 miles. Turn left (south) and follow signs back toward the visitors center. Turn left (east) over the boardwalk at 2.5 miles on the Ridge Connector Trail. Reach the Universal Trail and turn left (north) to hike 0.3 mile back to the visitors center.

DIRECTIONS

From downtown Newport, follow RI-138A to Purgatory Road. Bear left on Hanging Rock Road and then turn left on Third Beach Road. The well-marked and signed parking lot is on the left. Be sure to check in at the visitors center before hiking the trails.

GPS COORDINATES: 41°29'59.3"N 71°15'00.9"W

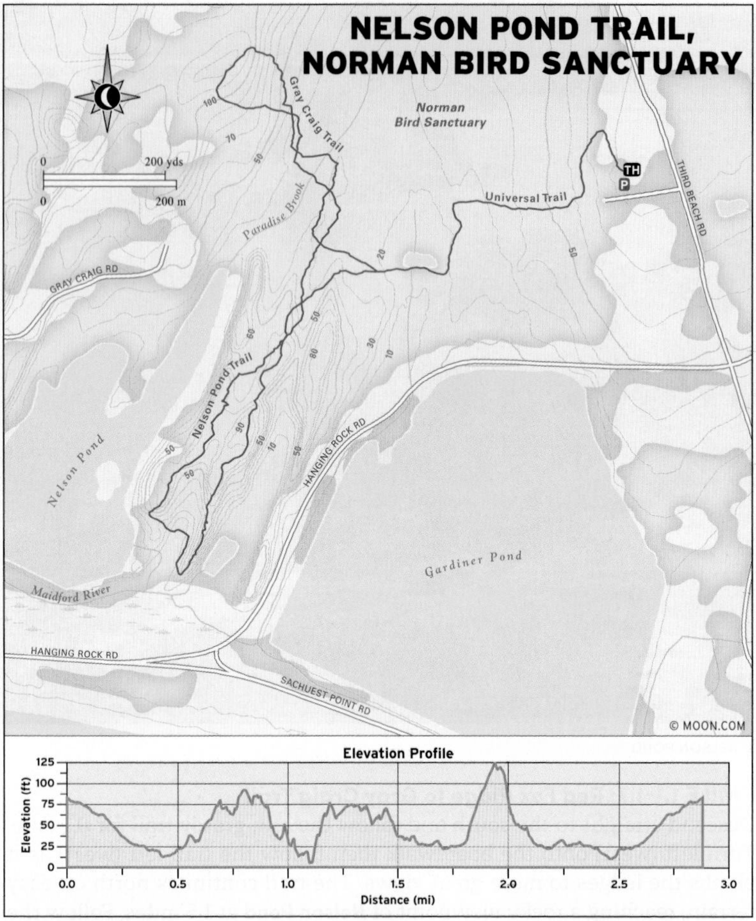

NELSON POND TRAIL, NORMAN BIRD SANCTUARY

Norman Bird Sanctuary
Gray Craig Trail
Universal Trail
Paradise Brook
Nelson Pond Trail
Nelson Pond
Gardiner Pond
Maidford River
GRAY CRAIG RD
HANGING ROCK RD
SACHUEST POINT RD
THIRD BEACH RD
TH
P
0 200 yds
0 200 m
© MOON.COM

Elevation Profile
Elevation (ft)
Distance (mi)

▲ BRIDGE OVER RED MAPLE POND

8 Pond, Coney Brook, and Flintlock Loops

TILLINGHAST POND MANAGEMENT AREA, WEST GREENWICH

Enjoy views of a pristine pond surrounded by field and forest on the trails of the Nature Conservancy's largest preserve.

BEST: Winter hikes

DISTANCE: 5.4 miles round-trip

DURATION: 2.75 hours

ELEVATION CHANGE: 204 feet

EFFORT: Easy

TRAIL: Dirt path

USERS: Hikers, paddlers

SEASON: Year-round

PASSES/FEES: None

MAPS: The Nature Conservancy "Tillinghast Pond Management Area"

CONTACT: The Nature Conservancy, 401/331-7110, http://nature.org

START THE HIKE

▸ MILE 0-0.1: Pond Loop Trailhead to Plain Road

Walk to the **Pond Loop** trailhead at the north corner of the parking lot and hike north, following the white blazes. Turn left (west) onto the orange-blazed **Coney Brook Loop** at 0.1 mile. The trail crosses straight west over **Plain Road,** then becomes narrow as it winds through a stand of pines.

▸ MILE 0.1-1.9: Plain Road to Cascades

Bear left (west) to stay on the orange-blazed Coney Brook Loop at 0.1 mile. The trail opens into a field of blueberries with views of the hills to the west, then turns into the woods after 0.3 mile. Hike along the slopes of a fern-covered mixed forest, then arrive at a frog-filled bog in 0.4 mile. Turn right (north) to stay on the Coney Brook Loop, which reaches Coney Brook at 1.7 miles. Follow the brook and hike east upstream along the gorge, descend the wooden staircase, and cross the bridge to reach a small series of **cascades.** At the dam, the trail turns right (south) around a pond. The trail may be slightly flooded here. Arrive at an open field of daisies and black-eyed Susans in 0.2 mile.

▸ MILE 1.9-3.4: Cascades to Flintlock Loop

Continue south along the edge of the field and reach the road in 0.2 mile. Turn left (north) onto the road and find the white-blazed **Pond Loop** where it enters the forest to the right (east). The Pond Loop trail alternates between fields of hay and the pine-forested shoreline as it traces Tillinghast's northern shore. Turn left (north) onto the yellow-blazed **Flintlock Loop** in 1.2 mile.

▲ TILLINGHAST POND

‣ MILE 3.4–4.7: Flintlock Loop to Ellis Homestead

The narrow path climbs slightly uphill to a fork in 0.4 mile. Turn right at the fork to follow the south spur to the "**Boulder Garden,**" where large rocks seem to sprout from tufts of grass. 0.2 mile east of the Boulder Garden, turn right (east) to return to the main Flintlock Loop. At the unsigned intersection with the Wickaboxet Trail at 4.3 miles, turn right (south) to follow the blue and yellow blazes through a corridor of large white pines. The blue-blazed trail diverges in 0.3 mile. Stay straight south, following the yellow-blazed Flintlock Loop, which opens into a grassy clearing and reaches Phillips Brook and the **Ellis Homestead** at 4.7 miles.

‣ MILE 4.7–5.4: Ellis Homestead to Pond Loop

Turn right at the homestead and follow the narrow trail west through thick growth. At 4.8 miles, the path passes the **Ellis Family Cemetery.** Continue west for 0.4 mile to the intersection with the **Pond Loop.** Hike straight west, following the white blazes between the pond and a stone wall for 0.2 mile back to the parking area.

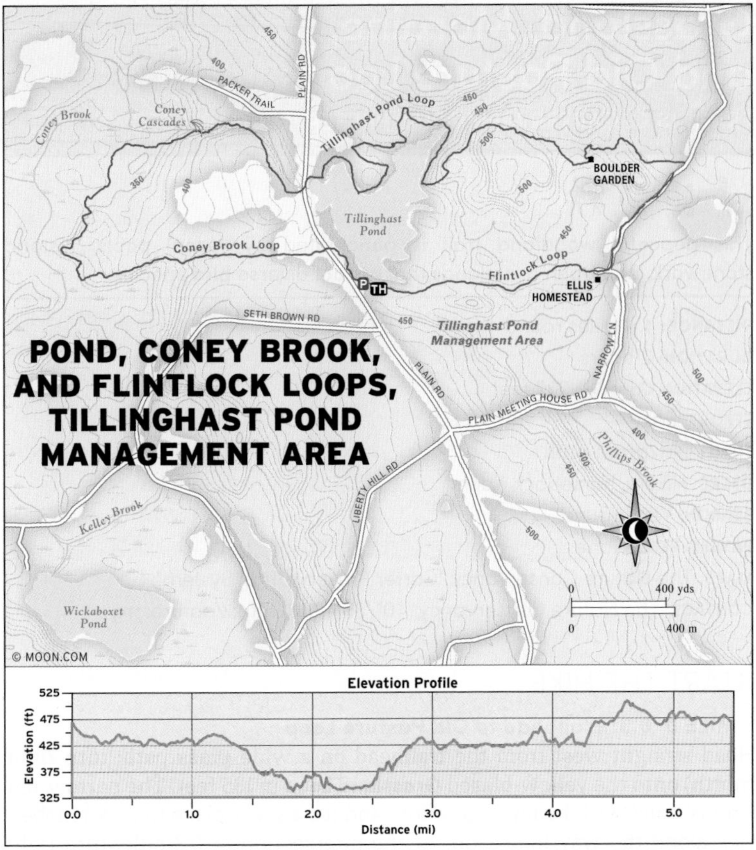

POND, CONEY BROOK, AND FLINTLOCK LOOPS, TILLINGHAST POND MANAGEMENT AREA

Coney Brook
Coney Cascades
Packer Trail
Plain Rd
Tillinghast Pond Loop
Boulder Garden
Tillinghast Pond
Coney Brook Loop
Flintlock Loop
Ellis Homestead
Seth Brown Rd
Tillinghast Pond Management Area
Narrow Ln
Plain Meeting House Rd
Phillips Brook
Liberty Hill Rd
Kelley Brook
Wickaboxet Pond
0 400 yds
0 400 m

Elevation Profile
Elevation (ft): 525, 475, 425, 375, 325
Distance (mi): 0.0, 1.0, 2.0, 3.0, 4.0, 5.0

DIRECTIONS

From West Greenwich on RI-102, turn left onto Plain Meetinghouse Road. At the four-way intersection, turn right onto Plain Road and continue for 0.5 mile. The large parking area on the right is marked with a Nature Conservancy sign and trailhead kiosk.

GPS COORDINATES: 41°38'47.2"N 71°45'28.7"W

▲ CONEY BROOK LOOP

9 Grassland, Moraine, and Old Pasture Loops

FRANCIS C. CARTER MEMORIAL PRESERVE, CHARLESTOWN

This peaceful woodland trail is punctuated by vernal pools, historic stonework, and open grasslands that attract diverse bird species.

DISTANCE: 4.4 miles round-trip

DURATION: 2 hours

ELEVATION CHANGE: 227 feet

EFFORT: Easy

TRAIL: Dirt/grass path

USERS: Hikers, horseback riders

SEASON: Year-round

PASSES/FEES: None

MAPS: The Nature Conservancy "Carter Preserve Trail System"

CONTACT: The Nature Conservancy, 401/331-7110, http://nature.org

START THE HIKE

▸ MILE 0-0.3: Trailhead to Old Pasture Loop

Head straight west from the trailhead on a wide grass path; turn right (north) onto the yellow-blazed **Grassland Loop** in 135 feet. The narrow, flat trail is lined with heavy vegetation, and it's a great place to pick blueberries along the way in season. At the intersection at 0.3 mile, turn right (north) onto the blue-blazed **Old Pasture Loop** trail.

▸ MILE 0.3-0.9: Old Pasture Loop to Moraine Loop

Cross the stone wall and then follow alongside it in a black oak forest dotted with fern and pitch pine. Reach a fork in another 0.3 mile and keep right (east) on the blue-blazed trail. When you reach the large boulder and intersection with the **Moraine Loop** at 0.9 mile, turn right (south) to follow the orange blazes.

▸ MILE 0.9-3.0: Moraine Loop to Grassland Loop

The trail climbs slightly uphill to the south before bending back northwest. At the intersection with the **Split Rock Loop** at 1.2 miles, stay left (east) on the orange-blazed trail. Pass the other end of the Split Rock Trail at 1.6 miles, then another spur trail at 2.2 miles, keeping left (north) at both intersections. Continue on the Moraine Loop and pass several giant boulders and a stone wall, then cross over the historic dam at 2.7 miles. Reach the intersection with the **Old Pasture Loop** and bear right (north) to follow the blue blazes. The trail winds along a bog and through a patch of tall ferns before it reaches the intersection with the **Grassland Loop** at 3.0 miles.

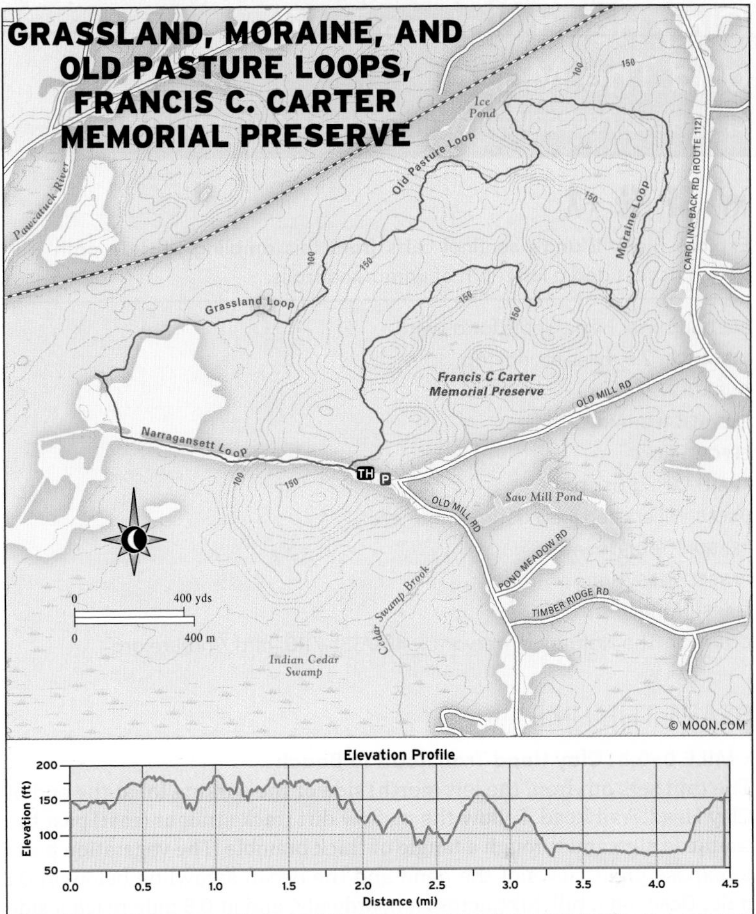

‣ MILE 3.0–4.4: Grassland Loop to Trailhead

Turn right (north) onto the yellow-blazed trail, which passes the bog and winds left uphill to a bench. The trail here can sometimes be brushy and overgrown, but it shortly emerges in an open field at 3.2 miles. At the field, turn right (west) onto the grass path and follow it along the northern border of the meadow. When you reach the intersection with the Narragansett Loop at 3.7 miles, keep left on the Grassland Loop, which eventually enters a pitch pine forest and leads straight southeast back to the parking area in 0.7 mile.

DIRECTIONS

From I-95, take exit 3 to RI-138 E and follow it to the intersection with RI-112. Follow RI-112 past a sign for Carter Preserve and take the next right onto Old Mill Road. At the next Carter Preserve sign, bear right onto the dirt road and follow it to the large parking area at the end of the drive.

GPS COORDINATES: 41°25'33.2"N 71°39'46.8"W

10 Clay Head Nature Trail and The Maze

CLAY HEAD PRESERVE, NEW SHOREHAM, BLOCK ISLAND

Explore Block Island's sentinel cliffs from this ambling seaside path with beach access and a labyrinth of unmarked trails.

BEST: Summer hikes, spots for a swim

DISTANCE: 2.9 miles round-trip

DURATION: 2 hours

ELEVATION CHANGE: 114 feet

EFFORT: Easy

TRAIL: Dirt/grass path

USERS: Hikers, leashed dogs, swimmers

SEASON: Year-round

PASSES/FEES: None

MAPS: None

CONTACT: The Nature Conservancy, 401/331-7110, http://nature.org

START THE HIKE

▸ MILE 0-0.5: Clay Head Trail Road to Beach

The trail sets out from the left (north) side of the parking lot at the end of Clay Head Trail Road. Follow the narrow dirt track straight (east) past the trailhead sign and through a tangle of thick bramble. The vegetation parts to expose great views of the pond and the ocean sprawling below in 0.1 mile. Descend a hill, hike across a boardwalk, and at 0.5 mile reach a side path opening to a gorgeous sandy beach on the right (east) side.

▸ MILE 0.5-1.0: Beach to Pond

Turn left (northeast) to stay on the sandy trail as it winds uphill. From here, the trail is marked with waist-high posts with blue arrows. You will pass several side paths to the left that lead into "The Maze," an unmarked network of intertwining trails lined with thick vegetation. Follow the blue arrows straight north to stay on the main Clay Head Trail, which emerges on a bluff at 0.7 mile to reveal ocean vistas from the top of the 800-foot clay cliffs. As the trail winds along, it passes lovely stone walls and meadows. Arrive at a secluded pond at 1.0 mile, which offers great chances to glimpse rare wildlife such as the yellow-crowned night heron.

▸ MILE 1.0-2.9: Pond to The Maze

Continue straight north from the pond and reach a fork at 1.2 miles. Bear left (northwest) to follow the red arrows for a brief tour of The Maze. This counterclockwise loop (keep turning left) will return you to the fork in about 0.6 mile. From here, backtrack straight south on the blue-arrow trail to return to the parking lot.

▲ VIEWS FROM THE CLAY HEAD BLUFF

DIRECTIONS

Take the ferry to New Shoreham, Block Island. Take Water Street north around the bend where it becomes Dodge Street. At the four-way intersection, turn right on Corn Neck Road and continue for 2.6 miles. Turn right onto Clayhead Trail Road and follow it until the end. The road ends in a large dirt parking lot with a Clay Head Nature Trail sign.

GPS COORDINATES: 41°12'30.7"N 71°33'43.8"W

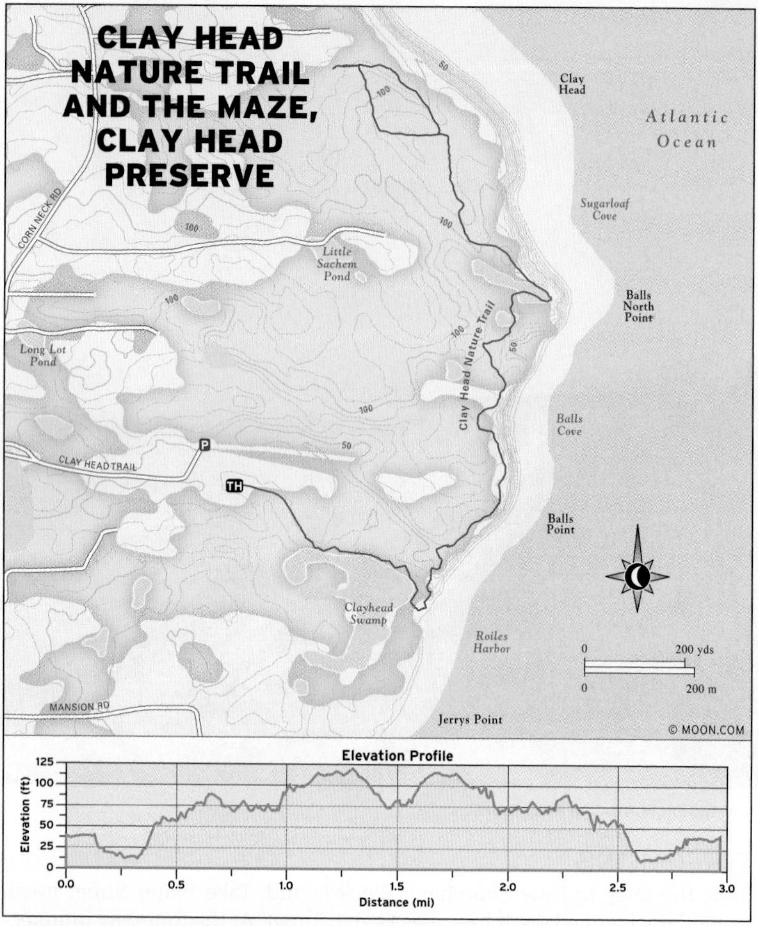

CLAY HEAD NATURE TRAIL AND THE MAZE, CLAY HEAD PRESERVE

Clay Head
Atlantic Ocean
Sugarloaf Cove
Balls North Point
Balls Cove
Balls Point
Roiles Harbor
Jerrys Point
Little Sachem Pond
Long Lot Pond
Clayhead Swamp
Clay Head Nature Trail
CORN NECK RD
CLAY HEAD TRAIL
MANSION RD
P
TH
0 200 yds
0 200 m
© MOON.COM

Elevation Profile

Elevation (ft): 0, 25, 50, 75, 100, 125
Distance (mi): 0.0, 0.5, 1.0, 1.5, 2.0, 2.5, 3.0

▲ THE CLAY HEAD BEACH

NEARBY CAMPGROUNDS

NAME	LOCATION	FACILITIES	SEASON	FEE
George Washington State Campground	2185 Putnam Pike, Chepachet, RI 02814	74 RV and tent sites, 2 shelters; restrooms	mid-April–October	$20-35
401/568-2085, www.riparks.com/Locations/LocationGeorgeWashington.html				
Fishermen's Memorial State Campground	1011 Point Judith Rd., Narragansett, RI 02882	182 RV and tent sites; restrooms	mid-April–October	$20
401/789-8374, www.riparks.com/Locations/LocationFishermens.html				
Burlingame State Campground	1 Burlingame State Park Rd., Charlestown, RI 02813	692 standard sites, 20 cabins, 1 shelter; restrooms	mid-April–mid-October	$20-35
401/322-8910, www.riparks.com/Locations/LocationBurlingameCampground.html				
Charlestown Breachway	Charlestown Beach Rd., Charlestown, RI 02813	75 RV sites	mid-April–October	$20
401/322-8910, www.riparks.com/Locations/LocationCharlestownBreachway.html				
East Beach Campground	E Beach Rd., Charlestown, RI 02813	20 sites for "camping unit" vehicles	late-September–late-May	$20
Permit-only, 401/322-8910, www.riparks.com/Locations/LocationEastBeach.html				
Second Beach Family Campground	474 Sachuest Point Rd., Middletown, RI 02842	RV sites; hookups; restrooms with showers	late-September–late-May	$70
401/846-6273, http://parks.middletownri.com/second-beach-family-campground/				

HIKING TIPS

Safety

Safety is paramount to making sure your day on the New England trails is an enjoyable experience for all. The best way to ensure safety is to plan for your hike ahead of time. Consider preparedness your first defense in the prevention of accidents and mishaps. If something does go wrong, have an emergency plan in place that will allow you to seek help while keeping all members of your group safe. A Wilderness First Aid class is a great resource for anyone who spends time outdoors. Check out the SOLO School of Wilderness Medicine for classes across New England.

BEFORE YOU GO

Before you set out on your hike, review a map and research your desired route. Keep in mind that a 2-mile hike straight up a mountain peak may require more time, effort, and resources than a gentle 2-mile hike along a beach. Consider your route's unique terrain and weather as well as the size and ability of your group when planning and packing for your hike. In addition to "The 10 Essentials" listed below, make sure you have any equipment required for enjoyment and comfort on your hike. It's also a good idea to double-check the fit and quality of essential gear ahead of time. Does your footwear give you uncomfortable blisters? Does that tear in your rain jacket let in excess moisture? If you foresee trouble with any of your supplies, repair or replace those items before the need to use them arises.

Always be sure to let someone know where you are traveling and when you plan to return, no matter how easy, close to home, or familiar a hike seems. If an accident happens on the trail, this valuable information could be the key to making sure you return home safely. Cell phones and communication devices are prone to battery failures and lapses in service, and should not be relied on as your sole method for obtaining help.

The 10 Essentials

No matter where you travel, experts agree that these "10 Essentials" should make their way into your backpack.

Hydration: Water bottle or hydration pack, plenty of water, and filtration/purification system

Nutrition: Plenty of food, plus extra snacks in case you are out longer than anticipated

Navigation: A detailed map and compass, a GPS device, and knowledge of how to use them

First Aid Kit: Be sure your kit includes enough supplies for the length of your trip and the size of your group

Illumination: A headlamp (even if you don't expect to be out after dark)

Sun Protection: Sunblock, a hat, and breathable layers to cover your skin

Insulation: Warm layers, preferably made of wool and synthetics that insulate even when wet

Fire: A lighter or waterproof matches in case you need to start a fire for warmth

Pocketknife/Repair Tools: A blade or multi-tool can come in handy throughout a trip, especially if your equipment needs repair or adjusting

Emergency Survival Gear: If stranded, an emergency blanket, tent, and sleeping bag can help protect you from the elements; a whistle and flares allow you to signal for help

Hiking Prep

Hiking is remarkable in that almost everyone can do it, regardless of age or body type. That said, it's important to know both your strengths and your limitations when choosing a trail in New England. Some of the trails listed in this book require a high baseline of existing physical fitness and endurance. Hikers should be trained and confident in their physical abilities before attempting trails marked "strenuous." We absolutely recommend that hikers challenge themselves mentally and physically when exploring New England, but it's a good idea to start small and work your way up to more challenging trails as your body is ready.

On the Trail

A good understanding of navigation is one of the best tools a hiker can have. In addition to map and compass skills, familiarize yourself with the various forms of trail markers. Most hiking trails use "blazes," colored markers painted or nailed along the route to mark the way (usually found on trees or rocks). Most trails are marked with a single color or symbol that differentiates that trail from other trails in a park. Some hikes, especially those above the tree line, utilize cairns—pyramid-like towers of rock that mark a pathway. While the majority of the hikes in this book are well marked, hikers should pay especially close attention at intersections to ensure they remain on the right track. If you're unsure which way to go, don't be afraid to reach out! Most hikers are friendly and more than willing to help.

Practice common courtesy on the trail. Respect other visitors by yielding and creating space where necessary, controlling your pets, and keeping voices at a polite volume.

WEATHER

There is a saying in New England that "if you don't like the weather, wait five minutes and it will change." In a nutshell, New England weather is unpredictable and often extreme. Summers (late May-September) bring pleasantly warm daytime temperatures and cooler evenings. Still, summer weather can be chilly, especially in the north and at high elevations, and thunderstorms are frequent in warmer weather. Spring and fall consist of cooler daytime temperatures and often cold nights. Spring also brings on the notorious New England "mud season" caused by excessive rain and snow runoff. Winters are long and cold, and snowfall is likely, especially in the mountainous northern states. Snow and frigid temperatures may begin as early as October and linger into April.

HIKING WITH CHILDREN

It's never too early for kids to hit the trail and start learning about the natural beauty that surrounds them. But remember, your young companions are depending on you to prepare for the day with supplies and information. Here are some tips to help turn first-timers into lifelong hikers.

- GEAR UP: While they may not be carrying as heavy a pack, kids should still have all the essential gear to keep them comfortable for a day on the trail. This includes appropriate footwear and plenty of layers to stay warm and dry in all conditions. For younger kids, consider a carrying pack for when they need a break.
- KNOW YOUR LIMITS: Visit shorter, less-steep trails when traveling with little legs, and factor in extra time for rest breaks, play, and exploration. You may also want to pick a hike with a special destination or activity (like swimming) so kids have something to look forward to.
- DOUBLE DOWN ON SNACKS: Proper hydration and nutrition is crucial to keeping us all energized on the trail, but children may be especially sensitive to missed snack times. Having plenty of tasty treats on hand can help improve energy and mood and provide necessary encouragement on tough trails.
- MAKE IT A LEARNING EXPERIENCE: Foster curiosity about the natural world by asking and answering questions about where you are, what you're doing, and why. Use events on the trail as "teaching moments." Even a tough day on the trail can help inspire tenacity and perseverance in young minds.

BEST HIKES WITH KIDS

- MAINE: Wells Reserve (page 107)
- NEW HAMPSHIRE: The Flume (page 178)
- MASSACHUSETTS: Bartholomew's Cobble (page 471)
- VERMONT: Devil's Gulch (page 393)
- RHODE ISLAND: Norman Bird Sanctuary (page 570)
- CONNECTICUT: Chauncey Peak (page 531)

Hikers should take extra precautions against weather-related incidents of hypothermia and frostbite, especially on New England's high peaks. Use additional caution in the event of thunder and lightning storms. Avoid high peaks, open spaces, and water during lightning events.

New England water can be quite cold, even in summertime, and coastal surf can be dangerous. Always heed local warnings regarding swimming and never swim alone.

WILDLIFE

While hikers are unlikely to encounter hostile wildlife on New England trails, it is important to take precautions to ensure your safety and the safety of any animals you encounter. Observe wild animals from a safe distance and do not attempt to approach or follow them. Be especially cautious around injured, mating, nesting, and young animals, and report any odd or aggressive behavior to local authorities. Always heed local signs regarding wildlife and avoid any restricted areas designated to protect them.

Avoid feeding wildlife intentionally or accidentally by storing and transporting your food and trash properly. A taste of human food can change the feeding behaviors of wild animals in ways that are dangerous for both humans and wildlife. This applies not only to large creatures, but smaller animals like rodents and birds.

Moose

Moose are gentle and elusive creatures, and most hikers are lucky to spot them in their natural habitat. However, moose are responsible for hundreds of car accidents each year. Use caution driving to and from the trailhead, especially in areas marked with Moose Crossing signs.

Bears

Black bears are common across Maine, New Hampshire, Vermont, and the western parts of Massachusetts and Connecticut, although they may be spotted elsewhere. In general, these creatures are harmless, but they may cause problems when they have been exposed to human food, or if they feel threatened. When camping, secure food and other scented items in a bear hang or a bear-proof box. If you encounter a bear on the trail, speak in calm tones and slowly wave your arms. This will help the bear identify you as human and it will usually flee. Move away slowly sideways. If the bear charges or makes aggressive movements towards you, stand your ground. Never run or climb a tree, and never place yourself between a mother bear and its cubs. As long as hikers behave respectfully, most bear encounters are exciting experiences that do not result in injury.

Snakes

Most species of snakes found in New England are harmless. However, although they are endangered and rarely encountered, timber rattlesnakes and northern copperheads are present throughout New England. These venomous pit vipers are marked by a triangular head. Timber rattlesnakes have black tails with a distinctive rattle at the end, and are most commonly found in rocky areas of western Massachusetts. Reddish-hued copperheads are most common from Massachusetts southward. Both species are wary of humans and are unlikely to strike unless provoked. When climbing, always look before placing your hand, and never attempt to pick up a snake. In the unlikely event you are bitten by a venomous snake, wrap the wound distally to proximally in an Ace bandage and seek immediate medical treatment.

Insects

Biting insects such as mosquitoes, blackflies, no-see-ums, and greenheads are a fact of life in New England. While cases of eastern equine encephalitis (EEE) and other mosquito-borne illnesses have occurred in the region, most insect bites are little more than an itchy nuisance. Biting insects usually reach their peak in midsummer, and can be especially vicious in the evening, in shady areas, and near water. Protect yourself with long-sleeved clothing and insect repellant. Various species of bees can also be found in New England. Beestings can be painful and uncomfortable, but they may also cause serious allergic reactions in some individuals. If someone in your party has a history of allergic reactions to beestings, carry an epinephrine injector and an antihistamine such as Benadryl in your first aid kit.

Ticks

Though some are only as big as a pinhead, ticks are one of the most ubiquitous hazards of hiking in New England. These ectoparasites feed on the blood of humans and other species and may transmit potentially serious illnesses including Lyme disease, babesiosis, and anaplasmosis. While deer ticks (also known as black-legged ticks) are implicated in the spread of most tick-borne diseases in New England, dog ticks and lone star ticks can also spread pathogens. To prevent tick-borne illness, use insect repellant and wear long clothing. Perform a "tick check" after spending time outdoors by scanning your body for crawling or embedded ticks, which prefer warm crevices in the skin. An embedded tick is no cause for alarm, but it should be removed as soon as possible to decrease the likelihood of disease transmission. Simply grasp the tick with a pair of tweezers as close to the skin as possible and pull the entire body straight out, firmly but gently. A little bit of irritation is normal, but if you notice a rash, fever, or flu-like symptoms following a tick bite, consult your physician immediately. Most tick-borne illnesses are mild when caught early and can be easily treated with antibiotics.

HAZARDOUS PLANTS

Rash-causing plants like poison ivy and poison sumac can put a serious damper on your experience of the great outdoors. These prevalent New England plants contain a compound called urushiol, which causes an extremely itchy, blistery contact dermatitis in most humans. The best defense against both plants is knowing how to identify and avoid them.

Poison ivy is the more common of the two plants. Most New Englanders stand by the rule "Leaves of three, let it be." The plant is notorious for its three almond-shaped leaves (sometimes notched) with a reddish dot where the leaves meet. Leaves are green in summer, reddish or yellow in fall, and may appear to have a shiny coat. Poison ivy is most often encountered on a hairy vine, but can also grow as a shrub or as individual sprouts. In late summer and fall, it produces clusters of whitish, waxy berries.

Poison sumac is also widespread in New England, though it is most commonly found in and surrounding wetlands. This woody shrub has long ovoid leaves that sometimes take on a reddish hue, and white clustered berries. While less common on the trail, poison sumac is even more toxic than poison ivy, and should be identified and avoided accordingly.

▲ POISON IVY

If you suspect you've come into contact with either of these plants, it's important to wash your skin and clothing as soon as possible to reduce the risk of rash. Specialty products like Tecnu can help break down urushiol, but most regular soaps will help remove the rash-causing oil. A typical laundry cycle will remove urushiol from clothing. If a rash breaks out, keep the area clean and ventilated, and avoid scratching. Topical over-the-counter anti-itch treatments can bring some relief, but if the rash is persistent, widespread, or on sensitive areas of the body, a prescription steroid may be necessary.

PROTECT THE ENVIRONMENT

Help preserve the beauty and tranquility of the natural spaces you visit by following the seven "Leave No Trace" principles as outlined by the Leave No Trace Center for Outdoor Ethics.

Plan Ahead and Prepare: Unprepared hikers are more likely to impact the environment if they become ill, injured, or lost. View the above sections to ensure you and your group have the right equipment, skills, and plan for an enjoyable and environmentally friendly trip.

Travel and Camp on Durable Surfaces: Trails do not only exist to mark the way and make hiking easier. Restricting foot traffic to designated areas helps reduce human impact, especially in frequently visited areas. Trail crews work hard to maintain safe, weather- and traffic-resistant trails—use them! Staying on-trail helps protect sensitive areas, such as alpine zones, from overuse.

Dispose of Waste Properly: Carry in, carry out! Most backcountry trails are not equipped with trash cans, so hikers should plan to pack out any waste with them. Make sure to scan your area for "microtrash"—items like bottle caps and wrapper corners that are easily left behind. While many trailheads are equipped with outhouses or restroom facilities, hikers should familiarize themselves with protocol for when nature calls on the trail. Bury solid human waste in a "cathole" 6 inches deep, at least 200 feet away from trails, water, or camping areas. Pack out toilet paper and hygiene products along with other trash.

Leave What You Find: Finding a beautiful flower, a shed antler, or a historical artifact is one of the many joys of hiking in New England. Let others enjoy the same experience by leaving what you find where you find it. This not only preserves history and natural spaces, but helps eliminate the introduction and transport of non-native species.

Minimize Fire Impacts: While there are other ways of cooking, staying warm, and finding entertainment outdoors, fires can be a great experience when enjoyed safely and sustainably. Where fires are allowed, keep them small, contain them to designated or low-impact areas, and extinguish them properly. Avoid transporting firewood from nonlocal areas to prevent the spread of pests and diseases.

Respect Wildlife: Treat wildlife and their habitats with caution and dignity. Observe wildlife from a distance and never feed wild animals. See also "Wildlife."

Be Considerate of Other Visitors: Allow other hikers to enjoy a peaceful and pleasant trail experience by sharing spaces, controlling volume, and practicing common courtesy and respect. See also "On the Trail."

PASSES, PERMITS, AND FEES

Veterans of the U.S. military can access most New England parks free of charge.

America the Beautiful Pass: Covers entrance fees to all U.S. national parks and national wildlife refuges, plus day-use fees to all national forests, grasslands, and lands managed by the Bureau of Land Management, Bureau of Reclamation, and U.S. Army Corps of Engineers for the driver and up to four adults per vehicle. Valid for one year from date of purchase. $80. Purchase at http://store.usgs.gov/pass, 888/275-8747, or at most park entrances.

Maine State Parks Annual Passes: Vehicle season pass admits pass holder and occupants of vehicle to day-use facilities at most Maine state parks and historic sites (some exclusions apply). $105. Individual season pass admits only pass holder. $55. Senior discounts available. Valid for one calendar year. Purchase at http://maine.gov/dacf/parks, 207/624-9950, or at most park entrances.

New Hampshire State Parks Annual Passes: Individual season pass admits pass holder to most day-use New Hampshire state parks (some exclusions apply). $60. Family season passes admit 2 adults and up to 4 dependents. $105 residents/$120 nonresidents. Youth and senior discounts available. Valid for one calendar year. Purchase at http://nhstateparks.org/planning/schedule-and-fees, 603/271-3556, or at most park entrances.

HIKING APPS

Smartphones can be useful both on the trail and while planning your trip. Not only can they help with navigation, they can be a fun way to learn more about the natural environment, whether it's identifying flora and fauna or predicting the weather. Though cell service is not always reliable in some hiking areas, many apps have offline components.

- GAIA GPS: This navigation app shows detailed topographic maps, hiking trails, and landmarks, but it also tracks your hike as you go along, providing information on distance, time, elevation, and more. Free. A $19.99 membership unlocks additional useful features. Available for Android and iOS.
- FIRST AID AMERICAN RED CROSS: Keep your cool in any medical emergency with this preloaded guide to treating common illnesses and injuries. English and Spanish translations. Free. Available for Android and iOS.
- WEATHER LIVE: One of the most accurate weather apps out there, Weather Live provides real-time forecast information complete with easy-to-read radar, maps, and helpful warnings regarding sudden weather changes. $2.99 iOS/$1.99 Android.
- PEAKVISOR: Get the most out of each mountain vista with PeakVisor, which helps users identify each summit in their line of sight using your phone's camera and GPS. $5.99 iOS/$4.49 Android.
- MERLIN BIRD ID: From the Cornell Lab of Ornithology, this acclaimed birding app allows users to identify avian species by uploading a picture or using the "Bird ID Wizard." Free. Available for Android and iOS.

Be sure to ask park staff if there is an app for the hiking area you're visiting. Many organizations have apps with additional maps and interpretive information.

Vermont State Parks Annual Passes: Season vehicle passes admit pass holder and up to 8 passengers to all Vermont state parks. $90. Individual season pass admits only pass holder. $30. Valid for one calendar year. Purchase at http://vtstateparks.com/fees, 888/409-7579, or at most park entrances.

Massachusetts State Parks Annual Passes: The DCR ParksPass covers parking fees at most Massachusetts state parks (park admission is free). $60 residents/$120 nonresidents. Valid for one calendar year. Senior lifetime pass: $10. Purchase at http://reserveamerica.com, 877/422-6762, or at most park entrances.

Connecticut State Parks Annual Pass: Nonresidents may purchase a season pass to cover parking fees at most Connecticut state parks (park admission is free). $112. No on-site charge for CT residents. Valid for one calendar year. Purchase at http://ct.gov/deep, 860/424-3105, or at most park entrances.

Rhode Island Beaches Season Pass: Covers admission and parking at all Rhode Island state beaches for the pass holder's vehicle and all passengers. $30 residents/$60 nonresidents. Senior discounts available. Valid for one calendar year. Purchase at state beach locations from opening day in May until Labor Day. Info at http://riparks.com.

Trustees of Reservations Membership: Provides free or discounted membership to all Trustees of Reservations properties in Massachusetts. Memberships start at $50 individual/$70 family. Additional parking permit needed for Crane Beach. Valid for one year from date of purchase. Purchase at http://thetrustees.org/membership, 978/921-1944, or at most Trustees park entrances.

White Mountain National Forest Season Pass: Covers parking and admission for one vehicle at developed White Mountain National Forest sites that require a recreation fee (most WMNF areas are free). Holders of the America the Beautiful Pass do not need to purchase an additional WMNF pass. $30 individual/$50 household. Valid for one year from date of purchase. Purchase at http://fs.usda.gov/detail/whitemountain, 603/536-6100, or WMNF offices and information centers.

Baxter State Park Season Pass: Admits vehicles to Baxter State Park for summer season. Additional fees apply for camping. $40. Purchase at park entrance. Info http://baxterstatepark.org, 207/723-5140.

Resources

CLUBS AND MEMBERSHIPS

Appalachian Mountain Club

A great resource for Appalachian Trail maps, lodging, and trail information, especially in the White Mountains. Annual membership saves pass holders 20 percent on AMC lodging, programs, and maps, plus gear discounts, a magazine subscription, and more. Valid for one year from date of purchase. Starting at $50. Purchase at http://outdoors.org/get-involved, 800/372-1758, or at most AMC locations.

Green Mountain Club

The best contact for maps and information about the Long Trail in Vermont. Annual membership gives the pass holder a discount on GMC gear, workshops, and publications, plus deals at participating retailers, inns, and B&Bs. Valid for one year from date of purchase. Starting at $45. Purchase at http://greenmountainclub.org, 802/244-5864, or at the GMC visitors center.

Appalachian Trail Conservancy

Provides helpful information and maps for the Appalachian Trail, especially for thru-hikers. Help protect the Appalachian Trail with an annual ATC membership. Benefits include a map, magazine subscription, retail/lodging discounts, and more. Starting at $50. Purchase at http://atctrailstore.org.

HIKING WITH DOGS

Man's best friend can double as man's best hiking buddy with a little extra preparation. Taking your dog for a hike is a great way for you and your pet to bond and get some exercise. Just be sure to follow the below measures to make sure your dog's day on the trail is safe and enjoyable for all.

- CHECK PARK GUIDELINES: While many parks allow dogs, others may impose rules to help protect local wildlife. Dogs can pose a risk to endangered species and delicate ecosystems, so some parks must limit dog visits entirely or during sensitive times of year.
- BRING A LEASH: Even the best-behaved dogs may make wildlife or other hikers feel uncomfortable. Keep your dog on a leash to ensure he or she stays on the trail and away from delicate habitats, and always control your dog as other hikers approach.
- CLEAN UP AFTER YOUR PET: Bring bags so you can pick up any dog poo and dispose of it in a proper waste receptacle. This is the best way to ensure that no waste finds its way into the environment or onto other hikers' boots.
- BRING EXTRA FOOD AND WATER: A vigorous hike can be taxing, even for a fit and energetic dog. Be sure to bring plenty of water, a drinking bowl, and snacks to keep your dog happy and healthy on the trail.
- CONSIDER PROTECTIVE CLOTHING: If it's particularly cold out, consider outfitting your dog with a sweater or jacket to keep him or her comfortable. During hunting season, it's a good idea to dress your dog in blaze orange or another bright color to distinguish him or her from other animals.
- TAKE PRECAUTIONS AGAINST TICKS AND POISON IVY: Do a thorough tick check on your dog after your hike to protect him or her from serious illnesses such as Lyme disease. Remove attached ticks with tweezers as you would from a human. While poison ivy does not cause a rash in dogs, pets may spread the rash-causing oil to humans. If you suspect your dog has come in contact with poison ivy, give him or her a bath.

Randolph Mountain Club

This beloved local group helps maintain trails and shelters in the White Mountains. A great resource for trail information. Members receive discounts on lodging, and fees directly benefit trails. $30 individual/$60 family. Purchase at http://randolphmountainclub.org.

Trustees of Reservations

A great resource for trail information and special events at select properties in Massachusetts. See "Passes, Permits, and Fees."

National Audubon Society

Aims to protect birds and manages conservation areas throughout the United States. Members receive a magazine subscription, membership in a local chapter, admission to special events, and more. Starting at $20. Purchase at http://audubon.org.

Mass Audubon

Independent of the National Audubon Society, this Massachusetts group is dedicated to protecting the nature of the commonwealth through conservation lands, programming, and more. Members receive free admission to properties and discounts on programs and gear. Starting at $48 individual/$65 family. Purchase at http://massaudubon.org.

Nature Conservancy

A membership with this conservation organization helps support many of the properties in this book. Members receive news, magazines, and more. Starting at $50. Purchase at http://nature.org.

WEATHER AND SAFETY

In case of emergency, dial 911.

National Oceanographic and Atmospheric Administration

Best resource for tidal and weather information nationwide. 1401 Constitution Avenue NW, Room 5128, Washington, DC 20230. http://noaa.gov.

Mount Washington Observatory

Best resource for weather information in the White Mountains. 2779 White Mountain Highway, P.O. Box 2310, North Conway, NH 03860. 603/356-2137, http://mountwashington.org.

HikeSafe

Great information on hiker preparedness and education. http://hikesafe.com.

NH Hike Safe Card

Purchase of this voluntary card helps support New Hampshire Fish and Game search and rescue efforts, and pass holders are not required to repay costs in the event they need rescue (not applicable in instances of negligence). $25 individual/$35 family. Purchase at http://nhfishandgame.com or at the Fish and Game office in Concord.

SOLO Wilderness Medicine

Provides classes for Wilderness First Aid, Wilderness First Responder, and Wilderness EMT certifications. 623 Tasker Hill Rd., Conway, NH 03818. 603/447-6711, http://soloschools.com.

NATIONAL PARKS, FORESTS, AND SEASHORES

White Mountain National Forest

71 White Mountain Drive, Campton, NH 03223. 603/536-6100, http://fs.usda.gov/main/whitemountain

Green Mountain National Forest

231 North Main Street, Rutland, VT 05701. 802/747-6700, http://fs.usda.gov/main/gmfl

Acadia National Park
PO Box 177, Bar Harbor, ME 04609; Hulls Cove Visitor Center, Route 3 Bar Harbor, ME 04609. 207/288-3338, http://nps.gov/acad

Cape Cod National Seashore
99 Marconi Site Road, Wellfleet, MA 02667. 508/771-2144, http://nps.gov/caco

FEDERAL WILDLIFE AGENCIES

United States Fish and Wildlife Service
1849 C Street NW, Washington, DC 20240. 800/344-WILD, http://fws.gov

STATE WILDLIFE AGENCIES

New Hampshire Fish and Game Department
11 Hazen Drive, Concord, NH 03301. 603/271-3421, http://wildlife.state.nh.us

Massachusetts Division of Fish and Wildlife (MassWildlife)
1 Rabbit Hill Road, Westborough, MA 01581. 508/389-6300, http://mass.gov/orgs/division-of-fisheries-and-wildlife

Maine Department of Inland Fisheries and Wildlife (Maine Warden Service)
284 State Street, Augusta, ME 04333. 207/287-8000, http://maine.gov/ifw/warden-service

Rhode Island Division of Fish and Wildlife
235 Promenade Street, Providence, RI 02908. 401/222-4700, http://dem.ri.gov/programs/fish-wildlife

Connecticut Department of Energy and Environmental Protection, Bureau of Natural Resources
79 Elm Street, Hartford, CT 06106, 860/424-3000, http://ct.gov/deep

Vermont Fish and Wildlife Department
1 National Life Drive, Dewey Building, Montpelier, VT 05620, 802/828-1000; http://vtfishandwildlife.com

STATE PARK AGENCIES

Massachusetts Department of Conservation and Recreation (DCR)
251 Causeway Street, 9th Floor, Boston, MA 02114. 617/626-1250, http://mass.gov/orgs/department-of-conservation-recreation

Maine Bureau of Parks and Lands
22 State House Station, 18 Elkins Lane, Augusta, ME 04333. 207/287-3821, http://maine.gov/dacf/parks

Vermont Department of Forests, Parks, and Recreation
1 National Life Dr., Davis 2, Montpelier, VT 05620. 888/409-7579, http://vtstateparks.com

New Hampshire Division of Parks and Recreation
172 Pembroke Road, Concord, NH 03301. 603/271-3556, http://nhstateparks.org

Connecticut Department of Energy and Environmental Protection, Bureau of Outdoor Recreation
79 Elm Street, Hartford, CT 06106, 860/424-3200, http://ct.gov/deep

Rhode Island Division of Parks and Recreation
1100 Tower Hill Road, North Kingstown, RI 02852. 401/667-6200, http://riparks.com

MAPS

United States Forest Service
http://nationalforestmapstore.com

United States Geological Survey
888/275-8747, http://usgs.gov/products/maps

Appalachian Mountain Club
10 City Square, Boston MA 02129. 800/262-4455, http://amcstore.outdoors.org

Appalachian Trail Conservancy
Kellogg Conservation Center, P.O. Box 264, South Egremont, MA 01258. 413/528-8002, http://atctrailstore.org

Green Mountain Club
4711 Waterbury-Stowe Road, Waterbury Center, Vermont 05677. 802/244-7037, http://store.greenmountainclub.org

NEW ENGLAND'S LONG TRAILS

Appalachian National Scenic Trail
2,180 miles from Georgia to Maine. Managed in New England by the Appalachian Trail Conservancy and the Appalachian Mountain Club. P.O. Box 50, Harpers Ferry, WV 25425. 304/535-6278, http://nps.gov/appa

New England National Scenic Trail
215 miles from the Connecticut coast through Massachusetts to the New Hampshire border. Managed by the Appalachian Mountain Club and the Connecticut Forest and Park Association. http://newenglandtrail.org

The Long Trail
273 miles through Vermont to the Canadian border. Managed by the Green Mountain Club. Waterbury-Stowe Road, Waterbury Center, VT 05677. 802/244-7037, http://greenmountainclub.org

The Wapack Trail
21 miles from north-central Massachusetts into southern New Hampshire. Managed by Friends of the Wapack Trail. P.O. Box 115, West Peterborough, NH 03468. http://wapack.org

Midstate Trail
92 miles through central Massachusetts from the Rhode Island border to the New Hampshire border. Managed by the Midstate Trail Committee. 2 Westinghouse Parkway, Worcester MA 01606. http://midstatetrail.org

North South Trail

77 miles from the Rhode Island coast to the Massachusetts border. Managed by the North South Trail Council and the Appalachian Mountain Club. http://outdoors.org/Narragansett

Bay Circuit Trail

230 miles circling the Boston area. Managed by the Bay Circuit Alliance. http://baycircuit.org

Cohos Trail

175 miles from the White Mountains to the Canadian border. Managed by the Cohos Trail Association. P.O. Box 82, Lancaster, NH 03584. http://cohostrail.org

Monadnock-Sunapee Greenway

48 miles through central New Hampshire. Managed by the Monadnock-Sunapee Greenway Trail Club. P.O. Box 164, Marlow, NH 03456. http://msgtc.org

INDEX

NO

P

QRS

TU

VWXYZ

NOTES

PHOTO CREDITS

Page 1 © Kelsey Perrett, page 4 © Miles Howard, page 6 © Miles Howard, page 7 © Kelsey Perrett (top), © [illegible] | Dreamstime.com (bottom), page 8 © Kelsey Perrett (top), © Sam Moore (bottom), page 9 © Miles Howard (top), © Kelsey Perrett (middle), © Long Trail Brewing/John Lindquist (bottom), page 10 © Kelsey Perrett (top), © [illegible] | Dreamstime.com (bottom), page 11 © Miles Howard, page 12 © Miles Howard, page 15 © Sam Moore, page 17 © Kelsey Perrett, page 19 © Miles Howard, page 20 © Kelsey Perrett, page 21 © Miles Howard, page 23 © Kelsey Perrett, page 24 © Miles Howard, page 25 © Kelsey Perrett

Maine

All photos by Miles Howard except page 28 © Mary Katherine Wynn | Dreamstime.com, page 31 © Claudine Van Massenhove | Dreamstime.com, page 43 © [illegible] | Shutterstock.com, page 47 © [illegible] | Dreamstime.com, page 55 © Luckydoor | Dreamstime.com, page 61 © Bar Harbor KOA, page 73 © Mike Cherim | Dreamstime.com, page 95 © [illegible] | Dreamstime.com, page 127 © [illegible] | Shutterstock.com, page 161 © Phil Dumond | Dreamstime.com

New Hampshire

All photos by Miles Howard except page 164 © Joseph Jacobs | Dreamstime.com, page 175 © [illegible] | Dreamstime.com, page 177 © Richard Howard, page 211 © Wangkun Jia | Dreamstime.com, page 216 © Yuriy Boyko | Dreamstime.com, page 217 © William Jusseaume | Dreamstime.com, page 218 © Ross Spradling | Dreamstime.com, page 231 © [illegible] | Dreamstime.com, page 232 © Jeffrey Holcombe | Dreamstime.com, page [illegible] © [illegible] | Dreamstime.com, page 265 © Annie [illegible] | Dreamstime.com, page [illegible] © Deborah Howard | Dreamstime.com, page 275 © Jon Bilous | Dreamstime.com, page 282 © Mikael Males | Dreamstime.com, page 287 © Matthew Benoit | Dreamstime.com

Vermont

All photos by Kelsey Perrett except page 290 © Sam Moore, page 292 © Sam Moore, page 294 © Sam Moore, page 297 © Jim Lowrance | Dreamstime.com, page 299 © Sam Moore, page 301 © Sam Moore, page 302 © Sam Moore, page 315 © Miles Howard, page 317 © Sam Moore, page 321 © Sam Moore, page 329 © George Schott, page 340 © Amanda Luiso Photography, page 344 © Miles Howard, page 358 © Miles Howard, page 359 © Miles Howard, page 363 © Miles Howard, page 365 © Miles Howard, page 367 © Miles Howard, page 371 © Ann Moore | Dreamstime.com, page 375 © Miles Howard, page 377 © Miles Howard, page 383 © Miles Howard, page 384 © Sam Moore, page 385 © Sam Moore (left), page 386 © Sam Moore, page 389 © Sam Moore, page 390 © Sam Moore, page 392 © Sam Moore, page 399 © Sam Moore, page 400 © Sam Moore

Massachusetts

All photos by Kelsey Perrett except page 404 © Sam Moore, page 407 © Sam Moore (right), page 429 © Sam Moore (left), page 439 © Sam Moore, page 448 © Sam Moore (left), page 450 © [illegible] | Dreamstime.com, page 465 © Sam Moore, page 468 © Sam Moore, page 470 © Sam Moore, page 471 © Sam Moore

Connecticut

All photos by Kelsey Perrett except, page 502 © Darryl Ferrante | Dreamstime.com

Rhode Island

All photos by Kelsey Perrett except, page 558 © Amanda Luiso Photography, page 564 © Rollsketter Tavern, Douglas and Miranda Brumley, page 578 © Amanda Luiso Photography, 580 © Amanda Luiso Photography

Background

© Kelsey Perrett

NOTES

PHOTO CREDITS

Page 1, © Kelsey Perrett, page 3 © Miles Howard, page 6 © Miles Howard, page 7 © Kelsey Perrett (top) © Justinhoffmanoutdoors | Dreamstime.com (bottom), page 8 © Kelsey Perrett (top), © Sam Moore (bottom), page 9 © Miles Howard (top), © Kelsey Perrett (middle), © Long Trail Brewing/John Lundquist (bottom), page 10 © Kelsey Perrett (top), © Detonn | Dreamstime.com (bottom), page 11 © Miles Howard, page 13 © Miles Howard, page 15 © Sam Moore, page 17 © Kelsey Perrett, page 19 © Miles Howard, page 20 © Kelsey Perrett, page 21 © Miles Howard, page 23 © Kelsey Perrett, page 24 © Miles Howard, page 25 © Kelsey Perrett

Maine
All photos by Miles Howard except: page 28 © Mary Katherine Wynn | Dreamstime.com, page 30 © Claudia M. | Dreamstime.com, page 45 © hawkeye978 | Shutterstock.com, page 47 © Kumpyashka | Dreamstime.com, page 55 © Luckydoor | Dreamstime.com, page 61 © Bar Harbor KOA, page 73 © Mike Chabre | Dreamstime.com, page 95 © Lynnemariehale | Dreamstime.com, page 127 © Salvan | Shutterstock.com, page 161 © Phil Dumond | Dreamstime.com

New Hampshire
All photos by Miles Howard except: page 164 © Joseph Jacobs | Dreamstime.com, page 175 © Joseph Jacobs | Dreamstime.com, page 177 © Richard Howard, page 211 © Wangkun Jia | Dreamstime.com, page 215 © Yuriy Barbaruk | Dreamstime.com, page 217 © William Jacovina | Dreamstime.com, page 218 © Paul Roedding | Dreamstime.com, page 221 © Salajean | Dreamstime.com, page 238 © Jeffrey Holcombe | Dreamstime.com, page 263 © Joseph Jacobs | Dreamstime.com, page 265 © Annilein | Dreamstime.com, page 271 © Deborah Hewitt | Dreamstime.com, page 275 © Jon Bilous | Dreamstime.com, page 283 © Mikael Males | Dreamstime.com, page 287 © Matthew Benoit | Dreamstime.com

Vermont
All photos by Kelsey Perrett except: page 290 © Sam Moore, page 292 © Sam Moore, page 294 © Sam Moore, page 296 © Jim Lawrence | Dreamstime.com, page 299 © Sam Moore, page 301 © Sam Moore, page 302 © Sam Moore, page 315 © Miles Howard, page 317 © Sam Moore, page 328 © Sam Moore, page 329 © George Bouret, page 349 © Amanda Luisa Photography, page 354 © Miles Howard, page 355 © Miles Howard, page 359 © Miles Howard, page 363 © Miles Howard, page 365 © Miles Howard, page 369 © Miles Howard, page 371 © Ann Moore | Dreamstime.com, page 375 © Miles Howard, page 381 © Miles Howard, page 383 © Miles Howard, page 384 © Sam Moore, page 385 © Sam Moore (left), page 386 © Sam Moore, page 389 © Sam Moore, page 390 © Sam Moore, page 397 © Sam Moore, page 399 © Sam Moore, page 400 © Sam Moore

Massachusetts
All photos by Kelsey Perrett except: page 404 © Sam Moore, page 407 © Sam Moore (right), page 429 © Sam Moore (left), page 439 © Sam Moore, page 445 © Sam Moore (left), page 448 © Joe Sohm | Dreamstime.com, page 461 © Sam Moore, page 469 © Sam Moore, page 470 © Sam Moore, page 473 © Sam Moore

Connecticut
All photos by Kelsey Perrett except: page 502 © Darya Petrenko | Dreamstime.com

Rhode Island
All photos by Kelsey Perrett except: page 550 © Amanda Luisa Photography, page 554 © Rathskeller Tavern/Douglas and Miranda Bramley, page 579 © Amanda Luisa Photography, 580 © Amanda Luisa Photography

Background
© Kelsey Perrett

TRAILS AT A GLANCE

PAGE	HIKE NAME	DISTANCE	DIFFICULTY
MAINE: ACADIA NATIONAL PARK			
34	Ocean Path	3.6 mi rt	Easy
37	The Beehive	1.6 mi rt	Moderate
40	South Bubble and Jordan Pond	3.6 mi rt	Moderate
43	Hadlock Falls	2 mi rt	Easy
46	Cadillac Mountain	4.6 mi rt	Strenuous
50	Perpendicular and Razorback Trails	2.6 mi rt	Moderate
53	Ship Harbor	1.4 mi rt	Easy
56	Penobscot Mountain via the Jordan Cliffs Trail	3.3 mi rt	Strenuous
MAINE: BAXTER, THE HIGHLANDS, AND THE CARRABASSETT VALLEY			
66	Poplar Stream Falls	4.4 mi rt	Easy
69	Mount Bigelow	10 mi rt	Strenuous
72	Gulf Hagas	8.2 mi rt	Strenuous
76	Mount Kineo	3.5 mi rt	Moderate
79	Orono Bog	1.6 mi rt	Easy
82	Little and Big Niagra Falls	2.4 mi rt	Easy
85	South Turner Mountain	3.6 mi rt	Moderate/Strenuous
88	Debsconeag Ice Caves	2 mi rt	Easy
91	Blueberry Ledges	3.6 mi rt	Easy
94	Mount Katahdin	9.4 mi rt	Stenuous
MAINE: MIDCOAST, CASCO BAY, AND THE MAINE BEACHES			
104	Mount Agamenticus	2.5 mi rt	Easy/Moderate
107	Wells Reserve	2.8 mi rt	Easy
110	Fore River Sanctuary and Jewell Falls	3.3 mi rt	Easy
113	Harpswell Cliff Trail	2.2 mi rt	Easy
116	Oven's Mouth Preserves	3.1 mi rt	Easy
119	Lane's Island	1 mi rt	Easy
122	Ragged Mountain	4.8mi rt	Moderate/Strenuous
125	Mount Megunticook	2.8 mi rt	Moderate

SEASONAL ACCESS	DOG-FRIENDLY	WATER FEATURES	WILDLIFE
May-Oct	X		X
June-Oct			X
June-Oct			X
May-Oct		X	
June-Oct		X	X
June-Oct	X		X
May-Oct			X
June-Oct			X
June-Oct		X	X
June-Sept	X		X
June-Sept	X	X	X
May-Oct			X
May-Nov			X
June-Oct		X	X
May-Oct			X
May-Sept			X
May-Sept		X	X
June-Sept		X	X
Apr-Oct	X		X
May-Oct			X
May-Nov	X	X	X
May-Nov	X	X	X
May-Oct	X		X
May-Nov	X		X
May-Nov	X		X
June-Oct	X	X	X

TRAILS AT A GLANCE (continued)

PAGE	HIKE NAME	DISTANCE	DIFFICULTY
MAINE: THE MAHOOSUCS, EVANS NOTCH, AND RANGELEY LAKES			
134	Caribou Mountain	6.7 mi rt	Strenuous
137	Bickford Slides	2.3 mi rt	Easy/Moderate
140	Lord Hill	4.3 mi rt	Easy
143	Old Speck	7.6 mi rt	Strenuous
146	Table Rock	2.1 mi rt	Moderate/Strenuous
149	Angel Falls	1.4 mi rt	Easy
152	Androscoggin Riverlands	7.2 mi rt	Moderate
156	Tumbledown Mountain	5.8 mi rt	Strenuous
NEW HAMPSHIRE: WHITE MOUNTAIN NATIONAL FOREST			
168	Mount Moosilauke	7.6 mi rt	Strenuous
171	Bridal Veil Falls	4.4 mi rt	Easy/Moderate
174	Mount Lafayette and Franconia Ridge	8.4 mi rt	Strenuous
178	The Flume	2 mi rt	Easy
181	Greeley Ponds	4.2 mi rt	Easty/Moderate
184	Zealand Valley and Thoreau Falls	9.4 mi rt	Moderate
187	Mount Willard	3 mi rt	Easy
190	Arethusa Falls via Bemis Brook	2.8 mi rt	Easy/Moderate
193	Mount Carrigan	10.4 mi rt	Strenuous
196	Basin Rim	4.4 mi rt	Moderate
199	Mount Chocorua	7.4 mi rt	Moderate/Strenuous
203	Mount Washington via Tuckerman Ravine	8.2 mi rt	Strenuous
207	Giant Falls	3 mi rt	Easy
210	Mount Adams	8.6 mi rt	Strenuous
NEW HAMPSHIRE: GREAT NORTH WOODS AND DIXVILLE NOTCH			
220	The Devil's Hopyward	2 mi rt	Easy
223	Table Rock	1.4 mi rt	Moderate/Strenuous
226	Magalloway Mountain	1.8 mi rt	Moderate

SEASONAL ACCESS	DOG-FRIENDLY	WATER FEATURES	WILDLIFE
June-Oct	X	X	X
June-Oct	X	X	X
May-Oct	X		X
June-Oct		X	X
June-Oct		X	
May-Oct	X	X	X
June-Oct			
June-Oct			X
June-Oct	X		X
May-Oct	X	X	X
June-Oct		X	X
June-Oct		X	X
June-Oct	X		X
June-Oct	X	X	X
June-Oct	X	X	X
May-Oct	X	X	X
June-Oct	X	X	X
June-Oct	X	X	X
June-Oct	X	X	X
June-Sept		X	X
May-Oct	X	X	X
June-Sept		X	X
June-Oct			X
May-Oct	X		X
June-Sept	X		X

TRAILS AT A GLANCE (continued)

PAGE	HIKE NAME	DISTANCE	DIFFICULTY
NEW HAMPSHIRE: GREAT NORTH WOODS AND DIXVILLE NOTCH (continued)			
230	Little Hellgate Falls	1.5 mi rt	Easy
233	Fourth Connecticut Lake	2.1 mi rt	Moderate
NEW HAMPSHIRE: WINNIPESAUKEE AND THE LAKES DISTRICT			
240	Belknap Mountain	2.5 mi rt	Moderate
243	Lake Solitude	3.8 mi rt	Easy/Moderate
246	Devil's Den Mountain	5.4 mi rt	Easy/Moderate
249	West and East Rattlesnake	3.8 mi rt	Easy/Moderate
252	Markus Wildlife Sanctuary	2 mi rt	Easy
255	Welch and Dickey	4.2 mi rt	Moderate/Strenuous
258	Welton Falls	2.6 mi rt	Easy
261	Mount Cardigan	3.4 mi rt	Moderate/Strenuous
NEW HAMPSHIRE: MONADNOCK, MERRIMACK VALLEY, AND THE SEACOAST			
270	Monte Rosa and Mount Monadnock	4.6 mi rt	Strenuous
273	Odiorne Point State Park	3.3 mi rt	Easy
276	Purgatory Falls	5 mi rt	Easy/Moderate
279	Madame Sherri's Forest	4 mi rt	Easy/Moderate
282	Skatutakee Mountain and Thumb Mountain	5 mi rt	Moderate
285	Sweet Trail	5.6 mi rt	Easy
VERMONT: NORTHERN GREEN MOUNTAINS			
297	Long Trail: Lincoln Gap to Mount Abraham	4.8 mi rt	Strenuous
300	Long Trail: Brandon Gap to Mount Horrid Great Cliff and Cape Lookout	1.8 mi rt	Moderate/Strenuous
303	Abbey Pound Trail	4.4 mi rt	Easy/Moderate
305	Skylight Pond Trail and Long Trail to Breadloaf Mountain	6.9 mi rt	Moderate
308	Bucklin Trail to Killington Peak	7.4 mi rt	Strenuous
310	Upper Meadow Road, Mountain Road, Mount Tom Road, and Precipice Trail to Mount Tom	3.6 mi rt	Moderate
313	Falls of Lana and Rattlesnake Cliffs	4.9 mi rt	Moderate

SEASONAL ACCESS	DOG-FRIENDLY	WATER FEATURES	WILDLIFE
June-Sept	X	X	X
June-Oct			X
May-Oct	X		X
June-Oct	X		X
May-Oct			X
June-Oct	X		X
May-Oct			X
June-Oct	X		X
May-Oct	X	X	X
June-Oct	X		X
May-Oct			X
Mar-Nov			X
Apr-Oct	X	X	X
May-Oct	X		X
May-Oct	X		X
Apr-Oct	X		X
May-Oct	X		X
May-Oct	X		
May-Oct	X	X	X
May-Oct	X		X
May-Oct	X		X
May-Oct	X		
June-Oct	X	X	X

TRAILS AT A GLANCE (continued)

PAGE	HIKE NAME	DISTANCE	DIFFICULTY
VERMONT: SOUTHERN GREEN MOUNTAINS			
322	Lake Trail and Long Trail to Baker Peak and Griffith Lake	8.4 mi rt	Strenuous
325	Old Town Road and Antone Road to Antone Mountain	5.2 mi rt	Moderate
327	Colby M Chester Memorial Trail to Haystack Mountain	3.2 mi rt	Moderate
330	Keewaydin Trail and Long Trail to White Rocks Cliffs	3.6 mi rt	Moderate/Strenuous
332	Blue Trail to Gettysburg Quarry and Gilbert Lookout	2.4 mi rt	Moderate/Strenuous
335	Blue Summit Trail to Mount Equinox and Lookout Rock	6 mi rt	Strenuous
337	Lye Brook Falls Trail	4.4 mi rt	Moderate
340	Stratton Pond Trail	7.4 mi rt	Easy/Moderate
342	West River Trail and Hamilton Falls Trail	5.6 mi rt	Easy/Moderate
345	Weathersfield Trail to Mount Ascutney	5.2 mi rt	Strenuous
348	Everett Path, Halloween Tree, Cave Trail, and Carriage Road to Everett Cave	2.7 mi rt	Easy
351	Haystack Mountain Trail	4.2 mi rt	Moderate
VERMONT: CHAMPLAIN VALLEY AND STOWE			
358	Stowe Pinnacle	3.4 mi rt	Moderate
361	Sterling Pond	2.6 mi rt	Moderate
364	Mount Mansfield via the Sunset Ridge Trail	5.2 mi rt	Strenuous
367	Little River History Hike	4 mi rt	Easy
370	Camel's Hump	6.8 mi rt	Strenuous
373	Mount Philo	2.2 mi rt	Moderate
376	Waterbury Trail to Mount Hunger	3.9 mi rt	Strenuous
379	Chazy Fossil Reef	1.5 mi rt	Easy

SEASONAL ACCESS	DOG-FRIENDLY	WATER FEATURES	WILDLIFE
May-Oct	X	X	X
Year-round	X		
May-Oct	X		
May-Oct	X		X
Apr-Oct			X
May-Oct	X		X
Year-round	X		X
Apr-Oct	X		X
May-Oct	X	X	
Apr-Nov	X	X	
Apr-Nov	X		
Apr-Nov	X		X
May-Oct	X		X
May-Oct	X		X
May-Oct	X	X	X
June-Oct	X	X	X
June-Oct	X		X
June-Oct	X		X
May-Oct	X	X	
June-Oct			X

TRAILS AT A GLANCE (continued)

PAGE	HIKE NAME	DISTANCE	DIFFICULTY
VERMONT: NORTHEAST KINGDOM			
388	North Trail to Mount Pisgah	4.3 mi rt	Strenuous
391	Long Pond Trail to Bald Mountain	4.2 mi rt	Moderate/Strenuous
393	Long Trail and Babcock Trail to Devil's Gulch	5.4 mi rt	Moderate/Strenuous
396	Long Trail: Jay Pass to Jay Peak	3.4 mi rt	Moderate/Strenuous
398	Little Loop and Peacham Bog Trail	5.9 mi rt	Moderate
401	Monadnock Mountain Trail	4.6 mi rt	Strenuous
MASSACHUSETTS: GREATER BOSTON, NORTH AND SOUTH SHORE			
410	Skyline Trail to Great Blue Hill	5.7 mi rt	Moderate/Strenuous
413	Carriage Paths	3.8 mi rt	Easy
416	Alternate Pond Loop and Emerson's Cliff	2.2 mi rt	Easy
419	Castle Neck Trails	5.6 mi rt	Moderate
422	Midstate Trail to Mount Wachusett	3.9 mi rt	Moderate
425	Wapack Trail to Mount Watatic	3 mi rt	Moderate
MASSACHUSETTS: CAPE COD AND THE ISLANDS			
432	Prospect Hill and the Great Sand Bank	3.1 mi rt	Easy/Moderate
435	Ocean Walk	5.7 mi rt	Easy
438	Great Island Trail	5.6 mi rt	Moderate
441	Marsh Trail	7.9 mi rt	Moderate
MASSACHUSETTS: THE BERKSHIRES			
449	Indian Monument, Squaw Peak, and Hickey Trails to Monument Mountain	2.4 mi rt	Moderate
452	Loop Trail	4.4 mi rt	Easy/Moderate
455	Pine Cobble, Appalachian, and Class of '98 Trails	4.9 mi rt	Moderate
458	Hoosac Range Trail to Spruce Hill	5.4 mi rt	Moderate
460	Money Brook, Appalachian, Hooper, Sperry Road, and Haley Farm Trails to Mount Greylock	11.8 mi rt	Strenuous

SEASONAL ACCESS	DOG-FRIENDLY	WATER FEATURES	WILDLIFE
May-Oct	X		
May-Oct	X		X
May-Oct	X	X	X
May-Oct	X		
May-Oct	X		X
May-Oct	X	X	X
Apr-Nov	X		X
Year-round	X		X
Year-round			
Year-round			X
Apr-Nov	X		X
Apr-Nov	X		X
Year-round	X		X
Year-round	X		X
Year-round	X		X
Year-round	X		X
Apr-Nov	X		
Year-round	X		
Apr-Nov	X		
Apr-Nov	X		X
Apr-Nov	X	X	X

TRAILS AT A GLANCE (continued)

PAGE	HIKE NAME	DISTANCE	DIFFICULTY
MASSACHUSETTS: THE BERKSHIRES (continued)			
463	Mahican-Mohawk and Indian Trails to Todd Mountain	5 mi rt	Strenuous
466	Alander Mountain Trail	6 mi rt	Moderate
468	Race Brook Falls and Appalachian Trail to Race Mountain	5.8 mi rt	Strenuous
471	Ledges, Bailey, Spero, Tulip Tree, and Tractor Path Trails	3.2 mi rt	Easy/Moderate
MASSACHUSETTS: THE PIONEER VALLEY AND NORTH QUABBIN			
478	Robert Frost Trail to Mount Toby	4.3 mi rt	Moderate
481	Metacomet-Monadnock Trail to Norwottuck Horse Caves and Rattlesnake Knob	3.9 mi rt	Moderate
484	Metacomet-Monadnock (New England) Trail	6.6 mi rt	Moderate
487	Tully Trail to Doane's Falls	6 mi rt	Easy/Moderate
489	Metacomet-Monadnock Trail to Hermit's Castle	5.7 mi rt	Moderate
492	Sanctuary Road Loop to High Ledges	3.3 mi rt	Easy
CONNECTICUT: LITCHFIELD HILLS			
503	Robert Ross and Agnes Bowman Trails	6.4 mi rt	Moderate
506	Appalachian Trail: Housatonic River Walk	7.6 mi rt	Easy
509	Pine Knob Loop	2.5 mi rt	Moderate
511	Appalachian Trail: Prospect Mountain and Rand's View	5.2 mi rt	Moderate
514	Macedonia Ridge Trail	6.4 mi rt	Moderate/Strenuous
516	Steep Rock Loop	4.4 mi rt	Moderate
518	Mattatuck and Little Pond Loop "Boardwalk" Trail	3.2 mi rt	Easy
520	Donkey Trail and Hodge Road Loop	3.3 mi rt	Moderate
522	Undermountain Trail, Appalachian Trail, and Paradise Lane Trail to Bear Mountain	6.1 mi rt	Strenuous

SEASONAL ACCESS	DOG-FRIENDLY	WATER FEATURES	WILDLIFE
Apr-Nov	X		X
Apr-Nov	X		X
Apr-Nov	X	X	X
Year-round			
Apr-Nov	X	X	X
Apr-Nov	X		
Apr-Nov	X		
Year-round	X	X	X
Apr-Nov	X	X	
Year-round			
May-Nov	X	X	X
Year-round	X		X
May-Nov		X	X
May-Nov	X		X
May-Nov	X		X
May-Nov	X		X
Year-round	X		X
May-Nov	X		
May-Nov	X		X

TRAILS AT A GLANCE (continued)

PAGE	HIKE NAME	DISTANCE	DIFFICULTY
CONNECTICUT: METACOMET RIDGE			
528	Preserve and Metacomet Trails to Ragged Mountain	5.3 mi rt	Easy
531	Mattabesett Trail to Lamentation Mountain and Chauncey Peak	3.8 mi rt	Moderate
534	Vista Trail	2.4 mi rt	Easy
537	Blue and Violet Trails	4.6 mi rt	Strenuous
540	Talcott Mountain Trail to Heublein Tower	2.4 mi rt	Easy/Moderate
543	Blue Trail to Wolf Den and Indian Chair	4.4 mi rt	Easy/Moderate
RHODE ISLAND			
555	North South Trail to Stepstone Falls	5.6 mi rt	Easy
557	Coventry and Foster Loops	6 mi rt	Easy
560	Foster Cove, Cross Refuge, and Grassy Point Trails	4.5 mi rt	Easy
562	Long and Ell Pond Trail	4.4 mi rt	Easy/Moderate
565	Walkabout Trail	7.8 mi rt	Easy/Moderate
567	Flint Point and Ocean View Loops	2.5 mi rt	Easy
570	Nelson Pond Trail	2.8 mi rt	Easy/Moderate
573	Pond, Coney Brook, and Flintlock Loops	5.7 mi rt	Easy
576	Grassland, Moraine, and Old Pasture Loops	4.4 mi rt	Easy
578	Clay Head Nature Trail and The Maze	2.9 mi rt	Easy

SEASONAL ACCESS	DOG-FRIENDLY	WATER FEATURES	WILDLIFE
Apr–Nov	X	X	
Apr–Nov	X		
Year-round	X	X	
Apr–Nov	X		
Apr–Nov	X		
Apr–Nov	X		X
Year-round	X	X	
Year-round			X
Year-round			X
Apr–Nov	X		
Year-round	X		X
Year-round			X
Year-round			X
Year-round	X	X	
Year-round	X		X
Year-round	X		X

MOON NEW ENGLAND HIKING

Avalon Travel
Hachette Book Group
1700 Fourth Street
Berkeley, CA 94710, USA
www.moon.com

Editors: Kimberly Ehart, Rachael Sablik, Rachel Feldman
Acquiring Editor: Nikki Ioakimedes
Series Manager: Sabrina Young
Copy Editors: Brett Keener and Kelly Lydick
Proofreader: Elizabeth Jang
Graphics and Production Coordinators: Megan Jones, Ravina Schneider, Kit Anderson
Cover Design: Kimberly Glyder Design
Interior Design: Megan Jones Design
Moon Logo: Tim McGrath
Map Editor: Mike Morgenfeld
Cartographers: Brian Shotwell, Lohnes + Wright, Mike Morgenfeld
Indexer: Greg Jewett

ISBN-13: 978-1-64049-023-9

Printing History
1st Edition — March 2020
5 4 3 2 1

Front cover photo: Fall colors in New England. © Reed Kaestner | Getty Images
Back cover photo: © Larry Gloth | Getty Images

Printed in China by RR Donnelley

ICON AND MAP SYMBOLS KEY

- Kid-friendly
- Historic landmarks
- Wildlife
- Wildflowers
- Dog-friendly
- Water features
- Public transit
- Wheelchair accessible

Expressway	Feature Trail	Park	City/Town
Primary Road	Other Trail	Unique Feature	Point of Interest
Secondary Road	Contour Line	Waterfall	Other Location
Unpaved Road	Parking Area	Camping	Airport
Rail Line	Trailhead	Mountain	Ski Area

QUICK-REFERENCE CHART: TRAILS AT A GLANCE